A Taste of the MEDITERRANEAN

A Taste of the MEDITERRANEAN

JACQUELINE CLARK AND JOANNA FARROW

southwater

This edition is published by Southwater

Distributed in the UK by
The Manning Partnership
251–253 London Road East
Batheaston
Bath BA1 7RL
UK
tel. (0044) 01225 852 727
fax. (0044) 01225 852 852

Distributed in Australia by
Sandstone Publishing
Unit 1, 360 Norton Street
Leichhardt
New South Wales 2040
Australia
tel. (0061) 2 9560 7888
fax. (0061) 2 9560 7488

Distributed in the USA by
Ottenheimer Publishing
5 Park Center Court
Suite 300
Owing Mills MD 2117-5001
USA
tel. (001) 410 902 9100
fax. (001) 410 902 7210

Distributed in New Zealand by
Five Mile Press NZ
PO Box 33-1071
Takapuna
Auckland 9
New Zealand
tel. (0064) 9 4444 144
fax. (0064) 9 4444 518

Southwater is an imprint of
Anness Publishing Limited

1 3 5 7 9 10 8 6 4 2

Publisher: Joanna Lorenz
Senior Cookery Editor: Linda Fraser
Designer: Nigel Partridge
Photography and styling: Michelle Garrett, assisted by Dulce Riberio
Food for photography: Jacqueline Clark and Joanna Farrow
Illustrator: Anna Koska

Previously published as *A Taste of the Mediterranean*

Printed and bound in Singapore

Notes

For all recipes, quantities are given in both metric and imperial measures and, where appropriate, measures are also given in standard cups and spoons. Follow one set, but not a mixture because they are not interchangeable.

Standard spoon and cup measures are level.
1 tsp = 5ml, 1 tbsp = 15ml, 1 cup = 8 fl oz

Size 3 (medium) eggs should be used unless otherwise stated.

Contents

INTRODUCTION

The countries bordered by the Mediterranean sea produce some of the finest food the world has to offer—set sail with us on a culinary tour.

ABOVE: A grove of old olive trees lit by the afternoon sun in Provence.

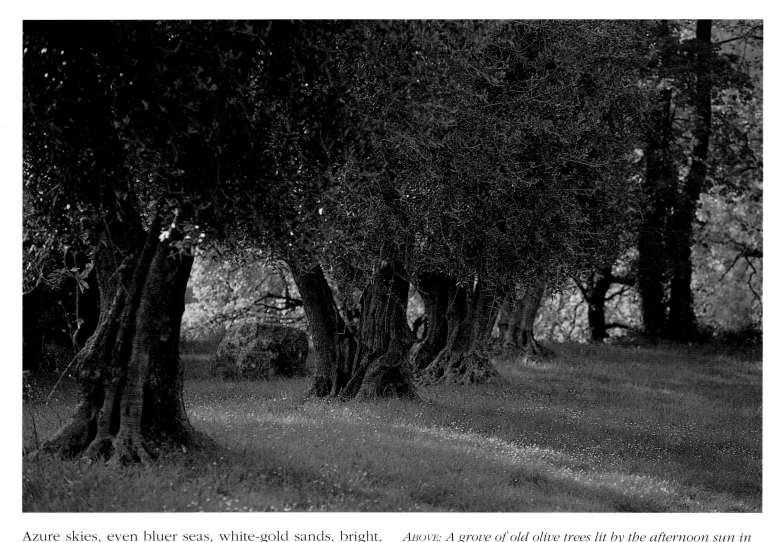

Azure skies, even bluer seas, white-gold sands, bright, whitewashed walls, the vibrant reds, greens, yellows, purples and oranges of the flowers, fruits and vegetables on display in the market—these are the paint palette colors of the Mediterranean. These evocative images are familiar to many of us, although, of course, we will not all be thinking of the same country—after all, there are fifteen to consider. A quick tour will take us from the shores of Spain, to France, Italy, Greece, Turkey, Syria, Lebanon, Israel, and into Africa to Egypt, Libya, Tunisia, Algeria and Morocco. The islands of Malta and Cyprus are truly Mediterranean, encircled by the sea. In many ways these fifteen countries are completely different from each other, but one thread links them all—the love of good food.

Centuries before Christ, the area surrounding the Mediterranean sea was colonized by the Phoenicians, Greeks and Romans, who shared a basic cultivation of wheat, olives and grapes. These, in turn, became bread, oil and wine, three components that are still very important in today's Mediterranean diet. With the building of ships came import and export, and the various countries began a sort of cross-pollination of crops, ingredients and recipes. Spices and flavorings were introduced through North Africa and Arabia, and saffron, cloves, chiles, ginger and allspice continue to be popular all over the Mediterranean, appearing in sweet and savory dishes. Nuts, too, are an ingredient common to many of the countries. Almonds, pistachios and pine nuts are perhaps the most popular, as they are native to the region.

When thinking of Mediterranean food, however, it is the fresh fruit, vegetables and herbs that immediately spring to mind. Open-air markets from Marseilles to Morocco are a feast for the senses. Fabulous arrays of

ABOVE: Melons, including the familiar tiger watermelons in the background, lie piled in the sun in a Greek market.

tomatoes, eggplant, zucchini, peaches, figs, garlic and pungent herbs such as basil and thyme are tantalizingly displayed; the experience is completed by the hot sun drawing out the flavors and aromas. Mediterranean cooking depends on the freshest of ingredients; it is honest, simple and prepared with respect.

Recent research has proved the Mediterranean diet to be a very healthy one, thus increasing its popularity. Olive oil is at the heart of this theory; it contains a high proportion of monounsaturated fats. Olive oils vary in color, from the golden Spanish varieties to the deep greens of some Greek, Provençal and Italian oils. Color is not really an indication of quality; the oils have to be tasted, and flavor, like color, varies immensely.

BELOW: Glossy green leaves shade juicy oranges in a grove near Seville.

The people of the Mediterranean have known great hardship and poverty. Although we may have images of endless sunny days, the weather can be wild and unjust. Lack of rain, terrible winds and a capricious sea ruin crops and the fishermen's haul; in the past, foreign domination and disease caused poverty and death. Because of this, the most basic foods are, even today, a celebration of life to the Mediterranean people. Bread is an important staple and always accompanies a meal, be it a bowl of soup or a platter of grilled fish.

Perhaps Mediterranean food could be described as "peasant food," not in a derogatory sense, but as an homage to the people who have provided and inspired us with such a vast and wonderful repertoire of recipes, ancient and new. In this book, we give you just a few of the countless dishes from around the Mediterranean. Some are traditional—for example, Gazpacho, Ratatouille, Greek Salad and Provençal Beef Daube, while others are more contemporary, using Mediterranean ingredients but creating something new. Among these recipes are Grilled Vegetable Terrine, Pan-fried Red Mullet with Basil, Mushroom and Pesto Pizza, and Turkish Delight Ice Cream.

As in the Mediterranean, ingredients should be fresh and of the highest quality, even if this means waiting for some of them, such as tomatoes or figs, to be in season. We hope to bring you a true taste of the Mediterranean.

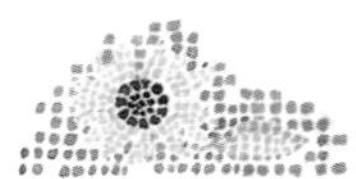

INGREDIENTS

VEGETABLES

ARTICHOKES There are two types of artichoke, in no way related: the globe, which belongs to the thistle family, and the Jerusalem, which is a tuber, belonging to the sunflower family. The globe artichoke is common throughout the Mediterranean, appearing as different varieties, depending on the country. When buying, choose firm, taut specimens. After boiling, the ends of the leaves and base are edible. Baby varieties are completely edible and are sometimes eaten raw. Jerusalem artichokes look like knobbly potatoes, and can be treated as such.

EGGPLANT Although eggplant originated in Asia, it is featured in dishes from every Mediterranean country. There are many different varieties, including green, white and yellow, but the plump purple variety is the most common. Look for firm, taut, shiny-skinned specimens with green stalks. Eggplant is sometimes salted and drained before cooking, which helps to extract bitter juices and makes it absorb less oil during cooking.

FAVA OR BROAD BEANS Fava beans were the only beans known in Europe before the discovery of the New World. When young, fava beans can be cooked and eaten, pods and all, or shelled and eaten raw with cheese, as in Italy. When the beans are older, they are shelled, cooked, and sometimes peeled. Dried fava beans are popular in the Middle East, where they are cooked with spices or added to stews.

Artichokes

Fennel

FENNEL This white bulb of overlapping leaves and green, feathery fronds has a fresh anise flavor and can be eaten cooked or raw. Its flavor complements fish and chicken, but it is also delicious served as a separate vegetable course, either roasted or baked with a cheese sauce. Choose firm, rounded bulbs, and use the fronds for garnishing. If using raw, toss the slices in lemon juice to prevent them from discoloring.

MUSHROOMS The varieties used in Mediterranean cooking are button, open-cup and flat, but regional wild species, such as cèpes, chanterelles and oyster mushrooms, can be found in the markets during autumn.

OKRA This African vegetable, sometimes called lady fingers, is a long five-sided green pod, with a tapering end. It has a subtle flavor and a gelatinous texture that helps to thicken and enrich certain dishes. Used in Middle Eastern and Greek cooking, its most successful partners are garlic, onion and tomatoes. Choose small, firm specimens and use sliced or whole in cooking.

Okra

Onions The starting point of so many dishes, the onion is invaluable to Mediterranean cooking. There are many varieties, differing in color, size and strength of flavor. For salads, or when onion is to be used raw, choose red or white-skinned varieties that have a sweet, mild flavor. The large Spanish onions have a mild flavor too, and are a good choice when a large quantity of onion is called for in a recipe. Pearl onions are perfect for adding whole to stews, or serving as a vegetable dish on their own.

Peppers Sweet bell peppers add color to markets across the Mediterranean region. To make the most of their flavor, broil peppers until the skins are charred, then rub off and discard the skins. Marinate the peppers in olive oil.

Radicchio This red chicory is very popular in Italy. There are several varieties, but the most common is the round variety that looks like a little lettuce. The leaves are crisp and pleasantly bitter and can be eaten raw or cooked. Radicchio is delicious broiled and drizzled with olive oil and sprinkled with black pepper, or shredded and stirred into risotto or spaghetti. The raw leaves make a colorful addition to salads.

Radishes These are best eaten raw to appreciate their peppery flavor—serve them as the French do, with salt and butter, or use them as a colorful addition to a platter of crudites.

Spinach This leaf vegetable is very popular in the Mediterranean countries. Cooked or raw, it is a good source of vitamins A and C. Young spinach leaves can be eaten raw and need little preparation, but older leaves should be washed in several changes of water and then picked over and the tough stalks removed. Spinach is used in Middle Eastern pastries, Spanish tapas, French tarts and many more dishes—eggs and fish, for example, make good partners. A little doesn't go a long way—if the spinach is to be cooked, allow 8 ounces raw weight per person.

Tomatoes Some of the best tomatoes are to be found in Mediterranean markets. Sun-ripened and full of flavor, they come in many varieties—beefsteak tomatoes for slicing, plum tomatoes, vine tomatoes, cherry tomatoes and baby pear-shaped ones. Cooked with onion and garlic, tomatoes make the universal sauce that so many Mediterranean dishes rely on. Canned and sun-dried tomatoes are invaluable items to keep in the pantry.

Radishes

Vine tomatoes

Grape Leaves These pretty leaves have been used in cooking for hundreds of years. They can be stuffed with a variety of fillings and also make perfect wrappers for meat, fish and poultry. Fresh leaves must be young and soft. If using brined grape leaves, soak them in hot water for 20–30 minutes before stuffing or wrapping.

Zucchini These green squashes are at their best when they are small. They can be eaten raw and have a good flavor and crisp texture. The larger they become, the less flavor they have. When buying, choose firm, shiny specimens. Yellow varieties are sometimes available and, although there is no difference in flavor, they make a pretty alternative to the usual green variety. In Italy and France, the golden flowers are stuffed and cooked, or deep-fried in batter.

Olives

The fruit of one of the earliest-known trees native to the Mediterranean. There are hundreds of varieties, differing widely in size, quality and taste. Color depends purely on ripeness—the fruit changes from yellow to green, violet, purple, brown and finally black when fully ripened. Fresh olives are picked at the desired stage of ripeness, then soaked in water, bruised and immersed in brine to produce the familiar-tasting result. They can be bought whole or pitted, sometimes stuffed with bell peppers, anchovies or nuts, or in jars with flavorings such as garlic, coriander, chile and herbs.

Dairy Products

Cheese The range of cheeses from Mediterranean countries is diverse—varieties are made from cow's, goat's, sheep's and, in the case of Italian mozzarella, water buffalo's milk. Cream cheese is also common to many countries, varying a little according to the milk and the method used for preparing it.

Yogurt This live product (pasteurized milk combined with two beneficial bacteria) is perhaps most associated with the Middle Eastern countries, where it is used extensively in cooking. Greek yogurt is thick and creamy, and French yogurt is traditionally of the set variety. It is used as a marinade, a dip and to enrich soups and stews, and can be made from goat's, sheep's or cow's milk.

Grains

Bulgur Also known as cracked wheat, this cereal has been partially processed, and so cooks quickly. It can be used in place of rice as an accompaniment to broiled meats, as a stuffing, mixed with ground meat to make patties, or in salads, such as tabbouleh.

Couscous This is a product made from semolina. The grains have been rolled, dampened and coated with the fine wheat flour. The commercial variety simply needs moistening, then steaming to swell the grains and produce a soft texture. It is the staple of the North African diet and is usually served with a spicy meat or vegetable stew, but it can also be used as a stuffing or in salads.

Rice There are many varieties of this worldwide staple food. In Italy there are at least four short-grained types used for risotto, and in Spain, Valencia rice is the preferred variety for paella. In the Middle East it is served with every meal, either plainly boiled or cooked with saffron and spices to create fragrant pilafs.

Fruit

Dates Although fresh dates are quite widely available today, the dried variety remains an invaluable addition to cakes and quick breads. Fresh dates should be plump

and slightly wrinkled and have a rich, honeylike flavor and dense texture. They are best treated simply, or pitted and served with thick strained yogurt.

Figs This fruit is associated with all the Mediterranean countries. Different varieties vary in skin color, from dark purple to green to a golden yellow, but all are made up of hundreds of tiny seeds surrounded by soft pink flesh. Choose firm unblemished fruit that just yield to the touch. Treat them simply, or serve with prosciutto or plain yogurt and honey.

Melons This fruit comes in many different sizes, shapes and colors—cantaloupe, charentais, galia, honeydew, ogen, orange- and green-fleshed varieties, and the wonderful pink watermelon. Ripe melons should yield to gentle pressure at the stem end and have a fragrant scent. Rarely used in cooked dishes, they are best eaten chilled by the slice or as part of a fruit salad.

Peaches and Nectarines Peaches need plenty of sun to ripen them. They grow in France, Spain and Italy. There are yellow-, pink- and white-fleshed varieties; some are clingstone, where the flesh clings to the pit, while others are of the freestone variety. Look for bruise-free specimens that just give when squeezed gently. Nectarines are smooth-skinned, with all the luscious flavor of the peach.

Figs

Sea Bass

Oranges This fruit is grown all over the Mediterranean, particularly in Spain. Seville oranges, the bitter marmalade variety, have a short season in January. The best of the flavor comes from the zest—the outer layer of the skin—and this is often included in recipes using oranges.

Fish and Seafood

Red Mullet Very popular along the coasts of the Mediterranean, the red mullet is a pretty fish. It is usually treated simply by grilling over a wood fire. It can also be filleted and pan-fried, or included in delicious fish soups. Snapper makes a good alternative.

Sea Bass This fish is usually sold and cooked whole. The flesh is soft and delicate and needs careful attention when cooking. Cooking methods include poaching, steaming, broiling and baking.

Squid Very popular in the Mediterranean, particularly in Spain, Italy and Portugal. Squid vary in size from the tiny specimens that can be eaten whole to the larger varieties, which are good for stuffing, broiling or stewing. The flesh is sweet and, when cooked for a short time, tender. Long cooking will also produce succulent results. Sometimes the ink is used to make a sauce for the squid.

Salt Cod Most salt cod is prepared in Norway, Iceland and Newfoundland and then exported to Mediterranean countries. It is gutted, cleaned and soaked in brine, then dried. The end result looks very unappetizing, with a

pungent smell, but after soaking for 48 hours and cooking in the Mediterranean style, it is delicious.

Tuna An oily fish belonging to the same family as the mackerel. The flesh, which is sold in steaks or large pieces, is richly flavored, firmly textured, dark red and very dense, and has a tendency to dry out when cooked. Marinating before cooking helps to keep the flesh moist, as does basting while cooking. Tuna can be baked, fried, broiled or stewed.

Crab There are thousands of species of crab around the world. In the Mediterranean countries, brown and spider crabs are the most common. The meat of the crab is divided into two types—brown and white. Crabs are often sold cooked and dressed, which means that the crab has been prepared and is ready to eat. Choose heavy cooked crabs, which should have a lot of meat.

Mussels Available in the Mediterranean from September to April, mussels usually need to be scrubbed and have the beard—the hairy tuft attached to the shell—removed. Any open mussels should be discarded if they do not close after a sharp tap. Mussels vary in size, and the shell can be blue-black to dappled brown. They are easy to cook—just steam for a few minutes in a covered pan.

Shrimp These vary enormously in size. The classic Mediterranean shrimp is large, about 8 inches, reddish brown in color when raw, and pink when cooked. When shrimp are cooked over strong heat, as on a barbecue, the shell is often left on to protect the flesh from charring.

Shrimp

Beans

Chickpeas These look like pale golden hazelnuts and are sold either dried or already cooked. Chickpeas have a nutty flavor and are used in stews from North Africa to Spain. In the Middle East they are made into flour, and in Greece they are puréed to produce a delicious dip. Soak them for at least 5 hours before cooking. They may have to be cooked for up to 4 hours before they become tender. This varies according to the age of the chickpeas.

Lentils These come in different sizes and can be yellow, red, brown or green. The tiny green Puy lentils are favored in France and the brown and red ones in the Middle East, where they are cooked with spices to make dhals. They are also used in soups and need no soaking time, cooking in under an hour.

Navy Beans These small, plump white beans, which are quite soft when cooked, are used in casseroles in Spain and Portugal, as well as the famous cassoulet in France. They need to be soaked for 3–4 hours before cooking, and are also good in soups and salads.

Pasta

Pasta is simply the Latin word for "paste," the flour-and-egg-based dough from which it is made. Although a staple of Italian cooking, pasta is widely used throughout the Mediterranean and has much in common with Chinese noodles, which filtered from China via the Middle Eastern trade routes. In Italy today there are countless varieties, from flat sheets of lasagne and ribbon noodles to pressed and molded shapes, specifically designed to pocket substantial amounts of the sauce they are served with. Dried pasta makes a good standby, but fresh pasta has a better flavor and texture and freezes well. Both can

Toasted pine nuts

be bought flavored with tomato, olive, spinach or mushroom paste. Black pasta, made with the addition of squid ink, is increasingly popular. Homemade pasta is easy to make if time is allowed for chilling the fresh dough. Rolling it can be done effortlessly using a pasta machine.

Nuts

Almonds Cultivated commercially in Spain, Italy and Portugal, the almond is widely used in the Arab-influenced countries. It is an important ingredient in sweet pastries and is often added to savory dishes, too. Almonds are sold fresh in their velvety green shells in the Mediterranean markets.

Pine Nuts These little nuts are used in both sweet and savory dishes, and are one of the principal ingredients in pesto, the basil sauce from Italy.

Pistachios This colorful nut originated in the Middle East. It has flesh that ranges from pale to dark green, and a papery, purple-tinged skin. Pistachio nuts have a subtle flavor and are used in a wide range of dishes, from pastries (both sweet and savory) to ice creams and nougat.

Walnuts This very versatile nut is used in both sweet and savory dishes. Walnut oil is a popular ingredient in salad dressings in France. Elsewhere, walnuts are chopped and added to pastries, ground to make sauces, or eaten fresh.

Herbs

Basil One of the herbs most crucial to Mediterranean cooking, particularly in Italian dishes. The sweet tender leaves have a great affinity for tomatoes, eggplant, peppers, zucchini and cheese. A handful of torn leaves livens up a green salad and can be packed into a bottle of olive oil to produce an aromatic flavor.

Bay These hardy leaves are taken from the bay shrub or tree and are widely used to flavor slow-cooked dishes like stocks, soups and stews. They are also added to marinades, threaded onto kebab skewers, thrown on the grill to invigorate the smoky flavor, or used for decorative purposes. One or two young bay leaves, infused with milk or cream in desserts, add a warm, pungent flavor.

Bouquet Garni A collection of herbs that traditionally includes parsley, thyme and bay, although other herbs, such as rosemary and marjoram, can be added. Available dried, tied in muslin bundles or in tea bag-like sachets. Fresh bouquet garni can be tied together with string for easy removal from the dish before serving.

Chervil This delicate, pretty-leaved, gentle herb is rather like a mild parsley and needs to be used generously to impart sufficient flavor. Widely used in French cooking, it works well in herb butters and with eggs and cheese.

Chives A grasslike herb that produces a beautiful purplish flower. Its flavor resembles that of mild onions.

Cilantro Huge bundles of fresh cilantro are a familiar sight in eastern Mediterranean markets, their warm, pungent aroma rising at the merest touch. The leaves impart a distinctive flavor to soups, stews, sauces and spicy dishes when added toward the end of cooking. They are also used sparingly in salads and yogurt dishes.

Dill Feathery dill leaves have a mild anise taste, popular in the eastern Mediterranean, particularly Greece and Turkey. It is chopped into fish and chicken dishes as well as stuffings and rice. Pickled gherkins and cucumbers are often flavored with dill.

Marjoram A versatile herb of which there are several varieties. It grows both wild and cultivated and goes very well with red meats, game and tomato dishes. Oregano is a wild form of marjoram.

Basket of herbs

Mint One of the oldest and most widely used herbs. In Greece, chopped mint accompanies other herbs to enhance stuffed vegetables and fish dishes, and in Turkey and the Middle East, finely chopped mint adds a cooling tang to yogurt dishes as well as teas and iced drinks.

Parsley Flat-leaf parsley is far more widely used in Mediterranean cooking than the tightly curled variety. Mixed with garlic and lemon zest, it makes a wonderfully aromatic gremolata a colorful, refreshing garnish for scattering over tomato and rice dishes.

Rosemary Cut from the pretty flowering shrub, rosemary grows well throughout the Mediterranean and is most widely used in meat cooking. Several sprigs, tucked under a roast chicken or lamb with plenty of garlic, impart an inviting warm, sweet flavor.

Sage Native to the northern Mediterranean, soft, velvety sage leaves have a strong, distinctive flavor and should be used sparingly in meat and game dishes. Sage can be added to stuffings or panfried with squab and liver to give an interesting flavor.

Tarragon Long, lank tarragon leaves have a very individual aroma and flavor, most widely appreciated in French cooking. It is used generously in egg and chicken dishes, and with salmon and trout. Tarragon-flavored vinegar makes a delicious ingredient in a good mayonnaise or bearnaise sauce.

Thyme A few sprigs of hardy thyme add a warm, earthy flavor to slow-cooked meat and poultry dishes as well as to pâtés, marinades and vegetable dishes.

Spices

Cardamom Usually associated with Indian cooking, the use of cardamom extends to the eastern Mediterranean. The black, green or white pods should be pounded to release the small black seeds, which can be bruised to accentuate the flavor. The pods are usually discarded.

Chiles These are the small, fiery relatives of the sweet pepper family. Mediterranean chiles are generally milder in flavor than the fiery South American ones, but should still be used with caution, because their heat is difficult to gauge. It is the oil in chiles that accounts for the heat and the irritation they can cause to sensitive skin.

Cinnamon Cinnamon sticks, the thin curled bark of the cinnamon tree, have an aromatic, sweet flavor that is used extensively in the eastern Mediterranean to flavor meat and pilaf dishes and to infuse milk and syrups for desserts. Ground cinnamon is more convenient but lacks the fresh, sweet flavor.

Coriander Seeds These seeds of the herb cilantro have a warm, slightly orange flavor that is essential to many dishes of the eastern Mediterranean. Their flavor can be accentuated by crushing and gently heating them in a frying pan before using.

Cumin Seeds These dark, spindly seeds are often married with coriander when making spicy dishes that are typical of North Africa and the eastern Mediterranean.

Mace This is the thin, lacy covering of nutmeg, available ground to a powder or as thin "blades." It has a gentler flavor than nutmeg.

Nutmeg Nutmeg's beautiful, sweet, warm aroma makes a good addition to sweet and savory dishes, particularly terrines and pâtés and those featuring spinach, cheese and eggs.

Pepper There are several different types of peppercorns, all of which are picked from the pepper vine, a plant unrelated to the capsicum family. Black peppercorns have the strongest flavor. Green peppercorns are the fresh unripe berries, which are bottled while soft.

Preserved lemons

Saffron This is by far the most highly prized spice, since it takes the handpicked stamens of about 70,000 saffron crocuses to make up one pound of the spice. Its exotic, rich color and flavor are indispensable in many Mediterranean dishes, particularly French fish stews, Spanish rice and chicken dishes and Italian risottos. To accentuate the flavor, the strands should be lightly crushed and soaked in a little boiling water before use.

Lemons and Limes The grated zest or squeezed juice of lemons and limes is widely added to fish, meat and poultry for a typically fresh flavor.

Oranges Thinly pared strips of orange zest give a fresh fragrance, particularly in the fish stews and soups of southern France.

Preserved Lemons and Limes Lemons or limes preserved in salt develop a mellow flavor and are much used in Mediterranean dishes. To make them, scrub and quarter almost through to the base and rub cut sides with salt. Pack tightly into a large sterilized jar. Half-fill the jar with more salt, adding some bay leaves, peppercorns and cinnamon if desired. Cover completely with lemon juice. Cover with a lid and store for two weeks, shaking the jar daily. Add a little olive oil to seal and use within one to six months, washing off the salt before use.

Rose Water This distilled essence of rose petals is used mainly in eastern Mediterranean desserts, giving a mild rose fragrance and flavor. The strength varies greatly, so add carefully at first.

Tahini A smooth oily paste ground from sesame seeds and used to give a nutty flavor to Middle Eastern dishes.

Tomato Paste A concentrated paste made from fresh tomatoes, perfect for boosting the flavor of bland tomatoes in soups, stews and sauces. Use sun-dried tomato paste for a richer flavor.

Flavorings

Capers Capers are the pickled buds of a shrub native to the Mediterranean region. The best are those preserved in salt rather than brine or vinegar. When capers are coarsely chopped, their sharp piquant tang is used to cut the richness of lamb, liven up fish sauces and flavor salads and pastes such as tapenade.

Garlic Sold in "braids" or as separate bulbs, the main consideration when buying garlic is that the cloves are plump and firm. Garlic is one of the most vital ingredients in Mediterranean cooking, and there are few recipes in which it would be out of place. Used crushed, sliced or even whole, garlic develops a smooth, gentle flavor with long, slow cooking. Used raw in salads, mayonnaise and sauces, garlic has a hot, fierce impact.

Harissa A fiery-hot paste used mostly in North African cooking, it is made from a blend of chiles, garlic, cumin, coriander and cayenne and can be bought in small jars.

Honey An ancient sweetener that depends on the flowers on which the bees have fed for its individual fragrance and flavor. The Turks and Greeks use it in their syrupy pastries and puddings, and small quantities are added to some savory dishes.

Olive Oil

Besides its healthy qualities, olive oil is indispensable to Mediterranean cooking for its fine flavor. Italy, France and Spain produce some of the best. The richest oil comes from the first cold pressing of the olives, producing an aromatic green "virgin" oil.

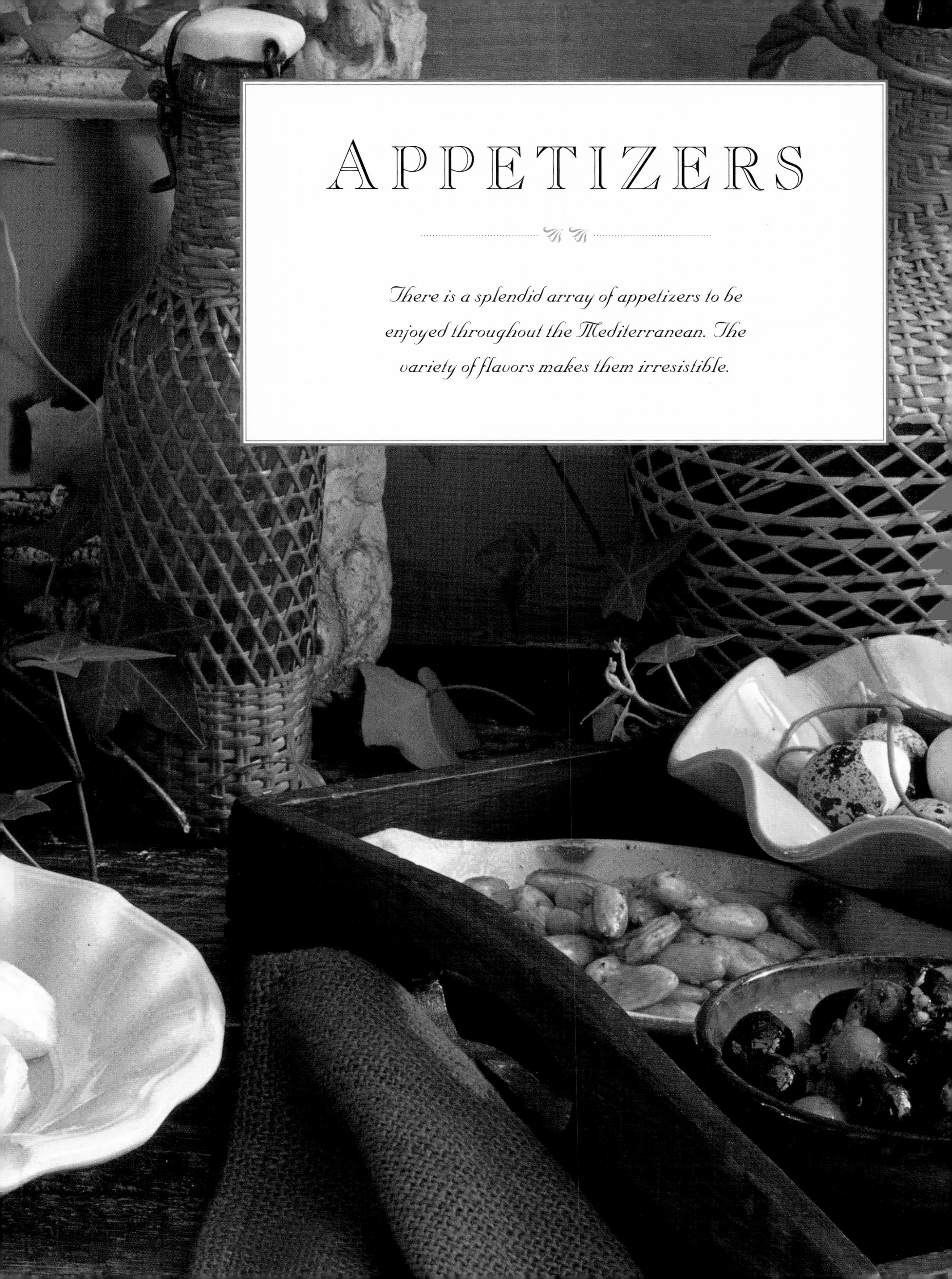

APPETIZERS

There is a splendid array of appetizers to be enjoyed throughout the Mediterranean. The variety of flavors makes them irresistible.

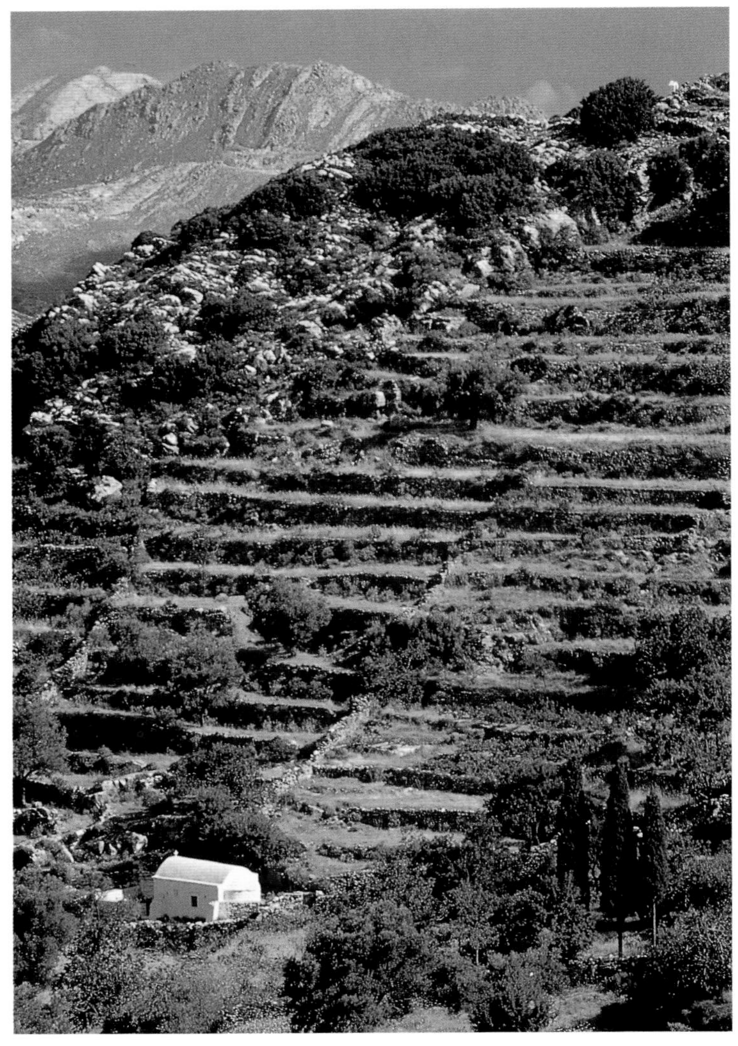

LEFT: On the mountainous Greek island of Naxos, arable land is precious, and hillsides are extensively terraced.

Tapas, apéritifs, mezze, mezedes—all these terms describe the inexhaustible and highly flavored range of appetizers that are served with drinks before a meal or as a light snack at almost any time of day. This is one of the most enticing aspects of Mediterranean cooking—the irresistible nibbles enjoyed in a casual, unhurried atmosphere, offering a culinary glimpse of the good things to follow. For the cook, the preparation of these savories can be as simple or as demanding as time and circumstances allow. Whether it is a selection of marinated olives, regional cheeses or fresh seafood or, on a more elaborate scale, delicious baked vegetables, pickles and spicy pastries, this informal style of enjoying food is quintessentially Mediterranean.

In Spanish, "tapa" means a lid, and it was the custom of bartenders to serve glasses of sherry covered with a slice of bread topped with sausage or ham that evolved into the fascinating and imaginative selection of "little dishes" served today. Tapas bars, particularly abundant in southern Spain, serve a variety of such dishes. In these bars you can enjoy predinner bites or thoroughly indulge yourself with a selection of dishes as a main meal. Fried new potatoes, chorizo sausage in olive oil, garlic shrimp and empanadillas are tapas classics. The tortilla, an omelet in which fried potatoes are layered in a pan, covered with beaten eggs and baked to a set "cake," is another well- established dish. It is served warm or cold, cut into wedges, and washed down with local chilled wines or, like other tapas, with sherry, port or beer.

In the eastern Mediterranean, in places like Turkey, Greece, Lebanon and North Africa, local and specialized variations of mezze are popular with both locals and visitors. Arak, raki and ouzo, as well as wine, are drunk with a wonderful selection of foods to whet the appetite. These are usually highly spiced and aromatic. In Greece, sheep's and goat's milk yogurt are strained to produce thickened cheeses that are preserved in spiced olive oil. Spread on warm toast, this delicious snack is good

RIGHT: Bent double, Moroccan farmworkers bring in the olive harvest.

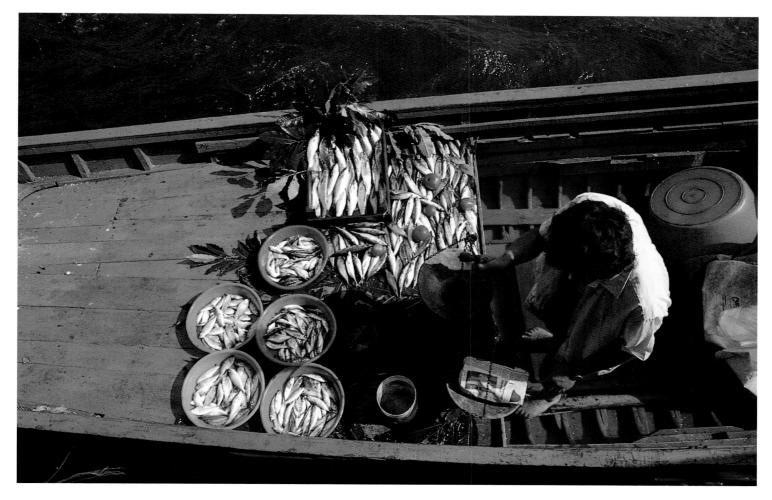

ABOVE: With his scales at the ready, a Turkish fisherman sets out his catch on his stall.

enough to enjoy as a complete meal. Stuffed tomatoes, fried halloumi or keflotyri cheese drizzled with lemon juice and pepper and a bowl of garlic-flavored Greek yogurt complete a mouthwatering spread.

Vegetables, salads and beans feature prominently in North African or Lebanese mezze. Simple vegetable crudités such as carrots, turnips and cucumber are scattered with coarse salt and left to marinate lightly before being moistened with lemon juice or wine vinegar. Miniature versions of national dishes such as kibbeh and little phyllo pastries are also ideal for whetting the appetite.

Sampling a selection of nibbles before a Turkish meal is almost compulsory, and the range of dishes is very extensive. A rich, thick sauce of tomato and chile and a refreshing cacik, or cucumber and yogurt salad, provide a stimulating contrast alongside specialties such as garlic mussels, broiled vegetables and stuffed bell peppers.

The classic Italian appetizer is the antipasto, usually an assortment of salami, prosciutto and other cured meats, served alongside roasted bell pepper salads, artichokes in olive oil, green bean vinaigrette, anchovy fillets and breads such as crostini and focaccia.

Tasty dips like tapenade, herb aïoli and a very garlicky vinaigrette are essential appetizers in France, often accompanied by a selection of raw or roasted crudités, herb salads and radishes with salt and butter.

Part of the pleasure of serving appetizers is that they can be as simple or as complicated as desired. Serve several as a light summer meal, two or three as a simple appetizer or a varied selection for a larger party. Added interest can be provided, with little extra effort, by serving a variety of olives, interesting Mediterranean breads and salted or spiced nuts.

Essentially, plenty of time must be allowed so that the nibbles can be enjoyed in the unhurried and relaxed atmosphere that is an integral part of the Mediterranean way of life.

DEEP-FRIED NEW POTATOES WITH SAFFRON AIOLI

Aïoli is a well-known garlic mayonnaise from Southern France; this Spanish version is very similiar. In this recipe, saffron adds color and flavor.

1 egg yolk
½ teaspoon Dijon mustard
1¼ cups extra virgin olive oil
1–2 tablespoons lemon juice
1 garlic clove, crushed
½ teaspoon saffron strands
20 very small new potatoes
vegetable oil for frying
salt and ground black pepper

SERVES 4

1 To make the aïoli, put the egg yolk in a bowl with the mustard and a pinch of salt. Beat together with a wooden spoon. Still beating, add the olive oil very slowly, drop by drop to begin with, then, as the aïoli gradually thickens, in a thin stream. Add the lemon juice and salt and pepper to taste, then beat in the crushed garlic.

2 Place the saffron in a small bowl, and add 2 teaspoons hot water. Press the saffron with the back of a teaspoon to extract the color and flavor, and let infuse for about 5 minutes. Beat the saffron and the liquid into the mayonnaise.

3 Cook the potatoes in boiling salted water for 5 minutes, then turn off the heat. Cover the pan and let sit for 15 minutes. Drain the potatoes, then dry them thoroughly.

4 Heat ½ inch oil in a deep pan. When the oil is very hot, add the potatoes and fry quickly, turning, until crisp and golden. Drain on paper towels and serve with the saffron aïoli.

DATES STUFFED WITH CHORIZO

A delicious combination from Spain, using fresh dates and spicy chorizo sausage.

2 ounces chorizo sausage
12 fresh dates, pitted
6 bacon slices
oil for frying
flour for dusting
1 egg, beaten
1 cup fresh bread crumbs
toothpicks for serving

SERVES 4–6

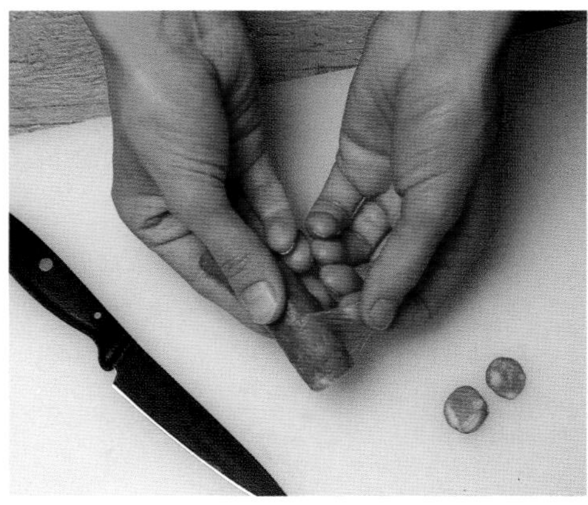

1 Trim the ends of the chorizo sausage and peel away the skin. Cut into three ¾-inch slices. Cut these in half lengthwise, then into quarters, giving 12 pieces.

2 Stuff each date with a piece of chorizo, closing the date around it. Stretch the bacon by running the back of a knife along each slice. Cut each slice in half crosswise. Wrap a piece of bacon around each date and secure with a toothpick.

3 In a deep pan, heat ½ inch of oil. Dust the dates with flour, dip them in the beaten egg, then coat in bread crumbs. Fry the dates in the hot oil, turning them, until golden. Remove the dates with a slotted spoon and drain on paper towels. Serve immediately.

SANLUCAR
L-123/5
AGENCIES LTD, LONDON

SPINACH EMPANADILLAS

These are little pastry turnovers, filled with ingredients that show a strong Moorish influence—pine nuts and raisins.

2 tablespoons raisins
1½ tablespoons olive oil
1 pound fresh spinach, washed and chopped
6 drained canned anchovies, chopped
2 garlic cloves, finely chopped
⅓ cup pine nuts, chopped
1 egg, beaten
12 ounces puff pastry
salt and ground black pepper

MAKES 20

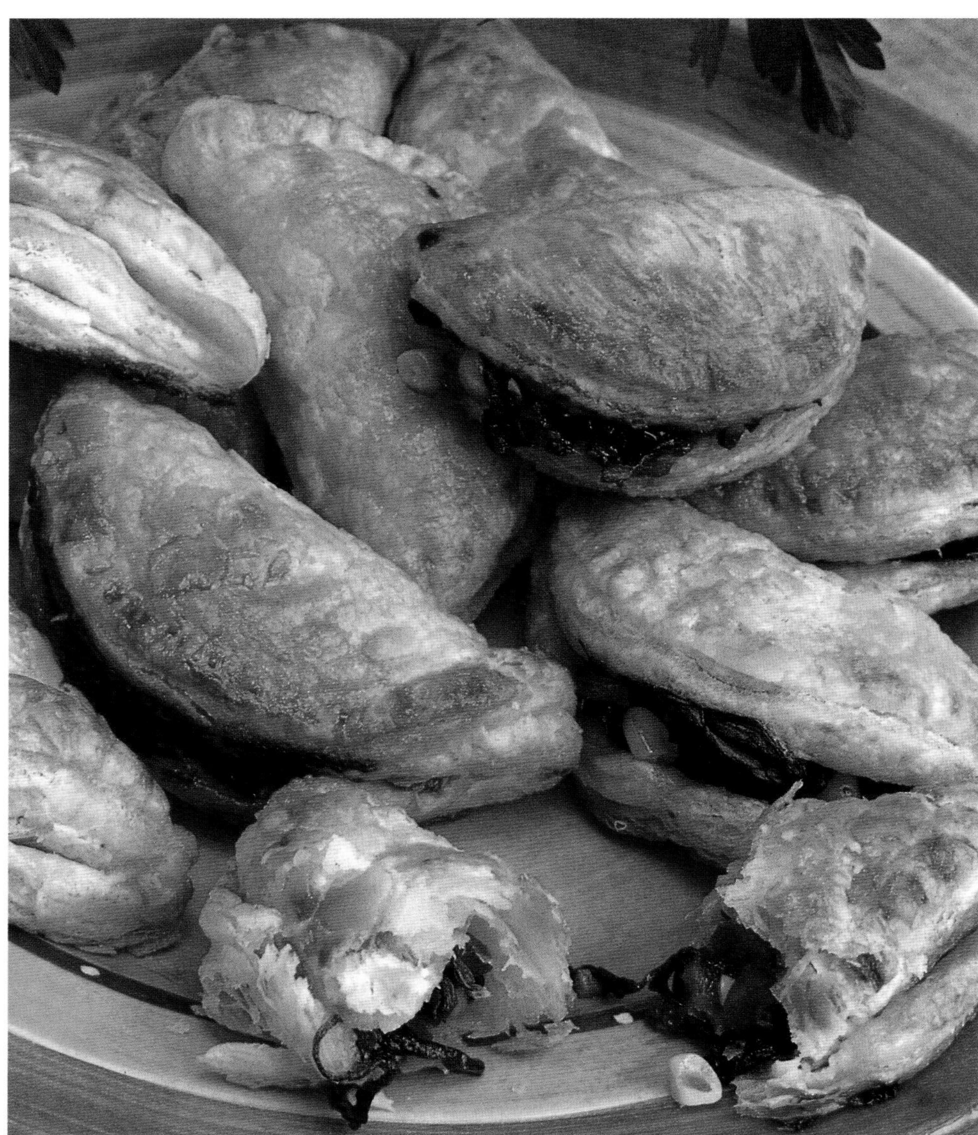

1 To make the filling, soak the raisins in a little warm water for 10 minutes. Drain, then chop them coarsely. Heat the oil in a large sauté pan or wok, add the spinach, stir, then cover and cook over low heat for about 2 minutes. Uncover, turn up the heat and let any liquid evaporate. Add the anchovies, garlic and seasoning. Cook, stirring, for another minute. Remove from the heat, add the raisins and pine nuts, and cool.

2 Preheat the oven to 350°F. On a floured surface, roll out the pastry to a ⅛-inch thickness.

3 Using a 3-inch pastry cutter, cut out 20 circles, re-rolling the dough if necessary. Place about 2 teaspoons of the filling in the middle of each circle, then brush the edges with a little water. Bring up the sides of the pastry and seal well (*left*). Press the edges together with the back of a fork. Brush with egg. Place the turnovers on a lightly greased baking sheet and bake for about 15 minutes, until golden. Serve warm.

SAUTEED MUSSELS WITH GARLIC AND HERBS

These mussels are served without their shells, in a delicious paprika-flavored sauce. Eat them with toothpicks.

2 pounds fresh mussels
1 lemon slice
6 tablespoons olive oil
2 shallots, finely chopped
1 garlic clove, finely chopped
1 tablespoon chopped fresh parsley
½ teaspoon sweet paprika
¼ teaspoon dried red pepper flakes
parsley sprigs, to garnish

SERVES 4

1 Scrub the mussels, discarding any damaged ones that do not close when tapped with a knife. Put the mussels in a large pan with 1 cup water and the slice of lemon. Bring to a boil and let boil for 3–4 minutes, removing the mussels as they open. Discard any that remain closed. Take the mussels out of the shells and drain them on paper towels.

2 Heat the oil in a sauté pan, add the mussels *(left)* and cook, stirring, for a minute. Remove from the pan. Add the shallots and garlic and cook, covered, over low heat for about 5 minutes, until soft. Stir in the parsley, paprika and red pepper flakes, then add the mussels with any juices. Cook briefly. Remove the pan from the heat, cover and let sit for 1–2 minutes to let the flavors mingle. Serve, garnished with parsley.

TAPAS OF ALMONDS, OLIVES AND CHEESE

These three simple ingredients are lightly flavored to create a delicious Spanish tapas medley that's perfect for a casual appetizer or nibbles to serve with cocktails.

FOR THE MARINATED OLIVES
½ teaspoon coriander seeds
½ teaspoon fennel seeds
1 teaspoon chopped fresh rosemary
2 teaspoons chopped fresh parsley
2 garlic cloves, crushed
1 tablespoon sherry vinegar
2 tablespoons olive oil
⅔ cup black olives
⅔ cup green olives

FOR THE MARINATED CHEESE
5 ounces goat cheese, or Spanish sheep's milk cheese
6 tablespoons olive oil
1 tablespoon white wine vinegar
1 teaspoon black peppercorns
1 garlic clove, sliced
3 fresh tarragon or thyme sprigs
tarragon sprigs, to garnish

FOR THE SALTED ALMONDS
¼ teaspoon cayenne pepper
2 tablespoons sea salt
2 tablespoons butter
4 tablespoons olive oil
1¾ cups blanched almonds
extra salt for sprinkling (optional)

SERVES 6–8

1 To make the marinated olives, crush the coriander and fennel seeds with a mortar and pestle. Combine with the rosemary, parsley, garlic, vinegar and oil and pour over the olives in a small bowl. Cover and chill for up to 1 week.

2 To make the marinated cheese, cut the cheese into bite-size pieces, leaving the rind on. Combine the oil, vinegar, peppercorns, garlic and herb sprigs and pour over the cheese in a small bowl. Cover and chill for up to 3 days.

COOK'S TIP
If serving with cocktails, provide toothpicks for spearing the olives and cheese.

3 To make the salted almonds, combine the cayenne pepper and salt in a bowl. Melt the butter with the olive oil in a frying pan. Add the almonds to the pan and fry, stirring, for about 5 minutes, until the almonds are golden.

4 Pour the almonds out of the frying pan into the salt mixture and toss together until the almonds are coated. Let cool, then store them in a jar or airtight container for up to 1 week.

5 To serve the tapas, arrange in small, shallow serving dishes. Use fresh sprigs of tarragon to garnish the cheese and sprinkle a little more salt on the almonds, if desired.

ROASTED BELL PEPPER ANTIPASTO

Jars of Italian mixed peppers in olive oil are now a common sight in many supermarkets. None, however, can compete with this colorful, freshly made version, perfect as an appetizer on its own, or with some Italian salamis and cold meats.

3 red bell peppers
2 yellow or orange bell peppers
2 green bell peppers
½ cup sun-dried tomatoes in oil, drained
2 tablespoons balsamic vinegar
5 tablespoons olive oil
few drops of hot pepper sauce
4 canned artichoke hearts, drained and sliced
1 garlic clove, sliced
salt and ground black pepper
basil leaves, to garnish

SERVES 6

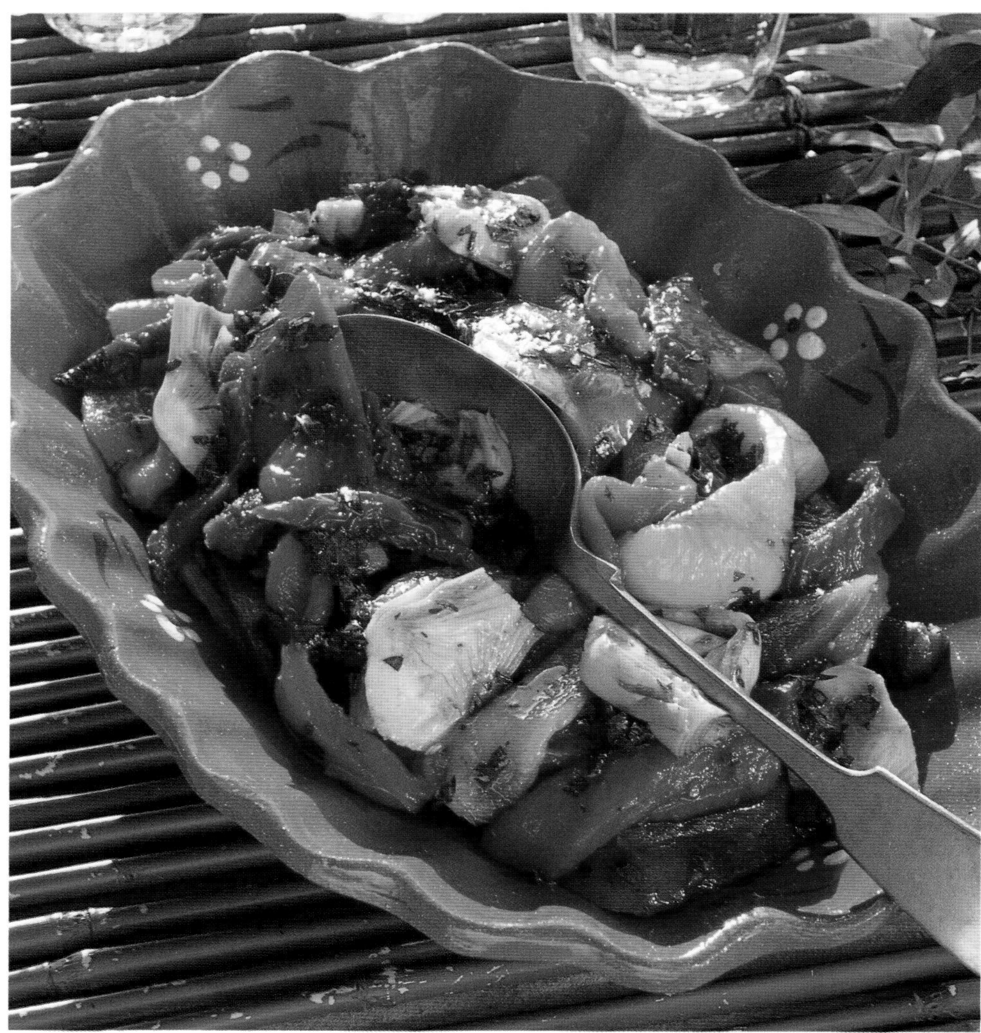

1 Preheat the oven to 400°F. Lightly oil a foil-lined baking sheet and place the whole peppers on the foil. Bake for about 45 minutes, until beginning to char. Remove from the oven, cover with a dish towel and let cool for 5 minutes.

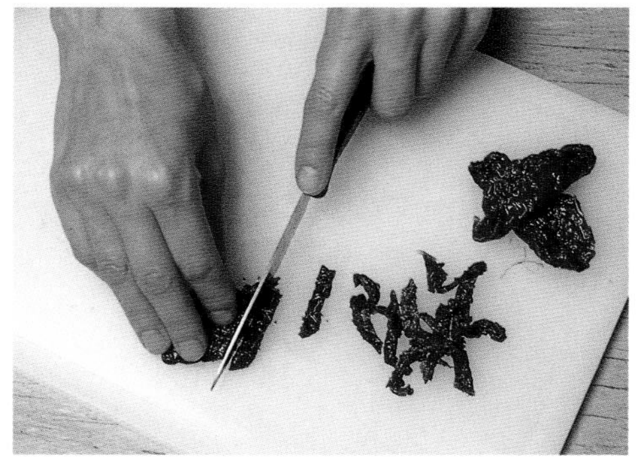

2 Slice the sun-dried tomatoes. Remove the core and seeds from the peppers and peel away the skins. Slice each pepper into thick strips.

3 Beat together the vinegar, oil and hot pepper sauce, then season with a little salt and pepper.

4 Toss the peppers with the sliced artichokes, tomatoes and garlic. Pour the dressing over and sprinkle the basil leaves on top.

FONDUTA

Fontina is a medium-fat Italian cheese with a rich salty flavor, a little like that of Gruyère, which makes a good substitute. This delicious cheese dip needs only some warm ciabatta or focaccia, an herb salad and some robust red wine to make a thoroughly enjoyable meal.

9 ounces fontina cheese, diced
1 cup milk
1 tablespoon butter
2 eggs, lightly beaten
ground black pepper

SERVES 4

1 Place the cheese in a bowl, add the milk and let soak for 2–3 hours. Transfer to a double boiler or a heatproof bowl set over a pan of simmering water.

2 Add the butter and eggs and cook gently, stirring, until the cheese has melted to a smooth sauce with the consistency of custard.

3 Remove from heat and transfer to a serving dish. Grind on some pepper and serve immediately.

COOK'S TIP

Don't overheat the sauce, or the eggs might curdle. Very gentle heat will produce a lovely, smooth sauce.

GARLIC SHRIMP

For this simple Spanish tapas dish, you really need fresh raw shrimp, which absorb the flavors of the garlic and chiles as they cook. Have everything ready for last-minute cooking so you can take the dish to the table still sizzling.

12 ounces—1 pound large raw shrimp
2 fresh red chiles
5 tablespoons olive oil
3 garlic cloves, crushed
salt and ground black pepper

SERVES 4

1 Remove the heads and shells from the shrimp, leaving the tails intact.

2 Halve each chile lengthwise and discard the seeds. Heat the oil in a flameproof pan, suitable for serving. (Alternatively, use a frying pan and have a warmed serving dish ready in the oven.)

3 Add all the shrimp, chiles and garlic to the pan and cook over high heat for about 3 minutes, stirring, until the shrimp turn pink. Season lightly with salt and pepper and serve immediately.

CHORIZO IN OLIVE OIL

Spanish chorizo sausage has a deliciously pungent taste; its robust seasoning of garlic, chile and paprika flavors the ingredients it is cooked with. Frying chorizo with onions and olive oil is one of its simplest and most delicious uses.

5 tablespoons extra virgin olive oil
12 ounces chorizo sausage, sliced
1 large onion, thinly sliced
coarsely chopped flat-leaf parsley, to garnish

SERVES 4

1 Heat the oil in a frying pan and fry the chorizo sausage over high heat until beginning to color. Remove from pan with slotted spoon.

2 Add the onion to the pan and fry until colored. Return the sausage slices to the pan and heat through for 1 minute.

3 Pour the mixture into a shallow serving dish and sprinkle with the parsley. Serve with warm bread.

VARIATION

Chorizo is usually available in large supermarkets or delicatessens. Other similarly rich, spicy sausages can be used as a substitute.

CROSTINI

These are Italian canapés, consisting of toasted slices of bread spread with various toppings. The following recipes are for a chicken liver pâté and a shrimp butter.

FOR THE CHICKEN LIVER PATE
10 tablespoons butter
1 small onion, finely chopped
1 garlic clove, crushed
8 ounces chicken livers
4 sage leaves, chopped
salt and ground black pepper

FOR THE SHRIMP BUTTER
8 ounces cooked, peeled shrimp
2 drained canned anchovies
4 tablespoons butter, softened
1 tablespoon lemon juice
1 tablespoon chopped fresh parsley
salt and ground black pepper

FOR THE CROSTINI
12 slices crusty Italian or French bread, cut ½-inch thick
6 tablespoons butter, melted

FOR THE GARNISH
sage leaves
flat-leaf parsley

SERVES 6

1 To make the chicken liver pâté, melt half the butter in a frying pan, add the onion and garlic, and fry gently until soft. Add the chicken livers and sage and sauté for about 8 minutes, until the livers are brown and firm. Season with salt and pepper and process in a blender or food processor with the remaining butter.

2 To make the shrimp butter, chop the shrimp and anchovies finely. Place in a bowl with the butter and beat together until well blended. Add the lemon juice and parsley and season with salt and pepper. Preheat the oven to 400°F. Place the bread slices on one or two baking sheets and brush with the butter.

3 Bake for 8–10 minutes, until pale golden. Spread half the hot crostini with the pâté and the rest with the shrimp butter, garnishing with sage and parsley, respectively. Serve the crostini immediately.

COOK'S TIP

Both the chicken liver pâté and the shrimp butter can be made ahead, but should be used within two days. Cover both toppings tightly and store them in the refrigerator.

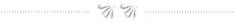

MARINATED BABY EGGPLANT WITH RAISINS AND PINE NUTS

Eggplant is popular in all the Mediterranean countries. This is a recipe with an Italian influence, using ingredients that have been included in recipes since Renaissance times. Make a day in advance, to let the sweet and sour flavors develop.

12 baby eggplant, halved lengthwise
1 cup extra virgin olive oil
juice of 1 lemon
2 tablespoons balsamic vinegar
3 cloves
⅓ cup pine nuts
2 tablespoons raisins
1 tablespoon sugar
1 bay leaf
large pinch of dried red pepper flakes
salt and ground black pepper

SERVES 4

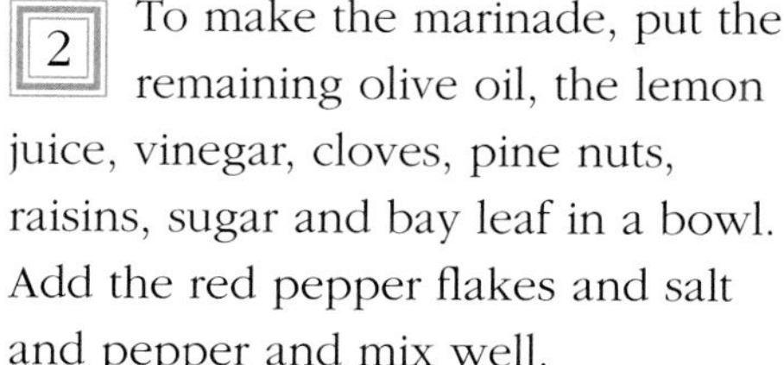

1 Preheat the broiler to high. Place the eggplant, cut side up, in the broiler pan and brush with a little of the olive oil. Broil for about 10 minutes, until slightly blackened, turning them over halfway through cooking.

2 To make the marinade, put the remaining olive oil, the lemon juice, vinegar, cloves, pine nuts, raisins, sugar and bay leaf in a bowl. Add the red pepper flakes and salt and pepper and mix well.

3 Place the hot eggplant in an earthenware or glass bowl, and pour the marinade over. Let cool, turning the eggplant once or twice. Serve cold.

YOGURT CHEESE IN OLIVE OIL

Sheep's milk is widely used in cheese making in the eastern Mediterranean, particularly in Greece, where sheep's milk yogurt is hung in cheesecloth to drain off the whey before being patted into balls of soft cheese. Here it's preserved in olive oil with chiles and herbs—an appropriate gift for a "foodie" friend.

1¾ pounds sheep's milk yogurt
½ teaspoon salt
2 teaspoons crushed dried chiles or chili powder
1 tablespoon chopped fresh rosemary
1 tablespoon chopped fresh thyme or oregano
1¼ cups olive oil, preferably garlic-flavored

FILLS TWO 1-POUND JARS

1 Sterilize a 12-inch square of cheesecloth by steeping it in boiling water. Drain and lay over a large plate. Mix the yogurt with the salt and pour onto the center of the cheesecloth. Bring up the sides of the cheesecloth and tie firmly with string.

2 Hang the bag on a kitchen cupboard handle or suitable position where the bag can be suspended with a bowl underneath to catch the whey. Leave for 2–3 days until the yogurt stops dripping.

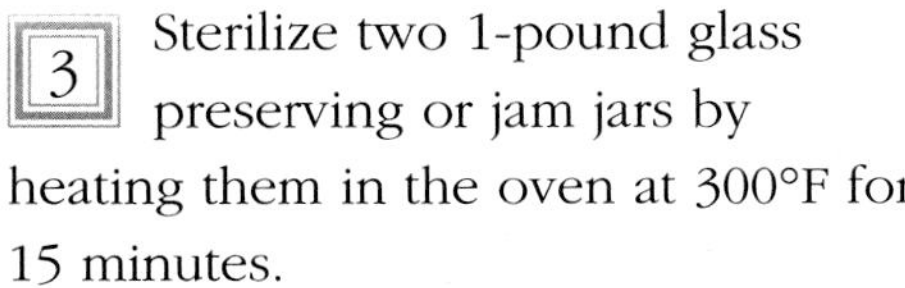

3 Sterilize two 1-pound glass preserving or jam jars by heating them in the oven at 300°F for 15 minutes.

4 Combine the chiles and herbs. Take teaspoonfuls of the cheese and roll into balls with your hands. Lower into the jars, sprinkling each layer with the herb mixture.

5 Pour the oil over the cheese until completely covered. Store in the refrigerator for up to 3 weeks.

6 To serve the cheese, spoon out of the jars with a little of the flavored olive oil and spread on lightly toasted bread.

COOK'S TIP

If your kitchen is particularly warm, find a cooler place to suspend the cheese. Alternatively, drain the cheese in the refrigerator, suspending the bag from one of the shelves.

TAPENADE AND HERB AIOLI WITH SUMMER VEGETABLES

A beautiful platter of salad vegetables served with one or two interesting sauces makes a thoroughly delicious and informal appetizer. This colorful French dish is perfect for entertaining, as it can be prepared in advance.

FOR THE TAPENADE
1½ cups pitted black olives
2-ounce can anchovy fillets, drained
2 tablespoons capers
½ cup olive oil
finely grated zest of 1 lemon
1 tablespoon brandy (optional)
ground black pepper

FOR THE HERB AIOLI
2 egg yolks
1 teaspoon Dijon mustard
2 teaspoons white wine vinegar
1 cup light olive oil
3 tablespoons chopped mixed fresh herbs, such as chervil, parsley or tarragon
2 tablespoons chopped watercress
5 garlic cloves, crushed
salt and ground black pepper

TO SERVE
2 red bell peppers, seeded and cut into wide strips
2 tablespoons olive oil
8 ounces new potatoes
4 ounces green beans
8 ounces baby carrots
8 ounces young asparagus
12 quail's eggs (optional)
fresh herbs, to garnish
coarse salt for sprinkling

SERVES 6

1. To make the tapenade, finely chop the olives, anchovies and capers and beat together with the oil, lemon zest and brandy if using. (Alternatively, lightly process the ingredients in a blender or food processor, scraping down the mixture from the sides of the bowl if necessary.)

2. Season with pepper and blend in a little more oil if the mixture is very dry. Transfer to a serving dish.

3. To make the aïoli, beat together the egg yolks, mustard and vinegar. Gradually blend in the oil, a trickle at a time, whisking well after each addition until thick and smooth. Season with salt and pepper to taste, adding a little more vinegar if the aïoli tastes bland.

4. Stir in the mixed herbs, watercress and garlic, then transfer to a serving dish. Cover and put in the refrigerator.

5. Put the peppers on a foil-lined broiler rack and brush with the oil. Broil under high heat until just beginning to char.

6. Cook the potatoes in a large pan of boiling salted water until just tender. Add the beans and carrots and cook for 1 minute. Add the asparagus and cook for another 30 seconds. Drain the vegetables.

7. Cook the quail's eggs (if using) in boiling water for 2 minutes. Drain and remove half of each shell.

8. Arrange all the vegetables, eggs and sauces on a serving platter. Garnish with fresh herbs and serve with coarse salt for sprinkling.

COOK'S TIP

Keep any leftover sauces for serving with salads. The tapenade is also delicious tossed with pasta or spread on warm toast.

Broiled Vegetable Terrine

A colorful layered terrine, using vegetables associated with the Mediterranean.

2 large red bell peppers, quartered, cored and seeded
2 large yellow bell peppers, quartered, cored and seeded
1 large eggplant, sliced lengthwise
2 large zucchini, sliced lengthwise
6 tablespoons olive oil
1 large red onion, thinly sliced
½ cup raisins
1 tablespoon tomato paste
1 tablespoon red wine vinegar
1⅔ cups tomato juice
2 tablespoons powdered gelatin
fresh basil leaves, to garnish

For the dressing
6 tablespoons extra virgin olive oil
2 tablespoons red wine vinegar
salt and ground black pepper

Serves 6

1 Place the prepared red and yellow peppers skin side up under a hot broiler and cook until the skins are blackened. Transfer to a bowl and cover with a plate. Let cool.

2 Arrange the eggplant and zucchini slices on separate baking sheets. Brush them with a little oil and cook under the broiler, turning occasionally, until tender and golden.

3 Heat the remaining olive oil in a frying pan and add the sliced onion, raisins, tomato paste and red wine vinegar. Cook gently until soft and syrupy. Let the mixture cool in the frying pan.

4 Line a 7½-cup terrine with plastic wrap (it helps to oil the terrine lightly first), leaving a little hanging over the sides.

5 Pour half the tomato juice into a saucepan and sprinkle with the gelatin. Dissolve gently over low heat, stirring.

6 Place a layer of red peppers in the bottom of the terrine and pour in enough of the tomato juice with gelatin to cover. Continue layering the eggplant, zucchini, yellow peppers and onion mixture, finishing with another layer of red peppers. Pour tomato juice over each layer of vegetables.

7 Add the remaining tomato juice to any left in the pan, and pour into the terrine. Give it a sharp tap, to disperse the juice. Cover the terrine and chill until set.

8 To make the dressing, whisk together the oil and vinegar and season with salt and pepper. Turn out the terrine and remove the plastic wrap. Serve in thick slices, drizzled with dressing. Garnish with basil leaves.

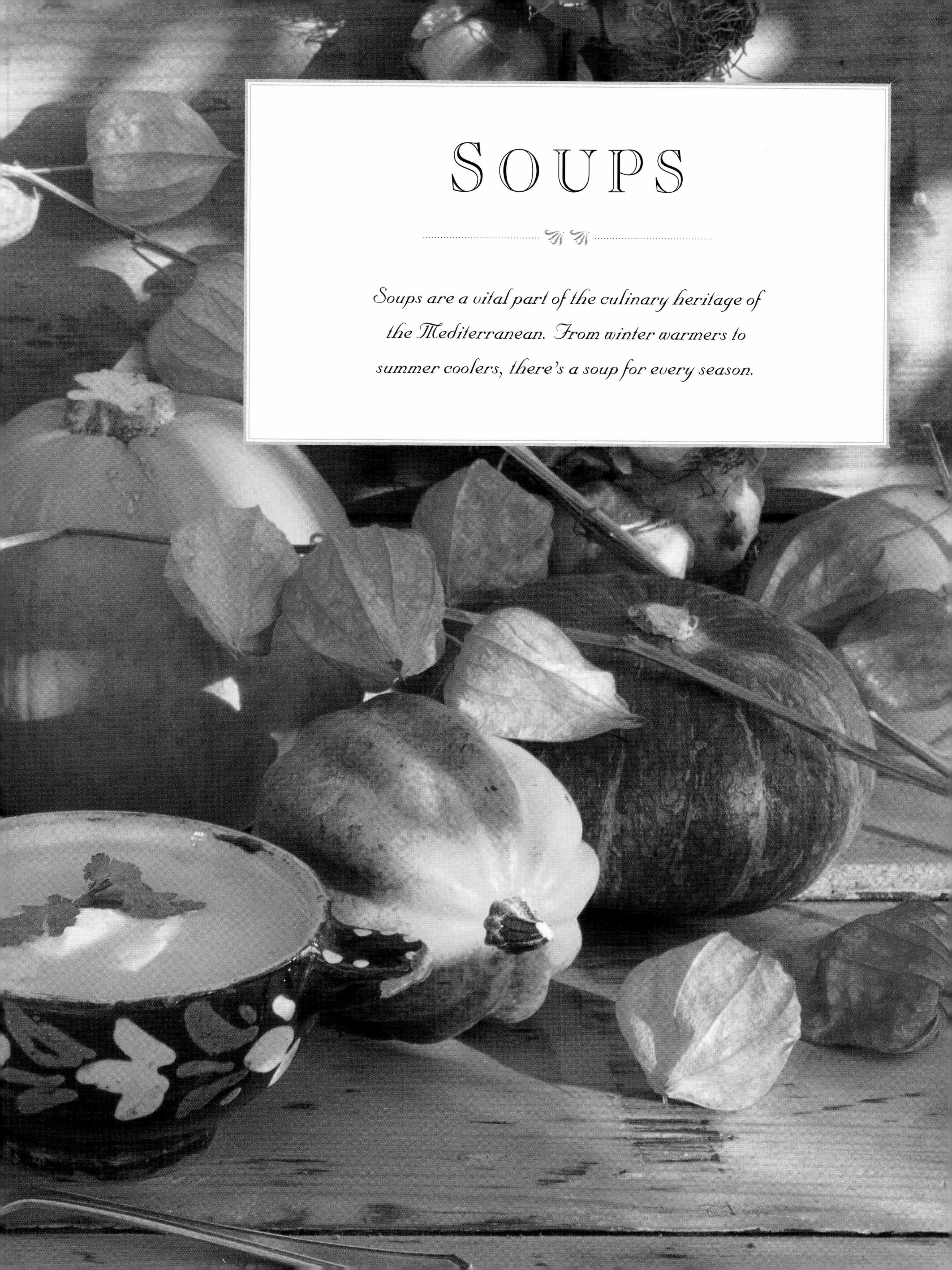

SOUPS

Soups are a vital part of the culinary heritage of the Mediterranean. From winter warmers to summer coolers, there's a soup for every season.

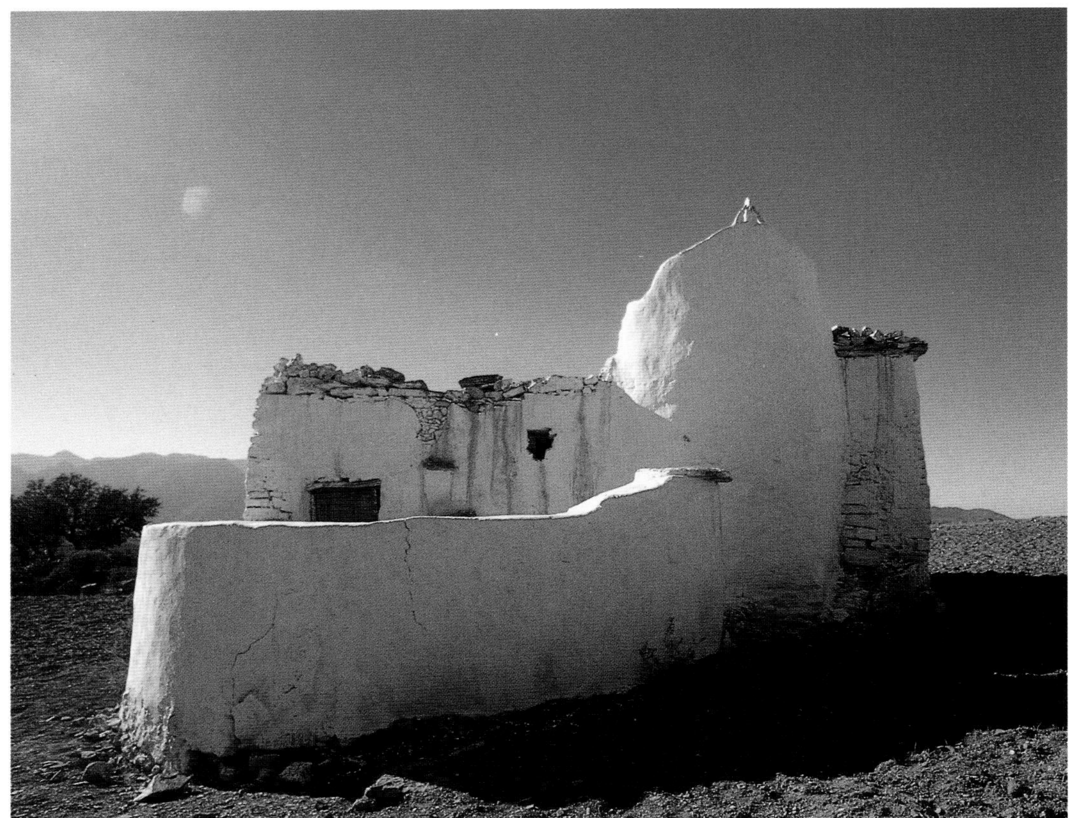

LEFT: In Morocco the nights can be bitterly cold, and a bowl of hot, spicy soup is very welcome.

BELOW: In autumn, when Majorca's almond trees are heavy with the delicious nuts, farmworkers spread nets on the ground and use long poles to knock them down. The reward for their labors is a delicately flavored soup.

Soups have long been an important part of the Mediterranean diet. In the past, when a lot of the countries were poverty-stricken, soup constituted a meal for many. These broths were made with dried beans, peas and lentils, particularly during the cold winter months. Eaten with plenty of bread, they were filling and provided nourishment. Fresh vegetables were added in season, and sometimes eggs. Many of these soups, therefore, were extremely simple. Some of the recipes that exist today have been passed down through the generations, only to be given new life, and new status, with the rising popularity of "peasant food" in restaurants and cookbooks. These are unfussy recipes, which rely for their success on the quality of the ingredients. Take garlic soup, for example, which is made in various ways throughout Spain and France; in its simplest form, it is nothing but garlic, water and seasoning, but with the best garlic, these basic ingredients are transformed into a delicious and fragrant liquor. This basic method is applied to many vegetables, with the water sometimes replaced with a meat stock, and the mixture sometimes put through a strainer, to produce a smooth soup.

Pumpkins, Jerusalem artichokes, tomatoes, bell peppers, asparagus and spinach are just a few of the many varieties of vegetables used to make soup.

Soups containing meat are usually hearty, combined as they are with pulses such as lentils or chickpeas, or potatoes, rice or pasta. In the Middle East, beef and lamb are used, and soups are seasoned with spices and herbs. There are special feast day soups, and soups to eat after sunset during the fast of Ramadan. However, the more typical Mediterranean soup is based on vegetables, beans,

ABOVE: Dawn in Corfu, and a fisherman prepares to head out to sea.

and of course, fish and shellfish. Wonderful fish soups come in numerous different guises; the now famous, and often poorly imitated, bouillabaisse is a "stew" of various varieties of fish and seafood native to the coast of the south of France. The dish originated in the port of Marseilles. Again, these soups serve as complete meals, sometimes with the fish and broth offered separately, accompanied by bread or toasted croutons.

Every country and coastal region has its own specialty, and the soup will never be quite the same, the ingredients depending on the fishermen's catch that day. Many of the recipes were originated by the fishermen themselves, who cooked them on their boats, using fish that they couldn't sell in the market, because it had no commercial value. Today, with a wide choice of fish available in fish stores and supermarkets, it is possible to re-create many of these wonderful dishes at home.

Chilled soups come from the south of Spain, where gazpacho is extremely popular—this is a delicious and refreshing mixture of raw tomatoes, bell peppers and cucumbers, which makes the perfect lunch for a hot summer day. Again, there are variations on this classic recipe, with such diverse ingredients as almonds and grapes. Cold soups are also featured in the Middle East—these are yogurt-based, usually mixed with cucumber and garlic, spiked with mint.

Tourists who travel to the Mediterranean seldom sample more than a few of the many different soups available, but it is worth investigating that delicious smell wafting from a restaurant kitchen, or asking the name of the delectable-looking soup that is being enjoyed at the next table.

Changing at the whim of the cook, or to take best advantage of the finest market produce, Mediterranean soups are certainly a cause for celebration.

BOUILLABAISSE

Perhaps the most famous of all Mediterranean fish soups, this dish, originating in Marseilles in the south of France, is a rich and colorful mixture of fish and shellfish, flavored with tomatoes, saffron and orange.

3–3½ pounds mixed fish and raw shellfish, such as red mullet, porgy, monkfish, red snapper, whiting, large shrimp and clams
8 ounces ripe tomatoes
pinch of saffron strands
6 tablespoons olive oil
1 onion, sliced
1 leek, sliced
1 celery stalk, sliced
2 garlic cloves, crushed
1 bouquet garni
1 strip pared orange zest
½ teaspoon fennel seeds
1 tablespoon tomato paste
2 teaspoons Pernod
4–6 thick slices French bread
3 tablespoons chopped fresh parsley
salt and ground black pepper

SERVES 4–6

1 Remove the heads, tails and fins from the fish and put them in a large pan with about 5 cups water. Bring to a boil and simmer for 15 minutes. Strain, reserving the liquid.

2 Cut the fish into large chunks. Leave the shellfish in their shells. Scald the tomatoes, then drain and refresh in cold water. Peel and coarsely chop them. Soak the saffron in 1–2 tablespoons hot water.

3 Heat the oil in a large pan, add the onion, leek and celery and cook until softened. Add the garlic, bouquet garni, orange zest, fennel seeds and tomatoes, then stir in the saffron and liquid and the fish stock. Season with salt and pepper, then bring to a boil and simmer for 30–40 minutes.

4 Add the shellfish and boil for about 6 minutes. Add the fish and cook for another 6–8 minutes, until it flakes easily.

5 Using a slotted spoon, transfer the fish to a warmed serving platter. Keep the liquid boiling, to allow the oil to emulsify with the broth. Add the tomato paste and Pernod, then check the seasoning. To serve, place a slice of French bread in each soup bowl, pour the broth on top and serve the fish and shellfish separately, sprinkled with the parsley.

Chilled Almond Soup

Unless you want to spend time pounding the ingredients for this dish by hand, a food processor is essential. Then you'll find that this Spanish soup is very simple to make and refreshing to eat on a hot day.

2 slices fresh white bread
1 cup blanched almonds
2 garlic cloves, sliced
5 tablespoons olive oil
1½ tablespoons sherry vinegar
salt and ground black pepper
toasted sliced almonds and seedless green and black grapes, halved and peeled, to garnish

Serves 6

1. Break the bread into a bowl and pour ⅔ cup cold water over it. Let sit for 5 minutes.

2. Put the blanched almonds and garlic in a blender or food processor and process until very finely ground. Blend in the soaked bread.

3. Gradually add the olive oil until the mixture forms a smooth paste. Add the sherry vinegar, then 2½ cups cold water, and process until smooth.

4. Transfer to a bowl and season with salt and pepper, adding a little more water if the soup is very thick. Chill for at least 2–3 hours.

5. Ladle the soup into bowls and sprinkle with the toasted almonds and peeled grapes.

GAZPACHO

There are many versions of this refreshingly chilled, pungent soup from southern Spain. All contain an intense blend of tomatoes, peppers, cucumber and garlic, perfect on a hot summer's evening.

2 pounds ripe tomatoes
1 cucumber
2 red bell peppers, seeded and coarsely chopped
2 garlic cloves, crushed
3 cups fresh white bread crumbs
2 tablespoons white wine vinegar
2 tablespoons sun-dried tomato paste
6 tablespoons olive oil
salt and ground black pepper

To finish
1 slice white bread, crust removed and cut into cubes
2 tablespoons olive oil
6–12 ice cubes
small bowl of mixed chopped garnishes, such as tomato, cucumber, red onion, hard-boiled egg and flat-leaf parsley or tarragon leaves

Serves 6

1 Plunge the tomatoes into boiling water for 30 seconds, then refresh in cold water. Peel away the skins and quarter. Peel and coarsely chop the cucumber. Mix the tomatoes and cucumber in a bowl with the peppers, garlic, bread crumbs, vinegar, tomato paste and olive oil and season lightly with salt and pepper.

2 Process half the mixture in a blender or food processor until fairly smooth. Process the remaining mixture and combine with the first.

3 Check the seasoning and add a little cold water if the soup is too thick. Chill for several hours.

4 To finish, fry the bread in the oil until golden. Spoon the soup into bowls, adding one or two ice cubes to each. Serve accompanied by the croutons and garnishes.

Cook's Tip
The sun-dried tomato paste has been added to accentuate the flavor of the tomatoes. You might not need this if you use a really flavorful variety.

SPICED MUSSEL SOUP

Chunky and colorful, this Turkish fish soup is like a chowder in its consistency. It's flavored with harissa, a spicy paste more familiar in North African cooking.

3–3½ pounds fresh mussels
⅔ cup white wine
3 tomatoes
2 tablespoons olive oil
1 onion, finely chopped
2 garlic cloves, crushed
2 celery stalks, thinly sliced
bunch of scallions, thinly sliced
1 potato, diced
1½ teaspoons harissa
3 tablespoons chopped fresh parsley
ground black pepper
thick yogurt, to serve (optional)

SERVES 6

1. Scrub the mussels, discarding any damaged ones or any open ones that do not close when tapped with a knife.

2. Bring the wine to a boil in a large saucepan. Add the mussels and cover with a lid. Cook for 4–5 minutes, until the mussels have opened wide. Discard any mussels that remain closed. Drain the mussels, reserving the cooking liquid. Reserve a few mussels in their shells for garnish and shell the rest.

3. Peel the tomatoes and dice them. Heat the oil in a pan and sauté the onion, garlic, celery and scallions for 5 minutes.

4. Add the shelled mussels, reserved liquid, potato, harissa and tomatoes. Bring just to a boil, reduce the heat and cover. Simmer gently for 25 minutes or until the potatoes are breaking up.

5. Stir in the parsley and pepper and add the reserved mussels. Heat through for 1 minute. Serve hot, with a spoonful of yogurt, if desired.

GREEN LENTIL SOUP

Lentil soup is an eastern Mediterranean classic, varying in its spiciness according to region. Red or puy lentils make equally good substitutes for the green lentils used here.

1 cup green lentils
5 tablespoons olive oil
3 onions, finely chopped
2 garlic cloves, thinly sliced
2 teaspoons cumin seeds, crushed
¼ teaspoon ground turmeric
2½ cups chicken or vegetable stock
salt and ground black pepper
2 tablespoons coarsely chopped
chopped cilantro

SERVES 4–6

1. Put the lentils in a saucepan and cover with cold water. Bring to a boil and boil rapidly for 10 minutes. Drain.

2. Heat 2 tablespoons of the oil in a pan and sauté two-thirds of the chopped onions with the garlic, cumin and turmeric for 3 minutes, stirring. Add the lentils, stock and 2½ cups water. Bring to a boil, reduce the heat, cover and simmer gently for 30 minutes, until the lentils are soft.

3. Sauté the remaining onion in the remaining oil until golden.

4. Use a potato masher to lightly mash the lentils and make the soup pulpy. Reheat gently and season with salt and pepper to taste. Pour the soup into bowls. Stir the chopped cilantro into the sautéed onion and sprinkle on the soup. Serve with warm bread.

MOROCCAN HARIRA

This is a hearty meat and vegetable soup, eaten during the month of Ramadan, when the Muslim population fasts between sunrise and sunset.

1 pound ripe tomatoes
½ pound lamb, cut into ½-inch pieces
½ teaspoon ground turmeric
½ teaspoon ground cinnamon
2 tablespoons butter
4 tablespoons chopped cilantro
2 tablespoons chopped fresh parsley
1 onion, chopped
¼ cup split red lentils
½ cup dried chickpeas, soaked overnight
4 baby onions or small shallots, peeled
¼ cup soup noodles
salt and ground black pepper
chopped fresh cilantro, lemon slices and ground cinnamon, to garnish

SERVES 4

1 Plunge the tomatoes into boiling water for 30 seconds, then refresh in cold water. Peel away the skins. Cut into quarters and remove the seeds. Chop coarsely.

2 Put the lamb, turmeric, cinnamon, butter, cilantro, parsley and onion into a large pan, and cook over medium heat, stirring, for 5 minutes. Add the chopped tomatoes and continue to cook for 10 minutes.

3 Rinse the lentils under running water and add to the pan with the drained chickpeas and 2½ cups water. Season with salt and pepper. Bring to a boil, cover, and simmer gently for 1½ hours.

4 Add the onions and cook for another 30 minutes. Add the noodles 5 minutes before the end of the cooking time. Garnish with the cilantro, lemon slices and cinnamon.

RIBOLLITA

Ribollita is a lot like minestrone. In Italy it is traditionally served ladled over bread and a rich green vegetable, although you could omit this for a lighter version.

3 tablespoons olive oil
2 onions, chopped
2 carrots, sliced
4 garlic cloves, crushed
2 celery stalks, thinly sliced
1 fennel bulb, trimmed and chopped
2 large zucchini, thinly sliced
14-ounce can chopped tomatoes
2 tablespoons homemade or store-bought pesto
3¾ cups vegetable stock
14-ounce can navy or pinto beans, drained
salt and ground black pepper

TO FINISH
1 pound young spinach
1 tablespoon extra virgin olive oil, plus extra for drizzling
6–8 slices crusty white bread
Parmesan cheese shavings

SERVES 6–8

VARIATION
Use other dark greens, such as chard or cabbage, instead of the spinach; shred and cook until tender.

1 Heat the oil in a large saucepan. Add the onions, carrots, garlic, celery and fennel and sauté gently for 10 minutes. Add the zucchini and sauté for another 2 minutes.

2 Add the chopped tomatoes, pesto, stock and beans and bring to a boil. Reduce the heat, cover and simmer gently for 25–30 minutes, until the vegetables are completely tender. Season with salt and pepper to taste.

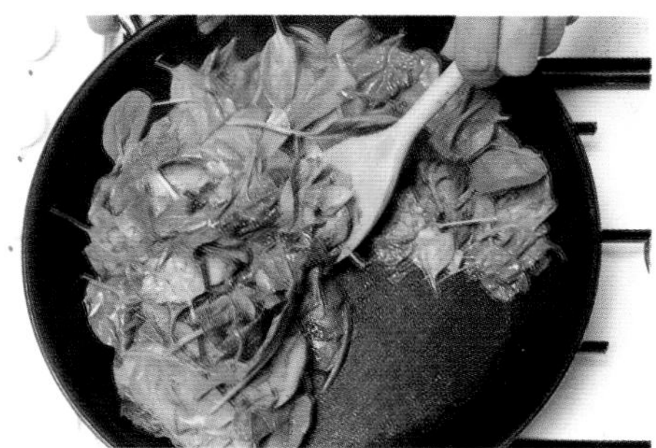

3 To serve, sauté the spinach in the oil for 2 minutes or until wilted. Spoon over the bread in soup bowls, then ladle the soup over the spinach. Serve with extra olive oil for drizzling onto the soup and Parmesan cheese to sprinkle on top.

SEAFOOD SOUP WITH ROUILLE

This is a chunky, aromatic mixed fish soup from France, flavored with plenty of saffron and herbs. Rouille, a fiery hot paste, is served separately for diners to swirl into their soup to flavor.

3 snapper or red mullet, scaled and gutted
12 large shrimp
1½ pounds white fish, such as cod, haddock, halibut or monkfish
½ pound fresh mussels
1 onion, quartered
1 teaspoon saffron strands
5 tablespoons olive oil
1 fennel bulb, coarsely chopped
4 garlic cloves, crushed
3 strips pared orange zest
4 thyme sprigs
1½ pounds tomatoes or 14-ounce can chopped tomatoes
2 tablespoons sun-dried tomato paste
3 bay leaves
salt and ground black pepper

FOR THE ROUILLE
1 red bell pepper, seeded and coarsely chopped
1 red chile, seeded and sliced
2 garlic cloves, chopped
5 tablespoons olive oil
¼ cup fresh bread crumbs

SERVES 6

1 To make the rouille, process the pepper, chile, garlic, oil and bread crumbs in a blender or food processor until smooth. Transfer to a serving dish and chill.

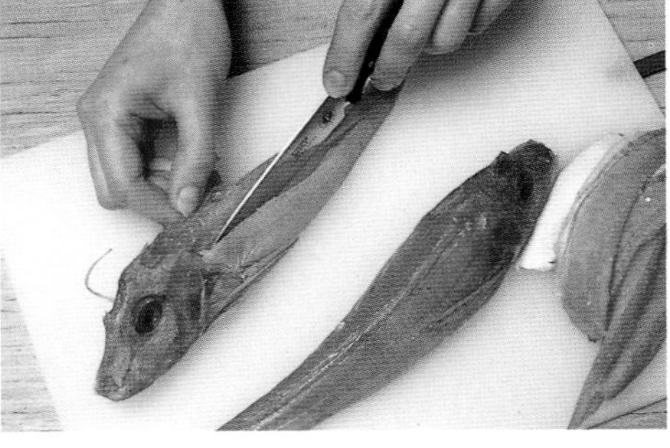

2 Fillet the snapper or mullet by cutting the flesh from either side of the backbone, reserving the heads and bones. Cut the fillets into small chunks. Shell half the shrimp and reserve the trimmings for the stock. Skin the white fish, discarding any bones, and cut into chunks. Thoroughly scrub the mussels, discarding any that are damaged or any open ones that do not close when tapped with a knife.

3 Put the fish heads and bones and shrimp trimmings in a large saucepan with the onion and about 5 cups water. Bring to a boil, then simmer gently for 30 minutes. Cool slightly and strain.

4 Soak the saffron in 1 tablespoon boiling water. Heat about 2 tablespoons of the oil in a large sauté pan or saucepan. Add the snapper or mullet and white fish and sauté over high heat for 1 minute. Drain.

5 Heat the remaining oil and sauté the fennel, garlic, orange zest and thyme until beginning to color. Make up the strained stock to about 5 cups with water.

COOK'S TIP
To save time, order the fish and ask the fish seller to fillet the snapper or mullet for you.

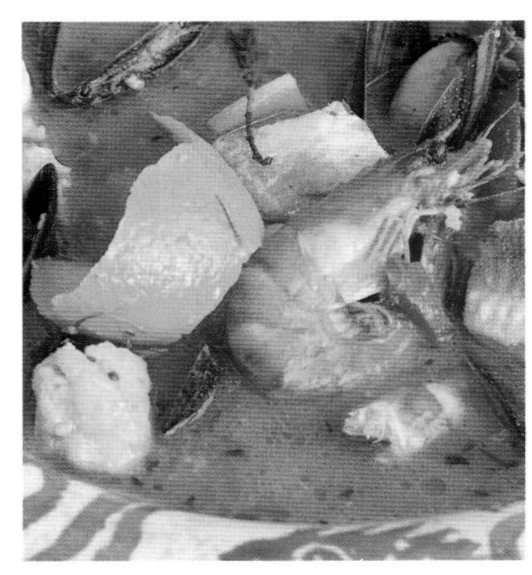

6 If using fresh tomatoes, plunge them into boiling water for 30 seconds, then refresh in cold water. Peel and chop. Add the stock to the pan with the saffron, tomatoes, tomato paste and bay leaves. Season, bring almost to a boil, then simmer gently, covered, for 20 minutes.

7 Stir in the snapper or mullet, white fish and shrimp and add the mussels. Cover the pan and cook for 3–4 minutes. Discard any mussels that do not open. Serve the soup hot with the rouille.

Spicy Pumpkin Soup

Pumpkin is popular all over the Mediterranean, and it's an important ingredient in Middle Eastern cooking, by which this soup is inspired. Ginger and cumin give the soup its spicy flavor.

2 pounds pumpkin, peeled and seeds removed
2 tablespoons olive oil
2 leeks, trimmed and sliced
1 garlic clove, crushed
1 teaspoon ground ginger
1 teaspoon ground cumin
3¾ cups chicken stock
salt and ground black pepper
cilantro leaves, to garnish
4 tablespoons plain yogurt, to serve

Serves 4

1 Cut the pumpkin into chunks. Heat the oil in a large pan and add the leeks and garlic. Cook gently until softened.

2 Add the ginger and cumin and cook, stirring, for another minute. Add the pumpkin and the chicken stock and season with salt and pepper. Bring to a boil and simmer for 30 minutes, until the pumpkin is tender. Process the soup, in batches if necessary, in a blender or food processor.

3 Reheat the soup and serve in warmed individual bowls, with a swirl of yogurt and a garnish of cilantro leaves.

MIDDLE EASTERN YOGURT AND CUCUMBER SOUP

Yogurt is used extensively in Middle Eastern cooking, and it is usually made at home. Sometimes it is added at the end of cooking a dish, so that it won't curdle, but in this cold soup the yogurt is one of the basic ingredients.

1 large cucumber, peeled
1¼ cups light cream
⅔ cup plain yogurt
2 garlic cloves, crushed
2 tablespoons white wine vinegar
1 tablespoon chopped fresh mint
salt and ground black pepper
sprigs of mint, to garnish

1 Grate the cucumber coarsely. Place in a bowl with the cream, yogurt, garlic, vinegar and mint. Stir well and season to taste.

2 Chill for at least 2 hours before serving. Just before serving, stir the soup again. Pour into individual bowls and garnish with mint sprigs.

PISTOU

A delicious vegetable soup from Nice in the south of France, served with a sun-dried tomato pesto and fresh Parmesan cheese.

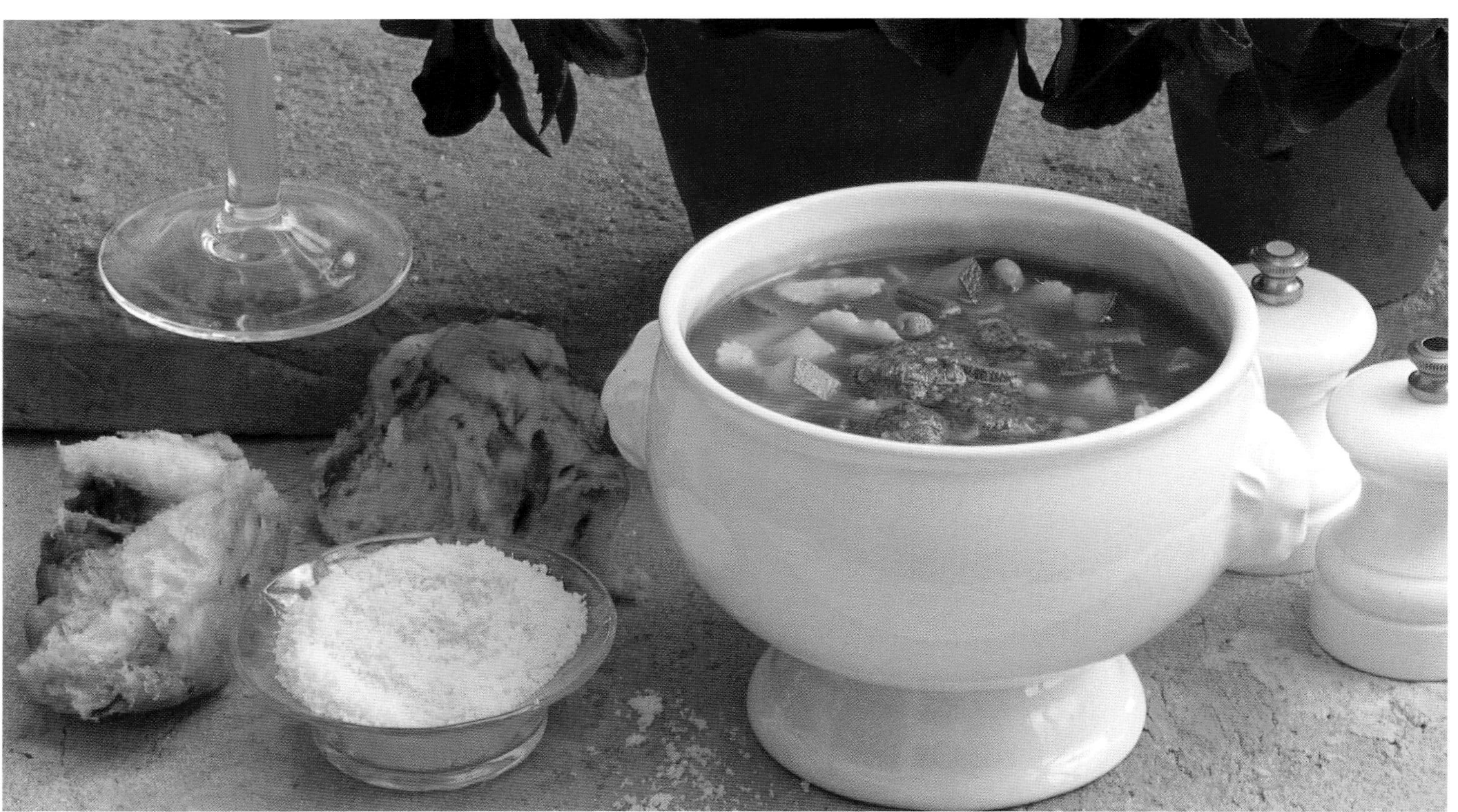

1 zucchini, diced
1 small potato, diced
1 shallot, chopped
1 carrot, diced
8-ounce can chopped tomatoes
5 cups vegetable stock
2 ounces green beans, cut into ½-inch pieces
½ cup frozen tiny peas
½ cup small pasta shapes
4–6 tablespoons homemade or bought pesto
1 tablespoon sun-dried tomato paste
salt and ground black pepper
freshly grated Parmesan cheese, to serve

SERVES 4–6

1. Place the zucchini, potato, shallot, carrot and tomatoes in a large pan. Add the vegetable stock and season with salt and pepper. Bring to a boil, then cover and simmer for 20 minutes.

2. Add the green beans, peas and pasta. Cook for another 10 minutes, until the pasta is tender. Adjust the seasoning.

3. Ladle the soup into individual bowls. Combine the pesto and sun-dried tomato paste and stir a spoonful into each serving. Serve with grated Parmesan cheese to sprinkle into each bowl.

AVGOLEMONO

he most popular of Greek soups. The name means egg and lemon, the two important ingredients, which ce a light, nourishing soup. Orzo is a Greek pasta shaped like rice, but you can use any small shape.

7¹ avorful chicken stock
cup orzo pasta
3 eggs
juice of 1 large lemon
salt and ground black pepper
lemon slices, to garnish

SERVES 4–6

1 Pour the stock into a large pan and bring to a boil. Add the pasta and cook for 5 minutes.

2 Beat the eggs until frothy, then add the lemon juice and a tablespoon of cold water. Slowly stir in a ladleful of the hot chicken stock, then add one or two more. Return this mixture to the pan, off the heat, and stir well. Season with salt and pepper and serve immediately, garnished with lemon slices. (Do not let the soup boil once the eggs have been added or it will curdle.)

GALICIAN BROTH

This delicious main-dish soup is very similar to the warming, chunky meat and potato broths of cooler climates. For extra color, a few onion skins can be added when cooking the smoked ham, but remember to remove them before serving.

1 pound smoked ham, in one piece
2 bay leaves
2 onions, sliced
2 teaspoons paprika
1½ pounds potatoes, cut into large chunks
½ pound collard greens
15-ounce can navy beans, drained
salt and ground black pepper

SERVES 4

1 Soak the smoked ham overnight in cold water. Drain and put in a large saucepan with the bay leaves and sliced onions. Pour in 6¼ cups cold water.

2 Bring to a boil, then reduce the heat and simmer very gently for about 1½ hours, until the meat is tender. Keep an eye on the pan to make sure it doesn't boil over.

3 Drain the meat, reserving the cooking liquid, and let cool slightly. Discard the skin and any excess fat from the meat and cut into small chunks. Return to the pan with the paprika and potatoes. Cover and simmer gently for 20 minutes.

4 Cut away the cores from the greens. Roll up the leaves and cut into thin shreds. Add to the pan with the beans and simmer for about 10 minutes. Season with salt and pepper to taste and serve hot.

COOK'S TIP

Ham hocks can be used instead of the smoked ham. The bones will give the juices a delicious flavor.

Fresh Tomato Soup

Intensely flavored sun-ripened tomatoes need little embellishment in this fresh-tasting soup. If you buy from the supermarket, choose the ripest-looking ones and add the amount of sugar and vinegar necessary, depending on their natural sweetness. On a hot day, this Italian soup is also delicious chilled.

3–3½ pounds ripe tomatoes
1⅔ cups flavorful chicken or vegetable stock
3 tablespoons sun-dried tomato paste
2–3 tablespoons balsamic vinegar
2–3 teaspoons sugar
small handful basil leaves
salt and ground black pepper
basil leaves, to garnish
toasted cheese croutons and sour cream, to serve

Serves 6

1 Plunge the tomatoes into boiling water for 30 seconds, then refresh in cold water. Peel away the skins and quarter the tomatoes. Put them in a large saucepan and pour in the chicken or vegetable stock. Bring just to a boil, reduce the heat, cover and simmer gently for 10 minutes, until the tomatoes are soft.

2 Stir in the tomato paste, vinegar, sugar and basil. Season with salt and pepper, then cook gently, stirring, for 2 minutes. Process the soup in a blender or food processor, then return to the pan and reheat gently. Serve in bowls topped with one or two toasted cheese croutons and a spoonful of sour cream, garnished with basil leaves.

CHILLED TOMATO AND SWEET PEPPER SOUP

A recipe inspired by the Spanish gazpacho, the difference being that this soup is cooked first, and then chilled.

2 red bell peppers, halved, cored and seeded
3 tablespoons olive oil
1 onion, finely chopped
2 garlic cloves, crushed
1½ pounds ripe tomatoes
⅔ cup red wine
2½ cups chicken stock
salt and ground black pepper
snipped fresh chives, to garnish

FOR THE CROUTONS
2 slices white bread, crusts removed
4 tablespoons olive oil

SERVES 4

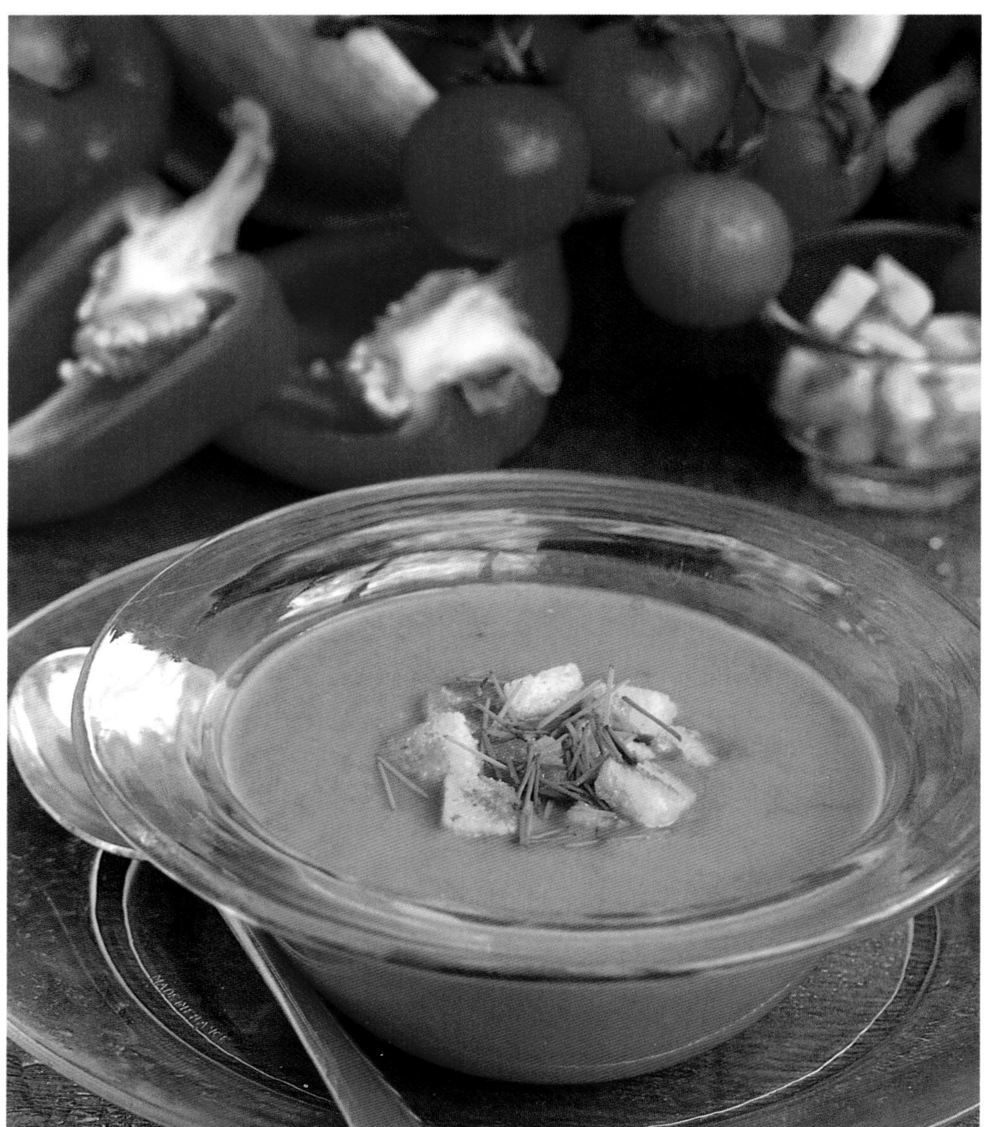

1 Cut each pepper half into quarters. Place skin side up on a broiler rack and cook until the skins have charred. Transfer to a bowl and cover with a plate.

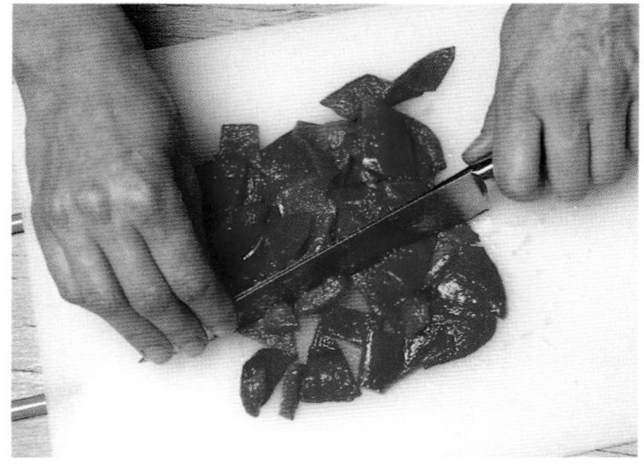

2 Heat the oil in a large pan. Add the onion and garlic and cook until soft. Meanwhile, remove the skin from the peppers and coarsely chop them. Cut the tomatoes into chunks.

3 Add the peppers and tomatoes to the pan, then cover and cook gently for 10 minutes. Add the wine and cook for another 5 minutes, then add the stock and salt and pepper and continue to simmer for 20 minutes.

4 To make the croutons, cut the bread into cubes. Heat the oil in a small frying pan, add the bread and sauté until golden. Drain on paper towels and store in an airtight box.

5 Process the soup in a blender or food processor until smooth. Pour into a clean glass or ceramic bowl and let cool thoroughly before chilling in the refrigerator for at least 3 hours. When the soup is cold, season to taste.

6 Serve the soup in bowls, topped with the croutons and garnished with snipped chives.

SPANISH GARLIC SOUP

This is a simple and satisfying soup, made with one of the most popular ingredients in the Mediterranean—garlic!

2 tablespoons olive oil
4 large garlic cloves, peeled
4 slices French bread, ¼ inch thick
1 tablespoon paprika
4 cups beef stock
¼ teaspoon ground cumin
pinch of saffron strands
4 eggs
salt and ground black pepper
chopped fresh parsley, to garnish

SERVES 4

1 Preheat the oven to 450°F. Heat the oil in a large pan. Add the whole garlic cloves and cook for a minute or two, until golden. Remove and set aside. Sauté the bread in the oil until golden, then set aside.

2 Add the paprika to the pan and sauté for a few seconds. Stir in the beef stock, cumin and saffron, then add the reserved garlic, crushing the cloves with the back of a wooden spoon. Season with salt and pepper, then cook for about 5 minutes.

3 Ladle the soup into four ovenproof bowls and break an egg into each. Set a slice of bread on top of each egg and place in the oven for 3–4 minutes, until the eggs are set. Sprinkle with parsley and serve immediately.

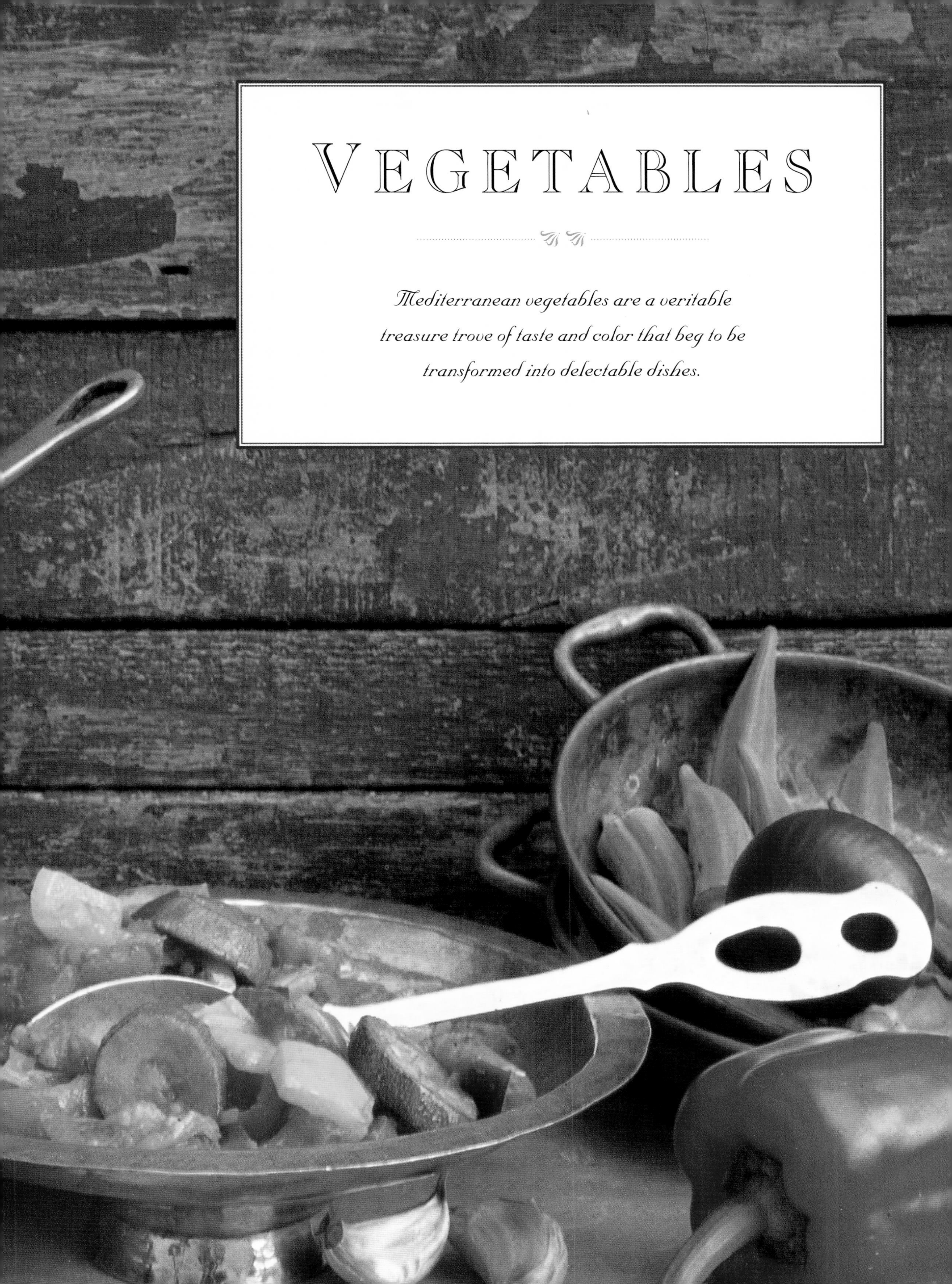

Vegetables

Mediterranean vegetables are a veritable treasure trove of taste and color that beg to be transformed into delectable dishes.

A Mediterranean street market is a fascinating vision of color and photo opportunities. The wonderful array of fruit and vegetable stalls in particular gives many vacationers the urge to swap their hotel rooms for a kitchen in which to cook a feast of sweet, juicy local produce. Mediterranean vegetables have an inviting irregularity about them. Uneven colorings, bumpy skins and asymmetrical shapes are a sure indication that the flesh inside will be full of flavor, a far cry from the mass-produced, artificially grown produce of colder climes. The dishes cooked using them are a joy to eat, and even the simplest tossed salad of tomatoes and greens, sprinkled with olive oil and seasoning, is worthy of serving solo—a meal in itself.

All around the Mediterranean, vegetables are the basis of everyday meals. This is due both to the expense of meat and to the religious obligations of fasting before the many festive occasions each year. This austerity has led to the development of many imaginative cooking skills. Deep-fried, roasted, baked, stuffed, marinated, broiled, steamed, added to pies, tarts, omelets, stews and stuffings: Vegetables are very versatile.

Below: At a finca—or farm—in Andalusia, vegetables grow alongside the grape-drying beds.

RIGHT: Tomatoes, chiles, potatoes and braids of garlic are just some of the vegetables on sale at this market in southern Turkey.

BELOW: A golden harvest: Pumpkins make delicious soups, pies and casseroles.

In France and Italy, vegetable fritters of zucchini or eggplant, deep-fried in a light crisp batter, make a very enjoyable dish, often served with a ripe tomato sauce or garlicky herb dressing. Even the zucchini flowers are battered and fried, making a visual and interesting garnish. Ratatouille, a wonderful stew of lightly cooked vegetables, is traditionally French, although similar recipes stretch across the Mediterranean.

No vegetable is considered too small to bother with; the smallest artichokes, turnips, eggplant and fava beans are put to good use in many dishes.

A stunning variety of mushrooms appears frequently in Italian and French cooking. In these countries, markets are filled with wild varieties in the spring and autumn. The lovely shapes and flavors make interesting risottos and salads and may even be used to flavor pasta. Many mushroom varieties are dried for year-round availability. A small quantity goes a long way and can be used to liven up the flavor of everyday button mushrooms.

Stuffed vegetables are greatly loved in many countries of the Mediterranean, particularly in Turkey, Greece and the Middle East. Tomatoes, eggplant, peppers, zucchini and onions are filled with couscous, rice, herbs, spices, dried fruits, nuts, cheese and sometimes meat. Large leaves like spinach, grape and cabbage are stuffed with interesting ingredients, packed in a pan and gently cooked so as to mingle all the flavors together.

Even the humble potato takes pride of place at the Mediterranean table. The Spanish make a delicious potato salad in which new potatoes are fried to give a crisp crust. Italian gnocchi is a distinctively shaped, puréed and poached potato dish flavored with a variety of herbs, cheese or mild spices.

MARINATED MUSHROOMS

This Spanish recipe makes a nice change from the classic French mushrooms à la Grecque. Make this dish the day before you eat it; the flavor will improve with keeping.

2 tablespoons olive oil
1 small onion, very finely chopped
1 garlic clove, crushed
1 tablespoon tomato paste
¼ cup dry white wine
2 cloves
pinch of saffron strands
½ pound button mushrooms, trimmed
salt and ground black pepper
chopped fresh parsley, to garnish

SERVES 4

1 Heat the oil in a pan. Add the onion and garlic and cook until soft. Stir in the tomato paste, wine, ¼ cup water, cloves and saffron and season with salt and pepper. Bring to a boil, cover and simmer gently for about 45 minutes, adding more water if the mixture becomes too dry.

2 Add the mushrooms to the pan, then cover and simmer for another 5 minutes. Remove from the heat and, still covered, let cool. Chill overnight. Serve cold, sprinkled with chopped parsley.

POTATO AND ONION TORTILLA

One of the signature dishes of Spain, this delicious, thick potato and onion omelet is eaten at all times of the day, hot or cold.

1¼ cups olive oil
6 large potatoes, peeled and sliced
2 Spanish onions, sliced
6 eggs
salt and ground black pepper
cherry tomatoes, halved, to serve

SERVES 4

1 Heat the oil in a large nonstick frying pan. Stir in the potato, onion and a little salt. Cover and cook gently for 20 minutes, until soft.

2 Beat the eggs in a large bowl. Remove the onion and potato from the pan with a slotted spoon and add to the eggs. Season with salt and pepper to taste. Pour off some of the oil, leaving about 4 tablespoons in the pan. (Reserve the leftover oil for other cooking.) Heat the pan again.

3 When the oil is very hot, pour in the egg mixture. Cook for 2–3 minutes. Cover the pan with a plate and invert the omelet onto it. Slide it back into the pan and cook for 5 more minutes, until golden brown and moist in the middle. Serve in wedges, with the tomatoes.

BROILED EGGPLANT PARCELS

These are delicious little Italian bundles of tomatoes, mozzarella cheese and basil, wrapped in slices of eggplant.

2 large, long eggplant
8 ounces mozzarella cheese
2 plum tomatoes
16 large basil leaves
salt and ground black pepper
2 tablespoons olive oil

FOR THE DRESSING
¼ cup olive oil
1 teaspoon balsamic vinegar
1 tablespoon sun-dried tomato paste
1 tablespoon lemon juice

FOR THE GARNISH
2 tablespoons toasted pine nuts
torn basil leaves

SERVES 4

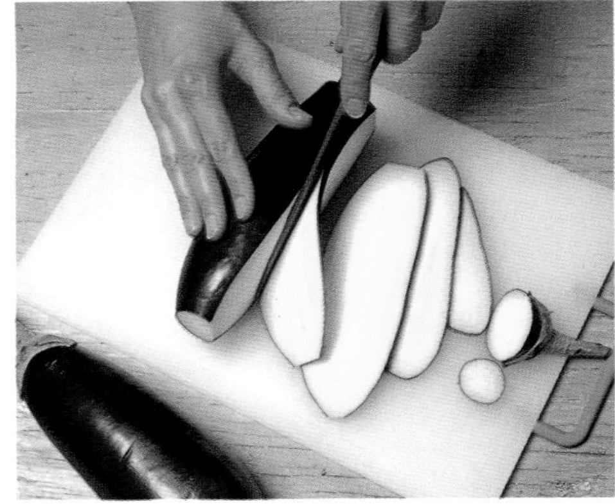

1 Remove the stems from the eggplant and cut the eggplant lengthwise into thin slices—the aim is to have a total of 16 slices, disregarding the first and last slices (each about ¼ inch thick). (If you have a mandoline, it will cut perfect, even slices for you; otherwise use a sharp, long-bladed knife.)

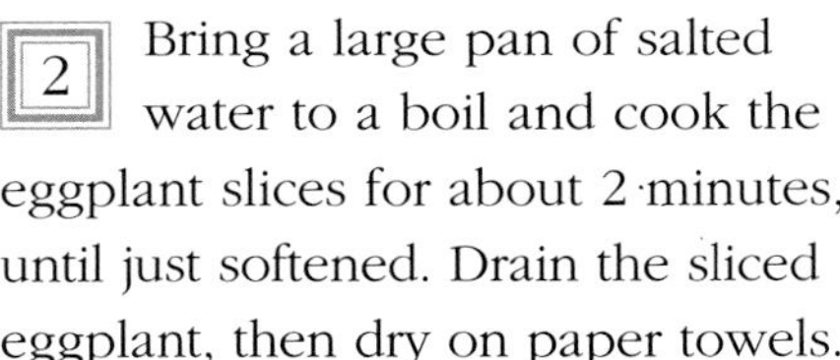

2 Bring a large pan of salted water to a boil and cook the eggplant slices for about 2 minutes, until just softened. Drain the sliced eggplant, then dry on paper towels.

3 Cut the mozzarella cheese into eight slices. Cut each tomato into eight slices, not counting the first and last slices.

4 Take two eggplant slices and place on an ovenproof baking sheet or dish in a cross. Place a slice of tomato in the center, season with salt and pepper, then add a basil leaf, followed by a slice of mozzarella, another basil leaf, a slice of tomato and more seasoning.

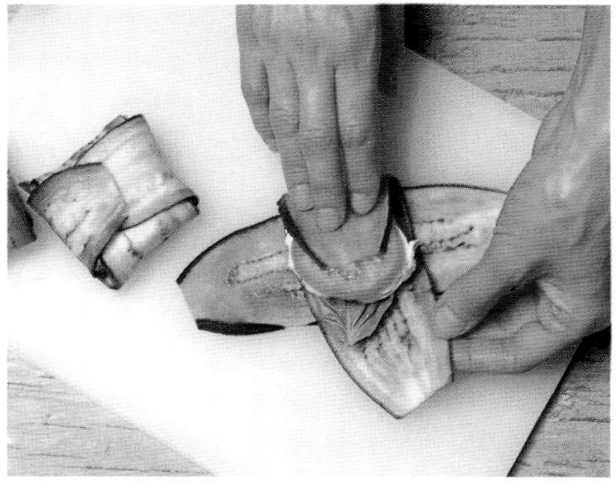

5 Fold the ends of the eggplant slices around the mozzarella and tomato filling to make a neat parcel (*left*). Repeat with the rest of the assembled ingredients to make eight parcels. Chill the parcels for about 20 minutes.

6 To make the tomato dressing, whisk together the olive oil, vinegar, sun-dried tomato paste and lemon juice. Season to taste.

7 Preheat the broiler. Brush the parcels with olive oil and cook for about 5 minutes on each side, until golden. Serve hot, with the dressing, sprinkled with pine nuts and basil.

SPINACH AND RICOTTA GNOCCHI

The success of this Italian dish lies in not overworking the mixture, to achieve delicious, light mouthfuls.

2 pounds fresh spinach
1½ cups ricotta cheese
¼ cup freshly grated
Parmesan cheese, plus extra to serve
3 eggs, beaten
¼ teaspoon grated nutmeg
3–4 tablespoons flour
8 tablespoons butter, melted
salt and ground black pepper

SERVES 4

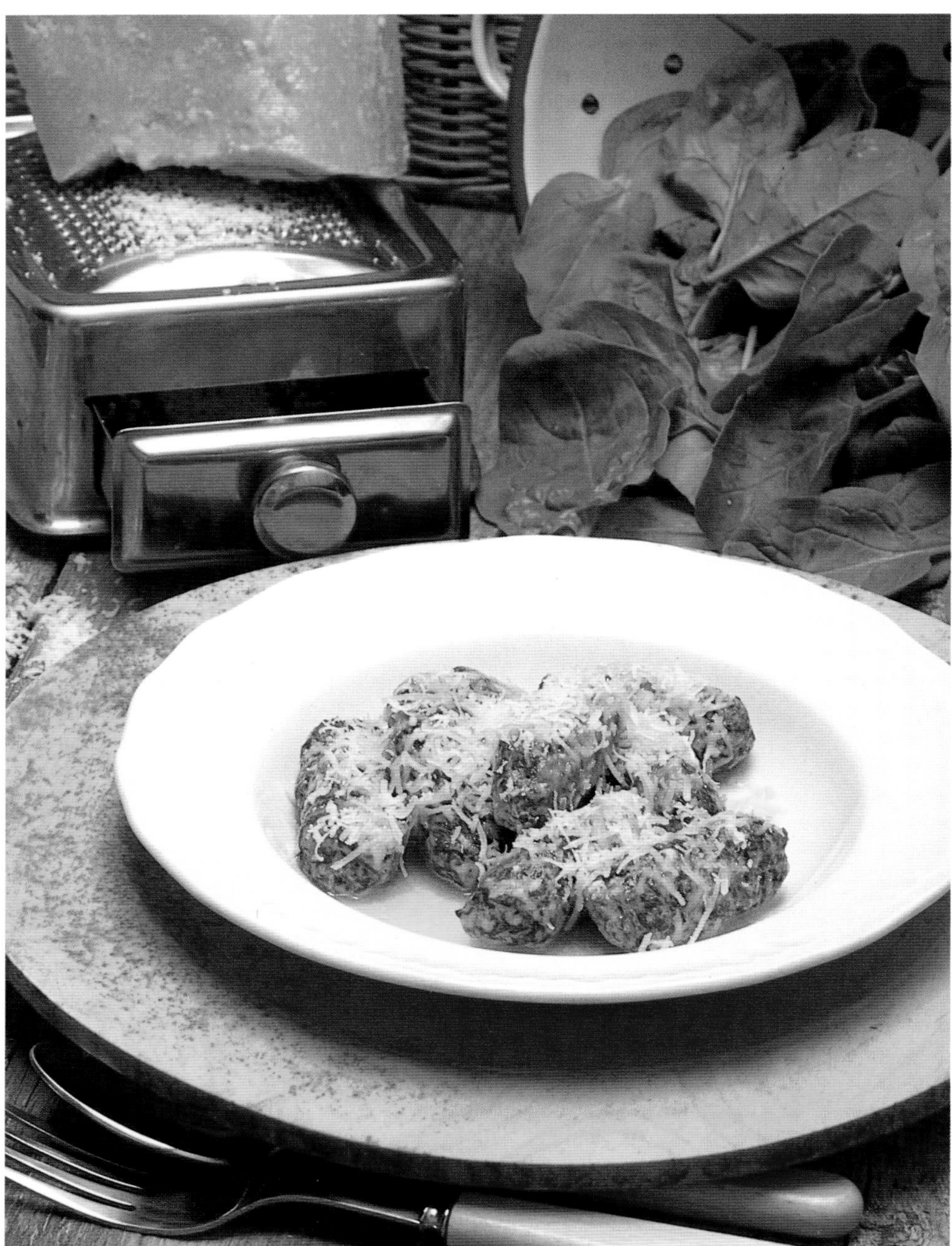

1 Place the spinach in a large pan and cook for 5 minutes, until wilted. Let cool, then squeeze the spinach as dry as possible. Process in a blender or food processor, then transfer to a bowl.

2 Add the ricotta, Parmesan, eggs and nutmeg. Season with salt and pepper and combine. Add enough flour to make the mixture into a soft dough. Using your hands, shape the mixture into 3-inch sausages, then dust lightly with flour.

3 Bring a large pan of salted water to a boil. Gently slide the gnocchi into the water and cook for 1–2 minutes, until they float to the surface. Remove the gnocchi with a slotted spoon and transfer to a warmed dish. Pour the melted butter over them and sprinkle with Parmesan cheese. Serve immediately.

POTATO CAKES

Delicious little fried morsels of potato and Greek feta cheese, flavored with dill and lemon juice.

1¼ pounds potatoes
4 ounces feta cheese
4 scallions, chopped
3 tablespoons chopped fresh dill
1 egg, beaten
1 tablespoon lemon juice
salt and ground black pepper
flour for dredging
3 tablespoons olive oil

SERVES 4

1 Boil the potatoes in their skins in lightly salted water until soft. Drain, then peel while still warm. Place in a bowl and mash. Crumble the feta cheese into the potatoes and add the scallions, dill, egg and lemon juice and season with salt and pepper. (The cheese is salty, so taste before you add salt.) Stir well.

2 Cover the mixture and chill until firm. Divide the mixture into walnut-size balls, then flatten them slightly. Dredge with flour. Heat the oil in a frying pan and fry the cakes until golden brown on each side. Drain on paper towels and serve immediately.

STUFFED TOMATOES AND PEPPERS

Colorful bell peppers and tomatoes make perfect containers for various meat and vegetable stuffings. This rice and herb version uses typically Greek ingredients.

VARIATION

Small eggplant or large zucchini also make good vegetables for stuffing. Halve and scoop out the centers of the vegetables, then oil the vegetable shells and bake for about 15 minutes. Chop the centers, sauté for 2–3 minutes to soften and add to the stuffing mixture. Fill the eggplant or zucchini shells with the stuffing and bake as for the peppers and tomatoes.

2 large ripe tomatoes
1 green bell pepper
1 yellow or orange bell pepper
4 tablespoons olive oil, plus extra for sprinkling
2 onions, chopped
2 garlic cloves, crushed
½ cup blanched almonds, chopped
scant ½ cup long-grain rice, cooked and drained
½ ounce mint, roughly chopped
½ ounce parsley, coarsely chopped
2 tablespoons golden raisins
3 tablespoons ground almonds
salt and ground black pepper
chopped mixed herbs, to garnish

SERVES 4

1 Preheat the oven to 375°F. Cut the tomatoes in half and scoop out the pulp and seeds using a teaspoon. Leave the tomatoes to drain on paper towels with cut sides down. Coarsely chop the tomato pulp and seeds and set aside.

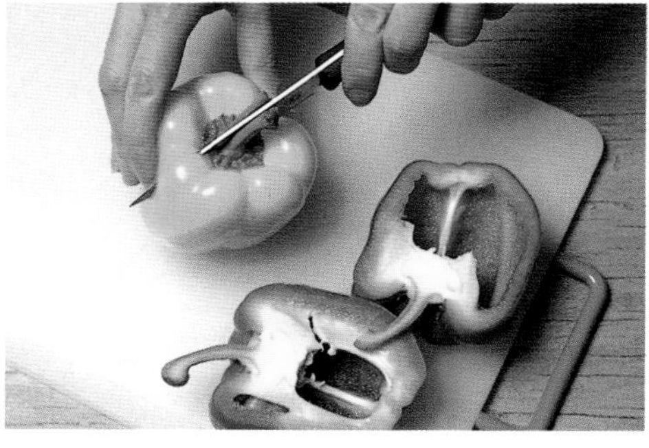

2 Halve the peppers, leaving the cores intact. Scoop out the seeds. Brush the peppers with 1 tablespoon of the oil and bake on a baking sheet for 15 minutes. Place the peppers and tomatoes in a shallow ovenproof dish and season with salt and pepper.

3 Sauté the onions in the remaining oil for 5 minutes. Add the garlic and chopped almonds and sauté for another minute.

4 Remove the pan from the heat and stir in the rice, chopped tomatoes, mint, parsley and golden raisins. Season well with salt and pepper and spoon the mixture into the tomatoes and peppers.

5 Pour ⅔ cup boiling water around the tomatoes and peppers and bake, uncovered, for 20 minutes. Scatter the ground almonds over them and sprinkle with a little extra olive oil. Return to the oven and bake for 20 more minutes, or until turning golden. Serve garnished with fresh herbs.

OKRA WITH CORIANDER AND TOMATOES

Okra is frequently combined with tomatoes and mild spices in various parts of the Mediterranean. Buy okra only if it is soft and velvety, not dry and shriveled.

1 pound tomatoes or 14-ounce can chopped tomatoes
1 pound fresh okra
3 tablespoons olive oil
2 onions, thinly sliced
2 teaspoons coriander seeds, crushed
3 garlic cloves, crushed
½ teaspoon sugar
finely grated zest and juice of 1 lemon
salt and ground black pepper

SERVES 4

1 If using fresh tomatoes, plunge them into boiling water for 30 seconds, then refresh in cold water. Peel off the skins and chop.

2 Trim off any stalks from the okra and keep whole. Heat the oil in a sauté pan and sauté the onions and coriander for 3–4 minutes, until beginning to color.

3 Add the okra and garlic and sauté for 1 minute. Gently stir in the tomatoes and sugar and simmer gently for about 20 minutes, until the okra is tender, stirring once or twice. Stir in the lemon zest and juice and add salt and pepper to taste, adding a little more sugar if necessary. Serve warm or cold.

STUFFED PEPPERS

Couscous is a form of pasta used extensively in the Middle East. It makes a good basis for a stuffing, combined with other ingredients.

6 red bell peppers
2 tablespoons butter
1 onion, finely chopped
1 teaspoon olive oil
½ teaspoon salt
1 cup instant couscous
2 tablespoons raisins
2 tablespoons chopped fresh mint
1 egg yolk
salt and ground black pepper
mint leaves, to garnish

SERVES 4

1 Preheat the oven to 400°F. Carefully slit each pepper and remove the core and seeds. Melt the butter in a small pan and add the onion. Cook until soft.

2 To cook the couscous, bring 1 cup water to a boil. Add the olive oil and the salt, then remove the pan from the heat and add the couscous. Stir and let stand, covered, for about 5 minutes. Stir in the cooked onion, raisins and mint, then season well with salt and pepper. Stir in the egg yolk.

3 Using a teaspoon, fill the peppers with the couscous mixture to only about three-quarters full, as the couscous will swell when cooked further. Place in a lightly oiled ovenproof dish and bake, uncovered, for about 20 minutes, until tender. Serve hot or cold, garnished with the mint leaves.

Zucchini Fritters with Pistou

These delicious fritters are a specialty of southern France. The pistou sauce provides a lovely contrast in flavor, but you could substitute other sauces, like a garlicky tomato sauce or an herb dressing.

For the pistou
½ ounce basil leaves
4 garlic cloves, crushed
1 cup grated Parmesan cheese
finely grated zest of 1 lemon
⅔ cup olive oil

For the fritters
1 pound zucchini, grated
⅔ cup flour
1 egg, separated
1 tablespoon olive oil
oil for shallow-frying
salt and ground black pepper

Serves 4

1. To make the pistou, crush the basil leaves and garlic with a mortar and pestle to make a fairly fine paste. Transfer the paste to a bowl and stir in the grated cheese and lemon zest. Gradually blend in the oil, a little at a time, until combined, then transfer to a small serving dish.

2. To make the fritters, put the grated zucchini in a strainer over a bowl and sprinkle with plenty of salt. Let sit for 1 hour, then rinse thoroughly. Dry well on paper towels.

3. Sift the flour into a bowl and make a well in the center, then add the egg yolk and oil. Measure 5 tablespoons water and add a little to the bowl.

4. Beat the egg yolk and oil, gradually incorporating the flour and water to make a smooth batter. Season and let sit for 30 minutes.

5. Stir the zucchini into the batter. Beat the egg white until stiff, then fold into the batter.

6. Heat ½ inch of oil in a frying pan. Add spoonfuls of batter to the oil and fry for 2 minutes, until golden. Drain the fritters on paper towels and keep warm while frying the rest. Serve with the sauce.

RATATOUILLE

A highly versatile vegetable stew from Provence, ratatouille is delicious hot or cold, on its own or with eggs, pasta, fish or meat—particularly roast lamb.

2 pounds ripe tomatoes
½ cup olive oil
2 onions, thinly sliced
2 red bell peppers, seeded and cut into chunks
1 yellow or orange bell pepper, seeded and cut into chunks
1 large eggplant, cut into chunks
2 zucchini, cut into thick slices
4 garlic cloves, crushed
2 bay leaves
1 tablespoon chopped young thyme
salt and ground black pepper

SERVES 6

1. Plunge the tomatoes into boiling water for 30 seconds, then refresh in cold water. Peel and chop coarsely.

2. Heat a little of the oil in a large, heavy pan and sauté the onions for 5 minutes. Add the peppers and sauté for another 2 minutes. Drain. Add the eggplant and more oil and sauté gently for 5 minutes. Add the remaining oil and zucchini and sauté for 3 minutes. Drain.

3. Add the garlic and tomatoes to the pan with the bay leaves and thyme and a little salt and pepper. Cook gently until the tomatoes have softened and are turning pulpy.

4. Return all the vegetables to the pan and cook gently, stirring frequently, for about 15 minutes, until fairly pulpy but retaining a little texture. Season with more salt and pepper to taste.

COOK'S TIP

There are no specific quantities for the vegetables when making ratatouille, so you can, to a large extent, vary the quantities and types of vegetables depending on what you have in the refrigerator. If the tomatoes are a little tasteless, add 2–3 tablespoons tomato paste and a dash of sugar to the mixture along with the tomatoes.

SPINACH WITH RAISINS AND PINE NUTS

Raisins and pine nuts are frequent partners in Spanish recipes. Here, tossed with wilted spinach and croutons, they make a delicious snack or main-dish accompaniment.

⅓ cup raisins
1 thick slice crusty white bread
3 tablespoons olive oil
⅓ cup pine nuts
1¼ pounds young spinach, stems removed
2 garlic cloves, crushed
salt and ground black pepper

SERVES 4

1. Put the raisins in a small bowl with boiling water and let soak for 10 minutes. Drain.

2. Cut the bread into cubes and discard the crusts. Heat 2 tablespoons of the oil and fry the bread until golden. Drain.

3. Heat the remaining oil in the pan. Sauté the pine nuts until beginning to color. Add the spinach and garlic and cook quickly, turning the spinach until it has just wilted.

4. Toss in the raisins and season lightly with salt and pepper. Transfer to a warmed serving dish. Sprinkle croutons on top and serve hot.

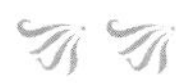

VARIATION

Use Swiss chard or beet greens instead of the spinach, cooking them a little longer.

Spiced Turnips with Spinach and Tomatoes

Sweet baby turnips, tender spinach and ripe tomatoes make tempting partners in this simple eastern Mediterranean vegetable stew.

1 pound plum or other ripe tomatoes
¼ cup olive oil
2 onions, sliced
1 pound baby turnips, peeled
1 teaspoon paprika
½ teaspoon sugar
4 tablespoons chopped cilantro
1 pound fresh young spinach, stalks removed
salt and ground black pepper

Serves 6

1 Plunge the tomatoes into a bowl of boiling water for 30 seconds, then refresh in a bowl of cold water. Peel away the tomato skins and chop coarsely. Heat the olive oil in a large frying pan or sauté pan and sauté the onion slices for about 5 minutes until golden.

2 Add the baby turnips, tomatoes and paprika to the pan with ¼ cup water and cook until the tomatoes are pulpy. Cover with a lid and continue cooking until the baby turnips have softened.

3 Stir in the sugar and cilantro, then add the spinach and a little salt and pepper and cook for another 2–3 minutes, until the spinach has wilted. Serve warm or cold.

STUFFED GRAPE LEAVES WITH GARLIC YOGURT

An old Greek recipe that comes in many guises. This meatless version is highly flavored with fresh herbs, lemon and a little chile.

8 ounces preserved grape leaves
1 onion, finely chopped
½ bunch of scallions, trimmed and finely chopped
¼ cup chopped fresh parsley
10 large mint sprigs, chopped
finely grated zest of 1 lemon
½ teaspoon crushed dried chiles
1½ teaspoons fennel seeds, crushed
scant 1 cup long-grain rice
½ cup olive oil
⅔ cup thick plain yogurt
2 garlic cloves, crushed
salt
lemon wedges and mint leaves, to garnish (optional)

SERVES 6

1 Rinse the grape leaves in plenty of cold water. Put in a bowl, cover with boiling water and let sit for 10 minutes. Drain thoroughly.

2 Combine the onion, scallions, parsley, mint, lemon, chiles, fennel, rice and 1½ tablespoons of the olive oil. Mix thoroughly and season with salt.

3 Place a grape leaf, veined side facing upward, on a work surface and cut off any stem. Place a heaping teaspoonful of the rice mixture near the stem end of the leaf.

4 Fold the stem end of the leaf over the rice filling, then fold over the sides and carefully roll up into a neat cigar shape.

5 Repeat with the remaining filling to make about 28 stuffed leaves. If some of the grape leaves are quite small, use two and patch them together to make parcels of the same size as the others.

6 Place any remaining leaves in the bottom of a large, heavy saucepan. Pack the stuffed leaves in a single layer in the pan. Spoon on the remaining oil, then add about 1¼ cups boiling water.

COOK'S TIP

To check that the rice is cooked, lift out one stuffed leaf and cut in half. The rice should have expanded and softened to make a firm parcel. If necessary, cook the stuffed leaves a little longer, adding boiling water if the pan is becoming dry.

7 Place a small plate over the leaves to keep them submerged in the water. Cover the pan and cook over very low heat for 45 minutes.

8 Combine the yogurt and garlic and place in a small serving dish. Transfer the stuffed leaves to a serving plate and garnish with lemon wedges and mint, if desired. Serve with the garlic yogurt.

SPICY CHICKPEA AND EGGPLANT STEW

This is a Lebanese dish, but similar dishes are found all over the Mediterranean.

3 large eggplant, cubed
1 cup chickpeas, soaked overnight
¼ cup olive oil
3 garlic cloves, chopped
2 large onions, chopped
½ teaspoon ground cumin
½ teaspoon ground cinnamon
2½ teaspoons ground coriander
3 14-ounce cans chopped tomatoes
salt and ground black pepper
cooked rice, to serve

FOR THE GARNISH
2 tablespoons olive oil
1 onion, sliced
1 garlic clove, sliced
sprigs of cilantro

SERVES 4

1 Place the eggplant pieces in a colander and sprinkle them with salt. Set the colander in a bowl and let sit for 30 minutes, to allow the bitter juices to escape. Rinse with cold water and dry on paper towels.

2 Drain the chickpeas and put in a pan with enough water to cover. Bring to a boil and simmer for 30 minutes or until tender. Drain.

3 Heat the oil in a large pan. Add the garlic and onions and cook gently, until soft. Add the spices and cook, stirring, for a few seconds. Add the eggplant and stir to coat with the spices and onion. Cook for 5 minutes. Add the tomatoes and chickpeas and season with salt and pepper. Cover and simmer for 20 minutes.

4 To make the garnish, heat the oil in a frying pan and, when very hot, add the sliced onion and garlic. Fry until golden and crisp. Serve the stew with rice, topped with the onion and garlic and garnished with cilantro.

SPANISH POTATOES

This is an adaptation of a peppery potato dish of which there are several versions. All of them are fried and mildly spiced with the added tang of wine vinegar. Serve with cold meats or as a tapa.

1½ pounds small new potatoes
5 tablespoons olive oil
2 garlic cloves, sliced
½ teaspoon crushed dried chiles
½ teaspoon ground cumin
2 teaspoons paprika
2 tablespoons red or white wine vinegar
1 red or green bell pepper, seeded and sliced
coarse sea salt, to serve (optional)

SERVES 4

1 Cook the potatoes in boiling salted water until almost tender. Drain and, if preferred, peel them. Cut into chunks.

2 Heat the oil in a large frying or sauté pan and fry the potatoes, turning them frequently, until golden.

3 Meanwhile, crush together the garlic, chiles and cumin using a mortar and pestle. Mix with the paprika and wine vinegar.

4 Add the garlic mixture to the potatoes with the sliced pepper and cook, stirring, for 2 minutes. Serve warm, or let sit until cold. Sprinkle with coarse sea salt, if desired, to serve.

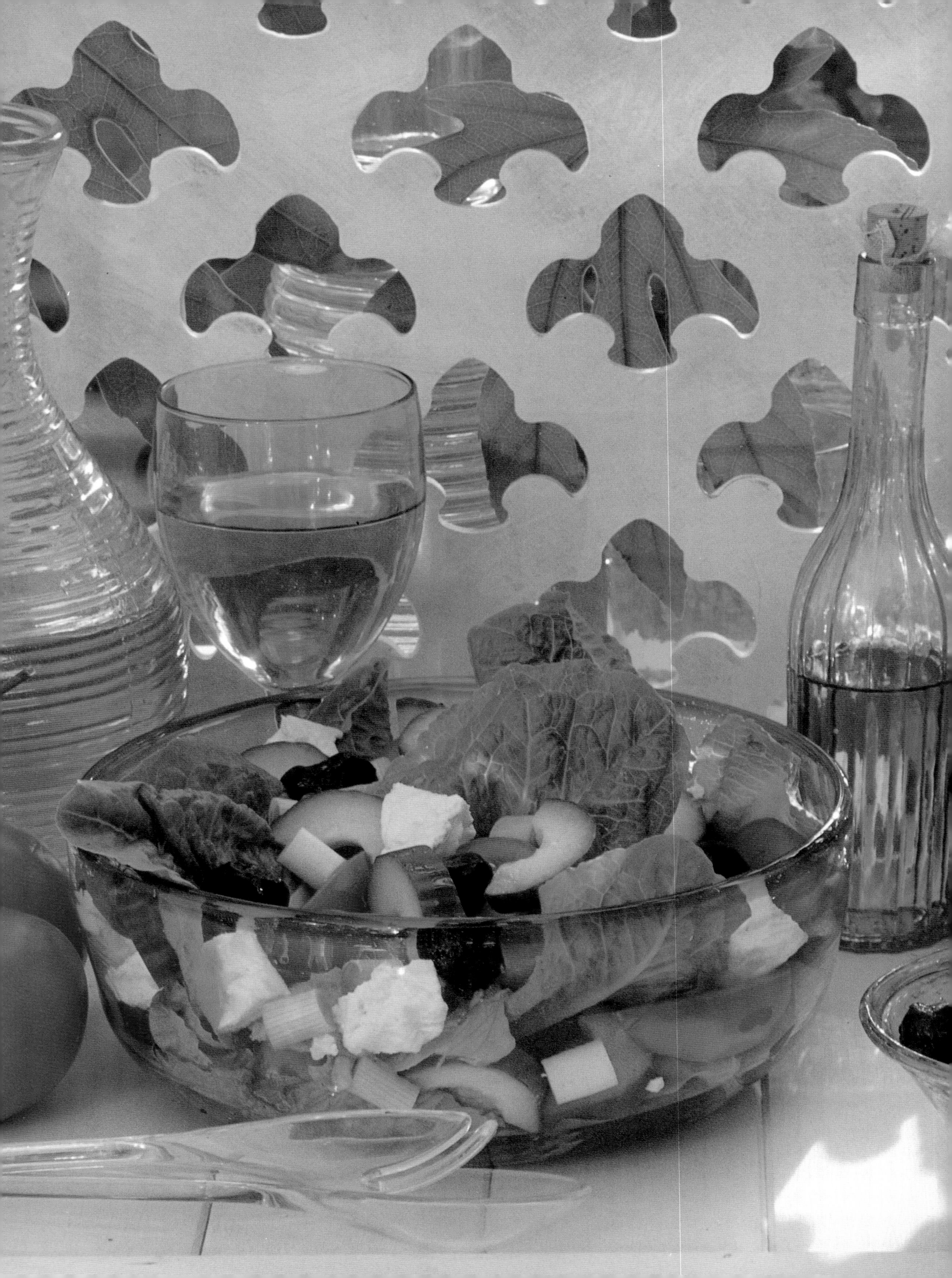

SALADS

Summer and salads are synonymous, and nowhere is there a wider variety of these flavorful dishes than in the Mediterranean.

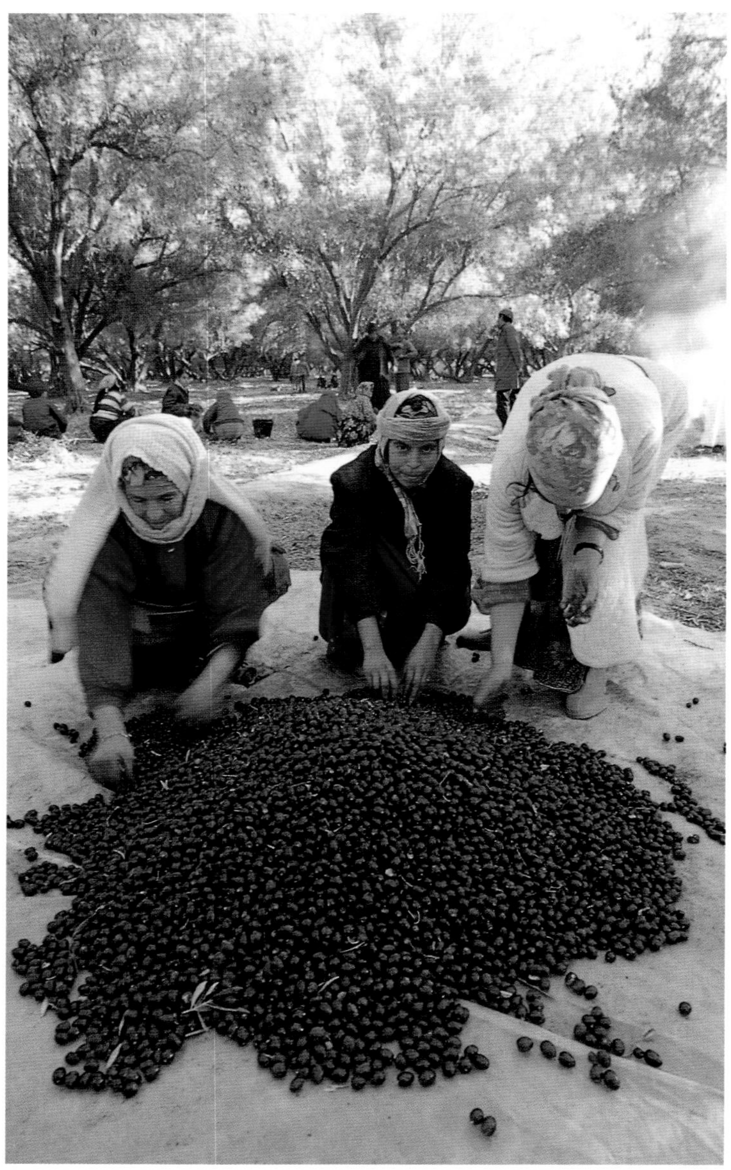

LEFT: Some of these plump Moroccan olives will find their way into salads, but the majority will be pressed for oil.

The climate of the Mediterranean countries has ensured that salads and cold dishes have always been popular. There is an abundance of wonderful ingredients, particularly vegetables, which are combined to produce delicious results. In its simplest form, a salad in France, Spain or Italy would consist of lettuce, or perhaps a mixture of a few different salad greens, dressed with vinaigrette. A salad may be eaten after the main course, often before the cheese is served. Vinaigrette is the basic salad dressing. Originally a French classic, it is now used worldwide. As its name suggests, vinegar is a main ingredient, combined with three times its quantity of olive oil, and seasoned with salt and pepper. There are many variations, using different ingredients such as lemon juice, mustard, herbs, garlic and cream; the types of oils and vinegars can be varied too. Extra virgin olive oil gives the finest flavor of all the olive oils, but a mixture of peanut oil and olive oil will produce a lighter dressing. Nut oils, such as walnut, complement salads containing nuts. The Italians favor a good red wine vinegar, but there is also the sour/sweet flavor of balsamic vinegar to consider—delicious with broiled vegetables. Spanish sherry vinegar is another good flavor to try. Herb-infused vinegars are also useful, particularly if the fresh herbs are unavailable.

There is an abundant variety of salad greens in the Mediterranean, ranging in color, taste and texture. The French favor a mixture of leaves called mesclun, which can be bought at markets by the handful. Dandelion greens are popular too, as well as frisée, Belgian endive, red leaf lettuce and many more. In Italy, radicchio and arugula are preferred, and the Spanish favor romaine lettuce. In

RIGHT: Visiting a Turkish market is more than a mere shopping trip; it's a chance to catch up on local news.

ABOVE: A quiet landscape near Carmona in the beautiful region of Andalusia in southern Spain.

the Middle East, however, green salads are less popular. Salads of cooked or raw vegetables, dressed with a lemony vinaigrette, are more typical of these countries. Fresh herbs also play an important part, sometimes served alone, between courses, to cleanse the palate. These basic salads are spontaneous, depending on what is available in the market, and need no recipes.

The markets of the Mediterranean offer some of the best vegetables and fruit in the world. From huge vine-ripened tomatoes to tiny artichokes, all are lovingly displayed, waiting to be picked up and dropped into a basket to be taken home. The inspiration for salads is endless. Fruit too, is included; grapes and oranges make refreshing additions to some of our recipes.

Apart from the simple salads, there are the composed salads—specific ingredients, with a special dressing, which are dishes on their own, to be eaten as a lunch dish, or perhaps an appetizer. These salads include all sorts of foods: olives, sausage, nuts, cheese, anchovies—morsels chosen for a contrast in taste, texture and color.

This chapter includes some of the classic salads of the region, including Salad Niçoise and Greek Salad, both of which are sure to transport anyone who has eaten them in their native countries straight to a little village on the coast of the Mediterranean. Some salads are substantial enough to be served as a main dish, such as Roasted Peppers with Tomatoes and Anchovies or Fava Bean, Mushroom and Chorizo Salad. Bread and a glass of wine should complete the picture!

ROASTED PEPPERS WITH TOMATOES AND ANCHOVIES

This is a Sicilian-style salad, using some typical ingredients from the Italian island. The flavor improves if the salad is made and dressed an hour or two before serving.

1 red bell pepper
1 yellow bell pepper
4 sun-dried tomatoes in oil, drained
4 ripe plum tomatoes, sliced
2 canned anchovies, drained and chopped
1 tablespoon capers, drained
1 tablespoon pine nuts
1 garlic clove, very thinly sliced

FOR THE DRESSING
5 tablespoons extra virgin olive oil
1 tablespoon balsamic vinegar
1 teaspoon lemon juice
chopped fresh mixed herbs
salt and ground black pepper

SERVES 4

1 Cut the peppers in half and remove the seeds and stems. Cut into quarters and cook, skin side up, under a hot broiler, until the skin chars. Transfer to a bowl and cover with a plate. Let cool. Peel the peppers and cut into strips.

2 Thinly slice the sun-dried tomatoes. Arrange the peppers and fresh tomatoes on a serving dish. Sprinkle the anchovies, sun-dried tomatoes, capers, pine nuts and garlic on top.

3 To make the dressing, combine the olive oil, vinegar, lemon juice and chopped herbs and season with salt and pepper. Pour over the salad just before serving.

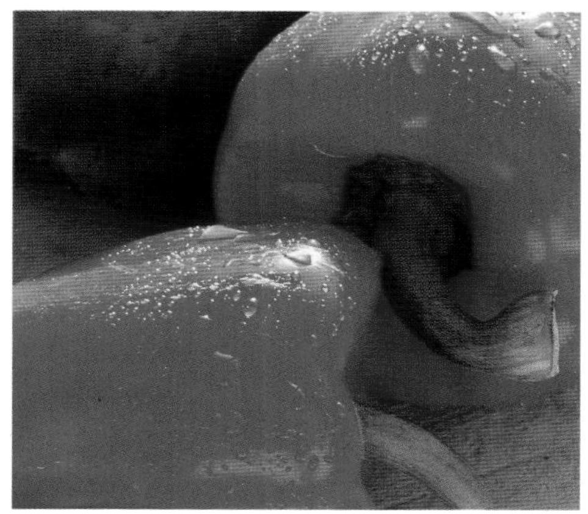

SWEET-AND-SOUR ONION SALAD

This recipe is primarily from Provence in the south of France, but there are influences from other Mediterranean countries, too.

1 pound baby onions, peeled
¼ cup wine vinegar
3 tablespoons olive oil
3 tablespoons sugar
3 tablespoons tomato paste
1 bay leaf
2 parsley sprigs
½ cup raisins
salt and ground black pepper

SERVES 6

1 Put all the ingredients in a pan with 1¼ cups water. Bring to a boil and simmer gently, uncovered, for 45 minutes or until the onions are tender and most of the liquid has evaporated.

2 Remove the bay leaf and parsley, check the seasoning and transfer to a serving dish. Serve at room temperature.

GREEK SALAD

Anyone who has spent a vacation in Greece will have eaten a version of this salad—the Greek equivalent of a mixed salad. Its success relies on using the freshest of ingredients and a good olive oil.

1 small head romaine lettuce, sliced
1 pound ripe tomatoes, cut into eighths
1 cucumber, seeded and chopped
7 ounces feta cheese, crumbled
4 scallions, sliced
½ cup black olives, pitted and halved

FOR THE DRESSING
6 tablespoons good olive oil
1½ tablespoons lemon juice
salt and ground black pepper

SERVES 6

1 Put all the main salad ingredients into a large bowl. Whisk together the olive oil and lemon juice, then season with salt and pepper, and pour the dressing on the salad. Mix well and serve immediately.

SPICED EGGPLANT SALAD

Serve this Middle Eastern-influenced salad with warm pita bread as an appetizer or to accompany a main-course rice pilaf.

2 small eggplant, sliced
5 tablespoons olive oil
¼ cup red wine vinegar
2 garlic cloves, crushed
1 tablespoon lemon juice
½ teaspoon ground cumin
½ teaspoon ground coriander
½ cucumber, thinly sliced
2 ripe tomatoes, thinly sliced
2 tablespoons plain yogurt
salt and ground black pepper
chopped flat-leaf parsley, to garnish

SERVES 4

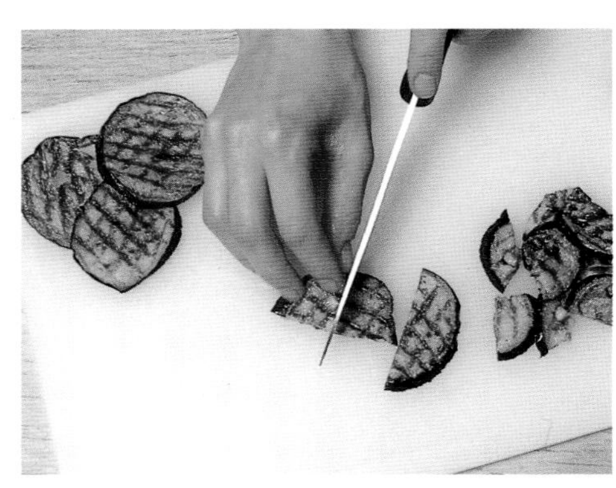

1 Preheat the broiler. Brush the eggplant slices lightly with some of the oil and cook under high heat, turning once, until golden and tender. Cut into quarters.

2 Combine the remaining oil, vinegar, garlic, lemon juice, cumin and coriander. Season with salt and pepper and mix thoroughly. Add the warm eggplant, stir well and chill for at least 2 hours. Add the cucumber and tomatoes. Transfer to a serving dish and spoon the yogurt on top. Sprinkle with parsley.

MOROCCAN DATE, ORANGE AND CARROT SALAD

A colorful and unusual salad with exotic ingredients—fresh dates and orange-flower water—combined with crisp greens, carrots, oranges and toasted almonds.

1 head Bibb lettuce
2 carrots, finely grated
2 oranges
4 ounces fresh dates, pitted and cut into eighths lengthwise
¼ cup toasted whole almonds, chopped
2 tablespoons lemon juice
1 teaspoon sugar
¼ teaspoon salt
1 tablespoon orange-flower water

SERVES 4

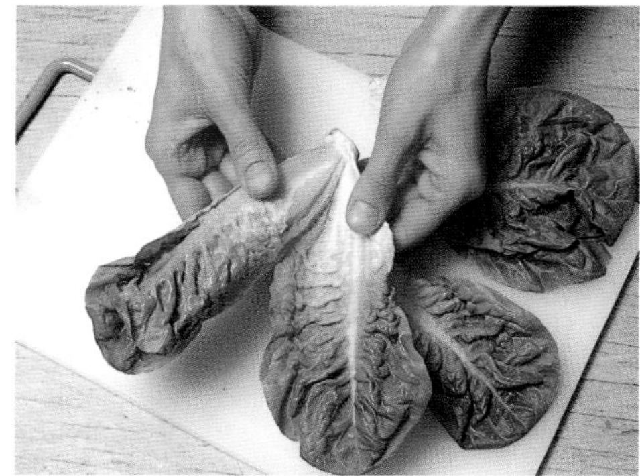

1 Separate the lettuce leaves and arrange them in the bottom of a salad bowl or on individual serving plates. Place the grated carrot in a mound on top.

2 Peel and segment the oranges and arrange them around the carrot. Pile the dates on top, then sprinkle with the almonds. Combine the lemon juice, sugar, salt and orange-flower water and sprinkle on the salad. Serve chilled.

MOROCCAN COOKED SALAD

A version of a North African favorite, this cooked salad is served as a side dish with a main course. Make this one the day before serving to improve the flavor.

2 ripe tomatoes, quartered
2 onions, chopped
½ cucumber, halved lengthwise, seeded and sliced
1 green bell pepper, halved, seeded and chopped
2 tablespoons lemon juice
3 tablespoons olive oil
2 garlic cloves, crushed
2 tablespoons chopped cilantro
salt and ground black pepper
sprigs of cilantro, to garnish

SERVES 4

1 Put the tomatoes, onions, cucumber and green pepper into a pan, add 1/4 cup water and simmer for 5 minutes. Let cool.

2 Combine the lemon juice, olive oil and garlic. Strain the vegetables, then transfer to a bowl. Pour the dressing over them, season with salt and pepper and stir in the chopped cilantro. Serve immediately, garnished with cilantro sprigs.

PANZANELLA

In this lively Italian specialty, a sweet, tangy blend of tomato juice, rich olive oil and red wine vinegar is soaked up in a colorful salad of roasted peppers, anchovies and toasted ciabatta.

8 ounces ciabatta (about ⅔ loaf)
⅔ cup olive oil
3 red bell peppers
3 yellow bell peppers
2-ounce can anchovy fillets
1½ pounds ripe plum tomatoes
4 garlic cloves, crushed
4 tablespoons red wine vinegar
¼ cup caperberries or capers
1 cup pitted black olives
salt and ground black pepper
basil leaves, to garnish

SERVES 4–6

1. Preheat the oven to 400°F. Cut the ciabatta into ¾-inch chunks and drizzle with ¼ cup of the olive oil. Bake lightly until a pale golden color.

2. Put the peppers on a foil-lined baking sheet and bake for about 45 minutes, until the skin begins to char. Remove from the oven, cover with a cloth and let cool slightly.

3. Pull the skin off the peppers and cut them into quarters, discarding the stem ends and seeds. Drain and then coarsely chop the anchovies. Set aside.

4. To make the tomato dressing, peel and halve the tomatoes. Scoop the seeds into a strainer set over a bowl. Using the back of a spoon, press the tomato pulp in the strainer to extract as much juice as possible. Discard the pulp and add the remaining oil, the garlic and vinegar to the juices.

5. Layer the toasted bread, peppers, tomatoes, anchovies, capers and olives in a large salad bowl. Season the tomato dressing with salt and pepper and pour it over the salad. Let stand for about 30 minutes. Serve garnished with plenty of basil leaves.

RADICCHIO, ARTICHOKE AND WALNUT SALAD

The distinctive, earthy taste of Jerusalem artichokes makes a lovely contrast to the sharp freshness of radicchio and lemon. Serve warm or cold as an accompaniment to broiled steak or grilled meats.

1 large head radicchio or 5 ounces radicchio leaves
6 tablespoons walnut pieces
3 tablespoons walnut oil
1¼ pounds Jerusalem artichokes
pared zest and juice of 1 lemon
coarse sea salt and ground black pepper
flat-leaf parsley, to garnish (optional)

SERVES 4

1. If using a whole radicchio, cut it into 8–10 wedges. Put the wedges or leaves in a flameproof dish. Sprinkle the walnuts on top, then spoon on the oil and season. Broil for 2–3 minutes.

2. Peel the artichokes and cut up any large ones so the pieces are all roughly the same size. Add the artichokes to a pan of boiling salted water with half the lemon juice and cook for 5–7 minutes, until tender. Drain. Preheat the broiler to high.

3. Toss the artichokes into the salad with the remaining lemon juice and the pared zest. Season with coarse salt and pepper. Broil until beginning to brown. Serve immediately garnished with torn pieces of parsley, if desired.

CACIK

This refreshing yogurt dish is served all over the eastern Mediterranean, whether as part of a mezze with marinated olives and pita bread or as an accompaniment to meat dishes. Greek tzatziki is very similar.

1 small cucumber
1¼ cups thick plain yogurt
3 garlic cloves, crushed
2 tablespoons chopped fresh mint
2 tablespoons chopped fresh dill or parsley
salt and ground black pepper
mint or parsley and dill, to garnish
olive oil, olives and pita bread, to serve

SERVES 6

1 Finely chop the cucumber and layer in a colander with plenty of salt. Let sit for 30 minutes. Wash the cucumber in several changes of cold water and drain thoroughly. Pat dry on paper towels.

2 Combine the yogurt, garlic and herbs and season with salt and pepper. Stir in the cucumber. Garnish with herbs, drizzle on a little olive oil and serve with olives and pita bread.

BROWN BEAN SALAD

Brown beans, sometimes called "ful medames," are widely used in Egyptian cooking and are occasionally seen in health-food stores here. Dried fava beans or black or red kidney beans make a good substitute.

1½ cups dried brown beans
3 thyme sprigs
2 bay leaves
1 onion, halved
4 garlic cloves, crushed
1½ teaspoons cumin seeds, crushed
3 scallions, finely chopped
6 tablespoons coarsely chopped fresh flat-leaf parsley
4 teaspoons lemon juice
6 tablespoons olive oil
3 hard-boiled eggs, shelled and coarsely chopped
1 dill pickle, roughly chopped
salt and ground black pepper

SERVES 6

1 Put the beans in a bowl with plenty of cold water and let soak overnight. Drain, transfer to a saucepan and cover with fresh water. Bring to a boil and boil rapidly for 10 minutes.

2 Reduce the heat and add the thyme, bay leaves and onion. Simmer very gently for about 1 hour, until tender. Drain and discard the herbs and onion.

COOK'S TIP

The cooking time for dried beans can vary considerably. They may need only 45 minutes or a lot longer.

3 Combine the garlic, cumin, scallions, parsley, lemon juice, oil and add a little salt and pepper. Pour over the beans and toss the ingredients together lightly.

4 Gently stir in the eggs and pickle and serve immediately.

WARM FAVA BEAN AND FETA SALAD

This recipe is loosely based on a typical medley of fresh-tasting Greek salad ingredients—fava beans, tomatoes and feta cheese. It's great warm or cold, as an appetizer or main-course accompaniment.

2 pounds fava beans, shelled, or 12 ounces shelled frozen beans
4 tablespoons olive oil
6 ounces plum tomatoes, halved, or quartered if large
4 garlic cloves, crushed
4 ounces firm feta cheese, cut into chunks
3 tablespoons chopped fresh dill
12 black olives
salt and ground black pepper
chopped fresh dill, to garnish

SERVES 4–6

1. Cook the fresh or frozen fava beans in boiling salted water until just tender. Drain and set aside.

2. Meanwhile, heat the oil in a heavy frying pan and add the tomatoes and garlic. Cook until the tomatoes are beginning to color.

3. Add the feta to the pan and toss the ingredients together for 1 minute. Mix with the drained beans, dill, olives and salt and pepper. Serve garnished with chopped dill.

HALLOUMI AND GRAPE SALAD

In Eastern Europe, firm, salty halloumi cheese is often served fried for breakfast or supper. Feta cheese makes a good substitute in this recipe.

FOR THE DRESSING
¼ cup olive oil
1 tablespoon lemon juice
½ teaspoon sugar
salt and ground black pepper
1 tablespoon chopped fresh thyme or dill

FOR THE SALAD
5 ounces mixed salad greens
3 ounces seedless green grapes
3 ounces seedless red grapes
9 ounces halloumi cheese
3 tablespoons olive oil
thyme leaves or dill, to garnish

SERVES 4

1. To make the dressing, combine the olive oil, lemon juice and sugar. Season. Stir in the thyme or dill and set aside.

2. Toss together the salad greens and the green and red grapes, then transfer to a large serving plate.

3. Thinly slice the cheese. Heat the oil in a large frying pan. Add the cheese and sauté briefly until turning golden on the underside. Turn the cheese with a spatula and cook the other side.

4. Arrange the cheese on the salad. Pour on the dressing and garnish with thyme or dill.

SALAD NIÇOISE

Made with good-quality ingredients, this Provençal salad makes a simple yet unbeatable summer lunch or supper dish. Serve with country-style bread and chilled white wine.

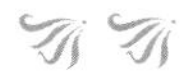

FOR THE DRESSING
6 tablespoons extra virgin olive oil
2 garlic cloves, crushed
1 tablespoon white wine vinegar
salt and ground black pepper

FOR THE SALAD
4 ounces green beans, trimmed
4 ounces mixed salad greens
½ small cucumber, thinly sliced
4 ripe tomatoes, quartered
7-ounce can tuna in oil, drained
2-ounce can anchovies, drained
4 eggs, hard-boiled
½ bunch radishes, trimmed
½ cup small black olives
flat-leaf parsley, to garnish

SERVES 4

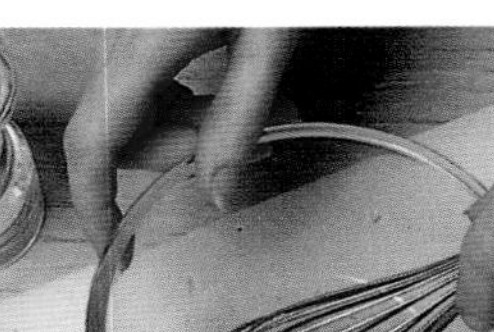

1 To make the dressing, whisk together the oil, garlic and vinegar and season to taste with salt and pepper.

2 Halve the green beans and cook in a saucepan of boiling water for 2 minutes, until only just tender; drain.

3 Mix the salad greens, cucumber, tomatoes and green beans in a large, shallow salad bowl. Flake the tuna. Halve the anchovies lengthwise. Shell and quarter the eggs.

4 Sprinkle the radishes, tuna, anchovies, eggs and olives on the salad. Pour the dressing over and toss together lightly. Serve garnished with parsley.

SPANISH ASPARAGUS AND ORANGE SALAD

Complicated salad dressings are rarely found in Spain—they simply rely on the wonderful flavor of a good-quality olive oil.

8 ounces asparagus, trimmed and cut into 2-inch pieces
2 large oranges
2 ripe tomatoes, cut into eighths
2 ounces romaine lettuce leaves, shredded
2 tablespoons extra virgin olive oil
½ teaspoon sherry vinegar
salt and ground black pepper

SERVES 4

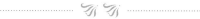

COOK'S TIP

Bibb lettuce can be used in place of romaine.

1 Cook the asparagus in boiling, salted water for 3–4 minutes, until just tender. Drain and refresh under cold water.

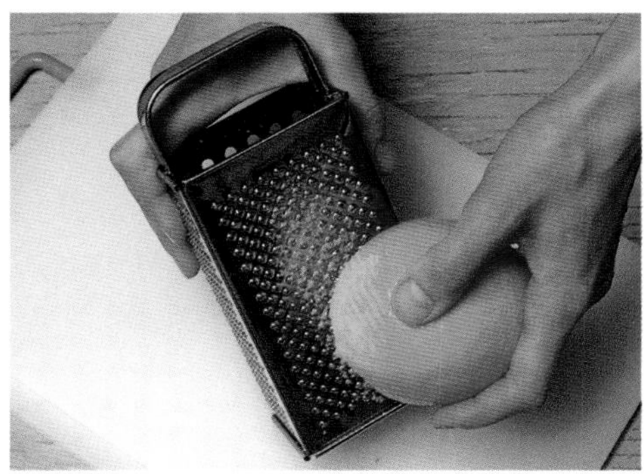

2 Grate the zest from half an orange and reserve. Peel all the oranges and cut into segments. Squeeze out the juice from the membrane and reserve the juice.

3 Put the asparagus, orange segments, tomatoes and lettuce into a salad bowl. Combine the oil and vinegar and add 1 tablespoon of the reserved orange juice and 1 teaspoon of the zest *(left)*. Season with salt and pepper. Just before serving, pour the dressing over the salad and mix gently to coat.

GLOBE ARTICHOKES WITH GREEN BEANS AND AIOLI

Just like the French aïoli, there are many recipes for the Spanish equivalent. This one is exceptionally garlicky, a perfect partner to freshly cooked vegetables.

FOR THE AIOLI
6 large garlic cloves, sliced
2 teaspoons white wine vinegar
1 cup olive oil
salt and ground black pepper

FOR THE SALAD
8 ounces green beans
3 small globe artichokes
1 tablespoon olive oil
pared zest of 1 lemon
coarse salt for sprinkling
lemon wedges, to garnish

SERVES 4–6

1 To make the aïoli, put the garlic and vinegar in a blender or mini food processor. With the machine switched on, gradually pour in the olive oil until the mixture is thickened and smooth. (Alternatively, crush the garlic to a paste with the vinegar and gradually beat in the oil using a hand whisk.) Season with salt and pepper to taste.

2 To make the salad, cook the beans in boiling water for 1–2 minutes, until slightly softened. Drain.

3 Trim the artichoke stems close to the base. Cook the artichokes in a large pan of salted water for about 30 minutes or until you can easily pull away a leaf from the base. Drain well.

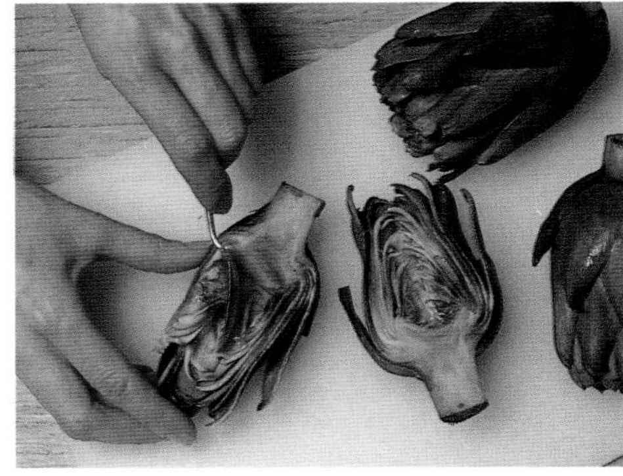

4 Using a sharp knife, halve the artichokes lengthwise and ease out the choke using a teaspoon.

5 Arrange the artichokes and beans on serving plates and drizzle with the oil. Sprinkle on the lemon zest and season with coarse salt and a little pepper. Spoon the aïoli into the artichoke hearts and serve warm, garnished with lemon wedges. To eat artichokes, pull the leaves from the base one at a time and use to scoop a little of the sauce. It is only the fleshy end of each leaf that is eaten, as well as the base or heart of the artichoke.

COOK'S TIP
Mediterranean baby artichokes are sometimes available and are perfect for this kind of salad, as unlike the larger ones, they can be eaten whole. Cook them until just tender, then cut in half to serve.
Canned artichoke hearts, thoroughly drained and sliced, can be substituted when fresh ones are not available.

FAVA BEAN, MUSHROOM AND CHORIZO SALAD

Fava beans are used in both their fresh and dried forms in various Mediterranean countries. This Spanish salad could be served as either a first course or a lunch dish.

8 ounces shelled fava beans
6 ounces chorizo sausage
4 tablespoons extra virgin olive oil
8 ounces cremini mushrooms, sliced
handful of fresh chives
salt and ground black pepper

SERVES 4

1 Cook the fava beans in boiling salted water for about 8 minutes. Drain and refresh under cold water.

2 Remove the skin from the sausage and cut it into small chunks. Heat the oil in a frying pan, add the chorizo and cook for 2–3 minutes. Pour the chorizo and oil into the mushrooms and mix well. Let cool. Chop half the chives. If the beans are large, peel off the tough outer skins. Stir the beans and snipped chives into the mushroom mixture and season to taste. Serve at room temperature, garnished with the remaining chives.

AVOCADO, ORANGE AND ALMOND SALAD

The Mediterranean is not particularly known for its avocados, but the climate is perfect for them and they are grown in many parts of the region. This salad has a Spanish influence.

2 oranges
2 ripe tomatoes
2 small avocados
¼ cup extra virgin olive oil
2 tablespoons lemon juice
1 tablespoon chopped fresh parsley
1 small onion, sliced into rings
salt and ground black pepper
¼ cup sliced almonds and
10–12 black olives, to garnish

SERVES 4

1 Peel the oranges and cut into thick slices. Plunge the tomatoes into boiling water for 30 seconds, then refresh in cold water. Peel off the skins, cut into quarters, remove the seeds and chop coarsely.

2 Cut the avocados in half, remove the pits and carefully peel off the skin. Cut into chunks.

3 Combine the olive oil, lemon juice and parsley. Season with salt and pepper. Toss the avocados and tomatoes in half of the dressing.

4 Arrange the sliced oranges on a plate and scatter the onion rings over them. Drizzle with the rest of the dressing. Spoon the avocados, tomatoes, almonds and olives on top.

Fish and Shellfish

Mediterranean fishermen reap a rich harvest of fish and shellfish, which are often simply broiled or fried, or used as the basis of a soup or stew.

The Mediterranean Sea is tiny in relation to the world's larger seas and oceans. It is also relatively shallow, warm, low in natural food supplies and more polluted. Despite all these factors, the Mediterranean has hundreds of different species of fish and crustacea, marketed in the Mediterranean and beyond. Visit a large fish market in any part of the region and you will be amazed by the fantastic variety of fish, many of which are completely unknown except to the locals and, of course, the fishermen themselves.

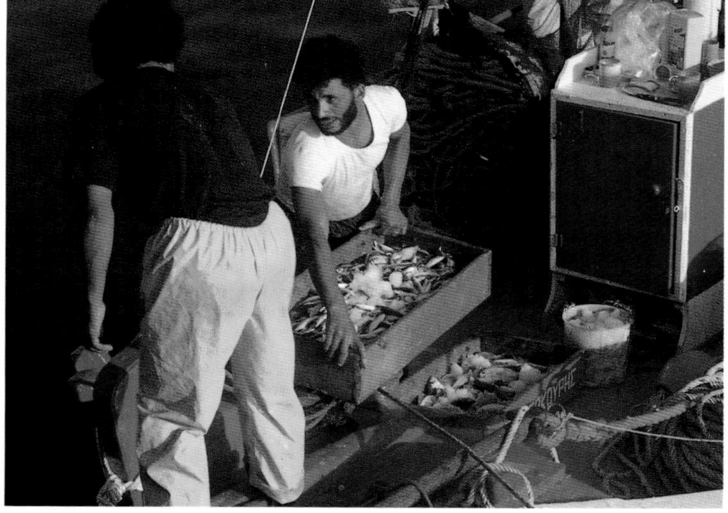

ABOVE: Fishermen in Crete bring home the day's catch, packed in salt.

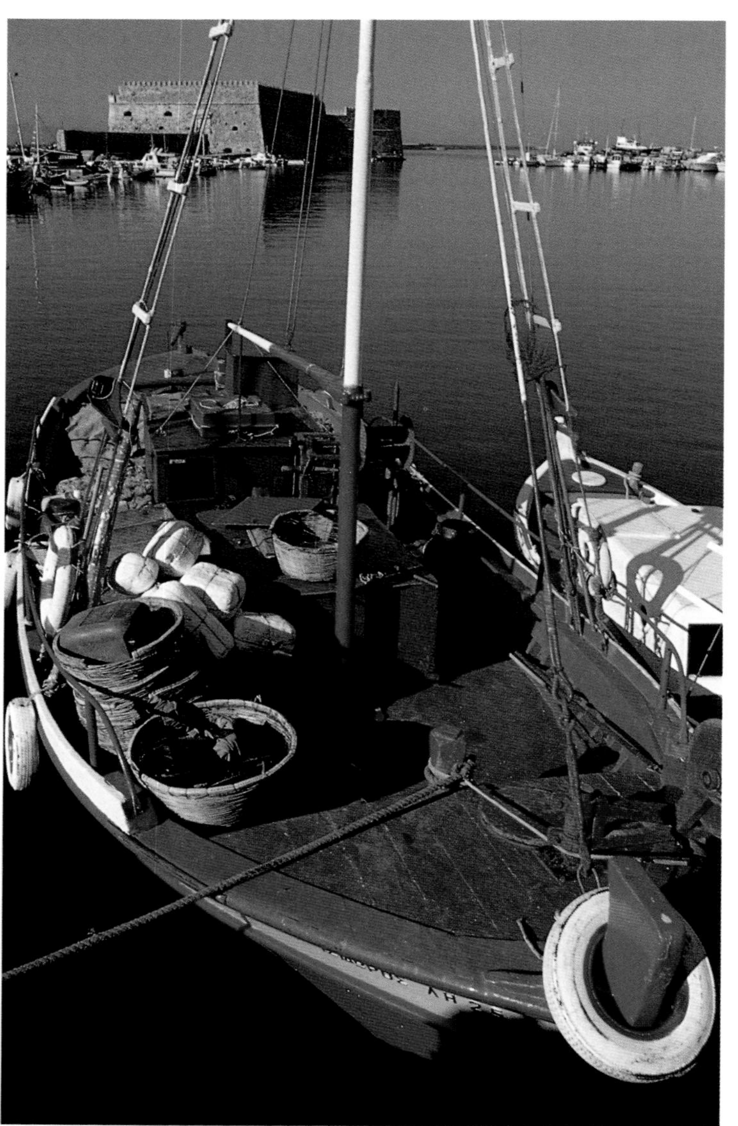

LEFT: Safely back in harbor, a Cretan fishing boat bobs gently on the calm sea.

A visit to a Mediterranean restaurant, bar or taverna illustrates how this freshly caught fish, cooked simply, can be quite unbeatable. Few of us ever forget the arrival of a hot, steaming bowl of garlicky mussels or crisp shrimp dripping in garlic and olive oil. Perfectly fresh fish, broiled or grilled with a basting of olive oil, garlic and herbs, needs little more embellishment, except perhaps a crisp salad and a light wine.

On a more elaborate scale, fish stews and soups are typically Mediterranean. A varied mixture of fish such as conger eel, gurnard, John Dory, monkfish, bass, bream and red mullet is combined with aromatic flavorings like saffron, herbs, garlic and orange peel and cooked in an intensely flavored fish stock made from fish trimmings. The bourride of France and the brodetto of Italy are classic examples but similar variations can be found all over the Mediterranean.

Small, oily fish thrive in the Mediterranean, and the

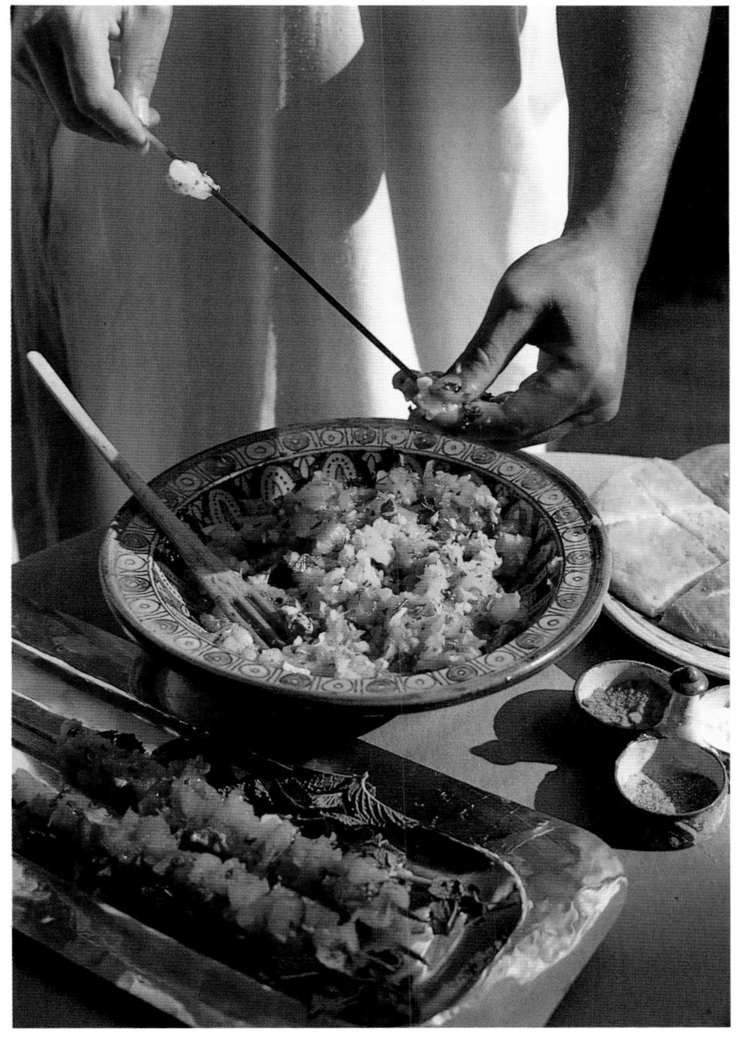

ABOVE: A Moroccan cook patiently prepares the family meal of fish kebabs.

freshly broiled or grilled sardines prepared in cafés and tavernas around the region cannot be rivaled anywhere else in the world. Sardines and large anchovies are sometimes stuffed with a slightly tangy mixture of ingredients, such as capers, olives, pine nuts, lemons and dried fruit, that provides a perfect contrast to the rich oiliness of the fish itself. Other interesting preparations are the short-term preserving of fried sardines in olive oil and vinegar or the delicious combination of sardines with fresh herbs and spaghetti or macaroni.

The technique of frying fish in a light batter is typical of the Mediterranean. Fritto Misto is an Italian version in which a medley of seafood, such as mussels, squid, red mullet, shrimp and whitebait, is coated in a light crisp batter and deep-fried. When served piping hot, this is delicious as a light snack or appetizer with a spinkling of gremolata (a blend of garlic, parsley and lemon zest), or simply squeezed with lemon. The Spanish also love fried fish and use much the same technique, sometimes simply dredging the fish with seasoned flour before frying in light olive oil.

Taking into consideration the availability of so much fresh produce, it is surprising that salt cod is so well loved in various parts of the Mediterranean; the kite-shaped, leathery pieces are a common sight in many market-places. The Spanish and Portuguese fished for cod in the Atlantic, salted it and sun-dried it at sea as a means of preservation. These familiar stiff, yellow-tinged boards of fish, which once were associated with the frugal eating of Lent, are now a highly esteemed luxury. Perhaps the most famous dish is the brandade of France, a smooth purée of salt cod flavored with garlic and olive oil.

On the eastern side of the Mediterranean the types of fish available are much the same, although the cooking methods vary. Baking fish whole is the most widespread practice, often on a bed of tomatoes, lemons, onions and herbs, and sometimes with slightly sweet and spicy flavorings such as raisins and cinnamon. The Greek plaki is a well-loved example, perfect for fish such as gray mullet, sea bream and bass, which absorb all the wonderful flavors of the accompanying ingredients. Middle Eastern and North African fish dishes emphasize the accompanying sauce—the choice of fish being the pick of the catch. A simple blend of tahini with olive oil and lemon juice is very traditional.

Squid and octopus both play an important role in Mediterranean cooking. Squid, from the tiniest, which are lovely seared in olive oil with garlic and herbs, to huge specimens, rich with stuffings, typify Mediterranean cooking techniques. Octopus, too, is highly esteemed, particularly in the eastern Mediterranean, where it is frequently stewed with red wine or used in salads.

PANFRIED RED MULLET WITH BASIL AND CITRUS

Red mullet is popular all over the Mediterranean. This Italian recipe combines it with oranges and lemons, which grow in abundance there.

4 red mullet (or snapper), about 8 ounces each, filleted
6 tablespoons olive oil
10 peppercorns, crushed
2 oranges, one peeled and sliced and one squeezed
1 lemon
2 tablespoons flour
1 tablespoon butter
2 drained canned anchovies, chopped
4 tablespoons shredded fresh basil
salt and ground black pepper

SERVES 4

1 Place the fish fillets in a shallow dish in a single layer. Pour the olive oil over them and sprinkle with the crushed peppercorns. Lay the orange slices on top of the fish. Cover the dish and let marinate in the refrigerator for at least 4 hours.

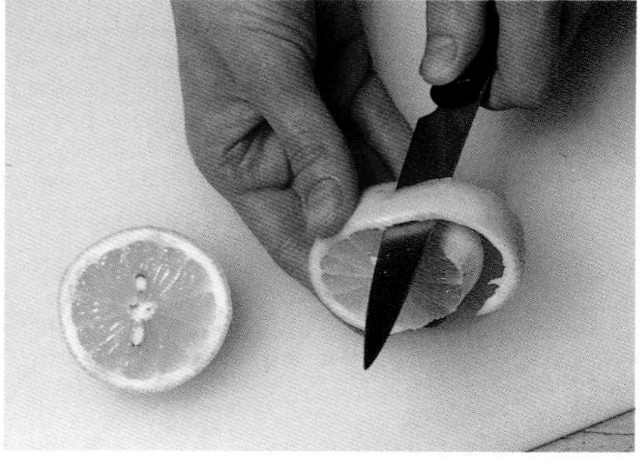

2 Halve the lemon. Remove the zest and pith from one half using a small sharp knife and slice thinly. Squeeze the juice from the other half.

COOK'S TIP

If you prefer, use other fish fillets for this dish, such as red snapper, lemon sole, haddock or hake.

3 Lift the fish out of the marinade and pat dry on paper towels. Reserve the marinade and orange slices. Season the fish with salt and pepper and dust lightly with flour.

4 Heat 3 tablespoons of the marinade in a frying pan. Add the fish and fry for 2 minutes on each side. Remove from the pan and keep warm. Discard the marinade that is left in the pan.

5 Melt the butter in the pan with any of the remaining original marinade. Add the anchovies and cook until completely softened.

6 Stir in the orange and lemon juice, then check the seasoning and simmer until slightly reduced. Stir in the basil. Pour the sauce on the fish and garnish with the reserved orange slices and the lemon slices.

Seafood Risotto

Risotto is one of Italy's most popular rice dishes, and it is made with everything from pumpkin to squid ink. On the Mediterranean shores, seafood is the most obvious addition.

¼ cup sunflower oil
1 onion, chopped
2 garlic cloves, crushed
generous 1 cup arborio rice
7 tablespoons white wine
6¼ cups hot fish stock
12 ounces mixed seafood, such as raw shrimp, mussels, squid rings or clams
grated zest of ½ lemon
2 tablespoons tomato paste
1 tablespoon chopped fresh parsley
salt and ground black pepper

Serves 4

1 Heat the oil in a heavy pan, add the onion and garlic and cook until soft. Add the rice and stir to coat the grains with oil. Add the wine and cook, stirring, over medium heat, for a few minutes until absorbed.

2 Add ⅔ cup of the hot fish stock and cook, stirring constantly, until the liquid is absorbed by the rice. Continue stirring and adding stock in ⅔ cup quantities, until half of the stock is left. This should take about 10 minutes.

3 Stir in the seafood and cook for 2–3 minutes. Add the remaining stock as before, until the rice is cooked. It should be quite creamy and the grains al dente.

4 Stir in the lemon zest, tomato paste and parsley. Season with salt and pepper and serve warm.

Italian Shrimp Skewers

Simple and delicious mouthfuls from the Amalfi Coast.

2 pounds raw shrimp, peeled
¼ cup olive oil
3 tablespoons vegetable oil
1¼ cups very fine dry bread crumbs
1 garlic clove, crushed
1 tablespoon chopped fresh parsley
salt and ground black pepper
lemon wedges, to serve

Serves 4

1 Slit the shrimp down their backs and remove the dark vein. Rinse in cold water and pat dry.

2 Put the olive oil and vegetable oil in a large bowl and add the shrimp, mixing them to coat evenly. Add the bread crumbs, garlic and parsley and season with salt and pepper. Toss the shrimp thoroughly to give them an even coating of bread crumbs. Cover and let marinate for at least 1 hour.

3 Thread the shrimp onto four metal or wooden skewers, curling them up as you do so, so that the tail is skewered in the middle.

4 Preheat the broiler. Place the skewers in the broiler pan and cook for about 2 minutes on each side, until the bread crumbs are golden. Serve with lemon wedges.

BLACK PASTA WITH SQUID SAUCE

Tagliatelle flavored with squid ink looks amazing and tastes deliciously of the sea. You'll find it at good Italian food stores.

7 tablespoons olive oil
2 shallots, chopped
3 garlic cloves, crushed
3 tablespoons chopped fresh parsley
1½ pounds cleaned squid, cut into rings and rinsed
⅔ cup dry white wine
14-ounce can chopped tomatoes
½ teaspoon dried red pepper flakes
1 pound squid ink tagliatelle
salt and ground black pepper

SERVES 4

1 Heat the oil in a pan and add the shallots. Cook until pale golden, then add the garlic. When the garlic colors a little, add 2 tablespoons of the parsley, stir, then add the squid and stir again. Cook for 3–4 minutes, then add the wine.

2 Simmer for a few seconds, then add the tomatoes and red pepper flakes (*right*) and season with salt and pepper. Cover and simmer gently for about 1 hour, until the squid is tender. Add more water if necessary.

3 Cook the pasta in plenty of boiling salted water, according to the instructions on the package, or until al dente. Drain and return the tagliatelle to the pan. Add the squid sauce and mix well. Sprinkle each serving with the remaining chopped parsley and serve immediately.

SICILIAN SPAGHETTI WITH SARDINES

A traditional dish from Sicily, with ingredients that are common to many parts of the Mediterranean.

12 fresh sardines, cleaned and boned
1 cup olive oil
1 onion, chopped
¼ cup dill sprigs
½ cup pine nuts
2 tablespoons raisins, soaked in water
½ cup fresh bread crumbs
1 pound spaghetti
flour for dusting
salt

SERVES 4

1. Wash the sardines and pat dry on paper towels. Open them out flat, then cut in half lengthwise.

2. Heat 2 tablespoons of the oil in a pan, add the onion and fry until golden. Add the dill and cook gently for a minute or two. Add the pine nuts and raisins and season with salt. Dry-fry the bread crumbs in a frying pan until golden. Set aside.

3. Cook the spaghetti in boiling salted water according to the instructions on the package until al dente. Heat the remaining oil in a pan. Dust the sardines with flour and fry in the hot oil for 2–3 minutes. Drain on paper towels.

4. Drain the spaghetti and return to the pan. Add the onion mixture and toss well. Transfer the spaghetti mixture to a serving platter and arrange the fried sardines on top. Sprinkle with the toasted bread crumbs and serve immediately.

GRILLED JUMBO SHRIMP WITH ROMESCO SAUCE

This sauce, from the Catalan region of Spain, is served with fish and shellfish. Its main ingredients are pimento, tomatoes, garlic and almonds.

24 raw jumbo shrimp
2–3 tablespoons olive oil
flat-leaf parsley, to garnish
lemon wedges, to serve

FOR THE SAUCE
2 ripe tomatoes
4 tablespoons olive oil
1 onion, chopped
4 garlic cloves, chopped
1 canned pimiento, chopped
½ teaspoon dried red pepper flakes
5 tablespoons fish stock
2 tablespoons white wine
10 blanched almonds
1 tablespoon red wine vinegar
salt

SERVES 4

1 To make the sauce, immerse the tomatoes in boiling water for about 30 seconds, then refresh them under cold water. Peel off the skins and coarsely chop the flesh.

2 Heat 2 tablespoons of the oil in a pan, add the onion and three-fourths of the chopped garlic and cook until soft. Add the pimiento, tomatoes, red pepper flakes, fish stock and wine, then cover and simmer for 30 minutes.

3 Toast the almonds under the broiler until golden. Transfer to a blender or food processor and grind coarsely. Add the remaining 2 tablespoons of oil, the vinegar and the remaining chopped garlic and process until evenly combined. Add the tomato and pimiento sauce and process until smooth. Season with salt.

4 Remove the heads from the shrimp, leaving them otherwise unshelled, and, with a sharp knife, slit each one down the back and remove the dark vein. Rinse and pat dry on paper towels. Preheat the broiler. Toss the shrimp in olive oil, then spread out in the broiler pan. Broil for 2–3 minutes on each side, until pink. Arrange on a serving platter with the lemon wedges, and place the sauce in a small bowl. Serve immediately, garnished with parsley.

GRILLED SEA BASS WITH FENNEL

This dish is served in almost every seafood restaurant on the French Mediterranean coast. Traditionally, fennel twigs are used, but as they are hard to find, this recipe uses fennel seeds.

1 sea bass, weighing
4–4½ pounds, cleaned
4–6 tablespoons olive oil
2–3 teaspoons fennel seeds
2 large fennel bulbs, trimmed and thinly sliced (reserve any fronds)
¼ cup Pernod
salt and ground black pepper

SERVES 6–8

1 With a sharp knife, make three or four deep cuts in both sides of the fish. Brush the fish with olive oil and season with salt and pepper. Sprinkle the fennel seeds in the stomach cavity and in the cuts. Set aside while you cook the fennel.

2 Preheat the broiler. Put the slices of fennel in an ovenproof dish or on the broiler rack and brush with oil. Broil for 4 minutes on each side, until tender. Transfer to a large platter.

3 Place the fish on the oiled broiler rack and position 4–5 inches away from the heat. Cook for 10–12 minutes on each side, brushing with oil occasionally.

4 Transfer the fish to the platter on top of the fennel. Garnish with fennel fronds. Heat the Pernod in a small pan, light it and pour it, flaming, over the fish. Serve immediately.

BRANDADE DE MORUE

Salt cod is popular in Spain and France, and it can be found cooked in a number of ways. This recipe is a purée flavored with garlic and olive oil that is made all over southern France.

1½ pounds salt cod
1¼ cups olive oil
1 cup milk
1 garlic clove, crushed
grated nutmeg
lemon juice, to taste
white pepper
parsley sprigs, to garnish

FOR THE CROUTONS
¼ cup olive oil
6 slices white bread, crusts removed
1 garlic clove, halved

SERVES 6

1. Soak the salt cod in cold water for at least 24 hours, changing the water several times. Drain.

2. To make the croutons, heat the oil in a frying pan. Cut the bread slices in half diagonally and fry in the hot oil until golden. Drain on paper towels, then rub both sides with garlic.

3. Put the cod in a large pan with enough cold water to cover. Cover and bring to a boil. Simmer gently for 8–10 minutes, until just tender. Drain and cool. Flake the fish and discard any skin and bones.

4. Heat the oil in a pan until very hot. In a separate pan, scald the milk. Transfer the fish to a blender or food processor and, with the motor running, slowly pour in the hot oil, followed by the milk, until the mixture is smooth and stiff. Transfer to a bowl and beat in the crushed garlic. Season with nutmeg, lemon juice and white pepper. Let the **brandade** cool and then chill until almost ready to serve.

5. Spoon the brandade into a shallow serving bowl and surround with the croutons. Garnish with parsley and serve cold.

MOUCLADE OF MUSSELS

This recipe is quite similar to Moules Marinière but has the additional flavoring of fennel and mild curry. Traditionally, the mussels are shelled and piled into scallop shells, but nothing beats a bowlful of steaming hot, garlicky mussels, served in their own glistening shells.

4½ pounds fresh mussels
1 cup dry white wine
good pinch of grated nutmeg
3 thyme sprigs
2 bay leaves
1 small onion, finely chopped
4 tablespoons butter
1 fennel bulb, thinly sliced
4 garlic cloves, crushed
½ teaspoon curry paste or powder
2 tablespoons all-purpose flour
⅔ cup heavy cream
ground black pepper
chopped fresh dill, to garnish

SERVES 6

1 Scrub the mussels, discarding any that are damaged or open ones that do not close when tapped with a knife.

2 Put the wine, nutmeg, thyme, bay leaves and onion in a large saucepan and bring just to a boil. Pour in the mussels and cover with a lid. Cook for 4–5 minutes, until the mussels have opened.

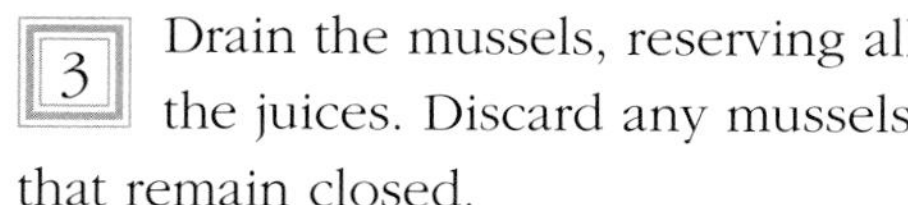

3 Drain the mussels, reserving all the juices. Discard any mussels that remain closed.

4 Melt the butter in a large clean pan and gently sauté the fennel slices and garlic for about 5 minutes, until softened.

5 Stir in the curry paste or powder and flour and cook for 1 minute. Remove from the heat and gradually blend in the cooking juices from the mussels. Return to the heat and cook, stirring, for 2 minutes.

6 Stir in the cream and a little pepper. Add the mussels to the pan and heat through for 2 minutes. Serve hot, garnished with dill.

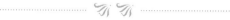

VARIATION

Saffron is a popular addition to a mouclade. Soak ½ teaspoon saffron strands in a little boiling water and add to the sauce with the stock.

Octopus and Red Wine Stew

Unless you're happy to clean and prepare octopus for this Greek dish, buy one that's ready for cooking.

2 pounds prepared octopus
1 pound onions, sliced
2 bay leaves
1 pound ripe tomatoes
¼ cup olive oil
4 garlic cloves, crushed
1 teaspoon sugar
1 tablespoon chopped fresh oregano or rosemary
2 tablespoons chopped fresh parsley
⅔ cup red wine
2 tablespoons red wine vinegar
chopped fresh herbs, to garnish
warm bread and pine nuts, to serve

Serves 4

1 Put the octopus in a saucepan of gently simmering water with a quarter of the onions and the bay leaves. Cook gently for 1 hour.

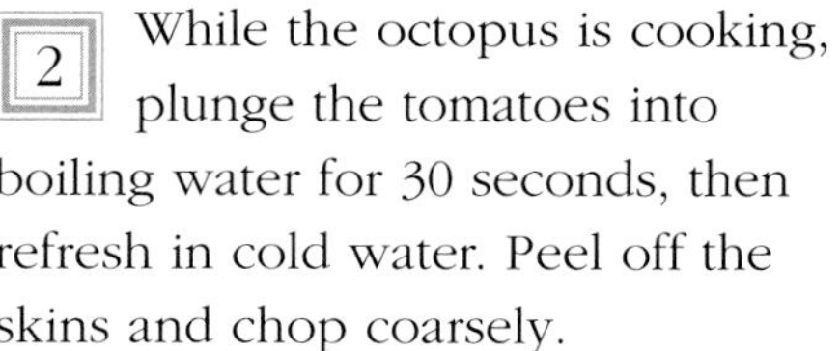

2 While the octopus is cooking, plunge the tomatoes into boiling water for 30 seconds, then refresh in cold water. Peel off the skins and chop coarsely.

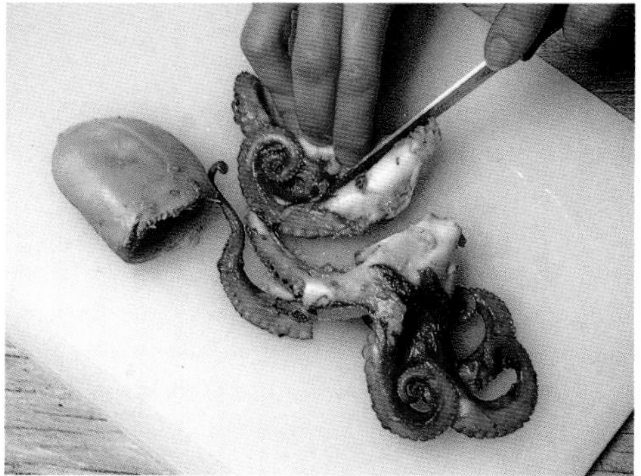

3 Drain the octopus and, using a sharp knife, cut it into bite-size pieces. Discard the head.

4 Heat the oil in a saucepan and sauté the octopus, the remaining onions and the garlic for 3 minutes. Add the tomatoes, sugar, oregano or rosemary, parsley, wine and vinegar and cook, stirring, for 5 minutes, until pulpy.

5 Cover the pan and cook over the lowest possible heat for about 1½ hours, until the sauce is thickened and the octopus is tender. Garnish with fresh herbs and serve with warm bread and pine nuts to sprinkle on top.

Variation

Use white wine instead of red and stir in ½ cup coarsely chopped black olives before serving.

Fresh Tuna and Tomato Stew

A deliciously simple dish that relies on good basic ingredients. For real Italian flavor, serve with polenta or pasta and an herb salad.

12 baby onions, peeled
2 pounds ripe tomatoes
1½ pounds fresh tuna
3 tablespoons olive oil
2 garlic cloves, crushed
3 tablespoons chopped fresh herbs
2 bay leaves
½ teaspoon sugar
2 tablespoons sun-dried tomato paste
⅔ cup dry white wine
salt and ground black pepper
baby zucchini and fresh herbs, to garnish

Serves 4

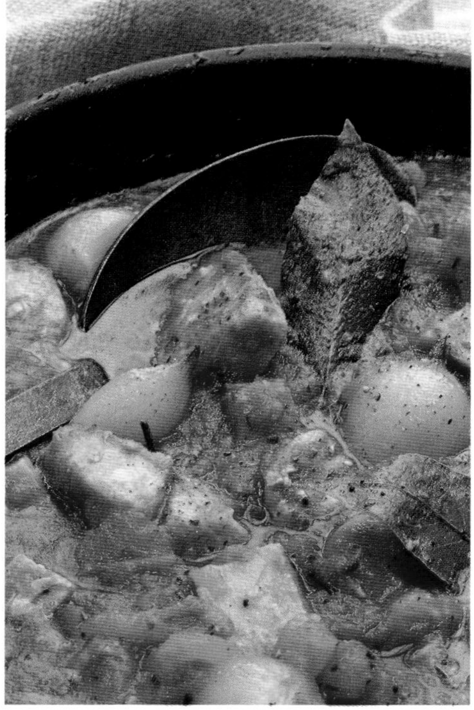

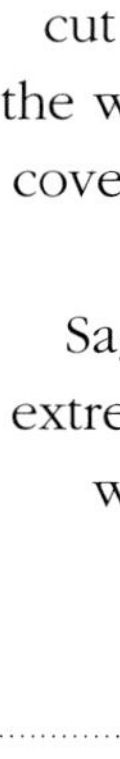

Variation

Two large mackerel make a nice alternative to the tuna. Fillet them and cut them into chunks or simply lay the whole fish on the sauce and cook, covered with a lid, until the mackerel is cooked through.

Sage, rosemary or oregano all go extremely well with this dish. Choose whichever you prefer, or use a mixture of one or two.

1 Leave the onions whole and cook in a pan of boiling water for 4–5 minutes, until softened. Drain.

2 Plunge the tomatoes into boiling water for 30 seconds, then refresh in cold water. Peel off the skins and chop coarsely.

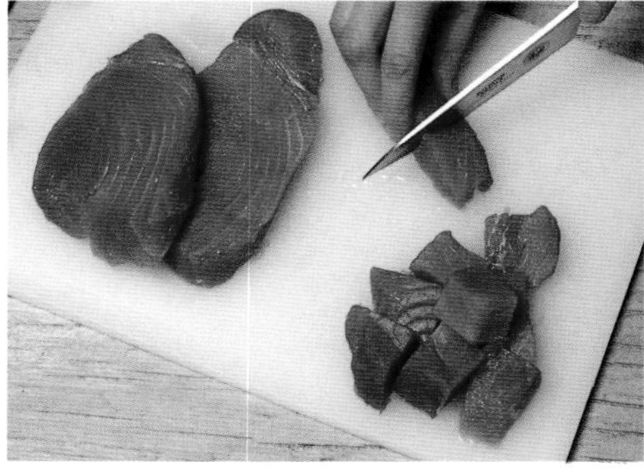

3 Cut the tuna into 1-inch chunks. Heat the oil in a large frying or sauté pan and quickly sauté the tuna until browned. Drain.

4 Add the onions, garlic, tomatoes, chopped herbs, bay leaves, sugar, tomato paste and wine and bring to a boil, breaking up the tomatoes with a wooden spoon.

5 Reduce the heat and simmer gently for 5 minutes. Return the fish to the pan and cook for another 5 minutes. Season and serve hot, garnished with baby zucchini and fresh herbs.

BRODETTO

The different regions of Italy have their own variations of this dish, but all require a good fish stock. Make sure you buy some of the fish whole so you can simply simmer them, remove the cooked flesh and strain the deliciously flavored juices to make the stock.

2 pounds mixed fish fillets or steaks, such as monkfish, cod, haddock, halibut or hake
2 pounds mixed conger eel, red or gray mullet, snapper or small white fish
1 onion, halved
1 celery stalk, coarsely chopped
½ pound squid
½ pound fresh mussels
1½ pounds ripe tomatoes
¼ cup olive oil
1 large onion, thinly sliced
3 garlic cloves, crushed
1 teaspoon saffron strands
⅔ cup dry white wine
6 tablespoons chopped fresh parsley
salt and ground black pepper
croutons, to serve

SERVES 4–5

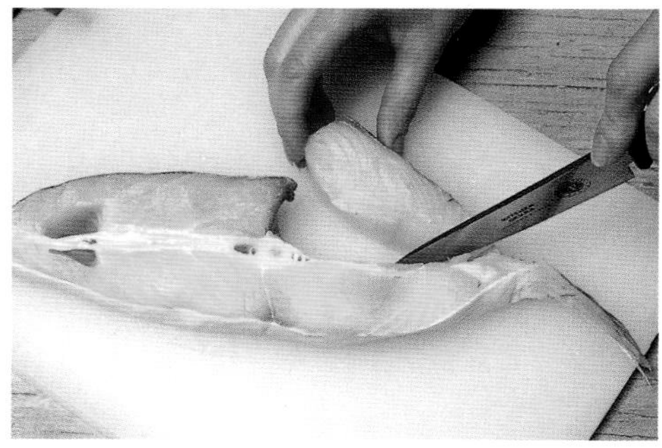

1 Remove any skin and bones from the fish fillets or steaks, cut the fish into large pieces and reserve. Place the bones in a pan with all the remaining fish.

2 Add the halved onion and the celery and just cover with water. Bring almost to a boil, then reduce the heat and simmer gently for about 30 minutes. Lift out the fish and remove the flesh from the bones. Reserve the stock.

3 To prepare the squid, twist the head and tentacles away from the body. Cut the head from the tentacles. Discard the body contents and peel off the mottled skin. Wash the tentacles and bodies and dry on paper towels.

COOK'S TIP

To make the croutons, cut thin slices from a long thin stick of bread and shallow-fry in a little butter until golden.

4 Scrub the mussels, discarding any that are damaged or open ones that do not close when tapped.

5 Plunge the tomatoes into boiling water for 30 seconds, then refresh in cold water. Peel off the skins and chop coarsely.

6 Heat the oil in a large saucepan or sauté pan. Add the sliced onion and the garlic and sauté gently for 3 minutes. Add the squid and the uncooked fish that you reserved earlier and sauté quickly on all sides. Drain.

7 Add 2 cups strained reserved fish stock, the saffron and tomatoes to the pan. Pour in the wine. Bring to a boil, then reduce the heat and simmer for about 5 minutes. Add the mussels, cover, and cook for 3–4 minutes, until the mussels have opened. Discard any that remain closed.

8 Season the sauce with salt and pepper and put all the fish in the pan. Cook gently for 5 minutes. Sprinkle on the parsley and serve with the croutons.

SARDINE GRATIN

In Sicily and other regions of the western Mediterranean, sardines are filled with a robust stuffing, flavorful enough to compete with the rich oiliness of the fish.

1 tablespoon light olive oil
½ small onion, finely chopped
2 garlic cloves, crushed
6 tablespoons blanched almonds, chopped
2 tablespoons golden raisins, coarsely chopped
10 pitted black olives
2 tablespoons capers, coarsely chopped
2 tablespoons coarsely chopped fresh parsley
1 cup bread crumbs
16 large sardines, scaled and gutted
⅓ cup grated Parmesan cheese
salt and ground black pepper
flat-leaf parsley, to garnish

SERVES 4

1 Preheat the oven to 400°F. Lightly oil a large, shallow ovenproof dish.

2 Heat the oil in a frying pan and sauté the onion and garlic gently for 3 minutes. Stir in the almonds, raisins, olives, capers, parsley and ¼ cup of the bread crumbs. Season lightly with salt and pepper.

ABOVE: Brodetto (top) and Sardine Gratin (bottom)

3 Make 2–3 diagonal cuts on each side of the sardines. Pack the stuffing into the cavities and lay the sardines in the prepared dish.

4 Mix the remaining bread crumbs with the cheese and sprinkle on the fish. Bake for about 20 minutes, until the fish is cooked through. Test by piercing one sardine through the thickest part with a knife. Garnish with parsley and serve immediately, with a leafy salad.

ZARZUELA

Zarzuela means "light opera" or "musical comedy" in Spanish, and the classic fish stew of the same name should be as lively and colorful as the zarzuela itself. This feast of fish includes lobster and other shellfish, but you can modify the ingredients to suit the occasion and availability.

1 cooked lobster
24 fresh mussels or clams
1 large monkfish tail
8 ounces squid rings
1 tablespoon all-purpose flour
6 tablespoons olive oil
12 large raw shrimp
1 pound ripe tomatoes
2 large mild onions, chopped
4 garlic cloves, crushed
2 tablespoons brandy
2 bay leaves
1 teaspoon paprika
1 fresh red chile, seeded and chopped
1¼ cups fish stock
2 tablespoons ground almonds
2 tablespoons chopped fresh parsley
salt and ground black pepper

SERVES 6

1 Using a large knife, cut the lobster in half lengthwise. Remove the dark intestine that runs down the length of the tail. Crack the claws using a hammer.

2 Scrub the mussels, discarding any that are damaged or open ones that do not close when tapped with a knife. Cut the monkfish fillets away from the central cartilage and cut each fillet into three pieces.

3 Toss the monkfish and squid in seasoned flour. Heat the oil in a large frying pan. Add the monkfish and squid and sauté quickly; remove from the pan. Sauté the shrimp on both sides, then remove from the pan.

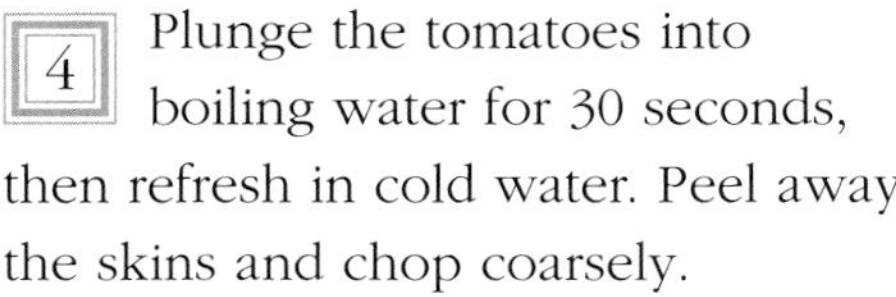

4 Plunge the tomatoes into boiling water for 30 seconds, then refresh in cold water. Peel away the skins and chop coarsely.

5 Add the onions and two-thirds of the garlic to the frying pan and, stirring thoroughly, sauté for about 3 minutes. Add the brandy and ignite. When the flames die down, add the tomatoes, bay leaves, paprika, chile and stock.

6 Bring to a boil, reduce the heat and simmer gently for 5 minutes. Add the mussels or clams, cover and cook for 3–4 minutes, until the shells have opened.

7 Remove the mussels or clams from the sauce and discard any that remain closed.

8 Arrange all the fish, including the lobster, in a large flameproof serving dish. Blend the ground almonds to a paste with the remaining garlic and parsley and stir into the sauce. Season with salt and pepper.

9 Pour the sauce over the fish and lobster and cook gently for about 5 minutes, until hot. Serve immediately with a green salad and plenty of warm bread.

Baked Fish with Tahini Sauce

This North African recipe evokes all the color and rich flavors of Mediterranean cuisine. Choose any whole white fish, such as sea bass, hake, bream or snapper.

1 whole fish, about 2½ pounds, scaled and cleaned
2 teaspoons coriander seeds
4 garlic cloves, sliced
2 teaspoons harissa
6 tablespoons olive oil
6 plum tomatoes, sliced
1 mild onion, sliced
3 preserved lemons or 1 fresh lemon
plenty of fresh herbs, such as bay leaves, thyme and rosemary
salt and ground black pepper

For the sauce
⅓ cup light tahini
juice of 1 lemon
1 garlic clove, crushed
3 tablespoons finely chopped fresh parsley or cilantro
extra herbs, to garnish

Serves 4

1. Preheat the oven to 400°F. Grease the bottom and sides of a large, shallow ovenproof dish or roasting pan.

2. Slash the fish diagonally on both sides with a sharp knife. Finely crush the coriander seeds and garlic with a mortar and pestle. Mix with the harissa and about 4 tablespoons of the olive oil.

3. Spread a little of the harissa, coriander and garlic paste inside the cavity of the fish. Spread the remainder over each side of the fish and set aside.

4. Scatter the tomatoes, onion and preserved or fresh lemon into the dish. (Thinly slice the lemon if using fresh.) Sprinkle with the remaining oil and season with salt and pepper. Lay the fish on top and tuck plenty of herbs around it.

5. Bake, uncovered, for about 25 minutes or until the fish has turned opaque—test by piercing the thickest part with a knife.

6. Meanwhile, make the sauce. Put the tahini, lemon juice, garlic and parsley or cilantro in a small saucepan with ½ cup water and add a little salt and pepper. Cook gently until smooth and heated through. Serve in a separate dish.

Cook's Tip

If you can't get a suitable large fish, use small whole fish such as red snapper or even cod or haddock steaks. Remember to reduce the cooking time slightly.

STUFFED SQUID

This Greek delicacy is best made with large squid, because they are less awkward to stuff. If you have to make do with small squid, buy about 1 pound.

FOR THE STUFFING

2 tablespoons olive oil
1 large onion, finely chopped
2 garlic cloves, crushed
1 cup fresh bread crumbs
4 tablespoons chopped fresh parsley
4 ounces halloumi cheese, grated
salt and ground black pepper

TO FINISH

4 drained squid, each about 7 inches long
2 pounds ripe tomatoes
3 tablespoons olive oil
1 large onion, chopped
1 teaspoon sugar
½ cup dry white wine
several rosemary sprigs
toasted pine nuts and flat-leaf parsley, to garnish

SERVES 4

1 To make the stuffing, heat the oil in a frying pan and sauté the onion for 3 minutes. Remove the pan from the heat and add the garlic, bread crumbs, parsley, cheese and a little salt and pepper. Stir until thoroughly blended.

2 Dry the squid on paper towels and fill with the prepared stuffing using a teaspoon. Secure the ends of the squid with wooden toothpicks.

VARIATION

If you would prefer a less rich filling, halve the quantity of cheese and bread crumbs in the stuffing and add 8 ounces cooked spinach.

3 Plunge the tomatoes into boiling water for 30 seconds, then refresh in cold water. Peel off the skins and chop coarsely.

4 Heat the oil in a frying pan or sauté pan. Add the squid and sauté on all sides. Remove from the pan.

5 Add the onion to the pan and sauté gently for 3 minutes. Stir in the tomatoes, sugar and wine and cook rapidly until the mixture becomes thick and pulpy.

6 Return the squid to the pan with the rosemary. Cover and cook gently for 30 minutes. Slice the squid and serve on individual plates with the sauce. Sprinkle the pine nuts on top and garnish with parsley.

HAKE AND CLAMS WITH SALSA VERDE

Hake (an Atlantic fish) is one of the most popular fish in Spain; here, it is cooked in a sauce flavored with parsley, lemon juice and garlic.

4 hake steaks, about ¾ inch thick
½ cup flour for dusting, plus 2 tablespoons
4 tablespoons olive oil
1 tablespoon lemon juice
1 small onion, finely chopped
4 garlic cloves, crushed
⅔ cup fish stock
⅔ cup white wine
6 tablespoons chopped fresh parsley
3 ounces frozen tiny peas
16 fresh clams
salt and ground black pepper

SERVES 4

1 Preheat the oven to 350°F. Season the fish with salt and pepper, then dust both sides with flour. Heat 2 tablespoons of the oil in a large sauté pan, add the fish and sauté for about 1 minute on each side. Transfer to an ovenproof dish and sprinkle with lemon juice.

2 Clean the pan, then heat the remaining oil. Add the onion and garlic and cook until soft. Stir in 2 tablespoons flour and cook for about 1 minute. Gradually add the stock and wine, stirring until thickened and smooth. Add 5 tablespoons of the parsley and the peas and season with salt and pepper.

3 Pour the sauce over the fish and bake for 15–20 minutes, adding the clams to the dish 3–4 minutes before the end of the cooking time. Discard any clams that do not open, then sprinkle with the remaining parsley before serving.

COD PLAKI

This is a traditional Greek preparation for fish, using onions, tomatoes, parsley and olive oil. Although cod is an Atlantic fish, it works very well in this recipe.

1¼ cups olive oil
2 onions, thinly sliced
3 large ripe tomatoes, coarsely chopped
3 garlic cloves, thinly sliced
1 teaspoon sugar
1 teaspoon chopped fresh dill
1 teaspoon chopped fresh mint
1 teaspoon chopped fresh celery leaves
1 tablespoon chopped fresh parsley
6 cod steaks
juice of 1 lemon
salt and ground black pepper
extra dill, mint or parsley, to garnish

SERVES 6

1 Heat the oil in a large sauté pan or flameproof dish. Add the onions and cook until pale golden. Add the tomatoes, garlic, sugar, dill, mint, celery leaves and parsley with 1¼ cups water. Season with salt and pepper, then simmer, uncovered, for 25 minutes, until the liquid has reduced by one-third.

2 Add the fish steaks and cook gently for 10–12 minutes, until the fish is just cooked. Remove from the heat and add the lemon juice (*left*). Cover and let stand for about 20 minutes before serving. Arrange the cod in a dish and spoon the sauce over. Garnish with herbs and serve warm or cold.

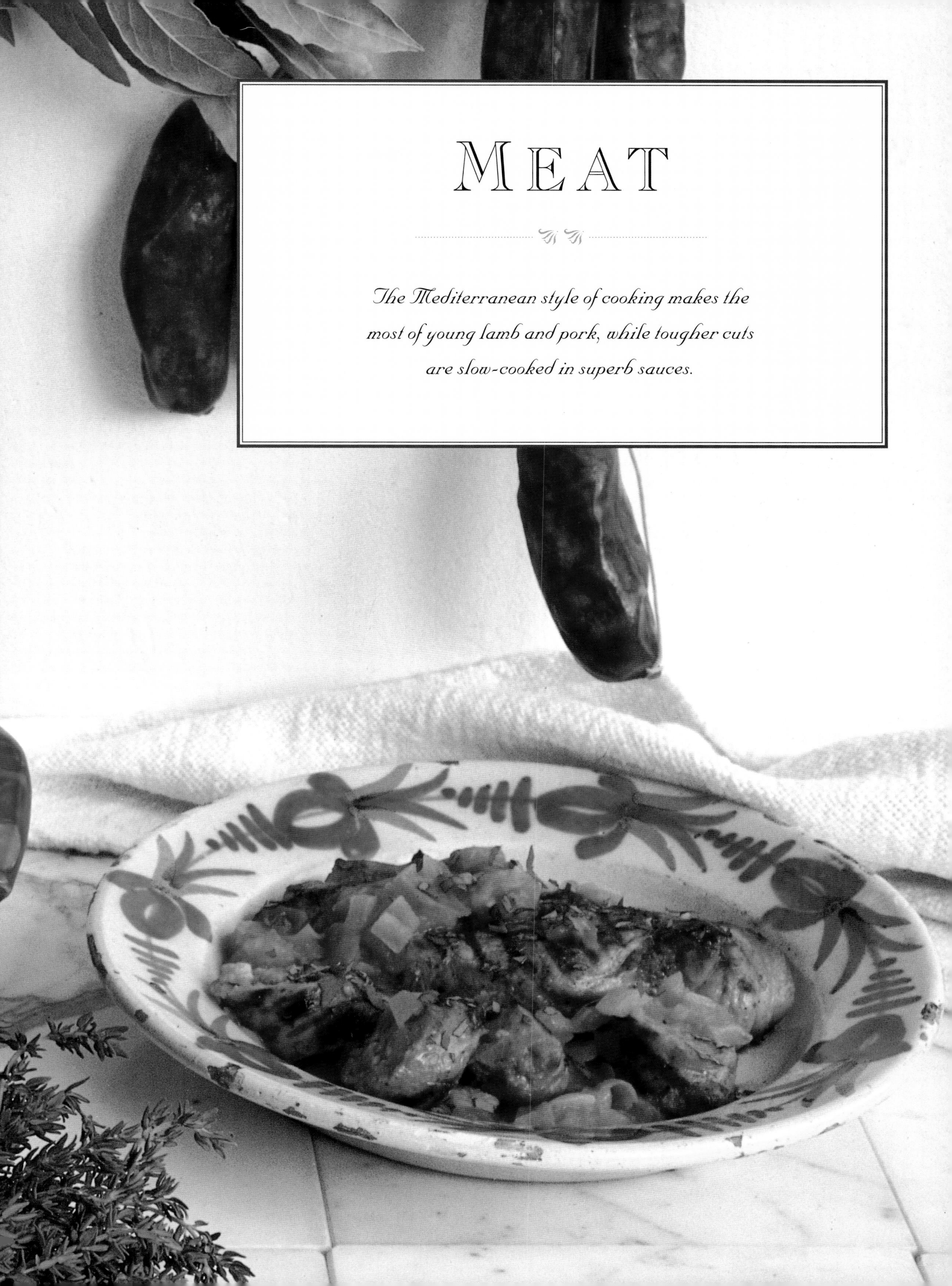

MEAT

The Mediterranean style of cooking makes the most of young lamb and pork, while tougher cuts are slow-cooked in superb sauces.

Above: Sunlight dapples the walls of this farmhouse overlooking Lake Trasimeno, in Umbria.

Unlike the vegetable and fish recipes from the Mediterranean, meat recipes do not readily spring to mind. The countryside around the Mediterranean can be quite harsh—no lush, green fields for animals to graze. Beasts are often slaughtered young, and baby lamb and goat are favorite meats. Traditionally, these animals were usually roasted whole on a spit, flavored with wild herbs, and eaten on feast days. The meat of the young kid is particularly popular in certain parts of the Mediterranean, such as Corsica, parts of Greece and the Middle East. Cattle are a rare sight and, in times past, beef was considered a luxury. Many rural families kept a pig, which was slaughtered and the meat preserved, to feed them through the chilly winter months. This, in turn, inspired the many wonderful dry sausages, like salami, and the cured hams, which are still popular today, and appreciated all over the world. Both Jews and Muslims were forbidden by their religion to eat pork, so there are no traditional pork recipes from their countries and regions.

In the Middle East, only lamb and mutton were eaten, although nowadays beef and veal are becoming more popular. The Roman Catholic and Greek Orthodox Churches used to have strict rules concerning "lean" days, when meat could not be consumed, and therefore many special feast dishes using meat were created to celebrate the ends of these regular fasts.

Meat was often of poor quality if the beast had not been properly fed, resulting in tough and stringy cuts. This was remedied by marinating the meat in wine or yogurt and cooking it slowly at a low temperature, to tenderize it and improve the flavor. These methods resulted in some of the most delicious recipes for casseroles and stews. Many are still cooked today, despite the fact that the meat is probably of better quality. Daubes from France, tagines from Morocco, estofados

RIGHT: This French shepherd has a magnificent view of the Provençal countryside.

BELOW: Sacks of spices and grains invite inspection at a Tunisian market.

from Spain—every country has its own version, recipes having been handed down through the generations. As meat was a luxury, beans, rice and potatoes were often added to the pot to make the meal go further.

Another popular method of cooking meat is broiling. Quite often the meat is threaded onto skewers, or sometimes a branch of rosemary or bay, with chunks of onion and other vegetables. This is a basic form of cooking, originating from cooking over the hot embers of an open fire, and it results in succulent, smoky-flavored meat. Greece and the Middle East have mastered this technique, and the smell of meat cooking on a wood fire is one associated with these countries. Using ground meat, in the form of patties, meatballs, sausages, sauces for pasta and fillings for savory pastries, is popular throughout the Mediterranean. This was another way of padding out meat with other ingredients to make a more economical dish. Bread crumbs, rice, bulgur and potatoes are all used to add more bulk, particularly when making meatballs and patties. Onion and tomatoes give flavor and volume to sauces. In the Middle East, spices, nuts and dried fruits are often mixed with ground meat, to make delicious fillings for little parcels of phyllo. Elsewhere, in Italy, garlic, wine, and herbs are added to slow-cooked meat sauces, to eat with pasta. In Greece, ground lamb is layered with eggplant, tomato sauce and béchamel sauce to create Moussaka, and in Turkey, ground lamb is used to stuff halved eggplant, the vegetable flesh being mixed with the ground meat. These versatile dishes are good for feeding a large crowd, often making a little go a long way.

Although there are no recipes for goat in this chapter (as it is not readily available), the selection varies from Sicilian Pork with Marsala to Turkish Lamb Pilaf and Greek Lamb Sausages with Tomato Sauce. As with most recipes in this book, all that is needed to accompany any of them, once cooked and ready to eat, is a glass of wine (in this case red) and some good bread!

TURKISH LAMB PILAF

Here we have a delicious combination of rice, lamb, spices, nuts and fruit—a typical Middle Eastern dish.

3 tablespoons butter
1 large onion, finely chopped
1 pound lamb fillet, cut into small cubes
½ teaspoon ground cinnamon
2 tablespoons tomato paste
3 tablespoons chopped fresh parsley
½ cup dried apricots, halved
¾ cup pistachios
1 pound long-grain rice, rinsed
salt and ground black pepper
flat-leaf parsley, to garnish

SERVES 4

1 Heat the butter in a large, heavy pan. Add the onion and cook until soft and golden. Add the cubed lamb and brown on all sides. Add the cinnamon and season with salt and pepper. Cover and cook gently for 10 minutes.

2 Add the tomato paste and enough water to cover the meat. Stir in the parsley, bring to a boil, cover and simmer very gently for 1½ hours, until the meat is tender. Chop the pistachios.

3 Add enough water to the pan to measure about 2½ cups liquid. Add the apricots, pistachios and rice, bring to a boil, cover tightly and simmer for about 20 minutes, until the rice is cooked. (You may need to add a little more water.) Transfer to a warmed serving dish and garnish with parsley before serving.

GREEK LAMB SAUSAGES WITH TOMATO SAUCE

The Greek name for these sausages is "soudzoukakia." They are more like elongated meatballs than the sausage shapes we are accustomed to. Passata is strained tomato pulp, which can be bought in cartons or jars.

1 cup fresh bread crumbs
⅔ cup milk
1½ pounds ground lamb
2 tablespoons grated onion
3 garlic cloves, crushed
2 teaspoons ground cumin
2 tablespoons chopped fresh parsley
flour for dusting
olive oil for frying
2½ cups passata
1 teaspoon sugar
2 bay leaves
1 small onion, peeled
salt and ground black pepper
flat-leaf parsley, to garnish

SERVES 4

1. Combine the bread crumbs and milk. Add the lamb, onion, garlic, cumin and parsley and season with salt and pepper.

2. Shape the mixture with your hands into little fat sausages, about 2 inches long, and roll them in flour. Heat about ¼ cup olive oil in a frying pan.

3. Fry the sausages for about 8 minutes, turning them until evenly browned. Remove and place on paper towels to drain.

4. Put the passata, sugar, bay leaves and whole onion in a pan and simmer for 20 minutes. Add the sausages and cook for 10 more minutes. Serve garnished with parsley.

ROAST LOIN OF PORK STUFFED WITH FIGS, OLIVES AND ALMONDS

Pork is a popular meat in Spain, and this recipe using fruit and nuts in the stuffing is inspired by Catalan cooking, where the combination of meat and fruit is quite common.

4 tablespoons olive oil
1 onion, finely chopped
2 garlic cloves, chopped
1½ cups fresh bread crumbs
4 dried figs, chopped
8 pitted green olives, chopped
¼ cup sliced almonds
1 tablespoon lemon juice
1 tablespoon chopped fresh parsley
1 egg yolk
2 pounds boned loin of pork
salt and ground black pepper

SERVES 4

1 Preheat the oven to 400°F. Heat 3 tablespoons of the oil in a pan, add the onion and garlic, and cook gently until softened. Remove the pan from the heat and stir in the bread crumbs, figs, olives, almonds, lemon juice, parsley and egg yolk. Season to taste.

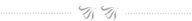

COOK'S TIP

Keep a container of bread crumbs in the freezer. They can be used frozen.

2 Remove any string from the pork and unroll the belly flap, cutting away any excess fat or meat to enable you to do so. Spread half the stuffing on the flat piece and roll up, starting from the thick side. Tie at intervals with string.

3 Pour the remaining oil into a small roasting pan and put in the pork. Roast for 1 hour and 15 minutes. Form the remaining stuffing mixture into balls and add to the roasting pan around the meat 15–20 minutes before the end of cooking time.

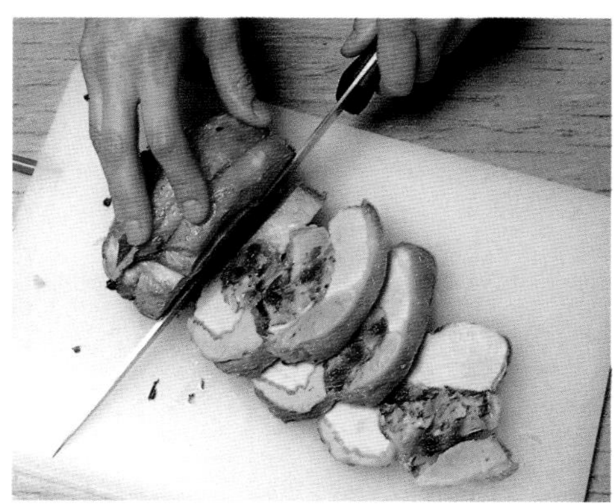

4 Remove the pork from the oven and let it rest for 10 minutes. Carve into thick slices and serve with the stuffing balls and any juices from the pan. This is also good served cold.

LAMB WITH RED PEPPERS AND RIOJA

Plenty of garlic, bell peppers, herbs and red wine give this lamb stew a lovely, rich flavor. Slice through the pepper stems, rather than removing them, as this makes it look extra special.

2 pounds lean lamb fillet
1 tablespoon all-purpose flour
¼ cup olive oil
2 red onions, sliced
4 garlic cloves, sliced
2 teaspoons paprika
¼ teaspoon ground cloves
1⅔ cups red Rioja wine
⅔ cup lamb stock
2 bay leaves
2 thyme sprigs
3 red bell peppers, halved and seeded
salt and ground black pepper
bay leaves and thyme sprigs, to garnish
green beans and saffron rice or boiled potatoes, to serve

SERVES 4

1 Preheat the oven to 325°F. Cut the lamb into chunks. Season the flour, add the lamb and toss lightly to coat.

2 Heat the oil in a frying pan and sauté the lamb, stirring, until browned. Transfer to an ovenproof dish. Lightly sauté the onions in the pan with the garlic, paprika and cloves.

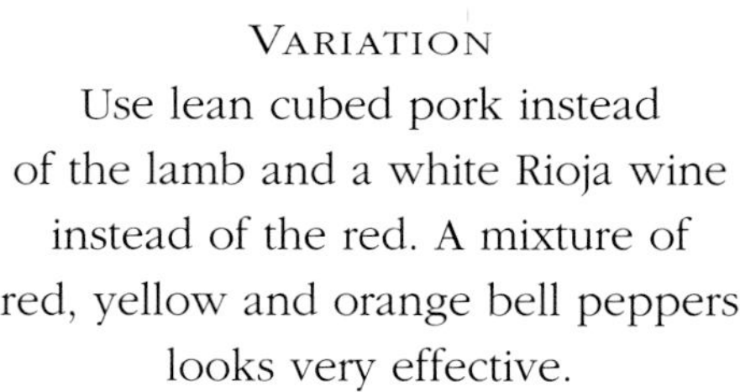

VARIATION

Use lean cubed pork instead of the lamb and a white Rioja wine instead of the red. A mixture of red, yellow and orange bell peppers looks very effective.

3 Add the Rioja, stock, bay leaves and thyme and bring to a boil, stirring. Pour the contents of the pan onto the meat. Cover with a lid and bake for 30 minutes.

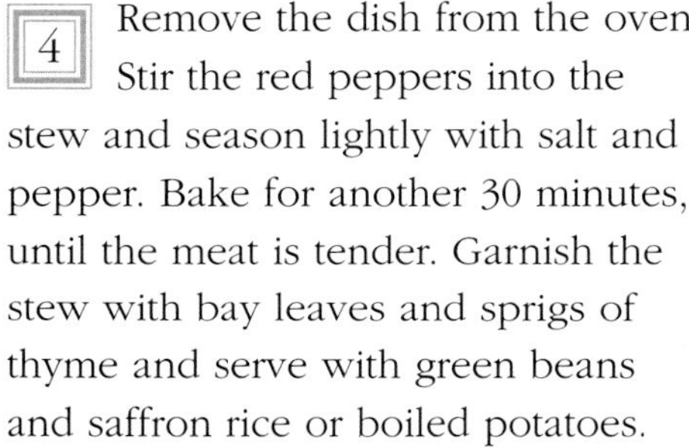

4 Remove the dish from the oven. Stir the red peppers into the stew and season lightly with salt and pepper. Bake for another 30 minutes, until the meat is tender. Garnish the stew with bay leaves and sprigs of thyme and serve with green beans and saffron rice or boiled potatoes.

Corsican Beef Stew with Macaroni

Pasta is eaten in many parts of the Mediterranean. In Corsica, it's often served with gravy as a sauce and, in this case, in a rich beef stew.

1 ounce dried mushrooms (cèpes or porcini)
6 garlic cloves
2 pounds stewing beef, cut into 2-inch cubes
4 ounces lardons, or thick bacon cut into strips
3 tablespoons olive oil
2 onions, sliced
1¼ cups dry white wine
2 tablespoons passata (or tomato sauce)
pinch of ground cinnamon
sprig of rosemary
1 bay leaf
2 cups large macaroni
⅔ cup freshly grated Parmesan cheese
salt and ground black pepper

Serves 4

1 Soak the dried mushrooms in warm water for 30 minutes. Drain, set the mushrooms aside and reserve the liquid. Cut three of the garlic cloves into thin strips and insert into the pieces of beef by making little slits with a sharp knife. Push the lardons or pieces of bacon into the beef with the garlic. Season the meat with salt and pepper.

2 Heat the oil in a heavy pan, add half the beef and brown well on all sides. Repeat with the remaining beef. Transfer to a plate. Add the sliced onions to the pan and cook until lightly browned. Crush the remaining garlic and add to the onions with the meat.

3 Stir in the white wine, passata, mushrooms, cinnamon, rosemary and bay leaf and season with salt and pepper. Cook gently for about 30 minutes, stirring often. Strain the mushroom liquid and add to the stew with enough water to cover. Bring to a boil, cover and simmer very gently for 3 hours, until the meat is very tender.

4 Cook the macaroni in a large pan of boiling salted water for 10 minutes or until al dente Lift the pieces of meat out of the gravy and transfer to a warmed serving platter. Drain the pasta and layer in a serving bowl with the gravy and cheese. Serve with the meat.

AFELIA

This lightly spiced pork stew makes a delicious supper dish served simply, as it would be in Cyprus, with warm bread, a leafy salad and a few olives.

1½ pounds pork fillet, boneless leg or loin chops
4 teaspoons coriander seeds
½ teaspoon sugar
3 tablespoons olive oil
2 large onions, sliced
1¼ cups red wine
salt and ground black pepper
cilantro, to garnish

SERVES 4

COOK'S TIP

A clean coffee grinder can also be used to grind the coriander seeds. Alternatively, use 1 tablespoon ground coriander.

1 Cut the pork into small chunks, discarding any excess fat. Crush the coriander seeds with a mortar and pestle until fairly finely ground.

2 Mix the coriander seeds with the sugar and salt and pepper and rub all over the meat. Let marinate for up to 4 hours.

3 Preheat the oven to 325°F. Heat 2 tablespoons of the oil in a frying pan over high heat. Brown the meat quickly, then transfer to an ovenproof dish.

4 Add the remaining oil to the pan and sauté the onions until beginning to color. Stir in the wine and a little salt and pepper and bring just to a boil.

5 Pour the onion and wine mixture over the meat and cover with a lid. Bake for 1 hour or until the meat is very tender. Serve sprinkled with cilantro.

MOUSSAKA

Like many popular classics, a real moussaka bears little resemblance to the imitations experienced in many Greek tourist resorts. This one is mildly spiced, moist but not dripping in grease, and encased in a golden baked crust.

2 pounds eggplant
½ cup olive oil
2 large tomatoes
2 large onions, sliced
1 pound ground lamb
¼ teaspoon ground cinnamon
¼ teaspoon ground allspice
2 tablespoons tomato paste
3 tablespoons chopped fresh parsley
½ cup dry white wine
salt and ground black pepper

FOR THE SAUCE
4 tablespoons butter
½ cup all-purpose flour
2½ cups milk
¼ teaspoon grated nutmeg
⅓ cup grated Parmesan cheese
3 tablespoons toasted bread crumbs

SERVES 6

1 Cut the eggplant into ¼-inch thick slices. Layer the slices in a colander, sprinkling each layer with plenty of salt. Let stand for 30 minutes.

2 Rinse the eggplant in several changes of cold water. Squeeze gently with your fingers to remove the excess water, then pat them dry on paper towels.

3 Heat some of the oil in a large frying pan. Sauté the eggplant slices in batches until golden on both sides, adding more oil when necessary. Let the eggplant slices drain on paper towels.

4 Plunge the tomatoes into boiling water for 30 seconds, then refresh in cold water. Peel away the skins and chop coarsely.

5 Preheat the oven to 350°F. Heat 2 tablespoons oil in a saucepan. Add the onions and lamb and sauté gently for 5 minutes, stirring and breaking up the lamb with a wooden spoon.

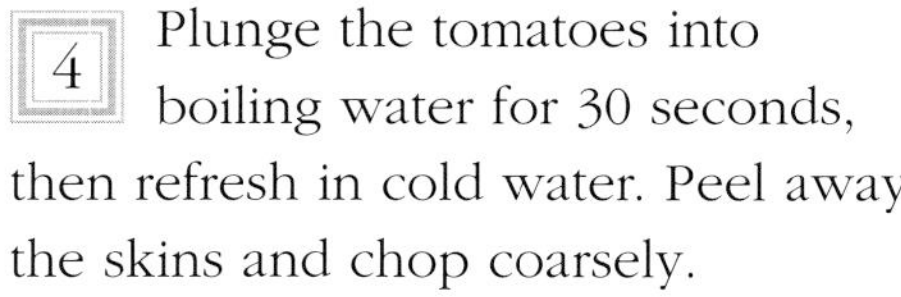

VARIATION

Sliced and sautéed zucchini or potatoes can be used instead of the eggplant in this dish.

6 Add the tomatoes, cinnamon, allspice, tomato paste, parsley, wine and pepper and bring to a boil. Reduce the heat, cover with a lid and simmer gently for 15 minutes.

7 Spoon alternate layers of the eggplant and meat mixture into a shallow ovenproof dish, finishing with a layer of eggplant.

8 To make the sauce, melt the butter in a small pan and stir in the flour. Cook, stirring, for 1 minute. Remove from the heat and gradually blend in the milk. Return to the heat and cook, stirring, for 2 minutes, until thickened. Add the nutmeg, cheese and salt and pepper. Pour the sauce on the eggplant and sprinkle with the bread crumbs. Bake for 45 minutes, until golden. Serve hot, sprinkled with extra black pepper, if desired.

BEEF ROLLS WITH GARLIC AND TOMATO SAUCE

Italy has many regional variations on the technique of wrapping thin slices of beef around a richly flavored stuffing. This recipe incorporates some classic ingredients. Serve with polenta, if desired.

4 thin slices of sirloin steak (about 4 ounces each)
4 slices smoked ham
5 ounces Pecorino cheese, grated
2 garlic cloves, crushed
5 tablespoons chopped fresh parsley
2 eggs, soft-boiled and peeled
3 tablespoons olive oil
1 large onion, finely chopped
⅔ cup passata or tomato sauce
⅓ cup red wine
2 bay leaves
⅔ cup beef stock
salt and ground black pepper
flat-leaf parsley, to garnish

SERVES 4

1 Preheat the oven to 325°F. Lay the steak slices on a sheet of waxed paper. Cover the steak with another sheet of waxed paper or plastic wrap and beat with a mallet or rolling pin until the slices are very thin.

2 Lay a ham slice over each. Mix the cheese in a bowl with the garlic, parsley, eggs and a little salt and pepper. Stir well until all the ingredients are evenly mixed.

3 Spoon the stuffing onto the ham and steak slices. Fold two opposite sides of the meat over the stuffing, then roll up the meat to form neat parcels. Secure with string.

4 Heat the oil in a frying pan. Add the parcels and sauté quickly on all sides to brown. Transfer to an ovenproof dish.

5 Add the onion to the frying pan and sauté for 3 minutes. Stir in the passata, wine, bay leaves and stock and season with salt and pepper. Bring to a boil, then pour the sauce over the meat in the dish.

6 Cover the dish and bake for 1 hour. Drain the meat and remove the string. Spoon onto warmed serving plates. Taste the sauce, adding extra salt and pepper if necessary, and spoon it over the meat. Serve garnished with flat-leaf parsley.

Pork with Marsala Wine and Juniper

Although most frequently used in desserts, Sicilian marsala gives savory dishes a rich, fruity tang. Use good quality butcher's pork that won't be drowned out by the flavor of the sauce.

1 ounce dried cèpes or porcini mushrooms
4 pork cutlets
2 teaspoons balsamic vinegar
8 garlic cloves
1 tablespoon butter
3 tablespoons marsala wine
several rosemary sprigs
10 juniper berries, crushed
salt and ground black pepper
noodles and green vegetables, to serve

Serves 4

1. Put the dried mushrooms in a bowl and just cover with hot water. Let stand.

2. Brush the pork with 1 teaspoon of the vinegar and season with salt and pepper. Put the garlic cloves in a small pan of boiling water and cook for 10 minutes, until soft. Drain and set aside.

3. Melt the butter in a large frying pan. Add the pork and cook quickly until browned on the underside. Turn the meat over and cook for another minute.

4. Add the marsala, rosemary, mushrooms, 4 tablespoons of the mushroom juices, the garlic cloves, juniper and remaining vinegar.

5. Simmer gently for about 3 minutes, until the pork is cooked through. Season lightly and serve hot with noodles and green vegetables.

SKEWERED LAMB WITH CILANTRO YOGURT

Although lamb is the most commonly used meat for Turkish kebabs, lean beef or pork work equally well. For color you can alternate pieces of bell pepper, lemon or onions, although this is not traditional.

2 pounds lean boneless lamb
1 large onion, grated
3 bay leaves
5 thyme or rosemary sprigs
grated zest and juice of 1 lemon
½ teaspoon sugar
⅓ cup olive oil
salt and ground black pepper
sprigs of rosemary, to garnish
broiled lemon wedges, to serve

FOR THE CORIANDER YOGURT
⅔ cup thick plain yogurt
1 tablespoon chopped fresh mint
1 tablespoon chopped cilantro
2 teaspoons grated onion

SERVES 4

1 To make the cilantro yogurt, combine the yogurt, mint, cilantro and grated onion and transfer to a small serving dish.

2 To make the kebabs, cut the lamb into small chunks and put in a bowl. Combine the grated onion, herbs, lemon zest and juice, sugar and oil, then add salt and pepper and pour over the lamb.

3 Combine the ingredients and let marinate in the refrigerator for several hours or overnight.

4 Drain the meat and thread onto skewers. Arrange on a broiler rack and cook under a preheated broiler for about 10 minutes, until browned, turning occasionally. Transfer to a plate and garnish with rosemary. Serve with the broiled lemon wedges and the cilantro yogurt.

COOK'S TIP
Cover the tips of wooden skewers with foil so they don't char.

KLEFTIKO

For this Greek recipe, marinated lamb steaks or chops are slow-cooked to develop an unbeatable flavor and meltingly tender texture. The dish is sealed, like a pie, with a flour dough lid to trap succulence and flavor; a tight-fitting foil cover, if less attractive, will serve equally well.

juice of 1 lemon
1 tablespoon chopped fresh oregano
4 lamb leg steaks or loin chops with bones
2 tablespoons olive oil
2 large onions, thinly sliced
2 bay leaves
⅔ cup dry white wine
2 cups all-purpose flour
salt and ground black pepper

SERVES 4

COOK'S TIP

They are not absolutely essential for this dish, but lamb steaks or chops with bones will provide lots of additional flavor. Boiled potatoes make a delicious accompaniment.

1 Combine the lemon juice, oregano and salt and pepper, and brush onto both sides of the lamb steaks or chops. Let marinate for at least 4 hours or overnight.

2 Preheat the oven to 325°F. Drain the lamb, reserving the marinade, and dry the lamb with paper towels. Heat the olive oil in a large frying pan or sauté pan and sauté the lamb over high heat until browned on both sides.

3 Transfer the lamb to a shallow baking dish. Scatter the sliced onions and bay leaves around the lamb, then pour on the white wine and the reserved marinade.

4 Mix the flour with enough water to make a firm dough. Moisten the rim of the dish. Roll out the dough on a floured surface and use to cover the dish so that it is tightly sealed.

5 Bake for 2 hours, then break open the dough crust and serve the lamb hot with boiled potatoes.

Black Bean Stew

This simple Spanish stew uses a few robust ingredients to create a deliciously intense flavor, something like a French cassoulet.

1⅓ cups black beans
1½ pounds bacon
¼ cup olive oil
12 ounces baby onions
2 celery stalks, thickly sliced
2 teaspoons paprika
5 ounces chorizo sausage, cut into chunks
2½ cups light chicken or vegetable stock
2 green bell peppers, seeded and cut into large pieces
salt and ground black pepper

Serves 5–6

1 Put the beans in a bowl and cover with plenty of cold water. Let soak overnight. Drain the beans in a saucepan and cover with fresh water. Bring to a boil and boil rapidly for 10 minutes. Drain.

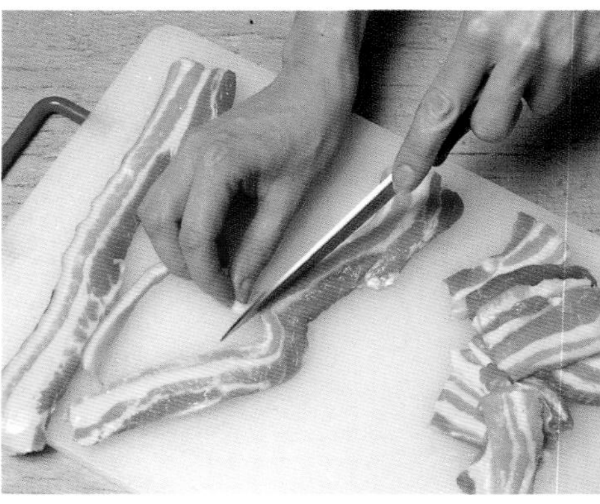

2 Preheat the oven to 325°F. Cut the bacon into chunks.

3 Heat the oil in a large frying pan and sauté the onions and celery for 3 minutes. Add the bacon and sauté for 5–10 minutes, until the bacon is browned.

4 Add the paprika and chorizo and cook for another 2 minutes. Transfer to an ovenproof dish with the beans and combine.

5 Add the stock to the pan and bring to a boil. Season lightly, then pour over the meat and beans. Cover and bake for 1 hour.

6 Stir the green peppers into the stew and return to the oven for 15 minutes more. Serve hot.

Cook's Tip

This is the sort of stew to which you can add a variety of winter vegetables, such as chunks of leek, turnip, celery root and even little potatoes.

PROVENÇAL BEEF AND OLIVE DAUBE

A daube is a French method of braising meat with wine and herbs. This version from the Nice area in the south of France also includes black olives and tomatoes.

3–3½ pounds top round roast
½ pound lardons, or thick bacon cut into strips
½ pound carrots, sliced
1 bay leaf
1 thyme sprig
2 parsley sprigs
3 garlic cloves
2 cups pitted black or green olives
14-ounce can chopped tomatoes
crusty bread, flageolet beans or pasta, to serve

FOR THE MARINADE
½ cup extra virgin olive oil
1 onion, sliced
4 shallots, sliced
1 celery stalk, sliced
1 carrot, sliced
⅔ cup red wine
6 peppercorns
2 garlic cloves, sliced
1 bay leaf
1 thyme sprig
2 parsley stalks
salt

SERVES 6

1 To make the marinade, heat the oil in a large shallow pan and add the onion, shallots, celery and carrot. Cook for 2 minutes, then lower the heat and add the red wine, pepper-corns, garlic, bay leaf, thyme and parsley. Season with salt, then cover and let simmer gently for 15–20 minutes. Set aside.

2 Place the beef in a large glass or earthenware dish and pour the cooled marinade over. Cover the dish and let marinate in a cool place or in the refrigerator for 12 hours, turning the meat once or twice.

3 Preheat the oven to 325°F. Lift the meat out of the marinade and fit snugly into an ovenproof casserole. Add the lardons or bacon and carrots, along with the herbs and garlic. Strain in all the marinade. Cover the casserole with waxed paper, then the lid, and bake for 2½ hours.

4 Remove the casserole from the oven and stir in the olives and tomatoes. Re-cover the casserole, return to the oven and cook for another 30 minutes. Serve the meat cut into thick slices, accompanied by crusty bread, beans or pasta.

LAMB CASSEROLE WITH GARLIC AND FAVA BEANS

This recipe has a Spanish influence and makes a substantial meal, served with potatoes. It's based on stewing lamb with a large amount of garlic and sherry—the addition of fava beans gives color.

3 tablespoons olive oil
3–3½ pounds lamb fillet, cut into 2-inch cubes
1 large onion, chopped
6 large garlic cloves, unpeeled
1 bay leaf
1 teaspoon paprika
½ cup dry sherry
4 ounces shelled fresh or frozen fava beans
2 tablespoons chopped fresh parsley
salt and ground black pepper

SERVES 6

1 Heat 2 tablespoons of the oil in a large flameproof casserole. Add half the meat and brown well on all sides. Transfer to a plate. Brown the rest of the meat in the same way and remove from the casserole.

2 Heat the remaining oil in the pan, add the onion and cook for about 5 minutes, until soft. Return the meat to the casserole.

3 Add the garlic cloves, bay leaf, paprika and sherry. Season with salt and pepper. Bring to a boil, then cover and simmer very gently for 1½–2 hours, until the meat is tender.

4 Add the fava beans about 10 minutes before the end of the cooking time. Stir in the parsley just before serving.

SPANISH PORK AND SAUSAGE CASSEROLE

Another pork dish from the Catalan region of Spain, which uses the spicy butifarra sausage. You can find these sausages in some Spanish food stores but, if not, sweet Italian sausages will do.

2 tablespoons olive oil
4 boneless pork chops, about 1 pound
4 butifarra or sweet Italian sausages
1 onion, chopped
2 garlic cloves, chopped
½ cup dry white wine
4 plum tomatoes, chopped
1 bay leaf
2 tablespoons chopped fresh parsley
salt and ground black pepper
green salad and baked potatoes, to serve

SERVES 4

1 Heat the oil in a large, deep frying pan. Cook the pork chops over high heat until browned on both sides, then transfer to a plate.

2 Add the sausages, onion and garlic to the pan and cook over medium heat until the sausages are browned and the onion softened, turning the sausages two or three times during cooking. Return the chops to the pan.

3 Stir in the wine, tomatoes and bay leaf, and season with salt and pepper. Add the parsley. Cover the pan and cook for 30 minutes.

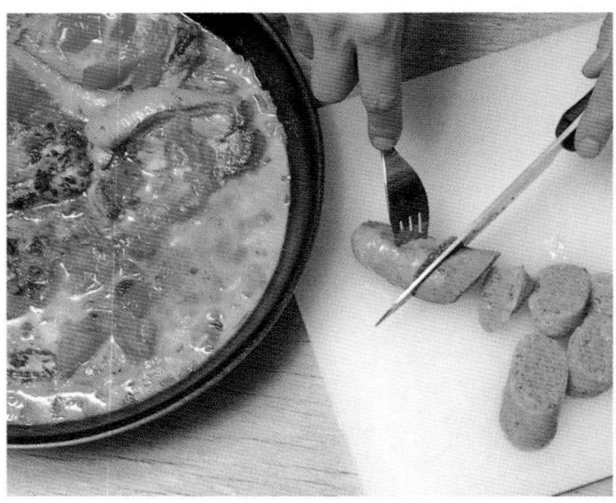

4 Remove the sausages from the pan and cut them into thick slices. Return them to the pan and heat through. Serve hot, accompanied by a green salad and baked potatoes.

COOK'S TIP

Vine tomatoes, which are making a welcome appearance in supermarkets, can be used instead of plum tomatoes.

MEATBALLS WITH MOZZARELLA AND TOMATO

These Italian meatballs are made with beef and topped with mozzarella cheese and tomato.

½ slice white bread, crusts removed
3 tablespoons milk
1½ pounds ground beef
1 egg, beaten
⅔ cup dry bread crumbs
vegetable oil for frying
2 beefsteak or other large tomatoes, sliced
1 tablespoon chopped fresh oregano
1 mozzarella cheese, cut into 6 slices
6 drained canned anchovies, cut in half lengthwise
salt and ground black pepper

SERVES 6

1 Preheat the oven to 400°F. Put the bread and milk in a small saucepan and heat very gently over low heat until the bread absorbs all the milk. Mash it to a pulp and let cool.

2 Put the beef into a bowl with the bread mixture and the egg and season with salt and pepper. Mix well, then shape the mixture into six patties. Sprinkle the bread crumbs on a plate and dredge the patties, coating them thoroughly.

3 Heat about ¼ inch oil in a large frying pan. Add the patties and fry for 2 minutes on each side, until brown. Transfer to a greased ovenproof dish in a single layer.

4 Lay a slice of tomato on top of each patty, sprinkle with oregano and season with salt and pepper. Place the mozzarella slices on top. Arrange two strips of anchovy placed in a cross on top of each slice of mozzarella.

5 Bake for 10–15 minutes, until the mozzarella has melted. Serve hot, straight from the dish.

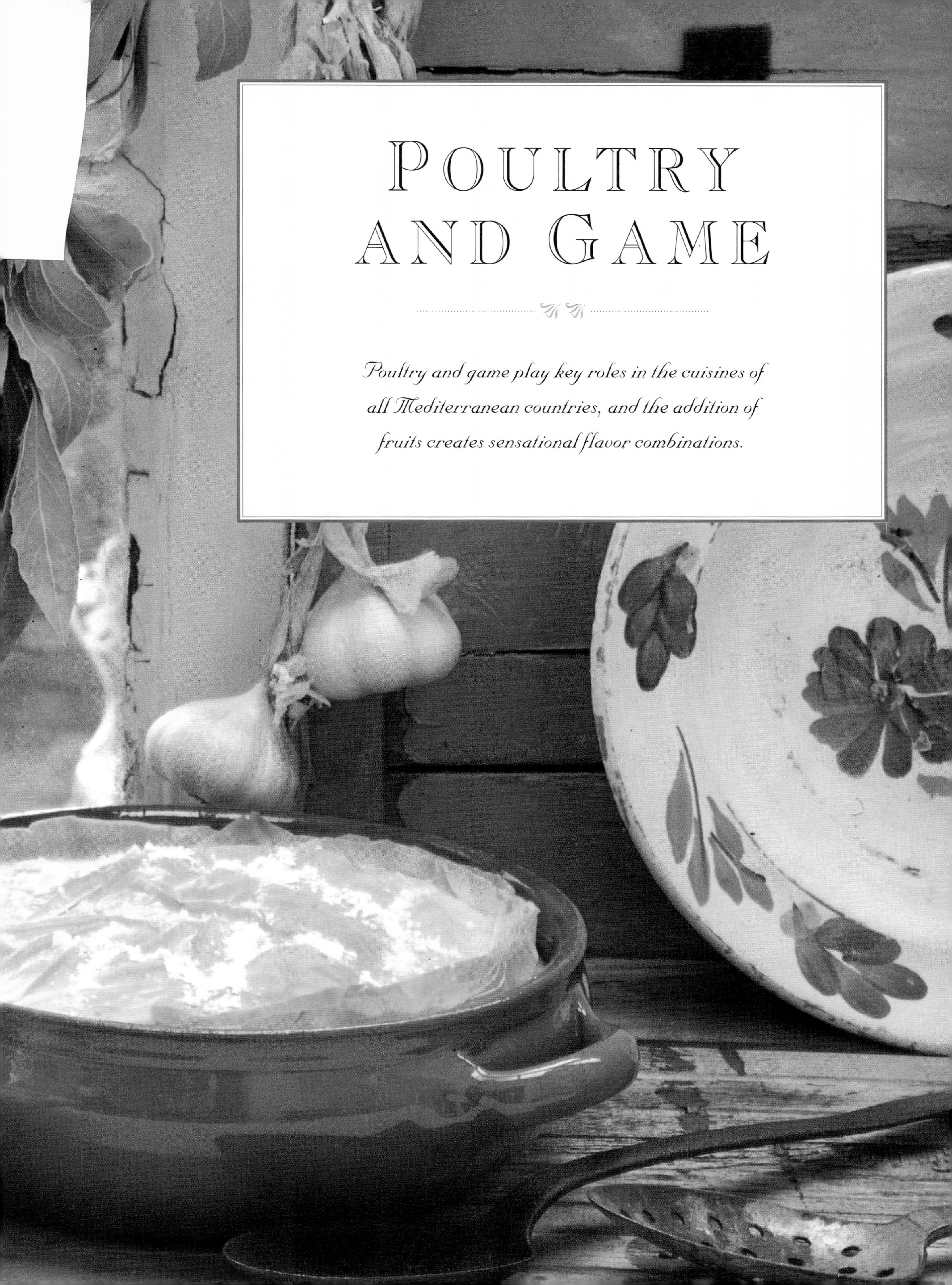

Poultry and Game

Poultry and game play key roles in the cuisines of all Mediterranean countries, and the addition of fruits creates sensational flavor combinations.

Poultry and game have always played an important role in Mediterranean cooking. This is largely due to the dry, rugged and, in some places, mountainous land that does not provide good pasture. Chickens and ducks are more accessible to the poorer people of the Mediterranean, who often raise them on their own land.

Chicken is without doubt the most popular type of poultry and is used creatively for Mediterranean dishes. Traditionally corn-fed, the poultry's flesh is rich in color and full of flavor, despite the fact that individual birds might look quite thin. The cooking methods are varied and interesting, but they have many similarities. In both the east and west Mediterranean cooks have acknowledged the fact that chicken is perfectly complemented by the tang of fresh, dried or preserved fruits, the rich earthiness of nuts and the lively warmth of spices.

In the Middle East, chickens were traditionally kept mainly for their eggs rather than meat, and generally only the older birds were cooked. This meant long, slow braising with highly flavored stuffings and sauces to add flavor. These recipes are now perfectly suited to improving the

BELOW: Verdant farmland rimmed by mountains in southern Spain.

RIGHT: Lord of all he surveys, this Greek cockerel patrols his perimeter wall.

BELOW: Lemons are a favorite flavoring for chicken dishes, notably in Chicken with Lemons and Olives.

mild taste of our mass-produced chickens. Preserved lemons tucked in or around a whole chicken impart a fresh, aromatic flavor that lacks the acidity of fresh lemons, although these can also be used successfully, adding a little sugar or honey for sweetness. Another popular flavoring for chicken is provided by glassy, jewellike segments of pomegranates, crushed and blended to a juice or made into a canned preserve, having been mixed with lemon, sugar and seasoning.

From the simplest roast, served with a raisin, pine nut and sherry sauce, to chorizo-flavored casseroles, Spain has numerous excellent chicken and rabbit recipes that are popular favorites throughout the country. Duck and goose feature prominently, cooked with pears, apples or figs to counteract the richness of the meat.

Small game birds are typically Mediterranean but are used more in winter, when the tourists have left. Squab and small game birds such as partridge and quail take their migratory route across the sea, and hunters from all quarters of the Mediterranean take full advantage of this. Italians are particularly fond of small game and prepare some delicious squab dishes, lightly cooked in rich sauces and accompanied by broiled or soft polenta.

CHICKEN THIGHS WITH LEMON AND GARLIC

This recipe uses classic flavorings for chicken. Versions of it can be found in Spain and Italy. This particular recipe, however, is of French origin.

2½ cups chicken stock
20 large garlic cloves
2 tablespoons butter
1 tablespoon olive oil
8 chicken thighs
1 lemon, peeled, pith removed and thinly sliced
2 tablespoons all-purpose flour
⅔ cup dry white wine
salt and ground black pepper
chopped fresh parsley or basil, to garnish
new potatoes or rice, to serve

SERVES 4

1 Put the stock into a pan and bring to a boil. Add the garlic cloves, cover and simmer gently for 40 minutes. Heat the butter and oil in a sauté or frying pan, add the chicken thighs and cook gently on all sides until golden. Transfer them to an ovenproof dish. Preheat the oven to 375°F.

2 Strain the stock and reserve it. Distribute the garlic and lemon slices among the chicken pieces. Add the flour to the fat in the pan in which the chicken was browned and cook, stirring, for 1 minute. Add the wine, stirring constantly and scraping the bottom of the pan, then add the stock. Cook, stirring, until the sauce has thickened and is smooth. Season with salt and pepper.

3 Pour the sauce over the chicken, cover and bake for 40–45 minutes. If a thicker sauce is required, lift out the chicken pieces and reduce the sauce by boiling rapidly until it reaches the desired consistency. Sprinkle the chopped parsley or basil on top and serve with boiled new potatoes or rice.

OLIVE OIL-ROASTED CHICKEN WITH MEDITERRANEAN VEGETABLES

This is a delicious French alternative to a traditional roast chicken. Use a corn-fed or free-range bird, if available. This recipe also works well with guinea fowl.

4½-pound roasting chicken
⅔ cup extra virgin olive oil
½ lemon
few sprigs of fresh thyme
1 pound small new potatoes
1 eggplant, cut into 1-inch cubes
1 red bell pepper, seeded and quartered
1 fennel bulb, trimmed and quartered
8 large garlic cloves, unpeeled
coarse salt and ground black pepper

SERVES 4

1 Preheat the oven to 400°F. Rub the chicken all over with olive oil and season with pepper. Place the lemon half inside the bird with a sprig or two of thyme. Put the chicken breast side down in a large roasting pan. Roast for about 30 minutes.

2 Remove the chicken from the oven and season with salt. Turn the chicken right side up and baste with the drippings from the pan. Surround the bird with the potatoes, roll them in the pan drippings and return the roasting pan to the oven to continue roasting.

3 After 30 minutes, add the eggplant, red pepper, fennel and garlic cloves to the pan. Drizzle with the remaining oil and season with salt and pepper. Add any remaining thyme to the vegetables. Return to the oven and cook for 30–50 more minutes, basting and turning the vegetables occasionally.

4 To find out if the chicken is cooked, push the tip of a sharp knife between the thigh and breast. If the juices run clear, it is done. The vegetables should be tender and just beginning to brown. Serve the chicken and vegetables from the pan, or transfer the vegetables to a serving dish, cut up the chicken and place it on top. Serve the skimmed juices in a gravy boat.

CHICKEN WITH CHORIZO

The addition of chorizo sausage and sherry gives a warm, interesting flavor to this simple Spanish casserole. Serve with rice or boiled potatoes.

1 medium chicken, cut up, or
4 chicken legs, halved
2 teaspoons ground paprika
4 tablespoons olive oil
2 small onions, sliced
6 garlic cloves, thinly sliced
5 ounces chorizo sausage, thickly sliced
14-ounce can chopped tomatoes
12–16 bay leaves
5 tablespoons medium sherry
salt and ground black pepper
rice or potatoes, to serve

SERVES 4

1 Preheat the oven to 375°F. Coat the chicken pieces in the paprika, making sure they are evenly covered, then season with salt. Heat the olive oil in a frying pan and sauté the chicken until brown.

2 Transfer to an ovenproof dish. Add the onions to the pan and sauté quickly. Add the garlic and chorizo and sauté for 2 minutes.

3 Add the tomatoes, two of the bay leaves and the sherry and bring to a boil. Pour over the chicken and cover with a lid. Bake for 45 minutes. Remove the lid and season to taste. Cook for another 20 minutes, until the chicken is tender and golden. Serve with rice or potatoes, garnished with bay leaves.

CHICKEN CASSEROLE WITH SPICED FIGS

The Spanish Catalans have various recipes for fruit with meat. This is quite an unusual one, but it uses one of the fruits most strongly associated with the Mediterranean—the fig.

FOR THE FIGS

⅔ cup sugar
½ cup white wine vinegar
1 lemon slice
1 cinnamon stick
1 pound fresh figs

FOR THE CHICKEN

½ cup medium-sweet white wine
pared zest of ½ lemon
3½-pound chicken, cut into eight pieces
2 ounces lardons, or thick bacon cut into strips
1 tablespoon olive oil
¼ cup chicken stock
salt and ground black pepper

SERVES 4

1 Put the sugar, vinegar, lemon slice and cinnamon stick in a pan with ½ cup water. Bring to a boil, then simmer for 5 minutes. Add the figs, cover, and simmer for 10 minutes. Remove from heat, cover, and let sit for 3 hours.

2 Preheat the oven to 350°F. Drain the figs and place in a bowl. Add the wine and lemon zest. Season the chicken. In a large frying pan, cook the lardons or bacon strips until the fat melts and they turn golden. Transfer to a shallow ovenproof dish, leaving any fat in the pan. Add the oil to the pan and brown the chicken pieces all over.

3 Drain the figs, adding the wine to the pan with the chicken. Boil until the sauce has reduced and is syrupy. Transfer the contents of the frying pan to the ovenproof dish and bake, uncovered, for about 20 minutes. Add the figs and chicken stock, cover and return to the oven for another 10 minutes. Serve with a green salad.

CHICKEN AND APRICOT PHYLLO PIE

The filling for this pie has a Middle Eastern flavor—chopped chicken combined with apricots, bulgur, nuts and spices.

½ cup bulgur
6 tablespoons butter
1 onion, chopped
1 pound chopped chicken
¼ cup dried apricots, finely chopped
¼ cup blanched almonds, chopped
1 teaspoon ground cinnamon
½ teaspoon ground allspice
¼ cup strained plain yogurt
1 tablespoon snipped fresh chives
2 tablespoons chopped fresh parsley
6 large sheets phyllo pastry
salt and ground black pepper
chives, to garnish

SERVES 6

1 Preheat the oven to 400°F. Put the bulgur in a bowl with ½ cup boiling water. Soak for 5–10 minutes, until the water is absorbed.

2 Heat 2 tablespoons of the butter in a pan and gently sauté the onion and chicken until pale golden.

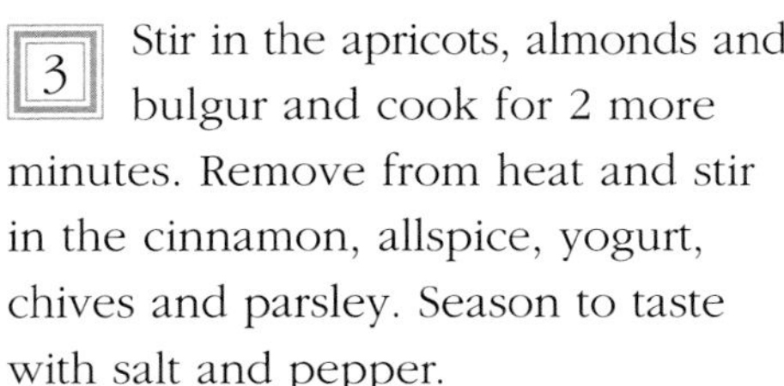

3 Stir in the apricots, almonds and bulgur and cook for 2 more minutes. Remove from heat and stir in the cinnamon, allspice, yogurt, chives and parsley. Season to taste with salt and pepper.

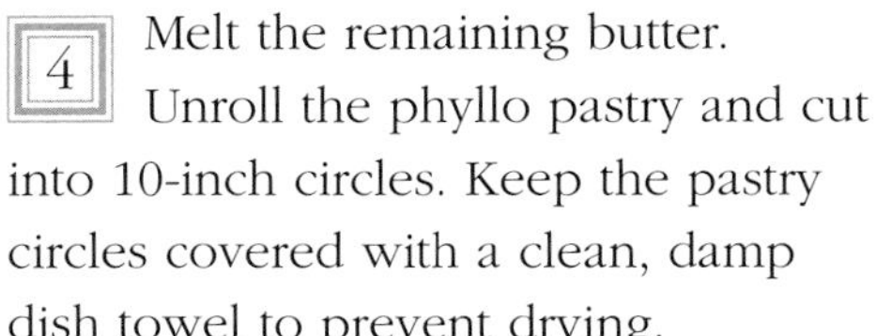

4 Melt the remaining butter. Unroll the phyllo pastry and cut into 10-inch circles. Keep the pastry circles covered with a clean, damp dish towel to prevent drying.

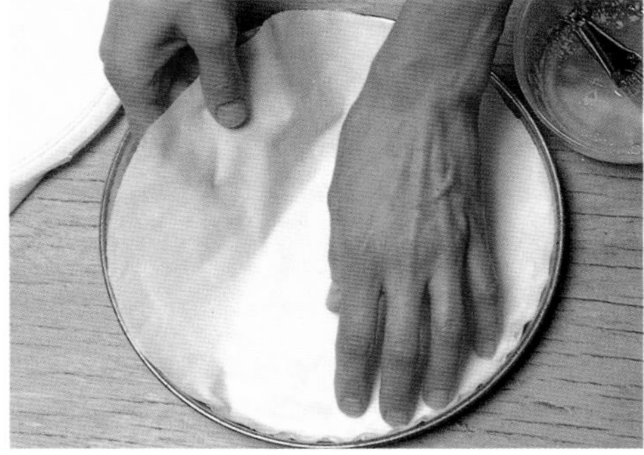

5 Line a 9-inch quiche pan with a removable bottom with three of the pastry circles, brushing each one with butter as you layer them. Spoon in the chicken mixture and cover with three more pastry rounds, brushed with melted butter as before.

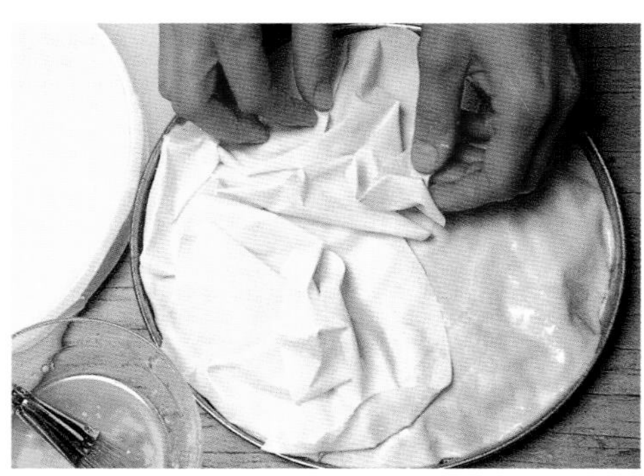

6 Crumple the remaining circles and place them on top of the pie, then brush on any remaining melted butter. Bake the pie for about 30 minutes, until the pastry is golden brown and crisp. Serve Chicken and Apricot Phyllo Pie hot or cold, cut into wedges and garnished with chives.

CIRCASSIAN CHICKEN

This is a Turkish dish that is popular all over the Middle East. The chicken is poached and served cold with a flavorful walnut sauce.

3½-pound chicken
2 onions, quartered
1 carrot, sliced
1 celery stalk, trimmed and sliced
6 peppercorns
3 slices bread, crusts removed
2 garlic cloves, coarsely chopped
3½ cups chopped walnuts
1 tablespoon walnut oil
salt and ground black pepper
chopped walnuts and paprika, to garnish

SERVES 6

1. Place the chicken in a large pan with the onions, carrot, celery and peppercorns. Add enough water to cover and bring to a boil. Simmer for about 1 hour, uncovered, until the chicken is tender. Let cool in the stock. Drain the chicken, reserving the stock.

2. Tear up the bread and soak in 6 tablespoons of the chicken stock. Transfer to a blender or food processor with the garlic and walnuts and add 1 cup of the remaining stock. Process until smooth, then transfer to a pan.

3. Over low heat, gradually add more chicken stock to the sauce, stirring constantly, until it is a thick pouring consistency. Season with salt and pepper, remove from the heat and let cool in the pan. Skin and bone the chicken, and cut into bite-size chunks.

4. Place in a bowl and add a little of the sauce. Stir to coat the chicken, then arrange on a serving dish. Spoon the remaining sauce over the chicken and drizzle with the walnut oil. Sprinkle with walnuts and paprika and serve immediately.

CHICKEN WITH LEMONS AND OLIVES

Preserved lemons and limes are frequently used in Mediterranean cooking, particularly in North Africa, where their gentle flavor enhances all kinds of meat and fish dishes.

½ teaspoon ground cinnamon
½ teaspoon ground turmeric
3½-pound chicken
2 tablespoons olive oil
1 large onion, thinly sliced
2-inch piece fresh ginger root, grated
2½ cups chicken stock
2 preserved lemons or limes, or fresh, cut into wedges
½ cup pitted black olives
1 tablespoon honey
¼ cup chopped cilantro
salt and ground black pepper
cilantro sprigs, to garnish

SERVES 4

1. Preheat the oven to 375°F. Mix the ground cinnamon and turmeric in a small bowl with a little salt and pepper and rub all over the chicken skin to give an even coating.

2. Heat the oil in a large sauté or shallow frying pan and sauté the chicken on all sides until it turns golden. Transfer the chicken to an ovenproof dish.

3. Add the sliced onion to the pan and sauté for 3 minutes. Stir in the grated ginger and the chicken stock and bring just to a boil. Pour over the chicken, cover with a lid and bake for 30 minutes.

4. Remove the chicken from the oven and add the lemons or limes, olives and honey. Bake, uncovered, for another 45 minutes, until the chicken is tender.

5. Stir in the cilantro and season to taste. Garnish with cilantro sprigs and serve immediately.

CASSOULET

Cassoulet is a classic French dish in which a feast of various meats is baked slowly with beans under a golden crumb crust. It is hearty and rich, perfect for a winter gathering.

3½ cups dried navy or Great Northern beans
2 pounds salt pork or pork pieces
4 large duck breasts
4 tablespoons olive oil
2 onions, chopped
6 garlic cloves, crushed
2 bay leaves
¼ teaspoon ground cloves
4 tablespoons tomato paste
8 good-quality sausages
4 tomatoes
1½ cups dried bread crumbs
salt and ground black pepper

SERVES 6–8

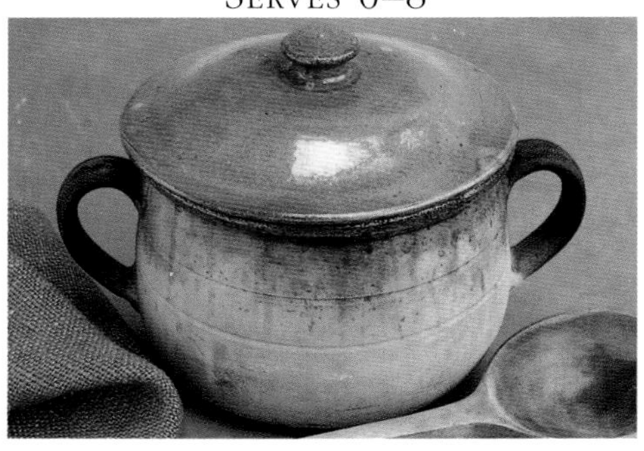

1 Put the beans in a large bowl and cover with plenty of cold water. Let soak overnight. If using salt pork, soak it overnight in water.

2 Drain the beans thoroughly and put them in a large saucepan with fresh water to cover. Bring to a boil and boil rapidly for 10 minutes. Drain and set the beans aside.

3 Cut the pork into large pieces, discarding the rind. Halve the duck breasts.

4 Heat 2 tablespoons of the oil in a frying pan and sauté the pork in batches until browned.

5 Put the beans in a large, heavy saucepan with the onions, garlic, bay leaves, ground cloves and tomato paste. Stir in the browned pork and just cover with water. Bring to a boil, then reduce the heat to the lowest setting and simmer, covered, for about 1½ hours, until the beans are tender.

6 Preheat the oven to 350°F. Heat the rest of the oil in a frying pan and sauté the duck breasts and sausages until browned. Cut the sausages into pieces.

7 Plunge the tomatoes into boiling water for 30 seconds, then refresh in cold water. Peel away the skins and cut them into quarters.

8 Transfer the bean mixture to a large earthenware pot or ovenproof dish and stir in the sausages, duck breasts and chopped tomatoes with salt and pepper to taste.

9 Sprinkle with an even layer of bread crumbs and bake for 45 minutes to 1 hour, until the crust is golden. Serve hot.

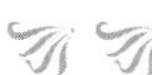

VARIATION

You can easily alter the proportions and types of meat and vegetables in a cassoulet. Turnips, carrots and celery root make suitable vegetable substitutes, while cubed lamb and goose can replace the pork and duck.

CHICKEN IN A SALT CRUST

Cooking food in a casing of salt gives a deliciously moist, tender flavor that, surprisingly, is not too salty. The technique is used in both Italy and France for chicken and whole fish, although chicken is easier to deal with.

4½-pound chicken
about 5 pounds coarse sea salt

FOR THE GARLIC PUREE
1 pound onions, quartered
2 large heads of garlic
½ cup olive oil
salt and ground black pepper

FOR THE ROASTED TOMATOES AND PEPPERS
1 pound plum tomatoes
3 red bell peppers, seeded and quartered
1 red chile, seeded and finely chopped
6 tablespoons olive oil
flat-leaf parsley, to garnish

SERVES 6

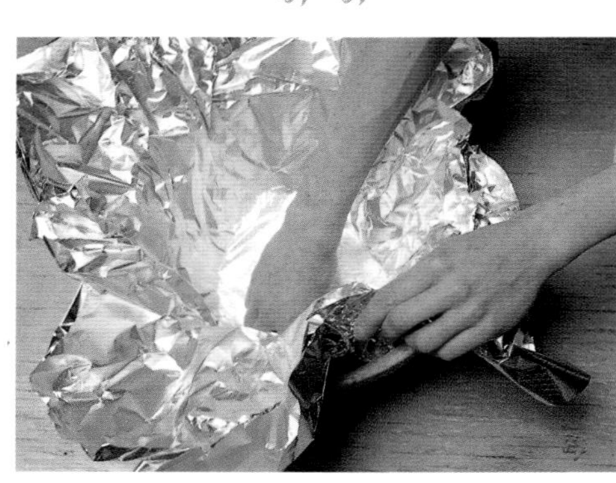

1 Preheat the oven to 425°F. Choose a deep ovenproof dish into which the whole chicken will fit snugly. Line the dish with a double layer of heavy foil, allowing plenty of excess foil to overhang the top edge of the ovenproof dish.

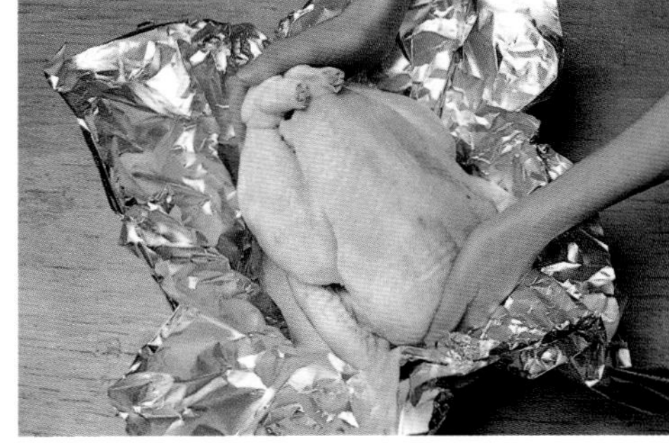

2 Truss the chicken tightly so that the salt cannot fall into the cavity. Sprinkle a thin layer of salt in the foil-lined dish, then place the chicken on top.

3 Pour the remaining salt all around and on the top of the chicken until it is completely encased. Sprinkle the top with a little water.

4 Cover tightly with the foil and bake the chicken on the lower oven shelf for 1¾ hours. Meanwhile, put the onions in a small, heavy saucepan. Break up the heads of garlic, but leave the skins on. Add to the pan with the olive oil and a little salt and pepper.

5 Cover and cook over the lowest possible heat for about 1 hour or until the garlic is completely soft.

COOK'S TIP

This recipe makes a stunning main course when you want to serve something a little different. Take the salt-crusted chicken to the table garnished with plenty of fresh mixed herbs. Once you've scraped off the salt, transfer the chicken to a clean plate to carve it.

6 Plunge the tomatoes into boiling water for 30 seconds, then refresh in cold water. Peel off the skins and quarter the tomatoes. Put the red peppers, tomatoes and chile in a shallow ovenproof dish and sprinkle with the oil. Bake on the shelf above the chicken for 45 minutes, or until the peppers are slightly charred.

7 Squeeze the garlic out of the skins. Process the onions, garlic and pan juices in a blender or food processor until smooth. Return the purée to the clean saucepan.

8 To serve the chicken, open up the foil and ease it out of the dish. Place on a large serving platter. Transfer the roasted pepper mixture to a serving dish and garnish with parsley. Reheat the garlic purée. Crack open the salt crust on the chicken and brush off the salt before carving and serving with the garlic purée and pepper mixture.

SPICED DUCK WITH PEARS

This delicious casserole is based on a Catalan dish that uses goose or duck. The sautéed pears are added toward the end of cooking, along with picarda sauce, a pounded pine-nut and garlic paste that both flavors and thickens.

6 duck portions, either breast or leg pieces
1 tablespoon olive oil
1 large onion, thinly sliced
1 cinnamon stick, halved
2 thyme sprigs
2 cups chicken stock

TO FINISH
3 firm, ripe pears
2 tablespoons olive oil
2 garlic cloves, sliced
⅓ cup pine nuts
½ teaspoon saffron strands
2 tablespoons raisins
salt and ground black pepper
young thyme sprigs or parsley, to garnish

SERVES 6

1 Preheat the oven to 350°F. Sauté the duck portions in the olive oil for about 5 minutes, until the skin is golden. Transfer the duck to an ovenproof dish and drain off all but 1 tablespoon of the fat left in the pan.

2 Add the onion to the pan and sauté for 5 minutes. Add the cinnamon stick, thyme and stock and bring to a boil. Pour over the duck and bake for 1¼ hours.

3 Meanwhile, peel, core and halve the pears and sauté quickly in the oil until beginning to turn golden on the cut sides. Pound the garlic, pine nuts and saffron in a mortar with a pestle to make a thick, smooth paste.

4 Add the paste to the casserole along with the raisins and pears. Bake for another 15 minutes, until the pears are tender.

5 Season to taste with salt and pepper and garnish with parsley or thyme. Serve with mashed potatoes and a green vegetable, if desired.

COOK'S TIP
A good stock is essential for this dish. Buy a large duck (plus two extra duck breasts if you want portions to be generous) and cut it up yourself, using the giblets and carcass for stock. Alternatively, buy duck portions and canned chicken stock.

RABBIT SALMOREJO

Small pieces of rabbit, conveniently sold in packages at some supermarkets, make an interesting alternative to chicken in this light, spicy sauté from Spain. Serve with a simple dressed salad.

1½ pounds rabbit pieces
1¼ cups dry white wine
1 tablespoon sherry vinegar
several oregano sprigs
2 bay leaves
6 tablespoons olive oil
6 ounces baby onions, peeled and left whole
1 red chile, seeded and finely chopped
4 garlic cloves, sliced
2 teaspoons paprika
⅔ cup chicken stock
salt and ground black pepper
flat-leaf parsley sprigs, to garnish

SERVES 4

1 Put the rabbit in a bowl. Add the wine, vinegar, oregano and bay leaves and toss together lightly. Cover and let marinate for several hours or overnight.

2 Drain the rabbit, reserving the marinade, and pat dry on paper towels. Heat the oil in a large sauté or frying pan. Add the rabbit and sauté on all sides until golden, then remove with a slotted spoon. Sauté the onions until beginning to color.

3 Remove the onions from the pan and add the chile, garlic and paprika. Cook, stirring, for about a minute. Add the reserved marinade, with the stock. Season lightly.

4 Return the rabbit to the pan with the onions. Bring to a boil, then reduce the heat and cover with a lid. Simmer very gently for about 45 minutes, until the rabbit is tender. Serve garnished with a few sprigs of flat-leaf parsley, if desired.

COOK'S TIP

If more convenient, rather than cooking on top of the stove, transfer the stew to an ovenproof dish and bake at 350°F for about 50 minutes.

DUCK BREASTS WITH A WALNUT AND POMEGRANATE SAUCE

This is an extremely exotic sweet-and-sour dish that originally came from Persia.

4 tablespoons olive oil
2 onions, very thinly sliced
½ teaspoon ground turmeric
3½ cups walnuts, coarsely chopped
4 cups duck or chicken stock
6 pomegranates
2 tablespoons sugar
¼ cup lemon juice
4 duck breasts, about 8 ounces each
salt and ground black pepper

SERVES 6

COOK'S TIP

Choose pomegranates with shiny, brightly colored skins. The juice stains, so be careful when cutting them. Only the seeds are used in cooking; the pith is discarded.

1 Heat half the oil in a frying pan. Add the onions and turmeric and cook gently until soft. Transfer to a pan, add the walnuts and stock, then season with salt and pepper. Stir, then bring to a boil and simmer the mixture, uncovered, for 20 minutes.

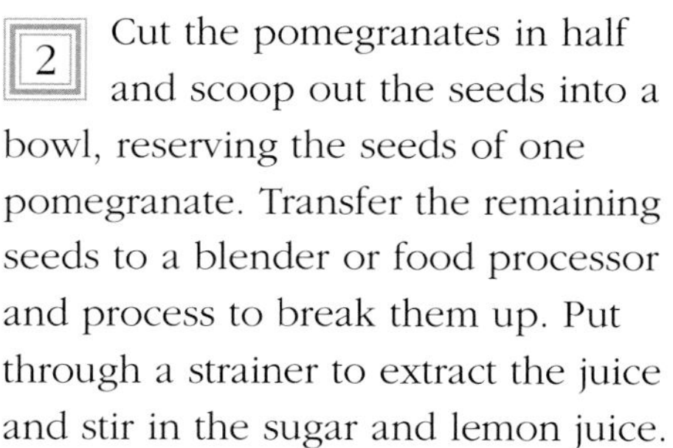

2 Cut the pomegranates in half and scoop out the seeds into a bowl, reserving the seeds of one pomegranate. Transfer the remaining seeds to a blender or food processor and process to break them up. Put through a strainer to extract the juice and stir in the sugar and lemon juice.

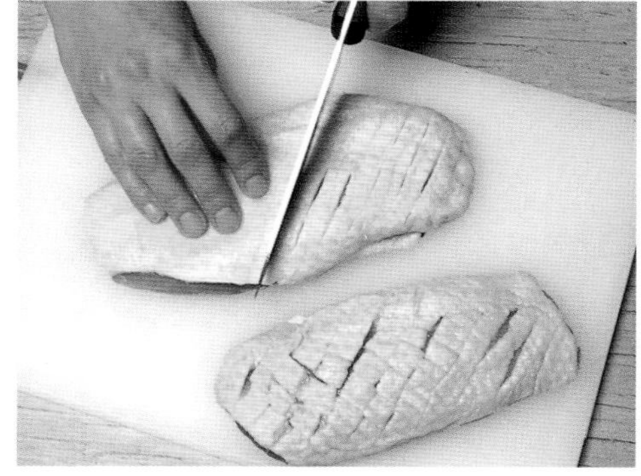

3 Score the skin of the duck breasts in a lattice fashion with a sharp knife. Heat the remaining oil in a frying pan or grill pan and place the duck breasts in it, skin side down.

4 Cook gently for 10 minutes, pouring off the fat from time to time, until the skin is dark golden and crisp. Turn the duck breasts over and cook for another 3–4 minutes. Transfer to a plate and allow to rest.

5 Deglaze the frying pan or grill pan with the pomegranate juice mixture, stirring with a wooden spoon, then add the walnut and stock mixture and simmer for 15 minutes, until the sauce has thickened slightly. Serve the duck breasts sliced, drizzled with a little sauce, and garnished with the reserved pomegranate seeds. Serve the remaining sauce separately.

SQUAB BREASTS WITH PANCETTA

Mild, succulent squab breasts are easy to cook and make an impressive main course for a special dinner. Serve this Italian-style dish with polenta and some simple green vegetables.

4 whole squabs
2 large onions
2 carrots, coarsely chopped
1 celery stalk, trimmed and coarsely chopped
1 ounce dried porcini mushrooms
2 ounces pancetta
2 tablespoons butter
2 tablespoons olive oil
2 garlic cloves, crushed
⅔ cup red wine
salt and ground black pepper
flat-leaf parsley, to garnish
cooked oyster mushrooms, to serve

SERVES 4

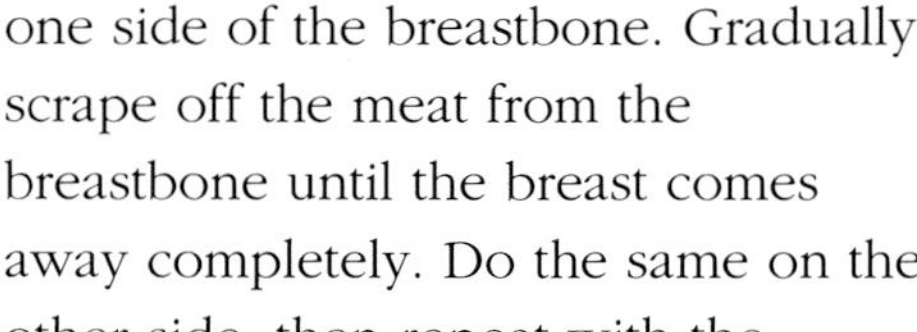

1 To prepare a squab, cut down the length of the bird just to one side of the breastbone. Gradually scrape off the meat from the breastbone until the breast comes away completely. Do the same on the other side, then repeat with the remaining squabs.

2 Put the squab carcasses in a large saucepan. Halve one of the onions, leaving the skin on. Add to the pan with the carrots and celery and just cover with water. Bring to a boil, reduce the heat and simmer very gently, uncovered, for about 1½ hours, to make a dark, rich stock. Let cool slightly, then strain into a bowl.

3 Cover the porcini mushrooms with ⅔ cup hot water and let soak for at least 30 minutes. Chop the pancetta.

4 Peel and finely chop the remaining onion. Melt half the butter with the oil in a large frying pan. Add the onion and pancetta and sauté very gently for 3 minutes. Add the squab breasts, skin side down, and sauté for 2 minutes, until browned. Turn over and sauté for another 2 minutes.

5 Add the mushrooms with their soaking liquid, garlic, wine and 1 cup of the stock. Bring just to a boil, then reduce the heat and simmer gently for 5 minutes, until the squab breasts are tender but still a little pink in the center.

6 Lift out the squab breasts and keep them hot. Return the sauce to a boil and boil rapidly to reduce slightly. Gradually whisk in all the remaining butter and season with salt and pepper to taste.

7 Transfer the squab breasts to warmed serving plates and pour on the sauce. Serve immediately, garnished with sprigs of parsley and accompanied by oyster mushrooms.

COOK'S TIP

If buying squab from a butcher, order them in advance and ask him to remove the breasts for you. You can also cut off the legs and sauté these with the breasts, although there is little meat on them and you might prefer to let them flavor the stock.

MOROCCAN PIGEON PIE

This recipe is based upon a classic Moroccan dish called Pastilla, which is a phyllo pastry pie filled with an unusual but delicious mixture of squab, eggs, spices and nuts. If squab is unavailable, chicken makes a good substitute.

3 squabs
4 tablespoons butter
1 onion, chopped
1 cinnamon stick
½ teaspoon ground ginger
2 tablespoons chopped fresh cilantro
3 tablespoons chopped parsley
pinch of ground turmeric
1 tablespoon sugar
¼ teaspoon ground cinnamon
1 cup toasted almonds, finely chopped
6 eggs, beaten
salt and ground black pepper
cinnamon and confectioners' sugar, to garnish

FOR THE PASTRY
12 tablespoons (1½ sticks) butter, melted
16 sheets phyllo pastry
1 egg yolk

SERVES 6

1 Wash the squabs and place in a pan with the butter, onion, cinnamon stick, ginger, cilantro, parsley and turmeric. Season with salt and pepper. Add just enough water to cover and bring to a boil. Cover and simmer gently for about 1 hour, until the squab is very tender.

2 Strain off the stock and reserve. Skin and bone the squabs, and shred the flesh into bite-size pieces. Preheat the oven to 350°F. Combine the sugar, cinnamon and almonds, and set aside.

3 Measure ⅔ cup of the reserved stock into a small pan. Add the eggs and mix well. Stir over low heat until creamy and very thick and almost set. Season with salt and pepper.

4 Brush a 12-inch diameter ovenproof dish with some of the melted butter and lay the first sheet of pastry in the dish. Brush this with butter and continue with five more sheets of pastry. Cover with the almond mixture, then half the egg mixture. Moisten with a little stock.

5 Layer four more sheets of phyllo pastry, brushing with butter as before. Lay the squab meat on top. Add the remaining egg mixture and more stock. Cover with the remaining pastry, brushing each sheet with butter, and tuck in any overlapping edges.

6 Brush the pie with egg yolk and bake for 40 minutes. Raise the oven temperature to 400°F and bake for 15 minutes more, until the pastry is crisp and golden. Garnish with a lattice design of cinnamon and confectioners' sugar. Serve hot.

Grains and Beans

Mediterranean countries deserve thanks for the creation of risotto, paella, pizzas and pasta, and the many salads and stews based on dried peas and beans.

The countries surrounding the Mediterranean produce a seemingly inexhaustible quantity and variety of grains, peas and beans. Wheat, the most ancient cereal grown in the region, predominates. It is the staple that provides for traditional and specialized local dishes, but from centuries of trading and travel come a great number of dishes that, although originally associated with one country, are often made using slightly different techniques and ingredients in many different areas of the Mediterranean.

Pasta, for example, although most widely consumed in Italy, is also made in the eastern Mediterranean under the name of **rishta**; it is known in Spain as **fideos**, and in Egypt as **macaroni or koshari**.

Bread is a staple food all over the Mediterranean. When you consider that it is made using the same basic ingredients, it is remarkable that there is such a variety of flavors and textures. There are the Italian olive breads—focaccia and ciabatta—and the dry breads like grissini and crostini, as well as a feast of soft breads, richly flavored with sun-dried tomatoes and herbs. Visit any part of France and see how important freshly baked breads, from rich brioches to crisp baguettes, are to the French. Bakeries stay open all through the day, turning out batch after batch of hot loaves. French bakers do not depend on preservatives, so bread has to be prepared fresh for every meal. Festive breads are also still widely enjoyed. The most elaborate is the braided Greek Easter Bread, flavored with nuts and fruit and adorned with hard-boiled eggs that are dyed red. According to legend, the eggs will keep those who eat them safe from harm.

Below: Spain produces a wide range of grains of all types, seen here at a typical market.

The unleavened or slightly leavened flat breads of the eastern Mediterranean and North Africa are eaten with every meal. The most common of these is the pita, which varies in shape and size. The Turks bake a huge, flat loaf that inflates like a balloon during baking. This is carried ceremoniously to the table, where it is shared by the diners; its soft, chewy dough is perfect for mopping up spicy sauces. Pita bread is often used instead of knives and forks; when slit, the empty pocket makes a perfect container for salads, bean dishes, falafel and meats.

Wheat flour is also used to make the highly popular phyllo pastries of North Africa, Lebanon, Greece and Turkey. It is skillfully shaped and stretched to form a transparent sheet, which is then brushed with olive oil or melted butter and folded into layers. When cooked, it is extremely flaky, light and crisp. Phyllo is used in many sweet or savory classics, such as the Moroccan pastilla, a spicy squab pie with cloves and cinnamon.

Regional classics like North African couscous are also made with wheat. Couscous is a kind of wheat pasta that gives its name to the traditional dish of either a spiced meat or vegetable sauce that covers the steamed pasta. At its most splendid it is served as a finale to a special feast when guests have already enjoyed several delicate courses. The couscous is piled high on a large platter and topped with meat or vegetables smothered in a delectable sweet, spicy sauce.

ABOVE: The fertile Guadalquivir valley near Carmona, in Spain.

Rice has been central to Mediterranean cooking for as long as twelve thousand years. The Moors brought rice to Europe in the eighth century through the eastern Mediterranean from Persia and Asia. With its strong Moorish tradition, southern Spain, particularly Valencia, remains the country's main producer of rice. The national dish, paella, originated in the coastal cities and fishing ports of Andalusia. But the uses for rice extend much further than one national dish. Many other rich, saffron-flavored risottos are widely popular and are good with zarzuela, an extravagant feast of fish and crustacea. Italians also consume a lot of rice, predominantly arborio, a short-grain, starchy rice that cooks down to a soft, creamy consistency. Arborio supplies the authentic taste of the classic subtle accompaniment Risotto alla Milanese, which is enriched with saffron, wine and Parmesan. In contrast, the fiery, dry pilafs of Turkey and the Middle East are heavily spiced and mixed with numerous herbs, dried fruits, nuts and vegetables.

Chickpeas are perhaps the most popular of the Mediterranean peas and form the basis of creamy pastes like hummus. Along with other peas and beans they are widely used in cold, garlicky dressed salads and as the base of many soups.

Traditionally a peasant food, beans are given long, slow cooking, and their taste is enhanced with cheap but flavorful meats or garlic-cured sausages. Served with locally produced vegetables, beans are the heart of many delicious soups and stews—for example, the traditional cassoulet of France. Before cooking dried beans, soak them in water overnight. Drain, cover with fresh water, then boil them rapidly for ten minutes to eliminate the sugars that cause indigestion. Reduce the heat and simmer for the rest of the recommended cooking time. Only add salt toward the end of the cooking time—if added too soon, salt will toughen the beans.

HUMMUS BI TAHINA

Blending chickpeas with garlic and oil makes a surprisingly creamy purée that is delicious as part of a Turkish-style mezze, or as a dip with vegetables. Leftovers make good sandwiches.

¾ cup dried chickpeas
juice of 2 lemons
2 garlic cloves, sliced
2 tablespoons olive oil
pinch of cayenne pepper
⅔ cup tahini paste
salt and ground black pepper
extra olive oil and cayenne pepper for sprinkling
flat-leaf parsley, to garnish

SERVES 4–6

1. Put the chickpeas in a bowl with plenty of cold water and let soak overnight.

2. Drain the chickpeas and cover with fresh water in a saucepan. Bring to a boil and boil rapidly for 10 minutes. Reduce the heat and simmer gently for about 1 hour, until soft. Drain.

3. Process the chickpeas in a food processor to a smooth purée. Add the lemon juice, garlic, olive oil, cayenne pepper and tahini and blend until creamy, scraping the mixture down from the sides of the bowl.

4. Season the purée with salt and pepper and transfer to a serving dish. Sprinkle with oil and cayenne pepper and serve garnished with a few parsley sprigs.

COOK'S TIP

For convenience, canned chickpeas can be used instead of dried. Use two 14-ounce cans and drain them thoroughly. Tahini paste can now be purchased at most supermarkets or health-food stores.

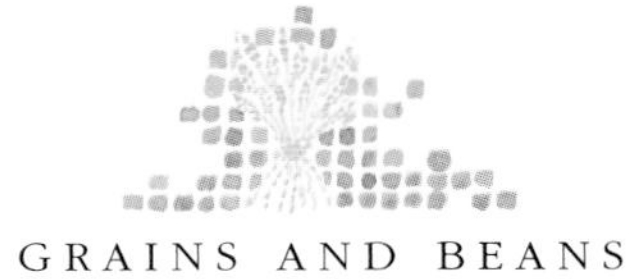

FALAFEL

In North Africa, these spicy fritters are made using dried fava beans, but chickpeas are much easier to find. Falafel are great served as a snack with garlicky yogurt or stuffed into warmed pita bread.

¾ cup dried chickpeas
1 large onion, coarsely chopped
2 garlic cloves, coarsely chopped
4 tablespoons coarsely chopped parsley
1 teaspoon cumin seeds, crushed
1 teaspoon coriander seeds, crushed
½ teaspoon baking powder
salt and ground black pepper
oil for deep-frying
pita bread, salad and yogurt, to serve

SERVES 4

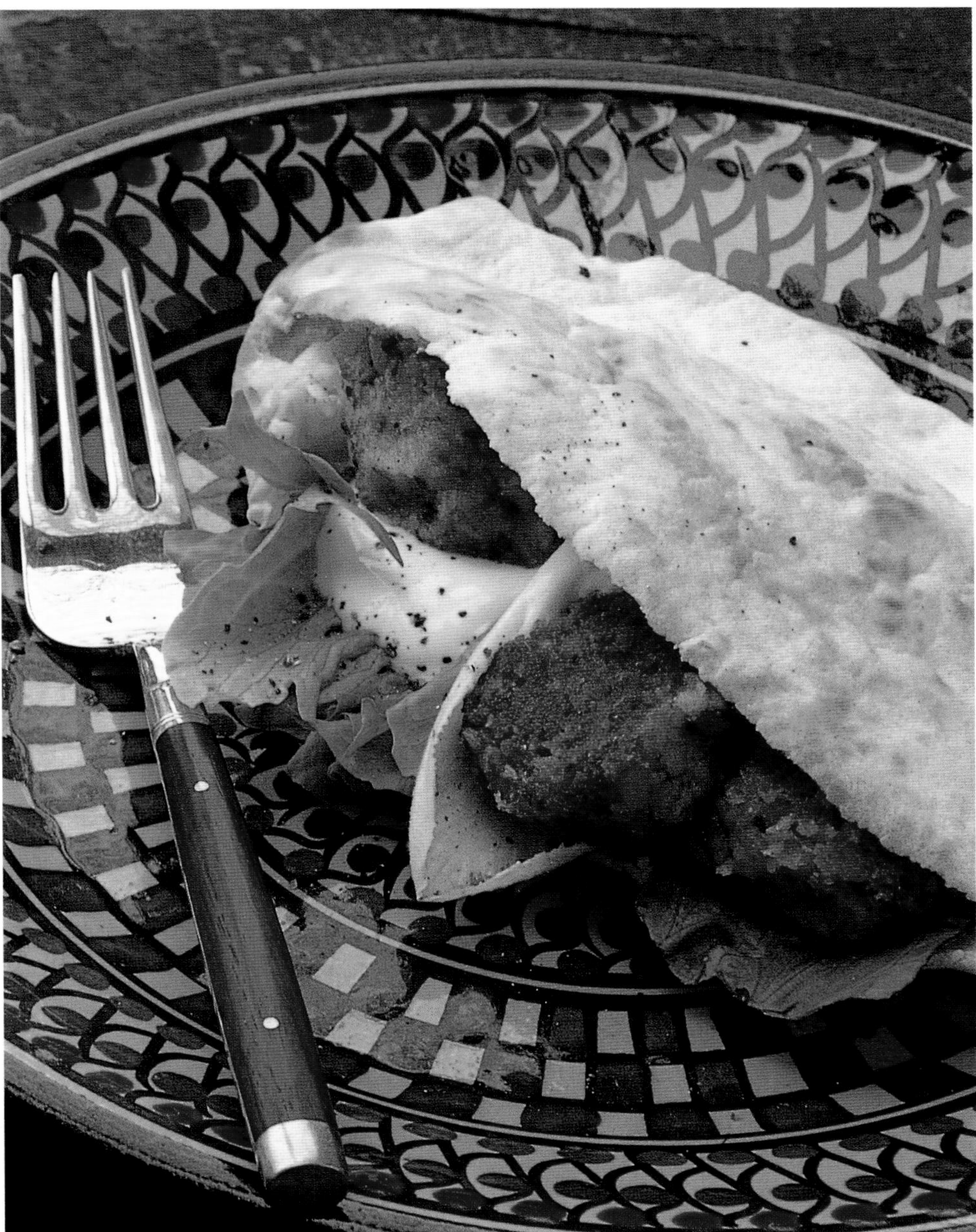

1 Put the chickpeas in a bowl with plenty of cold water. Let soak overnight.

2 Drain the chickpeas and cover with water in a pan. Bring to a boil. Boil rapidly for 10 minutes. Reduce the heat and simmer for about 1 hour, until soft. Drain.

3 Place in a food processor with the onion, garlic, parsley, cumin, coriander and baking powder. Add salt and pepper to taste. Process until the mixture forms a firm paste.

4 Shape the mixture into walnut-size balls and flatten them slightly. In a deep pan, heat 2 inches oil until a little of the mixture sizzles on the surface when added. Fry the falafel in batches until golden. Drain on paper towels and keep hot while frying the remainder. Serve warm, in pita bread, with salad and yogurt.

SUN-DRIED TOMATO BREAD

In the south of Italy, tomatoes are often dried in the hot sun. They are then preserved in oil, or hung up on strings in the kitchen, to use in the winter. This recipe uses the former type.

6 cups all-purpose flour
2 teaspoons salt
2 tablespoons sugar
1 package active dry yeast
1⅔–2 cups warm milk
1 tablespoon tomato paste
5 tablespoons oil from the jar of sun-dried tomatoes
5 tablespoons extra virgin olive oil
¾ cup drained sun-dried tomatoes, chopped
1 large onion, chopped

MAKES 4 SMALL LOAVES

1 Sift the flour, salt and sugar into a bowl, and make a well in the center. Mix the yeast with ⅔ cup of the warm milk and add to the flour.

2 Mix the tomato paste into the remaining milk until evenly blended, then add to the flour with the tomato oil and olive oil.

3 Gradually mix the flour into the liquid ingredients until you have a dough. Turn out onto a floured surface and knead for about 10 minutes, until smooth and elastic. Return to the clean bowl, cover with a cloth and let rise in a warm place for about 2 hours.

4 Punch down, and add the tomatoes and onion. Knead until evenly distributed through the dough. Shape into four loaves and place on a greased baking sheet. Cover with a dish towel and let rise again for about 45 minutes.

5 Preheat the oven to 375°F. Bake the bread for 45 minutes or until the loaves sound hollow when you tap them with your fingers. Let cool on a wire rack. Eat warm, or toasted with grated mozzarella cheese sprinkled on top.

COOK'S TIP

Use a pair of sharp kitchen scissors to cut up the sun-dried tomatoes.

GREEK EASTER BREAD

In Greece, Easter celebrations are very important and involve much preparation in the kitchen. This bread is sold in all the bakers' shops and also made at home. It is traditionally decorated with eggs dyed red.

1 package active dry yeast
½ cup warm milk
6 cups bread flour
2 eggs, beaten
½ teaspoon caraway seeds
1 tablespoon sugar
1 tablespoon brandy
4 tablespoons butter, melted
1 egg white, beaten
2–3 hard-boiled eggs, dyed red
½ cup split almonds

MAKES 1 LOAF

1 Mix the yeast with one or two tablespoons of warm water and set aside until it bubbles. Add the milk and 1 cup of the flour and mix to a creamy consistency. Cover with a cloth and let rest in a warm place to rise for 1 hour.

COOK'S TIP
For a nontraditional but festive variation, dye the eggs in different, spring-like colors.

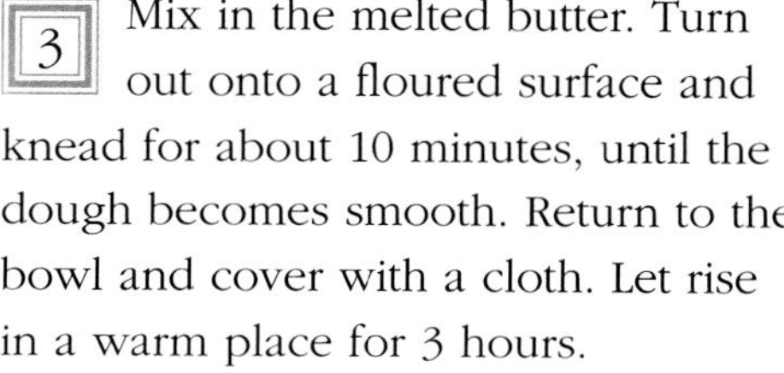

2 Sift the remaining flour into a large bowl and make a well in the center. Pour the risen yeast mixture into the well and draw in a little of the flour from the sides. Add the eggs, caraway seeds, sugar and brandy. Incorporate the remaining flour until the mixture begins to form a dough.

3 Mix in the melted butter. Turn out onto a floured surface and knead for about 10 minutes, until the dough becomes smooth. Return to the bowl and cover with a cloth. Let rise in a warm place for 3 hours.

4 Preheat the oven to 350°F. Punch down the dough, turn out onto a floured surface and knead for a minute or two. Divide the dough into three pieces and roll each piece into a long sausage. Make a braid, as shown above, and place the loaf on a greased baking sheet.

5 Tuck the ends under, brush with the egg white and decorate with the eggs and split almonds. Bake for about 1 hour, until the loaf sounds hollow when tapped on the bottom. Cool on a wire rack.

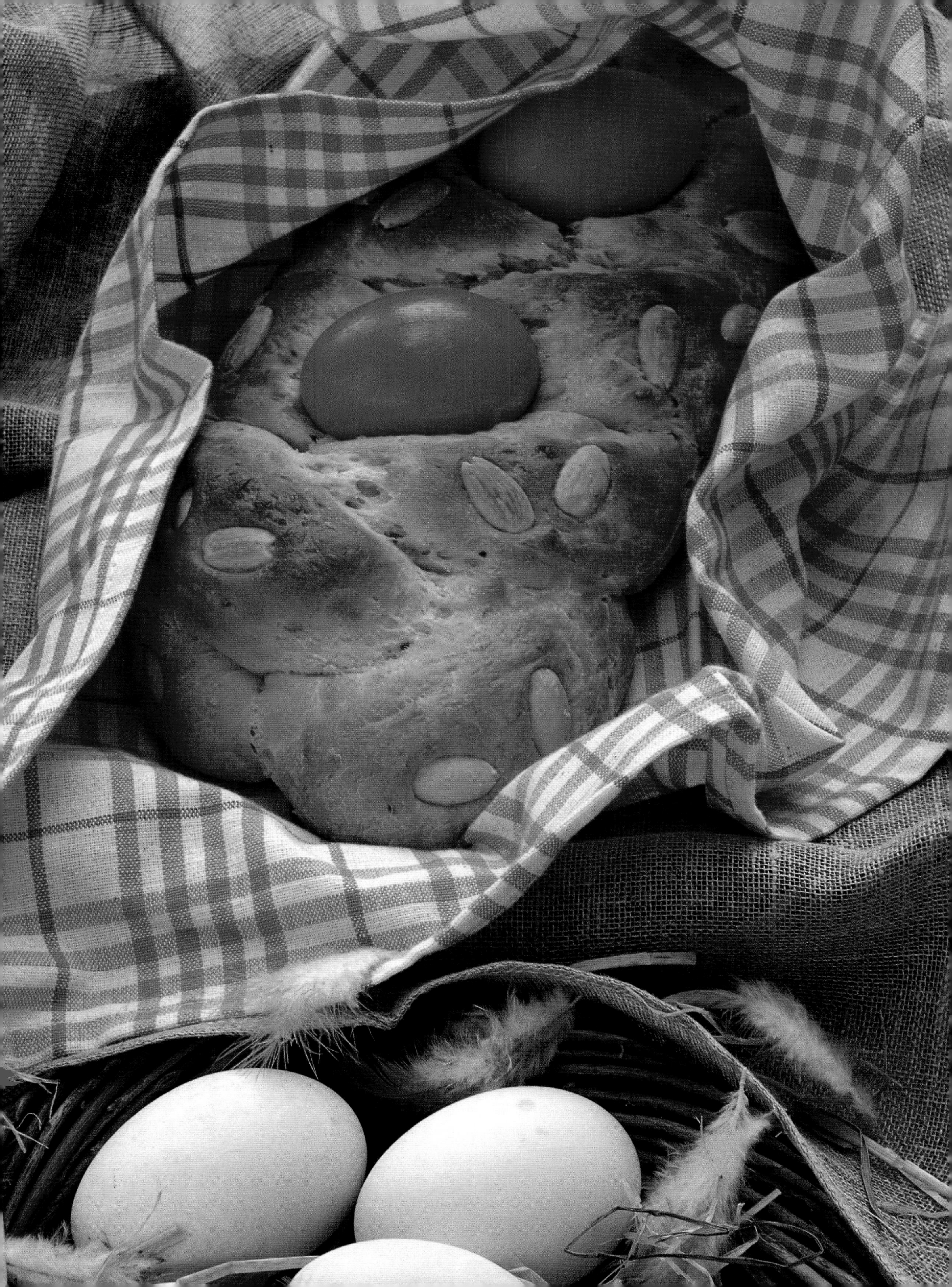

FOCACCIA

This is a flattish bread, originating in Genoa, Italy, made with flour, olive oil and salt. There are many variations from many regions, including stuffed varieties and versions topped with onions, olives or herbs.

1 package active dry yeast
3½ cups all-purpose flour
2 teaspoons salt
5 tablespoons olive oil
2 teaspoons coarse sea salt

MAKES 1 ROUND 10-INCH LOAF

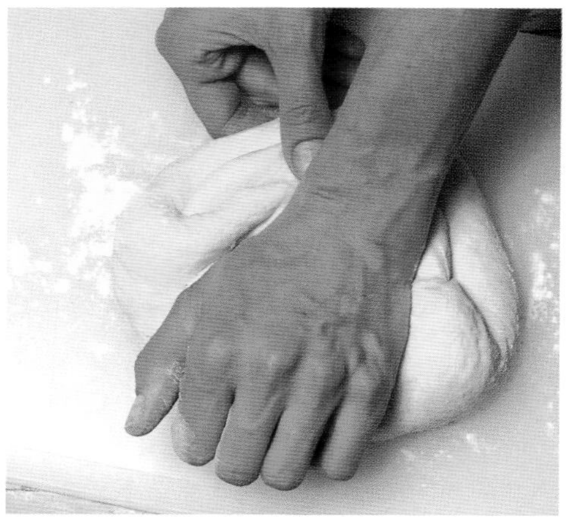

1. Dissolve the yeast in ½ cup warm water. Let stand for 10 minutes. Sift the flour into a large bowl, make a well in the center, and add the yeast mixture, salt and 2 tablespoons oil. Mix in the flour and add more water to make a dough.

2. Turn out onto a floured surface and knead the dough for about 10 minutes, until smooth and elastic. Return to the bowl, cover with a cloth, and let rise in a warm place for 2–2½ hours, until the dough has doubled in bulk.

3. Punch down the dough and knead again for a few minutes. Press into an oiled 10-inch tart pan and cover with a damp cloth. Let rise for 30 minutes.

4. Preheat the oven to 400°F. Poke the dough all over with your fingers to make little dimples in the surface. Pour the remaining oil over the dough, using a pastry brush to take it to the edges. Sprinkle with the salt.

5. Bake for 20–25 minutes, until the bread is pale gold. Carefully remove from the pan and let cool on a rack. The bread is best eaten on the same day, but it also freezes very well.

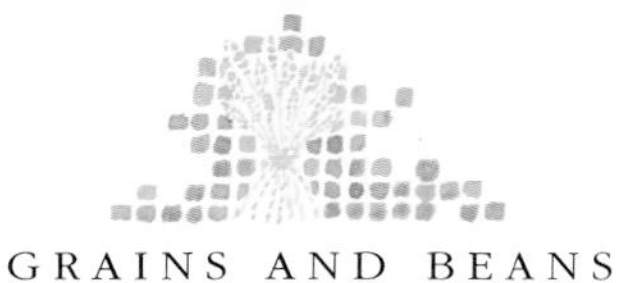

ONION FOCACCIA

This pizza-like flat bread is characterized by its soft, dimpled surface, sometimes dredged simply with coarse salt or with onions, herbs or olives. It tastes delicious served warm with soups and stews.

6 cups all-purpose flour
½ teaspoon salt
½ teaspoon sugar
1 tablespoon rapid-rise yeast
4 tablespoons extra virgin olive oil
2 cups warm water

TO FINISH
2 red onions, thinly sliced
3 tablespoons extra virgin olive oil
1 tablespoon coarse salt

MAKES TWO 10-INCH BREADS

1 Sift the flour, salt and sugar into a large bowl. Stir in the yeast, oil and water and mix to a dough using a round-bladed knife. (Add a little extra water if the dough is dry.)

2 Turn out onto a lightly floured surface and knead for about 10 minutes, until smooth and elastic.

3 Put the dough in a clean, lightly oiled bowl and cover with plastic wrap. Let rise in a warm place until doubled in bulk.

4 Place two 10-inch plain metal baking rings on baking sheets. Oil the insides of the rings and the baking sheets.

5 Preheat the oven to 400°F. Halve the dough and roll out each piece to a 10-inch circle. Press into the rings, cover with a dampened dish towel and let rise for 30 minutes.

6 Make deep holes, about 1 inch apart, in the dough. Cover and let rest for another 20 minutes.

7 Sprinkle the onions on top and drizzle with the oil. Sprinkle with the salt, then a little cold water, to prevent a crust from forming.

8 Bake for about 25 minutes, sprinkling with water again during cooking. Cool on a wire rack.

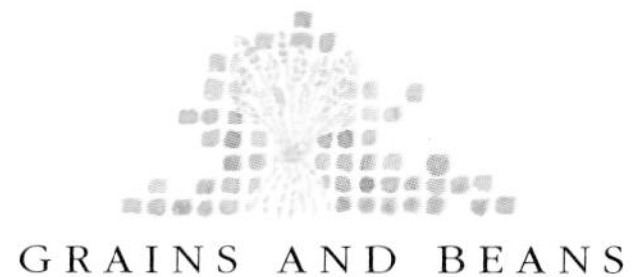

PAPPARDELLE WITH OLIVE AND CAPER PASTE

This homemade pasta is flavored with sun-dried tomato paste. The results are well worth the effort, but store-bought pasta can be substituted for a quick supper dish.

FOR THE PASTA

2½ cups all-purpose flour
¼ teaspoon salt
3 eggs
3 tablespoons sun-dried tomato paste

FOR THE SAUCE

⅔ cup pitted black olives
5 tablespoons capers
5 drained anchovy fillets
1 red chile, seeded and coarsely chopped
¼ cup coarsely chopped basil
¼ cup coarsely chopped parsley
⅔ cup olive oil
4 ripe tomatoes
salt and ground black pepper
flat leaf parsley or basil, to garnish
Parmesan cheese shavings, to serve

SERVES 4

1 To make the pasta, sift the flour and salt into a bowl and make a well in the center. Lightly beat the eggs with the tomato paste and pour the mixture into the well.

2 Combine the ingredients using a round-bladed knife. Turn out onto a work surface and knead for 6–8 minutes, until the dough is very smooth and soft, working in a little more flour if it becomes sticky. Wrap in aluminum foil and chill for 30 minutes.

3 To make the sauce, put the olives, capers, anchovies, chile, basil and parsley in a food processor or blender with the oil. Process very briefly until the ingredients are finely chopped. (Alternatively, you can finely chop the ingredients and then mix with the olive oil.)

4 Plunge the tomatoes into boiling water for 30 seconds, then refresh in cold water. Peel away the skins, remove the seeds and dice. Roll out the dough very thinly on a floured surface. Sprinkle with a little flour, then roll up like a jelly roll. Cut crosswise into ½-inch slices.

5 Unroll the pasta and lay out on a clean dish towel for about 10 minutes to dry.

6 Bring a large saucepan of salted water to a boil. Add the pasta and cook for 2–3 minutes, until just tender. Drain immediately and return to the saucepan.

7 Add the olive mixture, tomatoes and salt and black pepper to taste, then toss together gently over medium heat for about 1 minute, until heated through. Garnish with parsley or basil and serve sprinkled with Parmesan shavings.

SPANISH ONION AND ANCHOVY PIZZA

This pizza has flavors and ingredients brought to Spain by the Moors and still used today in many classic Spanish recipes.

2½ cups all-purpose flour
½ teaspoon salt
½ ounce rapid-rise yeast
½ cup olive oil
⅔ cup milk and water, in equal quantities, combined
3 large onions, thinly sliced
2-ounce can anchovies, drained and coarsely chopped
2 tablespoons pine nuts
2 tablespoons golden raisins
1 teaspoon red pepper flakes
salt and ground black pepper

SERVES 6–8

1 Sift the flour and salt together into a large bowl. Stir in the yeast. Make a well in the center, and add half of the olive oil and a little of the milk and water. Bring the flour mixture and liquid together, gradually adding the remaining milk and water, until a dough is formed. Knead on a floured surface for about 10 minutes. Return to the bowl, cover with a cloth, and set in a warm place to rise for about 1 hour.

2 Heat the remaining oil in a large frying pan, add the onions and cook until soft. Preheat the oven to 475°F.

3 Punch down the dough and roll out to a rectangle about 12 x 15 inches. Place on an oiled baking sheet. Cover with the onions. Sprinkle on the anchovies, pine nuts, golden raisins and red pepper flakes. Season. Bake for 10–15 minutes, until the edges are beginning to brown. Serve hot.

MUSHROOM AND PESTO PIZZA

Home-made Italian-style pizzas are a little time-consuming to make, but the results are well worth the effort.

FOR THE PIZZA CRUST

3 cups all-purpose flour
¼ teaspoon salt
½ ounce rapid-rise yeast
1 tablespoon olive oil

FOR THE FILLING

2 ounces dried porcini mushrooms
¾ cup fresh basil
⅓ cup pine nuts
1½ ounces Parmesan cheese, thinly sliced
7 tablespoons olive oil
2 onions, thinly sliced
8 ounces cremini mushrooms, sliced
salt and ground black pepper

SERVES 4

1. To make the pizza crust, put the flour in a bowl with the salt, yeast and olive oil. Add 1 cup warm water and mix to a dough using a round-bladed knife.

2. Turn out onto a work surface and knead for 5 minutes, until smooth. Place in a clean bowl, cover with plastic wrap and let rise in a warm place until doubled in bulk.

3. Meanwhile, make the filling. Soak the dried mushrooms in hot water for 20 minutes. Place the basil, pine nuts, Parmesan and 5 tablespoons of the olive oil in a blender or food processor and process to make a smooth paste. Set the paste aside.

4. Fry the onions in the remaining olive oil for 3–4 minutes, until beginning to color. Add the cremini mushrooms and fry for 2 minutes. Stir in the drained porcini mushrooms and season lightly.

5. Preheat the oven to 425°F. Lightly grease a large baking sheet. Turn out the pizza dough onto a floured surface and roll out to a 12-inch circle. Place the dough on the baking sheet.

6. Spread the pesto mixture to within ½ inch of the edges. Spread the mushroom mixture on top.

7. Bake the pizza for 35–40 minutes, until risen and golden.

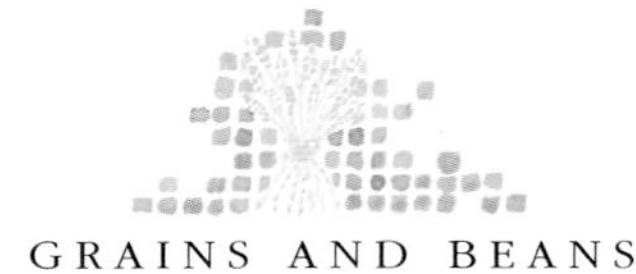

OLIVE BREAD

Olive breads are popular all over the Mediterranean. For this Greek recipe use rich, oily olives or those marinated in herbs rather than canned ones.

2 red onions, thinly sliced
2 tablespoons olive oil
1⅓ cups pitted black or green olives
7 cups all-purpose flour
1½ teaspoons salt
4 teaspoons rapid-rise yeast
3 tablespoons each coarsely-chopped parsley and cilantro or mint

MAKES TWO 1½-POUND LOAVES

1 Sauté the onions in the oil until soft. Coarsely chop the olives.

2 Put the flour, salt, yeast, parsley and cilantro or mint in a large bowl with the olives and onions and pour in 2 cups warm water.

VARIATION

Shape the dough into 16 small rolls. Slash the tops as above and reduce the cooking time to 25 minutes.

3 Mix to a dough using a round-bladed knife, adding a little more water if the mixture feels dry.

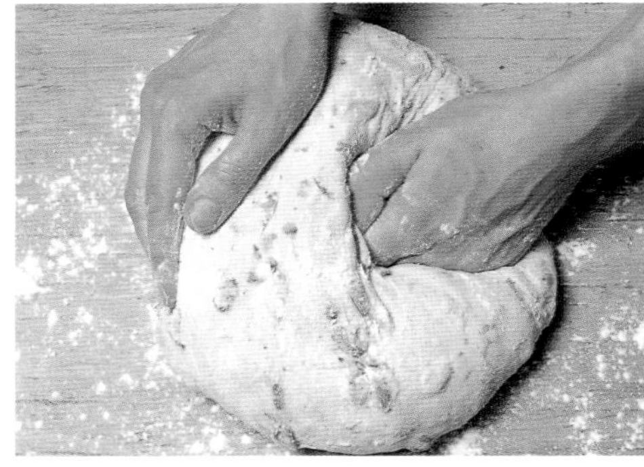

4 Turn out onto a lightly floured surface and knead for about 10 minutes. Put in a clean bowl, cover with plastic wrap and let sit in a warm place until doubled in bulk.

5 Preheat the oven to 425°F. Lightly grease two baking sheets. Turn the dough out onto a floured surface and cut in half. Shape into two loaves and place on the baking sheets. Cover loosely with lightly oiled plastic wrap and let rise until doubled in size.

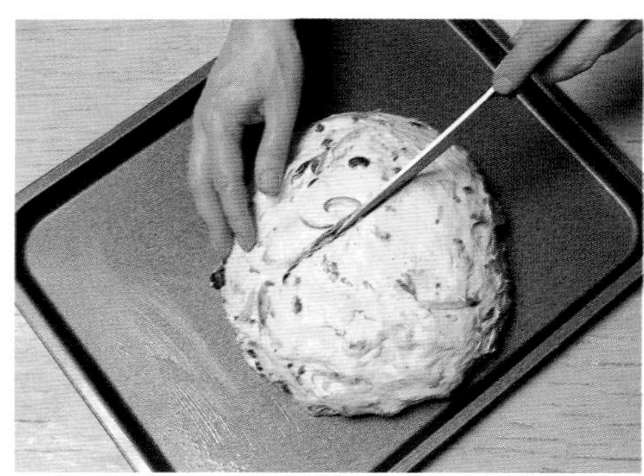

6 Slash the tops of the loaves with a knife, then bake for about 40 minutes or until the loaves sound hollow when tapped on the bottom. Transfer to a wire rack to cool.

STUFFED KIBBEH

Kibbeh is a tasty North African specialty of ground meat and bulgur. The patties are sometimes stuffed with additional meat and deep-fried. Moderately spiced, they're good with yogurt or cacik sauce.

1 pound lean lamb (or lean ground lamb or beef)
oil for deep-frying
avocado slices and cilantro sprigs, to serve

FOR THE KIBBEH
1⅓ cups bulgur
1 red chile, seeded and coarsely chopped
1 onion, coarsely chopped
salt and ground black pepper

FOR THE STUFFING
1 onion, finely chopped
⅔ cup pine nuts
2 tablespoons olive oil
1½ teaspoons ground allspice
¼ cup chopped cilantro

SERVES 4–6

1 If necessary, coarsely cut up the lamb and process the pieces in a blender or food processor until ground. Divide the ground meat into two equal portions.

2 To make the kibbeh, soak the bulgur for 15 minutes in cold water. Drain well, then process in the blender or food processor with the chile, onion, half the meat and plenty of salt and pepper.

3 To make the stuffing, fry the onion and pine nuts in the oil for 5 minutes. Add the allspice and remaining ground meat and fry gently, breaking up the meat with a wooden spoon, until browned. Stir in the cilantro and a little seasoning.

4 Turn the kibbeh mixture out onto a work surface and shape into a cake. Cut into 12 wedges.

5 Flatten one piece in the palm of your hand and spoon a little stuffing into the center. Bring the edges of the kibbeh up over the stuffing to enclose it. Make into a firm, egg-shaped mold between the palms of your hands, making sure that the filling is completely encased. Repeat with the other kibbeh.

6 Heat oil to a depth of 2 inches in a large pan, until a few kibbeh crumbs sizzle on the surface.

7 Lower half the kibbeh into the oil and fry for about 5 minutes, until golden. Drain on paper towels and keep them hot while cooking the remainder. Serve with avocado slices and cilantro sprigs.

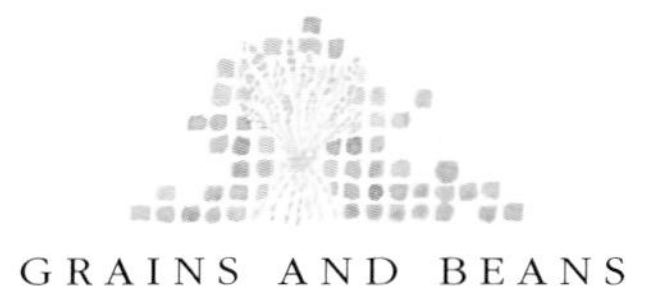

EGYPTIAN RICE WITH LENTILS

Lentils are cooked with spices in many ways in the Middle East. Two important staples come together in this dish, which can be served hot or cold.

1½ cups large brown lentils, soaked overnight in water
2 large onions
3 tablespoons olive oil
1 tablespoon ground cumin
½ teaspoon ground cinnamon
generous 1 cup long-grain rice
salt and ground black pepper
flat-leaf parsley, to garnish

SERVES 6

1 Drain the lentils and put in a large pan. Add enough water to cover by 2 inches. Bring to a boil, cover the pan and simmer for 40 minutes to 1½ hours or until tender. Drain thoroughly.

2 Finely chop one onion and slice the other. Heat 1 tablespoon oil in a pan, add the chopped onion and sauté until soft. Add the lentils, salt, pepper, cumin and cinnamon.

3 Measure out the rice and add it, with the same volume of water, to the lentil mixture. Cover and simmer for about 20 minutes, until both the rice and lentils are tender. Heat the remaining oil in a frying pan and cook the sliced onion until very dark brown. Pour the rice mixture into a serving bowl, sprinkle with the onion and serve hot or cold, garnished with flat-leaf parsley.

BAKED CHEESE POLENTA WITH TOMATO SAUCE

Polenta, or cornmeal mush, is a staple food in Italy. It is cooked like a sort of porridge, and eaten soft, or set, cut into shapes, then baked or broiled.

1 teaspoon salt
2¼ cups instant polenta
1 teaspoon paprika
½ teaspoon ground nutmeg
2 tablespoons olive oil
1 large onion, finely chopped
2 garlic cloves, crushed
2 14-ounce cans chopped tomatoes
1 tablespoon tomato paste
1 teaspoon sugar
salt and ground black pepper
3 ounces Gruyère cheese, grated

SERVES 4

1. Preheat the oven to 400°F. Line an 11 x 7-inch baking pan with plastic wrap. Put 4 cups water into a pan and bring to a boil with the salt.

2. Pour in the polenta in a steady stream and cook, stirring constantly, for 5 minutes. Beat in the paprika and nutmeg, then pour into the prepared pan and smooth the surface. Let cool.

3. Heat the oil in a pan and cook the onion and garlic until soft. Add the tomatoes, paste and sugar. Season. Simmer for 20 minutes.

4. Turn out the polenta onto a cutting board and cut into 2-inch squares. Place half the squares in a greased ovenproof dish. Spoon on half the tomato sauce, and sprinkle with half the cheese. Repeat the layers. Bake for about 25 minutes, until golden.

PILAF WITH SAFFRON AND PICKLED WALNUTS

Pickled walnuts have a warm, tangy flavor that is delicious in rice and bulgur dishes. This eastern Mediterranean pilaf is interesting enough to serve on its own or with broiled lamb or pork.

1 teaspoon saffron strands
½ cup pine nuts
3 tablespoons olive oil
1 large onion, chopped
3 garlic cloves, crushed
¼ teaspoon ground allspice
1½-inch piece fresh ginger, grated
generous 1 cup long-grain rice
1¼ cups vegetable stock
½ cup pickled walnuts, drained and coarsely chopped
¼ cup raisins
3 tablespoons coarsely chopped parsley or cilantro
salt and ground black pepper
parsley or cilantro, to garnish
plain yogurt, to serve

SERVES 4

1 Put the saffron in a bowl with 1 tablespoon boiling water and let stand. Heat a large frying pan and dry-fry the pine nuts until they turn golden. Set them aside.

2 Heat the oil in the pan and sauté the onion, garlic and allspice for 3 minutes. Stir in the ginger and rice and cook for 1 more minute.

3 Add the stock and bring to a boil. Reduce the heat, cover and simmer gently for 15 minutes, until the rice is just tender.

4 Stir in the saffron and liquid, the pine nuts, pickled walnuts, raisins and parsley or cilantro. Season to taste with salt and pepper. Heat through gently for 2 minutes. Garnish with parsley or cilantro leaves and serve with plain yogurt.

VARIATION

Use one small eggplant, chopped and sautéed in a little olive oil, instead of the pickled walnuts, if you prefer.

RISOTTO ALLA MILANESE

Italian risottos have a distinctive creamy texture that is achieved using arborio rice, a short-grain rice that absorbs plenty of stock but at the same time retains some texture. This risotto, sprinkled with cheese and gremolata, makes a delicious light meal or accompaniment to a meaty stew or casserole.

FOR THE GREMOLATA

2 garlic cloves, crushed
¼ cup chopped fresh parsley
finely grated zest of 1 lemon

FOR THE RISOTTO

1 teaspoon saffron strands
2 tablespoons butter
1 large onion, finely chopped
1½ cups arborio (risotto) rice
⅔ cup dry white wine
4 cups chicken or vegetable stock
salt and ground black pepper
Parmesan cheese shavings

SERVES 4

1 To make the gremolata, combine the garlic, parsley and lemon zest and reserve.

2 To make the risotto, put the saffron in a small bowl with 1 tablespoon boiling water and set aside. Melt the butter in a heavy saucepan and gently sauté the onion for 5 minutes.

3 Stir in the rice and cook for about 2 minutes, until it becomes translucent. Add the wine and saffron mixture and cook for several minutes, until the wine is absorbed.

4 Add 2½ cups of the stock to the pan and simmer gently until the stock is absorbed, stirring frequently.

5 Gradually add more stock, a ladleful at a time, until the rice is tender. (The rice might be tender and creamy before you've added all the stock, so add it slowly toward the end of the cooking time.)

6 Season the risotto with salt and pepper and transfer to a serving dish. Sprinkle lavishly with shavings of Parmesan cheese and the gremolata.

VARIATION

If preferred, stir plenty of grated Parmesan cheese into the risotto.

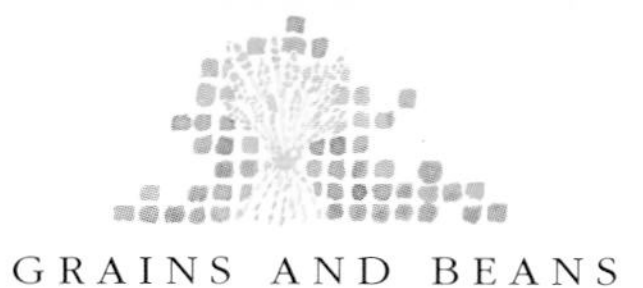

Spiced Vegetable Couscous

Couscous, a cereal processed from semolina, is used throughout North Africa, mostly in Morocco, where it is served with meat, poultry and vegetable stews or tagines.

3 tablespoons vegetable oil
1 large onion, finely chopped
2 garlic cloves, crushed
1 tablespoon tomato paste
½ teaspoon ground turmeric
½ teaspoon cayenne pepper
1 teaspoon ground coriander
1 teaspoon ground cumin
1½ cups cauliflower florets
8 ounces baby carrots, trimmed
1 red bell pepper, seeded and diced
4 beefsteak tomatoes
8 ounces zucchini, thickly sliced
14-ounce can chickpeas, drained and rinsed
3 tablespoons chopped cilantro
salt and ground black pepper
cilantro sprigs, to garnish

For the couscous
1 teaspoon salt
2⅔ cups couscous
2 tablespoons butter

Serves 6

1 Heat 2 tablespoons of the oil in a large pan, add the onion and garlic, and cook until soft. Stir in the tomato paste, turmeric, cayenne, ground coriander and cumin. Cook, stirring, for 2 minutes.

2 Add the cauliflower, carrots and pepper, with enough water to come halfway up the vegetables. Bring to a boil, then lower the heat, cover and simmer for 10 minutes.

Cook's Tip

Beefsteak tomatoes have excellent flavor and are ideal for this recipe, but you can substitute six ordinary tomatoes or two 14-ounce cans chopped tomatoes.

3 Plunge the tomatoes into boiling water for 30 seconds, then refresh in cold water. Peel away the skins and chop. Add the sliced zucchini, chickpeas and tomatoes to the other vegetables and cook for another 10 minutes. Stir in the cilantro and season with salt and pepper. Keep hot.

4 To cook the couscous, bring 2 cups water to a boil in a large saucepan. Add the remaining oil and the salt. Remove from the heat and add the couscous, stirring. Let swell for 2 minutes, then add the butter and heat through gently, stirring to separate the grains.

5 Turn the couscous out onto a warm serving dish and spoon the vegetables on top, pouring any liquid over. Garnish and serve.

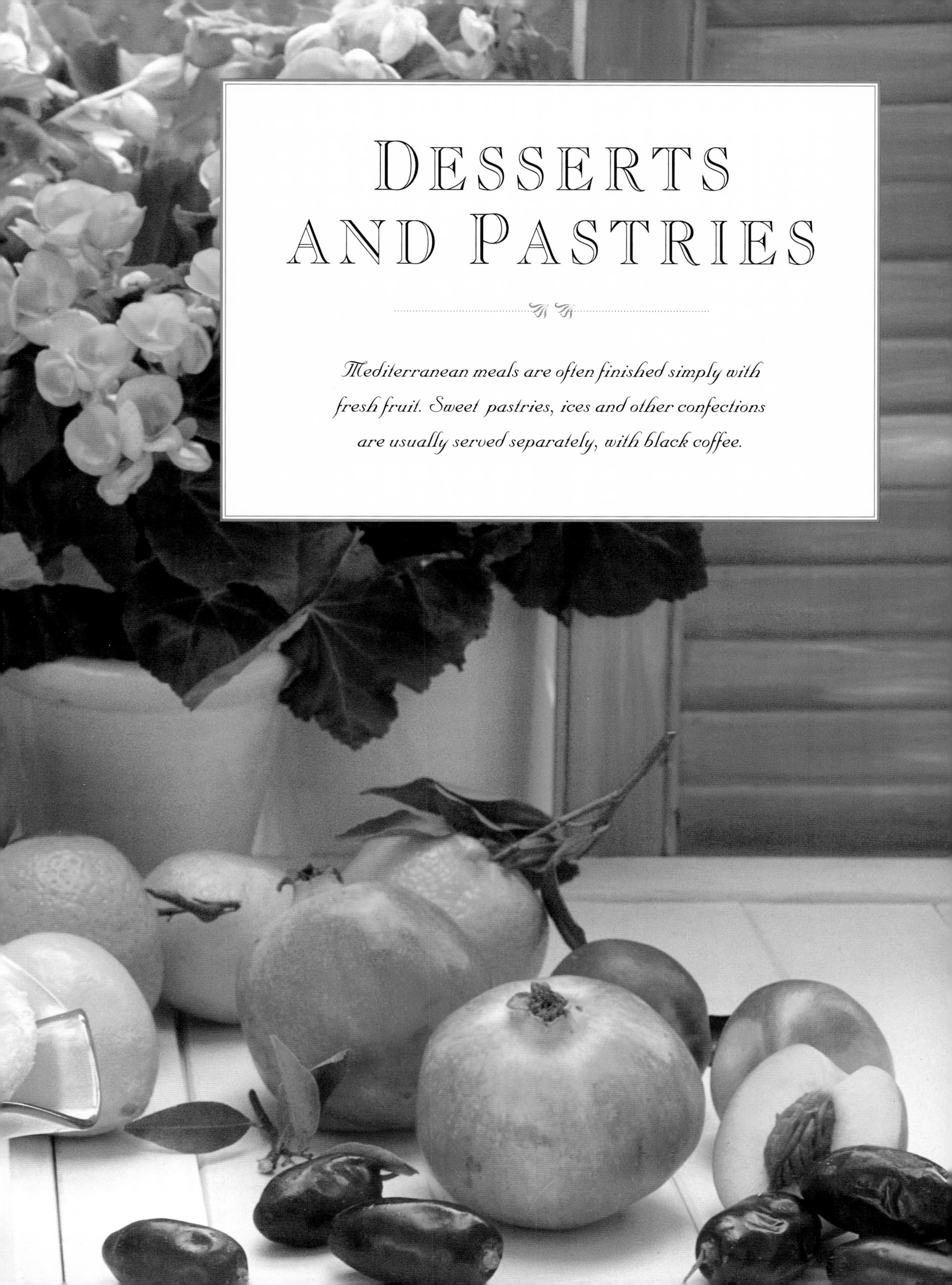

Desserts and Pastries

Mediterranean meals are often finished simply with fresh fruit. Sweet pastries, ices and other confections are usually served separately, with black coffee.

A peep in the glass display cabinets of any pâtisserie, confectioner or coffeehouse just about anywhere around the Mediterranean will reveal an absolute feast of sweet treats. From highly decorated cakes and tortes, lavishly finished with sugared decorations, to the painstakingly stuffed and glazed or candied fruits, all Mediterranean sweets offer an abundance of fabulous flavors. Many desserts, pastries and confections involve complex cooking techniques and need specialized ingredients, and they are perhaps best left to the skills of professional pastry chefs. These include some of the lavish, multi-flavored ice cream gâteaux of Italy and a number of the specialized pastries of the Arab world.

On a domestic level, most Mediterranean desserts take full advantage of the glorious abundance of fresh fruits. For a special occasion, a colorful selection of seasonal fruits such as figs, plums, apricots, peaches, melons and cherries makes a stunning finale. These can be arranged on a platter lined with grape or fig leaves with some of the fruits cut open decoratively, and the whole platter scattered with crushed ice. On a simpler scale, pomegranate seeds or sweet juicy oranges can be arranged in bowls, sprinkled with sugar and rose water or orange-

Below: Orange groves abound in this fertile valley near Jaén in Spain.

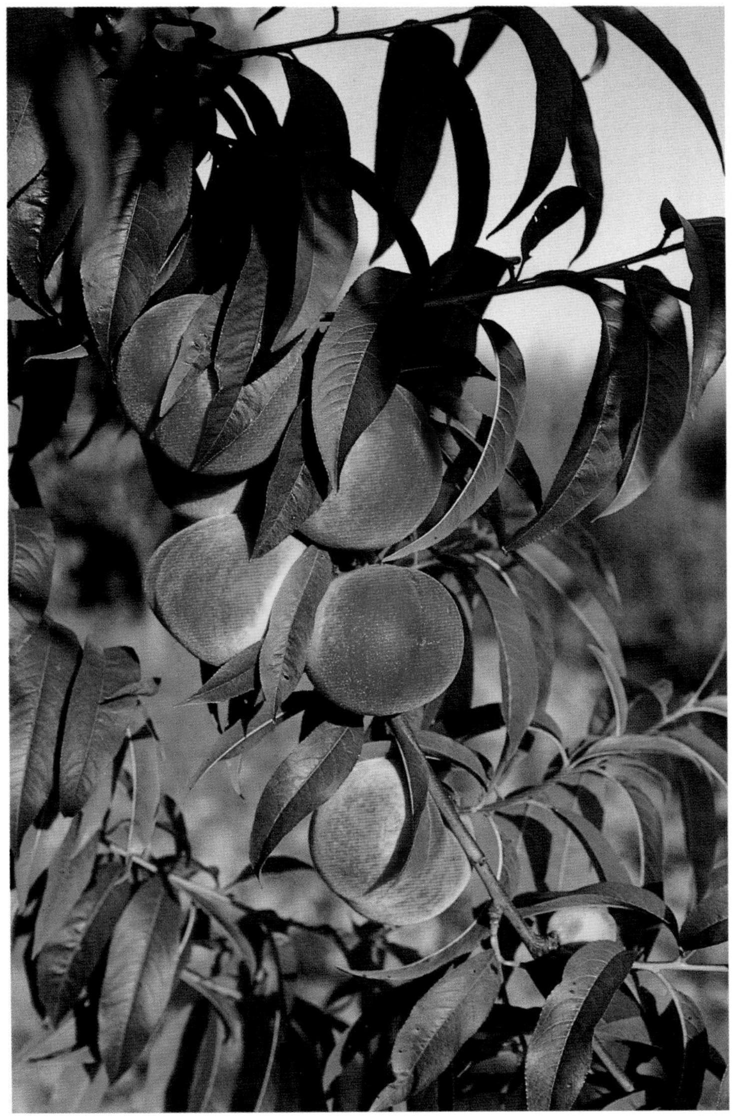

ABOVE: Plump, rosy and ready for picking, peaches make a perfect dessert, alone or with a delicious amaretto stuffing.

flower water and served iced. Fresh fruits can also be lightly poached in sugar- or honey-sweetened syrups, sometimes with the addition of mild spices. They'll store well for several days as the syrup becomes impregnated with the flavors of the fruit and spices. Pears, quinces, apricots and figs are typical examples. Other refreshing desserts are the smooth sorbets of France and the granitas of Italy, or the broiled or baked fruits that are so full of flavor. Sometimes these are sugared or topped with a scoop of mascarpone or ricotta and laced with a little liqueur. A selection of dried fruits, available in abundance and of good quality, makes an ideal end to a meal when served with dessert wine or liqueurs.

ABOVE: Pyramids of gorgeous fruit await the shopper at the covered market in Florence.

In Turkey, Greece, Lebanon and Egypt, small sweet pastries and confections are enjoyed as a between-meal snack with good strong coffee. These include the rich pastries, doughnuts, and semolina and nut cakes, drenched in spiced syrup and featuring flavors like honey, almonds, pistachios, sesame, pine nuts, rose water and orange-flower water. Served in small pieces, they make a wonderful contrast to the bitterness of the coffee. The Semolina and Nut Halva is a light version of a syrupy steeped cake which that is perfect with coffee or as a dessert with cream.

Other prominent Mediterranean desserts are the sweet milk-based puddings of both the east and the west. In North Africa and the Middle East these are made with ground or short-grain rice and spiced with cinnamon, cloves, anise or fennel. They are usually served cold, sometimes drizzled with a honey-and-orange-flavored syrup. One of Spain's classic desserts is the elegant Crema Catalana, a sweet, creamy custard that is absolutely delicious either on its own or accompanied by fresh or sweetened fruits.

Fresh Figs with Honey and Wine

Any variety of figs can be used in this recipe, their ripeness determining the cooking time. Choose ones that are plump and firm, and use them quickly because they don't keep well.

2 cups dry white wine
1/3 cup honey
1/4 cup sugar
1 small orange
8 whole cloves
1 pound fresh figs
1 cinnamon stick
mint sprigs or bay leaves, to decorate

For the cream
1 1/4 cups heavy cream
1 vanilla bean
1 teaspoon sugar

Serves 6

1 Put the wine, honey and sugar in a heavy saucepan and heat gently until the sugar dissolves.

2 Stud the orange with the cloves and add to the syrup with the figs and cinnamon. Cover and simmer very gently for 5–10 minutes, until the figs are softened. Transfer to a serving dish and let cool.

3 Put 2/3 cup of the cream in a small saucepan with the vanilla bean. Bring almost to a boil, then let cool and infuse for 30 minutes. Remove the vanilla bean and mix with the remaining cream and sugar in a bowl. Whip lightly. Transfer to a serving dish. Decorate the figs, then serve with the cream.

CHURROS

These Spanish doughnuts are commercially deep-fried in huge coils and broken off into smaller pieces for selling. Serve this homemade version freshly cooked with hot chocolate or strong coffee.

1¾ cups all-purpose flour
¼ teaspoon salt
2 tablespoons sugar
¼ cup olive or sunflower oil
1 egg, beaten
sugar and ground cinnamon for dusting
oil for deep-frying

MAKES 12–15

1 Sift the flour, salt and sugar onto a plate or piece of paper. Heat 1 cup of water in a saucepan with the oil until it boils.

2 Pour in the flour mixture and beat with a wooden spoon until the mixture forms a stiff paste. Let cool for 2 minutes.

3 Gradually beat in the egg until smooth. Oil a large baking sheet. Sprinkle plenty of sugar onto a plate and stir in a little cinnamon.

4 Put the dough in a large pastry bag fitted with a ½-inch plain piping nozzle. Pipe little coils or S shapes onto the baking sheet.

5 Heat 2 inches of oil in a large pan to 336°F or until a little dough sizzles on the surface.

6 Using an oiled metal spatula, lower several of the piped shapes into the oil and cook for about 2 minutes, until light golden.

7 Drain on paper towels, then coat with the sugar and cinnamon mixture. Cook the remaining churros in the same way and serve immediately.

WALNUT AND RICOTTA CAKE

Soft, tangy ricotta cheese is widely used in Italian desserts. Here, it is included along with walnuts and orange to flavor a sponge cake. Don't worry if it sinks slightly after baking—this gives it an authentic appearance.

1 cup walnut pieces
10 tablespoons unsalted butter, softened
⅔ cup sugar
5 eggs, separated
finely grated zest of 1 orange
⅔ cup ricotta cheese
6 tablespoons all-purpose flour

TO FINISH
¼ cup apricot jam
2 tablespoons brandy
2 ounces unsweetened or semisweet chocolate, coarsely grated

MAKES 10 SLICES

1 Preheat the oven to 375°F. Grease and line the bottom of a deep 9-inch round, removable-bottomed cake pan. Coarsely chop and lightly toast the walnuts.

2 Cream together the butter and ½ cup of the sugar until light and fluffy. Add the egg yolks, orange zest, ricotta cheese, flour and walnuts and combine.

3 Beat the egg whites in a large bowl until stiff. Gradually beat in the remaining sugar. Using a large metal spoon, fold a quarter of the beaten whites into the ricotta mixture. Carefully fold in the rest of the beaten whites.

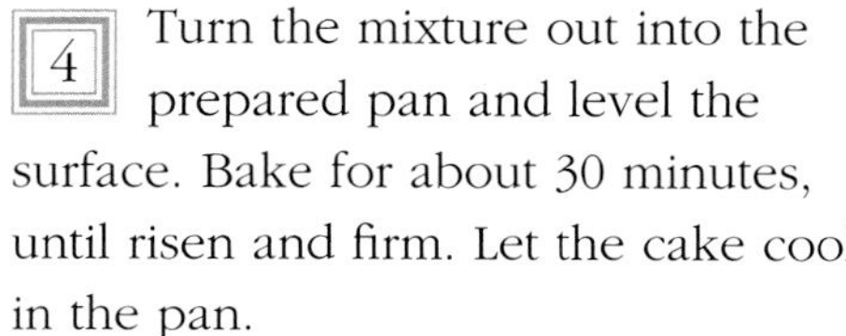

4 Turn the mixture out into the prepared pan and level the surface. Bake for about 30 minutes, until risen and firm. Let the cake cool in the pan.

5 Transfer the cake to a serving plate. Heat the apricot jam in a small saucepan with 1 tablespoon water. Strain and stir in the brandy. Use to coat the top and sides of the cake. Scatter grated chocolate generously over the cake.

VARIATION
Use toasted and chopped almonds in place of the walnuts.

BISCOTTI

These Italian cookies are baked, sliced to reveal a feast of mixed nuts and then baked again until crisp and golden. Traditionally they're served dipped in vin santo, a sweet dessert wine—perfect for rounding off a Mediterranean meal.

4 tablespoons unsalted butter, softened
½ cup sugar
1½ cups self-rising flour
¼ teaspoon salt
2 teaspoons baking powder
1 teaspoon ground coriander
finely grated zest of 1 lemon
½ cup polenta
1 egg, lightly beaten
2 teaspoons brandy or orange-flavored liqueur
½ cup unblanched almonds
½ cup pistachios

MAKES 24

1 Preheat the oven to 325°F. Lightly grease a baking sheet. Cream together the butter and sugar in a bowl.

2 Sift all the flour, salt, baking powder and coriander into the bowl. Add the lemon zest, polenta, egg and brandy or liqueur and combine to make a soft dough.

3 Stir in the nuts until evenly combined. Halve the mixture. Shape each half into a flat sausage about 9 inches long and 2½ inches wide. Bake for about 30 minutes, until risen and just firm. Remove from oven.

4 When cool, cut each sausage diagonally into 12 thin slices. Return to the baking sheet and cook for another 10 minutes, until crisp.

5 Transfer to a wire rack to cool completely. Store in an airtight jar for up to 1 week.

COOK'S TIP

Use a sharp, serrated knife to slice the cooled cookies, otherwise they will crumble.

SEMOLINA AND NUT HALVA

Semolina is a popular ingredient in many desserts and pastries in the eastern Mediterranean. Here it provides a spongy base for soaking up a deliciously fragrant, spicy syrup.

For the halva
8 tablespoons (1 stick) unsalted butter, softened
½ cup sugar
finely grated zest of 1 orange, plus 2 tablespoons juice
3 eggs
1 cup semolina
2 teaspoons baking powder
1 cup ground hazelnuts

To finish
1½ cups sugar
2 cinnamon sticks, halved
juice of 1 lemon
¼ cup orange-flower water
½ cup unblanched hazelnuts, toasted and chopped
½ cup blanched almonds, toasted and chopped
shredded zest of 1 orange
Serves 10

1 Preheat the oven to 425°F. Grease and line the bottom of a deep 9-inch square cake pan.

2 Lightly cream the butter in a bowl. Add the sugar, orange zest and juice, eggs, semolina, baking powder and hazelnuts and beat the ingredients together until smooth.

3 Put into the prepared pan and level the surface. Bake for 20–25 minutes, until just firm and golden. Let cool in the pan.

4 To make the syrup, put the sugar in a small, heavy saucepan with 2¼ cups water and the half cinnamon sticks. Heat gently, stirring, until the sugar has dissolved completely.

5 Bring to a boil and boil rapidly, without stirring, for 5 minutes. Measure half the boiling syrup and add the lemon juice and orange-flower water to it. Pour over the halva. Reserve the remainder of the syrup in the pan.

6 Leave the halva in the pan until the syrup is absorbed, then turn it out onto a plate and cut diagonally into diamond-shaped portions. Sprinkle with the nuts.

7 Boil the remaining syrup until slightly thickened, then pour it on the halva. Sprinkle the shredded orange zest on the cake and serve with lightly whipped cream.

Cook's Tip
Be sure to use a deep, solid cake pan rather than one with a removable bottom; otherwise, the syrup might seep out.

CREMA CATALANA

This delicious Spanish dessert is a cross between a crème caramel and a crème brûlée. It is not as rich as crème brûlée, but has a similar caramelized sugar topping.

2 cups milk
pared zest of ½ lemon
1 cinnamon stick
4 egg yolks
7 tablespoons sugar
1½ tablespoons cornstarch
ground nutmeg

SERVES 4

1 Put the milk in a pan with the lemon zest and cinnamon stick. Bring to a boil, then simmer for 10 minutes. Remove the lemon zest and cinnamon. Place the egg yolks and 3 tablespoons of the sugar in a bowl and whisk until pale yellow. Add the cornstarch and mix well.

2 Stir in a few tablespoons of the hot milk, then add this mixture to the remaining milk. Return to the heat and cook gently, stirring, for about 5 minutes, until thickened and smooth. Do not let it boil. There should be no cornstarch taste.

3 Pour into 4 shallow ovenproof dishes, about 5 inches in diameter. Let cool, then chill for a few hours or overnight if possible, until firm. Before serving, sprinkle each custard with a tablespoon of sugar and a little of the ground nutmeg. Preheat the broiler to high.

4 Place the custards under the broiler, on the highest shelf, and cook until the sugar caramelizes. This will only take a few seconds. Let cool for a few minutes before serving. (The caramel will only stay hard for about 30 minutes.)

MOROCCAN RICE PUDDING

A simple and delicious alternative to a traditional rice pudding. The rice is cooked in almond-flavored milk and delicately flavored with cinnamon and orange-flower water.

¼ cup blanched almonds, chopped
2¼ cups short-grain rice
¼ cup confectioners' sugar
3-inch cinnamon stick
4 tablespoons butter
pinch of salt
¼ teaspoon almond extract
¾ cup milk
¾ cup sweetened condensed milk
2 tablespoons orange-flower water
toasted sliced almonds and ground cinnamon, to decorate

SERVES 6

1. Put the chopped almonds in a food processor or blender with ¼ cup of very hot water. Process, then strain into a bowl. Return the almonds to the food processor or blender, add another ¼ cup very hot water, and process again. Strain into a saucepan.

2. Add 1¼ cups of water to the almond "milk" and bring to a boil. Combine the other milks. Add the rice, sugar, cinnamon and half the butter, the salt, the almond extract, and half the mixed milks.

3. Bring to a boil, then simmer, covered, for about 30 minutes, adding more milk if necessary. Continue to cook the rice, stirring and adding the remaining milk, until it becomes thick and creamy. Stir in the orange-flower water, then taste the rice pudding for sweetness, adding extra sugar, if necessary.

4. Pour the rice pudding into a serving bowl and sprinkle with the sliced almonds. Dot with the remaining butter and dust with ground cinnamon. Serve hot.

TURKISH DELIGHT ICE CREAM

Not strictly a traditional Middle Eastern recipe, but a delicious way of using Turkish delight. Serve scattered with rose petals, if you can find them.

4 egg yolks
½ cup sugar
1¼ cups milk
1¼ cups heavy cream
1 tablespoon rose water
6 ounces rose-flavored Turkish delight, chopped

SERVES 6

1 Beat the egg yolks and sugar until light. In a pan, bring the milk to a boil. Add to the egg and sugar, stirring, then return to the pan.

2 Continue stirring over low heat until the mixture coats the back of a spoon. Do not boil, or it will curdle. Let cool, then stir in the cream and rose water.

3 Put the Turkish delight in a pan with 2–3 tablespoons water. Heat gently, until almost completely melted, with just a few small lumps. Remove from the heat and stir into the cooled custard mixture.

4 Let the mixture cool completely, then pour into a shallow freezer container. Freeze for 3 hours, until just frozen all over. Spoon the mixture into a bowl.

5 Using a whisk, beat the mixture well, return it to the freezer container and freeze for 2 hours more. Repeat the beating process, then return to the freezer for about 3 hours or until firm. Remove the ice cream from the freezer 20–25 minutes before serving. Serve with thin almond cookies or meringues.

ICED ORANGES

These little sherbets served in the fruit shell were originally sold in the beach cafés in the south of France. They are pretty and easy to eat—a good picnic treat to store in the cooler.

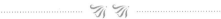

⅔ cup sugar
juice of 1 lemon
14 medium oranges
8 fresh bay leaves, to decorate

SERVES 8

1 Put the sugar in a heavy pan. Add half the lemon juice and ½ cup water. Cook over low heat until the sugar has dissolved completely. Bring to a boil and boil for 2–3 minutes, until the syrup is clear. Let cool.

2 Slice the tops off eight of the oranges to make "hats." Scoop out the flesh of the oranges and reserve. Put the empty orange shells and "hats" on a tray and place in the freezer until needed.

3 Grate the zest of the remaining oranges and add to the syrup. Squeeze the juice from the oranges and from the reserved flesh. There should be 3 cups. Squeeze another orange or add bought orange juice, if necessary.

4 Stir the orange juice and remaining lemon juice, with 6 tablespoons water, into the syrup. Taste, adding more lemon juice or sugar, as desired. Pour the mixture into a shallow freezer container and freeze for 3 hours.

5 Transfer the mixture into a bowl and whisk to break down the ice crystals. Freeze for 4 more hours, until firm but not solid.

6 Pack the mixture into the orange shells, piling it up, and set the "hats" on top. Freeze until ready to serve. Just before serving, push a skewer into the tops of the "hats" and push a bay leaf into each one.

COOK'S TIP

Use crumpled paper towels to keep the shells upright.

STUFFED PEACHES WITH MASCARPONE CREAM

Mascarpone is a thick, velvety Italian cream cheese made from cow's milk. It is often used in desserts or eaten with fresh fruit.

4 large peaches, halved and pitted
1½ ounces amaretti cookies, crumbled
2 tablespoons ground almonds
3 tablespoons sugar
1 tablespoon cocoa powder
⅔ cup sweet wine
2 tablespoons butter

FOR THE MASCARPONE CREAM
2 tablespoons sugar
3 egg yolks
1 tablespoon dessert wine
1 cup mascarpone cheese
⅔ cup heavy cream

SERVES 4

1 Preheat the oven to 400°F. Using a teaspoon, scoop some of the flesh from the cavities in the peaches, to make a reasonable space for stuffing. Chop the scooped-out peach flesh.

2 Combine the amaretti, ground almonds, sugar, cocoa and peach flesh. Add enough wine to make the mixture into a thick paste.

3 Place the peaches in a buttered ovenproof dish and fill them with the stuffing. Dot with the butter, then pour the remaining wine into the dish. Bake for 35 minutes.

4 To make the mascarpone cream, beat the sugar and egg yolks until thick and pale. Stir in the wine, then fold in the mascarpone. Whip the heavy cream to soft peaks and fold into the mixture. Remove the peaches from the oven and let them cool. Serve at room temperature, with the mascarpone cream.

CHERRY CLAFOUTI

When fresh cherries are in season this makes a deliciously simple dessert for any occasion. Serve warm with a little cream.

1½ pounds fresh cherries
½ cup all-purpose flour
pinch of salt
4 eggs, plus 2 egg yolks
½ cup sugar
2½ cups milk
4 tablespoons butter, melted
sugar for dusting

SERVES 6

1 Preheat the oven to 375°F. Lightly butter the bottom and sides of a shallow ovenproof dish. Pit the cherries and place in the dish.

2 Sift the flour and salt into a bowl. Add the eggs, egg yolks, sugar and a little of the milk and whisk to a smooth batter.

3 Gradually whisk in the rest of the milk and the rest of the butter, then strain the batter over the cherries. Bake for 40–50 minutes, until golden and just set. Serve warm, dusted with sugar, if desired.

VARIATION

Use two 15-ounce cans pitted black cherries, thoroughly drained, if fresh cherries are not available. For a special dessert, add 3 tablespoons kirsch to the batter.

COFFEE GRANITA

Granitas are like semi-frozen sherbets, but consist of larger particles of ice. Served in Italian cafés, they are very refreshing, particularly in the summer. Some are made with fruit, but the coffee version is perhaps the most popular and is often served with a spoonful of whipped cream on top.

1½ cups hot strong espresso coffee
2 tablespoons granulated sugar
1 cup heavy cream
2 teaspoons superfine sugar

SERVES 6–8

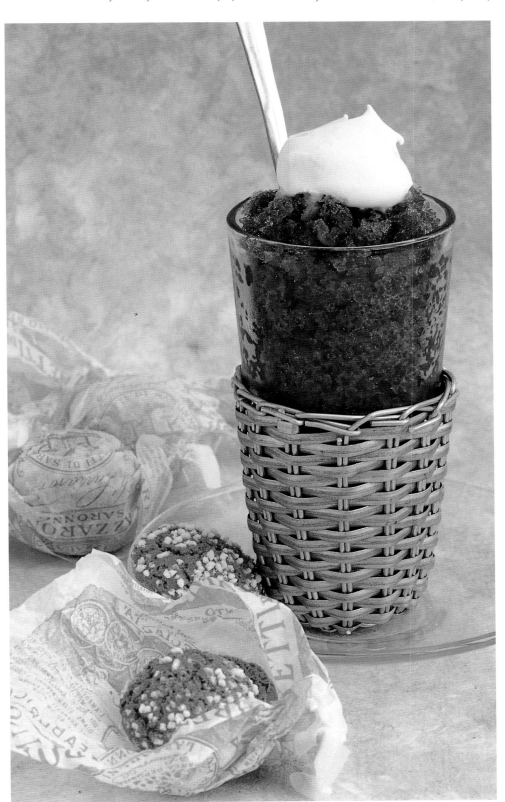

1. Stir the sugar into the hot coffee until dissolved. Let cool, then chill. Pour into a shallow plastic or metal freezer container, cover and freeze for about 1 hour.

2. The coffee should have formed a frozen crust around the rim of the container. Scrape this off with a spoon and mix with the rest of the coffee. Repeat this process every 30 minutes, using the spoon to break up the clumps of ice.

3. After about 2½ hours, the granita should be ready. It will have the appearance of small, fairly uniform ice crystals. Whip the cream with the superfine sugar until stiff. Serve the granita in tall glasses, each topped with a spoonful of cream.

DATE AND ALMOND TART

Fresh dates make an unusual but delicious filling for a tart. The influences here are French and Middle Eastern—a true Mediterranean fusion!

FOR THE PASTRY
1½ cups all-purpose flour
6 tablespoons butter
1 egg

FOR THE FILLING
scant 8 tablespoons (1 stick) butter
7 tablespoons sugar
1 egg, beaten
scant 1 cup ground almonds
2 tablespoons flour
2 tablespoons orange-flower water
12–13 fresh dates, halved and pitted
¼ cup apricot jam

SERVES 6

1 Preheat the oven to 400°F. Place a baking sheet in the oven. Sift the flour into a bowl, add the butter and work with your fingertips until the mixture resembles fine bread crumbs. Add the egg and a tablespoon of cold water, then work to a smooth dough.

2 Roll out the pastry on a lightly floured surface and use to line an 8-inch tart pan. Prick the bottom with a fork, then chill until needed.

3 To make the filling, cream the butter and sugar until light, then beat in the egg. Stir in the ground almonds, flour and 1 tablespoon of the orange-flower water, mixing well.

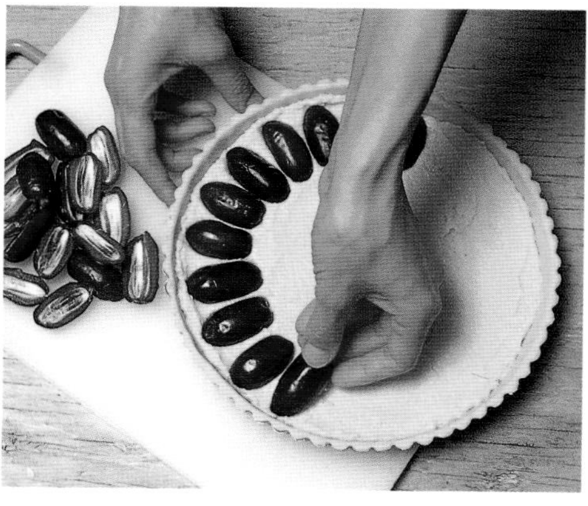

4 Spread the mixture evenly over the bottom of the pastry shell. Arrange the dates, cut side down, on the almond mixture. Bake on the hot baking sheet for 10–15 minutes, then reduce the heat to 350°F. Bake for another 15–20 minutes, until light golden and set.

5 Transfer the tart to a rack to cool. Gently heat the apricot jam, then strain. Add the remaining orange-flower water.

6 Brush the tart with the jam and serve at room temperature.

LEMON TART

This is one of the classic French desserts, and it is hard to beat—a rich lemon curd is encased in flaky pastry. Crème fraîche is an optional accompaniment.

FOR THE PASTRY
2 cups all-purpose flour
8 tablespoons (1 stick) butter
2 tablespoons confectioners' sugar
1 egg
1 teaspoon vanilla extract

FOR THE FILLING
6 eggs, beaten
1½ cups sugar
8 tablespoons (1 stick) unsalted butter
grated zest and juice of 4 lemons
confectioners' sugar, for dusting

SERVES 6

1 Preheat the oven to 400°F. Sift the flour into a bowl, add the butter and work with your fingertips until the mixture resembles fine bread crumbs. Stir in the 2 tablespoons of confectioners' sugar.

2 Add the egg, vanilla extract and a scant tablespoon of cold water, then work to a dough.

3 Roll the pastry out on a floured surface and use to line a 9-inch tart pan. Line with foil or waxed paper and fill with dried beans or rice, or baking beans if you have them. Bake for 10 minutes.

4 To make the filling, put the eggs, sugar and butter into a pan and stir over low heat until the sugar has dissolved completely. Add the lemon zest and juice and continue cooking, stirring constantly, until the lemon curd has thickened slightly.

5 Pour the mixture into the pastry shell. Bake for 20 minutes, until just set. Transfer the tart to a wire rack to cool. Dust with confectioners' sugar just before serving.

Honey and Pine Nut Tart

Wonderful tarts of all descriptions are to be found throughout France. This recipe recalls the flavors of the south.

For the pastry
2 cups all-purpose flour
8 tablespoons (1 stick) butter
2 tablespoons confectioners' sugar
1 egg

For the filling
¾ pound (3 sticks) unsalted butter, diced
½ cup granulated sugar
3 eggs, beaten
⅔ cup sunflower or other flower honey
grated zest and juice of 1 lemon
2⅔ cups pine nuts
pinch of salt
confectioners' sugar for dusting

Serves 6

1 Preheat the oven to 350°F. Sift the flour into a bowl, add the butter and work with your fingertips until the mixture resembles fine bread crumbs. Stir in the confectioners' sugar. Add the egg and 1 tablespoon of water and work to a firm dough that leaves the bowl clean.

2 Roll out the pastry on a floured surface and use to line a 9-inch tart pan. Prick the bottom with a fork and chill for 10 minutes. Line with foil or waxed paper and fill with dried beans or rice, or baking beans if you have them. Bake the pastry shell for 10 minutes.

3 Cream together the butter and sugar until light. Beat in the eggs one by one. Gently heat the honey in a small saucepan until runny, then add to the butter mixture with the lemon zest and juice. Stir in the pine nuts and salt, then pour the filling into the pastry shell.

4 Bake for about 45 minutes, until the filling is lightly browned and set. Let cool slightly in the pan, then dust generously with confectioners' sugar. Serve warm or at room temperature, with sour cream or vanilla ice cream.

GLAZED PRUNE TART

Generously glazed, creamy custard tarts are a pâtisserie favorite all over France. Plump prunes, heavily laced with brandy or kirsch, add a wonderful taste and texture to this deliciously sweet and creamy filling.

1 cup pitted prunes
¼ cup brandy or kirsch

FOR THE SWEET PASTRY
1½ cups all-purpose flour
pinch of salt
8 tablespoons (1 stick) unsalted butter
2 tablespoons sugar
2 egg yolks

FOR THE FILLING
⅔ cup heavy cream
⅔ cup milk
1 vanilla bean
3 eggs
¼ cup sugar

TO FINISH
¼ cup apricot jam
1 tablespoon brandy or kirsch
confectioners' sugar for dusting

SERVES 8

1 Put the prunes in a bowl with the brandy or kirsch and let sit for about 4 hours, until most of the liqueur has been absorbed.

2 To make the pastry, sift the flour and salt into a bowl. Add the butter, cut into small pieces, and rub in with the fingertips. Stir in the sugar and egg yolks and mix to a dough using a round-bladed knife.

3 Turn the dough out onto a lightly floured surface and knead to a smooth ball. Wrap tightly and chill for 30 minutes.

4 Preheat the oven to 400°F. Roll out the pastry on a lightly floured surface and use to line a 10-inch springform tart pan.

5 Line with waxed paper and fill with dried beans or rice, or baking beans if you have them. Bake for 15 minutes. Remove the beans and paper and bake for another 5 minutes.

6 Arrange the prunes, evenly spaced, in the pastry shell, reserving any liqueur left in the bowl.

7 For the filling, put the cream and milk in a saucepan with the vanilla bean and bring to a boil. Turn off the heat and let the mixture infuse for 15 minutes.

8 Whisk together the eggs and sugar in a bowl. Remove the vanilla bean from the cream and return the cream to a boil. Pour on the eggs and sugar, whisking to make a smooth custard.

9 Cool slightly, then pour the custard over the prunes. Bake the tart for about 25 minutes, until the filling is lightly set and turning golden around the edges.

10 Strain the apricot jam into a small pan. Add the liqueur and heat through gently. Use to glaze the tart. Serve warm or cold, dusted with confectioners' sugar.

COOK'S TIP
The vanilla bean can be washed and dried, ready for use another time. Alternatively, use 1 teaspoon vanilla or almond extract.

INDEX

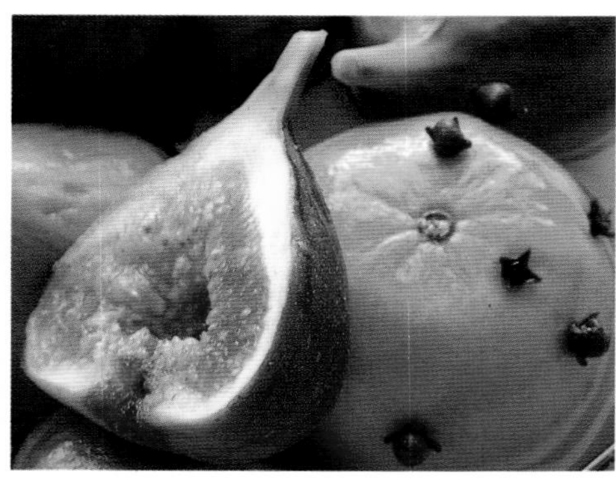

Photographs: With the exceptions noted below, all photographs by Michelle Garrett: Patrick McLeavey: p.10 (top right): The Image Bank: p.1, p.9 (bottom left), p.20 (top left), p.108 (left), p.198, p.227 (right); The Anthony Blake Photo Library: p.9 (top right), p.138, p.139, p.171 (top right), p.171 (bottom left), p.227 (left); Robert Estall: p.2, p.6–7, p.8; Michael Busselle: p.87, p.170, p.226

Arts and Crafts Architecture

Peter Davey

With love to my parents who brought me up in two Arts and Crafts houses (though none of us knew it at the time).

Phaidon Press Limited
Regent's Wharf
All Saints Street
London N1 9PA

First published in the UK 1980; in US as *Architecture of the Arts and Crafts Movement* 1980

First paperback edition 1997

A CIP catalogue record for this book is available from the British Library

ISBN 0 7148 2874 2 (hardback)

ISBN 0 7148 3711 3 (paperback)

Printed in Hong Kong

Frontispiece: Philip Webb. Design for a house for G. P. Boyes, Cheyne Row, Chelsea, London (1869)

Contents

Preface

I started to write this book because I needed it myself. There was no history of Arts and Crafts thinking as a whole with the exception of Gillian Naylor's pioneering work which scarcely touches on architecture. General histories of the period described the Arts and Crafts movement as no more than an aberrant offshore version of Art Nouveau or as the British John the Baptist for the messianic Modern Movement. Yet as that movement's most reductive phase waned, the ideas of Morris, the buildings of people like Voysey, Prior and Lutyens began to seem more and more relevant to a contemporary architecture fumbling to rediscover humanity and individualism.

What were all those half forgotten architects doing and thinking about a century ago? Why are their buildings so attractive? Why, suddenly and briefly, did British architecture become the cynosure of the Western world?

This book tries to explain, and, like all efforts to encapsulate real life, it has a heavy bias. People are so complicated, so illogical and contradictory that any attempt to describe a period fully would fill the world with paper. There are always alternative explanations – especially of something so ill defined as the Arts and Crafts movement, which never produced a manifesto to which all subscribed, nor a very recognizable style, nor a clear ideology.

I have tried to take a microscope section through the truth to show how, in architecture, the ideals of Pugin* and Ruskin and Morris grew from the Gothic Revival, interacted and, in the end, lost cohesion and fell apart to help generate quite other architectures. I hope that within its limits the story is truthful.

The account is as restricted in its coverage as in emphasis. Some architects and thinkers have been given star billing because I think they most clearly illuminate the period. Others like Sedding, Weir, Dawber, Cave, Troup, Ricardo and many more would, in a book five times this size, have merited treatment as long as I have given Lethaby, Voysey and Ashbee. I am sorry that such a lot of good architects can have no more than walk-on parts here but happily many monographs now exist.

Much has been published on individuals and particular aspects of the Arts and Crafts movement since the first edition of this book appeared. My debts to this work, and to conversations with many of the authors of it, are too numerous to mention in detail but are acknowledged in the notes and the bibliography. Nor is there space to reiterate my thanks to the many people who helped in the creation of the first edition, but I remain deeply grateful to them.

There are large changes and additions to the text of that edition, particularly in the much revised chapters on the United States and the Continent. In the general survey of British work in chapter nine much has been added. The small section on Arts and Crafts approaches to gardening in the original edition has been expanded into a whole new chapter (10) on the movement's theory and practice of landscape and gardens, based on an article which I wrote for *The Architectural Review* issue of September 1985.

Alan Crawford painstakingly read the first edition and provided a lot of helpful corrections and suggestions for this one. Many others have given advice about particular people and aspects of the period.

Julia Dawson has bravely fought through the sometimes incomprehensible thickets of computer incompatibilities, and my syntax and spelling, to bring consistency to the text. Much love and thanks.

I particularly want to thank, with love, my son Meredith for his help as research assistant and computer consultant.

And, above all, love and thanks again to my wife Carolyn Pulford who has been unfailingly supportive and kind with an author prone to fits of depression, mania and despair. This edition, like the first, would have been impossible without her.

LONDON AND LLANWRTHWL 1994

William Lethaby. Melsetter House, Hoy, Orkneys (completed 1900)

*Any history must begin arbitrarily, but my choice of Pugin to kick off with had some contemporary sanction. John Dando Sedding remarked in 1888 that 'we should have had no Morris, no Street, no Burges, no Shaw, no Webb, no Bodley, no Rossetti, no Burne-Jones, no Crane, but for Pugin'.

THIS IS THE PICTURE OF THE OLD
HOUSE BY THE THAMES TO WHICH
THE PEOPLE OF THIS STORY WENT
HEREAFTER FOLLOWS THE BOOK IT-
SELF WHICH IS CALLED NEWS FROM
NOWHERE OR AN EPOCH OF REST &
IS WRITTEN BY WILLIAM MORRIS

Once upon a time

1

Folk say, a wizard to a northern king
At Christmas-tide such wondrous things did show,
That through one window men beheld the spring,
And through another saw the summer glow,
And through a third the fruited vines a-row,
While still, unheard, but in its wonted way
Piped the drear wind of that December day.
So with this Earthly Paradise it is,
If ye will read aright, and pardon me,
Who strive to build a shadowy isle of bliss
Midmost the beating of the steely sea.

FROM THE EARTHLY PARADISE, *WILLIAM MORRIS 1868–70*

On a fine summer's morning in Hammersmith, a man awoke to find himself in the middle of a miracle. He had gone to bed on a winter night in 1890, but as he gathered his senses in the hot early sunshine, he gradually realized that not only had the season changed but the whole of society and its buildings had been wonderfully altered.

The hero of William Morris's *News from Nowhere* had, by a trick of time, entered the post-Revolutionary world. It was a world in which money did not exist, in which everyone freely laboured at the dreary tasks, allowing all to devote time to creating beautiful and useful artifacts which they gave to each other whenever they were asked.

A pellucid Thames flowed softly through a London freed of smoke and congestion, where gardens and orchards ran down to the river half hiding 'very pretty houses, low and not large, standing back a little way from the river; they were mostly built of red brick and roofed with tiles, and looked, above all, comfortable, and as if they were, so to say, alive and sympathetic with the life of the dwellers in them'.[1]

Frontispiece of *News from Nowhere* based on the east front of Kelmscott Manor

Rising above these little houses were the public buildings, and Morris's hero found himself lodging in one – the Guest House of Hammersmith. 'It was a longish building with its gable ends turned away from the road, and long traceried windows coming rather low down set in the wall that faced us. It was very handsomely built of red brick with a lead roof; and high up about the windows there ran a frieze of figure subjects in baked clay, very well executed, and designed with a force and directness which I had never noticed in modern work before.'[2]

Morris set his story more than a hundred years ahead of 1890, when it was first published in the *Commonweal*, the journal of the Socialist League. But, though the English Revolution has even now not occurred, when *News from Nowhere* was published, English architects and craftsmen were building a world that much resembled that seen by Morris's time traveller. These people centred around the Arts and Crafts Exhibition Society, founded in 1888 with the aim of initiating a new, original and vigorous approach to design. The approach was strongly rooted in the ideals of Morris as shown in the work of his firm and in his writings.

Arts and Crafts people were a highly individualistic lot but all

Kelmscott Manor, Oxfordshire, Morris's medieval house in the countryside, from the east

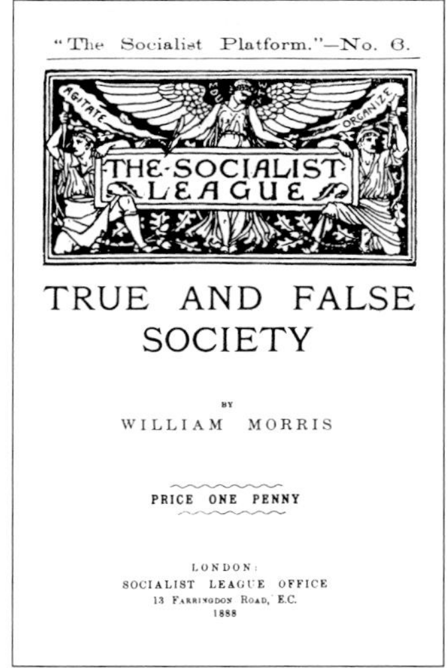

"The Socialist Platform."—No. 6.

THE SOCIALIST LEAGUE

TRUE AND FALSE SOCIETY

BY

WILLIAM MORRIS

PRICE ONE PENNY

LONDON:
SOCIALIST LEAGUE OFFICE
13 FARRINGDON ROAD, E.C.
1888

Morris as polemical visionary. Cover of *The Socialist Platform*

shared Morris's affection for simplicity, truth-to-materials, and the unity of handicraft and design. And they shared his affection for the Gothic – not the scholastic and religious Gothic of the High Victorians but for a Gothic spirit. It was a Gothic free of Rule, derived more from the unselfconscious cottages, almshouses and barns of ordinary medieval people than from palaces, town halls and churches. In an 1889 lecture on Gothic Morris spelt out the Arts and Crafts ideal: 'Now a Gothic building has walls that it is not ashamed of; and in those walls you may cut windows wherever you please; and, if you please may decorate them to show that you are not ashamed of them; your windows, which you must have, become one of the great beauties of your house and you have no longer to make a lesson in logic in order not to sit in pitchy darkness in your own house, as in the sham sham-Roman style; your window, I say, is no longer a concession to human weakness, an ugly necessity (generally ugly enough in all conscience) but a glory of the art of Building. As for the roof in the sham style: unless the building is infected with Gothic common sense, you must pretend that you are living in a hot country which needs nothing but an awning, and that it never rains or snows in these islands'.[3]

Hand in hand with these rather austere principles, a thoroughly Victorian affection for comfort and gentle ease ran throughout the Arts and Crafts movement. And there was a strong feeling for nationality – English and sometimes Scottish – as befitted a nation which had ruled the waves unhindered for the most part of a century.

The Arts and Crafts movement was of and for the Victorian upper

PSYCHE BORNE OFF BY ZEPHYRUS, DRAWN BY EDWARD BURNE-JONES & ENGRAVED BY WILLIAM MORRIS

NOTE BY WILLIAM MORRIS ON HIS AIMS IN FOUNDING THE KELMSCOTT PRESS.

I BEGAN printing books with the hope of producing some which would have a definite claim to beauty, while at the same time they should be easy to read and should not dazzle the eye, or trouble the intellect of the reader by eccentricity of form in the letters. I have always been a great admirer of the calligraphy of the Middle Ages, & of the earlier printing which took its place. As to the fifteenth-century books, I had noticed that they were always beautiful by force of the mere typography, even without the added ornament, with which many of them are so lavishly supplied. And it was the essence of my undertaking to produce books which it would be a pleasure to look upon as pieces of printing and arrangement of type. Looking at my adventure from this point of view then, I found I had to consider chiefly the following things: the paper, the form of the type, the relative spacing of the letters, the words, and the

Double-spread from *A Note by William Morris on his aims in founding the Kelmscott Press,* 1898

middle class. The inhabitants of William Morris's visionary world have all the nice characteristics of Victorian gentlefolk: they are kind, generous, polite, energetic, moral, nationalistic (in the best sense), intellectual, practical, comfort loving and fond of 'beauty'. They are purged of the reverse of the Victorian coin: hypocrisy, philistinism, selfishness, puritanism, arrogant chauvinism, indifference to others and terrible class consciousness.

The upper middle classes were the only people who could enjoy individual freedom in Victorian England; they were free of the grinding poverty of the lower orders, the inverted snobbery of the lower middle class and the increasingly rigid formality of the aristocracy. Because Britain was the richest and most powerful nation, they were probably the most free people in the world. It was for them that Arts and Crafts architects worked, evolving a new easy style which was most often seen in the small country houses of a free, proud, individualistic breed who, in three decades from 1880 to 1910, were the patrons of some of the finest and most original architecture and artifacts ever produced in Britain.

The achievements of Arts and Crafts architects were widely recognized by Continental contemporaries and by no-one more clearly than Hermann Muthesius, an architect attached to the German embassy in London between 1896 and 1903, who produced his monumental *Das englische Haus*, the definitive contemporary analysis of the domestic scene at the turn of the century, in 1904 and 1905.

Muthesius was clear that the mainspring of the British success was modest individuality. 'The Englishman builds his house for himself alone. He feels no urge to impress, has no thought of festive occasions or banquets and the idea of shining in the eyes of the world through lavishness in and of his house simply does not occur to him. Indeed, he even avoids attracting attention to his house by means of striking design or architectonic extravagance, just as he would be loth to appear personally eccentric by wearing a fantastic suit. In particular, the architectonic ostentation, the creation of "architecture" and "style" to which we in Germany are still so prone, is no longer to be found in England. It is most instructive to note...that a movement opposing the imitation of styles and seeking closer ties with simple rural buildings, which began over 40 years ago, has had the most gratifying results.'[4]

1 *Morris, William* News from Nowhere, *reprinted in* William Morris, *Nonesuch Press, New York, 1974, p9.*
2 Ibid, *p13.*
3 *Morris, William 'Gothic Architecture', reprinted in* William Morris, op cit, *p491.*
4 *Muthesius, Hermann* The English House, *Crosby Lockwood Staples, London, 1979, p10. The first English translation (by Janet Seligman).*

US SANCTUS

Gathering grounds

2

Forty years before Morris brought *News from Nowhere*, the Queen and Prince Albert had opened the Great Exhibition. Sixty thousand people a day flocked to the Crystal Palace crammed with locomotives, printing presses, electric telegraphs, Indian umbrellas, astronomical clocks, the Koh-i-noor, lighthouse lanterns, Turkish carpets and rows of the most sentimental sculpture the world has ever seen.

In the middle of the vast and chaotic collection of up-to-date inventions (condemned by *The Times* as exhibiting 'Universal infidelity in principles of design')[1] was one court devoted with firm principle entirely to the thirteenth and fourteenth centuries: there were embroidered copes, jewelled chains, stained glass windows, painted tiles, pews, silver and gilt vessels, great carved font covers, ironwork, screens and lamps, even, as *The Illustrated Exhibitor* commented, 'a pianoforte attempted in the Revived Style'.

'The Medieval Court', announced *The Illustrated Exhibitor*, 'in the strikingly-harmonious combination of its stained glass, hardware, woodcarving, hangings, encaustic tiles – all successful repetitions of Gothic models – will at least have the merit of suggesting to many, who would not otherwise have heard of such facts, the fullness of beauty and character, and the homogeneousness, of medieval design, however applied, to domestic as to ecclesiastic purposes...It is almost needless to say...that to the Messrs Pugin are due the entire design.'[2] *Messrs* Pugin was an exaggeration since Augustus Welby Northmore Pugin (1812-1852) had designed virtually everything in the court. He now had little more than a year to live before he died at 40 of overwork. He married three times, fathered eight children and designed more than a hundred buildings (mostly churches though many other building types as well), and great quantities of church ornament, plate, furniture and vestments. He drew virtually every line himself and, 'asked why he didn't give the mere mechanical part of his working drawings to a clerk, he riposted, "Clerk, my dear sir, clerk, I never employ one; I should kill him in a week"'.[3]

The taste for Gothic was very well established by the second quarter of the nineteenth century. Starting as an aristocratic fashion for picturesque Gothick country houses in the eighteenth century, by the time Pugin started to practise, Gothic was the accepted proper style for churches and widely used for other kinds of buildings. Pugin was himself deeply involved in the later years of Gothick. His father, A. C. Pugin, an aristocratic French émigré, had built up a flourishing practice from the 1790s onwards as a Gothic ghost who provided 'correct' detailing for picturesquely medieval country houses of architects like Nash. The younger Pugin was thought even more knowledgeable than his father and, at 15, he was delegated to design the Gothic furniture for Sir Jeffrey Wyatville's reconstructions of Windsor Castle. (He later called these designs 'enormities' and remarked that 'a man who remains any length of time in a modern Gothic room, and escapes without being wounded by some of its minutiæ, may consider himself extremely fortunate'.)[4]

In his late teens, Pugin set up a business which provided 'all the

A.W. N. Pugin. St Giles, Cheadle, Staffordshire (1841-6)

The Medieval Court of the Great Exhibition of 1851 by Louis Haghe (1806-85)

ornamental portions of buildings which could by possibility be executed apart from the structure and be fixed afterwards'.[5] The firm was needed because after the long reign of Classical architecture, there were very few craftsmen who could do Gothic work with correct feeling. The enterprise seems to have thrived for a short while but failed in 1831 because its proprietor was no businessman. In that year he designed sets for a ballet of Sir Walter Scott's *Kenilworth*.

He contrived intimate connections with craftsmen throughout his career. With his friends the manufacturers John Hardman, J. G. Crace and Herbert Minton, Pugin revitalized the crafts of ironwork, stained glass and ceramics; he was a partner* in Hardman's firm, doing most of the design work. Yet there was a contradiction; in the fourteenth century, a church was (in Pugin's theory) produced by craftsmen working together, sometimes for several generations. They worked to a general design but within it each mason, carpenter and smith produced his own details. Pugin's paradox was that because of the lack of good 'out workmen' he had to design down to the last nail to try to recreate the effect of a group of craftsmen working together. Pugin himself seems to have been unworried by the contradiction, but his paradox haunted succeeding generations of architects.

Pugin's satire on a modern Gothic room from which a man who escapes 'without being wounded by some of its minutiæ may consider himself extremely fortunate'. From *True Principles of Pointed or Christian Architecture* (1841)

The great turning point in Pugin's life was his conversion to Catholicism in 1834. Its immediate result was *Contrasts* (1836), in which Pugin preached the cause of Gothic as the only true Christian architecture by comparing a warm, Gothic pre-Reformation England with the buildings and institutions of his own day shown at their meanest, most cold hearted and Classical. 'Catholic England', he believed, 'was Merry England, at least for the humblest classes.'[6]

This interpretation of medieval life was in many ways ridiculously idealistic, for it left out the filth, plagues, brutality and appalling exploitation of the peasants and urban poor by the aristocracy and bourgeoisie. But this does not necessarily invalidate what Pugin was trying to do. He must have been aware of the horrors of the Middle Ages (though perhaps not as much as we are now), but he was concerned to promote their better aspects in a Gothic vision of community with which to fight the Benthamite Utilitarianism of the nineteenth-century Industrial Revolution. Yet if Gothic was to be the style of a truly Christian architecture, what was the real nature of Gothic?

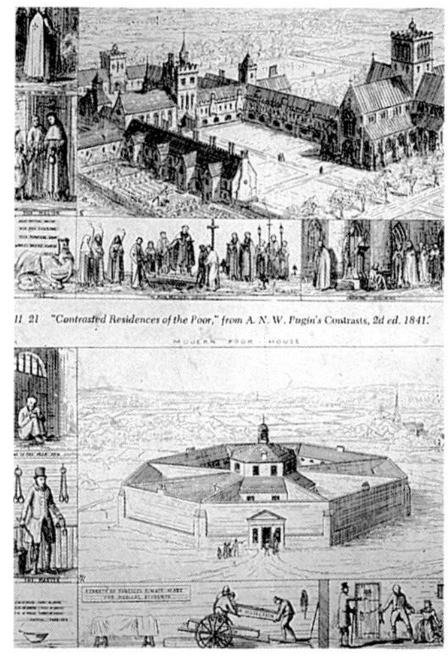

Pugin's *Contrasts* (1836) showing a medieval alms house and a modern Utilitarian work residence for the poor

Pugin provided the answer on the first page of his next book, *The True Principles of Pointed or Christian Architecture*. 'The two great rules for design are these: *1st, that there should be no features about a building which are not necessary for convenience, construction or propriety; 2nd, that all ornament should consist of the essential construction of the building.* The neglect of these two rules is the cause of all the bad architecture of the present time.'[7] These two principles were to influence the whole Arts and Crafts movement.

Pugin expounded: 'Architectural features are continually tacked on

*Several Victorian Gothic architects had to set up similar close links with manufacturers and craftsmen. For instance Sir George Gilbert Scott (1811-1878) worked closely with the Skidmore Art Manufacturers Company, metal craftsmen, and Clayton & Bell, stained glass manufacturers. His Albert Memorial (1863-1872) was in a sense a very early example of Arts and Crafts fusion of architecture, sculpture and craft work. (I am indebted to Gavin Stamp for this observation.) Integration of the arts was characteristic of the later Gothic Revival, brought to a luxuriant (and witty) high pitch by William Burges (1827-1881).

Pugin's first house, St Marie's Grange, Alderbury, Wiltshire (1838). Pioneering use of exposed red brick

buildings with which they have no connexion, merely for the sake of what is termed effect; and ornaments are *actually constructed*, instead of forming the decoration of *construction*, to which in good taste they should always be subservient'.[8] He went on, with surprising effect, to show how the individual elements of Gothic church architecture all had some functional purpose. And he emphasized that 'the architects of the Middle Ages were the first who *turned the natural properties of the various materials to their full account*, and made *their mechanism a vehicle for their art*'.[9]

In the early years of Queen Victoria's reign, 'How many objects of ordinary use are rendered monstrous and ridiculous simply because the artist, instead of seeking the *most convenient form*, and *then decorating it*, has embodied some extravagance to *conceal the real purpose for which the article has been made!* If a clock is required, it is not unusual to cast a Roman warrior in a flying chariot, round one of the wheels of which, on close inspection, the hours may be descried; or the whole front of a cathedral church reduced to a few inches in height, with the clock face occupying the position of a magnificent rose window'.[10]

A building and everything in it should be honest reflections of materials as well as of functions: 'all plaster, cast iron, and composition ornaments, painted like stone or oak, are mere impositions, and, although very suitable for a tea garden, are utterly unworthy of a sacred edifice'.[11]

It was not merely his approach to decorative details, but also Pugin's principles of domestic planning which foreshadowed the approach of the Arts and Crafts movement. 'An architect should exhibit his skill by turning the difficulties which occur in raising an elevation from a *convenient plan* into so many *picturesque beauties*; and this constitutes the great difference between the principles of Classic and pointed domestic architecture. In the former *he would be compelled to devise expedients to conceal these irregularities*; in the latter he has *only to beautify them*.'[12]

Pugin's practical and picturesque approach to planning and elevating is perfectly shown in his own cliff-top house at Ramsgate, the Grange, built in 1844. It is of plain buff local brick with stone dressings. The principal elevation overlooks the sea and is dominated by the tower from which Pugin (an ardent sailor who once exclaimed that, 'there is nothing worth living for but Christian Architecture and a boat')[13] used to watch in charity for ships in distress (and for the opportunity of making money from salvage). The tower is balanced by a double-height bay window at the other end of the elevation. This, in proper Gothic style, fronts the most important spaces – the drawing room and the study above. The rest is very quiet; all with square-headed windows, apart from the simple pointed lights of his private chantry next door to the church of St Augustine.

The exterior of St Augustine's, built at Pugin's own expense, reveals another doctrine – fidelity to place – adopted by the Arts and Crafts movement. Like the Grange, the facade of the church is very simple. It is made of local Kentish knapped black flints banded in brown Whitby stone which was traditionally brought down the coast by sea.

Pugin. St Augustine's, Ramsgate (1845-52). After a watercolour shown at the Royal Academy in 1849. The spire of the church and the bell tower were never built and the cloister was finished by E.W. Pugin with some changes. Pugin's house, the Grange, is next door, left

Perhaps because of his origins, Pugin had become an ardent English patriot: 'What does an Italian house do in England?', he railed against the prevailing fashion for Italianate villas. 'Is there any similarity between our climate and that of Italy? Not in the least...Another objection to Italian architecture is this – we are not Italians, we are Englishmen.' He raged against the international style of his day: 'a bastard Greek, a nondescript modern style has ravaged many of the most interesting cities of Europe'.[14]

As St Augustine's shows, Pugin wanted not only to escape from internationalism; he hoped to revive local as well as national architecture. 'I would...have travelling students but I would circumscribe their limits. Durham, the destination of some – Lincolnshire's steepled fens for others...each county should be indeed a school – for each *is* a school.'[15]

On Pugin's death, a memorial fund for travelling scholarships was set up on his model. It raised more than a thousand pounds, which was given to the Royal Institute of British Architects to provide the Pugin scholarship.* Most of the leading architects and critics of the day subscribed to the fund; even the young Norman Shaw put in his half guinea.[16]

One conspicuous absentee from the subscribers list was John Ruskin (1819-1900), by then the most widely acclaimed architectural critic of the age and the archpriest of Gothic. Despite a common

Pugin. St Augustine's, Ramsgate (1845-52) used vernacular materials and methods of building traditional to the locality

*Several Arts and Crafts architects benefited from the Pugin fund, including Lethaby and Stokes. The RIBA scandalously betrayed its trust and amalgamated the fund with others.

William Butterfield. St Saviour's vicarage, Coalpit Heath, Gloucestershire (now Avon) (1844-45). An early example of conscious changefulness?

Butterfield. Cowick vicarage, Yorkshire (1854): glazing bars have been altered in places but general form remains

dedication to Gothic, Ruskin was extremely hostile to Pugin, perhaps because he was thought by many to be a Puginite.

Ruskin vehemently denied any debt to Pugin and made the rather unlikely claim that 'I glanced at Pugin's *Contrasts* once in the Oxford architectural reading room during an idle forenoon. His "Remarks on Articles in *The Rambler*" were brought under my notice by some of the reviews. I never read a word of any other of his works, not feeling, from the style of his architecture, the smallest interest in his opinions'.[17]

He thundered against Pugin in an appendix to *The Stones of Venice*:* 'He is not a great architect but one of the smallest possible of conceivable architects'.[18] He savaged Pugin for 'being lured into the Romanist Church by the glitter of it...blown into a change of religion by the whine of an organ pipe; switched into a new creed by the gold threads of priests' petticoats; jangled into a change of conscience by the chimes of a belfry'.[19]

Ruskin, the son of a rich and cultivated but rather puritanical sherry merchant, was out to prove that Gothic, though it had originally been built by Catholics, was the true style for Protestants in England. Influenced perhaps by Thomas Carlyle's vision of the nature of English medieval life in *Past and Present* (1843), Ruskin performed this feat of intellectual sleight of hand in the great chapter in *The Stones of Venice* on 'The Nature of Gothic' which, through Morris, was to have a formative effect on the Arts and Crafts movement.† Ruskin emphasized that Gothic was the architecture of northern Europe and that, unlike Classical architecture built by slaves, it was the product of free craftsmen: in effect proto Protestants.

According to Ruskin, Classical architecture was the architecture of slavery, aiming at perfection of execution according to a series of clearly defined rules; in the end, any workman could produce it if he were beaten hard enough. But a truly Christian and humane architecture, Ruskin believed, *must* be imperfect – what he called 'Savage'. 'You can teach a man to draw a straight line, and to cut one; to strike a curved line, and to carve it; and to copy and carve any number of given lines and forms, with admirable speed and perfect precision; and you will find his work perfect of its kind: but if you ask him to think about any of those forms, to consider if he cannot find any better in his own head, he stops; his execution becomes hesitating; he thinks, and 10 to one he makes a mistake in the first touch he gives to his work as a thinking being. But you have made a man of him for all that. He was only a machine before, an animated tool.'[20]

This argument had profound consequences. Pugin was prepared to grant machinery a limited role provided it was not used to imitate handwork – machines were widely used in the Hardman workshops for instance – and he urged that 'We do not want to arrest the course of inventions, but to confine these inventions to their legitimate uses, and to prevent their substitution for nobler arts'.[21] Ruskin was far

*Ruskin later regretted his outburst, and the appendix was dropped from editions of *The Stones of Venice* published after Pugin's death.

†And a much wider public. It was published as a penny pamphlet for working men and was widely sold.

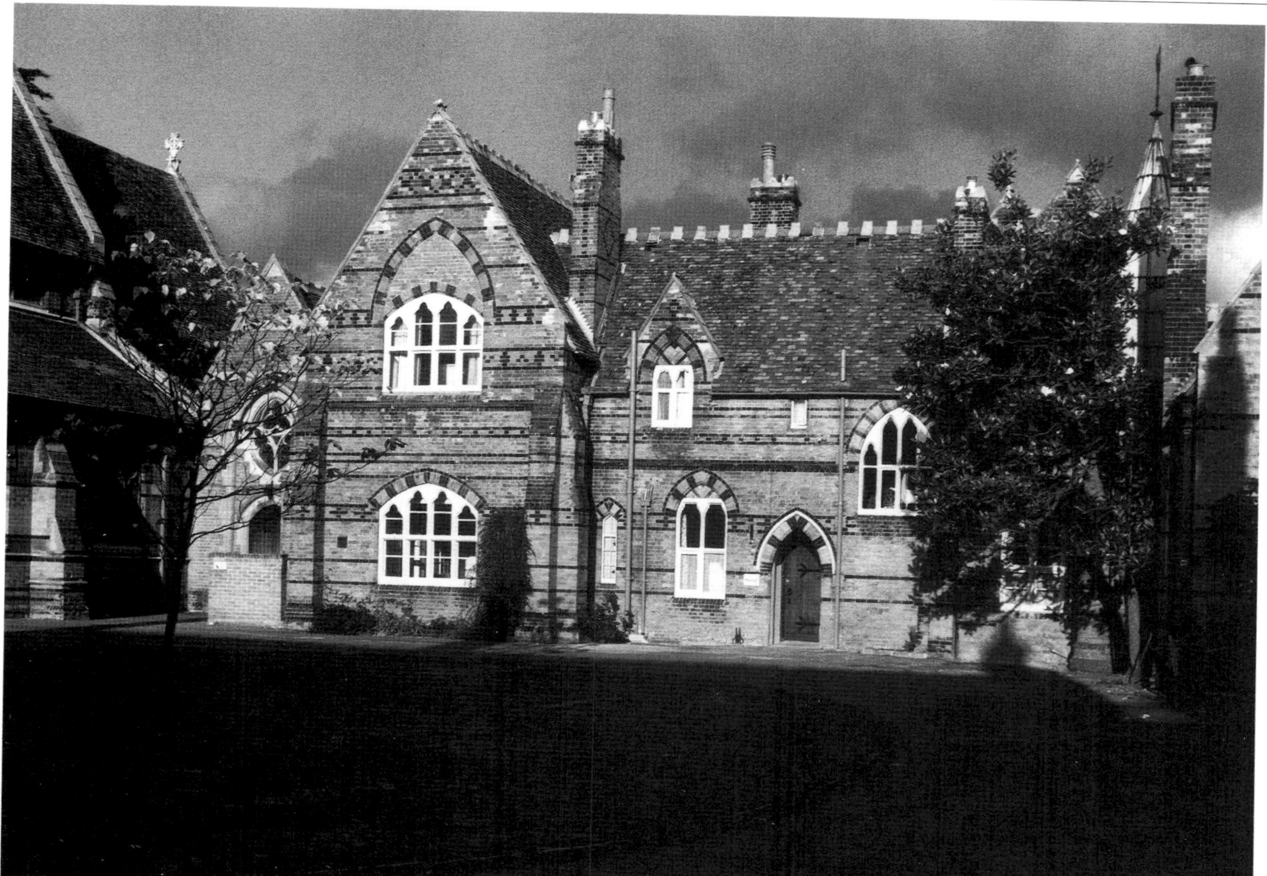

George Edmund Street. Vicarage, Boyne Hill, Maidenhead, Berkshire (started 1854). Structural polychromy in brick

more radical. In 'The Lamp of Truth' he had already proclaimed that 'all cast and machine work is bad, as work...it is dishonest'.[22] In *The Stones of Venice* he was more explicit: 'the great cry that rises from all our manufacturing cities, louder than their furnace blast, is...that we manufacture everything there except men...to brighten, to strengthen, to refine or to form a single living spirit, never enters into our estimate of advantages'.[23] The only remedy could be 'a determined sacrifice of such convenience, or beauty, or cheapness as is to be got only by the degradation of the workman; and by equally determined demand for the products and results of healthy and ennobling labour'. He laid down three rules for encouraging such products; '1: Never encourage the manufacture of any article not absolutely necessary in the production of which *Invention* has no share. 2: Never demand an exact finish for its own sake, but only for some practical or noble end. 3: Never encourage imitation or copying of any kind except for the sake of preserving record of great works'.[24] These were the rules of Ruskinian 'savageness' that for the next 50 years guided Arts and Crafts designers in everything they created from cathedrals to teapots.

Related to savageness was Gothic 'naturalism'. The Gothic craftsman, Ruskin believed, not only expressed his own imperfections in his art but, by close observation of nature, the imperfections of his subjects too. Unlike the Greek sculptor who 'could neither bear to confess his own feebleness nor to tell the faults of the forms that he portrayed',[25] the Gothic craftsman did not idealize, and struggled to render for instance the characteristics of foliage 'with as much accuracy [to nature] as was compatible with the laws of his design and the nature of his materials'.

Parallel to savageness in Ruskin's analysis of Gothic was 'changefulness'. Gothic was, he urged, the 'only rational' architecture, for it could fit itself to every use. 'Whenever it finds occasion for change in its form or purpose, it submits to it without the slightest sense of loss either to its unity or majesty.' Can he really only have spent an idle hour glancing at Pugin when he said, 'It is one of the chief virtues of the Gothic builders, that they never suffered ideas of outside symmetries and consistencies to interfere with the real use and value of what they did'? Ruskin believed that, 'If they wanted a window, they opened one; a room, they added one; a buttress, they built one; utterly regardless of any established conventionalities of external appearance, knowing...that such daring interruptions of the formal plan would rather give additional interest to its symmetry than injure it...Every successive architect, employed upon a great work, built the pieces he added in his own way, utterly regardless of the style adopted by his predecessors'.[26] This is a clear description of Pugin's 'picturesque beauties' and a definition of architectural virtue adopted by the leading Arts and Crafts architects whether they worked with Gothic motifs or not.

No mid-Victorian architect could be untouched by Pugin and Ruskin. Three in particular, Butterfield, Street and Devey, were of great importance to the Arts and Crafts movement. William Butterfield was born in 1814, two years after Pugin, and died in 1900,

the same year as Ruskin. George Edmund Street (1824-1881), like Butterfield, was an enormously successful church architect; but it is their secular buildings, less influenced by sectarian prejudices than their ecclesiastical work, that made the greater impact on Arts and Crafts people. George Devey (1820-1886) is a much more shadowy figure; he did not court publicity – a gentleman architect, most of his buildings were large country houses.[27]

In their parsonages and schools of the 1840s and '50s, Butterfield and Street took domestic architecture further towards informality than Pugin. As early as 1844 (the year Pugin's Grange was finished), Butterfield designed his first vicarage at Coalpit Heath, Gloucestershire in local stone. In outline, it is simple with a high gable terminating the main elevation. The Georgian sash windows are asymmetrical in a most un-Georgian manner and the first floor fenestration does not follow the windows on the ground floor. An enormous chimney crashes through the eaves to balance the gable. The chimney breast is half pierced with the window of an inglenook, and the massive porch barges into the window. These are the sort of changeful accidents that occur in vernacular building – and in a young architect's work.

Street's first efforts were more controlled. In the little village school at Inkpen, Berkshire, completed in 1850, all the windows are flat-topped (at Coalpit Heath, many of the main windows have pointed arches). Gables in the tiled roof emphasize the principal windows, which are crowned with pointed arches flush with the bricks of the wall; the spaces between the arches and the flat tops of the windows are filled with a pattern of decorative tiles common in the district, and the upper floor of the attached school house is completely covered in plain red tiles.

Street's next major secular work, the vicarage and schools at Boyne Hill, Maidenhead, begun in 1854, is much more varied, with all sorts of gables, chimneys and buttresses, all in local red brick with blue brick bands and patterns. In the vicarage, windows are surmounted by shallow pointed arches but elsewhere Street used several variations, including quite steep pointed arches with brickwork between them and the heads of the flat-topped windows.

Under the influence of Ruskin, Street had visited northern Italy in 1853 and the strong patterning at Boyne Hill shows the influence of the striped churches of Lombardy, and of Ruskin's teaching that the 'true colours of architecture are those of natural stone'.[28] Street could not afford stone so the colours of brick were the next best thing.

Butterfield had already shown a grave gaiety in the elaborate brick and stone patterning on All Saints, Margaret Street, London (started 1849). But in a series of Yorkshire parsonages and schools started in 1853, he adopted a much more restrained style. Cowick vicarage is typical: a four-square plain red brick house with a steeply pitched red tiled roof is terminated at one end by a hipped gable which is balanced by a smaller gable further along. The walls are pierced by all manner of windows, mostly flat-topped narrow sashes, sometimes grouped and arranged higgledy-piggledy with, over the wider ones, pointed arches flush with the rest of the brickwork.

Opposite and below: Butterfield. All Saints, Margaret Street, London (1849-59): gravely gay structural polychromy. Chancel wall decoration by William Dyce

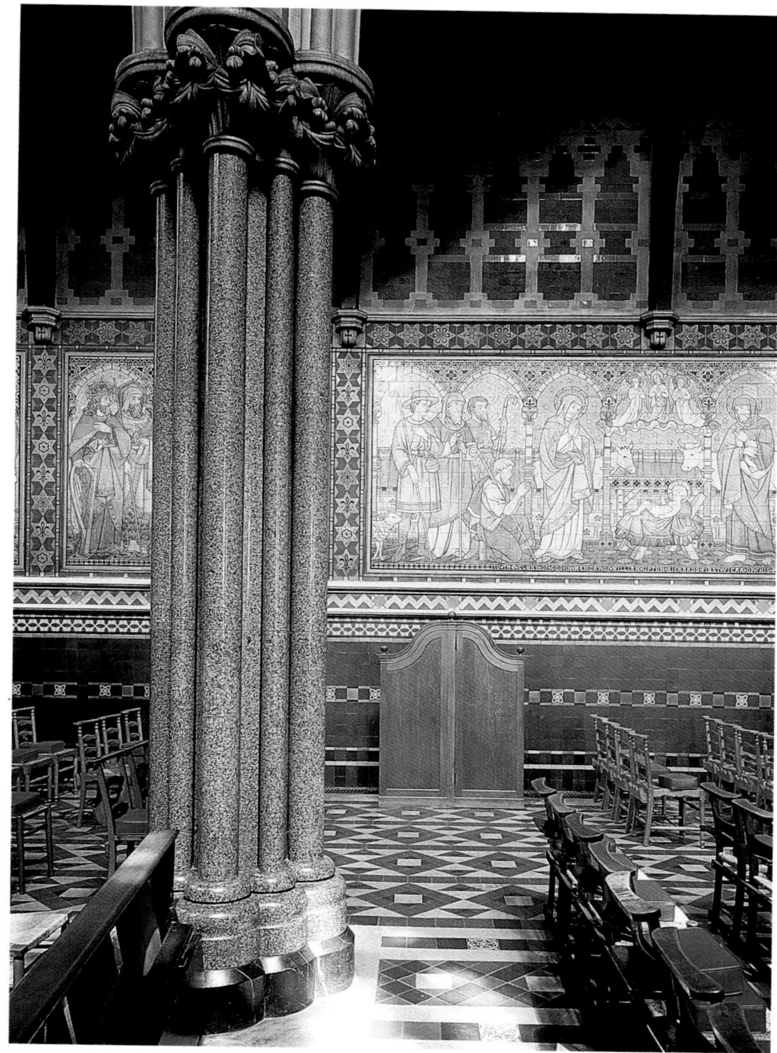

George Devey is quite a different kettle of fish. He too set up practice in the late 1840s, but he worked almost exclusively for large country landowners and produced at least 25 country houses, some of them very large, and innumerable estate cottages. His first important original work was restoring and adding to a group of cottages at the gate of Penshurst Place, Kent. With their red tiled roofs, half-timbering and roughcast, balanced over a ragstone ground floor, the cottages appear to be genuine vernacular buildings, yet only part of the delicately integrated group is truly old.

Devey trained as a watercolourist (under J. S. Cotman and J. D. Harding) as well as an architect; he never lost an exquisite sense of painterly picturesque, using native materials and techniques in a way Pugin would surely have admired. Devey's picturesqueness was much more locally based than that of the Gothick architects who built the *cottages ornés* of the early nineteenth century. As Mark Girouard has pointed out, 'these had been deliberate excursions into fancy dress, but Devey's kind of rural archaeology had never been tried before'.[29]

Top: George Devey. Cottages, Penshurst Place, Kent (1850): picturesque composition based on Devey's early training under Cotman

Above: Devey. Cottage, St Alban's Court, Nonington, Kent (1860s to 1880s): the impression of a new building in brick raised on the remains of an old stone one

Many of Devey's larger houses give the impression of having been built over many years, as indeed several were – St Alban's Court at Nonington in Kent, for instance, was built from the 1860s to '80s. But with its Elizabethan and Jacobean styling it looks as if it had been built over 200 years and finally finished 200 years before Devey. He even used a ground floor of local ragstone which meets the brick of the upper storeys in a most haphazard and irregular line, giving the impression that a brick house had been built upon the ruins of a much older stone building.

This kind of complex artificial aging, which requires much reticence and humour on the part of the architect, was increasingly loved by clients (particularly those with new money) in the second half of the nineteenth century, and it became an important ingredient in Arts and Crafts thinking, which simultaneously embraced Pugin's principle of fidelity to place and Ruskinian fidelity to function. The clash between the two approaches to design produced some of the most characteristic Arts and Crafts architecture.

Devey's love of local materials and techniques is clear, but there is no evidence that he was himself involved in practical work. Indeed, he almost certainly was not, for any obvious connection with trade could have caused him embarrassment with his grand clients. Butterfield is supposed to have been 'engaged in practical smithery'.[30] Street certainly learned smithing so that he could design ironwork properly, he painted murals in the Boyne Hill Church and believed that every architect 'should himself be able to decorate his own building with painting and sculpture'. But as his son remarked, 'rapidly increasing press of work...convinced him, I think, of the inapplicability of such views in our modern times'.[31] Street had, in effect, decided that he could not resolve Pugin's paradox of the relationship between designers and craftsmen in his own way of life and became noted for detailed control over the way in which his buildings were built.

Ruskin squarely faced this paradox: 'the painter should grind his own colours; the architect work in the mason's yard with his men'.

Butterfield. Milton Ernest Hall, Bedfordshire (1854-57)

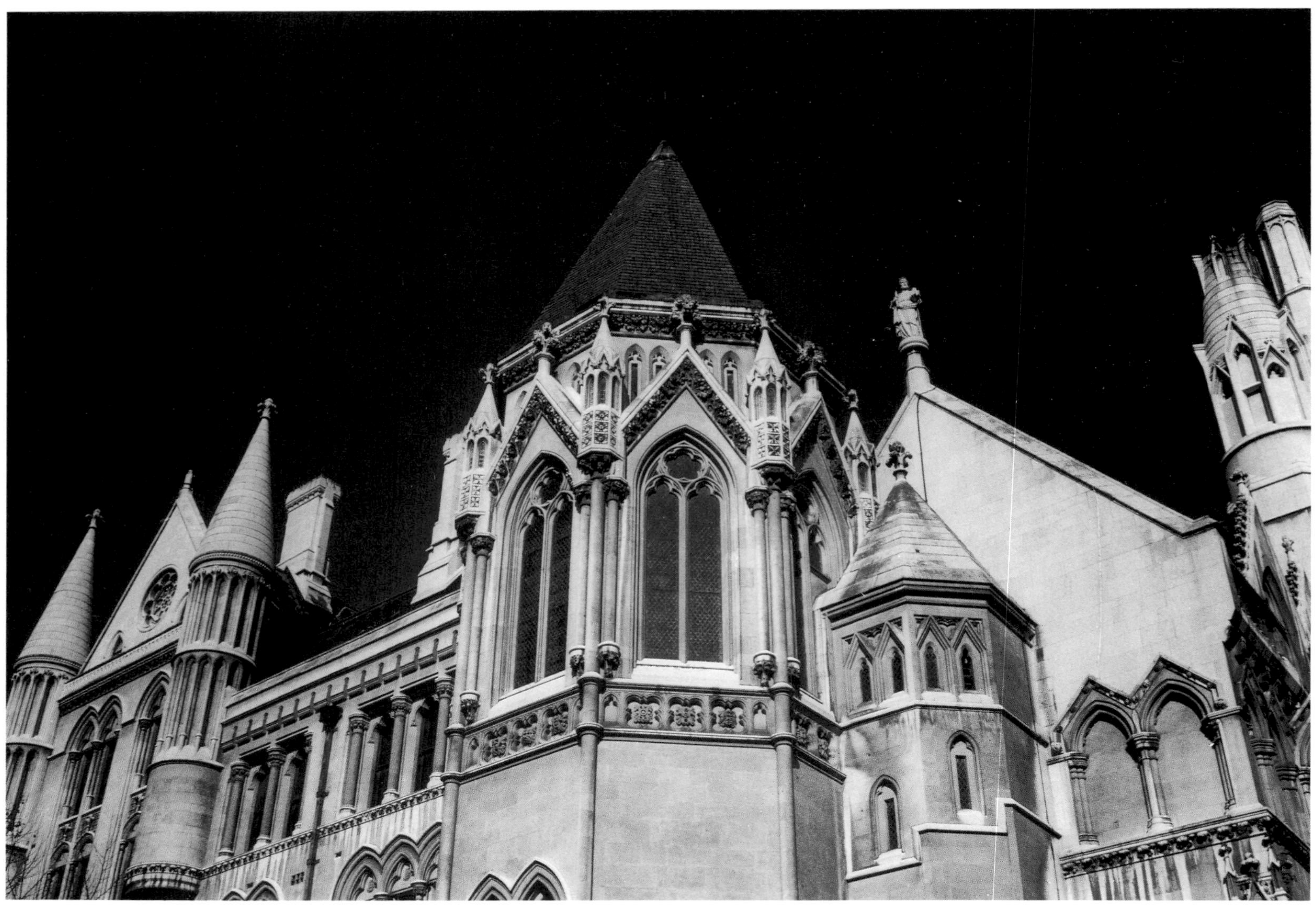

Formal High Victorian Gothic changefulness. G.E. Street's Law Courts, Strand, London (designed 1866, completed 1882). Underlying symmetries are obscured by the clash of functionally generated forms

Not that this should lead to equality, 'the distinction between one man and another [should] be only in experience and skill and the authority and wealth which these must naturally and justly obtain'.[32]

Ruskin's early political views were a more harshly expressed version of the neo-feudalism Pugin had preached in *Contrasts* 12 years before. Very similar to those of Carlyle in *Past and Present*, they stressed simultaneously the nobility and the dignity of decent work for the workman, and the importance of leadership by people like Carlyle's hero Abbot Samson of St Edmundsbury. The synthesis gave him a rather peculiar view of working people's freedom that was to echo down the decades in Arts and Crafts political thought.

In *The Stones of Venice*, Ruskin avowed that 'there might be more freedom in England, though her feudal lords' lightest words were worth men's lives...than there is while the animation of her multitudes is sent like fuel to feed the factory smoke'.[33]

By the 1860s Ruskin had begun to advocate a kind of state socialism, and in *Unto This Last*, he sketched out an ideal society almost as fierce as More's Utopia in which the old, sick and destitute are cared for, practical education is provided for all, there is a mixed economy, but the indigent are set 'under compulsion of the strictest nature...to the more painful and degrading forms of necessary toil'.[34]

In his last political stance, founding a society to pursue the ideals of the dignity of labour and fight against machines and their alienating effects, Ruskin anticipated the social experiments of the Arts and Crafts movement. In 1871 he founded the St George's Guild which aimed to give the example of a better life. Members were to be devoted 'first to the manual labour of cultivating pure land...and secondly together with this manual labour and much by its means they are to carry on the thoughtful labour of true education, in themselves and in others'.[35] Machinery was restricted to devices powered by wind and water – 'electricity perhaps not in future refused'. But 'steam is absolutely refused as a cruel and furious waste of fuel to do what every stream and breeze are ready to do costlessly'.[36]

The St George's experiment failed after three ill-starred communities were started in Worcestershire, at Barmouth and near Sheffield. Apart from Ruskin's progressive mental collapse, one of the main reasons for failure must have been his curiously contradictory attitude to authority. While embracing what he called socialism, Ruskin always stressed 'the impossibility of equality'. The St George's Guild communities were under the charge of wise overseers imposed from above and so could never be the free groupings of husbandmen and craftworkers for which half of Ruskin longed. It was the guild socialism which William Morris preached in *News from Nowhere* which provided the logical answer to Ruskin's political dilemma.

1 The Times *reprinted in* The Journal of Design, *1851, quoted by Naylor, Gillian in* The Arts and Crafts Movement, *Studio Vista, London, 1971, n18, p200.*
2 The Illustrated Exhibitor *John Cassell, 1851, p91.* The Illustrated Exhibitor *was published as a series during the course of the Great Exhibition.*
3 *Ferrey, Benjamin* Recollections of Pugin, *1861, Scolar Press, London, 1978, p187.*
4 *Pugin, A. W. N.* The True Principles of Pointed or Christian Architecture, *London, 1841, p47, Academy Editions facsimile, London, 1973, p47.*
5 *Ferrey* op cit, *p65.*
6 *Pugin A. W. N.* op cit, *p70.*
7 Ibid, *p1.*
8 Ibid.
9 Ibid, *p2.*
10 Ibid, *p27.*
11 Ibid, *p53.*
12 Ibid, *p72.*
13 The Builder, *Vol X, 1852, p605.*
14 *Pugin, A. W. N.* op cit, *pp64-65.*
15 *Pugin, A. W. N.* An Apology for the Revival of Christian Architecture in England, *London, 1843, reprint 1969, p20.*
16 *Ferrey* op cit, *pp470-473.*
17 *Ruskin, John* Modern Painters, *Vol III, Appendix 3, in Cook and Wedderburn* The Complete Works of John Ruskin, *London, 1904, Vol V, p429.*
18 *Ruskin, John* The Stones of Venice, *Vol I, Smith Elder, London, 1851, Appendix 12, p372. (This appendix was dropped in the second and all subsequent editions, which were published after Pugin's death.)*
19 Ibid, *p371.*
20 *Ruskin, John* The Stones of Venice, op cit, *Vol II, 1853, Chapter III 'The Nature of Gothic', p161.*
21 *Pugin, A. W. N.* An Apology for the Revival of Christian Architecture in England, op cit, *p41.*
22 *Ruskin, John* The Seven Lamps of Architecture, *Smith Elder, London, 1849, p48.*
23 *Ruskin, John* The Stones of Venice, op cit, *Vol II, p165.*
24 Ibid, *pp165-166.*
25 Ibid, *p198.*
26 Ibid, *p179.*
27 *See Allibone, Jill* George Devey, Architect 1820-1886, *Lutterworth Press, Cambridge, 1991 for a detailed discussion of the life and work. More architectural analyses are to be found in* The Architectural Review, *Vol XXI and Girouard (see below).*
28 *Ruskin, John* The Seven Lamps of Architecture, op cit, *p47.*
29 *Girouard, Mark 'George Devey in Kent',* Country Life, *Vol CXLIX, 1971, p745.*
30 *Thompson, Paul* William Butterfield, *Routledge & Kegan Paul, London, 1971, p501.*
31 *Street A. E.* Memoir of George Edmund Street RA, *John Murray, London, 1888, p13.*
32 *Ruskin, John* The Stones of Venice, op cit, *Vol II, p169.*
33 *Ruskin, John* The Stones of Venice, op cit, *Vol II, p162.*
34 *Ruskin, John* Unto This Last, *1862, in Cook and Wedderburn,* op cit, *Vol XVII, p22.*
35 *Quoted in Naylor, Gillian* op cit, *p93.*
36 Ibid.

The prophet

3

Virtually all the critics agreed that the standard of work shown at the second International Exhibition in 1862 had improved since 1851. But in the Medieval Court, the exhibits of one firm, Morris, Marshall, Faulkner & Co, were singled out for special hostility. *The Builder* denounced the Firm's furniture as 'unnecessarily rude and ugly'.[1] The *Building News* was much more explicit: 'If all modern inventions, luxuries, tastes and history are to be entirely ignored, and medieval art is required in its mingled purity and impurity, then undoubtedly Messrs Morris, Marshall & Faulkner take and well merit the foremost rank. Their works are almost perfect; their hangings, their music stand, their sofa, their chests, would all suit a family which might suddenly be awakened after a sleep of four centuries, and which was content to pay enormous prices suitably to furnish a barn. Standing on the opposite side of the Court and looking at the hangings, the harmony is exquisite; there is scarcely a false tone throughout them. The design of the ornament is also in keeping with the workmanship of the material. And all are thoroughly medieval; but they are no more adapted to the wants of living men, than medieval armour would be to modern warfare, Middle-Aged cookery to civic feasts, or Norman oaths to an English lady's drawing room. They would be all very well as curiosities in a museum, but they are fit for nothing else...The two doors of the lacquered cabinet are beautifully painted with single figures on a punctured gilt background. These pictures are decidedly the best of Messrs Morris, Faulkner & Marshall's work. If we possessed the cabinet, we should cut them out and put the rest behind the fire, *because* it gives us perfectly the rude execution and barbarous ornament of centuries ago. Messrs Morris, Faulkner & Marshall's works are the most complete, and the most thoroughly medieval of any in the Court. They are consequently the most useless'.[2]

Morris, Marshall, Faulkner & Co was the furnishing wing of the Pre-Raphaelite movement, which explained both the Ruskinian savageness of execution of the woodwork and the quality of the painting. The Firm, which was to have a prodigious effect on late nineteenth-century design,* had been founded only a year before the exhibition by a group of artists brought together by William Morris.

Morris (1834-1896) was born in Walthamstow, the son of a wealthy City businessman. In 1840, when Morris was six, his father acquired a fortune by speculating in a Devon copper mine, and the family moved to Woodford Hall on the fringe of Epping Forest, a world which had not changed greatly for hundreds of years. The household 'brewed its own beer and made its own butter; as much a matter of course as it baked its own bread'.[3] Morris rode his pony in the forest (sometimes clad in a specially made suit of armour): he fished and shot, gardened and learned the beauty of plants and birds. The Epping period ended

William Morris. Detail of Blue Bird woven fabric at Wightwick Manor, Staffordshire (late 1870s). Made on a Jacquard loom which used punched cards to reduce tedious hand labour. Webb designed the birds

*For all the magazine's hostility, the Firm was awarded two medals by the exhibition's jury – public acclaim enough to set the company on the track of prestigious commissions (for instance rooms in St James's Palace and the South Kensington Museum).

The great settle which was moved from Morris's Red Lion Square lodgings to the Red House. Present-day state

when Morris's father died in 1847 and his family, though still well off, had to move back to Walthamstow.

All his life, Morris tried to recreate the idyllic, almost medieval life of Woodford Hall: self-sufficient, financially secure, practical, in close contact with nature. But in Morris's vision, the ideal was to be shared by everybody, not just those who happened to be the owners of great houses in the country.

Love of medieval beauty was fostered by his undergraduate years in an Oxford little changed since the fifteenth century. It was confirmed when, with Edward Burne-Jones, his greatest university friend, he read the newly published *The Stones of Venice*. The effect of 'The Nature of Gothic' on the two young men was dramatic and made them resolve to give up their ambition to take the cloth. Burne-Jones decided to become a painter and Morris resolved to be an architect.

At 22, after obtaining a pass degree, Morris took articles with George Edmund Street, then architect to the Oxford diocese. Morris described Street as 'a good architect as things go now, and he has a good deal of business, and always goes for an honourable man'.[4] The relationship lasted only nine months, for Burne-Jones, who was already studying under Dante Gabriel Rossetti, introduced him to his master and Morris 'made up my mind to turn painter and studied the art but in a very desultory way for some time'.[5]

In 1857, he took rooms with Burne-Jones at 17 Red Lion Square, London, and, being unable to find suitable furniture, he sketched some designs, massive pieces which were made up by a local carpenter and painted with scenes from Chaucer and Dante by Rossetti and Burne-Jones. Savage furniture was born.

In the same year, Rossetti offered to paint the walls and roof of the new Oxford Union Building. A gang of painters including Morris and Burne-Jones took part in creating a transient Pre-Raphaelite masterpiece. (Rossetti had no real knowledge of how to work in fresco, and the paintings began to fade almost as quickly as they were done.) Morris had chosen as his subject 'How Sir Palimydes loved La Belle Iseult with exceeding great love out of measure and how she loved not him again but Sir Tristram'.

Morris's story was hidden behind a great mass of sunflowers, and his figures were so ill-proportioned that they caused Rossetti to burst into sarcastic laughter. But, behind the vegetation, Morris had found his own Iseult, Jane Burden, a groom's daughter, a 'stunner', with a long neck, vast dark eyes and a great mane of dark hair, who had been persuaded by Rossetti to sit as a model for the frescoists. William and Jane were engaged in 1858, and in the same year Morris's friend from the Street days, Philip Webb, was commissioned to design a house for the couple. This was the Red House at Bexley Heath which is described in the next chapter. It was as difficult for a convinced Ruskinian to furnish his new home as it had been to fit out Red Lion Square. Webb had to design much of the furniture, and the interior was decorated by Morris and his friends.

The experience determined Morris's final choice of career. He was to be a designer and interior decorator. In April 1861, the firm of

Mural at the Oxford Union Library by William Morris (1857)

Morris, Marshall, Faulkner & Co was set up with, as partners, Morris, Burne-Jones, Webb, Rossetti, Ford Madox Brown (the Pre-Raphaelite painter who had already dabbled in furniture design), Charles Faulkner (one of Morris's Oxford friends, a mathematics don), and Marshall (a surveyor friend of Brown). Morris was general manager. The Firm was set up at 8 Red Lion Square and offered furniture, wall paintings, stained glass, embroidery, table glass, metalwork, jewellery and sculpture. Although its work had received such a drubbing from the critics at its first public appearance in the 1862 exhibition, the Firm quickly secured work: the partners bought things for themselves; Webb persuaded his clients to commission decorative schemes, and Gothic church architects like Street, White and Bodley ordered stained glass and wall decorations. It was on these ecclesiastical commissions that the Firm survived the '60s to blossom into domestic success in the '70s.*

As a Ruskinite, Morris was bound to become involved in craft work as well as design. He explained to an admirer, 'almost all the designs we use for surface decoration, wallpapers, textiles and the like, I design myself. I have had to learn the theory and to some extent the practice of weaving, dying and textile printing: all of which I must admit has given me and gives me a great deal of enjoyment'.[6]

*Success and Morris's declining private income caused the dissolution of the original partnership. In 1875 Morris, whose money and energy had carried the company, reorganized it under his sole proprietorship as Morris & Co. This caused a split with Rossetti and Brown, but Burne-Jones and Webb remained faithful friends and continued to contribute designs. The quarrel between the original partners was later made up with the help of Georgiana Burne-Jones, Edward's wife.

Morris and Company's Merton Abbey workshop – an old mill to which the firm moved textile manufacture in 1881

Morris and Company. Sussex settee (1870s). Developed from traditional Sussex rush-bottomed chair and virtually mass produced

Secretaire cabinet designed by George Jack and made by Morris and Company. Mahogany with marquetry of sycamore and other woods

His own designs for wallpapers, textiles, tapestries, embroideries and carpets are too well known and well loved to need description here. Their power emerged from a creative tension between Pugin's rule that the designer should be truthful to his materials (for this reason Pugin argued that wallpaper patterns must always be flat, with no hint of perspective) and Ruskin's doctrine of naturalism under which the (imperfect) designer should struggle as hard as possible to depict (imperfect) nature. Of all Morris's splendid designs, the most joyous combine Pugin's stiff heraldic structure and a loving, delicate observation of leaves, fruits and flowers.

For all his skill as a designer, Morris never tried architecture. His experience in Street's office had not been happy: he had been set to copying a drawing of a doorway in St Augustine's church, Canterbury (by Butterfield) and 'suffered much tribulation in delineating the many arch mouldings "and at last the compass points nearly bored a hole through the drawing board"'.[7] The mechanical part of nineteenth-century architectural work did not at all suit Morris's temperament, but he was quite clear that architecture was the mother of the arts and crafts, that it should be a 'union of the arts mutually helpful and harmoniously subordinated to one another'.[8]

His ideal was an architecture altogether free of imposed style, one which would grow unselfconsciously from its surroundings and the needs of ordinary people. 'If the old cottages, barns and the like, are kept in good repair from year to year, they will not need to be pulled down to give place either to the red-brick, blue-slated man-sty, or the modern Tudor lord-bountiful cottage. And where...new buildings must be built, by building them well and in a common sense and unpretentious way, with the good material of the countryside, they will take their place alongside of the old houses and look, like them, a real growth of the soil.'[9] He hoped that 'it will be from such necessary, unpretentious buildings that the new and genuine architecture will spring, rather than from our experiments in conscious style, more or less ambitious or those for which the immortal Dickens has given us the never-to-be-forgotten adjective "Architectooralooral"'.[10]

A clean sparseness should be the aim, for 'simplicity of life, even the barest, is not misery, but the very foundation of refinement'. The choice was between 'a sanded floor and white-washed walls, and the green trees and flowering meads and living waters outside; or a grimy palace with a regiment of housemaids always working to smear the dirt together so that it may be unnoticed'.[11]

If the Arts and Crafts architects had ever felt the need to write a manifesto, these passages might well have formed its core, so widely were their principles accepted. The architects' work is often accused of being backward looking, and it often was so. Yet for those who took the teachings of Ruskin and Morris really seriously, Classical architecture was forbidden as were experiments with machine-made products like steel and cast iron. They were restricted to a range of traditional materials, used in a more or less traditional way but without Classical rules. So, even if they had not wanted affinities with pre-Classical late medieval and Tudor building, it would have been almost impossible to

Wightwick Manor, Staffordshire. The Great Parlour (1893). One of the most complete Morris & Co interiors with decorations, light fittings, wall-coverings, embroidery and upholstery by the firm, which worked on the house on and off for 40 years

Great Coxwell barn, Gloucestershire. Morris thought it 'unapproachable in its dignity, as beautiful as a cathedral, yet with no ostentation of the builder's art'. He believed that such structures could be the pattern of new public buildings

have escaped them, just as William Morris could envision the post-industrial, post-hierarchical society of *News from Nowhere* only through a translucent screen of idealized medievalism as painted by Carlyle, Walter Scott and Ruskin. No architect can be free of influences from the past and most Arts and Crafts people welcomed and exploited obvious connections with late medieval architecture in their own work.* At the same time some of the more adventurous spirits were prepared to experiment with new materials like concrete which could be adapted to craftsmanly techniques.

Morris's vision of the town was as potent as his ideas on architecture, and foreshadowed the Garden City Movement of the turn of the century. Cities, he believed, should be quite different from 'our great sprawling brick and mortar country of London...the centre with its big public buildings, theatres, squares and gardens; the zone round the centre with its lesser guildhalls grouping together the houses of the citizens; again with its parks and gardens; the outer zone again, still its district of public buildings, but with no definite gardens to it because the whole of this outer zone would be a garden thickly besprinkled with houses and other buildings. And at last the suburb proper, mostly fields and fruit gardens with scanty houses dotted about till you come to the open country with its occasional farm-steads'.[12]

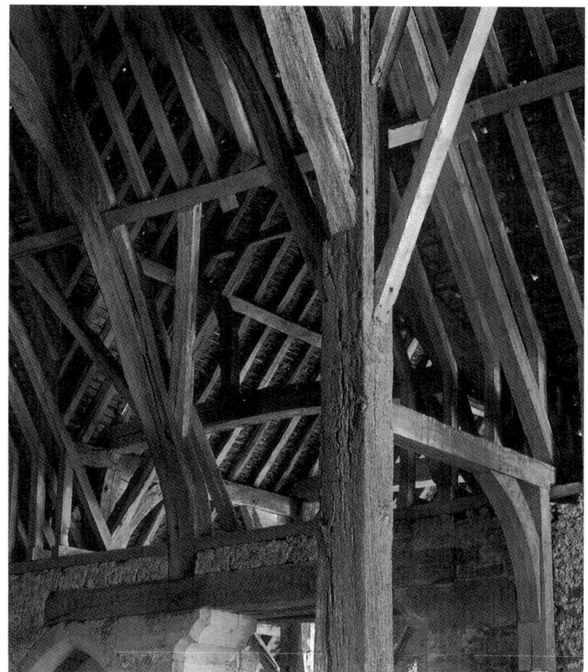

Detail of the oak roof in the thirteenth-century Cistercian tithe barn at Great Coxwell, Gloucestershire

If the new architecture and planning were to draw inspiration from the old, preservation of old work was vitally important – not just as a model but as a reminder of the continuity of the past, present and future. In 1877, Morris was outraged by a proposal by Sir George Gilbert Scott to restore Tewkesbury Abbey. Earlier restorations by High Victorian architects which were honestly but ruthlessly intended to return buildings to their original state had, in Morris's eyes, ruined much fine medieval architecture, partly through ignorance and partly through having to use nineteenth-century work methods, under which it was impossible for carvers to express true Gothic savageness.

The Tewkesbury proposal caused Morris to found the Society for the Protection of Ancient Buildings, which, with Morris's crusading zeal and Philip Webb's quiet technical competence, popularized the doctrine of honest repair rather than wholesale restoration to a state of perfection which often had reality not in history but in the architect's imagination. In the late nineteenth century SPAB saved many old buildings from the process of skimming off the accretions of time normally practised by the High Victorians. Many Arts and Crafts architects were members of SPAB, and the Society's gentle, honest approach did much to form their attitudes to old work which, whenever occasion demanded, was lovingly incorporated into new construction.

In the SPAB Manifesto, Morris urged his contemporaries 'to treat our ancient buildings as monuments of a bygone art, created by bygone manners, that modern art cannot meddle with without destroying. Thus, and thus only...can we protect our ancient buildings and hand them down instructive and venerable to those that come after us.'[13]

The understanding that the heritage of the past belonged to every-

*At first occasionally, then increasingly, vernacular Georgian, Palladianism's relaxed little brother, was also seen as a native architecture, and a suitable source of inspiration.

Kelmscott: a medieval manor growing unselfconsciously from its surroundings

man was one of the milestones on Morris's long march towards communism. The impetus came very largely from Ruskin. Ruskin had seen the imperative of allowing every craftsman freedom to make his own contribution, no matter how ham-fisted. He had understood the importance of creative work and the need to give nobility to the degraded lives of the Victorian poor by offering everybody the chance of creativity. And he had stressed the need for beauty and health in the lives of the whole community. Morris believed that Ruskin, 'by a marvellous inspiration of genius...attained at one leap to a true conception of medieval art...The essence of what Ruskin taught us was simple enough...It was really nothing more recondite than this, that the art of any epoch must of necessity be an expression of its social life, and that the social life of the Middle Ages allowed the workman freedom of individual expression, which on the other hand our social life forbids him'.[14] But Ruskin, as the St George's Guild showed, had refrained from the last logical step – acceptance that if everyone could be creative, society must be reorganized in a way that would give everyone an equal chance to create.

William Morris took this step in 1883 when he joined the Democratic Federation, the only socialist body then in existence. It was the start of a commitment to the socialist movement to which, through numerous vicissitudes, he remained faithful to the end of his life. He was never just a passive supporter but supported the Federation's weekly, *Justice,* both by working for it and paying its debts. He lectured all over the country and founded a local branch of the re-named Social Democratic Federation in 1884.

When I joined the Communist folk, I did what in me lay
To learn the grounds of their faith. I read day after day
Whatever books I could handle, and heard about and about
What talk was going amongst them; and I burned up doubt
after doubt,
Until it befel at last that to others I needs must speak.[15]

By 1889 Morris was prepared to declare that, 'I call myself a Communist and have no wish to qualify that word by joining any other to it. The aim of Communism seems to me to be the complete equality of condition for all people; and anything in a Socialist direction which stops short of this is merely a compromise with the present conditions of society; a halting place on the road to the goal'.[16]

Morris believed that the only way of resolving the Puginian paradox was by revolution – bloody if need be* – for 'if people were once to accept it as true, that it is nothing but just and fair that every man's work should have some hope and pleasure always present in it, they must try to bring the change about that would make it so'.[17]

Morris inherited Ruskin's hatred of machines but he was far from the popular picture of a late Victorian intellectual Luddite trying to smash machinery with a single stick, carpenter's chisel and embroidery needle that has been painted by some historians. Morris did not hate machines as such – just the way in which they were used by Victorian

*In Chapter XVII of *News from Nowhere,* Old Hammond relates that the change in society came about through 'war from beginning to end: bitter war, till hope and pleasure put an end to it'.

Attic room, Kelmscott Manor. Simple but decent furniture for a servant

capitalism. For him, Victorian machinery, like Classical architecture, reduced workers to slavery as machine minders or carvers-to-rote.

Morris's ideal society resembled that of his friend, the anarchist Peter Kropotkin. Creative work would be offered to everybody but, concomitantly, everyone would have to take a turn at the essential but unpleasant jobs like cleaning sewers or coal mining. He could not conceive, as we can, of machines that would accomplish these tasks, but he would undoubtedly have welcomed them, for he argued that 'if the necessary reasonable work be of a mechanical kind, I must be helped to do it by machine, not to cheapen my labour, but so that as little time as possible may be spent upon it and that I may be able to think of other things while I am tending the machine'.[18]

'Yet for the consolation of the artists I will say that I believe that a state of social order would probably lead at first to a great development of machinery for really useful purposes, because people will still be anxious about getting through the work necessary to holding society together; but that after a while they will find that there is not so much work as they expected...and if it seems to them that a certain industry would be carried on more pleasantly as regards the worker, and more effectively as regards the goods, by using hand work rather than machinery, they will certainly get rid of their machinery, because it will be possible for them to do so...I have a hope...that the elaboration of machinery in a society whose purpose is not the multiplication of labour as it now is, but the carrying on of a pleasant life, as it would be under social order – that the elaboration of machinery...will lead to

William Morris's bed, Kelmscott. Hangings designed by William and embroidered by his daughter, May, with Lucy Yeats

Arlington Row, Bibury, Gloucestershire. This Cotswold village was described by Morris as 'surely the most beautiful hamlet in England'

the simplification of life, and so once more to the limitation of machinery.'[19]

Morris was well aware that he was in a contradictory predicament. When he was working on Philip Webb's house, Rounton Grange, in 1874, the client Sir Lowthian Bell heard Morris 'talking and walking about in an excited way', and went to inquire if anything was wrong. 'He turned on me like a wild animal – "It is only that I spend my life ministering to the swinish luxury of the rich".'[20] Morris was a capitalist who preached communism; a designer of mass-produced art who believed in the freedom of individual craftsmen; a manufacturer of machine-made ornament who preferred utter simplicity.

These contradictions, which echo through the whole Arts and Crafts movement, were the product of a visionary trapped by circumstances in a very different world from the one he wanted to see. William's daughter May recalled that when preparing to visit a client to discuss some elaborate scheme of decoration 'he would often remark laughing that it would not answer, in the interests of the Firm, if he were to say what he really liked – white walls and no furniture and no pictures or stuffy curtains: that is for ordinary houses; for fine arras tapestry was the one decoration for stately buildings in our northern countries, "Wall papers are a poor makeshift" said the designer of them many a time'.[21]

This seems cynical and reinforces the view of contemporaries like Norman Shaw who believed that Morris was a money-grubbing hypocrite. But the alternative of fully enacting his social ideals in his own way of life would not only have impoverished his family without changing society in the least, but it would have deprived Morris of the time and energy he needed to imagine what the world could be like, freed from the fetters of capitalism.

Paul Thompson has analysed Morris's predicament: 'Morris had in fact considered a complete scheme of profit sharing...Morris calculated that in 1884 his own income from the Firm was £1,800 while Wardle [the manager] received £1,200 and four others about £500 each. Two of the foremen were given bonuses. The rest, except for two or three "lame dogs", were paid by piece work, rather above their trade rates. If he paid himself a foreman's wage he could distribute £1,600 a year to the other workmen, £16 a year each. But the utmost this income could do would be to help "a few individuals more creep out of their class into the middle class". True co-operation could never be organised within capitalism; and the gesture itself would cripple the support he now gave the socialist cause'.[22]

Morris's communism was that of a man freed by his membership of the upper middle class. His intense individualism would never have allowed him to accept collectivism. The man whose volcanic energy caused him to gnaw the dinner table and twist the tines of his fork in his mouth when thwarted* was not likely to accept consensus quietly. Morris was never much at home with groups of people of any sort.

*The strength of Morris's teeth occasionally had odd repercussions. Visiting, on behalf of SPAB, a church which was in the process of destructive restoration, Morris saw some vile new oak stalls about to be installed. 'Call that carving', he shouted, 'I could gnaw it better with my teeth.'[23] The vicar was not impressed.

George Bernard Shaw, who, though a non-revolutionary Fabian socialist, sometimes appeared with Morris at street corner meetings, recalled that 'he was an ungovernable man in a drawing room. What stimulated me to argument, or at least repartee, made him swear'.[24]

Yet Morris knew that, if working people got power in his lifetime, his privileged vision was unlikely to be accepted. 'I have always believed that the realization of Socialism would give us the opportunity of escaping from that grievous flood of utilitarianism which the full development of the society of contract has cursed us with; but that would be in the long run only; and I think it quite probable that in the early days of Socialism the reflex of the terror of starvation, which so oppresses us now, would drive us into excesses of utilitarianism...So that it is not unlikely that the public opinion of a community would be in favour of cutting down all the timber in England, and turning the country into a big Bonanza farm or market garden under glass. And in such a case what could we do?'[25]

C. R. Ashbee, a young apprentice architect toying with socialism, was introduced to Morris in 1886. He 'received us kindly and invited us all in to supper. Everything in his house is beautiful – such Rossettis, and such a harmony of colours and tones! Miss Morris in a plain crimson velvet dress with red glass beads and a silver ornament, looked like an Italian châtelaine of the fifteenth century. Sitting at table one felt like one of the people in Millais's Pre-Raphaelite picture of Isabella. Everything was harmonious...'Old Morris was delightful, firing up with the warmth of his subject, all the enthusiasm of youth thrilling through veins and muscles; not a moment was he still, but ever sought to vent some of his immense energy. At length banging his hand on the table: "No", said he "the thing is this; if we had our Revolution tomorrow, what should we Socialists do the day after?"

'"Yes...what?" we all cried. And that he could not answer. "We should all be hanged, because we are promising the people more than we can ever give them".'[26]

In fact, Morris was regarded as safely respectable by the class he spent so much energy in trying to overthrow. So much so that in spite of having been twice arrested at Socialist demonstrations, he was seriously canvassed for the Laureateship when Tennyson died in 1892. He smartly turned down the offer – though he derived some pleasure from receiving it.

It is this respectable Morris who presides in bronze over the Pantheon of the Arts and Crafts movement, the Hall of the Art Workers' Guild; his ebullient rug of curly hair is tamed and his douce expression can rarely have been seen in life. Below are written in letters of gold the names of the members. They gave him the place of honour because his example, in art and in life, had inspired them all: more than any other single man, Morris shaped the nature of the Arts and Crafts movement.

1 The Builder, *Vol XX, 1862, p420.*
2 Building News, *Vol IX, 1862, p99.*
3 *Mackail, J. W.* The Life of William Morris, *Longmans Green, London, 1922 (5th edition), p9.*
4 *Lethaby, W. R.* Philip Webb and His Work, *Oxford, 1935, p14.*
5 *Letter to Andreas Scheu; quoted in Morris, May* William Morris, Artist, Writer, Socialist, *Vol II, Basil Blackwell, Oxford, 1935, p10.*
6 Ibid, *p12.*
7 *Lethaby, W. R.* Philip Webb, op cit, *p15.*
8 *Morris, William 'The Prospects of Architecture', lecture to the London Institution, 1881. Printed in May Morris* Works of William Morris, *Vol XXII, p119.*
9 *Morris, William 'On the External Coverings of Roofs', lecture, 1890,* Works of William Morris, op cit, *Vol XXII, p408.*
10 *Morris, William 'Address to Birmingham Art Students', 1894,* Works of William Morris, op cit, *Vol XXII, p429.*
11 *Morris, William 'The Prospects of Architecture',* op cit, *p149.*
12 *Morris, William 'Makeshift' (1894), in May Morris* William Morris, op cit, *Vol II, p474.*
13 *Morris, William* SPAB Manifesto, *1877. Still required to be signed by every recruit to the Society today.*
14 *Morris, William 'The Revival of Architecture', lecture, 1888,* Works, op cit, *Vol XXII, p323.*
15 *Morris, William* The Pilgrims of Hope *section VI. Quoted by E. P. Thompson in* William Morris: Romantic to Revolutionary, *Merlin Press, London, 1977, p270.*
16 *Morris, William letter in* Commonweal, *18.5.89. Quoted in May Morris* William Morris, op cit, *Vol II, p313.*
17 *Morris, William 'The Prospects of Architecture',* Works, op cit, *Vol XII, p140.*
18 *Morris, William 'How We Live and How We Might Live' (1885),* Works, op cit, *Vol XXIII, p20.*
19 Ibid, *p24.*
20 *Lethaby, W. R.* Philip Webb, op cit, *p94.*
21 *Morris, May* William Morris, op cit, *Vol III, p616.*
22 *Thompson, Paul* The Work of William Morris, *Quartet Books, London, 1977, p50.*
23 *Morris, May* William Morris, op cit, *Vol II, p621.*
24 *Shaw, G. B. in May Morris* William Morris, op cit, *Vol II, pxviii.*
25 *Morris, William in May Morris* William Morris, op cit, *Vol II, p315.*
26 *Ashbee, C. R.* Memoirs, *typescript in the Victoria and Albert Museum Library, Vol I, p19.*

Lamplighters

4

When Morris entered G. E. Street's Oxford office in 1856, the chief clerk was a tall, thin rather serious young man called Philip Webb. They were to be lifelong friends, committed alike to the causes of art and socialism.

Phillippe Speakman Webb (1831-1915) was the son of a country doctor. He grew up in an Oxford almost untouched by the Industrial Revolution: a virtually medieval city in an idyllic landscape. Looking back, he wrote, 'I was born and bred in Oxford and had no other teacher in art than the impressive objects of the old buildings there, the effect of which on my natural bent has never left me'.[1] His teacher in the business of architecture was John Billing, a Reading architect whom he served from 1849 to 1852 after which he spent an unhappy period as clerk in Wolverhampton.

Street's invitation to return to Oxford must have been a godsend to Webb, who was never happy unless surrounded by old buildings. From Street, Webb imbibed iron self-discipline and a love of the craft of building. But it was Morris who ignited the fire. Webb was always withdrawn yet Morris could bring him out – to the extent of taking part in a battle of soda syphons when the two, with Faulkner, rowed down the Seine from Paris to Ste Opportune in 1858. On the back of a map in the Murray guide used by the three on the Seine trip was a sketch by Webb for his first large commission, a house for Morris.

Both had gone to London when Street moved his practice from Oxford in 1856. Morris drifted away from architecture and into the arms of the Pre-Raphaelites in the next two years. Webb remained with Street until 1858 and, in the early months of the next year, he designed the Red House at Bexley Heath for the newly married William and Jane – it turned out to be the only house Morris ever built for himself, and in later times, he thought of his five years there as the happiest period of his life. (He had to sell it because the income from his copper shares sank and he was forced to choose between his house and the Firm.) In the house, both owner and architect began to put their theories into practice, to such effect that when, 50 years later, Lawrence Weaver published *Small Country Houses of Today*, which contains a virtual roll call of Arts and Crafts architects, he felt bound to include the Red House because 'It stands for a new epoch of new ideals and practices. Though the French strain which touched so much of the work of the Gothic Revivalists is not absent, and the Gothic flavour itself is rather marked, every brick in it is a word in the history of modern architecture'.[2]

The Gothic flavour is to be seen in the pointed arches over some of the main windows, in the very steeply pitched roofs, and in the stair tower (into which the entrance hall projects at ground level) that is topped by a French leaded lantern. These are virtually the only motifs that have been directly copied from Gothic. Yet the house is Gothic in spirit, in direct descent from the domestic work of Street and Butterfield (who was one of Webb's few heroes).

Its windows are sized and proportioned and placed to suit what

Philip Webb. The Red House, Bexley Heath, Kent (designed 1859). The well is the ceremonial, if not functional, *fons* of the house

goes on inside the house and are not arranged regularly to suit an imposed style. The red bricks and tiles, which made the house so unusual to contemporaries used to stucco, were carefully chosen to give variation of colour and to avoid any impression of mechanical perfection. Outside there is virtually no ornament except for the pointed arches over the doors and sash windows, an echo of Butterfield's parsonages and Street at Boyne Hill. Overt Gothicism is fading away, for the arches are flush with the rest of the brickwork as if they are trying to disappear – as they do in most of Webb's more mature work.

In plan, the house was revolutionary. The most logical layout for an architect wanting to fulfil the ideal of Ruskinian changefulness is a long thin strip of rooms in which the functions of each can be clearly shown on the outside. Webb adopted this chain-like plan with the addition of a corridor down the side which connected all the rooms and obviated the need for walking through one room to get to another, common in medieval planning, but potentially embarrassing for nineteenth-century Britons (though not, apparently, for their American contemporaries).

Webb bent this one-room-and-a-corridor strip into an L-shape forming a courtyard round the well (necessary because no mains water was available). The result is like a Butterfield parsonage cut down the middle with the two halves set at right-angles to each other. Butterfield himself had occasionally experimented with L-shaped plans but never honed them down to the room-and-a-corridor width. For this, there were precedents in the vast castellated country houses of architects like Anthony Salvin, but Webb was one of the first to apply the scheme to a quite small house. It was to be echoed in innumerable Arts and Crafts plans before the end of the century though Webb himself never re-used it with such clarity.

If the layout was a powerful precedent, the orientation was not. All the principal rooms faced north in the Georgian fashion (though the drawing room has a delightful cantilevered oriel which receives light from the south and west as well). The kitchen faced west (which gave it the maximum amount of heat from the sun just when dinner was being prepared); and the garden round the well was faced by no more than the long corridor. Later, as his friend and assistant George Jack recorded, 'Webb often said that he never wanted to see [the Red House] or hear about it again, and that no architect ought to be allowed to build a house until he was 40'.[3]

In fact, as Peter Blundell Jones has pointed out, the corridor facing the garden was developed by Webb when, in 1864, he designed an (unbuilt) extension for Burne-Jones and Georgiana. The route became part of an enclosed cloister, and the whole would have made three sides of a court open to the south and focused on the well (which was largely symbolic for its water was drawn into the kitchen by a pipe and hand pump).[4]

The interior of the house that was built was restrained but greatly enlivened by Burne-Jones and Rossetti murals. There was massive furniture designed by Morris and Webb, including a settle from Red Lion Square: a mad and splendid combination of cupboard, bookshelf and

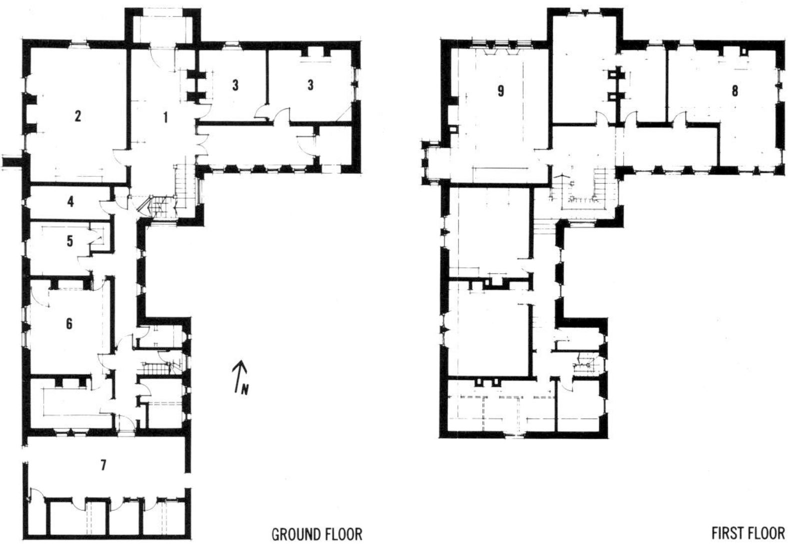

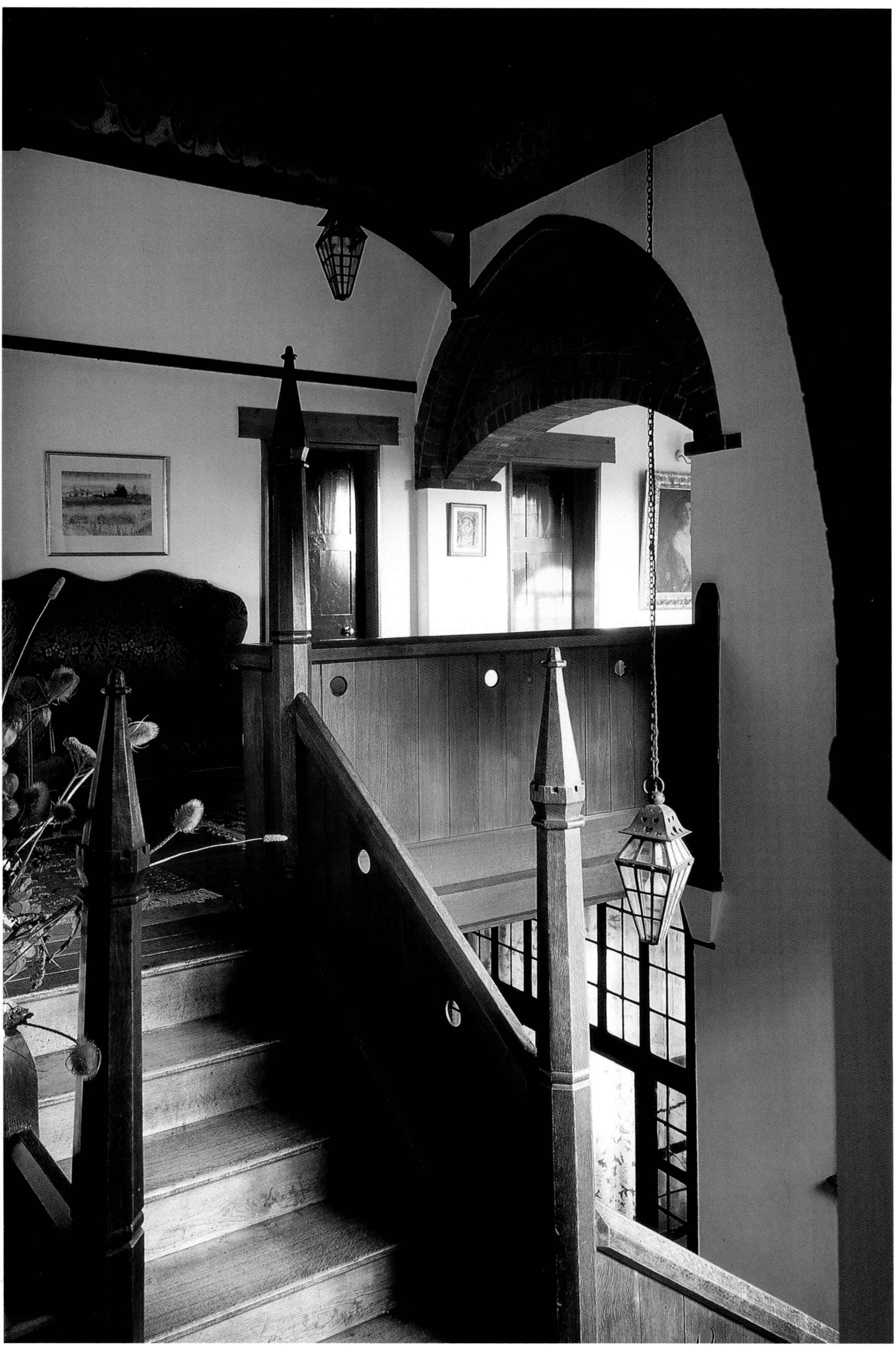

Opposite top: Philip Webb. West front of the Red House with the drawing room oriel
Opposite centre: Red House plans. The prototypical long, thin, room-and-a-corridor Arts and Crafts plan
Opposite bottom: Entrance door detail, Red House
Left: Oak staircase and balustrade, Red House

KEY TO PLANS:
1: Hall
2: Dining-room
3: Sitting-rooms
4: Lavatory
5: Pantry
6: Kitchen
7: Kitchen court
8: Studio
9: Drawing-room

Webb. 19 Lincoln's Inn Fields, London (1869). Urban decorum meets changefulness

sitting bench, very plain joinery but illuminated with panels designed by Rossetti. There was stained glass in the leaded lights of the corridors and above the staircase in its corner tower was what Weaver called a 'tall pyramidal roof left open on the inside and patterned in blue and green, a little Persian in feeling'.[5] Besides his furniture, Webb contributed designs for table glass and metal work, none of which Morris could find on the market to fit his exacting standards. There is no evidence to show how much influence each of the collaborators had on the design of the Red House, but it is probably safe to say that the dark glowing interiors owed more to Morris while the rather austere exterior had more of Webb in it.

While Morris was fierce, ebullient, febrile, and eloquent, Webb was his alter ego. Gentle, modest, patient and deeply reserved in public, he usually refused to have his buildings published, and practically the only light so far shed on Webb as a whole person (though it leaves out the politics) is the biography by his disciple William Lethaby. Yet in private he was affectionate and kindly, fond of jokes, good claret and snuff which in moments of stress he would take in enormous quantities. He was generous – for instance though he did not smoke, he always had an inexhaustible supply of cigars for his friends. George Jack, writing of Webb after his death said, 'it is like trying to remember past sunshine – it pleases and it passes, but it also makes things to grow and herein Webb was like the sunshine, and as little recognized and thanked'.[6]

Unthanked he may have been, but his buildings were enormously influential. Of his largest town house, 1 Palace Green, Kensington, completed in 1869 for George Howard the future Earl of Carlisle, Lethaby wrote that it was remarkable 'as having furnished precedents for fashionable house builders for a whole generation. Here first, so far as I know, cut-and-rubbed brickwork forming moulded and dentilled cornices was used in recent times.* Here too, are pilaster strips in brickwork, "aprons" under the window sills, a coved cornice, a carved panel, ornamental arrangements of brickwork, silver-grey slating, wrought-iron balconies, big sash windows with wide wood-frames, some little circular windows and a firm lead-covered dormer. All these things came in naturally in their places and grew out of the circumstances without effort, but this house furnished a pattern-book of "features" for architects who designed by compilation from cribs'.[7]

Webb himself had a horror of copying. Yet he was unwilling to divorce himself entirely from the past. The Palace Green house has great Gothic pointed arches as well as eighteenth-century sash windows. Number 19 Lincoln's Inn Fields, designed in the same year, is much more Georgian in feeling (it was after all set in an eighteenth-

*Lethaby was wrong, as Gavin Stamp has pointed out to me. Bodley and Nesfield, for instance, had both used rubbed brick cornices earlier. George Frederick Bodley (1827-1907) was one of the greatest later Victorian ecclesiastical architects. He was one of the early (1863) and constant patrons of the Morris Firm for stained glass. His career was crowned, a year before his death, with the commission for the Episcopal Cathedral, Washington (still building to modified designs).
His domestic architecture was often a blend of brick-and-gabling with symmetrical planning and windows with Georgian sashes. Bodley and Webb were close – so much so that when, for instance, Bodley fell temporarily, but seriously, sick, he asked Webb to complete Abermule, Montgomeryshire (1869), a house that had much in common with Webb's architecture of the next decade, with severe rubbed brick detailing, virtually symmetrical main fronts, Georgian windows and interior detailing. Changefulness was confined to the less important elevations and the stable block.

George Frederick Bodley (with Webb). Abermule, Montgomeryshire (1869). Finely crafted brick, symmetrical planning, gabled roofs

Webb. Joldwynds, Surrey (1873, now destroyed): local materials with Georgian overtones

century terrace), but with its gable-hooded porch and central stone bay projecting from its reserved brickwork on either side, it is very far from being a Neo-Georgian building.

During the '70s, Webb elaborated the symmetry first seen in Lincoln's Inn Fields. Houses like Rounton Grange near Northallerton, Yorkshire (1872-76), Joldwynds near Dorking, Surrey (1873), Four Gables, Brampton, Cumbria (for George Howard's agent, mid 1870s) and Smeaton Manor, Yorkshire (1876) were all variants of symmetrical planning, with the main accommodation crammed into a big rectangular block. The exteriors of this period were all more or less derived from Georgian – but the details were much simplified and were used with the same kind of austere insouciance that makes Lincoln's Inn Fields so distinctive.

Much of the '80s (during which Webb earned less than £320 a year, only slightly more than a master mason)[8] was taken up with designing and building Clouds and its ancillary buildings at East Knoyle near Salisbury which was burnt down soon after completion and then rebuilt. Now half destroyed and much mutilated, the house was partly symmetrical but its huge size allowed more freedom than the comparatively smaller country houses of the previous decade. In it, the Arts and Crafts plan was bent round a central top-lit hall, where people on the first floor could look down onto the central social life of the house through the leaded lights of the first floor corridor.

Clouds was a foretaste of the freedom of Webb's masterpiece, Standen, near East Grinstead, Sussex, designed in 1891 and completed by 1894. Unlike many of the houses of the '70s and '80s, Standen was not designed for a landed family but for J. S. Beale, a successful solicitor, which may explain its lack of formality. There is no tinge of symmetry about Standen, which has a long, thin L-shaped plan two rooms deep with a corridor in the middle. This allowed all rooms to be orientated in the way late Victorians preferred: main family spaces, conservatory, drawing and dining rooms face south; the morning room and kitchen face east and the servants' hall looks west to catch the evening sun and obtain a view of visitors arriving in the forecourt.

Outside, the building is an exemplar of Ruskinian changefulness and Puginian fidelity to place. The existing old farm house was retained at Webb's insistence. Its traditional tile hanging is echoed in the new work and complemented by all sorts of local materials and techniques: roughcast, clapboard, brick and stone, each of which enabled Webb to emphasize different functions. Even the windows are carefully differentiated, with leaded lights to show the circulation spaces (hall, corridor and so on) and big sash windows to indicate the rooms. Apart from these windows, all references to past styles have disappeared; the only mouldings are the minimum needed to keep the building waterproof.

The result is a big house that looks as if it grew up in stages over many years – the effect that George Devey had tried so hard to produce, but without any of Devey's curious picturesque jumbles. At Standen, each change of material is sharp, showing exactly where internal arrangements stop and start.

Above: Webb. Standen, Sussex (1891-94): the south (garden) front, in which each detail indicates the inner life of the house and each material is drawn from local precedent
Right: Ground floor plan

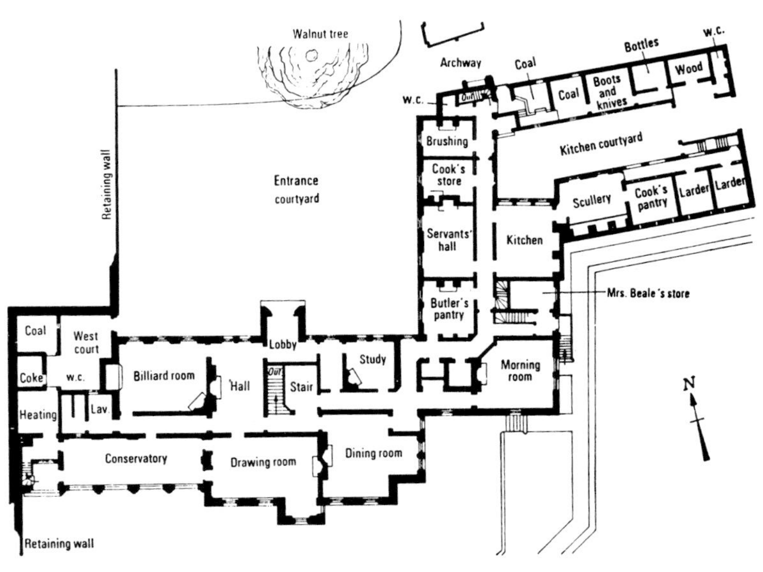

Standen dramatically illustrates Webb's abiding passion for traditional building and local materials which was strong even in his most classicizing days – the roof of Rounton Grange for instance was a north Yorkshire combination of pantiles and stone slates; Joldwynds, like Standen, was in a mixture of local brick, hung tiles and weather-boarding; Brampton was in local rosy stone; at Smeaton Manor the bricks were fired from clay found near the site.

Webb was passionate about good building; he spent much time discussing technique with the craftsmen of his day who still built as their forebears had done for hundreds of years. Lethaby remembered that 'He was deeply interested in limes and mortars, the proper ways of laying roof tiles and forming chimneys, of finishing plaster ceilings and mixing whitewash. He forced himself to become an expert in ventilation and drainage'.[9]

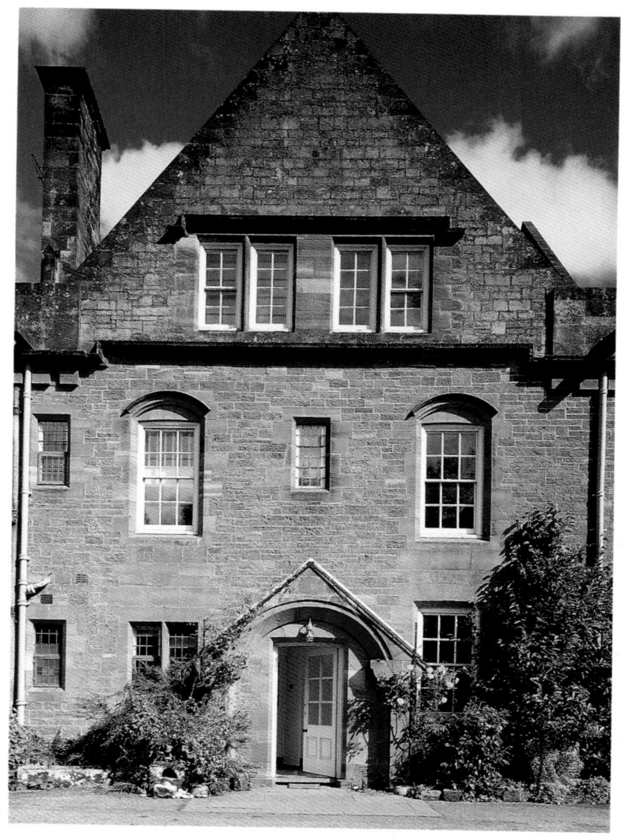

Webb. Four Gables, Brampton, Cumbria (mid 1870s): four square with simplified detailing in local stone

Webb's love of right construction and the necessity of relating his building to the site, and to local traditions, could go to great lengths. In a letter to a client at Arisaig, Argyll (1882) he urged: 'if you should fail in getting whinstone of sufficient size to do the memorial from stone got from your own ground, it would seem hardly to the purpose to get that sort of stone from elsewhere – unless it could be got from somewhere near by. Still, I think, in the rude little churchyard, with its ancient ruins standing by, the native stone would look more congruous than any imported stone would; but if the whinstone is not to be come at I think *unpolished* granite would be the next best, though in that case I should have to make a fresh design as the design you have is quite unsuited to the working of granite'.[10] Truth to materials and respect for locality could not go much further – yet curiously, Webb was prepared to make compromises in both structure and construction. Standen for instance has a concealed steel frame,[11] and the windows of St Martin's church at Brampton project higher than the ceiling inside so that their upper lights open into the roof space.[12] With such sanction from Webb, it is not surprising that unPuginian deceptions were sometimes practised by Arts and Crafts architects: everything is not always quite what it seems in the work of some of the master's admirers.

To get the effects of traditional craftsmanship that he wanted, Webb could be as stubborn as Pugin. Building the house at Arisaig, he found that few of the men could understand English. 'He managed however, to make them understand one thing – that he meant to have his own way; for he set them to building experimental slabs of walling, in order to settle the kind of facing the house was to have...The old traditional way of using this stone had died out in favour of imported stone and fancy surfaces. Webb got his way, however, more or less, as he always did, for he was an obstinate man. He taught the masons their business, much to their disgust at the interfering foreigner.'[13] He could be autocratic with clients too and would threaten to reduce the size of the drawing room if a client would not allow enough space for the servants. (Mrs Wyndham, the client of Clouds, remarked after the fire had destroyed the main block and she had to be temporarily housed during rebuilding that 'It is a good thing

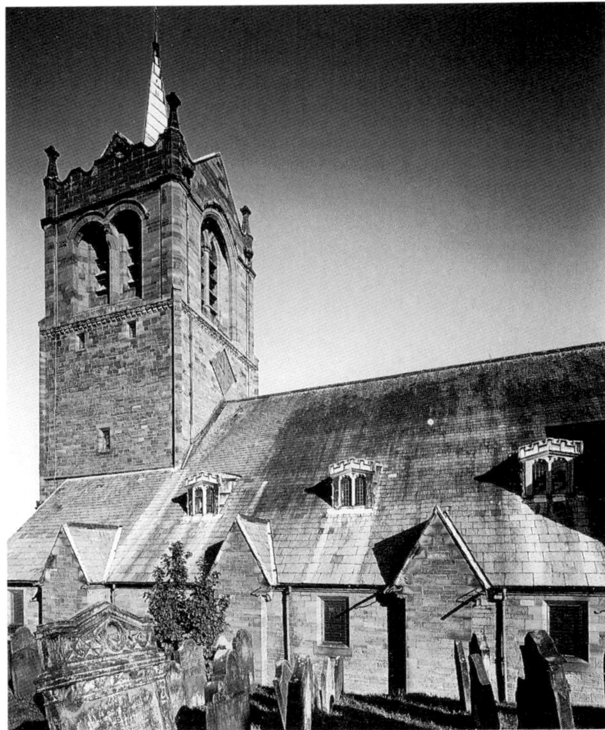

Webb. St Martin's church, Brampton, Cumbria (completed 1878, tower 1905). South front and south aisle: a complex and not always totally clear interaction of stone and wood

that our architect was a socialist because we find ourselves just as comfortable in the servants' quarters as we are in our own'.)[14]

Webb's autocracy was not aimed at building monuments to himself – or, apart from his symmetrical gestures, to his clients. In everything he did, including the beautiful animals and birds drawn for Morris's designs (the originals of which have a tenderness and accuracy which recall Dürer), Webb was concerned to let the object speak for itself and to withdraw his own personality as much as possible. George Jack recalled, 'I remember one design he did for a house that was never built, wonderfully elaborate and interesting. As the days went on, I found he had been using his india rubber very freely and he made the remark to me "Whatever you do, cut out, cut out"'.[15]

He wanted to achieve the commonplace, to be at one with the old craft traditions. Like Morris, he saw that this was only possible after a social revolution. Like Morris, he was condemned by the contradictions of his ideals to serving the luxury of the rich and to dictating design to his workmen. His last years of practice, before he retired in 1900 to a country life of increasing poverty and cheerfulness, were much devoted to the Society for the Protection of Ancient Buildings which, under Webb's gentle tutelage became 'a real school of practical building – architecture with all the whims which we usually call "design" left out'.[16]

Almost his last commission was for memorial cottages to William Morris at Kelmscott. The little grey houses, true in every detail to Cotswold tradition, varied only by a relief carved by Jack, are a fitting monument to Morris and to his architect – 'the best man that he had ever known'.[17]

Influential though he was on Lethaby and the next generation, Webb left no direct architectural descendants. Of his very few assistants, only Jack made a career for himself and that was as furniture designer for Morris & Co rather than as architect. It was Richard Norman Shaw (1831-1912) – Webb's almost exact contemporary – whose office became the most fruitful nursery of Arts and Crafts talent. Shaw followed Webb as Street's chief clerk in 1859 and he shared some of his predecessor's reserve. Yet he was free of Webb's puritanism and he never shunned publicity. His prodigious volume of ever changing work figured large in the magazines of the '70s and '80s, while Webb's relatively small output of buildings was only rarely seen and had to be searched out by devotees. Webb survived on the patronage of a few sympathetic clients. Shaw set himself up to cater for the taste of the *nouveaux riches*, initially producing a neo-medieval world for a generation raised on Walter Scott, then changing to take in new fashions of the class. Webb he respected, but he could not stomach his austerity. Webb was, he thought, 'a very able man indeed, but with a strong liking for the ugly'.[18]

Before joining Street, Shaw had trained under William Burn, an eclectic Scottish Classicist, and under the last great Gothick country house architect, Anthony Salvin. His work owed much to his early years under these two masters of the picturesque.

A digression is worth while to see the office that Shaw entered as an assistant at 28, an unusually late age for an up and coming

Shaw. Bradford Exchange competition entry (1864): Old English tries to come to town – and fails

Victorian architect. It shows the pattern of training of many Arts and Crafts people. Shaw told Street's son: 'We worked hard – or thought we did – we had to be at the office at nine o'clock and our hour of leaving was six o'clock – long hours – but he never encroached on our own time and as a matter of fact I am sure I never stayed a minute past six o'clock.

'There were some interesting men in the office, and we were thoroughly happy. I am sure we were loyal, and believed in our master entirely, so that our work was really a pleasure; [Street] was our master – and let us know it – not by nagging or in an aggressive spirit, but by daily showing that he knew more than any of us and could in a given time do about twice as much. When a new work appeared, his custom was to draw it out in pencil in his own room – plans, elevations and sections – even putting in the margin lines and places where he wished the title to go; nothing was sketched in; it was drawn and exactly as he wished it to be, so that really there was little to do except to ink in his drawings and tint and complete them.'[19] Street's own T-square rattled long into the night. Shaw's assistant Lethaby remembered him saying, 'Street, you know, would not let us design a keyhole'.[20]

If a mid-Victorian architect was to rise above being a tracer and a copier of his master, he had to seek further inspiration. Immediately after leaving Street in 1862, Shaw went on sketching trips to west Kent and Sussex with his old friend from Burn and Salvin days, William Eden Nesfield (1835-88). They sketched Devey's work at Penshurst Place and, like Devey, extensively studied local vernacular cottages. As Andrew Saint, Shaw's biographer, records 'immediately the "Old English" style emerges'.[21]

Old English was a Deveyan mixture of half-timbered or tile-hung upper storeys surmounting brick or stone ground floors with mullioned windows and leaded lights, all dominated by tall clusters of decorative brick chimneys. The style is both savage and changeful in Ruskin's sense. The first example of Shaw's personal style is a tiny cottage design of 1862 which in its crashing juxtaposition of porch and gable has the studied clumsiness of Butterfield's Coalpit Heath parsonage of nearly 20 years before. And it was from Butterfield, not Devey, that Shaw learned his use of fake timbering and of the hipped gable, both of which were to become important ingredients of Old English.

By 1864, Shaw felt sufficiently confident to submit an entry for the Bradford Exchange competition. It started off on the ground floor as a sort of Gothic with pointed arches and gradually rose through a carefully controlled series of irregular windows punched in a plain stone wall to a complex of hips, gables, balconies and half-timbering on top. The whole is dominated by a picturesquely irregular tower capped by a series of pitched French hats. Old English tried to come to town but was not acceptable; the design was placed sixth in a field of eight.

But the style was at home in the country. By the late '60s, Shaw was building really large country houses, Glen Andred and Leys Wood at Groombridge in Sussex, for instance, which show Old English at its

Shaw. Kate Greenaway's house, Frognal, London (designed 1884): changeful, relaxed suburban (note how top floor studio is twisted)

Shaw. Leys Wood, Groombridge, Sussex (1867-69): Old English at its most confident

purest and most confident. In both, a masonry lower storey is topped with a medley of tile-hung walls and roofs terminating in a riot of gables and dormers. The wall planes project and recede, and the levels subtly change. The great intricate mass is held together by the mullioned windows and pinned down by the gigantic vertical shafts of the great chimneys.

Like Webb, Shaw began to adopt a free Classical style in the '70s, particularly for the London work he was then beginning to attract. Webb's use of Renaissance motifs was always extremely idiosyncratic but Shaw was a much more clear-cut exponent of the Queen Anne style which had been pioneered by, among others, Nesfield, Shaw's partner of the early years. Mark Girouard, the style's historian, defines it as 'a kind of architectural cocktail, with a little genuine Queen Anne in it, a little Dutch, a little Flemish, a squeeze of Robert Adam, a generous dash of Wren and a touch of Francois 1er'.[22]

With its great range of expression, Queen Anne was eminently suitable for use by architects who continued to believe in Ruskinian changefulness but who wanted to enrich the diet of Gothic and vernacular models. Shaw's own house at 6 Ellerdale Road, Hampstead, London, designed in 1874, is largely composed of Renaissance elements but they are assembled in such a free manner that the result would have made the hair of even the most uncultivated eighteenth-century country builder stand on end. The main elevation starts off being apparently symmetrical under a cornice above which rise two gables, but from there down everything is free. The up-hill end with its oriel windows is, almost perversely, four storeys high, while the lower end, with its brick bay, has only three main floors, dominated by the great one-and-a-half storey dining room window. Between the oriels and bay, windows of several shapes and sizes are disposed round a big staircase light to maximize the clash between the two series of floor levels.

The dining room, Saint says, is 'the house's *pièce de résistance*. It is almost a cube, a storey and a half in height. It has high panelling, quarry tiles round the carpet and a massive inglenook to the west, the first to be used in town...Above, it accommodates the precious workroom or "den" where Shaw's drawing was done'.[23] This was reached by a little private stair; it had a porthole window looking down the road and another internal window so that Shaw could communicate with his family below.

In 1877, when Shaw was alternating between Old English and Queen Anne, he got what must have seemed to him one of his least important commissions, yet it was to have a profound effect on domestic architecture of the next four decades. In the mid '70s, a speculator called Jonathan Carr bought an estate, Bedford Park,[24] near the new railway station at Turnham Green, and asked E. W. Godwin and the firm of Coe & Robinson for house designs for a development of small detached and semi-detached villas.

Godwin's designs were attacked in the *Building News* and Carr turned to Shaw for a new set of standard drawings. Shaw produced house designs but did not supervise the works. He started with tile-hung variants of Old English, echoing Godwin, but moved towards

Shaw. Bedford Park,
Turnham Green, London.
Shaw house types arranged
on a typical avenue
(*Building News*,
21 December 1877)

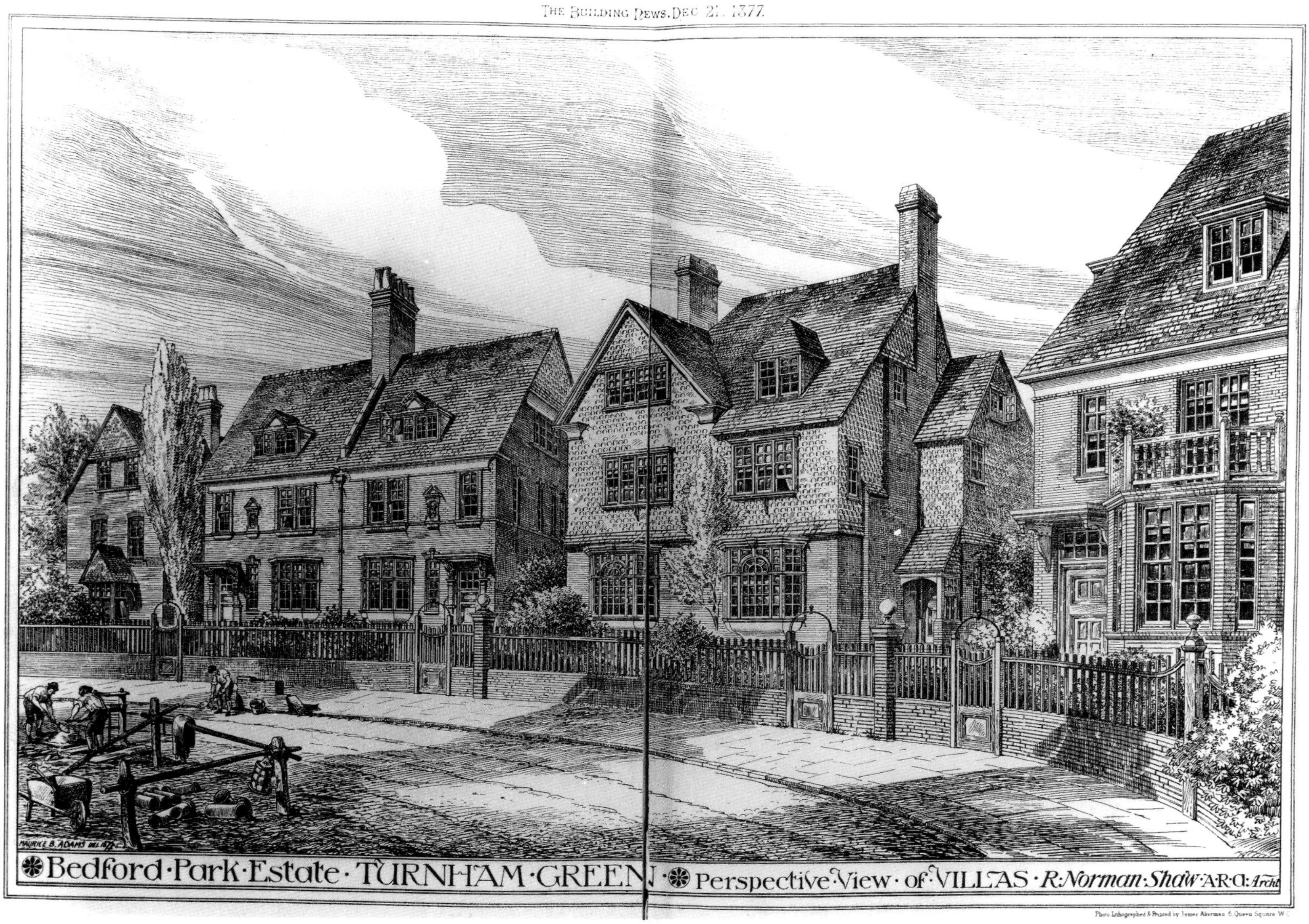

THE BUILDING NEWS. DEC 21. 1877.
MAURICE B. ADAMS del 1877
Bedford·Park·Estate·TURNHAM·GREEN· Perspective·View·of·VILLAS·R:Norman:Shaw·A.R.A: Archt

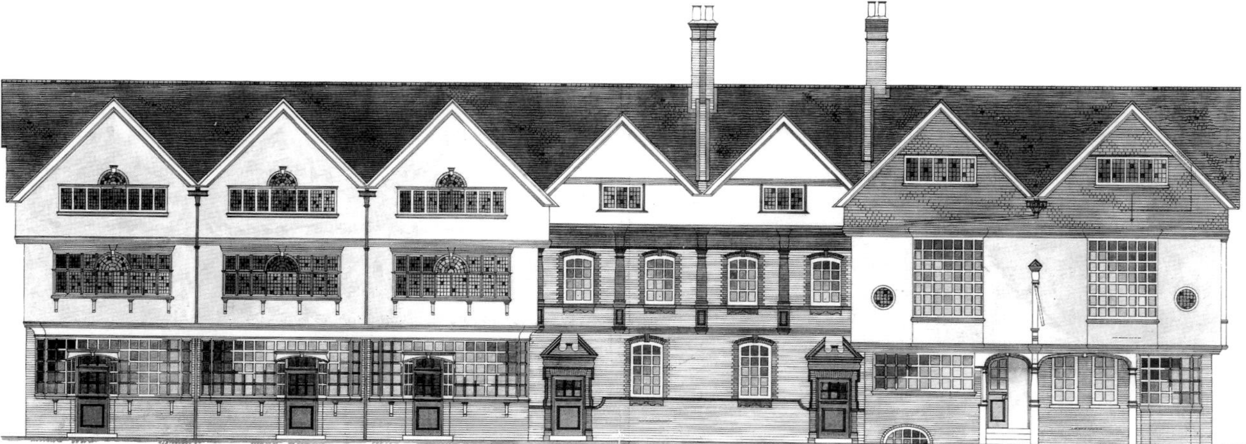

Shaw. The Tabard Inn,
Bedford Park, the suburb's
Old English pub (1879-80)

R. Norman Shaw. 180 Queen's Gate, Kensington, London (1884-85, destroyed 1970): Shaw's grand Queen Anne style

the cheaper Queen Anne as the economics of speculative building began to bite. Only for the Tabard, a mixture of pub, coffee house and department store, was enough cash available to do a more or less pure Old English job.

The cultural impact of Bedford Park was tremendous; writers and artists flocked to live in the jolly red houses along tree-lined streets, and the new suburb was given the widest publicity. Its (quite) low density pattern of basementless brick houses in a bosky setting became the model for the late nineteenth-century suburb and eventually for the Garden City movement.

By the mid '80s, Shaw was still working in both the Old English and the Queen Anne styles. His house for the illustrator Kate Greenaway at 39 Frognal, a few hundred yards from Shaw's own, is tile-hung on a brick base with a gable and mullioned windows: it is a cottage compressed into a small tower with, on top, a studio ingeniously diagonally orientated to obtain north light and to complicate the outline. The design of the Greenaway house started in 1884, and the year before Shaw had designed 180 Queen's Gate, a mighty, full-blown example of Queen Anne, much more obviously organized than the Ellerdale Road house but still very free, with the main rooms emphasized by a bay and by an arch-covered recess. Terminated with symmetrical tall pilaster-clad chimney stacks and great scrolled gables, the Queen's Gate house foreshadowed Shaw's transition to more orthodox formality in the decades around the turn of the century.

As the Frognal and Queen's Gate houses show, Shaw's work was still extraordinarily free and full of variety in the mid '80s. At the time, his office was staffed by men who were to become leading figures of the next generation. But before going on to them, it is worth glancing at a couple of contemporaries whose practices were also breeding grounds for Arts and Crafts talent.

Ernest George. Market Hall, Moreton in Marsh, Gloucestershire (1887): George at his most rural

Shaw's near contemporary Ernest George (1839-1922) set up on his own at the age of 22, after training under the obscure Samuel Hewitt. His extremely successful practice, which continued virtually until his death, handled work of all kinds but the bulk was country houses, some of which were based on local traditions of building, handled with gentleness and sympathy by George and his succession of partners: Thomas Vaughan, Harold Peto and Alfred Yeates.

But George was by no means a convinced vernacular revivalist. He was a picturesque architect with a great armoury of styles, and he would as happily adopt the Romanesque for a crematorium as French Renaissance for a music school. Lutyens, one of his many distinguished Arts and Crafts pupils and assistants,* remembered that in the '80s George was 'a distinguished architect who took each year three weeks' holiday abroad and returned with overflowing sketch books. When called on for a project he would look through these and choose some picturesque turret or gable from Holland, France or Spain and round it weave his new design. Location mattered little and no provincial formation influenced him, for at that time terracotta was the last word in building'.[25]

*Others included Robert Weir Schultz, Herbert Baker and Guy Dawber.

Another successful late Victorian architect, Thomas Graham Jackson (1835-1924) had a distinguished Oxford career before being apprenticed to Sir George Gilbert Scott like Street and Bodley. From that High Goth, Jackson acquired a passion for medievalism, on which he wrote a spirited apologia *Modern Gothic Architecture*. His secular Gothic buildings, for instance the Oxford Examination Schools and the Brasenose Master's house, were highly regarded by contemporaries for their toughness and masculinity, earning him the nickname Anglo-Jackson. Yet he could be delicate and charming as his design for workmen's cottages at Sevenoaks shows.

Like Webb, Jackson had a remarkably flexible definition of Gothic, 'I regard all buildings which conform to the conditions of English climate, material and habit as Gothic'.[26] This allowed him to adopt a wide range of elements, including Flemish gables and even, when he was feeling particularly perverse, large chunks of Renaissance architecture. As *The Architectural Review* remarked censoriously, 'his work seems to us varied to the verge of eclecticism'.[27] It was from the eclecticism and freedom of men like Webb, Shaw, George and Jackson that the Arts and Crafts architects set out to find a new direction.

Thomas Graham Jackson. Design for cottages at Sevenoaks, Kent (before 1897): Jackson in gentle mood

1 *Lethaby W. R.* Philip Webb and his Work, *Oxford, 1935, p7. The book is a collection of articles first published in* The Builder *during 1925.*
2 *Weaver, Lawrence* Small Country Houses of Today, *First Series, Country Life, London, nd, p180.*
3 *Jack, George 'An Appreciation of Philip Webb',* The Architectural Review, *Vol XXXVIII, 1915, p3.*
4 *Blundell Jones, Peter 'Red House',* The Architects' Journal, *Vol CLXXXIII, 15 January 1986, pp36-51.*
5 *Weaver, L.* op cit, *p182.*
6 *Quoted in Lethaby, W.R.* Philip Webb, op cit, *p194.*
7 *Lethaby, W.R.* Philip Webb, op cit, *p88.*
8 *Dakers, Caroline* Clouds, The Biography of a Country House, *Yale University Press, New Haven and London, 1993, p64.*
9 *Lethaby, W.R.* Philip Webb, op cit, *p122.*
10 *Ibid, p129.*
11 *Ford, Edward R.* Details of Modern Architecture, *MIT Press, Cambridge, Mass. and London, 1990, pp129-131.*
12 *McEvoy, Michael 'Webb at Brampton',* The Architects' Journal, *Vol CXC, 25 October 1989, pp40-63.*
13 *Jack* op cit, *p4.*
14 *Quoted in McEvoy* op cit, *p60.*
15 *Quoted in Lethaby* Philip Webb, op cit, *p137.*
16 *Lethaby, W. R.* Ernest Gimson, his Life and Work, *Stratford, London and Oxford, 1924, p3.*
17 *S. C. Cockrell quoted in Lethaby, W.R.* Philip Webb, op cit, *p230.*
18 *Lethaby, W.R.* Philip Webb, op cit, *p75.*
19 *Quoted in Street, A. E.* Memoir of George Edmund Street RA, *John Murray, London, 1888, p283.*
20 *Lethaby, W.R.* Philip Webb, op cit, *p75.*
21 *Saint, Andrew* Richard Norman Shaw, *Yale University Press, New Haven and London, 1976, p28.*
22 *Girouard, Mark* Sweetness and Light: the 'Queen Anne' Movement 1860-1900, *Oxford, 1977, p2.*
23 *Saint* op cit, *p179.*
24 *Saint* op cit *gives a detailed explanation of the development of Bedford Park on pp201-210.*
25 *Quoted in Hussey, Christopher* The Life of Sir Edwin Lutyens, *Country Life, London, 1950, p17.*
26 The Architectural Review, *Vol I, 1897, p140.*
27 *Ibid.*

The Guilds are forged

5

'Early in 1883, the pupils of R. Norman Shaw, RA, formed a Society for the discussion of Art and Architecture. Its members', recalled Edward Prior, 'though trained as Architects took the name of Art for the Association, and called themselves the "St George's Art Society" as meeting under the shadow of St George's Church Bloomsbury'[1] – and perhaps under that of Ruskin's St George's Guild.

Shaw's Bloomsbury Square office was the main nursery of the young men who founded the Arts and Crafts movement, and they owed much to his training. Shaw was much more liberal than his own master Street. W. R. Lethaby, who was Shaw's chief assistant from 1879, recalled, 'Mr Shaw was extraordinarily generous to his clerks, sometimes letting them "design" minor matters, not because of any gain to him but because he thought it would make their work more interesting and be a training'.[2] However much Shaw's own style changed, his assistants remained fondly indebted to him for their grounding in the craft of architecture.

The St George's Society was the first association to emerge from the fizzing and often rumbustious atmosphere generated by four of Shaw's pupils. Lethaby at 26 was senior to the 31 year old Edward Prior, Mervyn Macartney, 30, and Gerald Callcott Horsley, 21. The four were made five by Ernest Newton in whose Hart Street rooms they met. Newton had been Shaw's chief clerk until Lethaby took over.

J.D. Sedding. Holy Trinity, Sloane Street, London. Fusion of the arts and crafts. Grilles and altar rails by Wilson, altar relief by Harry Bates, chancel stalls and screen by F.W. Pomeroy, Burne-Jones glass, Nelson Dawson metalwork.

By October 1883, the Society had become aware that meetings of young architects were not enough. Prior recalled that 'Art and Architecture were drifting asunder. Was it possible to bring them together again? Close connection had been historically necessary to both. Was this now to be accepted as mere ancient history?'[3]

On one hand, the Royal Academy was 'now giving its favour almost entirely to oil painting', selecting members 'more often on the basis of culture or professional success, than in view of the merit of their art. On the other there was the Institute of British Architects, whose theory of architecture had driven from its doors most of those architects whose art was acknowledged; which had forbidden to Artists a personal interest in their handicrafts and had opened its doors so widely to business interests that Surveyors had become the largest element of its body'.[4]

Macartney and Horsley were deputized to ask Shaw for advice. Prior reported his reply that, 'In France, Architects, Painters and Sculptors were trained together in one common school of the Arts. If Architecture in England was missing its way, it was for the young men to bring her back from professionalism. The Architects of this generation must make the future for themselves and knock at the door of Art until they were admitted'.[5]

This is worth a digression. In the '80s and '90s there was a great row about whether architecture should, as the Royal Institute of British Architects hoped, be put on a professional footing, like law, medicine or divinity, with a central professional body setting educational and

John Ruskin. Unexecuted window design for the Oxford Museum (between 1855 and 1859)

ethical standards, or whether it ought to remain essentially a craft – taught by masters to apprentices in a way little changed since the Middle Ages.

Not surprisingly, Shaw and his pupils took the side of art and craft. In 1891 the imbroglio was brought to the attention of the public by a manifesto in *The Times* opposing a move to make architecture 'a close profession' by law with entry regulated by examination which 'by raising artificial barriers, would have a tendency still further to alienate'[6] painting and sculpture from architecture. Among the manifesto's signatories were Shaw and contemporaries such as Webb, Jackson, and Bodley; Lethaby and his generation, Macartney, Newton, Prior, Horne and Ricardo; and among the non-architects, Morris and the Pre-Raphaelites: Madox Brown, Burne-Jones and Holman Hunt were for once prepared to make cause with academicians like Alma-Tadema.

Shaw and Jackson edited a book, *Architecture, a Profession or an Art*, published a year later, in which essays by the editors, and Lethaby, Prior, Newton, Bodley and others aired the argument further. The objection to the examination system was explained to be not only that it would sever architecture from the other arts, but that it would also give the training of architects an entirely wrong bias towards business and theory. The proposals of the RIBA and its allies to allow architects to practise only after examination, would, the authors believed, actually reduce standards of design and competence for 'if he cannot properly direct the execution of his design, discriminate between good and bad materials, and judge of the qualities of workmanship, [no-one] has claim to be looked on as an architect however much he knows of law, surveying, "business" and all the routine of professional practice'.[7]

The objectors to the proposed law had nothing against formal architectural education. Indeed Jackson and Shaw both taught in the Royal Academy Schools, and the men of Lethaby's generation attended classes there or at the Architectural Association. Shaw wrote to a friend, 'by the time they have worked in their respective offices from 9.30 to 5.30, and then three days a week from 6 to 8 in the schools, getting home about 9, you could hardly expect them to throw themselves with much ardour into the study of "descriptive geometry applied to scientific masonry"'.[8]

In the end, the breach between the RIBA and the protagonists of architecture as an art (and craft) was largely healed when, in 1906, the RIBA set up a board of inspection for schools (on principles agreed by the two sides) and encouraged design work in school studios.[9] But for Shaw, there was no forgiveness and, after an early resignation from the Institute, he twice turned down the Royal Gold Medal for architecture which was (and is) in the RIBA's gift.*

Back in 1883, after Macartney and Horsley had got their answer from Shaw, the Five canvassed their friends and acquaintances and, at eight o'clock on 8 January 1884, 21 architects, artists and designers met in the Board Room of the Charing Cross Hotel under the chairmanship of John Belcher (1841-1913), an architect of the generation between Shaw and his clerks. As well as the Five, the meeting included architects such as John Dando Sedding (1838-1891) who, like Shaw, had been with Street, and Basil Champneys (1842-1920), another late Gothic Revival architect. There were painters, Alfred Parsons and J. McLure Hamilton, sculptors Hamo Thornycroft and Blackall Simonds and one designer, Lewis F. Day.**

The meeting agreed to set up a society which should consist of 'Handicraftsmen and Designers in the Arts' aimed at reuniting the arts and crafts. There was a good deal of controversy about whether the society should seek publicity, with Macartney and Ernest Newton calling for a series of public exhibitions. Lethaby was vehement for 'the institution of a National Gallery of Representative Modern Painting and Sculpture'. But Prior and Horsley carried the day with the motion that 'at present the proposed Society shall not aim at publicity'. It was a temporary proviso of great permanence: through its period of influence in the decades around the turn of the century to today, the society has always shunned publicity.

By the end of 1884 the society had a name – the Art Workers' Guild – and had agreed to meet for practical demonstrations of craft techniques, discussions and for small private exhibitions. Of its first 55 members, 26 were painters, four sculptors, 11 craftsmen and 15 architects.† It was a strange blend of academic artists with revolutionary architects and designers, between whom the only link was Ruskin.

*On the first occasion, the only previous refusee had been Ruskin, and the wits remarked that the one 'had turned it down because he was not an architect, the other because he was'.[10]

**The last two, with Sedding, and Walter Crane (the illustrator) belonged to a group called 'the Fifteen' who had been meeting since 1880 in each other's houses to discuss papers on the decorative arts.

†These figures – and total – are Prior's.

John Brett. 'The Stonebreaker' (1857-58). Ruskin's call for truth to nature, faithfully followed by painter members of the Art Workers' Guild, conflicted with his axioms on changefulness and savageness, followed by the architects and craftsmen

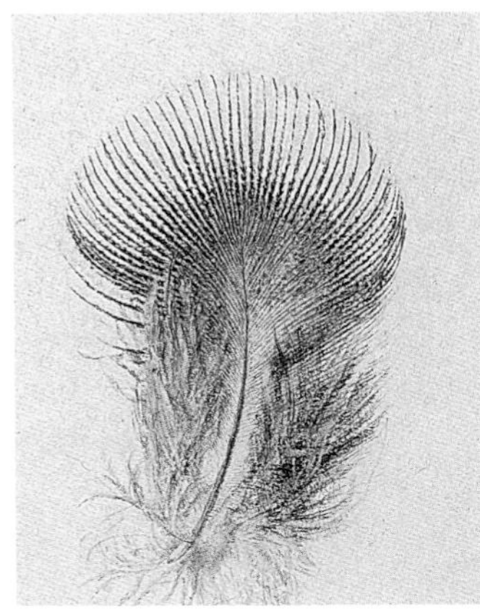

Ruskin. Watercolour of a peacock's feather (1875). In his own graphic work, Ruskin could conjure a sense of magic realism

Ruskin had called for a new relationship between designer and craftsman with the craftsman's mistakes being welcomed as a sign of honesty. But, virtually simultaneously, he had demanded the most scrupulous naturalism in painting and sculpture: 'no artist [can] be graceful, imaginative or original, unless he be truthful'.[11] The marriage between Ruskin's theories of architecture and painting attempted by the Art Workers' Guild created confusions that were never resolved.

A much more straightforward realization of Ruskin's Gothic principles had been proposed a couple of years before by Arthur Heygate Mackmurdo (1851-1942), an architect of the same generation as the Five but from a completely different background.

Arthur Heygate Mackmurdo. Writing table (1886): one of the products of the Century Guild

Mackmurdo, the son of a wealthy chemical manufacturer, trained under T. Chatfield Clarke but left in 1869, 'as ignorant of architecture as when I entered this architect's office'.[12] He persuaded James Brooks, whose Gothic Revival churches he had admired when involved in social work in East London, to take him as an assistant. Brooks was as hard a taskmaster as Street and designed 'every single incidental object and ornament', but there were 'constant failures in getting these designs carried out with any degree of artistic sympathy' which 'well nigh drove the man mad'.

'I realized that in the same way I should suffer did I not build a bridge to overreach the void. I must become personally acquainted with the technique of those arts most naturally acquainted with architecture. Some knowledge might enable me to design with that technical propriety essential for the complete marriage of the imagination and the material.'[13]

Mackmurdo's determination to achieve the consummation of design and craft so compellingly urged in 'The Nature of Gothic' must have been reinforced by a trip to Italy with Ruskin himself in 1874, after which Mackmurdo stayed on to study in Florence. Travelling with the arch-priest of the Gothic had a strange effect on Mackmurdo. He returned with a strong taste for the Italian Renaissance which he never abandoned, and the conflict between the two ideals frequently doomed Mackmurdo's architecture to quirky mediocrity; but his allegiance to Ruskinian architectural principles bore far more impressive fruit.

After he returned from Italy, Mackmurdo taught with Ruskin at the Working Men's College. In 1882, he started the Century Guild of Artists, 'to render all branches of art the sphere no longer of the tradesman but of the artist'. He had previously schooled himself in the 'technique of modelling and carving, trying my hand at some ornamental stonework for the first house I built. I learned to do repoussé work in brass and mastered sufficiently the elements of embroidery to enable me to design for this art. Under a skilful cabinet maker, I learnt enough about materials and constructive processes to enable me to design pieces of furniture, with one or two of which I took a hand in making'.[14] He had become the perfect Ruskinian architect, capable of designing with true understanding of craft.

But even this formidable combination of skills was not enough, and he decided that for the execution of design 'which I was not capable of' he must attract 'young men who were already working in the applied arts'. The Century Guild was founded by Mackmurdo, aged 31, and Selwyn Image, 33, designer of stained glass, book illustrations and embroidery. They were joined by the 18 year old Herbert Horne (later to become architect, typographer and biographer of Botticelli), Clement Heaton, a stained glass artist and Benjamin Creswick whom Gillian Naylor describes as 'the self-taught sculptor who as a boy had worked in a Sheffield knife factory'.[15] Designer Heywood Sumner was also associated with the Guild, and William de Morgan, already established as a distinguished ceramicist, was said offhandedly by Mackmurdo to have 'assisted me by executing my designs for tile work'. Workshops were set up for metal work and furniture and, in 1884, the Guild contributed a complete music room to the Health Exhibition in London. The same room, with small variations, was seen at the Liverpool International Exhibition of 1886 and the Manchester Jubilee show of 1887.

The room was distinguished by thin columns capped by a series of wafer-thin squares, one of Mackmurdo's hallmarks. Another was the intertwined forms of vegetation fretted into the backs of chairs and the brackets of shelves and printed on wallpapers and fabrics. The sinuous motifs had some influence on the Arts and Crafts work – particularly on Voysey's early textile designs. But most members of the movement preferred stiffer patterns; Mackmurdo's interlaced curves are supposed to have had a formative influence on Art Nouveau, the Continental contemporary of Arts and Crafts.*

Mackmurdo's thin square-topped columns had more influence; Voysey adopted them in his furniture and, through him, they were picked up by Mackintosh. Mackmurdo used similar elongated effects in his most original architecture: they appear for instance in his curious house, 8 Private Road, Enfield (1883). The building is in a stripped Classical style but in Mackmurdo's masterpiece, 25 Cadogan Gardens, London (1899), they are used with great delicacy in a sort of elegant Queen Anne style which is neither Classical nor Gothic. Mackmurdo's last buildings, for instance his own house Great Ruffins in Essex (1904), are in a complicated and clumsy Classicism – sadly disappointing after such an extraordinarily promising beginning.

In 1884, the Century Guild had started *The Hobby Horse*, a magazine devoted to a revival of arts and crafts which, itself, did much to re-awaken the art of printing. The first issue was edited by Mackmurdo with woodcut illustrations involving curved plant forms designed by Image and Horne cut by Arthur Burgess. Image and Horne took the editorial chair in later editions.

The magazine was intended by Mackmurdo to publicize Ruskinian ideals of design and production, and its early editions are studded with articles by a carefully chosen cast of nineteenth-century progressives: Ford Madox Brown, the Rossettis, May Morris (William's embroiderer daughter), Matthew Arnold, G. F. Watts and Oscar

Selwyn Image. Frontispiece of *The Hobby Horse* (1886), the Century Guild's magazine: proto Art Nouveau squirm?

Mackmurdo. Century Guild stand at the Liverpool Exhibition of 1886: the thin square finials on the columns influenced Voysey and Mackintosh

*Northern architects had been bidden to eschew the relaxed, sinuous line by Ruskin, one of whose definitions of Gothic was *rigidity*: 'the Gothic ornament stands out in prickly independence and frosty fortitude, jutting into crotchets, and freezing into pinnacles...alternately thorny, bossy, and bristly, or writhed into every form of nervous entanglement; but, even when most graceful, never for an instant languid, always quickset: erring, if at all, ever on the side of brusquerie'.[16] But Ruskin warned against excessive rigidity.

Mackmurdo.
8 Private Road, Enfield, Middlesex (1883): early abstracted Classicism

Wilde. Whatever the direct impact of the words (which seems to have been little), the image of the magazine was, according to Mackmurdo, so powerful that it inspired William Morris to begin printing and set up the Kelmscott Press.

The Century Guild was a commercial venture, rather like the Morris Firm, and a different kind of association from the Art Workers' Guild in which architect Edward Warren (Guild Master in 1913) explained that 'we neither seek public recognition, nor try to teach the world, nor even, definitely to teach each other; yet we are not without aims. Each member learns from each'.[17]

T. G. Jackson remembered the AWG's evening meetings: 'Morris once giving us an evening on paper-making, and bringing his paper-maker, Bachelor, who made a sheet for us in the room, showing how by a dextrous handshake, difficult to acquire and sometimes, strange to say, lost again, the workman secures that interlacing of the linen fibres which makes the durable hand-made article...The great feature of these evenings were the demonstrations by which the papers were illustrated. When enamelling was the subject there was a gas-stove in the room and enamels were prepared and burned. When plaster work was under discussion modelling and casting were going on before our eyes. I remember reading a paper on Intarsiatura, which was afterwards published, and showing a large number of tracings from old examples and also having one of Bessant's men cutting out and mounting veneers in the room. We also had exhibitions of all kinds of art and for some years an annual display of the members' own work in various crafts. This was superseded by the Arts and Crafts Exhibition which grew out of the Guild'.[18]

C. R. Ashbee recalled less formal evenings. At one of these in the '90s, the Guild 'held a mock trial, Mrs Grundy *v* the AWG. Mrs Grundy was indicting the Society for indecency and for flaunting Art in divers colours in the Voysey manner – Prior was Council for the Defence; Selwyn Image for the Prosecution – Voysey himself was Mrs Grundy and Cecil Brewer was her little boy...Cecil with his cheeks rouged, with short white stockings and pantaloons sat on a cornice in the Hall at Cliffords Inn sucking oranges with the peel of which he occasionally pelted his friends, and as he dangled a pair of long spindly legs he shouted mimic childish satire in his high pitched voice'.[19]

Such behaviour was not the only reason why the Guild was reluctant to appear in public. There were fundamental differences between members. In 1891, Mackmurdo (who had joined in 1888) tried to get the Guild to take corporate action against decorations being undertaken in St Paul's. The trouble was that the scheme was being carried out by painter W. B. Richmond, Master of the Guild for that year. Two contradictory Guild resolutions were sent to the Dean, and, to avoid similar embarrassments, the Guild's rules on public action were gradually tightened.

As early as 1885, members of the Art Workers' Guild who believed in a Ruskinian fusion of art and craft realised that a new organization which did not include the academic painters and sculptors was needed if the message was to be carried to the public. W.A.S. Benson, metal

Mackmurdo. 25 Cadogan Gardens, London (1899): his most successful urban building

worker and cabinet maker, and one of the members of the Guild, produced a scheme for the 'Combined Arts'. This took shape as the Arts and Crafts Exhibition Society which held its founding show in autumn 1888, when the term 'Arts and Crafts' (reputedly coined by bookbinder T. J. Cobden-Sanderson) first entered general currency.

The Society quickly collected the progressive element of the Art Workers' Guild and attracted new blood, some of which was transfused back into the Guild, for relations between the two associations were cordial and the membership overlapped (for instance, Walter Crane was simultaneously Master of the Guild and President of the Society in 1888). Most notable among the new recruits was William Morris himself, who, after doubts about the financial success of the Society, threw himself into the project. (He was elected to the Art Workers' Guild at the same meeting as Mackmurdo on 2 November 1888.) By the early 1890s, the Society combined the talents of the Five and their group, Mackmurdo's Century Guild people and Morris's circle of Pre-Raphaelites (including non-academic painters like Holman Hunt and Ford Madox Brown) and a large number of craftsmen. The only obvious omissions from this extraordinarily rich gathering were Shaw, Ruskin (who was by then going mad, and was not a designer), and Webb, who though he faithfully soldiered through the nightmare maze of late nineteenth-century Socialist associations with Morris, was congenitally anti-corporate.*

*Both Shaw and Webb's work was exhibited in the shows though.

The Society's first exhibition brought a very favourable notice from *The Builder* which reported that 'it represents the views and tastes of a sect; but the amount of beauty and variety in the work exhibited says a great deal for the talent and artistic feeling in the ranks of the sect, and it is impossible to go over it without reflecting what real progress has been made in decorative design during the last quarter of a century.

'Twenty-five years ago, such an exhibition as this – so full of fine colour and outline, and so devoid of anything which can be regarded as vulgar, or in bad taste, would have been impossible.'[20] The Society's shows (held at the New Gallery, Regent Street) were not simply exhibitions of work but included lectures and demonstrations as well; in every sense, it was an extension of the Guild.

Cobden-Sanderson remembered 'William Morris, on a raised platform, surrounded by products of the loom, at work on a model loom specially constructed from his design...to show how the wools were inwrought, and the visions of his brain fixed in colour and in form; Walter Crane, backed by a great black board, wiped clean alas! when one would have had it for ever still adorned by the spontaneous creations of his inexhaustible brain...Selwyn Image...with sweet reasonableness depicting...the bright new Jerusalem; Lethaby entrancing us with the cities which crowned the hills of Europe'.[21]

The Society's aims were expressed in a series of papers, many of which had previously been published in its catalogues, collected in 1893 as a small, stout book edited by Morris. His introduction set the

Above: J.D. Sedding and Henry Wilson. Holy Trinity Church, Sloane Street, London (from 1888), detail of rail
Right: Detail of entrance door to choir room

theme: 'we can expect no *general* impulse towards the fine arts till civilization has been transformed into some other condition of life...Our business as artists [is] to supply the lack of tradition by diligently cultivating in ourselves the sense of beauty,...skill of hand, and niceness of observation, without which only a *makeshift* of art can be got'. The Society's exhibitors, he believed, showed that 'there is still a minority with a good deal of life in it which is not content with what is called utilitarianism'; they called attention to that 'most important side of art, the decoration of utilities by furnishing them with genuine artistic finish in place of trade finish'.[22]

Morris's contribution to the first Arts and Crafts Exhibition Society's exhibition was hailed by *Today*, the Fabian magazine, as one of his 'best services to Socialism'.[23] But by 1893 he was a tired man with only three years of crowded life left. His somewhat bathetic conclusion was expanded by Walter Crane in sentiments which rivalled those of Morris at his height in an essay 'On the Revival of Design and Handicraft': 'The movement...represents in some sense a revolt against the hard mechanical conventional life and its insensibility to beauty (quite another thing to ornament). It is a protest against that so-called industrial progress which produces shoddy wares, the cheapness of which is paid for by the lives of their producers and the degradation of their users. It is a protest against the turning of men into machines, against artificial distinctions in art, and against making the immediate market value, or possibility of profit, the chief test of artistic merit. It also advances the claim of all and each to the common possession of beauty in things common and familiar'.[24]

Industrialization was reluctantly accepted by Crane, but, 'we have reached the *reductio ad absurdum* of an impersonal artist or craftsman trying to produce things of beauty for an impersonal and unknown public...Under such conditions it is hardly surprising that the arts of design should have declined'.[25] The aim of the Society's exhibitions was to break this vicious circle. 'At present, indeed, an exhibition may be said to be but a necessary evil; but it is the only means of obtaining a standard, and giving publicity to the works of Designer and Craftsman.'[26] And it asserted 'the principle of the essential unity and interdependence of the arts'.[27]

This ferment of Arts and Crafts activity quickly had results in buildings, one of the first and most magnificent of which was Holy Trinity, Sloane Street, Chelsea (1888 on), by John Dando Sedding (1838-1891), finished by his pupil Henry Wilson. Sedding had worked in Street's office with Webb and Shaw and was a very early member of the Guild and the Society. Horsley commented that the two associations 'were the means of bringing Mr Sedding into touch with many artists and prompted him to gather round him to help him in his last work, the great church of the Holy Trinity in Upper Chelsea, some of the foremost craftsmen of the day'.[28] The most important artists (apart from Sedding and Wilson) were all members of both associations: Harry Bates, sculptor (relief of Entombment on the altar); F. W. Pomeroy, sculptor (chancel stalls and screen); Nelson Dawson, metal

Burne-Jones's east window glass in John Dando Sedding's Holy Trinity Church, Sloane Street, London (1888-90). Made by Morris and Company

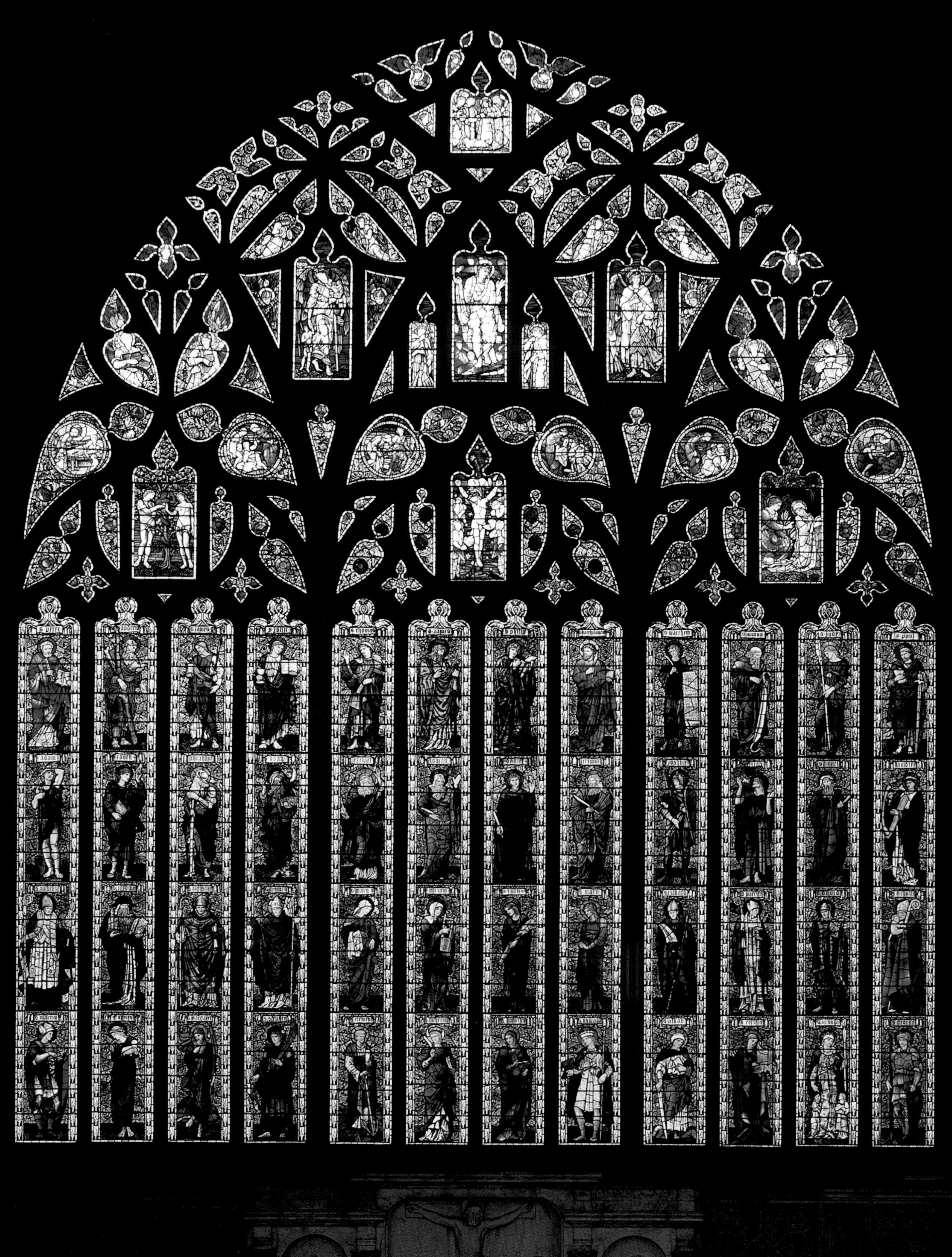

Sedding. Rood Screen, St Mary's Church, Stamford, Lincolnshire. Perspective by A.H. Powell

worker (who made Wilson's screens); and Burne-Jones (a member of the Guild fleetingly and an early exhibitor at the Society).

Those who visit the church now, expecting to be encrusted with Arts and Crafts gems, are initially disappointed. Of the thousands who pass it every day, few must notice its recessed dusky brick facade in which two thin towers frame a giant clear glass window which is contained by an ogee arch. The only relief is a certain luxuriance in the tracery of the window and a jolly, almost jangling, fussiness in the stone strap-work above the top of the arch and in the stone frills at the top of the towers.

Inside, the first impression is of equal austerity. The nave and chancel are formed into one great room, wide and high and very light from the mighty west window. The pale stone columns soar towards the vaults* with scarcely a break, only corbelled angels where, in traditional Gothic, the capitals would be. The simplicity is due to lack of money and to Sedding's early death (the church was started only a couple of years before). For instance, a Burne-Jones frieze which was to have run between the arcade and clerestory was never executed. Nor was the banded masonry Sedding originally intended for the nave and aisles. But Gerald Horsley's perspective of the design shows that Sedding's intention was to create a simple big well-lit space in which the plain structure dominated and knit together the contributions of individual artists – the effect we get today.

Throughout the '90s, Arts and Crafts artists contributed to the church – wherever you look, the details are exquisite. Burne-Jones designed (and the Morris Firm made) the east window with panel after panel of elegant Pre-Raphaelite saints. Richmond was responsible for the windows of the north aisle and Christopher Whall those of the south with their linear naturalistic scenes above abstract chevrons of coloured glass, equal to anything produced by Mackintosh or Wright in the same period (1904-23). Pomeroy did the angels on the chancel columns. Sedding and Wilson as well as Dawson were responsible for the metal work – which ranges from delicate, Italianate tracery in the chancel gates (by Sedding) to robust, heraldic gilded strap-work in the organ screen (by Wilson and Dawson).

Of course, the whole effect is Gothic – but of a special kind. It was stripped to its structural essentials. The carefully placed ornament was not executed by ordinary craftsmen, as it should have been according to the theories of Pugin, Ruskin and Morris, but by fellow members of the Guild and of the Exhibition Society, who were enlightened and agreeable enough to be trustworthy and avoid the potential catastrophes of real Ruskinian savageness.

Sedding at Holy Trinity got as near to resolving the Puginian paradox as any Arts and Crafts architect. The church was a precursor of many simple yet rich, rather introverted Arts and Crafts ecclesiastical buildings built in the two decades around the turn of the century.

*Rebuilt after destruction in the Second World War.

1 *Prior, E. S. 'The Origins of the Guild', lecture to the Guild, 6 December 1895. Printed in H. J. L. J. Massé* The Art Workers' Guild 1884-1934, *Oxford, 1935, p6.*
2 *Lethaby, W. R.* Philip Webb and His Work, op cit, *p75.*
3 *Prior* op cit, *p7.*
4 Ibid.
5 Ibid.
6 The Times *3.3.1891, quoted in* Architecture, a Profession or an Art, *eds Shaw, R. N. and Jackson, T. G., John Murray, London, 1892, ppxxxiii-xxxiv.*
7 *Shaw, R. N. and Jackson, T. G. ibid, p7.*
8 *Saint, A.* Richard Norman Shaw, *Yale University Press, New Haven and London, 1976, p316.*
The quotation is from a letter from Shaw to Frederic Eaton 9.11.90.
9 *The development of the controversy is discussed in detail in my 'Profession or Art' in* The Architectural Review, *Vol CLXXXV, 1989, pp59-66.*
10 *Saint* op cit, *p318.*
11 *Ruskin, John* Modern Painters, *Vol I, in Cook and Wedderburn,* Complete Works, op cit, *Vol III, p138.*
12 *Mackmurdo, A. H.* History of the Arts and Crafts Movement, *typescript in William Morris Museum, Walthamstow, chapter VIII.*
13 Ibid.
14 Ibid.
15 *Naylor, Gillian* The Arts and Crafts Movement, op cit, *p117.*
16 *Ruskin, John* The Stones of Venice, *Vol II, Smith Elder, London, 1853, p204.*
17 *In Massé* op cit, *p4.*
18 *Jackson, T. G.* Recollections, *ed Basil H. Jackson, Oxford, 1950, p218.*
19 *Ashbee, C. R.* Memoirs, *typescript in the Victoria and Albert Museum library, Vol II, p59.*
20 The Builder, *Vol LV, 1888, p241.*
21 *Cobden-Sanderson, J. T.* The Arts and Crafts Movement, *Hammersmith Publishing Society, London, 1905, p17.*
22 Arts and Crafts Essays *by members of the Arts and Crafts Exhibition Society, Rivington Percival & Co, London, 1893, pxii.*
23 *Quoted in Thompson, E. P.* William Morris, op cit, *p540.*
24 *Crane, W. 'Of the Revival of Design and Handicraft', in* Arts and Crafts Essays, op cit, *p12.*
25 Ibid, *p10.*
26 Ibid.
27 Ibid.
28 *Horsley, G. C. 'The Unity of Art', in Shaw, R. N. and Jackson, T. G. (eds)* op cit, *p202.*

The guide

6

Among all the intense talk of Art and Beauty in the Guild and the Exhibition Society, no one seems to have had much time to think out what the words meant. William Richard Lethaby (1857-1931) set himself the task of producing definitions for the late nineteenth century.

In the summer of 1879, Norman Shaw went into his assistants flourishing a copy of *Building News* in which some of Lethaby's drawings had appeared, asking 'What do you think of this? I am going to write and ask him to come here'.[1] Shaw was taking a gamble: up to then Lethaby had spent his whole life in the provinces and had no academic training of any kind.

He was the son of a Barnstaple frame maker and was apprenticed to a local man, Alexander Lauder, painter turned architect, who must have had much influence on Lethaby's early years, for Lauder was an inventor of new technical devices such as ventilators and drainage systems, as well as being a vigorous artist craftsman who, as his grandson recalled, 'would decorate many of the houses he built with huge sgraffito murals, terracotta friezes and high-relief ceramic tiles, all carved and modelled with his own hand'.[2] And 'he used to insist that all the men working on his own buildings should have an understanding of one another's craft, so that each might feel that he was building a house and not just practising carpentry, bricklaying or plumbing'.[3]

Leaving Lauder, Lethaby worked briefly in Derby and Leicester before entering the Shaw office at 21. It was another world: the big, fashionable metropolitan practice in which older, university educated men like Edward Prior and Mervyn Macartney were at home. The shock must have increased Lethaby's natural diffidence and modesty, but in a very short time he was a leader in the larking which so surprised Robert Weir Schultz when he joined the firm in the early 1880s after apprenticeship in the dour Glasgow office of Rowand Anderson.[4] One singularly dull afternoon Shaw and Lethaby held a cricket match in the office with T-squares and an india rubber;[5] it was a very different place from Shaw's own nursery in Street's office.

W.R. Lethaby. High Coxlease, Lyndhurst, Hampshire (1900-01)

But it was Lethaby's design talent that made him Shaw's chief clerk – and perhaps more: on one occasion an acquaintance referred to Lethaby as Shaw's pupil, '"No", said Shaw, "on the contrary it is I who am Lethaby's pupil"'.[6]

For all his prolific artistic talent, it was as a teacher that Lethaby made his impact. In *Architecture, Mysticism and Myth* published in 1891, two years after he had left Shaw, Lethaby set out to ask 'what...are the ultimate facts behind all architecture which has [sic] given it form? Mainly three: *First*, the similar needs and desires of men; *secondly* on the side of structure, the necessities imposed by materials, and the physical laws of their erection and combination; and *thirdly* on the side of style, nature. It is of this last that I propose to write'.[7]

In *Cosmos* (Lethaby's nickname for the book), he expanded Ruskin's concept of 'naturalism' and put it forward as the origin of style in architecture: 'if we trace the artistic forms of things, made by man, to their origin, we find a direct imitation of nature'.[8] From a vast magpie's nest of myths drawn from peoples as different as the

Byzantines and the Abyssinians, the Chinese and the Incas, Lethaby pulled out what he believed to be the guiding principles of symbolism and form of all previous architecture, for instance the sun as the sign of going out and coming in, 'pavements like the sea' and 'ceilings like the sky'.

But Lethaby was quite clear that man's past perceptions of the macrocosmos should not be a guide to the future of architecture. The high architectures of past ages were the products of tyranny, 'each stone cemented in the blood of a human creature...such an architecture is not for us, nor for the future.

'What then will this art of the future be? The message will still be of nature and man, of order and beauty, but all will be sweetness, simplicity and freedom, confidence and light; the other is past, and well is it, for its aim was to crush life: the new, the future is to aid life and to train it "so that beauty may flow into the soul like a breeze".'[9]

Lethaby. Window, Church of St John the Baptist, Symondsbury, Dorset (early 1880s). An example of Lethaby's early design work. Prior designed the tracery, Lethaby the glass

This vision is virtually identical to that of *News from Nowhere* (first published in instalments in the *Commonweal* the year before). By the early '90s Lethaby was very much under the influence of Morris and Webb and was drawing away from Shaw, who was by then becoming increasingly formal and Classical.

In his earliest years as a practitioner in his own right, Lethaby filled in his time and augmented his income by making drawings and designs for Morris & Co.[10] And his rooms were near to Webb's in Gray's Inn. Lethaby had met Morris and Webb through SPAB and, while still in Shaw's office, had become converted to their view of society. Shaw distrusted Morris whom he regarded as 'just a tradesman, whose only object was to make money, and as for his Socialism, that was just a pose. He thought that instead of producing expensive textiles and wallpapers...Morris as a Socialist should devote himself to the manufacture of cheap chests of drawers and wallpapers at 10½d a piece'.[11] But for Lethaby's socialism, Shaw had a good-humoured tolerance; the father of one of his pupils with whom Lethaby had agreed to go on a sketching tour 'rushed up to see Shaw in a great state: "I hear my boy is going sketching with a socialist", to which Shaw replied, "he's perfectly harmless, I assure you, perfectly harmless"'.[12]

Lethaby's architecture must also have seemed harmless to Shaw, for the first building Lethaby completed by himself, Avon Tyrrell near Christchurch, Hampshire (the commission was Shaw's setting-up present), is a very Shavian house. Completed in 1891, its main rooms face south and are divided from the entrance and servants' quarters by a long internal corridor running from east to west, which is intersected at right angles by a huge hall that cuts across the house from north to south – in essence very similar to some of Shaw's large country house plans of the 1880s. Similarly Shavian are the great mullioned windows of the hall next to the entrance and the three Queen Anne bay windows on the south front. These are not unlike the oriel windows in Shaw's own house with leaded lights, timber frames, a curved transom over the centre and bands of moulded plasterwork between the glazed areas (now replaced at Avon Tyrrell by tiles). But at the top of the same elevation is a row of four projecting gables, not so very different from those which Lethaby's neighbour Webb was designing for

Lethaby. Avon Tyrrell, Hampshire (completed 1891), south front: almost wilfully irregular

Detail of Avon Tyrrell chimney with its use of local materials

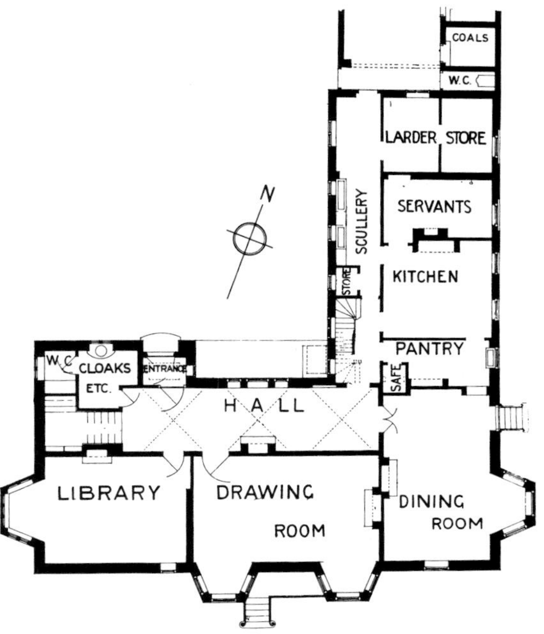

Above: Lethaby. The Hurst, Four Oaks, Sutton Coldfield, Warwickshire (1893-94, now demolished)
Right: Ground floor one-room-and-a-corridor plan

Standen in the same years. With what seems conscious idiosyncrasy, Lethaby placed the bays, not centrally under the gables, but – almost yet not quite – under the valleys between them, emphasizing the difference between the Webbian top-hamper and the Shavian base. The north (entrance) front is much less formal, with windows of all sizes and shapes arranged over a series of receding planes closely mirroring the functions within.

Lethaby's next house, the Hurst, at Four Oaks, Sutton Coldfield, near Birmingham, was much smaller, but it also had many Queen Anne motifs. For instance, on the south front, two large bays with segmentally headed sash windows rose up from the drawing room through the eaves of the roof. But the plan was remarkably different, much more like Webb's Red House – L-shaped and one-room-and-a-corridor deep, though the Hurst's hall was wide enough to use as a sitting room, unlike the comparatively narrow corridor at the Red House. Lethaby's client, Colonel Wilkinson, was plainly more fond of sun than Morris, for the Hurst's orientation was the reverse of the Red House, with the main rooms facing south and west. Sadly the effect of this orientation on the open space enclosed by the two wings cannot now be seen, for the house has been demolished. It was one of only six major buildings put up by Lethaby.*

His next commission was for another Birmingham businessman, Thomas Middlemore, who decided to retire to Hoy in the Orkneys. Melsetter House was completed in 1900. Its plan is a most sophisticated development of Webb's additive layout. Two thin Ls interlock in the living hall, and ingeniously incorporate, at half levels, the existing laird's house. The arrangement allows the main spaces – library, dining and drawing rooms – to obtain both the main views and sunlight from the south and west.[13] The exterior is as closely modelled on local tradition as even Webb would have wished, with white harled (roughcast) walls, high gables (crow-stepped and plain) and greenish Caithness flags on the steeply pitched roofs. (Orkney shares a tradition of building with the north-east coast of Scotland.) The fenestration, with bold stone surrounds to the small paned sash windows, resembles that of an eighteenth-century Scottish vernacular mansion, but with Ruskinian changefulness in its disposition.

May Morris (who, like William, was a friend of the Middlemores) described Melsetter as, 'a sort of fairy palace on the edge of the great northern seas, a wonderful place, this building which was remotely and romantically situated with its tapestries and its silken hangings and its carpets, which came from my father's workshop. It seemed like the embodiment of some of those fairy palaces of which my father wrote with great charm and dignity. But, for all its fineness and dignity, it was a place full of homeliness and the spirit of welcome, a very lovable place. And surely that is the test of an architect's genius: he built for home life as well as dignity'.[14]

Lethaby built several other works on Hoy for the Middlemores, including a shooting lodge on the east side of the island, a couple of

*Apart from those discussed in this chapter, there were the Eagle Insurance Company offices, Birmingham (chapter 11) and High Coxlease, a house near Lyndhurst, Hampshire (p64).

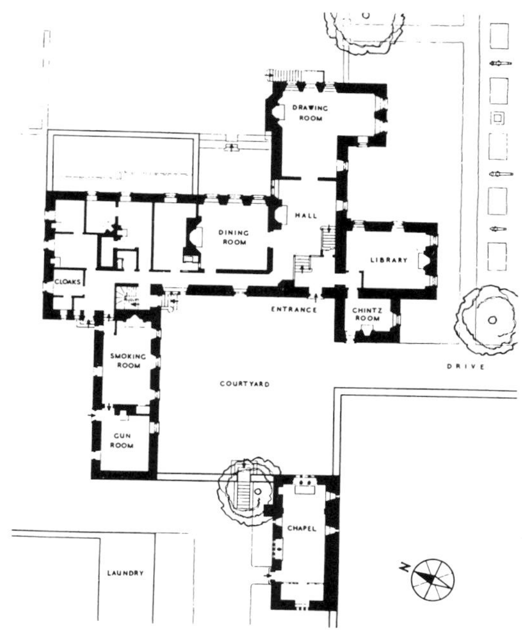

Above: Lethaby. Melsetter House, Hoy, Orkneys (completed 1900): extension and adaptation of existing farmhouse
Right: Ground floor plan

bridges and the chapel of SS Margaret and Colm, completed in 1900, part of the main complex. This is an extraordinary, intimate little building with a mass concrete roof covered with Caithness stone slates, supported on dressed rubble wall; windows are by Burne-Jones, Madox Brown and Christopher Whall.[15]

The chapel foreshadows Lethaby's last work, All Saints Church, Brockhampton in Herefordshire, and it is his most curious. Built during 1901 and 1902, it is constructed like no other church on earth. The thick walls are plain, of local red sandstone, and the nave roof is carried on high simple pointed stone arches that spring from just above floor level. But the curve of the roof is made of unreinforced concrete, which outside is covered by thatch dressed in the local domestic tradition. This stone, thatch, and concrete structure* is topped by a bell tower over the south porch, the upper half of which is clapboarded and capped by a pyramid covered in shingles. This is surprisingly taller than the square stone crossing tower, which, though it has dramatic effects on the interior, is not stressed as it would be in a traditional church. Presumably, Lethaby wished to emphasize the rituals of summons and assembly; as Peter Blundell Jones has pointed out,[16] the congregation walks past the bellringers in the porch, a gentle but clear moment of arrival and welcome.

Spatially, the church is like a miniature cathedral. The nave is rather dark, with triple square windows set in deep embrasures between each arch. The windows have clear leaded panes, so that if the sermon is dull, the congregation can look out onto God's creation. The space is slightly constricted and much intensified by the arch leading to the crossing tower that dramatically shoots light down onto the chancel, which is slightly raised from the nave. Beyond, at the east end, the sanctuary is raised by another small change in level so that the altar gently dominates the whole spatial composition under three lancet windows which symbolize the Trinity below the star of hope and faith. Simple though the building is externally (though quietly relieved by *Cosmos*-like symbolism), the interior is rich, with choir stalls carved in local flowers like bluebells and buttercups, Burne-Jones tapestries and Christopher Whall's stained glass.

The church is one of the greatest monuments of the Arts and Crafts movement, combining changefulness, savageness (craftsmen were given a good deal of freedom in the creation of decorative details), fidelity to place and structure with a mastery of space, light and occasion. Yet it nearly broke Lethaby, who had insisted on being master builder as well as architect. He used Randall Wells as site clerk who made several unauthorized changes during construction; costs overran and at one point the foundations started to move, a problem

*The mixture of concrete and thatch, bizarre as it seems at first, was not simply picturesque. As well as giving visual reminders of local buildings, the thatch was an excellent water-proofing material and, with the layer of breeze concrete into which the thatching irons were driven over the structural concrete, it provided very good thermal insulation. Combined with the high thermal mass of the concrete, the insulative thatch gave the roof properties (for instance slow response to sudden changes of external conditions, absence of condensation) that are still being pursued today: indeed a mixture of thatch and concrete would still be an excellent combination if thatching were not now so expensive. Thermally, the Brockhampton roof was one of the most sophisticated constructions of its day – and more so than many of our own.

Above: Lethaby. Melsetter House: split levels relate old and new parts of house

that Lethaby felt bound to rectify at his own expense. John Brandon-Jones says that 'So much responsibility was thrown on Lethaby himself that the strain brought him to the verge of a breakdown and he never repeated the experiment'.[17]

A parallel career had opened to Lethaby in 1896 when he was appointed first Principal of the London County Council's Central School of Arts and Crafts. Lethaby the teacher began to emerge. The school was described by Esther Wood shortly after it opened. Studios were open during the day but 'teaching is done entirely in the evenings...the students assemble in their various departments; each branch of study being open to men and women equally, with the exception of the life class for men. Some curious varieties of personality and character may be seen in almost every room. Young and middle-aged men, strong manual labourers, refined and scholarly-looking craftsmen, quiet, earnest girls and smart little lads scarcely out of their fourth standard, are gathered together round the tables and desks or thinking out their designs plodding steadily on at some set task'.[18]

This was the realization of Lethaby's ideal of a school for everyone involved in building, which he described in a 1904 essay on architectural education. 'The highly artificial separation of the present system is obviously most disastrous to progress in building, and I feel most strongly that up to a stage all who are to be engaged in building in any skilled capacity should meet in schools common to all.'[19] But what was progress in building? Where was that future that Lethaby left undefined at the end of *Cosmos*? Gradually Lethaby evolved the answer.

By 1896 he was a disciple of Morris, decreeing that 'beauty can only be brought back to common life by our doing common work in an interesting way'.[20] This thesis was gradually refined: 'All work of man bears the stamp of the spirit with which it was done but this stamp is not necessarily "ornament". The unadorned indeed can never stand as low as that which is falsely adorned in borrowed, brazen bedizenments. High utility and liberal convenience for the noble life are enough for architecture...Consider any of the great forms of life activity – seamanship, farming, housekeeping – can any-one say where utility ends and style, order, clearness, precision begin?'[21]

Utility and need for Lethaby were the key: 'there is...a brown-bread and dewy-morning ideal of beauty, and a late champagne-supper ideal. Who would say which was the right one were it not for Necessity's "You must"? We have to love the health ideal, or cease to exist'.[22] To fulfil this ideal in architecture, 'experiment must be brought back once more into the centre of architecture and architects must be trained as engineers are trained...The modern way of building must be flexible and vigorous, even smart and hard. We must give up designing the broken-down picturesque which is part of the ideal of make-believe'.[23] Yet innovative as the new architecture should be, 'no art that is only one man deep is worth much; it should be a thousand men deep. We cannot forget our historical knowledge, nor would we if we might. The important question is, can it be organized or must we continue to be betrayed by it? The only agreement that seems possible is

Melsetter House: local materials lovingly used

18
98

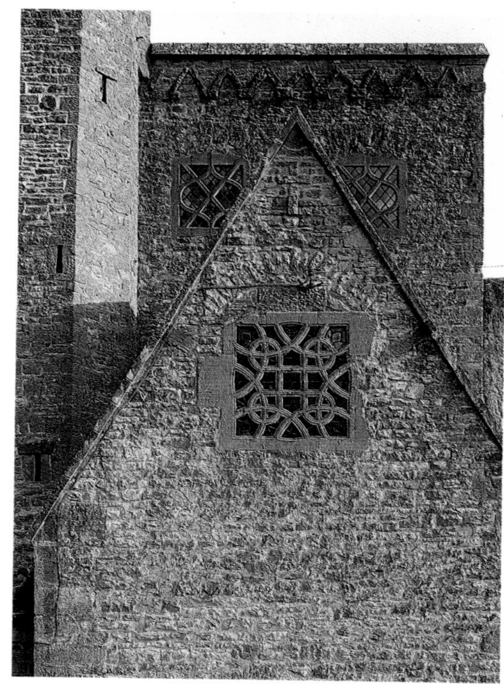

Lethaby. All Saints Church, Brockhampton (1901-02). East window and tower, a combination of rough local craftsmanship and sophisticated symbolism

agreement on a scientific basis, on an endeavour after perfect structural efficiency. If we could agree on this we need not trouble about beauty for that would take care of itself'.[24]

The thousand men had come to Lethaby's elbow when he led the cohorts of the Arts and Crafts movement to produce a design for the Liverpool Cathedral competition (1902-03). Lethaby, Henry Wilson, Halsley Ricardo, F. W. Troup and Weir Schultz were joined by sculptor Stirling Lee and Christopher Whall, the stained glass artist. The building was to consist of a gigantic aisled nave-and-choir, roofed by a series of concrete vaults folded together in a curved corrugated carapace. The walls were buttressed by a series of chapels surmounted by concrete semi-domes, and the whole composition was dominated by a stupendous, tapering detached campanile. If you ignore this entirely original feature, the effect is curiously Middle Eastern, and, as John Brandon-Jones has pointed out, it 'must have been based on the Byzantine studies made by Lethaby and Weir Schultz'.[25]

Lethaby. Concrete vault with stone ribs, Chapel, Melsetter (1900)

Lethaby later said of concrete that it 'is only a higher power of the Roman system of construction. If we could sweep away our fear that it is an inartistic material, and boldly build a railway station, a museum, or a cathedral, wide and simple, amply lighted, and call in our painters to finish the walls, we might be interested in building again almost at once'.[26] But the assessors of the competition, Shaw and Bodley, were not impressed, and the scheme was not even placed.

Liverpool Cathedral was Lethaby's last venture into designing buildings. He not only found himself in emotional difficulties organizing the work on Brockhampton as he believed it ought to be done, but he believed himself too ignorant to continue. 'It is absurd...that the writer should have been allowed to study cathedrals from Kirkwall to Rome and from Quimper to Constantinople; it would be far better to have an equivalent knowledge of steel and concrete construction.'[27]

The rest of his life was devoted to teaching at the Central School, then at the Royal College of Art, and to looking after Westminster Abbey, to which he was appointed surveyor in 1906, after which for

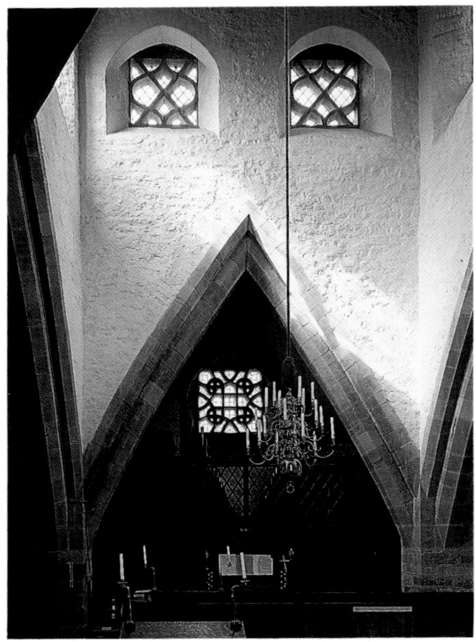

Lethaby. All Saints Church, Brockhampton
Left: looking towards altar through tower.
Below: looking west down concrete vaulted nave

20 years Lethaby looked 'upon myself here as the family butler'[28] and cared for the fabric according to the strictest SPAB principles.

It was writing rather than building that made him one of the most influential architects of the turn of the century. And it was through his essays that Lethaby, talented, kindly, erudite, persuasive, perceptive and forward-looking, yet always prepared to temporize, became one of the betrayers of the gospel of Ruskin and Morris. As he became more and more divorced from the realities of ordinary building, his theories became increasingly opposed to many of the original Arts and Crafts ideals. By 1915, perhaps because of the pressures of the War and the example of Germany's successful industrial use of some of these ideals, Lethaby was preaching that 'We must bring our new Chippendales, Flaxmans and Cranes into our industrial commerce'.[29] The Puginian paradox of the relationship between designer and craftsman was to be resolved firmly in favour of the designer who could harness the machine and make the craftsman an unnecessary part of the process.

Ideologically, Lethaby had removed one of the two basic objections to machines raised by Ruskin and Morris. For the Ruskinian objection to machine production of grotesque facsimiles of craftsmanship could be countered by Lethaby's argument that ornament was no longer necessary in ordinary building and, where it was needed, it would be a natural outcome of everyone living the good Arts and Crafts life. Yet Lethaby's 'brown-bread and dewy-morning' ideal could scarcely be enjoyed by factory hands, roused in the dark by the mill hooter and required to spend nine or 10 hours a day labouring intensely as appendages to machines. This was the reality of most industrial life in the first decades of this century and nowhere did Lethaby come to terms with the argument of Ruskin and Morris that minding a machine reduced the minder to slavery.

Certainly, he had an excuse, for, as the comprehensive historians of technology have written, 'scientific industry, even during the second half of the nineteenth century, did much to diminish danger, hardship and squalor'.[30] But the relationship of man and machine had not fundamentally changed.

To change that relationship, a revolution was necessary – either social (which Lethaby, socialist though he was, would not accept) or technological (which he could not foresee). His acceptance of the early twentieth-century industrial status quo was a reversal of his early ideals, in which a young architect would 'associate with himself, not 30 draftsmen in a back office (a number which I understand has [in 1892] been exceeded) but a group of associates and assistants on the building itself and in its decoration'.[31]

It is unfair to suggest that Lethaby was the Iscariot of the Arts and Crafts movement, for, being the most articulate of the generation which succeeded Morris, he provided a mirror to the development of the movement, and his later essays were the reflection of a revolution which had lost its impetus.

He had, after all, been one of the leaders of the movement: in setting up the associations, in carrying forward the messages of Ruskin and Morris, in producing innovative buildings, in methods of work

Lethaby. All Saints Church, Brockhampton, Herefordshire (built 1901-02): from south-west, with clapboarded bell tower on south porch and thatch above concrete over nave and chancel

Liverpool Cathedral competition design (1902-03), produced by a team of Arts and Crafts workers captained by Lethaby: unbuilt Arts and Crafts concrete manifesto

and teaching in generating a body of ideas which came nearest to being the movement's manifesto. His leadership was of the best, most natural kind.

On Lethaby's death, Alfred Powell recollected, 'he was about the jolliest companion anybody could dream of, always full of life. It seemed as though his five wits were multiplied by eight or 10, he had so much sensation, and his senses were all so continuously alive. It was that which made him so sympathetic to everybody; there was no kind of person he could not sympathize with'.[32] Mackail (Morris's biographer) recalled that Lethaby lived, 'not with his head in the clouds, but with his head in air which had something superterrestrial about it; and when he descended to the ordinary levels of earth he was often like someone who had strayed into darkness'.[33]

Lethaby lived long enough to know that the new architecture of the 1920s had no more achieved real functionalism and escaped from iconographic imperatives than had Pugin fully succeeded when he found in purest Gothic the answer to his search for a truly practical architecture. The Modern Movement, he said, was 'only another design humbug to pass off with a shrug – ye olde modernist style – we must have a style to copy – what funny stuff this art is'.[34]

Lethaby's life, for all its turns and twists, was totally devoted to art. On his grave is the epitaph 'love and labour are all', yet a truer memorial is perhaps to be found in the hall of the Art Workers' Guild, where Lethaby looks across the ranks of the Arts and Crafts movement to confront William Morris at the other side. Morris's shaggy majesty gazes at a rather sad Pooterish face, walrus moustached and close cropped, with deep-set, kindly thoughtful eyes. It is the confrontation of idealism and disillusion.

1 *Weir, Robert W. Schultz 'William Richard Lethaby', paper read before the Art Workers' Guild on 22 April 1932 and published by the Central School of Arts and Crafts in 1938. This architect's name is confusing. Before the First World War, he called himself Robert Weir Schultz, which he then changed to Robert Weir Schultz Weir.*
2 *Thomas, Brian* RIBA Journal, *Vol LXIV, 1957, p218.*
3 Ibid.
4 *Weir* op cit.
5 *Robert Shaw quoted in Saint, A.* Richard Norman Shaw, op cit, *p187.*
6 *Weir* op cit.
7 *Lethaby, W. R.* Architecture, Mysticism and Myth, *republished by The Architectural Press, London, 1974, p3.*
8 Ibid, *p4.*
9 Ibid, *p8.*
10 *Brandon-Jones, John* The RIBA Journal, *Vol LXIV, 1957, p220.*
11 *Blomfield, Sir Reginald* Richard Norman Shaw, *Batsford, London, 1940, p12. Blomfield is here paraphrasing notes by Robert Shaw, the son of R.N.S.*
12 *Weir* op cit.
13 *The plans were first published by John Brandon-Jones in* The AA Journal, *March 1949, pp168-169. Brandon-Jones, who was stationed in Orkney during the Second World War, gives a beautifully evocative description of the house. The most recent and extensive description of this remote building is Blundell Jones, Peter, 'Melsetter House',* The Architects' Journal, *Vol CXCII, 10 October 1990, pp36-56.*
14 *Morris, May, in* The RIBA Journal, *Vol XXXIX, 1932, p303. She was speaking at the memorial symposium in the year after Lethaby's death.*
15 *Rubens, Godfrey* William Richard Lethaby, his Life and Work 1857-1931, *Architectural Press, London, 1986, pp148-153.*
16 *Blundell Jones, Peter 'All Saints Brockhampton',* The Architects' Journal, *Vol CXCII, 15 August 1990, pp24-43. A detailed description which makes use of original drawings.*
17 *Brandon-Jones, John* The RIBA Journal, *Vol LXIV, 1957, p220.*
18 *Wood, Esther* The Architectural Review, *Vol II, 1897, p241.*
19 *Lethaby, W. R. 'Architectural Education',* The Architectural Review, *Vol XVI, 1904, p161.*
20 *Lethaby, W. R. 'Arts and the Function of Guilds', first published in* The Quest, *Birmingham 1896; reprinted in Lethaby, W. R.* Form in Civilization, *Oxford, 1957, p162.*
21 *Lethaby, W. R. 'Architecture as Form in Civilization' (1920), in* Form in Civilization, *op cit, p7.*
22 *Lethaby, W. R. 'What Shall We Call Beautiful?' Originally published in* Hibbert Journal, *1918; reprinted in* Form in Civilization, *op cit, p121.*
23 *Lethaby, W. R.* Architecture, *Williams and Norgate, London 1911. The quotation comes at the end of Lethaby's excellent succinct little history of architecture for laymen.*
24 Ibid, *p249.*
25 *Brandon-Jones, John* The RIBA Journal, *Vol LXIV, 1957, p220.*
26 *Lethaby, W. R.* Architecture, op cit, *p249.*
27 Ibid, *p247.*
28 *Quoted by Powell, Alfred, in* The Times Literary Supplement, *17 April 1973.*
29 *Lethaby, W. R. 'Design and Industry', an address delivered to the Design and Industries Association in 1915. Reprinted in* Form in Civilization, op cit, *p44.*
30 *Singer, Charles et al* A History of Technology, *Vol V, Oxford, 1970, pvii.*
31 *Lethaby, W. R. 'The Builder's Art and the Craftsman', in* Architecture, a Profession or an Art, *ed Shaw, R. N. and Jackson, T. G., John Murray, London, 1892, p168.*
32 *Powell, A. H.* The RIBA Journal, *Vol XXXIX, 1932, p311.*
33 *Mackail, J. W.* op cit, *p312.*
34 *Quoted in Macleod, Robert* Style and Society, *RIBA Publications, London, 1971, p67.*

Let there be a firmament
in the midst of the waters
AND·THE·EARTH·WERE·FINISHED
ON·THE·SEVENTH·DAY·GOD·ENDED·HIS

The explorer

7

There is a legend that when Lethaby was confronted by an irate woman client saying, 'I cannot see, Mr Lethaby, that you have done a single thing that I asked you to do', he replied, 'Well, you see, my first duty as an artist is to please myself'.[1] If even the diffident and mild mannered Lethaby could take such a high-handed aesthetic line, the lady could count herself lucky that she was not dealing with the much more fiercely independent Edward Schroder Prior (1852-1932), a co-founder of the Art Workers' Guild with Lethaby and perhaps the most brilliantly original of all Shaw's pupils.

At first sight, Prior appears to be a typical late Victorian hearty. A Harrovian and son of a barrister, he was a Cambridge blue (high jump, long jump, hurdles) and was amateur high jump champion before entering Shaw's office in 1874. There he joined in the horse-play with more than ordinary vigour. 'He could take off his trousers one day in the office because they were wet, or on another occasion he could tie up O'Neill, one of the dimmer pupils, in a brown paper parcel and leave him in the lobby.'[2]

The tough, bullying manner never left him: *The Architect and Building News* commented when he died, 'He could be something of a grizzly bear at times for he was pertinacious, and his opinion, once formed was hardly to be changed...Yet it was a kindly bear withal, that would emerge, honours divided, from a wordy warfare with a joyous twinkle in its eye; and for any small personal attention or service, it would be immensely grateful and appreciative'.[3] Inside the bear's skin was a scholar and artist. His books on Gothic architecture and sculpture, widely acclaimed in their day, helped him achieve the Slade Professorship of Fine Art in Cambridge in 1912, a post which he used to found the Cambridge school of architecture.

By then his creative life was virtually at an end. It had started 30 years earlier with a series of architectural essays in Norman Shaw's styles: Carr Manor in Meanwood, Leeds (1879-82), a remodelling of an original house, has in the ancillary buildings touches of Old English half-timbering and big plastered coved eaves a bit like those Shaw was using 15 years before; High Grove, Harrow (1880-81) is Queen Anne at its most formal, and the Red House, Harrow (1883-84) is an example of half-timbered Queen Anne.

Shaw had been right when he wrote to Prior's mother about Edward that 'it really does not matter when a man begins. He is certain to do but little for a year or two, barely perhaps making both ends meet, and the sooner he gets over this dull period the better...but once he gets a bit of a start, he won't want much help from anyone'.[4] Prior's start was at Carr Manor, but even at this early stage there is evidence of the mature architect. Shavian touches are kept to the stables and cottages. The main block is a many gabled, irregular composition in local stone, pierced by long rows of leaded windows divided by stone mullions. One of its sources is plainly Old English, but the dark stone severity is all West Riding – owing much to local seventeenth-century halls like those at Riddlesden and Sowerby. In this, Prior's earliest work

E.S. Prior. Sanctuary of St Andrew's Church, Roker, nr Sunderland (1906). Sky ceiling by Macdonald Gill (1927)

Prior. Carr Manor, Leeds, West Yorkshire (1879-82). Shaw with a dash of West Riding flavour in Prior's first major work

Prior. Pier Terrace elevation, West Bay, Dorset (1885). Local idioms and subtle geometry

(it seems to have been Shaw's setting-up commission), he showed a tremendous Puginian affection for local materials and techniques which distinguished all his later work.

In 1885, at West Bay, near Bridport, Dorset, Prior built Pier Terrace along one side of the harbour. He took up local themes: squared warm limestone rubble for the lower two storeys with, on the second floor and round the oriels of the first, slates cut to an almost (but not quite) hexagonal pattern which can be seen on many older buildings in the area. The whole is topped by a mansard of Roman tiles, under which the fenestration, at first appearing to be regular, moves up and down according to the dictates of slope and internal need.

Not very much later (1885-87), Prior was building the Henry Martyn Hall, Cambridge, an impeccably Gothic building but one which, again, showed much knowledge of local building techniques. Pugin would have been pleased with its string courses of ashlar separating broad bands of pebble, flint and rubble mixed higgledy-piggledy in the manner of Cambridgeshire churches. The stair in the turret is made visible by allowing its treads to emerge on the outside. It is a building of great savageness and changefulness in which the external effect is as much due to the craftsmen as the architect.

Prior, for all his belief in the individuality of the artist, was perhaps closer to Ruskin's ideal of the building designer than any other Arts and Crafts architect of the first generation. He made his position quite clear in 1901 when discussing the Liverpool Cathedral competition. He advocated that the client (the Church of England) should decide on the overall dimensions, lighting, access and furniture requirements and then the building should be produced by a team of craftsmen working together under the direction of an administrative ('planning') architect who, at all costs, must not design himself. For Prior believed that 'there are now no Gothic architects, but no Classic either – or any of other designation able to impress upon building that individuality of earnestness which the great architects of the nineteenth century achieved'.[5] An architect of some sort was necessary to cope with 'the complexities of modern life, the varied requirements of denser population, the by-laws of controlling authorities'.[6]

But he should make it his business only 'to find and quarry the best stone, make the best brick, forge the best iron, cut the best timber, so season and dress and build as wili make the best construction...Cannot an architect be found who will so consent to be builder without thought of design?' It is only what many would wish to be – what, whenever they have a chance many are.

'In this way, the full proportions of a great cathedral construction could be achieved, and then its painting, its glass, its wood and ironwork would follow, not laboriously and imperfectly calculated beforehand and imagined to be art, but in execution only trade production.'[7]

The design and making of the work would be left to 'masons skilled to work and lay stone, bricklayers to build, carpenters, plumbers and ironworkers expert in the crafts to make a building'.[8] Never, in any of his work, did Prior achieve this easy, direct relationship between architect and craftsman, so perhaps his Liverpool manifesto was not

Prior. Henry Martyn Hall, Cambridge (1885-87): changeful Gothic in local materials

supposed to apply fully to ordinary building but was particularly intended for a great cathedral where Prior, quoting Matthew Paris, urged that *'congregati sunt artifices'* – or at least they ought to be.

The highest flowering of architecture, Prior believed, happens when 'instead of art being the province of a sect, the whole people combines in the pursuit of beauty and becomes endowed with the faculties of artists'.[9] Yet in the imperfect late Victorian world, where this revolution had not yet occurred, Prior was totally opposed to the growing practice of 'professional' architects employing collective platoons of assistants who did the real work. In *Architecture, a Profession or an Art*, Prior's essay on 'The Profession and its Ghosts' was scathing about such architects, in whose practices the problems of keeping the organization running meant that 'little time can be left for even that directorate of architectural "designing" which is the ostensible groundwork of all this business...Pecksniffs go unabashed in these days'.[10]

'So the mechanical look of our architecture is readily explained. The world, by employing the professional architect, does not admit of Architecture being an art.'[11] The architect must be an artist (except when designing cathedrals) but Prior had nothing but contempt for the nineteenth-century concept of the artist: 'Our art is always the expression of strong individuality; so that each artist is a school of himself – with a rise, a flourish, perhaps a decadence – and then complete extinction: he can hand on no torch to his successor'.[12]

The way forward, for Prior, was not traditionalism. He was sure that 'the "styles" are dead...such things are gone by. The saviour of his art to the architect is no longer in knowledge but in experiment, in the devices of craftsmanship, in going back to the simple necessities of Building and finding in them the power of beauty'.[13]

Prior, the individual artist who wanted to be simply the chief supervisor of craftsmen, the traditionalist who believed the future lay in experiment, emerged as an integrated architect when he designed the Barn on a hill overlooking Exmouth in 1896.

The plan was revolutionary. Prior took the basic long, thin Arts and Crafts layout, one room and a corridor deep, and broke it like a chicken's leg, snapping back the two limbs to 90 degrees of each other. They are joined by the cartilage of the entrance hall at 45 degrees to each limb, and the knuckles, the drawing room and dining room, stick out on either side of the centre. The intentions were to obtain wide views of the sea from the principal rooms, to provide a sun trap in the angle between them and to reduce the amount of circulation space necessitated in a long thin plan by keeping the corridor on the inside of the angle. It is said by some historians[14] to have been modelled on Norman Shaw's Chesters (1891-93), a huge Classical house in Northumberland which has elements of an X-plan but which had (partly because it was a late great nineteenth-century palace) none of the virtues of prospect or economy which Prior achieved in the Barn.* Prior's butterfly plan was to have great influence in the next two decades.

*An equally probable source was a house by the French architect Hector Horeau in Avenue Road, near Prior's St John's Wood house. Built in 1856, it had two wings set at 45 degrees to the central irregular hexagon containing the drawing room and circulation spaces. The house (demolished in the 1950s) was published in *The Builder* in 1859.

Top: Prior. The Barn, Exmouth, Devon (designed 1896). The original thatch was burned and replaced by slate in 1905
Above: Detail of savage walls of sea-shore stone
Right: The butterfly plans

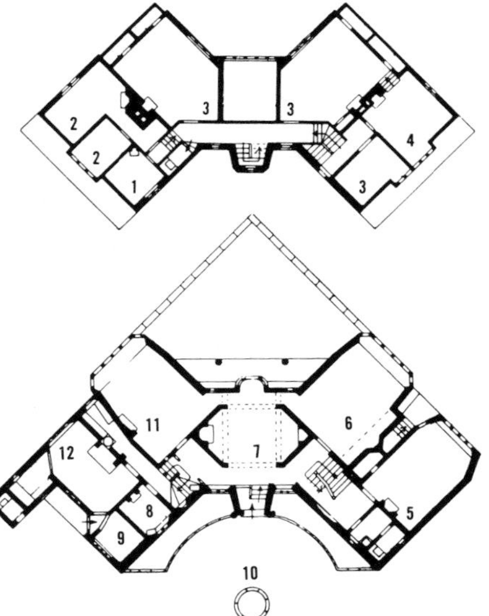

1: Bath
2: Maid's room
3: Bedroom
4: Dressing-room
5: Study
6: Drawing-room
7: Hall
8: Pantry
9: Scullery
10: Front drive
11: Dining-room
12: Kitchen

Externally, Prior expounded his beliefs in Puginian fidelity to place and Ruskinian savageness in a great, soft tea-cosy roof of local thatch supported by walls of local stone. Warm grey ashlar is mixed haphazardly with passages of red boulders and little arpeggios of sea pebbles, all combined to give a wonderfully varied texture that could never have been exactly specified by the architect but which must have come at least as much from the craftsman's sensibilities as from the drawing board. Sadly, there are no records of Prior's relationships with his masons, but letters from the local estate office show that Prior was fiercely living up to his ideal of the architect as specifier of good materials and was closely supervising the works from his father-in-law's rectory at Bridport.[15]

Prior, the experimental architect, tried two novel techniques at the Barn: a concrete first floor reinforced by tree trunks (an eminently sensible fireproofing and sound deadening technique in an area where timber was cheap) and, to obtain approval from the local council, he treated the thatch with an 'incombustible solution'. Neither was of much help when the Barn burnt down on 4 October 1905. It was re-roofed in slate and re-floored in timber, but the main lines of the house (now a private hotel) can still be seen; the rather run-of-the-mill Queen Anne fenestration was restored and the texture of the unique walls was unaffected.

Prior's next butterfly house, Kelling (now Home) Place (1903-05) near Holt in north Norfolk, was symmetrical not only at front and back but on the entrance side as well. Each of these symmetrical elevations faced an axially arranged garden. The house showed Prior in his most savage mood. It was built of solid concrete* faced with pebbles found on the site, zigzag patterns of thin tiles (showing their edges only) and, at the corners, cut local stone. The effect is aggressively restless, almost hiding the symmetrical formality of the plan and even overwhelming the horrid modern porch, which has subsequently been slapped onto the main front, and the standard metal window frames that have replaced many of Prior's casemented leaded lights. The result is confusing because, though all the materials were local and the patterns used all had precedents in local vernacular building, the whole effect had a strangely foreign exuberance, compared by Pevsner to Gaudí's daring.[17]

It was in techniques of building that Prior got nearest to the Ruskinian ideal. Instead of using a contractor, Prior himself took the responsibility for building and used Randall Wells as site clerk; Wells must have been a concrete expert for he had already supervised Lethaby's Brockhampton church. He hired labour and bought materials as they were needed and ensured that the services subcontractor fitted his work in with the rest.

*Both Prior and Lethaby were interested in concrete, which became quite a popular Arts and Crafts material. They must have learned about it in Shaw's office, for in the '70s and early '80s, Shaw was experimenting with concrete in various ways, following his own master, Street, who had used Roman concrete for economy as far back as 1870.[16] Prior's willingness to experiment with new materials could be very adventurous, particularly in his earlier years. There is a design from the '90s for a club at West Bay in which a swimming pool, library, shops and covered promenade are covered with a rolling wave-like roof of transparent green felt, a material which has not been heard of before or since. The project was not built. (See Richardson, Margaret *Architects of the Arts and Crafts Movement,* Trefoil, London, 1983, p53.)

The aggregates for the concrete at Kelling Place, and the pebbles for the building's exterior, were found by excavating a flower garden an acre in extent and six feet deep in front of what was to be the main elevation. (Prior believed that by using his own materials, the client had virtually covered the cost of digging this enormous hole.) Construction of the concrete walls was Roman fashion, 'without planking'[18] and the concrete upper floors were reinforced by 'iron chainage' instead of the then common steel joists. Roof timbers and the rest of the carpentry were of oak, which 'for this use could be obtained locally at a cost hardly above that of good deal'. Prior claimed with glee that by not using a builder 'the expenditure...has been kept to the sum of the estimate, £8,000' but warned readers of *The Architectural Review* that his direct labour system had some disadvantages – principally not having a contractor to blame for the size of the final bill. Yet Prior's toughness was not daunted by such problems, as Lethaby's gentler nature had been after his similar experiment at Brockhampton, and he went on to complete his masterpiece, the church of St Andrew at Roker, a suburb of Sunderland, in 1906 using the labour system he believed in so passionately, with Randall Wells as site clerk again.

Prior had started his church building career with Holy Trinity, Bothenhampton, Dorset, built between 1887 and 1889. It is a small church, made very simply. From the outside, it seems quite conventional, a quiet nineteenth-century exercise in Early English Gothic

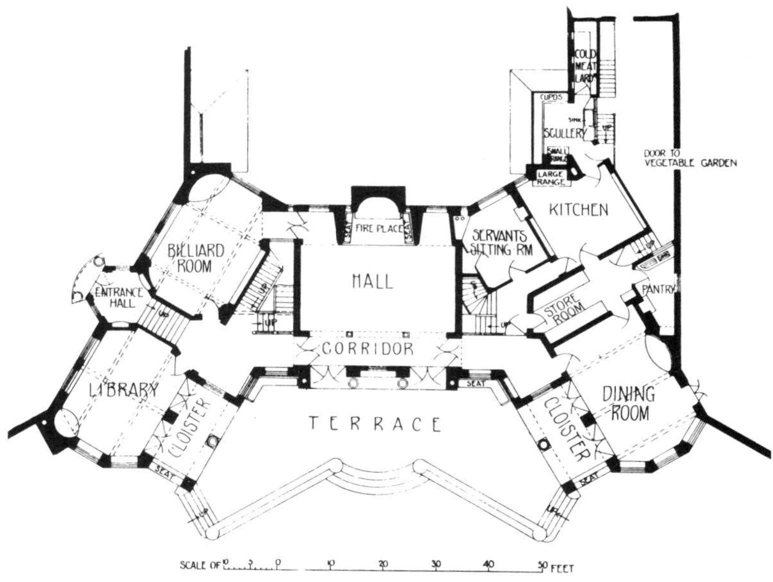

Top: Prior. Home Place, Holt, Norfolk (1903-05), built out of materials from the site itself
Above: Home Place, ground floor plan

Prior. Bothenhampton Church, Dorset (1887-89). Prior's first essay in ecclesiastical design – Gothic taken to essentials

Prior. Tower and sanctuary, St Andrew's Church, Roker, nr Sunderland (1906). Fortress-like simplified Gothic

with lancets in the chancel and narrow coupled windows between the buttresses of the nave. Inside, the space is very simple, with the unadorned timber roof of the nave supported on three plain stone arches which follow the external buttresses and spring smoothly out of the walls very low down.

The chancel is a little more complicated, with similar stone arches springing high up between strange corbel-like structures which are virtually the only decoration: there is scarcely a moulding to be seen anywhere except in the hood over the pulpit.

As at Lethaby's Brockhampton church, the effect at Bothenhampton is of great serenity: because the arches spring so low, just above waist height, the space is comfortably enclosing, like a big benevolent cave. The cave-like feeling is enhanced by the very deep embrasures of the windows through which light ripples, muted and never glaring, across the warm limestone. Then, beyond is the narrow high chancel in which the eye is drawn heavenwards by the corbels and the little trefoil window over the lancets at the east end.

The Roker church is a much bigger affair. It was built for a committee of which the main benefactor was Sir John Priestman, a local man who had risen from labourer to shipbuilding magnate and was doubtless used to getting his own way. He was prepared to contribute £6000 but on certain conditions: the church should seat 700 people, all of whom should have a clear view of the altar; the tower was to be a landmark from the sea; and the interior had to have good acoustical properties for the organ (Priestman remained organist until the '20s).[19]

This was the kind of clear brief that Prior had called for in the Liverpool Cathedral competition: functional without being stylistically prescriptive. He seized the opportunity of placing the solid castellated tower over the sanctuary at the east end to be as near as possible to the cliff-top a quarter of a mile away. This is the most immediately obvious departure from medieval precedent (in which the tower would have normally been at the west end or over the crossing). But closer inspection reveals many subtle innovations. The buttresses which prop the nave arches are expressed, not as extrusions of the rough local limestone walls, but by carving the wall back from 3'6" to 2'6" above the height at which the arches spring internally. So the buttresses rise smooth out of the base, giving the building a gracefully contained solidity. Between the buttresses, in the thinner part of the wall, the windows have all the curves of traditional tracery straightened out to become simple diagonals of stone supported on unadorned polygonal mullions. This kind of tracery is used throughout the church, and is particularly obvious in the east window where the sanctuary projects a few feet beyond the tower, retaining the ridge height of the nave so that it seems as if the church has been punched through its tower from west to east – a true if rather wilful expression of Ruskinian changefulness.

The buttresses, which are so muted on the outside, are very much in evidence in the nave where they support the high, almost parabolic arches that in turn carry concrete purlins under oak rafters. Priestman's wishes were carried out by making a large columnless

St Andrew's Church, nave. Note aisles under arch springings. Arches are concrete with stone cladding. Purlins are expressed in reinforced concrete

space that focuses on the altar through the chancel and the narrow sanctuary. The latter is spliced onto the nave in typical robust Prior fashion with a pair of round arches canted in plan.

The basic proposition is very similar to that at Bothenhampton, but the larger size of Roker necessitated some ingenious innovations. The nave buttresses are cut off virtually in mid-air just above head height and their inner edges are supported on simple hexagonal columns. This allows a low aisle or passageway between the columns and the wall – the cave effect is enhanced by these little tunnels under the buttresses which allow access to the northern and southern ends of the pews.

Such untraditional devices required unconventional building techniques. The arches, which are apparently made of stone, are in fact of concrete reinforced with iron rods covered with stone cladding. The walls, too, are stiffened with reinforced concrete, as are the lintels which span from the paired columns to the wall under the buttresses. (The purlins and the ridge, which are clearly concrete, are reinforced with steel.) Replying to those who criticised the work for being less than honest, Wells argued that 'rough stonework in any masses implies a core. The inference in these days would naturally be a cement core. In heavy arches in which economy has been effected by constructing them not of worked voussoirs but of roughly dressed quoins and wall stones, and which are connected together by concrete beams, it should be apparent that advantage has been taken of the one important addition to building materials – reinforced concrete'.[20]

St Andrew's Church. Pulpit, choir stalls and panelling are by Ernest Gimson

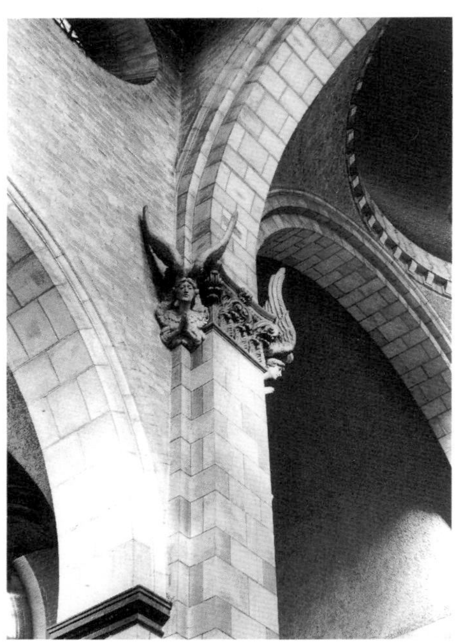

Prior (with Arthur Grove). Interior of St Osmund's, Parkestone, Poole (1913-16). Concrete barrel vaults and terracotta angels

The roughness of the stone facings and masonry is ameliorated by decoration and applied finishes like the oak planks that line the wall side of the aisles up to lintel height. In the sanctuary, there is finer fielded oak panelling, designed by Ernest Gimson, that runs up to the base of the east window. The fixed furniture, for instance the choir stalls and pulpit, was designed by Gimson and executed by Peter Waals with simplicity and elegance. Gimson was responsible for the lectern, candlesticks and crosses. There was stained glass by Henry Payne. The Morris Firm made the sanctuary carpet and the tapestry reredos; the Star of Bethlehem was by Burne-Jones. In 1927, the shallow concrete dome under the tower and over the sanctuary was painted by Macdonald Gill (a relation of Eric Gill who carved the foundation stone). This ceiling-like-a-sky broadly followed a sketch by Prior made at the time of the original works which showed a large central electrically-lit hemispherical sun in a blue sky full of stars and a crescent moon.[21] (Prior also hoped for painted decoration on the purlins which was never executed.)

The conjunction of so many artistic and craftsmanly talents was exactly what Prior had called for in his Liverpool Cathedral manifesto. That their work is to be found in a building which incorporated some of the most up-to-date technology may seem to us to be incongruous, but for Prior, there was no inconsistency: he wanted to use the best craftsmanship, the best techniques and the best local materials to create a noble place of worship for the people of his age.

Prior. Cambridge Medical Schools (1904). Restless Edwardian Baroque in formal urban context

For his last big church, St Osmund's at Parkestone in Poole, Dorset (1913-16), Prior must have been puzzled to find a suitable material, for he was building round an existing brick structure in the Byzantine style by G.A.B. Livesay. In the end he 'persuaded makers of simple pottery by the shores of Poole Harbour to turn their clay to bricks of every colour from purple to vivid orange'.[22] Again Prior (who was working with Arthur Grove) used simple arches, round this time, to roof the nave. But they are supported on mighty columns topped by terracotta Byzantine capitals and flanked by aisles covered by concrete barrel vaults. The simple interior (so kind to Livesay's work that you cannot see the join) is of roughcast relieved by terracotta. Outside, the building wears a fantastic but muted coat of many colours and patterns in which Prior's special bricks are made to dance in diapered and patterned work. The lines are as usual simple, with windows topped by semi-circular arches and roundels in the clerestory. The great west rose window consists of two concentric circles connected by straight glazing bars – a reminder of the straightened Gothic of Roker.

The use of (idiosyncratic) Byzantine motifs is an echo of Prior's use of overt stylism in the Cambridge Medical Schools (finished in 1904, only three years after his polemic on the Gothic principle for Liverpool had been published in *The Architectural Review*). In 1904 the same magazine* reported of the building that 'classic forms have been used to ornament the fronts, but the work is plain towards the courtyards, upon which the large microscope rooms look'.[23]

*Presumably the article was written by Prior himself.

The heavily rusticated street fronts of the building are inexplicable within Ruskinian canons – though the plan is changeful, with the medical museum darting out at an angle to the main body of the work, and the Classicism of the elevation is full of wit and surprise. The only possible Arts and Crafts justification for the building's style is its context: a Neo-Classical street in central Cambridge, which therefore possibly deserved the grand Classical manner.

Perhaps formality was important to Prior when he was working for official clients. His unbuilt design for the government medical school at Netley in Hampshire (1900), in no way subject to a context, was to have been executed in most rigorous Neo-Classical symmetries.

After the War, Prior's practice evaporated, partly because of his academic commitments. Yet he never lost his early inspiration. A former student recalled that, 'His ideal to make the Cambridge School in fact what it was called – a school of architectural studies – had something in it deeper and wider than any dallying with the crafts. It aimed, through cultural training, at a recognition of the whole field of art as *practice*, not theory; the production of a world of builders (not architects) who would build with direct knowledge of working conditions, controlling workmen (not contractors), yet fully cognisant of the business of building and the implications of a contract with the client. An impossible ideal, perhaps [but] with him it was the conviction of a lifetime'.[24] It was this unyielding adherence to an ideal that made Prior the man he was and gave his architecture such an individual stamp.

To his excessively successful Classical contemporary Reginald Blomfield, Prior 'of all Shaw's men...was the strongest personality. Somehow I think his real ability should have taken him further than it did; perhaps he was too unyielding, constitutionally incapable of accepting the *via media*'.[25]

Yet in the end, which went further? Every one of Prior's buildings repays study with delight and interest. Can anyone say that of the endless acres of Blomfield's work?

1 *Saint, A.* Richard Norman Shaw, op cit, *p145. Saint is quoting from notes left by Robert, Richard Norman Shaw's son.*
2 Ibid, *p186. Again from Robert Shaw's notes.*
3 The Architect and Building News, *Vol CXXI, 1932, p23.*
4 *Blomfield, R.* Richard Norman Shaw, op cit, *p88.*
5 *Prior, E. S. 'The New Cathedral for Liverpool',* The Architectural Review, *Vol X, 1901, p145.*
6 Ibid.
7 Ibid, *p146.*
8 Ibid.
9 *Prior, E. S.* A History of Gothic Art in England, *George Bell & Sons, London, 1900, p7.*
10 *Prior, E. S. in Shaw, R.N. and Jackson, T.G. (eds)* Architecture, a Profession or an Art, op cit, *pp107-108.*
11 *Prior, E. S. 'Church Building As It Is And As It Might Be',* The Architectural Review, *Vol IV, 1898, p108.*
12 Ibid, *p106.*
13 Ibid, *p158.*
14 *For instance Franklin, Jill 'Edwardian Butterfly Houses',* The Architectural Review, *Vol CLVII, April 1975, pp220-225.*
15 *The correspondence between Prior and the Rolle estate is extensively quoted in Hoare, Geoffrey and Geoffrey Pyne* Prior's Barn and Gimson's Coxen, *privately published by the authors, Seaforth, Little Knowle, Budleigh Salterton, 1978.*
16 *Saint, A.* Richard Norman Shaw, op cit, *pp165-171 gives an interesting description of Shaw's use of concrete.*
17 *Pevsner, N.* Buildings of England: North East Norfolk and Norwich, *Penguin, Harmondsworth, 1973, p169.*
18 *This and the following short quotations on construction are taken from* The Architectural Review, *Vol XIX, 1906, pp70-82*
19 *Walker, Angela 'The Church of St Andrew',* Northern Architect, *Vol XVII, 1979, pp19-24. Walker analyses the inception and construction of the church.*
20 *Wells, Randall,* The Builder, *Vol XCIII, 23 November 1907, p563.*
21 *Hawkes, Dean, 'St Andrew's Roker', in* Timeless Architecture, *ed Dan Cruickshank, Architectural Press, London, 1985, pp7-22. Hawkes also analyses the heating system which is at least as innovatory as the structural one.*
22 *Huges, H. C.* The RIBA Journal, *Vol XXXIX, 1932, p859. Huges was one of Prior's earliest students at Cambridge.*
23 The Architectural Review, *Vol XV, 1904, p159.*
24 *Fyfe, Theodore* The RIBA Journal, *Vol XXXIX, 1932, p814.*
25 *Blomfield, R.* Richard Norman Shaw, op cit, *p90.*

The pathfinder

8

Sometime during 1894, Edward Prior, then living in Melina Place, St John's Wood, acquired a new next-door neighbour who was just as fiercely independent and incapable of taking the *via media*.

Charles Francis Annesley Voysey (1857-1941) was one of the few major Arts and Crafts architects born in the '50s who did not belong to the apostolic succession of Street and his pupils: Morris, Webb and Shaw and through Shaw to his pupils, Lethaby, Prior, Newton and Macartney. But, the same age as Lethaby, Voysey was an early member of the Art Workers' Guild (elected in December 1884, the Guild's first year), and he must have known Prior for several years before they became neighbours.

Though similar in their fierce independence and strength of character, and in their reverence for Pugin and Ruskin, Prior and Voysey were unalike in almost every other way. Prior had been through the mill of conventional English upper middle class education; Voysey was almost completely privately educated. Prior, as far as his political opinions can be discerned, seems to have been a Whig; Voysey was definitely a high Tory – but of libertarian temperament. Prior was a conventional Anglican; Voysey was strongly religious. Prior always attempted great fidelity to local materials and building traditions; Voysey evolved a style which, though susceptible to local variation, was universally applicable.

Voysey was born at Hessle in the East Riding of Yorkshire where his father, the Rev Charles Voysey, ran a school. When Voysey was 14

C.F.A. Voysey. Broadleys, Windermere, Cumbria (1898)

his father was dismissed from the Church of England in one of the great ecclesiastical scandals of the nineteenth century; his heresy was that he did not believe in the doctrine of eternal damnation or, as his son put it, 'he believed in a good God rather than an angry one'.[1]

The influence of the Rev Charles was always strong. Voysey was educated by him at home in the Yorkshire years and his father's kindly puritanism permeated his life. 'If he had to punish any of his children', Voysey wrote, 'he would creep up to the bedside before the culprit was asleep, and gently stroking the head, with tears in his eyes, would soften the little heart with a few kind words and leave it in peace. His suffering in causing pain in order to do good could not be doubted and is the experience of all noble parents, surgeons, doctors, dentists and others. And surely of the Creator likewise?'[2]

Voysey's early years must have been very happy, if strictly regulated, and, perhaps as a result, there is an element of what some have condemned as childishness in all his work: a delight in simple jokes, such as designing an iron bracket to the profile of a client's face, and a love of obvious symbolic imagery: hearts, bull's-eye windows and big green water butts. Perhaps it is only in retrospect that his buildings themselves seem to have a childlike quality, but with their big roofs, wide doorways and low walls, they are models of what many children, particularly country-bred ones, first draw when they make their first pictures of houses.

In 1871, the year of his trial in the Lords, Charles Voysey moved to Dulwich to set up his own Theistic Church, and his son was sent to

Left: Voysey. House design, elevation and plans (published in *The British Architect* 1889, though designed before). Voysey cramming as many Deveyan idioms into a small a compass as possible

Right: George Devey. St Alban's Court, estate cottage (1870s to 1880s). Devey was Voysey's master and in his less grand work the lines of Voysey's later style can be discerned

Dulwich College, where he stayed for 18 months. The tough régime of a public school did not suit him, and he was withdrawn to study under a private tutor.

Though his art master at Dulwich had dubbed him incompetent for any artistic profession, Voysey was articled for five years to the Victorian Gothic architect J. P. Seddon in 1873. The relationship was a success, and Seddon introduced him to the writings of Pugin, who was to be one of his guiding stars. He probably already knew something of Ruskin, who taught drawing at a school which Voysey's sisters attended. In 1879 he worked briefly for Saxon Snell, an innovator in sanitation techniques, before being asked to join the office of George Devey, a member of his father's church.

In 1880, Devey's practice was wide and flourishing. Voysey learned much from him about designing houses in the country – which, on a different scale, were to be his main contribution to architecture. And he learned a style – or rather two styles.

Voysey set up his own practice in about 1882, and supported himself by undertaking surveys, alterations and designs for furniture, fabrics and wallpapers. As a designer he was both influenced and helped by Mackmurdo, whose flat, sinuous designs of birds and leaves, and furniture with tall, tapering verticals topped by thin square capitals, were to echo through much of Voysey's work. But the architectural influence was Devey. In a design for a house, published in *The British Architect* in 1889[3] but probably designed some years before, Voysey seems to be trying to introduce as many Deveyan idioms into as small a compass as possible. The walls have a stone base course with brick on top. They are pierced by rows of stone mullioned windows, patterned in all kinds of diapers and chequers, and bulge out into square, polygonal and semi-circular bays. On top is an exuberant roof which heaves up and down, with hips, gables both Dutch (in masonry) and English (in timber framing), and a series of little dormers. It was never built – perhaps because it would have been extremely expensive for the amount of space it would have provided.

Devey had a quiet approach for cottages which was to be the foundation of Voysey's mature style. On the St Alban's Court estate, where work was proceeding during Voysey's time in Devey's office, are several groups of cottages; they are the architectural forefathers of Voysey's small country houses. The floors are clearly delineated, usually by projecting the upper one; windows are in mullioned bands pushed up against the projection of the upper floor, the eaves or the projecting gables. Doors are simple, low and wide and the effect would be strongly horizontal but for the massive chimney stacks. The materials are different from those Voysey commonly used – Devey's cottages are covered in hung tiles, half-timbering and patterned brickwork. But imagine the effect of moving the mighty chimney stack round to the end of the cottage shown above, strip off the Old English clothing and replace it with roughcast and you have something strikingly similar to a mature Voysey house.

Voysey's mature style began to emerge in 1888 when he published a design for a cottage in *The British Architect*. He had made the draw-

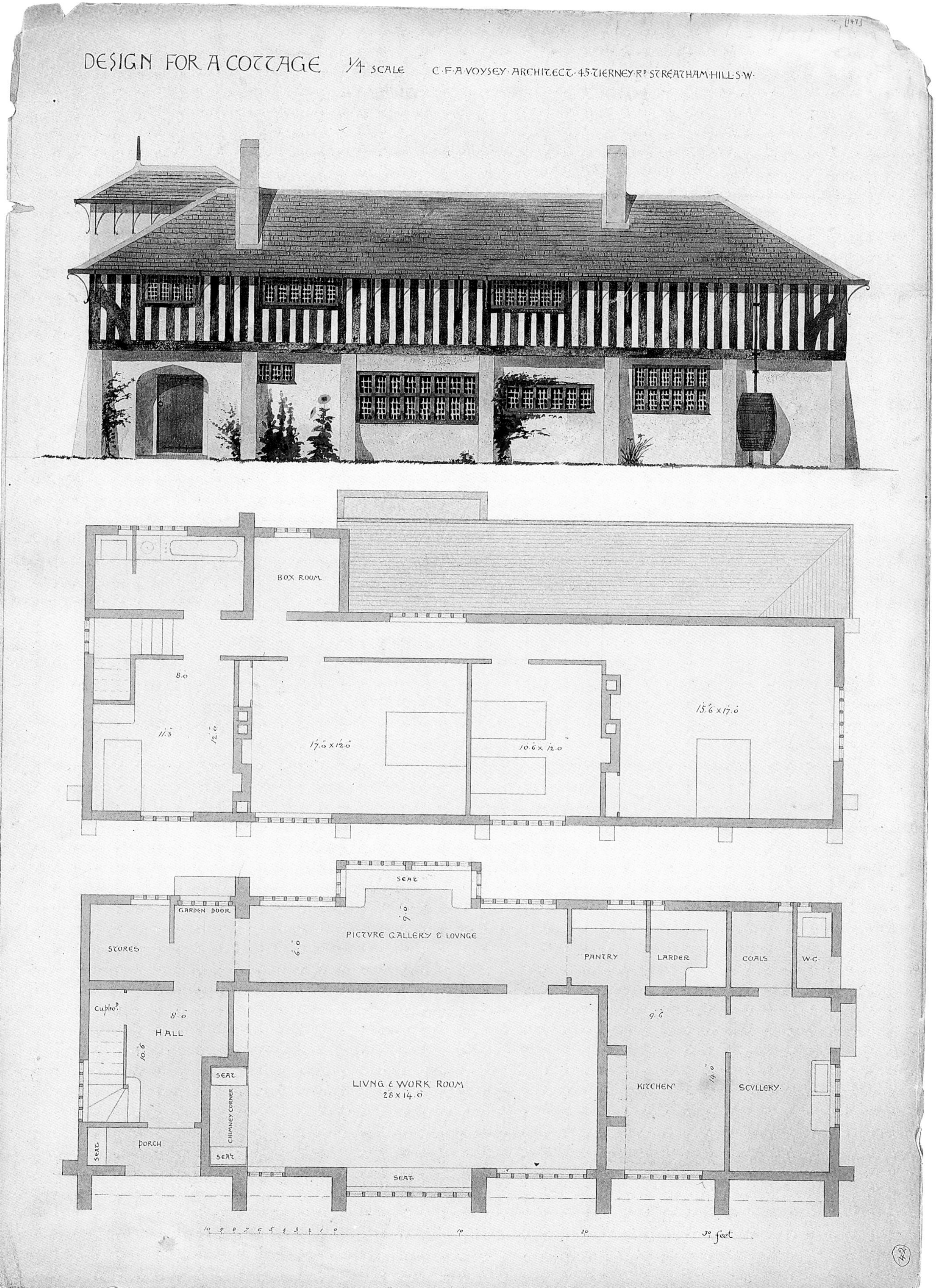

Voysey. Cottage design, elevation and plans c1885, published in *The Architect* XL, 1888). Voysey finds his mature style in a design intended for himself and his wife

Left: Voysey. Walnut Tree Farm, Castlemorton, Hereford and Worcester (1890): Voysey develops the sweeping roof – half timbering is fading away

Above: Voysey. Cottage, Bishop's Itchington, Warwickshire (1888): Voysey's first important commission

Right: Voysey. Tower house, Bedford Park, London (1891): the architect's tall response to a restricted site

ings in 1885 in the hope that he could build a house for himself and his new wife. The cottage was completely asymmetrical, long and low with its horizontality emphasized by recessing the ground floor. Its leaded windows were in long mullioned bands, the upper ones hard up against the wide eaves (themselves supported on delicate curved iron brackets) and the lower windows anchored visually between buttresses. The wide door was recessed behind a Tudorish arch and balanced by a water butt at the other end of the elevation. The whole composition is pinned down by a little tower over the stairs. The plan is economical; though long and thin, it is compact, with the major circulation space on the ground floor doubling as a 'picture gallery and lounge'.[4] It is the Arts and Crafts one-room-and-a-corridor plan in one of its most compressed forms.

All these themes were to be the basis of Voysey's later work.* His buildings were never symmetrical, for he was a firm believer in Ruskinian changefulness and praised Gothic architecture because 'outside appearances are evolved from internal fundamental conditions; staircases and windows come where most convenient for use. All openings are proportioned to the various parts to which they apply'.[5] The horizontality of most of his work derived from a belief in the symbolic importance of long low straight lines: 'When the sun sets horizontalism prevails, when we are weary we recline, and the darkness covers up the differences and hides all detail under one harmonious veil, while we, too, close our eyes for rest. What, then, is obviously necessary for the effect of repose in our houses, [is] to avoid angularity and complexity in colour, form or texture, and make our dominating lines horizontal rather than vertical'.[6]

The buttresses of the lower floor were, so he claimed, the result of economy. In 1897, an article in *The Studio*, presumably published with his approval, explained that 'Mr Voysey employs these buttresses to save the cost of thicker walls for the lower storey of his buildings. That they chance to afford pleasant-looking shelters for a garden seat and break up the wall-surface happily, giving the facade a certain architectural pattern of shadows he realizes, and is, beyond doubt delighted by the picturesque qualities...[But] Mr Voysey would no more dream of adding a superfluous buttress than he would add an unnecessary panel of cheap ornament'.[7] The roughcast, too, was an economy. Horace Townsend explained in another *Studio* article (Voysey was a favourite of the magazine from its foundation) that 'Mr Voysey's preference for [roughcast]...which is marked by the way – is based, so he tells me, mainly on its economy. He considers a nine inch brick wall faced with cement roughcast is as warm and weather-tight as any much more expensive construction'.[8]

The wide door had particular symbolic importance for Voysey who believed that doors should be 'wide in proportion to height, to suggest welcome – not stand-offishly dignified, like the coffin lid, high and narrow for the entrance of one body only'.[9]

*I have been free in juxtaposing Voysey's opinions of different dates in the quotations which follow, because, once he had achieved maturity, his ideas and architecture changed little until the end. The quotations are chosen as the most apt expressions of often uttered beliefs.

Right: Voysey. Sketch for a house on the Hog's Back, near Guildford, Surrey (1896). Sweeping roofs unite complicated plans and sections

Right: Voysey. Perrycroft, Colwall, Hereford and Worcester (1893-94): garden front from south-west. The half-timbering has disappeared and the house addresses the landscape with many different opportunities for perceiving it

And the long, thin Arts and Crafts plan was adopted partly because of his belief that servants should not be kept in dungeons as was common in many Victorian houses. 'In offices for servants' use, let them be cheerful, and not shabby and dark, as if it did not matter how you treated your servants because you were paying for their services. Some day men will be ashamed to do ugly things and cheap and nasty treatment of servants will be regarded as dishonouring to the master.'[10]

In 1888, the immediate result of publication of the design was Voysey's first important commission – for a similar cottage at Bishop's Itchington, Warwickshire which, when built, was quite like the original, though the half-timbering was omitted, a projecting porch added and the eaves line was broken by hipped dormers over the principal upstairs rooms.

Voysey was off, and during the next 20 years he built a multitude of houses, most of which used the themes he had brought together at Bishop's Itchington. There were, of course, exceptions: a charming little tower house for a narrow site in Bedford Park (1891), some houses in Hans Road (chapter 11), and there was a curious flirtation with Classical detailing in the late '90s in houses like New Place, Haslemere (1897). But all these buildings bear a Voysey stamp.

The basic vocabulary was gradually added to and refined. Voysey's next commission after Bishop's Itchington was Walnut Tree Farm (now Bannut Tree Farm) at Castlemorton near Malvern (designed 1890), where the roof pitch is increased and the eaves are pulled down to the bottom of the first floor windows, which are expressed as a series of gables. This gives a much greater expanse of roof and reduces the apparent height – a device used in many of Voysey's later buildings, in which steep sweeping roofs united quite complicated plans and sections, for example in the beautiful Sturgis House (1896) on the Hog's Back near Guildford (ruined by Herbert Baker's 1913 additions). Tucked under the first floor at the east end of Walnut Tree Farm is the half octagonal bay of the morning room, an instance of Voysey's rectangular, polygonal and semi-circular bays, which were often capped by the projecting horizontal of the first floor but sometimes allowed to crash up through the eaves to end up as a kind of dormer (for instance at Broadleys, Windermere, 1898). Walnut Tree Farm shows Voysey's last extensive use of half-timbering which he abandoned because 'bureaucratic bye-laws' necessitated half-timbering to be executed as boarding on rendered brickwork which Voysey refused to use because it was a sham.[11]

Perrycroft at Colwall in the Malvern Hills (designed 1893-94) was Voysey's first large commission and shows his mature approach to perfection, with buttresses rising the full height of the walls to the wide eaves which cover the shallow bays in front of the principal bedrooms. The hipped roof is of green Westmorland slates (a favourite Voysey material), penetrated by big, tapering rectangular chimneys (the chimney pots are modern).

The entrance side has an open porch shielding double doors with long strap hinges. A long band of small paned windows just under the eaves lights the first floor corridor. The composition is pinned down

Voysey. Stair hall, Norney Grange, Eashing, Surrey (1897). Voysey's interiors were as fine-honed and simple as his outsides

by a little tower, capped by a lead covered ogee-shaped roof with a weathercock on a high slender spike.

The siting is very carefully considered with bays and seats built between the buttresses to take advantage of magnificent views over the green hills to south-west and north-west. Voysey was always very considerate of his sites. 'The character of the site', he wrote, 'will suggest many limitations and conditions as to aspect and prospect. The contour of the ground obviously controls the arrangement, and the colour, shape and texture of hills and trees suggest the colour, form and texture of our building. That is, provided we have no preconceived notions of Classical *façades*, or a deep rooted preference for a particular style of architecture.'[12]

The remarks about the locality determining the colour and texture of the building may seem odd in a man who was prepared to bring Westmorland slates to Herefordshire, but Voysey, always a symbolist, was making a visual analogue with the smooth green shapes of the hills themselves. At least he avoided the paradox of Prior's Home Place – a building created out of materials from the very site itself but which manages to look extraordinarily foreign.

Yet after a while, Voysey became trapped by his own style. *The Studio* reported in 1904 that 'it is a matter of regret to the artist should a client insist on having what he or she deems a thoroughly characteristic house instead of one more properly native to the soil'.[13] He was certainly prepared to exploit local materials – for instance where he could get really good brick as in the Wentworth Arms, Elmesthorpe, Leicestershire (1895), he left it exposed. He made designs for houses in local stone (mostly unbuilt) and, at Hill Close near Studland, Dorset (1896), he used rough-hewn Portland stone round the windows and large local stone flags on the roof.

Hill Close was designed for the Edwardian animal painter, Alfred Suto, and had a large studio with a great window (sadly now replaced by modern patent glazing) looking out over the magnificent view over Studland Bay and Poole Harbour. The studio itself was a high room with a little library gallery over the door.* Most Voysey rooms were much lower, like the Hill Close dining room, which is not much more than eight feet high but looks lower because of its deep plaster frieze of stylized trees. Voysey believed that 'an eight foot room may be better ventilated and more comfortable to live in than a room 12 or 15 feet high and is certainly more easy to light and warm'[14] – because the lower ceiling reflected more light to the back of the room and so obviated the need for large areas of glass. The cold from large windows could lead to unsightly horrors, 'hot water pipes and various demonical contrivances for heating...like tombs to the memory of cremated air'.[15] (Voysey usually relied on open fires for heating, with special connections to the outside air to provide draughts for the chimneys and to avoid them in the rooms.)

Voysey's objections to central heating were largely aesthetic. He believed that most contemporary commercial artifacts were hideously ugly, and, given a chance, he would, like Webb, design everything for a house from the forks to the door hinges. His ideal was 'a well proportioned room, with whitewashed walls, plain carpet and simple oak furniture, and nothing in it but necessary articles of use, and one pure ornament in the form of a simple vase of flowers'.[16]

This image of a white box containing a few exquisite objects seems strange from a man who was one of the most successful wallpaper designers of the turn of the century. He explained that 'a wallpaper is of course only a background, and were your furniture good in form and colour a very simple or quite undecorated treatment of the walls would be preferable; but as most modern furniture is vulgar or bad in every way, elaborate papers of many colours help to disguise its ugliness'.[17] Voysey was rather less extreme in practice and, for instance, used his wallpapers in the house he designed for his wife at Chorleywood (1899) where, presumably, he did like the furniture.

To achieve the simple effects he wanted, Voysey had to go to some trouble, particularly at first. In the Bedford Park tower house, 'it was found necessary, in order to prevent the builder from displaying the usual "ovulo mouldings", "stop chamfers", fillets, and the like, to prepare 18 sheets of contract drawings to show where his beloved ornamentation *was to be omitted*...Great pains have to be taken to prevent the workmen from unconscious "decoration" as is their wonted habit'.[18]

Voysey had firmly resolved the Puginian paradox in favour of the designer rather than the craftsman and he was also prepared to accept

Voysey. The Homestead, Frinton-on-Sea, Essex (designed 1905-06): the full vocabulary of details of Voysey's mature exteriors

*Alexander Hamilton Fletcher has pointed out to me that the original gallery has been replaced with woodwork taken from Austin Reed's shop in Exeter.

Voysey. Platt's Lane, Hampstead, London (1895). House for his father in which the scope of the site was maximized by making an L-shaped plan on the perimeter

Voysey. The house he designed for his wife, The Orchard, Chorleywood, Hertfordshire (1889)

the machine – but tentatively, rather as Pugin himself had accepted it. 'The human quality in familiar objects has in many cases been driven out by the machine. Nevertheless, the machine has come to liberate men's minds for more intellectual work than was provided for them by the sawpit.'[19] But he was insistent that 'we are far too keen on mechanical perfection. That love of smooth, polished surfaces is very materialistic [a quality that Voysey abhorred]; it can be produced without brains and in most cases can only be produced by the elimination of all human thought and feeling'.[20]

From the earliest years, Voysey enlivened the general austerity of his houses with occasional jokey details: brackets bent to form his clients' profiles, lead hearts let into wooden balusters and little grotesque finials, caricatures of the architect or his client. They were the echoes of Ruskinian savageness in the work of a man who designed every detail and allowed little scope for intervention by craftsmen.

As he grew older, he became increasingly hostile to machine production. John Betjeman, who as a young editor of *The Architectural Review* discovered Voysey in retirement during the early '30s, recalled that 'he disliked machinery as "unnatural" and would always advocate the use of craftsmen – from the craftsman who made his pipes to those who built his houses'.[21]

But Voysey rarely had an opportunity to use craftsmanship lavishly. He was, after all, building houses that 'compare favourably in cost with the miserable shams of the jobbing builder',[22] and, as a Tory, he believed that there were certain qualities that were 'essential to all classes of homes, but there are certain other qualities like grandeur, splendour, pomp, majesty and exuberance which are suitable only to comparatively few. In the category of general need, we should put repose, cheerfulness, simplicity, breadth, warmth, quietness in storm, economy of up-keep, evidence of protection, harmony with surroundings, absence of dark passages or places, evenness of temperature'.[23] But where he did have what he believed to be an appropriate client, Voysey was prepared to indulge in some splendour and exuberance – for instance in his design for a house for the Earl of Lovelace (1894-95), where the white walls are relieved by a bay with carved ornament. It was not built, nor did he ever build a big house for a grandee.

His clients were generally comfortably-off members of the middle class like his own father, for whom he built a house in Platt's Lane, Hampstead (1895), and H. G. Wells, the rising young novelist, who in 1899 chose Voysey as the 'pioneer in the escape from the small snobbish villa residence to the bright and comfortable pseudo cottage'.[24] In Wells, incidentally, Voysey for once had a client as strong minded as he was about some aspects of design. 'Voysey wanted to put a large heart-shaped letter plate on my front door [by then virtually a Voysey trademark], but I protested at wearing my heart so conspicuously outside and we compromised on a spade'[25] (*ie*, by turning the heart upside down). Despite disagreements, the two must have remained on good terms, as Voysey was asked to add an extra bay in 1903.

Voysey's way of building could cope with almost any problem. The Platt's Lane house shows how his approach could be accommodated to

Voysey. Miners' cottages, Whitwood, Yorkshire (1904-05). Housing for working people with tower of Miners' Institute in background

Voysey. Lodge Style, Coombe Down, nr Bath. Overt Gothic detailing reappears in Voysey's last architectural work in his battle against Classicism

a small suburban plot (by running an L-shaped plan along the north and east sides of the site and by putting the entrance facing south-west in the angle so that all rooms had a sunny orientation). Wells's Spade House, on the cliff top at Sandgate in Kent, reveals how Voysey could run his buildings up a quite steeply sloping site.

He could even, without too much difficulty, adapt his style to a factory for Sandersons, the wallpaper manufacturers, at Chiswick (1902), with white glazed brick piers taking the place of buttresses and big small-paned windows with white spandrels between them. (The tops of the piers, which also act as ventilation shafts, are reminiscent of Voysey's furniture, complete with little Mackmurdoish capitals.)

And the technique could be adapted to quite large housing schemes – for example the row of cottages at Whitwood, Yorkshire (1904-05) in which pairs of cottages with low walls and hipped dormers in the roof are set in a terrace between seven cottages with big gables facing the road. The planning is extremely economical in circulation space and yet commodious in living area; the cottages must have been most desirable miners' residences (the complex was built for Briggs & Sons colliery). The terrace is dominated by the tower of the miners' institute, which is topped by simple crenellations.

This was one of the first instances of overt Gothic detailing which developed after 1905 in Voysey's work, perhaps as a counter-blast to the growing popularity of the Classical styles. By 1909 he was designing a stone courtyard house at Coombe Down near Bath in which almost every detail was taken from Gothic precedents. But there, the client, T. S. Cotterell, had particularly requested something to remind him of his old college, Merton, and Voysey's white houses continued in a thin trickle until they ceased with High Gault, St Margaret's-at-Cliffe, Kent in 1914. Voysey, though he lived to 1941, built nothing after the First World War apart from a couple of alterations and some war memorials. Yet he continued to design, in Gothic and Tudor; and even produced an unbuilt Tudor tower block scheme in 1923.

Increasingly, he thought of himself as one of the last disciples of Pugin and Ruskin. He echoed Pugin in calling for a real English architecture. 'Why...should England turn her back on her own country and pretend that she is such a born mongrel she can have no truly national architecture? Has she no national climate? Are her geological and geographical conditions the same as all other countries? Is there no difference between English and Italian men?...No one denies strong national character to the British people. Why, then, do we so persistently try to ape the manners of foreigners?'[26] But, at the same time, he was an individualist who despised excessive reverence for tradition, believing that 'if we are to try and harmonize with the laws of Nature and help her to progress we must leave the door perpetually open to progress and welcome (critically if you like) all attempts to improve our traditional modes and methods, whatever they may be'.[27]

His was such a strong character that he was accused of not allowing his clients' personalities to influence their houses. There is some truth in the allegation. Voysey wrote to his client, Cecil Fitch, 'all artistic questions you must trust me to decide. No two minds ever pro-

Voysey. Factory for Sanderson & Sons, Chiswick, London (1902): Voysey's rational approach applied to a non-domestic building type. The buttresses incorporate ventilation ducts and the walls are of self-washing white glazed bricks

duced an artistic result'.[28] But he was loved; in reply to a wounding article about his relationships with his clients published after a retrospective exhibition of his work organized by Betjeman in 1931, Voysey wrote to the RIBA librarian, 'out of 246 clients I have worked for, 53 have returned with fresh commissions, and I have built 108 private houses, only one of which I should care to live in, and that is the house I built for my wife'.[29] It was an unusually good record.

His last years were fraught with money worries. (As early as the First World War he had to approach James Morton, who printed many of his fabrics, for financial assistance.)[30] But he ended life as a Civil List pensioner and a pensioner of the Royal Academy and of the RIBA,[31] all of which, with fees and royalties for his designs, helped him keep afloat.

Gordon Russell remembered him in the early '20s. Voysey had only one job: 'It's a house for a lunatic', he said, 'such a nice man, and his doctor thought he might take an interest in the building of it. But I find it difficult. None of my friends can tell me how to deal with a client who, when the contract should be signed, gets under the table and refuses to come out'.[32] Not surprisingly, the bizarre commission came to nothing.

His spirit was unimpaired. Betjeman gave a beautiful obituary picture of a man who changed little once he reached maturity. 'He was a little below middle height and with an ascetic, clean shaven countenance...His dress was of his own design. He wore dark suits with no lapels to the coat, blue shirts and collars and a tie through a gold ring. He was always scrupulously neat and clean and his appearance never altered for all the time I knew him. He took snuff and smoked clay pipes that were made at a curious old pipe hospital in Soho.'[33] Robert Donat, who married Voysey's niece, recalled, 'You may have got the impression that butter wouldn't melt in his mouth. It certainly wouldn't unless it happened to be the very best butter. But if there was the slightest defect in the butter I'm afraid, without more ado, he would have spat it out. He liked only the best of everything'.[34]

Voysey believed to his dying day in his father's good God and that 'simplicity, sincerity, repose, directness and frankness are moral qualities as essential to good architecture as to good men'.[35]

1 *Much background information on Voysey is given in two essays by Brandon-Jones, John, in 'C. F. A. Voysey: a Memoir',* The Architectural Association Journal, *London, 1957, and in* C. F. A. Voysey: Architect and Designer, *Lund Humphries, London, 1978. The latter is the catalogue of the 1978 exhibition held in the Brighton Art Gallery and Museum.*
2 *Quoted by Brandon-Jones, J. in* The Architectural Association Journal, op cit, *p241.*
3 The British Architect, *Vol XXXI, 1889, p248.*
4 The British Architect, *Vol XXX, 1888, p407.*
5 *Voysey, C. F. A. 'The English Home',* The British Architect, *Vol LXXV, 1911, p60.*
6 *Voysey, C. F. A.* Individuality, *Chapman & Hall, London, 1915, p111.*
7 The Studio, *Vol XI, 1897, p20.*
8 *Townsend, Horace 'Notes on Country and Suburban Houses Designed by C. F. A. Voysey',* The Studio, *Vol XVI, 1899, p158.*
9 *Voysey, C. F. A. 'The English Home',* op cit, *p70.*
10 Ibid.
11 The Studio, *Vol XXXI, 1904, p128.*
12 *Voysey, C. F. A.* Reason as a Basis of Art, *Elkin Matthews, London, 1906, p11.*
13 *Vallance, Aymer 'Some Recent Work by Mr C. F. A. Voysey',* The Studio, *Vol XXXI, 1904, p127.*
14 *Voysey, C. F. A. 'Remarks on Domestic Entrance Halls',* The Studio, *Vol XXI, 1901, p243.*
15 Ibid, *p244.*
16 *Voysey, C. F. A. 'The English Home',* op cit, *p69.*
17 *'An Interview with Mr Charles F. Annesley Voysey, Architect and Designer',* The Studio, *Vol 1, 1893, p233.*
18 The Studio, *Vol XI, 1897, p25.*
19 *Voysey, C. F. A. 'Ideas in Things', one of a series of essays in* The Arts Connected With Building, *ed Davison, Raffles, Batsford, London, 1909, p107. The essays were a series of lectures given to the Carpenters' Company.*
20 Ibid.
21 The Architects' Journal, *Vol CXIII, 1941, pp193-194.*
22 The Studio, *Vol XI, 1897, p16.*
23 *Voysey, C. F. A. 'The English Home',* op cit, *p69.*
24 *Wells, H. G.* Experiment in Autobiography, *Victor Gollancz, London, republished 1966, p638.*
25 Ibid.
26 *Voysey, C. F. A. 'The English Home',* op cit, *p60.*
27 *Voysey, C. F. A. 'Tradition and Individuality in Art', 1928, unpublished paper in RIBA library.*
28 *Voysey to Cecil Fitch, 4 December 1899. Published by John Brandon-Jones in a collection of correspondence in* The Architect and Building News, *Vol CXCV, 1949, pp494-498.*
29 *Voysey to Edward Carter, 21 October 1931. Manuscript in the RIBA library.*
30 *Morton, Jocelyn* Three Generations in a Family Textile Firm, *Routledge & Kegan Paul, London, 1971, p286.*
31 The Times, *13 February 1941.*
32 *Russell, Gordon* Designer's Trade *Allen and Unwin, London, 1968, p126.*
33 *Betjeman, John* The Architects' Journal, *Vol XCIII, 1941, pp257-258.*
34 *Donat, Robert* The Architects' Journal, *Vol XCIII, 1941, pp193-194.*
35 *Voysey, C. F. A. 'The English Home',* op cit, *p69.*

Into the country

9

'There is still much of the peasant in every Englishman', wrote Muthesius, 'although in England, of course, the peasant as a class has practically disappeared from the scene. But the natural, unaffected intelligence, the generous dose of common-sense, that we find in the Englishman, his fondness for his native place with its fields and ploughed land, his love of fresh air and open country – all this shows that some of the best qualities of the country-dweller have persisted in him. In no country in the world has so strong a sense of the natural and the rural been passed down to modern times as in the land of the greatest traditional wealth...Naturalness makes up the best part of the Englishman's character. And we see this character in its present-day form reflected in the English house more truly and clearly, perhaps, than in any other manifestation of English culture.'[1]

Nowhere is Muthesius's idealized portrait of the English country house as the flower of national culture more true than in the work of Lethaby, Prior and Voysey, their contemporaries and followers. Their patrons were the upper middle classes; they rarely built big houses for really grand aristocracy or for the most flamboyant members of the new plutocracy. Nor were they often hired by the burgeoning late Victorian public and private institutions. The irony of Morris and Webb, both convinced socialists, being forced to work solely for the rich was echoed in the lives of their disciples, however much some of the younger men lacked their masters' political commitment. They had to work for the most economically free people. For late Victorians,

C.H. Townsend. St Mary the Virgin, Great Warley, Essex (1902-04)

one of the greatest freedoms was cheap and efficient public transport which had enabled the middle classes to move away from town centres, so their architects were usually required to build in the country or the suburbs. It is most unusual to find an Arts and Crafts house more than a couple of miles from a Victorian railway station. When Holmes and Watson were not wheeling up to a real medieval house in the station fly, they were approaching an Arts and Crafts version.

For the landed class, employing an Arts and Crafts architect to modernize country houses was a matter of course, unless an ostentatious splash was wanted. For instance, in 1888, when Lord Redesdale, the grandfather of the Mitfords, decided to renovate his country seat, he employed Arts and Crafts forerunner Ernest George. But in his exhaustive memoirs, in which no opportunity of dropping a name was lost, Redesdale merely remarked, 'I was now a free man, and...I sold my London house, took possession of Batsford and made up my mind to become a country squire'.[2] Redesdale makes no mention of the architect or his works.

Yet for less grand people, the image of the Arts and Crafts house with its calm, uncluttered interiors and rambling, steep-roofed exterior, quietly fitting into the countryside, was more important. It was exactly appropriate for a middle class aspiring to the landed values of the aristocracy. Vera Ryder was brought up in Copseham at Esher, a house which her father, a wealthy city businessman, had ramblingly altered by Guy Dawber:* 'A new nursery wing [was] added, with schoolroom, pantry and servants' hall. The old dining room and the

Below: Ernest Newton. Buller's Wood, Chislehurst, Kent (1889). His first style, much influenced by Shaw's Old English

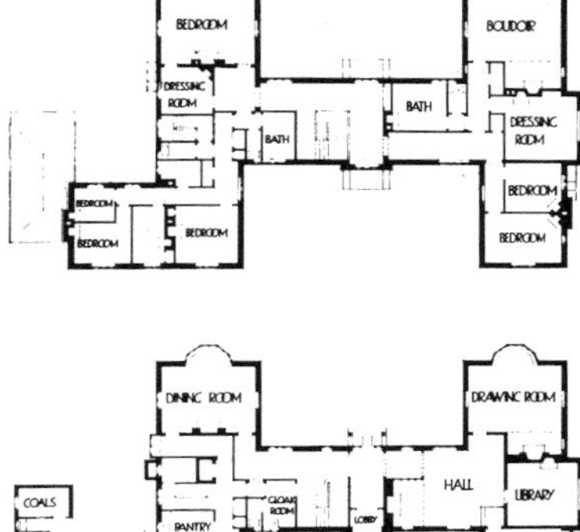

Above: Newton. Luckley, Wokingham, Berkshire (1907). Delicate Neo-Georgian with gentle reference to local tradition Left: Ground and first floor plans.

drawing room...[were] made into one big dining room. Finally a music room...was built at right angles to the drawing room and gave an imposing delightful finish to the place.

'The music room was a good room for sound with its high vaulted ceiling, and it was the focal point of our activities, both solemn and frivolous. Mother had no use for a drawing room as such, it would have cramped her style. For Mother...had big ideas; there was nothing immature about her inspirations. She needed a place to entertain her friends with no restrictions and no cluttering up with the usual drawing room knick-knacks'.[3]

Another, less relaxed aspect of middle class Arts and Crafts living was satirized by E. F. Benson in his description of the home of his heroine, super-snob Lucia Lucas, whose house, The Hurst, was in a village which suspiciously resembles Broadway in the Cotswolds. It 'presented a charmingly irregular and picturesque front'. It was formed of three cottages: 'Two were of the grey stone of the district, and the middle one, to the door of which led the paved path, of brick and timber. Latticed windows with stout mullions gave illumination to the room within [which had panelled walls and a white-washed ceiling with exposed beams]...To the original windows certain new lights had been added; these could be detected by the observant eye, for they had a markedly older appearance than the rest. The front door, similarly, seemed amazingly antique, the fact being that the one which Mrs Lucas had found there was too dilapidated...She had therefore caused to be constructed an even older one made from oak planks in a dismantled barn, and had it studded with large worn nails of antique patterns fashioned by the village blacksmith...Over the door hung an inn-sign, and into the space where once the sign had swung was now inserted a lantern, in which was ensconced, well hidden from view by its patinated glass sides, an electric light'.[4] Lucia Lucas's rich husband was, incidentally, the founder of a hand printing press at 'Ye Sign of Ye Daffodil' on the village green which existed mainly to print his prose poems 'in blunt type on thick yellowish paper'. This kind of behaviour was enough to give the Arts and Crafts movement a bad name; for several decades after the First World War, 'Arty Crafty' was synonymous with twee gentility.

The Arts and Crafts country house image was immensely influential on the upper middle class, and not only at home. In the United States of America, the great nineteenth-century cities all have their complement of Arts and Crafts suburbs. In 1904, Langford Warren commented in the Boston *Architectural Review* that 'it is not too much to say that no other nation has succeeded in developing a domestic architecture having the subtle and intimate charm which in the English country house makes so strong an appeal to the love of home as well as to the love of beauty'. Warren's article, which showed the work of Ernest George, Voysey and other contemporary English architects, praised the 'notable revivication of the old traditions and... application of the old forms to the needs of modern domestic life'.[5]

*Dawber was incidentally Ernest George's site clerk at Batsford before starting his own practice.

Newton. Steephill, Jersey (1902-04): Anglo-Français for Les Isles Normandes

Bedford & Kitson. Red House, Chapel Allerton, Leeds (before 1904)

And he was quite clear that 'our own best work, like that of England, will be done by founding it on the sound traditions of England's past, modifying these traditions frankly and fearlessly in the spirit of the old work to meet our new wants and new conditions'.[6]

The blend of English tradition and modernity had its adherents on the Continent too. Muthesius worked for years on his monumental book which so thoroughly expounded British domestic architecture to the German speaking world. The book's influence can be seen all over northern Europe in country houses reminiscent of England.

Even in provincial little Switzerland, industrialist Theodor Bühler was so impressed with the style that he hired the English architect Baillie Scott to create a house which 'should have the charm of a country seat...the general aspect of the house I should like to be simple, quiet and yet artistic, the facade not too irregular'.[7] The result was a perfect Arts and Crafts manor complete with gables, half-timbering, roughcast, ashlar, leaded lights and a tall tiled roof which still stands at Uzwil today, a piece of turn-of-the-century England transported to east Switzerland.

At home, the relaxed changeful Arts and Crafts country houses eventually became so closely identified with the values of the upper middle class that they became anathema to anyone with a claim to being in the forefront of taste. When H. G. Wells commissioned Voysey to design what Henry James called his 'stately treasure house on the sea shore'[8] in 1899, it was as a rebellion against the 'small snobbish villa residence'. But, a dozen years later, when Roger Fry, the critic and art impresario who mounted the first Post-Impressionist exhibition in London, was showing Virginia Woolf the Surrey landscape, he burst out, 'My house is neighboured by houses of the most gentlemanly picturesqueness, houses from which tiny gables with window slits jut out at any unexpected angle'. Their path 'avoided these gentlemanly residences, but his talk did not altogether avoid the inhabitants of those houses – their snobbery, their obtuseness, their complacency and their complete indifference to any kind of art'.[9]

If the clients were obtuse and indifferent, the architects did not resemble them. Quietly they fostered the ancient traditions of craftsmanship; faithfully they followed Ruskin's injunction to let appearance be determined by the plan; sensitively they obeyed Pugin's dictum that architecture should reflect its locality.

If between 1900 and 1910 you had taken a balloon from Brighton and floated north-west above England, you would have seen drift after drift of Arts and Crafts buildings: first the large houses of wealthy City men in Sussex and on the Surrey ridge between Guildford and Redhill, then, passing the metropolis, there was another belt of brick and tile houses in south Hertfordshire and Middlesex. Further north, a pattern emerged: each large town had a crescent of suburbs, usually running from south-west to north to take advantage of the prevailing winds which blew urban smoke away to the east. In north Oxford, the more adventurous dons were living in Arts and Crafts houses, and young Naomi Mitchison was envying the newest houses 'with lower ceilings and more bay windows with smaller panes which I thought

William Bidlake. Woodgate, Four Oaks, Birmingham. His own house (1906)

much nicer than our own big sash windows'.[10] In Birmingham, rich businessmen were building some of England's most beautiful suburbs at Four Oaks in Sutton Coldfield.

Away to the east, a strong telescope might have picked out the summer cottages of Leicester magnates built on the edge of the Charnwood Forest. Near Manchester, there was Middleton and in Leeds the newly developed suburbs of Adel and Roundhay. Then north again to the wastes of the Scottish border with a glance at the retreats of rich Lancashire cotton men in the Lakes. Beyond, in Glasgow, the pattern was repeated, with new, adventurous houses springing up to the north-west and on the banks of the Clyde.

Between these major cities, and always near to the knots of the Victorian railway network which knitted the country in a ravelled pattern, were the larger country mansions, the artists' houses and the estate cottages from which so many Arts and Crafts architects derived their income. Here and there was a new church or a village hall, the public works of the richer private house patrons.

In this chapter, the balloon, taking a much more errant course in space and time, descends now and then to give closer glimpses of the Arts and Crafts country work. Ernest Newton leads, partly because his career, as a founder-member of the Art Workers' Guild who developed a flourishing practice, shows the pattern for many successful architects of his generation, and partly because the delicacy, respect for tradition and gentle innovation of his work are typical of Arts and Crafts architects in the country. After Newton, the glimpses are alphabetical.

Ernest Newton (1856-1922) was Lethaby's predecessor as Norman Shaw's chief clerk and one of the founder members of the Art Workers' Guild. His work spans from the year he left Shaw, 1879, to the War, and virtually all of it was in the country. He started with quite small suburban houses in Shaw's Old English style, but as his practice grew he adopted two styles, one derived from Tudor and vernacular models, the other from Georgian.

Buller's Wood at Chislehurst, Kent (1889) is an early and large example of the first manner. He enclosed a stuccoed early Victorian house in a brick building with stone string courses; leaded, stone mullioned windows; crow-stepped gables and tall rectangular chimneys. At Redcourt, near Haslemere, Surrey (1894), he was much more formal with round-topped sash windows set into a Georgian brick carapace. The elevations are at first glance symmetrical, and only a vestige of almost wilful Ruskinian changefulness keeps them from being totally so.

In the next decade Newton was producing completely symmetrical elevations, for instance at Luckley, Wokingham, Berkshire (1907), a charming mixture of Wrenian roof and cornice on top of low brick walls relieved by leaded lights in wooden casements. Yet Luckley retains the thin room-and-corridor Arts and Crafts plan, cunningly bent into an H-shape, and the symmetry is relieved by a service wing which cranks round from the main entrance to the west.

Newton was at his most relaxed when adding to old houses – for example Upton Grey Manor, Hampshire (1907), for the editor of *The*

HOUSES·AT·FROGNAL·HAMPSTEAD FOR·T·J·COBDEN-SANDERSON·AND REGINALD·BLOMFIELD·1892·

THE·PLAN·

Reginald Blomfield. Houses at Frognal, Hampstead, London (1892). A pair for the architect and bookbinder T. J. Cobden-Sanderson

W. H. Brierley. Bishopsbarns, St George's Place, York (1905)

Detmar Blow. Happisburgh Manor, Cromer, Norfolk (1900)

Studio, where he added traditional half-timbering and tile hanging in exactly the spirit of the original building. He did the same at Oldcastle, Dallington, Sussex (1910) to produce a late (for Newton) irregular, asymmetrical complex of breathtaking horizontal sweep and simplicity; the brick ground floor is topped by a tile-hung upper storey, with the tile roof cramming hard down over the eaves and sometimes swooping down to top the bricks. Again, it was an extension to an old house from which Newton adapted idioms. At Oldcastle, the servants' quarters were cranked right round a courtyard with the corridor on the inside. Newton used this device again in his most formal house – Burgh Heath, Surrey (1912) where, without an old model to develop, he created an almost Palladian front for the main rooms in totally symmetrical ashlar relieved by knapped flint wings. But the house is as usual thin, and all the offices are stuck out in a great quadrangular block at one side surrounding a glazed courtyard.

However symmetrical, however Palladian, Newton became, the plan was always paramount; Pugin's principles were never entirely forgotten. 'I emphasize the plan', he wrote 'as that is really the house...Building must fall into some sort of style – memory, inherited forms, and ideas. But this must be accepted, not sought. Pass all through the mill of your mind and don't use forms unmeaningly, like the buttons on the back of a coat.'[11]

Charles Edward Bateman (1863-1947) was articled to his father, John Jones Bateman, but worked for Verity & Hunt in London before returning to Birmingham to join the family firm. In C. E.'s time, Bateman & Bateman was celebrated for numerous houses in the West Midlands, in particular the Sutton Coldfield area, which had a strong Cotswold feel. But the practice was general, and some of C. E.'s most original projects were for commercial premises in Birmingham, designed round the turn of the century.

Francis W. Bedford (1866-1904) and **Sydney Kitson (1871-1937)** were as influential in creating the new suburbs of Leeds as Bidlake in Birmingham or Wood in Manchester. Muthesius commented that 'their exteriors are more or less traditional in design, but inside they experiment in more independent ways, though without becoming fantastic...and give an impression of quiet refinement'.[12] Bedford & Kitson were free eclectics, drawing on both local and southern models, and were early into the game of reintroducing Classical idioms.

Bedford was articled in Leeds and was an assistant to Ernest George & Peto before returning there. After Bedford's early death, Kitson devoted himself to scholarship and collecting. He retired young.

William Henry Bidlake (1861-1938) set a tone of simplicity and restraint in the great suburban expansion of Birmingham round the turn of the century. *The Studio* reported in 1902 that: 'There is probably no architect in Birmingham who has influenced and guided the younger men of his profession to the same extent as Mr W. H. Bidlake'.[13] By then, Bidlake had been teaching at Birmingham's architecture school for 10 years after training in Bodley's office and being RIBA Pugin Scholar in 1885.

Bidlake's models were vernacular but he avoided 'the suburban villa with samples of every manner of building – brick, half-timber, tile hanging and roughcast'.[14] His houses had strong shapes, usually restricted to a combination of two main materials: brick and stone; roughcast and brick; tile hanging and half-timbering. His St Agatha's church at Sparkbrook has this restraint in materials but is relieved by bands of joyous carving.

Reginald Theodore Blomfield (1856-1942), though he became the arch-protagonist of Classicism in the early years of the twentieth century, was much involved in the Arts and Crafts movement. He was one of the young men who gravitated to the Lethaby and Prior group in the '80s and he was involved, with Lethaby, in Kenton & Co, the short-lived Arts and Crafts furniture firm. For all his love of Classical architecture he was prepared to compromise in the country. Even as late as 1909, long after he had started to preach the virtues of the Beaux Arts, he designed Wyphurst near Cranleigh, Surrey, a very complicated mixture of an existing house with a large new wing, all in diapered brickwork and half-timbering. It is a symmetrical Victorian Tudor building struggling to emerge from a vernacular complex of gables and hung tiles.

Detmar Blow (1867-1939) met Ruskin as a young man and was introduced to the Morris circle. He was Pugin Scholar of the Royal Institute in 1892. In the late '90s he was Gimson's site clerk on the wonderfully rustic Stoneywell cottage. In 1900 he built Happisburgh Manor on the sea-front near Cromer in Norfolk, a butterfly plan which geometrically out-Priors Prior's nearby (and slightly later) butterfly house at Holt by making the house angled on all four sides like an X with a stretched centre. Incidentally, Blow claimed that the inspiration for Happisburgh did not come from Prior's Exmouth Barn but 'originated with my friend Mr Ernest Gimson who sent the little butterfly device on a postcard'.[15]

He was as faithful to local materials as Prior but used them in more conventional local fashion – thick flint walls are patterned and quoined in brick and capped by a thick thatched roof.

Blow's work during the next decade moved from a free interpretation of local idioms towards Classicism of various kinds. By the '20s he had an extremely successful practice which built throughout the Empire – for instance Government House in Salisbury, Rhodesia. He was surveyor to the Grosvenor Estate for 17 years, encouraging creeping Neo-Georgianism over Mayfair. He died as the Lord of the Manor of Painswick, Gloucestershire.

Walter Henry Brierley (1862-1926) was articled to his father in York and his mature practice was conducted there. He ranged from country houses which freely interpreted local idiom through Neo-Classical banks and Gothic churches to racecourse buildings. His obituary in *The Builder* aptly summarizes the influence of Arts and Crafts thinking on a successful provincial practitioner: 'He was a master of detail, and upheld the principle that no single item, however small, in the composition of a building was outside the scope of the architect's most scrupulous care and consideration. He insisted on the employment of the very best materials and workmanship that the means placed at his disposal allowed. He had a great admiration of the craftsmanship of the past, and skilfully employed and adapted old

W.A. Harvey. Infants' school, Bournville model village, nr Birmingham (1910)

W.A. Forsyth. Dovecote. Illustrated in Muthesius's *Das englische Haus*

Guy Dawber. Foord Almshouses, Rochester (1926-27)

methods...directing and interesting the workmen, and encouraging them to revive forgotten details of their craft, in order to secure that harmony between the design and execution of it on which the successful portrayal of his ideas so much depended'.[16]

Walter Frederick Cave (1863-1939) was an archetypal hearty Edwardian. The son of a baronet, he was articled to Sir Arthur Blomfield (Reginald's uncle). He built many robust country houses, usually in local materials. Muthesius likened him to Voysey and thought that 'the external appearance of his houses is almost more successful than Voysey's; his surfaces have a broader sweep and the whole is more expressive'.[17] His furniture was highly regarded. His practice became very large and he had much urban work as well as the country buildings for which he was best known.

Ethel Mary Charles (1871-1962) was elected to being the first woman member of the Royal Institute of British Architects in December 1898, against a good deal of curmudgeonly opposition. (Some of the more old-fashioned members were astounded to find that anyone who had passed the examinations was eligible for membership.) She trained in the Ernest George & Peto office, then with Walter Cave.

She made an entry to the Letchworth Cheap Cottages Exhibition in 1905, and carried on a flourishing, mostly domestic, practice in Falmouth, London and Letchworth. Her sister, Bessie Ada, became the second woman member of the RIBA in 1900; they practised together.

William Harrison Cowlishaw (1869-1957) designed one of the weirdest products of the Arts and Crafts movement as virtually his only independent work: The Cloisters, Letchworth, which was made for Miss A. J. Lawrence as a private school of psychology for 20 students. A huge brick affair full of savage touches with a rambling plan of many axes pinned down by a rather municipal tower, the place offered its inmates no proper separation between inside and out. Instead as the architect enthusiastically recorded, they 'will sleep on flat frame hammocks, slung from vaulting around the cloisters. By means of the exterior curtains and the divisional curtains complete privacy is ensured'.[18]

Such a programme might have worked in the physical and idealistic climate of Southern California, but not surprisingly it failed in the Home Counties. The building was never completed. Cowlishaw worked for the Imperial War Graves Commission in France in the War, and stayed there until 1930, after which he returned to London to work for Holden.

Edward Guy Dawber (1862-1938) was a King's Lynn man who attended the Royal Academy Schools. He served his articles in Lynn and became an assistant to Ernest George & Peto, by whom he was sent, during a fit of bad sight in 1887, to be site clerk for building Batsford Park, Gloucestershire.[19]

One of the first Arts and Craftsmen to discover the Cotswolds, he started his own practice two or three years later at Bourton-on-the-Hill, from where he walked miles to his first jobs – all informed by the vernacular building of the district and built on long, thin Arts and Crafts plans. He set up in London in 1891 but retained his Gloucestershire

Gerald Horsley. Design for a country house (published in *The Builder* 1894)

P. Morley Horder. Spyways. Hartfield, Sussex

connection and became one of the most successful country house architects, practising all over England well into the '20s, often blending local idioms with the Classical forms he increasingly preferred. He was president of the RIBA in 1925-27 and founded the Council for the Preservation of Rural England.

Francis Charles Eden (1864-1944) was an almost perfect SPAB architect. He was the son of a wealthy barrister and, perhaps because of inherited money, spent most of his life in rather humble work on improvement of country churches, designing stained glass windows, and works in other crafts. On occasion, he could be a good domestic architect, for instance at Ardeley, Hertfordshire, where he worked on the church, built the village hall, and made some delightful thatched cottages. He died a Neo-Georgian, after living in bachelor splendour in Bedford Square.

William Adam Forsyth (1872-1951) was a distinguished preservationist and a devoted custodian of notable buildings like Salisbury Cathedral and St George's Chapel, Windsor. His original work was often for public schools ranging from Eton to Oundle where he usually offered heavy handed stripped variants of the Cotswold style. As a young man, he was inventive in garden design, and his work was illustrated by both Mawson and Muthesius.

Arthur Grove (1870-1929) was articled to J. D. Sedding and stayed on in the office when Henry Wilson inherited it on Sedding's death. He was principally a church architect and, before the War worked much with Prior, culminating in their collaboration on St Osmund's, Parkstone. His own work was mainly in Wales; the practice collapsed after 1915.

Arthur Jessop Hardwick (1867-1948) was articled to the relatively unknown R. W. Collier. He practised from Kingston-upon-Thames and his many house designs in a rather chaste Old English were widely published in England and Germany before the War.

William Alexander Harvey (1875-1951) was articled to a small Birmingham architect and then trained at the city's art school under Bidlake. He had a very extensive practice ranging from country houses to factories, was much involved in the Garden City Movement, and was architect to the Bournville Village Trust, the Cadbury chocolate company's model settlement near Birmingham, from 1895 to 1907, when he worked out overall planning principles on picturesque lines and contributed some housing and public buildings in a rather heavy Neo-Tudor.

Percy Morley Horder (1870-1944) was trained in George Devey's office. He designed many large country houses and was favoured by *The Studio*. Some of his houses have characteristics in common with the work of Voysey – another product of the Devey office. But though Horder's buildings often have sweeping roofs, low eaves and rows of casement windows, houses like Spyways, Hartfield, Sussex, are more lush and jumbled than Voysey's and they are usually executed in local materials rather than Voysey's ubiquitous roughcast. Horder's practice was varied and included much work for universities.

Gerald Callcott Horsley (1862-1917) was the youngest of Norman

Shaw's young men who founded the Art Workers' Guild. He was the son of a painter and, after being with Shaw, he worked for Sedding for a year before travelling to Italy and France in 1886 and to Sicily 1887-88 (under RIBA studentships). He was a fine draughtsman and illustrated, among other books, Prior's *History of Gothic Art in England*. His own architectural work (1889 to his early death) varied from romantic Old English country houses to Queen Anne buildings in town. As Arthur Keen, a fellow pupil in Shaw's office, remembered: 'His regard for his master amounted almost to veneration and it led him, perhaps, into following the actual forms of Norman Shaw's work in preference to breaking new ground for himself, but he invested all that he touched with his own sense of beauty and fitness'.[20]

Robert Lorimer. Laverockdale, nr Edinburgh (1912-14)

His delicate individual touch is clear in his design for a country house* where sweeping hips and gables top walls of diapered brick-work, hung tiles and stone mullioned windows with leaded lights all set off by large relief panels of Pre-Raphaelite pastoral scenes – few designs are closer to Morris's image of the Hammersmith Guest House. The St Paul's School for Girls, Hammersmith (1904-07), his chief London work, is Queen Anne at its most relaxed – ample, generous and much encrusted with the reliefs that his country clients could not afford.

Robert Stodart Lorimer (1864-1929) was the father of a school of Scottish vernacular building much less original than Mackintosh's work but more faithful to traditional seventeenth- and eighteenth-century models. Muthesius was very impressed: 'Scotland will not achieve what England has already achieved – a completely national style of house-building based on the old vernacular architecture – until it follows the lead given by Lorimer'.[21]

Geoffry Lucas. Housing (now Lucas Square), Hampstead Garden Suburb (c1906)

Laverockdale, on the Pentlands near Edinburgh, is typical of Lorimer's large country houses. It is like a large border tower complete with crow-stepped gables and steep slated roofs, and small sash windows pocking the massive walls of local rubble. It has long thin Arts and Crafts wings.

Thomas Geoffry Lucas (1872-1947) was essentially a suburban architect who built up a successful pre-war domestic and ecclesiastical practice north of London, where he built in Hampstead Garden Suburb and Broxbourne. In this period, he largely followed Gothic and vernacular forms. After the War, he went into partnership with the very successful H. V. Lanchester and was involved in designs for mighty Classical civic buildings such as the University of Leeds. He left Lanchester for obscurity because, as the latter said, 'the extent of our activities did not offer T. G. Lucas the scope he desired for giving an intensive study to specific undertakings'.[22]

Charles Rennie Mackintosh. Windyhill, Kilmalcolm, Renfrewshire (1899-1901)

Mervyn Edmund Macartney (1853-1932) was the least Ruskinian of Norman Shaw's young men who founded the Art Workers' Guild. The son of a Northern Irish doctor, he entered Shaw's office a year before Lethaby, with whom he was to be associated in Kenton & Co.

He started in practice in 1882 with a design for an Old English country house, Kent Hatch, and this vein persisted well into the 1900s

*Published in the *The Builder* LXVI, 3 February 1894.

Mackintosh. Hill House, Helensburgh, Dunbartonshire (1902-04). Scots vernacular, abstracted, and incorporating details from the English Arts and Crafts school

Edward Brantwood Maufe. Kelling Hall, Norfolk. (Drawing by J. B. Scott 1912.) Kelling was the last great butterfly house

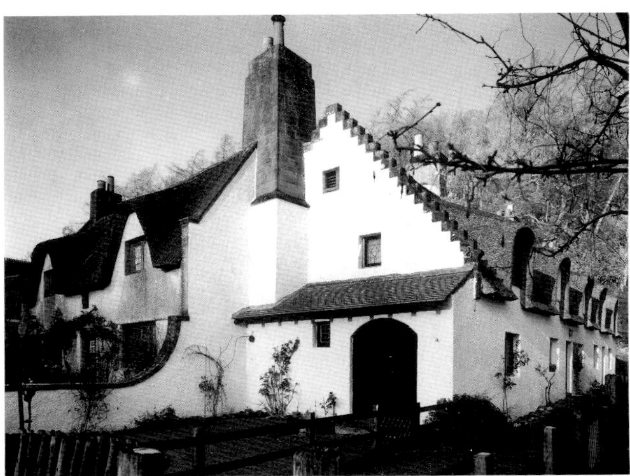

James Marjoribanks MacLaren. Kirkton Cottages, Fortingall (1889)

with soft, gentle houses like Rosebank, Silchester Common, Hampshire. But he became a strong protagonist of conventional Neo-Georgian, rarely achieving Newton's inventiveness in the style.

His *annus mirabilis* was 1906 when he beat Blomfield to the post of Architect to St Paul's Cathedral and became editor of *The Architectural Review* in succession to D. S. MacColl and a board which included Blomfield. The *Practical Exemplar of Architecture*, a series which showed 'correct' eighteenth-century detailing, was published in *The Architectural Review* between 1906 and 1913 and became one of the most influential forces in the movement towards Classicism.

Charles Rennie Mackintosh (1868-1928) was, according to Muthesius, 'The real driving force of the Scottish movement'. The essence of the art of the Glasgow group 'in fact rests in an underlying emotional and poetical quality. It seeks a highly charged...atmosphere of a mystical symbolic kind. One cannot imagine a greater contrast in this respect than that between the London architects working in the new forms, the most sedulous of whom is Voysey, and the Scottish architects round Mackintosh'.[23]

Yet, F. H. Newbury, under whom Mackintosh studied at the Glasgow School of Art, suggested that Voysey was the young Mackintosh's chief inspiration.* Voysey himself disliked the work of the Glasgow artists and called them the 'spook school', but elements of his work are clear in Mackintosh's country houses.

*There is certainly a continuity in decorative elements like the long tapering verticals capped by wafer thin finials that stretches from Mackmurdo through Voysey to Mackintosh.

The life of Mackintosh has been so excellently told[24] that the career of the Glasgow policeman's son, who rose to such heroic European stature that he was dragged by architectural students through the streets of Vienna in a flower-covered carriage, does not need to be covered here.

His architectural genius flowered for only 10 years from 1896 to about 1906, when it faded under the combined influence of work and whisky. During this period he built two outstanding country houses: Windyhill, Kilmalcolm, Renfrewshire (1899-1901) and Hill House, Helensburgh, Dunbartonshire (1902-04). Both derived much from Scottish eighteenth-century models and had slate roofs, white harlinged walls, drum stair towers and sash windows. Both had long thin Arts and Crafts plans. And both incorporated Voyseyish details – tall chimney stacks with sloping sides, strips of dormer windows (Windyhill only) and polygonal, projecting bay windows with wooden sashes.

Yet the result was more changeful than anything Voysey ever wished to achieve (after he had started to build). Hill House, particularly, achieved a stark vertical grandeur that is very Scottish yet quite original. The rooms were good but not especially remarkable for their period – except that they were made magical by Mackintosh's delicate and inventive furniture and ornament.

It was the sort of furniture and decoration that Mackintosh, his wife Margaret MacDonald and her sister Frances exhibited at the 1896 Arts and Crafts Exhibition Society show. They were met with English incomprehension. *The Studio* commented that 'no doubt in Glasgow there is a Rosetta stone, which makes clear the tangled meanings of these designs...One thing however is clear, that in their own way, unmoved by ridicule, or misconception, the Glasgow students have thought out a very fascinating scheme to puzzle, surprise and please'.[25]

James Marjoribanks MacLaren (1853-1890) was born near Stirling and was apprenticed to James Salmon in Glasgow before moving to J. J. Stevenson's office in the capital (known as 'the stepping stone to London' by young Scots draughtsmen, and the nursery of several Arts and Crafts architects including F. W. Troup).

He entered partnership with Cornishman Richard Coad in the early '80s and worked with him on various commissions in the West Country. Independently, he won the competition for extending Stirling High School in 1886, which led to Scottish commissions, many for Sir Donald Currie, a shipping magnate, for whom he designed estate buildings at Fortingall, Perthshire in the late '80s and early '90s. These were in a blend of Scottish and Cornish fishing village idioms, with white harled walls, crow-stepped gables and thatched roofs, and are held[26] to have foreshadowed Mackintosh's work.

MacLaren's London buildings were largely houses in an idiosyncratic Queen Anne style. His early death ended a career which promised much.

Charles Edward Mallows. Design for a country house near Severn Upton (1888)

Charles Edward Mallows (1864-1915) was a Bedford architect deeply interested in garden design as well as building. He illustrated *Gardens for Small Country Houses* by Gertrude Jekyll and Lawrence Weaver and worked with Thomas Mawson on *The Art and Craft of Garden Making*. In partnership with various architects at different times, principally George Grocock, Mallows executed numerous new country buildings as well as alterations and extensions to existing country houses all over the south of England. His work, as draughtsman, garden designer and architect, was always delicate and sensitive with deep respect for local tradition.

Edward Maufe (1883-1974) was one of the youngest architects who can reasonably be called a member of the Arts and Crafts movement. He trained under W. A. Pite. Before the War, he built several large country houses, the most grand of which was Kelling Hall, Norfolk, a butterfly house like Prior's Home Place further round the coast. His treatment of materials was not as radical as Prior's, but just as much based on local precedent. In the '20s and '30s, Maufe built up a flourishing practice, gaining Guildford Cathedral in 1932 with a stripped Gothic design. He became very stolid.

Arnold Mitchell. Own house, Lyme Regis (1920s)

Arnold Mitchell (1863-1944) was trained under Ernest George. He was much illustrated in *The Studio* in the first decade of this century, showing large country houses in England, Wales and Scotland, mostly with symmetrical elements, though he preferred variations on the typical Arts and Crafts plan. He moved from free interpretations of Tudor and vernacular motifs to almost proper Wren. His practice became very large; he put up the main stations for the (British financed) Argentinian railways as well as buildings in Germany, Austria, Belgium and at the Aswan Dam. And he designed Lotts playbricks, composition blocks in white, pink and blue with which virtually

Niven and Wigglesworth. Design for a country house at Wrotham, Kent (c1902)

Alfred Powell. Long Copse, Ewhurst, Surrey (1897). G.F. Watts thought it the most beautiful house in Surrey

every middle class child for three generations was brought up to make primitive Classical buildings.

When he retired to Lyme Regis in the '20s, Mitchell returned to his first love and built himself one of the last, most beautiful and original small Arts and Crafts houses. A tall, thin five storey building in local limestone rubble, with a flat top, it is dominated by a hooded bay window with neat, stone dressed mullions and leaded lights. A big ornamental sundial enriches the lower part of the oriel which has a broad, shallow hipped slate hat tying it to the rest of the fenestration. It is the house of a grown-up who has never forgotten childhood; a sea-shore tower studded with superb examples of local fossil ammonites.

David Barkley Niven (1864-1942) was a Scot and an Aston Webb man, who went into partnership with Herbert Hardy Wigglesworth (1866-1949) who had trained under Ernest George & Peto. Niven & Wigglesworth produced elegant and changeful house designs in the '90s, many of which were presented in Niven's beautiful perspectives in *The Studio*. They made a design for the Letchworth Cheap Cottages Exhibition in 1905. After the turn of the century, the practice acquired a good deal of City work which was mostly Neo-Georgian – for instance Hambro's Bank, Bishopsgate (1925). The partnership was dissolved in 1927.

Segar Owen (born in 1874) was articled to his father William and trained at the Royal Academy Schools. He had a flourishing practice in Warrington and throughout Lancashire. With his father, he was involved in the planning of Port Sunlight, Lever Brothers' model settlement near Birkenhead. Owen built some of the cottage groups in modified northern Old English, making workers' housing of a very high standard for the time. He also designed some of the public buildings, notably the Lady Lever Art Gallery (1914-22) in a grand Beaux Arts manner.

Alfred Powell (c1865-1960) seems to have had little formal training or apprenticeship but G. F. Watts, the painter, described Long Copse at Ewhurst as the most beautiful house in Surrey. It was a combination of an existing thatched cottage and a new wing covered in stone slates. The iron casement windows with leaded lights were divided by simple stone mullions. The plan was similar to Gimson's Stoneywell cottage, a series of rooms linked in line which crank round a curved staircase. The austerity was relieved by a sgraffito picture of peacocks in light red and white on the verandah.

Powell was both architect and contractor, and 'the craftsmen (save the plumbers – an entertaining exception) were University men who worked with him'.[27] Powell did little architecture and (with his wife Louise) concentrated on decorative painting for Gimson and Sidney Barnsley's furniture, and for the Wedgwood pottery firm. He was active in the Society for the Protection of Ancient Buildings, producing pamphlets explaining how country buildings should be restored and repaired.

Ernest Turner Powell (1859-1937) was a moderately successful country house architect. Much of his work was in Surrey and Sussex, though he had some foreign clients. He had a lush Old English touch.

Ernest Turner Powell. West Chart, Limpsfield, Surrey (before 1909)

Alfred Noble Prentice. Design for stables at Cavenham Hall, Suffolk (before 1904)

Fond of local materials, he used clapboarding, patterned hung tiles and brick in the home counties. He was inventive with gables.

Alfred Noble Prentice (1866-1941) was a Scot, articled in Glasgow, after which he worked for Colcutt. He built up a prosperous practice which included interior decoration for some of the large early twentieth-century steamships. Though an early advocate of Classicism (he published *Renaissance Architecture and Ornament in Spain* in 1893), he was happy to adopt vernacular models in the country – for instance in his unexecuted design for a house at Willersey, Gloucestershire (1908) which has all the local characteristics.

Charles Henry Bourne Quennell (1872-1935) was described by Muthesius as one of the architects 'for the most part concerned with interior decoration and furniture design' and the 'master of pen-and-ink drawing'.[28] As a young man he worked at a joiner's shop as Ruskinian training. Like Baillie Scott, he designed standardized Arts and Crafts furniture (particularly inglenooks and fireplaces) for J. P. White of Bedford, but he had quite a large architectural practice as well, mostly devoted to small country and suburban houses based on vernacular and Georgian models.

Quennell is most widely known for his *History of Everyday Things in England* (1918) in which, with his wife Marjorie, he gave an endlessly entertaining story for children of the development of English design, ranging over everything from architecture to jewellery from the Norman Conquest to 1899 (it was supplemented by later volumes taking the story back to the Stone Age and up to the '30s). The book's exposition of the interaction of everyday life, symbolism and design must have delighted Lethaby. After the War, Quennell became a devotee of industrialization and designed work in Essex for Crittalls, the steel window manufacturers.

Halsey Ricardo (1854-1928) was the son of a Bristol banker, and rich enough to take only the commissions he really wanted; he worked entirely by himself at home. After school at Rugby, he was articled in Chelmsford and worked for Basil Champneys, after which he fell under Philip Webb's spell. He started on his own in 1881 and went into partnership with William de Morgan, the Arts and Crafts potter, between 1888 and 1898. He was devoted to Persian-coloured glazed tiles in his urban work.

Ricardo alternated between Classical and vernacular idioms. In the country, he tended towards many gabled houses in brick, stone or stucco with wooden casement windows. His radical ideas on town building, where he was mostly Classical, are described in chapter 11.

Robert Weir Schultz (1860-1951), after training in Scotland under Rowand Anderson (whose office provided Lorimer with his first steps in architecture), moved south to join Norman Shaw in early 1884. There he befriended Lethaby and his circle: the founders of the Art Workers' Guild, Gimson and the Barnsley brothers. In 1886, he moved to Ernest George & Peto, where he overlapped with Dawber and Baker. Evening study at the RA schools won him a scholarship which he used for study in Italy. In 1889 Schultz was in Greece studying Byzantine architecture with Sidney Barnsley. A common interest in Byzantine

Halsey Ricardo. House for William Chance (1898)

architecture was probably the point of contact between Schultz and the third Marquess of Bute,[29] perhaps the most fantastic builder of Victorian times, who had commissioned some of Burges's best work. Bute became Schultz's patron, giving him work in rural Scotland, where, in the early '90s, the architect adopted local traditional building techniques – though when necessary (for instance when adding to the Adams' Dumfries House) he was not averse to adopting a more Classical approach.

A strong taste for symmetry permeated Schultz's mature work but it was usually leavened with an affection for local vernacular motifs and, where necessary, a freedom in planning which would have upset strict Classicists. His largest – and perhaps best – building was St Anne's Hospital, Canford Cliffs, Bournemouth (1909-1912) designed with F. W. Troup. It is almost perfectly symmetrical with two lines of room-and-corridor cranked to get the best views from the top of the cliffs; the two banks are linked by chains of rooms to form courtyards. The building was certainly institutional but with its bending, changeful, light-filled corridors and its careful maximization of sun and view for patients, it demonstrated what freedom the Arts and Crafts movement could bring to large buildings when it was given the chance. The exterior is (like some other Schultz buildings) in a kind of austere Queen Anne with big Dutch gables topping bays, all executed in simple, straightforward brickwork with stone dressings.

Schultz built the Khartoum Cathedral between 1906 and 1928, carefully executed on the principles laid down in Lethaby's *Cosmos* and with techniques suitable for local builders, many of which were based on Byzantine models.

Schultz changed his name by adding another Weir to R. W. S. Weir during the anti-German hysteria of 1914. His practice declined during the War and afterwards it gradually faded away. On retirement in 1939 he went into nominal partnership with his more successful friend Troup. He had always refused to accept full-blown Classicism, and, like those of his contemporaries who stuck by their early beliefs, he paid dearly for his devotion to Arts and Crafts freedom.

George John Skipper (1854-1948) was the leading Norfolk architect of the early years of this century and had a flourishing practice which employed a great variety of styles ranging from fruity Edwardian Baroque used for the headquarters of the Norwich Union insurance company to simple cottages for rural local authorities. Surprisingly, he continued to build these well into the 1920s, and at their best, they add to existing villages with sympathy and sensitivity. Skipper experimented in some of them with traditional building methods such as clunch and knapped flint.

Arnold Dunbar Smith (1866-1933) and **Cecil Brewer (1871-1918)** set up in practice together in 1895 and are best known for the Passmore Edwards Settlement in Bloomsbury (chapter 11). Smith & Brewer built some distinguished country houses. For example, Fives Court, near Pinner, Middlesex was a roughcast, deep-roofed version of Voysey without his pronounced horizontality; Acremead, Crockham Hill, Kent, was a rubble house with fine cut stone dressings and many

Smith & Brewer. Fives Court, Pinner, Middlesex, the garden front (c1905)

Robert Weir Schultz. St Anne's Hospital, Canford Cliffs, Bournemouth, Dorset (1909-12)

gables, some banded. Both had long thin plans. The Smith and Brewer practice became very successful, building the Edwardian Baroque National Museum of Wales in 1910. After Brewer's death, Smith continued a country house practice.

Leonard Stokes (1858-1925) was one of the most successful Arts and Crafts architects. He started in practice in 1883 after working for Street, Collcutt and Bodley. He was irascible and swore much, despite which he did a lot of work for Roman Catholic institutes. His most notable country work was All Saints Convent, London Colney, Hertfordshire (1899-1903), a free interpretation of late Tudor models in brick, strongly gridded in stone. There is a fine sculpted frieze over the main door in the tower designed by Henry Wilson.

His country houses usually followed the Arts and Crafts plan. He designed many telephone exchanges (see chapter 11) and, in towns, felt the need to adopt free Classical forms which were increasingly carried into his country work. Muthesius commented that 'in his non classicizing houses at least, he also treats the few details entirely as he pleases, in a free and witty manner that is attractive in its mixture of forcefulness and charm'.[30]

Charles Harrison Townsend (1851-1928) did most of his most interesting work in London (discussed in chapter 11), but he was a successful and original designer in the country too. Articled in Liverpool, he moved to London in about 1880 and had set up on his own by the end of the decade.[31]

In his larger country houses, he favoured the Arts and Crafts plan but his elevations – as for instance at Blatchfield, Blackheath near Guildford (probably about 1894) – are more changeful than most, with many variations of plane and materials; it is Shaw and Nesfield's Old English style stretched out in a long line. Some of his later large houses, like the design for Cliff Towers, Salcombe, Devon, retained the long plan and the variety of materials but are more unified.

Muthesius thought that if he had had more opportunities to build houses, he would have been the most important of the post-Shaw domestic architects.[32] In fact, his practice withered in the first decade of this century because he refused to bow to Neo-Classicism.

Before defeat set in, Townsend designed a triumph of the Arts and Crafts spirit. St Mary the Virgin, at Great Warley, near Brentwood, Essex (begun 1902) could at first glance be taken for a typical Essex country church with low, ample proportions, apsed end and buttressed roughcast walls pierced by simple, undecorated stone window surrounds; tiled roofs sweep down into broad eaves, and, at the west end, they are crowned by a little stubby square shingled bell tower and spire. All is quite in the local tradition, done with a simplicity and humility that would have delighted Pugin and Morris. The external unconventionalities are in the west front (which faces away from the road) with its big rose window floating over slits set in plain ashlar (the latter theme being a hallmark of Townsend's town work – see chapter 11).

The inside is big, welcoming and simple, like Prior's early churches. Only a small change of level separates nave from chancel, and at first

LOVE
PEACE
THE RECTORS

the small chapel that emerges on the south side cannot be seen. The space focuses on the figure of Christ in the centre of the silvered apse onto which light from the rose window shines.

As the eye becomes accustomed to the comparative gloom of the interior, great richness gradually unfolds: angels and flowers are everywhere. Most of the ornament is by William Reynolds-Stephens (1852-1943), Townsend's collaborator. The simple boarded roof is supported on wide ribs decorated with white York roses on silver stems and foliage. The ribs terminate in panels of white lilies on a silver ground.*

Everywhere, the church is a mixture of plain setting and pearl ornament – squares of mother-of-pearl in Townsend's walnut panelling and in the mother-of-pearl flowers which, with glowing ruby glass pomegranates, decorate the building's glory – its bronze rood-screen. The flowers and fruits are set among the glittering and green foliage of six heraldically stiff bronze Arts and Crafts trees. From the crown of each tree emerges an angel – a subject which, judging by its frequent occurrence in the rest of the church, was a favourite of Reynolds-Stephens at the time.

All the church's ornament, however luxurious, is stiff, heraldic and symmetrical. Like the surrounding garden of rest with its straight axial gravel paths, cypress avenue and pleached lime groves, the ornament expresses the Englishness of a building that has too often been claimed to be a triumph of the Art Nouveau. Townsend and Reynolds-Stephens could not compromise with the advancing wave of Neo-Classicism nor could they embrace the *risqué* 'squirm' of Continental Art Nouveau.

At Great Warley, the Arts and Crafts movement achieved the integration of ecclesiastical art that Sedding's Holy Trinity had sketched on a much larger scale 10 years before. But, by 1906, when Reynolds-Stephens had completed the decorations, few clients wanted such a humble yet gorgeous building. Taste was gradually beginning to turn to the more obviously prestigious results of one form or another of Neo-Classicism.

Francis William Troup (1859-1941) was pictured by Ashbee as a 'dour, uncompromising Scot, who clucks like a hen and roars like a lion yet seldom seems to have anything to say'.**[33] An Aberdeenshire man, he was apprenticed to a Glasgow firm and worked for Rowand Anderson. He went to London, and worked for J. J. Stevenson and others before setting up on his own in 1891.

Troup was a close friend of Henry Wilson. His early work had a Gothic flavour; for instance the walls of the heavy gabled Sandhouse (now Kingwood), Sandhills, Surrey (1902) are so extremely strongly diapered with blue vitrified headers that the effect of the overall massing is muted. His little village hall at Wooton Fitzpaine, Dorset (1906) has splendid simple timber arches and a remarkably complicated angu-

Charles Harrison Townsend. St Mary the Virgin, Great Warley, Essex (1902-04). Interior, with Reynolds-Stephens's rood screen

Townsend. Cliff Towers, Salcombe, Devon. Design (c1898)

*When the church was first built the effect must have seemed even more strange and exotic for the silver is achieved in aluminium, a metal that had been in commercial production only since 1896. The lily panels and the decoration of the ribs are of fibrous plaster silvered in aluminium leaf.

**Mrs Levson, Troup's niece, has told me that the roaring and clucking was her uncle's party trick for children.

Francis William Troup. Sandhouse, Sandhills, Surrey (1901-03)

George Walton. The Leys, Elstree, Hertfordshire (1901)

lar chimney. He was very fond of lead, which he called 'the English metal', and got excellent leadwork – in drainpipes everywhere, and, at Wooton, in frilly little friezes over the door canopy. Even as early as Sandhills, the plan is symmetrical and there are Classical columns supporting the entrance porch. His hall for the Art Workers' Guild (1913) in Queen Square is in inventive, free Neo-Georgian.

Troup became immensely respectable: supervising architect under Baker for rebuilding the Bank of England, and consulting architect to official bodies like the Home Office and Metropolitan Police for whom he designed asylums for the criminally insane.

Hugh Thackeray Turner (1850-1937) was articled in the Scott office and followed Morris as secretary of the Society for the Protection of Ancient Buildings, a post he occupied from shortly after SPAB's foundation in 1876 for 29 years. In that capacity he helped save many notable buildings from excessive restoration. His practice (with Eustace Balfour – a brother of the future Prime Minister A. J.) was partly urban; they were architects to the Grosvenor Estate in Mayfair which involved much Neo-Georgian work. Of his extensive country house work, his own Westbrook, overlooking Godalming in Surrey was, according to Troup,[34] the most notable. 'Here...is shown Turner's intimate knowledge of the building crafts...and his success in making every part of the structure not merely equal to its task, but to look sufficient for its work.'

George Walton (1876-1933) was a virtually self-taught Glasgow designer, who was discovered by Kate Cranston in the late 1880s. She set him up with some of her tea rooms (Walton was the main designer of the Buchanan Street branch where Mackintosh earned so much fame). He started a company, modelled on the Morris firm, which was very successful at the turn of the century, with large numbers of commissions for domestic and commercial interiors (the latter principally for the emerging Kodak photographic company). Muthesius called him 'the artist who has understood the interior as a work of art best'.[35] His style was individual, with elements of Christopher Dresser, the Aesthetic Movement, as well as Arts and Crafts influences. His showrooms for Kodak (all now destroyed) were scattered all over Europe.

After the turn of the century, he practised as an architect, and produced a small number of idiosyncratic buildings (largely houses for directors of Kodak). The architectural work was much less assured than the design. It perhaps shows the difference between the conception of changefulness produced by an untrained architect and those who had gone through apprenticeship. The Leys at Elstree has a remarkable atrium hall but a rather dull symmetrical exterior. Two of his most interesting houses were finished in 1908 for George Davison. Wern Fawr, near Harlech, is solid local stone, a cross between a Classical eighteenth-century mill and a castle. The White House at Shiplake on the Thames, is a blend of Regency with Arts and Crafts vernacular, dominated by an elegant bow with delicate metalwork and thin lines. For the latter, Walton was hailed on dubious grounds as a pioneer of the Modern Movement by the young *Architectural Review* polemicists of the '30s.

Above: Randall Wells. Kempley Church, Hereford and Worcester (1904). Right: Interior with pews by architect, Barnsley lectern. Wells carved the ornament on the rood truss

Randall Wells (1877-1942) was a model Arts and Crafts architect. He worked as site clerk for Prior at Holt and Roker and also did the same for Lethaby at Brockhampton. His little church at Kempley, which was built for Lord Beauchamp in 1904, is near Brockhampton and, in it, Wells took the principles of Pugin and Ruskin further than Lethaby ever did.

The roof was of Forest of Dean stone, local stone roofing quarries had fallen into disuse. It is now replaced by tiles. Their weight is carried on mighty oak trusses cut from trees from the Beauchamp estate and used green. The eaves are about head height and the walls of reddish local sandstone. There is no decoration in the stonework, apart from a few mouldings round the openings to throw off water and a relief sculpted into the tower over the door by the architect. The tracery of the great west window is even more simple than Prior's at Roker. It is a regular diagonal grid of stone.

Inside, there is a feast of Arts and Crafts work. The simple pews, prayer desk and altar were designed by Wells. Ernest Barnsley made the lectern and the main candelabra were designed by Ernest Gimson. All these pieces are fine, but the glory of the church is its rood-screen – an elaborate ornamented truss.

The Architectural Review reported that 'the edges of the Rood principal were ornamented by the carpenters with draw-knife and chisel in the traditional village manner. The pattern was gouged and cut into the oak by the architect, assisted by his brother, Mr Linley Wells, so that it could be easily repainted by the village painter. After gouging the whole principal was given a thin coat of ivory black, the pattern was then grounded in with broken white and the colours were filled in on top. The colours used were Chinese vermilion, ruby madder, golden ochre, chrome yellow, chrome green, permanent blue and indigo'.[37] Figures on the beam were made by the only ships' figurehead carver left in London but were removed by a priggish Bishop of Gloucester. Their modern replacements (shown here) are crude without being vigorous.

Wells was not prolific. He designed a few cottages and a country house or two. He ran off with Lady Noble, the wife of one of his clients, and married her in 1917. The two set up a late Arts and Crafts guild, the St Veronica's Workshop. During and after the War, Wells designed large reinforced concrete buildings for London sites, using the expertise he had acquired with Lethaby and Prior. None was built. He did manage to put up a bank at Teddington and a remarkable concrete church at Halton near Leeds. Most of his buildings incorporated concrete and everything he did was individualistic.[38]

Henry Wilson (1864-1934) studied under John Oldrid Scott and Belcher and became John Dando Sedding's chief assistant, inheriting the practice after Sedding's death in 1891. Most of his architectural work was ecclesiastical (he finished Sedding's Holy Trinity Church, Chelsea in 1900) and he added the splendid tower to St Clement's in the Bournemouth suburbs (1895). His domestic work was rare; his main job was the library and chapel of Welbeck Abbey (1890-96) for the Duke of Portland.

Henry Wilson. Tower, St Clement's, Bournemouth, Dorset (1895), added to Sedding's church after the master's death

Wood and Sellers. Upmeads, Stafford (1908): Arts and Crafts at its most rational

His career was very varied. He was the first editor of *The Architectural Review* (between 1896 and 1901), which he made an Arts and Crafts magazine. Increasingly, from the early 1900s, he concentrated on metalwork, church plate, enamel and jewellery (he was the first designer to introduce small electric batteries to make jewellery sparkle). He designed the immense sculpted bronze monument to Bishop Elphinstone in King's College, Aberdeen and the bronze doors of the Cathedral of St John the Divine, New York. Perhaps his greatest work was the gorgeous Byzantine interior of Edmund Scott's St Bartholomew's, Brighton (1895-1910). Wilson was associated with Lethaby in the Liverpool Cathedral competition design and taught with him at the Royal College of Art. Refusing to compromise with Neo-Georgianism, he retired to France in 1922.

Edgar Wood (1860-1935) and **James Henry Sellers (1861-1954)** were the leading Mancunian Arts and Crafts architects. Both were born near Manchester and trained in local offices. Edgar Wood started his own practice in about 1885, and his work spread over south Lancashire and west Yorkshire – mostly country buildings with a great feeling for place. Inside, they were sensitive too. Muthesius said of Wood's rooms that they 'do not merely interest or stimulate, they transport one into an agreeable, warm atmosphere to which one is glad to submit. Every room has its extremely attractive fireplace in the form of an inglenook, in which a sculptured overmantel is the *pièce de résistance*'.[39]

After he was joined by Sellers in the early 1900s, Wood's work became more formal and axial and his rooms less cosy. And it was probably under Sellers's influence that Wood took the radical step of introducing flat roofs to some of his later houses. The first of these, Upmeads at Stafford (1908), was described by Lawrence Weaver in *Small Country Houses of Today* as 'fortress like. It not only lacks anything approaching prettiness, which is all to the good, but presents an air of austerity, which shows the designer's devotion to extreme simplicity and restraint'.[40] In fact, the effect now seems comical, as if the whole top-hamper of a rather austere brick-and-stone-trim Arts and Crafts house had been raggedly sliced off with a celestial razor, for to make the skyline less than boringly horizontal, Wood had to introduce uneasy little jumps in his perimeter walls. He had moved the concrete first floor, so loved by Prior, up to the roof and justified the innovation to Weaver by explaining that, with a flat roof, it was much easier to cover a complicated plan shape than with conventional roofs. In fact, Wood's plans of this period are simple assemblies of rectangles, very easy to roof under pitches. At Upmeads, the roof was a simple slab of concrete with neither insulation nor weatherproofing. Only with hindsight can we pity the owners who must have faced vast maintenance and heating bills.

The entrance elevation of Upmeads is symmetrical but the others retain Ruskinian changefulness. Wood was spared the necessity of adopting Neo-Georgian, to which, in an eccentric manner, he was tending, by coming into a legacy in 1910 which allowed him to devote the latter part of his life to painting.

1 *Muthesius, Hermann* Das englische Haus, *published as* The English House, *Crosby Lockwood Staples, London, 1979, p239.*
2 *Redesdale, Lord* Memories, *Hutchinson, London, 1915, p710.*
3 *Ryder, Vera* The Little Victims Play, *Robert Hale, London, 1974, pp18-19.*
4 *Benson, E. F.* Queen Lucia, *London, 1920, republished Heinemann, London, 1970, p20.*
5 *Warren, H. Langford 'Recent Domestic Architecture in England',* The Architectural Review, *Boston, Vol XI, 1904, p5.*
6 Ibid, *p12.*
7 *Medici-Mall, Katharina* Das Landhaus Waldbühl, *Gesellschaft für Schweizerische Kunstgeschichte, Bern, 1979, p85.*
8 *Henry James in conversation with Ford Madox Hueffer. Ford, Ford Madox* Ford Madox Ford, *Vol V, The Bodley Head, London, 1971, p416.*
9 *Woolf, Virginia* Roger Fry, a Biography, *Hogarth, London, 1940, pp163-164.*
10 *Mitchison, Naomi* All Change Here: a Girlhood and Marriage, *Bodley Head, London, 1975, p14.*
11 *Newton, William Godfrey* The Work of Ernest Newton RA, *The Architectural Press, London, 1925, p16.*
12 *Muthesius* op cit, *p58.*
13 The Studio, *Vol XXV, 1902, p245.*
14 Ibid.
15 *Weaver, Lawrence* Small Country Houses of Today, *Second Series, Country Life, London, 1919, p24.*
16 The Builder, *Vol CXXXI, 1926, p365.*
17 *Muthesius* op cit, *pp43-44.*
18 *'The Cloisters Letchworth',* The Architectural Review, *Vol XXIII, 1908, p204.*
19 *Reilly, C. H.* Representative British Architects of the Present Day, *Batsford, London, 1931, p86.*
20 *Keen, Arthur* The RIBA Journal, *Vol XXIV, 1917, p221.*
21 *Muthesius* op cit, *p62.*
22 The RIBA Journal, *Vol LV, 1948, p39.*
23 *Muthesius* op cit, *p51.*
24 *Principally in Howarth, Thomas* Charles Rennie Mackintosh and the Modern Movement, *Routledge & Kegan Paul, London, 1952, and Macleod, Robert* Charles Rennie Mackintosh, *Hamlyn, Feltham, 1968.*
25 The Studio, *Vol IX, 1897, p204.*
26 *Calder, Allen* James MacLaren 1853-1890, Arts and Crafts Architect, *RIBA Publications, London, 1990.*
27 *Weaver, Lawrence* Small Country Houses of Today, *First Series, Country Life, London, nd, p122.*
28 *Muthesius,* op cit, *p46.*
29 *Ottewill, David,* Architectural History, *Vol XXII, 1979, pp88-115.*
30 *Muthesius,* op cit, *p46.*
31 *A detailed account of Townsend is given in Service, Alastair* Edwardian Architecture and its Origins, *The Architectural Press, London, 1975, pp162-182.*
32 *Muthesius* op cit, *p41.*
33 *Ashbee, C. R.* Memoirs, *typescript in Victoria and Albert Museum, Vol VII, p332.*
34 The RIBA Journal, *Vol XLV, 1938, p258.*
35 *Muthesius* op cit, *p53.*
36 *Moon, Karen in* George Walton, Designer and Architect, *White Cockade, Oxford, 1993, catalogues as much as is known of Walton's architectural and interior design work.*
37 The Architectural Review, *Vol XVI, 1904, pp184-185.*
38 *The best published description of Wells's work is still Pevsner, Nikolaus and Enid Radcliffe, 'Randall Wells',* The Architectural Review, *Vol CXXXVI, 1964, pp366-368.*
39 *Muthesius* op cit, *p47.*
40 *Weaver, Lawrence* Small Country Houses of Today, *First Series,* op cit, *p187.*

The garden path

10

Love of a mythical old England was the source of Arts and Crafts architects' affection for formal gardening, as it was of their devotion to informal, free-style architecture. Of the many Arts and Crafts paradoxes, none is so puzzling at first sight as the contrast between the Movement's passion for irregular buildings and its mania for surrounding them with clipped and pleached Euclidian patterns. Ruskin's doctrine of changefulness inspired the informality of the architecture. Round some of Morris's ideas grew the belief that, if new buildings were to resemble the Gothic in their process of composition, so new gardens should be made like those of the English Middle Ages and early Renaissance. As early as 1880, Morris had argued that 'a garden should be well fenced from the outside world. It should by no means imitate either the wilfulness or the wildness of Nature, but should look like a thing never to be seen except near a house'.[1]

Nature, and man's conscious interpretation of it, was the key to Arts and Crafts gardening. Everyone of the school who wrote about gardening was convinced, like J. D. Sedding, that 'any garden whatsoever is but Nature idealised...real nature exists outside the artist and apart from him'[2] – and that it is 'not everything in Nature that can, or that may be, artificially expressed in a garden'.[3]

Sedding's book, *Garden Craft Old and New*, is the first of several Arts and Crafts discussions of gardening which violently attack the eighteenth-century landscape ideal as virtually impious: 'man's imitation of Nature is bound to be unlike Nature' so 'it were wise to be frankly inventive in gardening on Art lines'.[4] But by the last decade of the nineteenth century, the British landscape school was dead as an artistic force so it often seems that Sedding and his contemporaries are stamping on a grave. And they frequently seem to be supporting the fashion for the formal, Italianate, geometric, gardening of the rich which had swept Britain in the second half of the century. Yet, as Reginald Blomfield pointed out in *The Formal Garden in England*, contemporary critics of the new Old English gardening seem 'to consider the English Renaissance as identical with the Italian, and the public, seeing such dismal fiascoes in the Italian style as the Crystal Palace Gardens...confuse these with the old English garden in one wholesale condemnation of the formal style'.[5]

Arts and Crafts gardeners were vehemently opposed to both artificial Italianate formality and the artificial English eighteenth-century pursuit of ideal nature based on the Italian visions of Claude and Poussin. They were just as adamantly hostile to the ideas of William Robinson (1839-1936), the immensely influential father of 'natural' gardening (and mentor of Gertrude Jekyll). He advocated that gardens were properly the preserve of the plantsman: that horticulturists, drawing on the wealth of the vast variety of temperate Empire plants, should be able to create an enhanced naturalistic English Elysium.

Blomfield urged that 'a distinction should be laid down between garden design and horticulture. The landscape gardener treats the two indiscriminately, yet they are entirely distinct, and it is evident that to

Edwin Lutyens with Gertrude Jekyll. Deanery Garden, Sonning, Berkshire. The iris rill (1899)

plan out a garden the knowledge necessary is that of design, not of the best method of growing a gigantic gooseberry. Mr Robinson justly remarks that "the profession of an architect has no one thing in common with that of horticulture"...But the question is not one of horticulture at all, but of design...The horticulturist and the gardener are indispensable, but they should work under control'.[6]

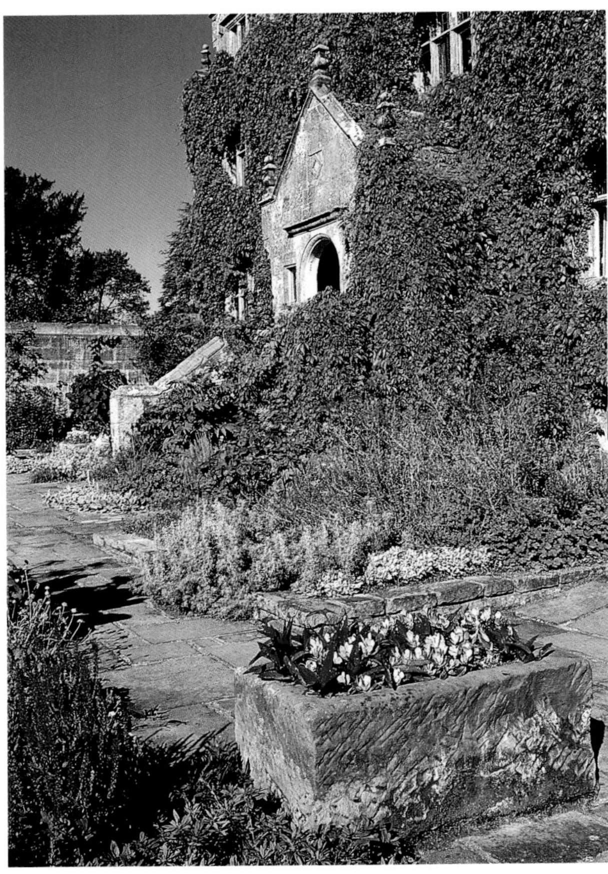

William Robinson. Terrace, Gravetye Manor, Sussex: 'the true flower garden near the house'

Robinson replied to this sort of argument spiritedly: 'geometrical gardens of a deplorable type are things of our own time...In all the newer houses we see the stereotyped garden often made in spite of all the needs of the ground, whereas in really old times it was not so'.[7]

Following eighteenth-century theory, Robinson believed that garden structure should follow the curved lines of natural landscape, no matter how much real nature had to be artificially manipulated to create picturesque effects. (At his house, Gravetye in Sussex, Robinson undertook mighty earthworks and introduced thousands of exotic plants – many of which failed.)

Sedding fiercely objected to this kind of false naturalism by pointing out that, in formal gardening, 'every natural good point, every tree, mound, declivity, stream or quarry, or other chance feature, shall be turned to good account, and its consequence heightened, avoiding the error of giving the thing mock importance, by...lowering declivities, raising prominences, planting dark foliaged trees to intensify the receding parts'.[8]

In fact, there was a good deal in common between the Arts and Crafts people and the Robinson school. Both deplored carpet bedding of annuals in which, as Robinson said 'the beautiful forms of flowers are degraded to crude colour without reference to the natural forms or beauty of the plants'.[9] This kind of drawing-board gardening became particularly hateful to both sides when flowers were dispensed with altogether and designers of the previous generation like Barry and Nesfield used broken brick, different coloured gravels and paints to achieve elaborate geometrical effects. And Robinson was by no means opposed to formal gardens – in their place. At Gravetye he had a little south garden, a formal place, 'a small square embraced by walls. I...have given all my days to save the flower garden from the ridiculous'. The 'true flower garden near the house' should be saved from 'being torn up twice a year to effect what is called spring and summer "bedding"'.[10]

Both horticulturists and architects agreed that the general arrangement should follow the seventeenth-century prescription of Francis Bacon (1561-1626) that gardens should be divided into three parts: 'a green at the entrance; a heath or desert in the going forth; and the main garden in the midst'.[11]

Outside the immediate formal purlieus of the house, Nature should be allowed to reign with (a good deal of) help from Robinson or, as Sedding argued, in perfect freedom.[12] The relationship of formal and wild was summed up by Clough Williams-Ellis (1883-1978), one of the last Arts and Crafts architects, who took me round his garden at Plas Brondanw in North Wales when he was a very old man and pointed out with great pride how the long alley he had planted when he was very young focused on a mountain. 'But I think you can use a

Gravetye Manor garden: Robinson's manifesto for the natural garden achieved with huge expenditure on earth moving and exotics

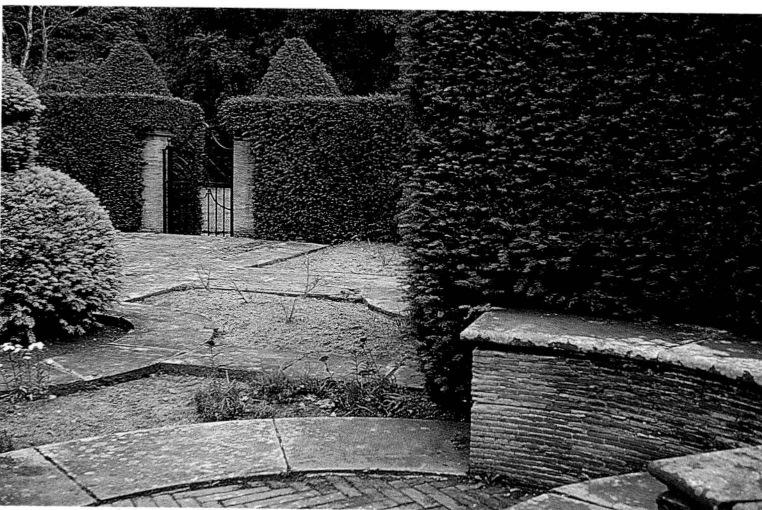

Above: Lutyens and Jekyll. Orchards, Munstead, Surrey (1897-99)

Below: Lutyens. Pergola, Little Thakeham, Pulborough, Sussex (1902). Pergolas were a favourite space-dividing device in Arts and Crafts gardens

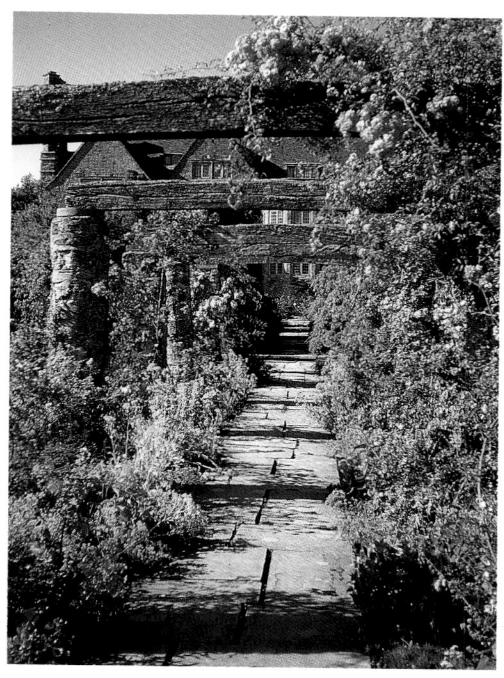

mountain as a garden ornament' – an elegant gesture – 'provided that you own it yourself': a late but succinct summary of Arts and Crafts garden sensibilities – and of the economic and class system that produced the movement.

It was Muthesius who, as usual, analysed the essence of the Arts and Crafts approach: 'the garden is seen as a continuation of the rooms of the house, almost a series of...outdoor rooms, each of which is self-contained and performs a separate function. Thus the garden extends the house into the midst of nature...This means that the regularly laid-out garden must not extend merely to one side of the house, but all the way round it, so that the house appears from all angles to rest on an adequate base'.[13] After 20 years, Morris's dictum that a garden should 'look like part of the house' and 'that no private pleasure garden should be very big'[14] had been deeply assimilated by turn-of-the-century architects.

A chief characteristic of the Arts and Crafts garden was the wall or hedge, enclosing (ideally) a square of ground and creating a boundary between the demesne and God- (or neighbour-) made territory beyond. Terraces round the house were generally agreed to be essential to hold the building down to the ground. They were either paved or covered with lawn incorporating a paved strip. Terraces were easy to create if the site sloped but if flat, a change of level was needed which, as Muthesius noticed, architects made 'by excavating the ground in front of the terrace by some 30 to 50 cm, thus creating a kind of sunk flower-garden. Sunk gardens, a favourite motif of early garden-designers, have acquired a certain popularity'.[15]

Opposite: Lutyens. Great Dixter (1909-11). Living walls and Euclidian layout

On a sloping site, terracing would be continued to achieve the series of rooms. The rooms, whether on the flat or in terraces, should be divided by vertical partitions but, as Prior pointed out in a series of articles in *The Studio*, these room boundaries could save capital outlay (compared to walls, for instance) and need not be 'expensive or elaborate...grass banks with a cresting of Mirabelle plum or of box, cut to make a parapet, may, with excellent results, take the place of masonry'.[16]

This economic reason for clipping plants into geometric shapes partly explains the paradox of the Arts and Crafts love of attacking with shears virtually every member of the vegetable kingdom that grew taller than three feet while leaving smaller, flowering plants to flourish in a natural way. But there were other reasons as well. Prior pointed out that shrubs, allowed to grow naturally, drain the soil of goodness and so prevent the full development of lawns and flowers: 'flower gardening and shrub-culture go badly together, unless the latter is ordered into due subordination'.[17]

And, of course, there was the precedent for topiary in the few remaining real old English gardens themselves, though these, to the turn-of-the-century minds, were not always satisfactory. Muthesius castigated the mysterious yew sculptures of Levens Hall which, with their symbolism long forgotten, seemed to him to 'give the whole thing a rather childish, almost idiotic appearance'. For Muthesius and the Arts and Crafts architects, 'the point about topiary work is its

Levens Hall, perspective by F. Inigo Triggs from Blomfield's *The Formal Garden in England*. This early eighteenth-century garden, planted on the Dutch model, was both loved and ridiculed by Arts and Crafts critics

Thomas Mawson. Garden design 'Terrace Walk and Herb Garden'. The border between man-made and nature is clearly articulated at the end of the path

ordered architectonic form...Clipped hedges are the walls by means of which the garden-designer delimits his areas. They also lend themselves to rhythmic repetition' establishing 'certain points in the geometric composition of the garden...Topiary work is...the indispensable means of establishing form'.[18]

Other ways of creating outdoor rooms included masonry, of course, and pergolas, over which flowering climbers like roses and wisteria were allowed to sprawl unchecked. The rooms themselves were often floored simply with lawn which Bacon had praised because 'nothing is more pleasant to the eye than green grass kept finely shorn'.[19] But many other treatments were possible, ranging from the introduction of paving (which had to be of brick or stone, unglazed tile – or gravel)[20] to, for wealthy clients, elaborate recreations of Renaissance knot gardens. These were particularly championed by Blomfield who devoted much of a chapter of his garden book to them,[21] but were not very often created in practice because less labour-intensive effects could be achieved by laying down paving in a geometric pattern (usually a grid) and planting the spaces either with roses or a variety of herbaceous plants. Other room treatments included the severely practical (kitchen gardens and orchards), the sporting (bowling and tennis lawns), to the frankly picturesque. Provided that they were severely enclosed, even naturalistic rock gardens were allowed within the pale*

Lutyens design, Jekyll planting: the Great Plat, Hestercombe, Somerset (1906)

*Surprise and unusual juxtaposition were sought-after qualities by Arts and Crafts gardeners – a taste shared with the later Picturesque gardeners a century before.

by Gertrude Jekyll and Lawrence Weaver in their immensely influential book, *Gardens for Small Country Houses*.[22]

Water was often used – always carefully constrained into Euclidian boundaries by stone or brick edging, though aquatic plants like water lilies, irises and bulrushes were often allowed to grow almost unchecked in the ponds as they still are today in many of the products of the Lutyens/Jekyll partnership like Deanery Garden and Hestercombe. Fountains were common, partly to increase architectonic effect and partly to reduce the perils of flies and frogs which, according to Bacon, were evils that attend the creation of an ordinary, stagnant pool.[23]

Thomas Mawson. Design for a hillside garden, Windermere, Cumbria: articulation into alleys and rooms

Blomfield urged that fish waters should provide a source of food, like the medieval stew ponds. This was part of his campaign to unite the practical and the pleasurable aspects of gardening: 'You either get a kitchen garden, useful but ugly, or a pleasure garden not useful, and only redeemed from ugliness by the flowers themselves'.[24] He advocated devices like nut hedges and pleached fruit trees to define rooms and pointed out that 'in the ground of a medieval tapestry, all beautiful flowers and fruits grow together, the strawberry next the violet, and columbines among the raspberries...It is more of this unsophisticated liking for everything that is beautiful that ought to be allowed full play'.[25]

The Arts and Crafts selection of plants was far from unsophisticated, however. By the end of the nineteenth century, British nurserymen offered an unrivalled collection of species gathered from all over the world, and an amazing variety of elaborately cultivated varieties.

Hestercombe – the formal rill in the west garden: water carefully contained in masonry edging

Nurserymen's varieties were decried as artificial, following Morris who had urged 'be very shy of double flowers; choose the old columbine where the clustering doves are unmistakable and distinct, not the double one, where they run into mere tatters'.[26] Equally, exotics like dahlias and gladioli, which need to be taken up in winter, were usually decried as being unnatural. But plants from more temperate climates like the Chinese wisteria, peony and even bamboo were allowed and so, inconsistently, were annuals like the marigold and sunflower (which came from South Africa and America) because they had long been part of the cottage garden tradition. Jekyll allowed such exotics as yuccas but plants of this kind were not generally acceptable to the architects.

For most Arts and Crafts garden designers, the touchstone of approval was tradition. Bacon's seventeenth-century list of appropriate plants was the foundation of many late nineteenth-century ones: in deep mid-winter, garden effects could only be achieved with evergreens (another reason for the love of topiary, for nothing can look so boring as a herbaceous border in January). But Bacon's calendar of plants was intended to show that it is possible to have a succession of flowers and fruit from the latter part of January and February with 'crocus vernus, both the yellow and the grey; primroses; anemones; the early tulippa; hyacinthus orientalis; chamaïris; fritilleria' to the beginning of November with 'services; medlars; bullises; roses cut or removed to come late...'[27] The old English herbaceous border was recognised by both the Robinson school and the Arts and Crafts advocates of the formal as an essential ingredient of the new garden.

Sissinghurst Castle, Kent. Looking towards ancient tower across the White Garden. Sissinghurst, by Vita Sackville-West, is a late example of Arts and Crafts garden design (started 1930)

Plate from Thomas H. Mawson's *The Art and Craft of Garden Making* (1900), showing all the elements of an Arts and Crafts garden: pool, terraces, green walls, herbaceous borders, clipped trees and the wild wood beyond the pale

Sedding observed that 'while the master of the "old formality" can give intricate harmonies of interwoven colours in geometric beds...he knows the value of the less as well as the more, and finds equal room for the unconstrained melodies of odd free growths in the border-beds, where you shall enjoy the individual character, the form, the outline, the colour, the tone of each plant'.[28]

Gertrude Jekyll (1843-1932) evolved an elaborate theory and practice of organizing borders in which it was important 'to keep the flowers in rather large masses of colour. No one who has ever done it, or seen it done, will go back to the old haphazard sprinkle of colouring without any thought of arrangement, such as is usually seen in a mixed border'.[29] Her partnership with Lutyens in making the gardens of great houses created some of the best and most influential designs of the turn of the century. Lutyens provided the architectural armature, Jekyll the planting. Her sense of colour had been developed by her training as a painter. She knew Ruskin and most of the well-known painters of the second half of the century.

The trouble with Arts and Crafts formal gardens (and the Jekyll/Lutyens blend of Robinson and formality) was that they were very expensive to maintain;* at one time Jekyll employed 17 gardeners

Sissinghurst. Herbaceous border: at this level plants are free to express their natural forms

Sissinghurst. Cottage Garden and Yew Walk

*And to make. As Jane Brown has pointed out, the early Sussex houses and gardens of the Lutyens/Jekyll partnership cost between £6000 and £10 000, at a time when a very handsome family income was £1000 a year.[30]

Sissinghurst. A Lutyens seat in paved room defined by clipped hedge with cottage garden beyond

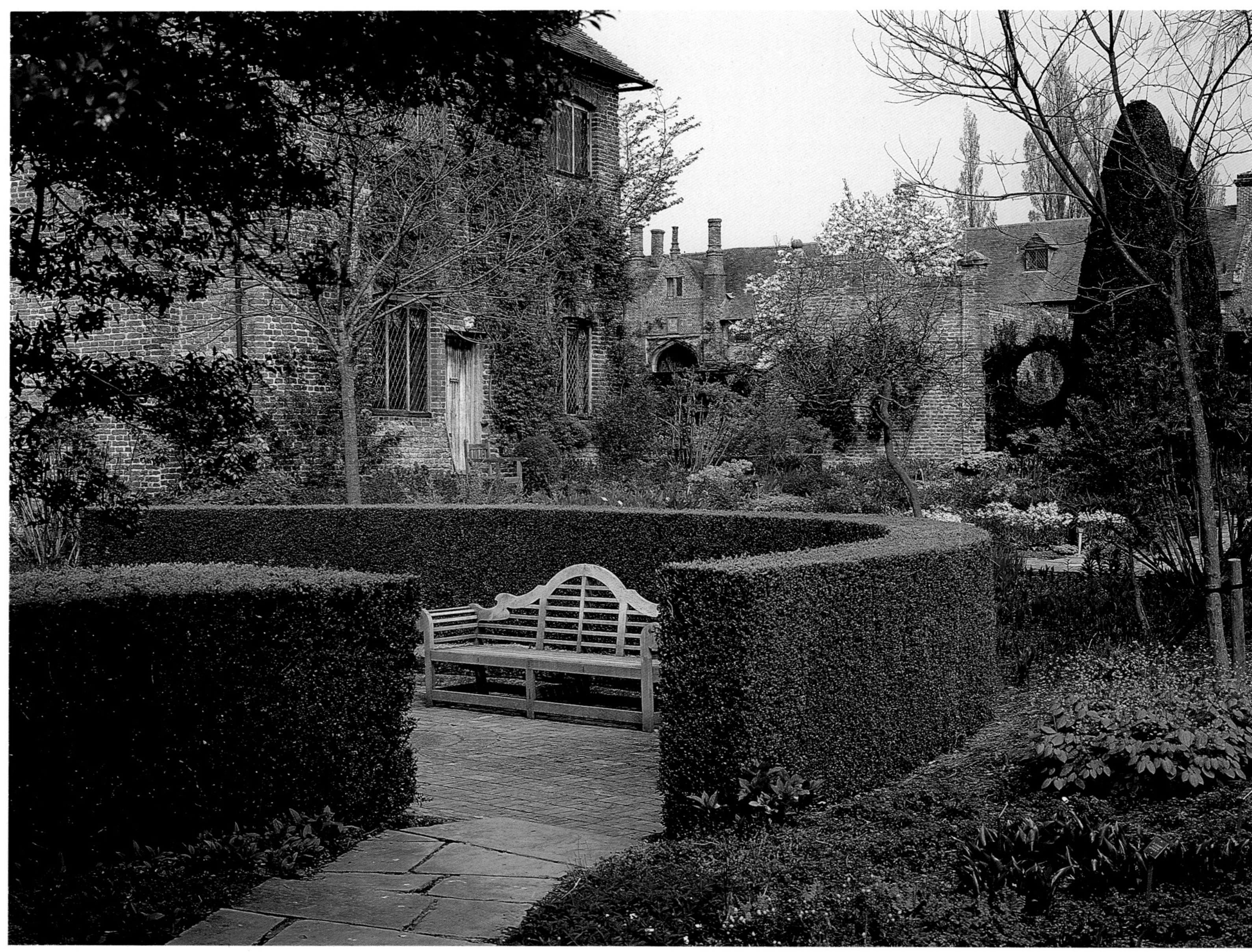

and boys in her Munstead Wood garden.[31] All that clipping and pleaching, and the continual tending of herbaceous borders, needed a lot of work and, as labour became more expensive after the First World War, the fashion for formal gardening faded as paths became overgrown and clipped shrubs lost their shape.

Yet, some very fine gardens in the tradition were created after the War, notably Sissinghurst, started in 1930 by Vita Sackville-West and Harold Nicolson in the overgrown relics of a Tudor demesne. Though the Nicolsons knew Lutyens well (he had helped design the garden of their previous house Long Barn),[32] Sissinghurst avoids the over richness, the flavour of Robinsonism, which characterizes some of the gardens of the Lutyens/Jekyll partnership. Its wonderfully varied rooms, and alleys defined by topiary, pleached limes and real old pink brick contain a profusion of flowers chosen and organized with a restraint and Englishness of which Prior and Sedding would have approved.

But by the time Sissinghurst was being created, taste and economics had caused many garden designers to swing back to a renewed affection for the eighteenth-century landscape school. In the last very large private gardens of England like Knightshayes Court and Dartington Hall, formal elements are fading into grass and trees. In the 1930s Neo-Georgian and Modern taste were united in at least one thing – fondness for ideal buildings surrounded by a 'natural' landscape. The complex gradation of outdoor space from terrace, through the green rooms to wilderness beyond the pale was forgotten. And architects gave up to landscape architects their role as organisers of the outdoors, so systemizing divorce between treatment of internal and external space. Arts and Crafts architects had produced the last comprehensive theory which united buildings, gardens and landscape.

1 *Morris, William 'Hopes and Fears for Art',* Making the Best of Things *Lectures delivered in Birmingham, London and Nottingham 1878-1881, Ellis and White, London, 1882, p128.*
2 *Sedding, John Dando* Garden Craft Old and New, *Kegan Paul, Trench, Trübner, London, 1891, p29.*
3 Ibid, *p37.*
4 Ibid, *p113.*
5 *Blomfield, Reginald and Thomas, F. Inigo* The Formal Garden in England, *Macmillan, London, 1892, p17. Inigo Thomas drew the illustrations.*
6 Ibid, *p19.*
7 *Robinson, William* The English Flower Garden, *John Murray, London, 1933, p27. This is the 15th edition of a book first published in 1883. Because it had remained in print so long, Robinson was able to set up his argument in the early editions and answer his critics in later ones.*
8 *Sedding* op cit, *p134.*
9 *Robinson* op cit, *p24.*
10 Ibid, *p28.*
11 *Bacon, Francis* Essayes, *Everyman edition, Dent & Dutton, London and New York, 1906, p139. Bacon's early seventeenth-century essay on the ideal garden was a key text to late nineteenth-century garden designers. Other sources of inspiration for English formalism included Gervaise Markham's* English Husbandman *(1614), William Lawson's* A New Orchard and Garden *(1618), and John Evelyn's* Compleat Gardener *(1693). Blomfield* (op cit) *gives a complete guide to the early sources of importance to turn of the nineteenth-century architects on pp242-244.*
12 *See Sedding* op cit, *ch VIII.*
13 *Muthesius, Hermann* The English House, *Crosby Lockwood Staples, London, 1979, p107.*
14 *Morris* op cit, *p128.*
15 *Muthesius* op cit, *p114.*
16 *Prior, Edward Schroder 'Garden Making',* The Studio, *Vol XXI, 1901, p184. In three Studio essays Prior expounds Arts and Crafts garden theory to a lay public.*
17 Ibid, *p186.*
18 *Muthesius* op cit, *p117. In calling Levens childish, Muthesius was echoing Blomfield* op cit, *p72. But Sedding* op cit *pp86-89, sings the praises of Levens as being perhaps the least spoiled old garden.*
19 *Bacon* op cit, *p139.*
20 *Prior* op cit, *p181-182.*
21 *Blomfield* op cit, *pp125-132.*
22 *Jekyll, Gertrude, and Weaver, Lawrence* Gardens for Small Country Houses, *Country Life, London, 1912, pxlv.*
23 *Bacon* op cit, *p140.*
24 *Blomfield* op cit, *p144.*
25 Ibid, *p229.*
26 *Morris* op cit, *p126.*
27 *Bacon* op cit, *pp137-138.*
28 *Sedding* op cit, *p172.*
29 *Jekyll, Gertrude* Wood and Garden, *Longmans Green, London, 1899, p110. Jekyll's first book,* Wood and Garden, *describes her early relationship with Lutyens and sets out her Robinsonian beliefs. Jane Brown, the present day analyst of the Jekyll/Lutyens partnership, is most helpful on Jekyll's planting and colour theory in* Gardens of a Golden Afternoon, *Allen Lane, London, 1982, pp41-50.*
30 *Brown* op cit, *p158.*
31 Ibid, *p38.*
32 Ibid, *p175.*

The lost city

11

Just where Regent Street curves into Portland Place, the curiously named Riding House Street snakes away eastward in the direction of Bloomsbury. On a corner, about halfway along this tall narrow thoroughfare, are the offices of T. J. Boulting & Sons, Sanitary and Hot Water Engineers, whose name is emblazoned high on both faces with elegant elongated Edwardian capitals in gold on green mosaic panels.

Apart from these, the building is almost severe. Above the ground floor, plain brick walls are relieved by bays of windows (originally all with leaded lights) in very simple square-section stone frames and mullions. The bays rise to a varied series of dormers, silhouetted against a slate mansard roof with great square chimney stacks stretching up into the sky behind.

The ground floor is equally simple but more changeful with some of the bays carried down to pavement level, others corbelling out to ease pedestrian traffic round the corner and provide an entrance (now hideously disfigured). The plain brick panels terminate over large, mullioned display windows. If you ignore the green and gold mosaics, the building (designed in 1903 by H. Fuller Clark) is the corner of a Tudorish Arts and Crafts country house set down in the middle of London. Boulting & Sons is a fragment of the lost Arts and Crafts city.

This rich and wonderful city is lost for several reasons. First of all, the attitude of the Arts and Crafts movement to cities was ambivalent. *News from Nowhere* articulated a long-held distrust of urbanism fuelled by revulsion from the squalor of nineteenth-century cities, many of which had exploded unplanned from tiny villages during the Industrial Revolution. Arts and Crafts architects built mainly in the countryside, partly because their work was of a kind that attracted country clients, partly because they wanted to anyway.

C. R. Mackintosh. Scotland Street school, Glasgow (1904-06)

It is no coincidence that the main Arts and Crafts contribution to planning – the Garden City movement – was at least to some extent intended to destroy cities as they then were: to create new independent communities* so that pressures on existing conurbations could be reduced and they could be remodelled on healthier lines.

But remaking existing cities was never fully explored by the movement. Arts and Crafts theorists spent little time on discussing what should be done, and the ideas that were propounded were so gentle that they could (mistakenly) be interpreted as a lack of determination to reform urban life. Lethaby, for instance, lecturing to the Arts and Crafts Exhibition Society in 1896, suggested that 'we should begin on the humblest scale by sweeping streets better, washing and whitewashing the houses, and taking care that such railings and lamp-posts as are required are good lamp-posts and railings, the work of the best artists available'.[1]

Lethaby repudiated the fashionable 'idea of grandifying London at a *coup*, or to any extent formalising it' by striking great avenues between important buildings. But he was prepared to recommend one major scheme – cutting a grand pedestrian avenue between Waterloo Bridge and the British Museum – which he regarded as the apex of the

*See chapter 14.

**H. Fuller Clark.
Boulting & Sons,
Riding House Street, London
(designed 1903):
the corner of a country
house brought to the city**

triangle of central London, the other two angles of which were to be found at Westminster Abbey and St Paul's. This one project would, he thought, allow 'all future improvements...[to] fall into place, without any large and violent change in the direction of the streets'.[2] This half mile of avenue, and a green belt round the city, were the only grand proposals Lethaby produced for planning great cities.

Again and again, he returned to his theme that urban improvement should start humbly and gradually develop, with increasing civic consciousness, into a movement for improving every aspect of a citizen's life. 'A town', he said, 'is a work of art according to its quality as a dwelling-place for men. Its art is its service and stimulus to life.'[3]*

Lethaby's call for gradual but deep and thorough city reform was echoed by the other Arts and Crafts theoretician, C. R. Ashbee, who urged that improvement should take place 'little by little and from within...Let us have a wise body of ordinances, a park or lung here, the gradual development of a Zone-system first in this, then in that city; let us have green belts round all our cities'.[5]

The buildings in which this programme of improvement would take form would, according to Lethaby, not be 'betrayed by the mysterious word Architecture away from reality into a realm of pretence about styles and orders and proportions and periods and conception and composition'.[6]

Those Arts and Crafts architects who did work in cities found that their buildings, country bred and free of orders, were not in great demand. Most of the major competitions of the '90s were judged by men like the great Gothic formalist Waterhouse and Shaw (then a firm Classicist), so free, changeful designs were rarely chosen for public buildings. Increasingly, formal styles were preferred (see chapter 13). One result was that those urban Arts and Crafts buildings that did get built were, like Boulting & Sons, quite small, so they are lost among their surroundings and are rarely noticed.

The formal tendency was reinforced because, stemming from as far back as Pugin, one of the ideals that had inspired the movement was the notion that a new building should fit in with its surroundings. In the country and in small country towns, this idea was relatively easy to achieve, for existing vernacular forms and materials could be adapted. But in cities, the model was not vernacular Gothic but (in the South at least) vernacular Georgian. So most Arts and Crafts architects were torn between Ruskinian savageness and changefulness (which, when faithfully followed, led to buildings of great originality) and an attempt to achieve fidelity to place: one of the reasons for the rise of Neo-Georgian architecture.

Neo-Georgian emerged from the more genteel wing of the Arts and Crafts movement, and it was a style with which most Arts and Crafts

*In his rejection of large-scale city reorganization, fashionable in the wake of the boulevards of Paris and Vienna's Ringstrasse, Lethaby was being true to the spirit of London, that vast and varied agglomeration of distinct villages. Only Nash, 90 years before, and by the turn of the century very much out of fashion, had tried to impose a great Baroque organization on Britain's capital. Lethaby's avenue was in intention a bow to Nash's grand design. At the time when he was speaking, the City Beautiful Movement in the USA was driving axes through cities like Philadelphia to link monuments by great vistas. It was against such thinking that Lethaby was arguing. He was not always consistent; though he normally preached gentle change, on at least one occasion he urged that 'except for a hundred or two of buildings, London needs to be rebuilt from end to end'.[4]

Herbert Baker. Church House, Westminster, west front (1937-40), his least formal urban building

architects at least toyed, apart from those completely dedicated to the Gothic spirit such as Lethaby, Voysey, Townsend and Mackintosh.

The irony is that as society threw up more and more functions, forms were adopted that were intrinsically inflexible. Although many architects used Georgian forms with some freedom, particularly initially, there was an underlying tendency to order. Many of the rules of Georgian, and hence of Neo-Georgian, building are strict – for instance there must be a gradation of window size from medium windows on the entrance floor to very large ones on the first floor to smaller and smaller windows as attic is piled upon attic. The lighting and size of rooms is determined by the rules of elevation. Pugin and Ruskin had demanded the precise opposite. 'Queen Anne' had shown a way of adapting Classical forms to new needs – Norman Shaw's own house is a particularly good example of how this could be done – but such freedom was increasingly forgotten in the pursuit of Rule and propriety.

The career of a successful turn of the century architect of no fixed principle is exemplified by Herbert Baker (1862-1946). Baker was one of the most productive architects of his generation – only Lutyens outstripped him in the Establishment acclaim. His training was in the office of Ernest George where he overlapped with Dawber and Schultz. He was chief draughtsman when Lutyens made his brief appearance as apprentice.

Baker emigrated to South Africa in the early '90s, and met Cecil Rhodes, under whose patronage he gained much official work. By the time he was 40, Baker had already built three cathedrals, Government House and the Union Buildings in Pretoria. He worked in many styles, notably a heavy stripped Classicism enlivened by ornament executed by local craftsmen.

His other styles included, for domestic work, references to vernacular building – for instance in South Africa, he adapted colonial Dutch motifs. In 1903 Ashbee was greatly taken with 'Baker's own house...springing like a jewel castle from out of the rock...it is one of the most exquisite pieces of architecture I have ever seen'.[7] Baker's Government House in Pretoria was tinged with Boer vernacular, just as his Delhi Secretariats (which flank Lutyens's Viceregal Lodge) have reminders of Mogul ornament.

He returned to England before the War to carry on a large and varied practice. His big buildings were usually Neo-Classical – or nearly so – in plan but he never quite forgot the lessons of Pugin and sometimes attempted to fit the bulk of his huge commissions quietly into context; for instance his Church House (1937-1940). This Westminster Abbey complex with its squared flints and patterned brick was intended to harmonize with the disparate architecture of the area and to evoke the original building of 1758. Ruskinian savageness was remembered too. Even Baker's highly Classical South Africa House (1935) in Trafalgar Square has a profusion of sculptured detail – particularly animal heads – a last echo of the belief in free craftsmanship.

One compelling reason why designing to Rule became increasingly popular was explained by H. S. Goodhart-Rendel, doyen of ordered

Philip Webb. Row of shops, Worship Street, Islington, London (1860s), transition from country to city

J.D. Sedding. All Saints' Vicarage, Plymouth, Devon (1880), a country type brought to town

architecture between the wars: free-style building was simply uneconomic. 'If', he said, 'we wished now to build in [an] informal and unhurried manner, we should find its cost prohibitive, not to the employer but to the architect. Just as in building itself, our methods have changed owing to the enormously increased cost of labour in relation to that of materials, so in...practice we now must save all we can of the principal's time and that of his draughtsmen if any profit at all is to be got out of the six per cent fee'. Yet even Goodhart-Rendel was prepared to admit that, 'In its results, however, the old method was better than is any of the same kind achieved by other means. The man of the future may prefer that his house should be no more visibly peculiar to himself than his suit of clothes or the body of his motor-car, but at present to most men home-building still means, as it meant in Victorian times, a competition in self expression between themselves and their architects'.[8]

In the '20s and '30s Neo-Georgian was stretched and stretched to cover acres of offices and flats until, in the impoverished days after the Second World War, the thin, taut crust was cracked off, revealing the concrete bones behind – which, in an uneasy marriage with Neo-Classical Modernist sinews introduced from the Continent, produced some of the crudest commercial architecture ever seen.

It is unfair to judge a style in its decadence and decay. Neo-Georgian started as a kindly, gentle response to the cities in which Arts and Crafts architects found themselves working. In architects' terms it had a fine pedigree, going back to 'Queen Anne' and to Webb's Georgian days, and from it came some of the minor masterpieces of Arts and Crafts people, particularly when they transplanted the style to the country.

But their greatest city successes emerged when they tried to use the full panoply of Puginian and Ruskinian theory in the urban context. From the relatively few works that were so produced, we can catch a glimpse of what the lost Arts and Crafts city would have been like if the confidence of British culture had not begun to change dramatically under the economic pressures of the first decade of the twentieth century.

The easiest transition from the country to the city was in buildings common to both. Webb built a row of shops in Worship Street, Islington during the '60s. Small-paned shop fronts project from a terrace that looks like Georgian relieved with Gothic touches. You enter each little unit past an inclined part of the glazed front and up a few steps. It is almost as if a bit of a village street has been brought to London and made rather taller and more appropriate for a dense urban context.

John Dando Sedding's All Saints' Vicarage, Harwell Street, Plymouth (1880) is a country vicarage brought to town. It is a Butterfield parsonage seen through Old English spectacles, with complicated gables and patterned tile hanging, but its tall polygonal bays stretching up from basement to a tiled hat over the first floor foreshadow later urban Arts and Crafts work.

Eleven years later, Voysey made his only two really urban houses, a

C.F.A. Voysey. Houses, Hans Road, Kensington, London (1891), one of Voysey's few urban works

gentle intrusion into Hans Road, a curving little street in Knightsbridge just behind Harrods. At first sight, 14 and 16 Hans Road are symmetrical, with a pair of polygonal, close mullioned bay windows. Voysey's favourite simple square-section stone mullions and leaded lights are set in brickwork which matches the rest of the terrace. The first design was indeed perfectly symmetrical, but on closer examination of what was built, subtle asymmetries emerge: there are only three oriel windows above the doors instead of the four symmetry would have required. And the bay of number 16 terminates at the bottom with a row of little windows, revealing a complicated series of floor levels within, while the bay of number 14 shows a much more regular disposition of floors; even though the room heights were lower than most of the rest of the houses in the terrace except number 12, designed by Mackmurdo in 1894, after Voysey and his client had quarrelled. This house picks up Voysey's floor heights, his oriel and his brick but in its details shows Mackmurdo's strong Renaissance affections. Mackmurdo's most free London house was 25 Cadogan Gardens, Chelsea, which has three tall oriel bays, complete with leaded lights which top a complicated ground floor fenestration and are capped by a wide, carved, curving early Shavian cornice. The side elevation repeats the oriel motif but is flat. It is a design of great elegance and wit.

An equally elegant but much more dramatic Arts and Crafts town house was Halsey Ricardo's 8 Addison Road, Kensington (1905-07). The building goes much further towards Classicism than conventional Neo-Georgian; it has pilasters and capitals, arches, roundels and elaborate cornices. Its prime attraction is the glazed turquoise and green brickwork. Between 1888 and 1898, Ricardo was a partner of William De Morgan, the great Arts and Crafts potter. And, as a disciple of Butterfield, he was a great believer in colour and glazed materials for city building: 'In the country and those favoured cities where houses have gardens, where creepers hang in rich festoons...the local building materials will probably supply us with colour enough to set off and harmonize with the palette set by Nature. But in the street, where all the colour there is of man's own making, it should be full and strong'.[9] Ricardo's belief that colour could enable the British architect to 'dispense with much of the architectural frippery felt to be requisite to prevent the surface of ungraduated plain tint appearing too bald'[10] was sadly not shared by many of his contemporaries: the streets of the lost city shine only in the imagination.

The Addison Road house is so large that, in any other town but London, it could be a great public building. When they did design for smaller cities, Arts and Crafts architects were more true to type. For instance, in 1892 Ricardo himself had produced a design for the Oxford Town Hall competition which involved a great bank of Jacobean glass in simple stone mullions between asymmetrical stone stair towers – a very early and elegant design for a glazed office block which, because of the size and mass of the stone mullions and transoms might have avoided the problems of modern glass-and-metal offices: over-heating in summer and freezing in winter.

**Charles Holden.
A market hall,
Soane Medallion design
(1896). Modification
of an age-old type**

**Holden.
Bristol Central
Reference Library
(1905-06). Large-scale
urban free style**

Charles Holden's Soane Medallion competition design for a provincial market hall, published in the first issue of *The Architectural Review* (1896), was a much more humble affair. It was basically a buttressed and pitched medieval market hall covering an open undercroft (with curiously Classical arches) all enlivened by an asymmetrical front door and tower. The austerity of the design was set against rich bands of Arts and Crafts relief sculpture that linked hall and tower.

In practice, Holden (1875-1960) was rarely able to use such expensive decoration. By the time he could, in the British Medical Association building in the Strand (1907) where Epstein was commissioned to do the relief sculptures, Holden was becoming Classical. But before he evolved the stripped heavily Muscovite style which balanced him uneasily between Modern Movement and Classicism in the '20s and '30s, Holden was a most free and inventive Arts and Crafts architect. His Belgrave Hospital for Children at the Oval (designed when he was chief assistant to Percy Adams in 1900) is a Grimm but Webbian monument of the lost city, and his Bristol Central Reference Library (1905-06) is a most ingenious symmetrical Jacobean series of stone planes and broad, flat, mullioned polygonal bays which is said by some to have had a good deal to do with the origins of Mackintosh's celebrated masterpiece, the west wing of the Glasgow School of Art.

Quieter than the Bristol library and built 10 years previously was the Passmore Edwards Settlement in Tavistock Place, Bloomsbury (now Mary Ward House). Designed by Smith and Brewer in 1895 and completed in 1898, it was a new type of building, part hostel, part community centre. As *The Studio* reported, it was intended to bring together 'persons of kindred tastes and interests, more especially those engaged in social and educational work in a given neighbourhood to form a home in which the conveniences of family life shall be combined with individual seclusion and liberty'.[11] Morris's Hammersmith Guest House had taken real shape. Many of the inhabitants were young architects and both Dunbar Smith and Cecil Brewer had been residents of the Passmore Edwards Settlement that preceded the Tavistock Place building (the settlement was founded by the successful novelist Mary Ward, but was then named after Edwards, the main benefactor).[12]

The worthy inhabitants lived in a rather spartan atmosphere enriched by Arts and Crafts elegance. The main rooms were basically undecorated except by the odd semi-Classical moulding and a few fine pots; the furniture, when not designed by the architects, was modelled on simple country styles; fireplaces were designed by Lethaby, Voysey, Newton, Troup and Dawber with grates by the architects based on chaste eighteenth-century models. Where any special work was needed – for instance in the dining hall fireplace designed in 'Lethaby brick' – the work was 'carried out by the ordinary manufacturers from instructions and sketches supplied by the architects', which was welcomed by *The Studio* because 'it is only by bringing modern design to bear directly upon ordinary production that any aesthetic growth can be effected in the commercial world; and thereby upon the public taste'.[13]

Holden. Belgrave Hospital for Children, Oval, London (1900). A Grimm and Webbian monument to the lost city

Smith & Brewer. Passmore Edwards Settlement (now Mary Ward House) (1895). Detail. A complex building integrated into a basically Georgian setting

The public was initially wary of the outside of the building. The front elevation is extremely simple: projecting wings at each end frame the blank brick wall of the hall, which has very deep projecting eaves over a deep plain white-rendered cornice. The white rendering is picked up again in the upper storey of the towers which are themselves completely symmetrical, with the stair windows forming opposing diagonals at each end of the composition. The design is saved from total symmetry by the entrance to the residential part which grows smoothly out of the curves of the balustrading to form a massive stone block projecting forward to the pavement, penetrated by a broad welcoming arched opening. The stone eggs on top of the porch derive from Lethaby's *Cosmos*, in which eggs are identified as symbols of creation.

Lethaby's only urban building, the Eagle Insurance office in Colmore Row, Birmingham (1899-1900), designed with J. L. Ball, is also topped by mystic ornament: an eagle surrounded by circles and wavy lines – symbols of the sun and clouds. But below this deep cornice, the building is extraordinarily spare. The top three storeys have five simple bays of full-height sash windows divided by a grid of mullions and transoms moulded only enough to ensure that water would be thrown off so the stone would not stain. This top-hamper sits on a storey and a half which is completely different but equally simple. An ashlar wall is dominated by the big window of the main office, stone gridded in almost Tudor proportions, flanked symmetrically by doors for public and staff with ample flattish arches. Behind is a completely asymmetrical plan, which, among other ingenuities, gives the director's office a glass tent for a ceiling.

It is unlikely that Lethaby would have fully approved of the overtly Classical detailing of Leonard Stokes's telephone exchanges. Yet stripped of their swags and their heavy bracketed cornices, the best of Stokes's many exchanges have all Lethaby's simplicity and freshness. The Southampton exchange (1900), for example, was five bays of simple windows between massive plain brick pilasters. In Stokes's masterpiece, Gerrard Street, London (1904), four wide bays of leaded windows sat on top of massive semi-circular arches. The basic material was brick, tied together with Stokes's favourite bands of stone. Now destroyed, the building showed how successfully, given the chance, Arts and Crafts architects could cope with the large single function buildings which have been the hallmark of this century's commercial clients' requirements.

Perhaps even more daring was C. E. Bateman's 1899 design for a printing works in Cornwall Street, Birmingham. Brick piers support a three-storey gabled roof in which the offices are lighted by dormer windows in the slopes. Between the piers, huge square gridded windows light the machine halls which rise above a base course infilled with glass blocks. It is one of the most daring designs for an industrial building of the period.

The Classical motifs on the Gerrard Street telephone exchange and the Hanseatic outline of the Cornwall Street works were not the only ways in which Arts and Crafts architects attempted to achieve rich-

Stokes. Gerrard Street telephone exchange, London (1904, now destroyed): Arts and Crafts response to twentieth-century type

ness in urban building. Henry Wilson won the competition for the public library at Ladbroke Grove, Kensington in 1890, while he was still working for Sedding. Big, stone mullioned windows and a wide, shallow arched entrance were to have been set within thin projecting brick towers, thinly reeded and increasingly elaborated by relief sculpture until their crowning cupolas were united with the walls in an intricate, sinuous, swooping band of intertwined figures and foliage, all crowned with the high pitch of a roof topped by a complicated spire. Sadly, much of the decoration had to be abandoned for lack of money, but enough survived of the original design to give a notion of what might have been, even if the result looks rather like a well decorated board-school.

A much smaller example of decorated urban Arts and Crafts work is The Black Friar pub (1905) in Queen Victoria Street, London, where H. Fuller Clark (the architect of Boulting & Sons) redesigned the ground floor of a mid-Victorian office block. Here, the architect's intentions were carried out in full. Rarely can such a quantity of Arts and Crafts design have been compressed into such a small space. The result is extraordinarily jolly. The scheme is basically very simple – only two sides of the thin wedge-shaped site can be seen; they are faced in smooth granite with big windows divided into leaded squares by stone mullions and transoms topped with a deep fascia announcing the name of the pub in Clark's favourite green and gold mosaic.

Onto this monastically chaste undercoat, no opportunity for imposing friars has been missed. The composition is dominated by a three-dimensional gigantic black friar beaming from the apex of the triangle towards Blackfriars Bridge; the door surrounds and the brackets which support the cornice are carved with grotesque friars in every stage of inebriation; the panels above the doors are of coloured mosaic showing sober friars preparing liquor, and at eye level between the windows are delicate bronze reliefs of kindly friars pointing the way to the different bars. The interior is more restrained with simple chunky Arts and Crafts furniture, a big coppery inglenook and some lively narrative bronze friezes (friars again) designed by Henry Poole. Anyone who believes that the Arts and Crafts movement was excessively solemn should take a drink at The Black Friar.

The man who brought decorated Arts and Crafts buildings to town in a big way was C. H. Townsend. The first of his three major London buildings was the Bishopsgate Institute designed in 1892, two years after Wilson's library scheme with which, as Alastair Service has pointed out,[14] it shares many features; it has shallow projecting towers, capped with cupolas, enclosing a large area of glass and the whole is topped with a steeply pitched roof. But (perhaps because he was required by his clients to keep the inside utterly simple) Townsend was able to find the money to decorate the outside with bands of relief in his favourite motif: trees of life with short, slender trunks and large overlapping leaves, which in this building are laced together by sinuous branches.

Townsend's next major design was for a very similar long site with a narrow street frontage – the Whitechapel Art Gallery, a proposal for which he exhibited at the Royal Academy in 1896. It was like an expanded version of the Bishopsgate elevation with two ampler towers symmetrically flanking a large arched doorway. Over this was a row of wide windows with semi-circular heads, topped by a deep pictorial frieze.

The final design (completed in 1901) had to be squashed to fit onto a much narrower site than was originally intended. The entrance arch was pushed off centre to allow a less obtrusive exit doorway to be accommodated by its side. So the whole of the ground floor became asymmetrical and the original symmetry only gradually reasserts itself as the building rises through a band of plain rectangular leaded windows on the first floor to two projecting towers enriched by Townsend's trees on the second. They flank a large rectangular area of dirty grey rendering (the rest of the elevation is in buff terracotta like the Bishopsgate Institute). The rectangle was intended to hold the elevation's crowning glory, a mosaic frieze by Walter Crane depicting 'the sphere and message of art'. Cash ran out so it was never constructed, and the panel itself was penetrated by mean little windows (now closed up) to light the caretaker's room – the inadequate lighting of which caused *The Architectural Review* to make one of its few criticisms of the ingenious planning of the building.[15]

Townsend's third major London building was the Horniman Free Museum at Forest Hill in south London, where he did manage to get

Halsey Ricardo. 8 Addison Road, London (1905-07). The gorgeous hall of one of the few buildings in which Ricardo was able to use his beloved turquoise and green glazed bricks

Henry Wilson. Ladbroke Grove Library, London (designed 1890)

H. Fuller Clark. The Black Friar, Blackfriars Bridge, London (1905)

a large mosaic put up. Unlike the other two buildings which were constructed for charities, the museum was built for a rich philanthropic tea merchant, F. J. Horniman, who commissioned Townsend to design a special gallery for his anthropological collections in 1896, after being driven nearly to distraction by allowing the public to visit them in his own house.

Again the site was long and thin, but this time it sloped uphill from the road. So Townsend arranged the entrance at the top of a flight of cranked stairs which carried the visitors up under the mosaic panel (by Robert Anning Bell). This covered the thin end of the gallery and was surmounted by a row of leaf-capped pilasters under the curve which fronted the long glazed barrel vault. At the top of the steps, you faced one of Townsend's big arched doorways in the side of the tower which dominates the elevation. Once inside, you emerged on to the balcony of the south gallery through which you moved to the north (uphill) gallery before going downstairs to the lower part of the south gallery and out again at the front of the tower. It was one of Townsend's most ingenious plans, although sadly it has been mauled by the present proprietors.

The tower is still extraordinary. It starts off as a square plan with rounded corners and gradually tapers until the radius of each corner turns into a little circular turret surrounding a round tower. On the way up, it passes large clocks (a philanthropic gesture by Horniman to the non-watch-wearing poor), a drift of leafy trees and a massive circular cornice. When first built, the design must have seemed to many grotesquely unusual, for *The Studio* felt impelled to produce a spirited defence: 'the architecture, whether liked or disliked, is not in the least degree an imitation, an echo of some old master's merit. It stands there at Forest Hill as a new series of frank and fearless thoughts expressed and co-ordinated in stone'.[16]

If the citizens of Forest Hill were disturbed by Townsend's tower, those of Huddersfield must have felt just as worried when, in 1902, Edgar Wood's clock tower at nearby Lindley was unveiled from its scaffolding. Wood's tower is as strange as Townsend's but its idiom is completely different: a four-square plan has a diagonal buttress at each corner so the effect is sharp and slightly reeded and not at all rounded apart from the drum stair for the clock winder. The buttresses rise past gargoyles to provide sharp pinnacles round the octagonal metal warlock's hat which gracefully terminates the tower.

Were it not for this roof, the tower would resemble that of an Arts and Crafts church – Gothic but straightened out and simplified. Wood's earlier designs for town buildings, for instance his George and Dragon Inn, Castleton, Derbyshire of 1898, were almost excessively medievalist. But, during the first years of this century Wood became less historically inclined.

His First Church of Christ Scientist at Victoria Park, Manchester (1903-08) is in a sort of stripped Gothic with a great Townsendish arched door under a crucifix shaped window, set into the tall, thin, white rendered gable. From this, two stone semi-Gothic wings project diagonally *à la* Prior and the composition is completed (and made

Townsend. Horniman Free Museum, Forest Hill, London (designed 1896)

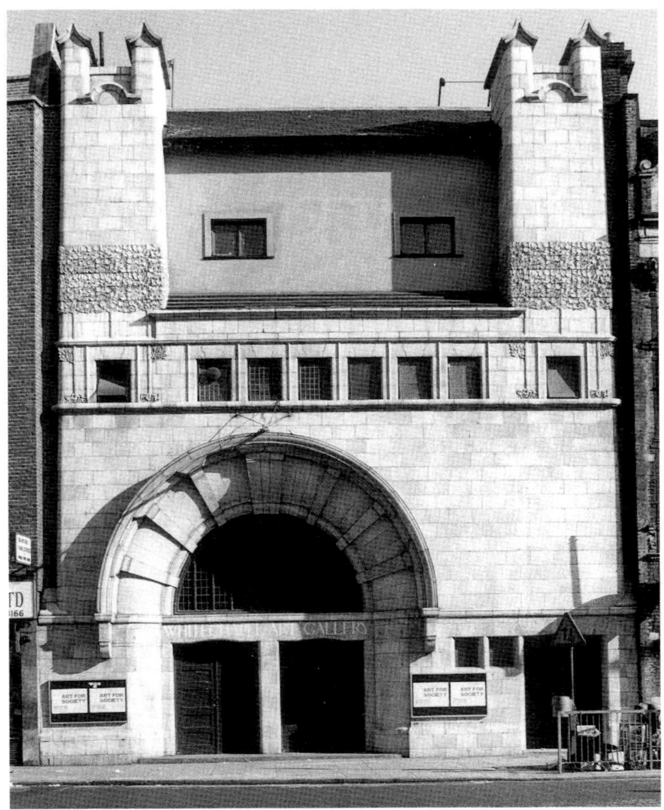

Townsend. Whitechapel Art Gallery, London (designed 1901)

more Hansel-and-Gretelish) by a squat, conically capped, round stone tower nestling against the right-hand side of the gable. The building shows the freedom that Arts and Crafts architects might have achieved in ecclesiastical architecture if they had not usually worked for the established church.

A similar kind of freedom was shown in Wood's Wesleyan school, Long Street, Middleton (1899-1902), a composition in which the white walls, leaded lights and interlocking gables owe something to Voysey; but its use of tall, thin motifs under the gables was new, as was the higgledy-piggledy arrangement of a school round a courtyard. The adjoining chapel is in restrained Arts and Crafts Gothic.

Composition became more formal after Henry Sellers (who was a devoted flat roof man) joined Wood's practice. Under its roof planes, the Durnford Street School, Middleton (1908-10) is a curious amalgam of board-school architecture with wide, high windows let into a background of brick from which stone-clad bays, many mullioned and finely detailed, project Tudor-like from a semi-industrial backdrop.

Two hundred miles further north, Mackintosh had already experienced the difficulties of trying to give life to stereotyped school design. His Scotland Street school in Glasgow (1903-06) had to be designed on a conventional board-school plan, but, in elevation, it was enlivened with small paned windows (rather than the ubiquitous sheet glass). And it had two conically capped semi-circular stair towers in the Scottish tradition; these are not really what they seem to be, for instead of containing a winding staircase, each drum encloses a perfectly conventional pair of straight flights terminating at landings which come out only as far as the main walls, leaving a great vertiginous semi-circular chute of space soaring from top to bottom of the building. Sadly, the local school board denied Mackintosh his small paned windows (except on the drums) because they were more expensive than sheet glass.

Mackintosh's Glasgow School of Art is one of the great works of Arts and Crafts genius of the turn of the century. It was built in two stages, 1897-99 and 1907-09, and is, in effect, three or four buildings. The first, on the north side, is a big windowed, big paned row of studios, much like a board-school, but relieved by Art Nouveauish wrought-iron brackets supporting the mullions. This regular and conventional elevation is penetrated by an asymmetrical ashlar entrance bay of great originality. The roofline breaks and a small tower suddenly appears over an irregular set of windows in a series of ashlar planes dominated by a Smith and Brewer shallow arch over the entrance. (This was the termination of the first phase which started at the east end.)[17]

The east elevation is quite different, a great plane relieved by a tall, flat, polygonal bay and a curious curved and ornately coved hood over the windows of the lower school. The south side is an amalgam of the original studio windows and the projecting 'hen-run', a long glazed loggia, added after the original building was completed.

The most remarkable part of this wonderfully changeful building is the west elevation (1907-09) which towers above one of Britain's

Edgar Wood. Lindley tower, near Huddersfield, Yorkshire (1902)

Left: Wood. First Church of Christ Scientist, Victoria Park, Manchester (1903-08)

Right: Wood. Wesleyan school and chapel, Long Street, Middleton, nr Manchester (1899-1902). The school buildings are through the arch

most steeply sloping streets. The double-height library of the art college rises behind three soaring bays full of small paned iron-framed lights (now replaced in bronze) starting stark out of the ashlar. The full-height bays are carried on in a sub-rhythm of careful projections until one turns the corner and meets the relative sobriety of the north front again.

Internally, the building is as varied and exciting as it is outside. Spaces vary from the almost domestic, like the director's suite and the boardroom calm and white, through grand public spaces, which like the school's museum are top-lit through great decorative trusses, to the almost Piranesian staircases and the hen-run. The high point is the library, a space of great subtlety, tall and etiolated, yet intimate; austere and almost dark, yet relieved by shafts of light and colour; made of ordinary materials, yet made rich by deft detailing.

The west elevation of the Glasgow School of Art has an almost equally inventive but less controlled precedent in England: the Euston Road fire station by the London County Council architect's department (1901-02).

By the late '90s the LCC department was responsible for designing housing and some public buildings including fire stations. Most of its fine pre-War work was coloured by Arts and Crafts motifs – in housing schemes, for instance, it is easy to see the influence of Webb and of Smith and Brewer's Passmore Edwards Settlement; in the fire stations there are elements of Webb again, and of Voysey.

The influence of Arts and Crafts was not limited to copying details. Some of the younger members of the department were in direct contact with Lethaby, Webb and Morris through the Society for the Protection of Ancient Buildings. The influence of Arts and Crafts socialism must have been strong for, at the time, only pronounced idealism could have made such a group of powerful talents work virtually anonymously for a public office. Their housing for the poor, such as the Millbank Estate, looks pretty grim now, but at the turn of the century it was a notable improvement not only on the slums but on many of the model dwellings provided by private charity.[18] The architects in charge, Thomas Blashill (up to 1899) and W. E. Riley (until 1920) deserve praise for setting up the system which allowed individual talent to flower but less for allowing credit for individual works to be obscured to the general public.

The chief designer of the Euston Road fire station, the department's masterpiece, was Charles Canning Winmill. He was faced with a difficult problem: that of combining a complicated barrack block with offices and with big halls for the fire engines – a large and varied bulk which all had to be eased onto a small site in central London.

The solution showed how details adapted from vernacular buildings and combined under the principle of Ruskinian changefulness could produce an architecture sufficiently flexible to cope with the most complicated set of urban requirements, while retaining dignity and domestic character.

The building is of brick over a stone ground floor which is occa-

Mackintosh. Scotland Street school, Glasgow (1904-06)

225
BOYS

THE GLASGOW
SCHOOL
OF ART
167
ART
SCH
OOL
167

Mackintosh. Library, west front, Glasgow School of Art (1907-09)

LCC Architect's Department. Euston Road fire station, London (1901-02)

sionally enlivened with semi-Classical details. Above this level, it relies entirely on Gothic domestic precedents: the brick is relieved by bands of stone and a regular series of leaded casement windows. Against these planes of brick is a quite irregular rhythm of bays, both square and three-sided, which gradually builds up to a collar topped by wide eaves and (to turn the corner) little gables with circular windows like the one Ashbee had used a couple of years before in his first Cheyne Walk house.

Mackintosh. Main entrance, north front of Glasgow School of Art (1897-99)

As at Boulting & Sons, if a few details were stripped from the Euston Road fire station, it could be the corner of a (very large) Arts and Crafts country house. It shows that, at its best, Arts and Crafts architecture knew no differentiation between public and private buildings and none between provision for the rich or the poor. The lost city of the Arts and Crafts movement would have been less grand than the Edwardian cities that were actually built. But it would have been a city with a human face; gentle, witty, occasionally dramatic, kind to its surroundings and responsive to the needs of its citizens.

1 *Lethaby, W. R. 'Of Beautiful Cities' in* Art and Life and the Building and Decoration of Cities, *lectures at the fifth Arts and Crafts exhibition 1896, Rivington Percival, London, 1897, pp103-104.*
2 *Ibid, p108.*
3 *Lethaby, W. R. 'Towns To Live In' first published in the* Hibbert Journal, *1918, republished in* Form in Civilization, *Oxford, 1957, p19.*
4 *Lethaby, W. R.* Architecture, *Williams and Norgate, London, 1911, p245.*
5 *Ashbee, C. R.* Where the Great City Stands, *Essex House Press, London, 1917, p67.*
6 *Lethaby, W. R. 'Towns To Live In',* op cit, *p25.*
7 *Ashbee, C. R.* Memoirs, *typescript in the Victoria and Albert Museum, Vol II, p195.*
8 *Goodhart-Rendel, H. S. 'The Work of Beresford Pite and Halsey Ricardo',* The RIBA Journal, *Vol XLIII, 1935, p118.*
9 *Ricardo, Halsey R. 'The Architect's Use of Colour',* The RIBA Journal, *Vol III, 1896, p366.*
10 Ibid, *p367.*
11 *Morris, G. L. and Wood, Esther 'The Architecture of the Passmore Edwards Settlement',* The Studio, *Vol XVI, 1899, p11.*
12 *Forty, Adrian, 'The Mary Ward Settlement',* The Architects' Journal, *Vol CXC, 2 August 1989, p34.*
13 *Morris and Wood* op cit, *p17.*
14 *Service, Alastair (ed)* Edwardian Architecture and its Origins, *Architectural Press, London, 1975, p169.*
15 *'The Whitechapel Art Gallery',* The Architectural Review, *Vol IX, 1901, p130.*
16 *'The Horniman Free Museum',* The Studio, *Vol XXIV, 1902, p198.*
17 *Buchanan, William (ed),* Mackintosh's Masterwork, the Glasgow School of Art, *Richard Drew, Glasgow, 1989, p38.*
18 *Beattie, Susan,* A Revolution in London Housing: LCC Housing Architects and their Work, 1893-1914, *GLC and Architectural Press, London, 1980, details the idealistic struggles, and the results of some of the first architects' involvement in mass housing for the poor.*

The attempt on the summit

12

By far the most original thinker of the later Arts and Crafts movement emerged in the darkest heart of the Victorian city – London's East End. Charles Robert Ashbee (1863-1942) did more than any other Arts and Crafts architect to try to turn Morris's ideals into practice.

As a young man, a Wellingtonian just down from King's College, Cambridge, Ashbee was articled to G. F. Bodley, friend of Webb and one of the first patrons of the Morris Firm. While Bodley's apprentice he lived at Toynbee Hall, a pioneer university settlement in the East End set up to enable young graduates to pass on something of their education to the poor. Ashbee's social conscience seems to have wakened early. In a semi-autobiographical novel he recalled, 'One of the most dreadful recollections of an otherwise happy childhood [he was the son of a prosperous merchant]* was when I heard in the London streets a chant – a slow marching chant – it was always the same, and went tramp, tramp, tramp, tramp, tramp:

"We've got no work to do-oo
We've got no work to do-oo".

When you looked you saw some 30 or 40 men; they may have been agricultural labourers...they were well built, kindly, humble, haggard, willing to do as they were bid. It was a dreadful sight'.[1]

At Toynbee Hall he started a Ruskin class in 1886 which originally consisted of three pupils. Inspired by Ruskin's *Fors Clavigera*, Ashbee expanded his activities to start a school which taught, in conjunction with Ruskinian theory, painting, modelling, plaster casting and 'the study of heraldic forms'.[2] To be truly Ruskinian, he had to associate the school with a practical workshop: 'the men in this workshop should be the teachers in the school, and...the pupils of the school should be drafted into the workshop'.[3] The school was formally opened by the Minister of Education in 1888. The workshop was established at the same time. It became the foundation of the Guild of Handicraft, the most interesting of all the Arts and Crafts guilds.

Morris, by then a fierce revolutionary, was highly sceptical of the venture. Ashbee recorded in his diary that when he went to see the Great Man he was told that, 'It is useless and that I am about to do a thing with no basis to do it on...I could not exchange a single argument with him till I granted his whole position as a Socialist and then said, "Look, I am going to forge a weapon for you: – and thus I too work with you for the overthrow of Society". To which he replied, "the weapon is too small to be of any value"'.[4] From the first, Ashbee realized that what he was starting must be 'a workman's movement; that it shall be one for the nobility and advance of English Art and Handicraft; that it shall be developed not on the basis of mastership in the ordinary sense, but co-operatively as an industrial** partnership

Ernest Gimson. Bedales School library interior (1920)

*His childhood may have been happy but his early manhood was not. His father was in the Hamburg trade, married one of the daughters of the great merchant house with which he dealt and prospered exceedingly. He was also the notorious Victorian pornographile 'Pisianus Fraxi'. The marriage broke up (which explains why Ashbee's first house was for his mother), and he was disinherited by his father.
**Ashbee's use of the word industrial is contradictory and confusing. Here from the context, he intended to mean no more than 'systematically economic', a use common in Arts and Crafts circles of the '90s (see for instance *The Studio*, Vol XVIII, 1900, p120). But sometimes he used the word in its modern sense of machine dominated.

C.R. Ashbee. Writing cabinet (c1898-99). Made by the Guild of Handicraft

Ashbee. Writing cabinet (1901-2). Made by the Guild of Handicraft

and that the arts and crafts, united in the Guild, shall be the children of the mother art of architecture'.[5]

The Guild's original three members started by selling woodwork, metalwork (Ashbee was a distinguished designer of silverware and jewellery) and decorative painting, but its scope quickly grew to cover all the arts and crafts. Increasing affluence allowed the Guild and School to move in 1891 to Essex House in the Mile End Road, an early eighteenth-century building which the Guild adapted and extended into classrooms, workshops and clubrooms. In 1898, Ashbee opened a shop in Brook Street and set up the Essex House Press.

By the end of the decade, the venture was an established success, and it appeared to be living up to its principles. *The Studio* reported of the 1899 Arts and Crafts Exhibition Society show that 'the work to which the name of Mr C. R. Ashbee is attached ought to be regarded less as his individual work than as that of the Guild of Handicraft in its collective capacity. For between the productions of Essex House and those issuing from elsewhere there is broadly this difference, that whereas many contemporary artists cause their designs to be carried out by artisans working under them and implicitly obeying their orders, Mr Ashbee, as head of the Guild founded by him, seeks rather to elicit the potential talent of the workshop; his responsibility being comprised in general supervision, sometimes merely in advice or suggestion, as distinct from absolute dictation; and in so acting he claims, indeed, to be fulfilling in its most literal sense the original purpose for which the Arts and Crafts Society was called into existence'.[6]

Quite early in his career, the practical problems of running the Guild convinced Ashbee of the importance of coming to terms with machine production. As a 'constructive' rather than revolutionary socialist, Ashbee did not follow Morris in advocating the violent destruction of Victorian capitalism and its machinery.

In 1894 he explained that 'the industrial organization of the mine, the mill and the dockyard must always remain quite a different thing from that of the builder's yard, the cabinet maker's, jeweller's or blacksmith's shop, or any form of production in which the hand and its individuality may prevail over the machine, but I believe that object lessons from the reconstruction of the latter may be drawn for the use of the former'.[7]

Fourteen years later he was more explicit. 'What I seek to show is that this Arts and Crafts movement, which began with the earnestness of the Pre-Raphaelite painters, the prophetic enthusiasm of Ruskin and the titanic energy of Morris, is not what the public has thought it to be, or is seeking to make it: a nursery for luxuries, a hothouse for the production of mere trivialities and useless things for the rich. It is a movement for the stamping out of such things by sound production on the one hand and the inevitable regulation of machine production and cheap labour on the other...To the men of this movement, who are seeking to compass the destruction of the commercial system, to discredit it, undermine it, overthrow it, their mission is just as serious and just as sacred as was that of their great grandfathers who first helped raise it into being...They want to put into the place of the old order that is passing away, something finer, nobler, saner; they

Ashbee. Norman Chapel, Broad Campden. Ashbee's conversion of a derelict building dating back to the eleventh century

want to determine the limitations of the factory system, to regulate machinery, to get back to realities in labour and human life.'[8]

He was never opposed to using machinery in craftwork itself: 'thus a timber plank [the Guild held] could be sawn by a circular saw but it should not be subsequently carved by machinery'; the client should not 'be put off with the machine-made article on the score of cheapness, neatness or trade finish'.[9]

If machinery was really to be regulated, if craftsmanship was to be an example to the factory system, craftwork would have to be able to compete on more equal terms with the machine so that its products were not just expensive luxuries for the rich but could be freely chosen by everyone. So the economic basis of craftsmanship had to be rethought and reorganized.

The Guild's co-operative workshop was one way of doing this. But it was not enough, and, in 1902 when the Essex House lease expired, Ashbee took the revolutionary and extremely brave step of leading the Guild (150 men, women and children from the East End accompanied him after a democratic vote) to Chipping Campden, a 'little forgotten Cotswold town of the Age of the Arts and Crafts where industrialism had never touched, where there was an old silk mill and empty cottages ready to hand, left almost as when the Arts and Crafts ended in the eighteenth century'.[10]

The motives were many, not least to establish the poetic relationship between people, craftsmanship and the land described in *News from Nowhere*. It later became clear that living off the land could provide a subsidy for craftwork. As smallholders, the workers could produce much of their own food, pigs and chickens as well as vegetables, which, coupled with the cheaper rents of country property, was supposed to allow them to charge less for their craft objects and so to allow these to compete with machine products.

At first, the project prospered. About half the craftsmen and their families took to cultivation seriously; new cottages were built and old ones improved; a school of higher education was founded on the lines of Essex House; all kinds of recreation were started: a drama society, a swimming club with its own bathing lake, and the town band was revitalized. Yet the Cockneys were never really accepted by the country folk, gentry and peasants alike. In 1905 trade began to fall off and by the end of 1907 the position was so desperate that the Guild had to be wound up as a limited company.

Ashbee attributed the failure partly to the decreasing purchasing power of the Guild's established clients and to the growing fashion for buying antiques instead of new made objects. But some of the difficulties were inherent in working in the country: it was difficult to keep in proper touch with clients in London from the heart of Gloucestershire; the Guild was at the mercy of the railway companies which appear to have been just as inefficient and rapacious as British Rail is now; and isolation in the countryside meant that Guildsmen could not exploit a wider labour market as they had been able to in London. In the bad times at Essex House, craftsmen had simply found work elsewhere, to return when the Guild was in better straits.

Ashbee. Magpie and Stump, Cheyne Walk, Chelsea, London (1894, now destroyed). Entrance hall

Magpie and Stump, light fitting. Exposed wires impressed *The Studio*

After the crash, some craftsmen had to leave Chipping Campden altogether and, though the Guild was reconstituted with the help of the American socialist millionaire Joseph Fels (it paid him four and a half per cent on his investment), neither the Guild nor Ashbee seems to have fully recovered self-confidence. The Guild staggered on until 1919* when, as a late casualty of the War, it was finally disbanded, though several of the original craftsmen stayed on in Chipping Campden until their deaths.

In fact, the realities of Guildwork may have been rather different from the idyll painted by Ashbee. Alec Miller, who joined the Campden group, wrote to Ashbee afterwards that, 'The Guild was never a real Guild...since I knew it in 1902. Most of the Guildsmen...regarded the Guild as a nuisance...The higher ideals of Craftsmanship also, as I soon saw, were not in the craftsmen – but were in you – and, if you as a director said that beaten and hammered silver work was better than spun work they accepted it...The Guild never produced things co-operatively since I knew it – it produced things working under your direction'.[11] Miller thought that in the successful years at Campden, the Guild was too big to allow any real co-operation between all members.

Ashbee continued to believe that 'the Standard of work and the Standard of life are one; that beauty of work and goodness are for craftsmen best expressed in the making of things that are serviceable; that this implies the acceptance by the Community of Standard...and that the Socialistic State or the State at which we are aiming is not possible without the recognition of Standard'.[12] If agriculture would not suffice to sustain the Arts and Crafts to fight on equal terms with machine production, other means must be found. Ashbee, the lifelong educationist, saw the answer in the schools of art and design.

In *Should We Stop Teaching Art* published in 1911, he proposed reconstituting these in association with workshops on the lines of the Guild and School of Handicraft. But there was to be an essential difference. The state would put up an interest-free capital fund (of quite modest size) which would provide, free, all the materials needed by the craftsmen and pay up to half their labour costs. In return, a craftsman would accept at least one apprentice from the school. Once the system was working properly, the state could withdraw, for the profits from the sale of craftwork could be used to re-endow the fund and sponsor more and more craftworkers.

Ashbee's attitude to machinery changed. He continued to believe that, though it was immoral to produce certain types of metal work, furniture or clothing by machine, 'it is just as immoral to keep men making mechanical things by hand – chains, for instance, in which the links have to be exact – when the machine would do the work better'.[13] The Standard should be still set by craftwork, yet here too machines had an increased part to play – but machines of a particular

*Felicity Ashbee, C.R.'s daughter, tells me that the family had to leave Campden during the War because of strong anti-German sentiment. Ashbee never returned.

Ashbee. 38 and 39 Cheyne Walk, Chelsea, London (completed 1899). Magpie and Stump, an adaptation, is the house on right edge

38~39 CHEYNE WALK
CHELSEA : S·W:
C·R·ASHBEE ·M·A · ARCHITECT:
MAGPIE & STUMP HOUSE:
37 CHEYNE WALK · CHELSEA ·

Ashbee and Holden. Danvers Tower, unbuilt design for Cheyne Walk, London (1897)

Ashbee. Shrewsbury Court, design for Cheyne Walk (c1911): Ashbee's most ambitious London design (unbuilt)

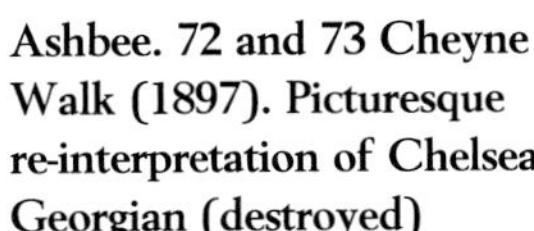

Ashbee. 72 and 73 Cheyne Walk (1897). Picturesque re-interpretation of Chelsea Georgian (destroyed)

sort. 'The whole tendency of what is known in America as "fine machine tool production" is in the direction of personal skill, and the use by the individual of the tool, and the power behind it under his direct control. All mechanism that helps individuality may also help the Arts'.[14]

Ashbee's understanding of machinery was far more profound than that of many of his contemporaries. In a sense, his insistence that 'there is a way of distinguishing between the good and the bad in machine production' so that 'it becomes much more difficult to be revolutionary'[15] brings Morris into the twentieth century. But perhaps Ashbee's qualified acceptance would have been less emphatic had he realized then how long it would take for machines which aid individuality to become readily available and how often, once they did, forms of contract would ensure that workers remained enslaved to what he called Mechanism. Certainly in his lifetime, Ashbee saw little progress. Governments were so uninterested in Standard that they preferred to pay people to remain unemployed rather than to experiment with Ashbee's system for subsidizing the crafts. They do still.

Ashbee had practised as an architect from the early '90s and in building, as in everything else, he firmly adhered to Guild principles. 'The first duty of the architect', he believed, 'is to interpret his client's wishes, and the first duty of a builder is honesty.' And he despised 'the relationship in which modern industrial development has placed the architect and the builder towards one another, setting the former to check the latter'.[16]

'Architecture, the "Mother Art" which should be guardian and helper of all Arts and Crafts, has, through the agency of industrial machinery and the contract system become in large measure the instrument of their destruction – an evil mother, destroying her little ones.'[17] So Ashbee often did away with the general contractor and worked direct as builder and architect with Guildsmen, 'a group of conscientious workmen, say a joiner or two, a few masons, and a couple of blacksmiths, all of whom were intimate with me, knew my ways and worked in my spirit'.[18]*

The first fruit of this kind of collaboration was Ashbee's Magpie and Stump (his mother's house and his own offices) in Cheyne Walk, Chelsea. Completed in 1894 it was** a tall, thin London house with a large three-storey oriel, all quietly clad in soft red brick with stone dressings, not unlike Voysey's houses in Hans Road. Inside, the house was simple but relieved by touches of rich craftsmanship. The chimney breast in the hall, for instance, ran without a mantelshelf from floor to frieze covered in copper squares, many of which, said *The Studio*, were 'enriched by the results of various experiments in enamels. Thus spots of gorgeous crimsons, purples and greens, inserted apparently by chance among the plain copper squares, give a jewelled effect to the whole'.[19] Roger Fry (a friend of Ashbee from Cambridge

*Alan Crawford tells me that, under what Ashbee called the Guild system of building, Guild workmen did the wood and metal work while bricklayers and masons were employed for the duration of each job.

**The building was scandalously demolished in the '70s to make way for an elephantine monument to greed and mediocrity.

Ashbee. Little Coppice, Iver Heath, Buckinghamshire (1905): an economical small house in the country

Ashbee. Norman Chapel, Broad Campden, Gloucestershire (1906): the old is old, the new, new

days) painted the mural over the drawing-room fireplace, and the curtains and piano cover were embroidered by Ashbee's mother. *The Studio* was particularly keen on the light fittings. 'Mr Ashbee has avoided the attempt to imitate gaseliers...Recognizing that a wire and not a tube was the essential factor, he has shown you the structure of the fittings boldly...In the drawing-room the corona is further enriched by pendulous balls of jewel-like enamel which catch the light and sparkle in spots of superb colour purely as ornament'[20] – a perfect summary of Ashbee's attitude, always ready to welcome new technology and express it directly, yet always insistent on impressing the stamp of craftsmanship.

The much less gorgeous craftsmanship of the exterior is the hallmark of Ashbee's architecture. Almost every building he designed was carefully, almost humbly, made to fit in with its surroundings – yet all show individuality. His work was divided between town houses in Chelsea, country cottages and loving restorations (for instance those of Turner's and Carlyle's houses in Chelsea and of his own first house in Chipping Campden, the Woolstapler's Hall).

Ashbee built several other houses in Cheyne Walk, but only two, numbers 38 and 39 (1899), remain. They originally formed a very free group, dominated by the white-rendered asymmetrical gable that fronted number 39's studio. The gable was pierced by a circular window, a motif occasionally taken up by other Arts and Crafts architects. Simple but decorative ironwork protected those areas with a design of verticals imposed on large semi-circles, all topped with gold finials. Even more free was his design (1897) for Danvers Tower, an unexecuted group of studio flats which was to have been built on the corner of Cheyne Walk and Danvers Street. Here, a great white tower, divided asymmetrically by a vertical strip of windows and finished with a shallow metal hat, was to have terminated a lower block in brick and stone with pronounced horizontals and irregular strips of window, topped by a great green pitched roof. Many of the motifs are similar to Voysey's but they are used with a freedom at which Voysey never aimed.*

The early Cheyne Walk designs have materials, detailing and, to some extent, window proportions in common with the undistinguished Georgian artisans' dwellings they replaced. But, even when they were grouped as at the Magpie and Stump, each was consciously individual – nearly always asymmetrical, they had odd, completely un-Georgian emphases, like 39's gable or the lozenge-shaped windows of numbers 72 and 73 (1897).

Ashbee was trying to create a new, picturesque, changeful Chelsea in place of Georgian regularity and uniformity. But he was gradually infected with the growing fashion for Classical building and he acquired a humbler attitude to the Georgian nature of Cheyne Walk. He designed a block of flats which was to have terminated against Cheyne Walk in two identical five-storey, nearly Neo-Georgian blocks connected by a colonnade. It was never built and nor was Ashbee's

*In his *Memoirs*, Ashbee said 'the drawings and much of the invention were by Charles Holden, then working in my office'.[21]

Ernest Barnsley. Upper Dorval House, Sapperton, Gloucestershire (1902). Original cottage in centre, with added wings

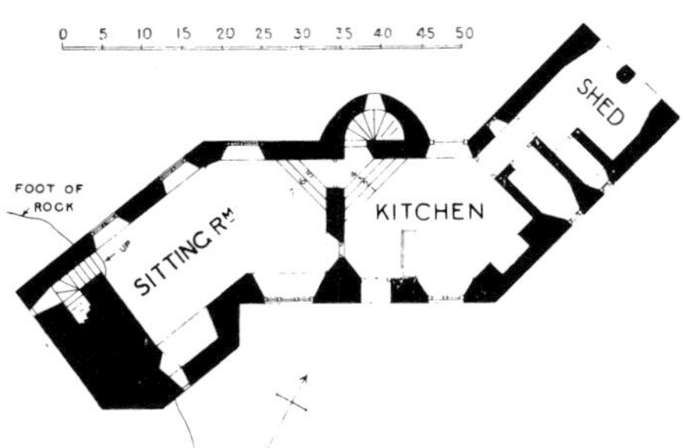

Top: Gimson. Stoneywell Cottage, nr Leicester (1898). Arts and Crafts at its most earthy
Above: Ground floor plan

Sidney Barnsley. Beechanger, Sapperton (1902). Lean-to and right hand gable are additions

most interesting big design of this period, Shrewsbury Court, a complex of student dwellings which was to have fronted Cheyne Walk with the mighty machicolated tower of the men's hostel joining an arched entrance gate; it was an elevation as inventive as many of Mackintosh's. But in the courts beyond the gate were two large hostels for women and married students designed in strictest symmetrical stripped Classical style.

This affection for Classical architecture is very rarely seen in Ashbee's country work. On new, open sites he tended to use white roughcast or brick for the same reason as Voysey – economy. And on occasion he would use Voysey-like buttresses, for instance in Little Coppice at Iver Heath, Buckinghamshire (1905), where he adopted a remarkably economical square plan with white-rendered ground floor walls irregularly pierced with windows. The upper floor is in a pyramidal roof covered with a grey-green slate which, he thought, 'certainly looks well against the dark wall of pines at the side of the garden'.[22]

Most of his country work was in and around Chipping Campden, much of which he rebuilt and restored for Guild members after 1902. Izod's Cottage* in the High Street is typical. Partly built from materials found in the two dilapidated cottages on the site, it has stone mullions and iron casements, stone walls coursed so that the largest blocks are at the bottom, and a dormered roof on which the stone slates are 'laid in gradation – the larger and heavier at the eaves, the smaller near the ridge. The beauty of old masonry and roofing lies in observing details of this kind'.[23] Now, it is almost impossible to distinguish between Ashbee's buildings and those hundreds of years older.

His most ambitious amalgam of old and new work was Norman Chapel at Broad Campden, done for the Ceylonese philosopher Coomarswamy, a house eventually occupied by Ashbee himself. He found an eleventh-century church, converted into a house in the fourteenth century, all derelict. (The Cotswolds were very different before they were invaded by rich Midlands businessmen and aristocrats escaping from the Irish troubles after the First World War.) Ashbee scrupulously preserved the old work 'while adapting it to modern needs' and brought his new 'into harmony with it without in any way working to a period or falsifying history – the old work is old and the new new'.[24] Today it stands as a higgledy-piggledy mixture of building bound together by materials unchanged over 900 years and a community of craftsmanship down the centuries. In its savageness and changefulness, its truth to tradition and to contemporary need, it is one of the most telling achievements of that side of Arts and Crafts building which tried tenderly and humbly to fulfil Pugin's plea for local English architectures.

While Ashbee began to settle his band of craftsmen in north Gloucestershire, a similar group was already celebrating its ninth birthday on the southern edge of the county. Ashbee visited it just before war broke out and commented enthusiastically that, 'the future of the arts must be in groups and schools and this little Sapperton group stands for something live and fine...I've not discovered yet which of

*Now regrettably called Shreelaine.

these three men, Ernest or Sidney Barnsley or Gimson, has the inspiration. All work in the same mood. Perhaps they inspire each other, that is as it should be'.[25]

Ernest Gimson (1864-1919) was the son of a wealthy Leicester engineer and had met Morris in his parents' house. Morris advised him to go to London to train as an architect under J. D. Sedding (whose office was then next door to the Morris shop in Bond Street). There, in 1886, he met Ernest Barnsley (1861-1926), the son of a successful Birmingham builder, and through Barnsley's brother Sidney (1863-1926), who was in Shaw's office, he was gradually introduced to the inner Arts and Crafts circle.

In 1890, Gimson and Sidney Barnsley set up a furniture firm in partnership with Lethaby, Macartney, Blomfield and a Colonel Mallet. Kenton & Co flourished for a couple of years until it had to be wound up for lack of capital.[26] The architects acted as designers for Kenton & Co and did not make the furniture themselves; but this was not enough for Gimson, who apprenticed himself to a firm of plasterers and to an old-fashioned furniture maker near Ledbury who produced high-backed chairs turned on a pole lathe.

His plaster-work was put to immediate use by Lethaby who employed him to design and execute the elaborate ceilings in the main rooms at Avon Tyrrell, where Lethaby recalled that in the summer of 1872, 'he lodged for months in a cottage close by, and after my visits to the "works" in the morning we played cricket with the children in the afternoon'.[27]

The attractions of country life were too strong to be resisted and, in 1893, Gimson and Sidney Barnsley moved to Ewen in south Gloucestershire and persuaded Ernest, who was practising as an architect in Birmingham, to join them. A year later they moved to nearby Pinbury Park and in 1902 they transferred to Sapperton. Throughout this period, all three were involved in furniture production in a workshop which they ran jointly, Gimson mainly as a designer, though Sidney Barnsley made all his own furniture himself. Gimson believed in handwork but, like Ashbee, he was prepared to allow machines such as circular saws. And, like Ashbee, he was prepared to let machine production look after itself. Alfred Powell recalled that, 'He desired [that] commercialism might leave handiwork and the arts alone and make use of its own wits and its own machinery. Let machinery be honest, he said, and make its own machine-buildings and its own machine furniture; let it make its chairs and tables of stamped aluminium if it likes: why not?'[28] But Gimson lacked Ashbee's understanding that machine production would inevitably win unless society could be radically changed.

Gimson's architecture was mostly designed in the '90s. There are two houses in Leicester done for members of his family in a free Georgian style, one with a most ingenious compact plan. Near Leicester, on the edge of Charnwood Forest which rises hummocky, dark and mysterious in the middle of one of England's most pastoral counties, Gimson built three summer houses for the same clients. Henry Wilson commented in *The Architectural Review*, when Gimson showed photographs and drawings at the 1899 Arts and Crafts show,

Gimson. Bedales School library (1920). Built by Geoffrey Lupton and Edward Barnsley, under Sidney Barnsley's supervision, after Gimson's death

'The buildings look as solid and lasting as the pyramids, and though they are built with almost stern rudeness, yet they look gracious and homelike'.[29]

Stoneywell Cottage, the best of the three, was built for Gimson's brother Sidney. It cranks up and round the curve of one of the heathery Charnwood hummocks and grows out of the rock more like a series of imposed strata than a building. Great flat stones project from the masonry both outside and in (where they are used as shelves). It was roofed in dark thatch* which rose to a ridge capped with straw, giving the back of the building the impression of a crested and amiable dragon worming its way round the hill. Inside, the bare rock was exposed in the sitting room, and partitions were made of halved tree trunks with plaster and lath between. 'The actual building was done by Mr Detmar Blow...captaining a little band of masons and gaining that practical knowledge of the crafts which has since stood him in good stead.'[30]

The cottage is Arts and Crafts architecture at its most earthy – if nature made buildings, they would surely look something like Stoneywell. Gimson built little else: a few buildings at Kelmscott as a memorial to William Morris, his own house at Sapperton and a cottage near Budleigh Salterton made out of local thatch and cob (rammed earth). He only once caught the naturalism of Stoneywell again, in his

*There was a fire in 1938, after which the roof was replaced with slates by another Gimson. Most of the internal timber remains and the walls were unaffected – though some of the windows were enlarged.

Ernest Barnsley. Rodmarton Manor, Gloucestershire (started 1909, completed by Norman Jewson 1929). One of the most thoroughly anti-industrial buildings created by the Arts and Crafts movement

last job, the library of Bedales School, finished by Sidney Barnsley after Gimson's early death. Outside, the building is conventionally neo-Tudor, brick with leaded casements. Inside, the roof is supported on great rough-sawn timbers which branch tree-like at gallery level into curved supports for the roof forming a covered grove of beautiful stateliness and simplicity.

Like Gimson, Ernest Barnsley often worked as an architect. He did work for the SPAB, his own house at Sapperton which, like Norman Chapel, was a beautifully harmonious extension of an existing building, and he produced one of the largest and last Arts and Crafts country houses, Rodmarton Manor, Gloucestershire, on which the client, the Hon Claude Biddulph, spent £5000 a year between 1909 and Barnsley's death in 1926, interrupted only by the War. At first sight the house, warm, mullioned and many-gabled, seems vast. It *is* big, but the Arts and Crafts plan, one-room-and-a-corridor deep, which wanders over the site, makes it seem much larger than it really is.

It is built in strictest Cotswold tradition with virtually no new motifs. All the timber was found locally and all the stone quarried on the estate. And it was built by hand – even the circular saw was eschewed and the wood was sawn in a pit. It is one of the most determined applications of Ruskinian precepts. Ashbee, who visited the works in October 1914, said that 'I've seen no modern work to equal it...And when I ask why, I find the answer in the system, the method rather than the man. It is a house built on the basis not of contract but of confidence...The English Arts and Crafts Movement at its best is here'.[31] Rodmarton is magnificent* but it is a dead end; a medieval house created in a medieval way in one of the last pockets of feudalism in England. Barnsley was lucky to have a rich client prepared to take his time. By 1914 time was critical.

Of his visit to Sapperton, Ashbee recalled that 'Gimson took me over his workshops and his house. He glowed...at having a kindred spirit to confide in [and said] "It's a frightful problem to keep things going: how to keep the men employed, how to keep your standard up"...In the middle of our talk Gimson suddenly seized the iron fire clippers. "There", he said, "can any smith of yours make a piece like that?...It's the most difficult double joint you can forge." I thought of Bill Thornton and Charley Downer also at work in their Cotswold valley. "It's all a matter of time" [I replied]. "Ah yes", he said, "time. That's it. Time. Let's forget these d-d economics and get to constructive facts again"'.[32]

Ashbee, less well insulated by a handsome private income than Gimson and the Barnsleys, and much more socially idealistic, was never one to forget the d-d economics. He was becoming more optimistic in the first half of 1914. The Campden community seemed to be a real Guild again; there was plenty to do and the partnership of craft and agriculture was apparently working. Yet it was a false dawn; 'The War and its aftermath was to reveal what we did not then know, how limited and precarious was the patronage'[33] – there was no time left, and the experiment was soon to end forever.

*It also shows the worst side of the Arts and Crafts dislike of machinery. While Gimson and the Barnsleys were having an idyllic time combining creative work and close contact with the countryside, two men, a father and son, spent a large portion of their lives in the backbreaking repetitive labour of sawing planks by hand. The task would have been much more easily and less demeaningly done with a circular saw, as architects like Ashbee and Voysey realized.

1 *Ashbee,* C. R. Trivialities of Tom, Being Reflections on a Victorian Boyhood, *typescript in the Victoria and Albert Museum, 1940-41, p7.*
2 *Ashbee,* C. R. Transactions of the Guild and School of Handicraft, *Vol I, 1890, p19.*
3 Ibid.
4 *Ashbee,* C. R. Memoirs, *typescript in the Victoria and Albert Museum, Vol I, p45.*
5 Transactions, op cit, *p22.*
6 The Studio, *Vol XVIII, 1900, p118.*
7 *Ashbee,* C. R. A Few Chapters on Workshop Reconstruction and Citizenship, *Guild and School of Handicraft, Essex House, London, 1894, p10.*
8 *Ashbee,* C. R. Craftsmanship in Competitive Industry, *Essex House Press, London and Campden, Gloucestershire, 1908, p9.*
9 Ibid, *p18.*
10 Ibid, *p42.*
11 *Letter from Alec Miller to Ashbee, 1911, quoted in* Memoirs, op cit, *Vol III, p190.*
12 Craftsmanship, op cit, *p224.*
13 *Ashbee,* C. R. Should We Stop Teaching Art, *Batsford, London, 1911, p13.*
14 Ibid, *p98.*
15 Ibid, *p115.*
16 *Ashbee,* C. R. A Book of Cottages and Little Houses, *Batsford, London, 1906, p97.*
17 *Ashbee,* C. R. Craftsmanship, op cit, *p125.*
18 Ibid, *p142.*
19 The Studio, *Vol V, 1895, p72.*
20 Ibid, *p74.*
21 *Ashbee,* C. R. Memoirs, op cit, *Vol I, p111.*
22 *Ashbee,* C. R. *'On the Bromleigh Estate at Iver Heath',* The Studio, *Vol XXXVI, 1905, p50.*
23 *Ashbee,* C. R. A Book of Cottages and Little Houses, op cit, *p9.*
24 *Ashbee,* C. R. *'The Norman Chapel Buildings at Broad Campden',* The Studio, *Vol XLI, 1907, p290.*
25 *Ashbee,* C. R. Memoirs, op cit, *Vol III, p366.*
26 *The history of Kenton & Co is summarized in Lethaby's contribution to* Ernest Gimson, his Life and Work, *Stratford, London and Oxford, 1924, p6, and in Blomfield's* Memoirs of an Architect, *Macmillan, London, 1932, pp76-78.*
27 *Lethaby, W. R. (ed)* Ernest Gimson, op cit, *p7.*
28 *Powell, Alfred H., in Lethaby, W.R. (ed)* Ernest Gimson, ibid, *p14.*
29 *Wilson, H. 'The Arts and Crafts Society's Exhibition',* The Architectural Review, *Vol VI, 1899, p214.*
30 *Weaver, Lawrence* Small Country Houses of Today, *Second Series,* op cit, *1919, p16.*
31 *Quoted by Clive Aslet,* Country Life, *Vol CLXIV, 1978, p1181.*
32 *Ashbee,* C. R. Memoirs, op cit, *Vol IV, p71.*
33 Ibid, *Vol III, pp367-368.*

The descent

13

The War virtually killed Arts and Crafts architecture. Ashbee very rarely practised as architect afterwards – though he did sterling service as civil adviser to the Palestine government between 1917 and 1923, repairing Jerusalem's walls according to SPAB principles.

A few anachronistic clients clung to the free-style after the War, but Arts and Crafts architecture had been dying for a decade before 1914. Without a radical change in society, it was impossible for the movement to have any more permanent basis than the production of luxuries for the rich. When upper middle class taste began to change, the architect and designer had to change too. As the social ideals of Morris and Ruskin lost their force in the imagination of the time, the Gothic spirit withered, and architects turned increasingly to Classical styles for inspiration. The few Arts and Crafts people who stuck to Gothic principles were increasingly left out.

After 1906, for instance, Voysey received few architectural commissions, and those he did get were not large; he began to use overtly Gothic detailing which must have made him increasingly less popular. Lethaby built nothing after 1902. Prior gradually faded out as an architect. The lesser followers of Pugin, Ruskin and Morris: people like Troup, Blow and Ricardo, gradually changed their style to Classical symmetry and severity in the decade around the War, though almost all of them returned to less formal designs occasionally.

The change in style was related to a change in the status of England. In the two middle quarters of the nineteenth century, Britain had been the workshop of the world, achieving her economic pre-eminence by unparalleled commercial exploitation of the machinery against which Ruskin and Morris had railed so fiercely. But from the 1870s, Britain's success became her undoing; the newly industrialized nations began to erect tariff walls against British goods, and by 1900 the Continent, the USA and even the white colonies such as Australia and Canada were protected by high import levies. Real incomes in Britain, which had grown throughout the last decade of the nineteenth century, virtually stagnated between 1900 and 1914.

E.L. Lutyens. Folly Farm, Sulhamstead, Berkshire (1906)

The prosperous middle classes on whom the Arts and Crafts movement had relied so much had the butter taken off their bread – particularly after the Liberal government of 1906 increasingly introduced reforms to alleviate the lot of working people, a process that culminated in Lloyd George's notorious 1909 budget which raised death duties, income tax from one shilling to a grievous one shilling and twopence, introduced super-tax and (abortively) Land Value duties. If you were wealthy and middle class, the years after 1906 were not a good time to build. But even if you felt secure enough to do so, your attitude to what was proper in building was likely to be very different from that of the previous generation.

To ensure a balance of trade and to finance reforms at home, Britain was increasingly forced to exploit colonies in Asia and Africa and semi-colonies like China. With the colonization of Africa a new element had entered British imperialism; economic necessity forced Britain to promote forms of serfdom and near slavery. Instead of being

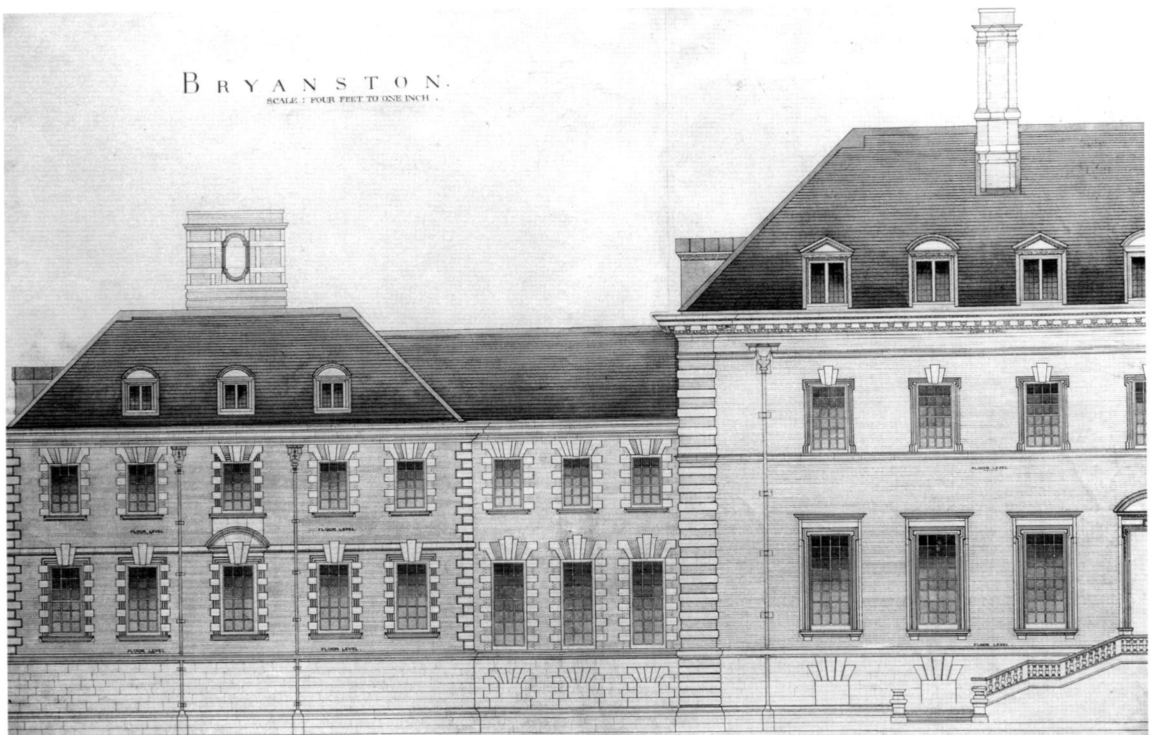

**R. Norman Shaw.
Bryanston, Dorset
(1889-94).
Half main elevation.
Shaw's late great
Classical manifesto**

left to the doubtful mercies of the market, indigenous people were exploited by government. For instance, all the land in Kenya was declared forfeit in 1898, forcing natives by a punitive system of taxation into overcrowded reserves on inferior soil whence they were obliged to toil on farms owned by Europeans. In South Africa, the last war of Victoria's reign was fought to obtain control of the Johannesburg gold fields; when Britain won, indentured Chinese labour was imported on a massive scale to work the mines.

This was the dark side of an Empire on which Britain was ever more dependent. Large parts of London were rebuilt as an imperial capital in the first decade of the century and Ruskin would not have been surprised to find that the great schemes – for example Admiralty Arch, built by Aston Webb between 1906 and 1911 – were all erected in high Classical styles which he had so scathingly decried as the architecture of slavery.*

Throughout middle class life, from the boy scout movement to the Stock Exchange, there was new emphasis on order and leadership, on things established, ordered, old looking and tested. Antique collecting became the rage to the detriment of working craftsmen. In architecture, the main spokesman of the new mood was Reginald Blomfield. Though a member of the Art Workers' Guild and the Arts and Crafts Exhibition Society from their earliest years, and a friend of Lethaby and Gimson, Blomfield had long been a Classicist and published several books calling for increased formality in building. His *Short History of Renaissance Architecture in England* (1897) paralleled Prior's book on English Gothic, and in the 1900 edition Blomfield made his position clear. Commenting on the late nineteenth century, he urged that because 'the co-operative art of the Middle Ages was no longer possible, some-one must take the lead. A strong individual intelligence was needed to restore order in this chaos of eclecticism'.[1]

Made professor of architecture at the Royal Academy in 1906, Blomfield was in a strong position to proselytize. He hoped 'against hope to divert students from the fashion for the picturesque and abundance of ornament prevalent at the time to a loftier conception of architecture as the art of *ordonnance*'.[2] In his lectures, he stressed that the student 'need not concern himself with dogmatic theories of the relation of art and morality in studying architecture':[3] it was the perennial conservative plea that art has nothing to do with politics and that it should implicitly support the status quo. His ideal was a return to eighteenth-century traditions of craftsmanship in which the workman could be guaranteed to turn out work by rote without any troublesome individuality creeping in. 'When an architect can depend on his men, he is spared the necessity of spending half his time in explaining to builders details which ought to be matters of common knowledge, he has leisure to devote his energy to his real business of thinking out the central conception of his design.'[4]

*Classicism was not limited to London. It permeated the whole empire. Herbert Baker was sent by the great imperialist Cecil Rhodes, to 'visit the old countries of the Mediterranean to get inspiration for any "thoughts" he might "undertake"'. Rhodes's 'thoughts' included war memorials and a great Greek temple halfway up a mountain. (Baker, Herbert 'Architecture and Personalities', *Country Life*, London, 1944, p35)

John Belcher. Institute of Chartered Accountants, London (1889-93). Edwardian Baroque enriched by Arts and Crafts sculpture by Hamo Thornycroft

In 1906, Classical architecture was no recent introduction. From about 1890 on, Shaw was almost entirely a Classicist, creating buildings of great formality like Bryanston (1889-1894) and the Lower Regent Street Quadrant (finished by Blomfield after many vicissitudes). By 1902, Shaw believed that 'we have now no proper traditional architecture, for it died away imperceptibly at the beginning of the last century...From the date of the Exhibition of 1851 until recently we were all intensely Gothic – and intensely wrong. We were trying to revive a style which was quite unsuited to the present day. Since 1880, however, we have been gradually awakening to this fact. After spending millions of pounds we came to the conclusion that it had been to no purpose. The Gothic Revival, for all practical purposes, is dead, and the tendency of late years has been to return to the English Renaissance. I was trained on the older Gothic lines, I am personally devoted to it, admire it in the abstract, and think it superb; but it is totally unsuited to modern requirements. When it came to building, especially in places like the City, we found it would not answer'.[5]

Another early user of Classical forms was John Belcher (1841-1913), who had sat in the chair at the meeting which founded the Art Workers' Guild. He produced the Institute of Chartered Accountants building between 1889 and 1893. With its mansard roof, free use of Tuscan columns and heavy rustication, it was immensely influential. Less influential was the way in which, in proper Art Workers' Guild fashion, it incorporated an intricate frieze of figure sculpture above the windows of the piano nobile (by Hamo Thornycroft, another AWG man) and delicate female figures above the ground floor columns. Inside, Belcher and his assistant Beresford Pite gave the newly respectable accounting profession an appropriately grand setting in a council chamber lined with vast murals and topped by a staggeringly tall drum and dome. The building was the work of an older generation of Guildsmen than Prior and Lethaby but it was one which demonstrated all their love of working together and incorporating painting and sculpture into architecture. That it lacked any allegiance to the principles of Ruskin and Morris, so revered by the younger men, showed the contradictory nature of the Guild.

In the next two decades, free Neo-Baroque became a major style for new civic architecture throughout Britain, with many grandiose buildings to its credit – Deptford Town Hall (1902-1904) by Lanchester and Rickards for instance, and their Central Hall, Westminster (1905).

Other Classical idioms emerged. There was a Wrenaissance following Bryanston in which Wren became a model for country houses and less grand town buildings. Early in this century, a much more severe and correct Classical style emerged – based on the French Renaissance (the style was not unrelated to the monarch's Continental predilections). One of the first examples was the Ritz Hotel in Piccadilly by Mewès and Davis (1906). It made a tremendous impression. Charles Reilly, professor of architecture at Liverpool from 1904, recalled that when the Mewès and Davis work first appeared, 'they seemed to set a new, and for an Englishman, an almost impossible standard of elegance'.[6] The schools had joined the profession in support of Classicism.

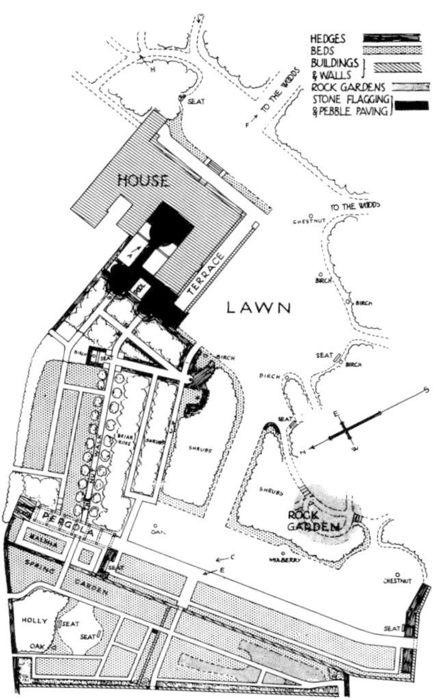

Gertrude Jekyll. Garden plan for Munstead Wood (1896)

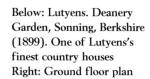

Below: Lutyens. Deanery Garden, Sonning, Berkshire (1899). One of Lutyens's finest country houses
Right: Ground floor plan

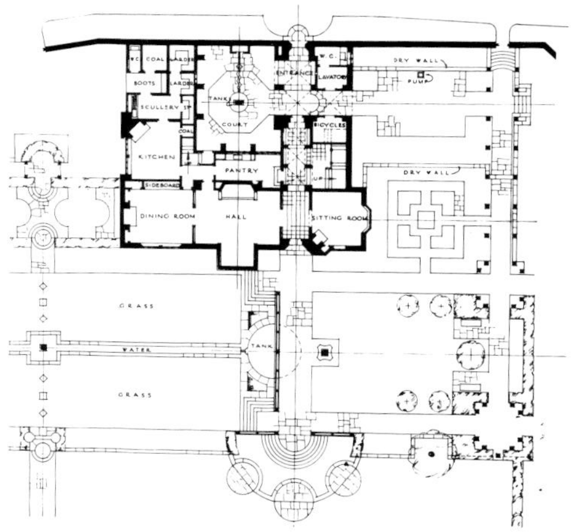

Yet against this background, two Arts and Crafts architects, Lutyens and Baillie Scott, continued to get work and even increase their practices. Each coped with the new climate in his own way.

Edwin Landseer Lutyens (1869-1944) was the 11th of 14 children of an army captain who retired from the service to train under Landseer and became a moderately successful sporting painter. Because of illness and the relative poverty of his parents, Ned (as Edwin not surprisingly preferred to be known) was educated at home. He was virtually self-taught in the Surrey countryside, until at 16 he was sent to what became the Royal College of Art to study architecture. At about this time, he met Norman Shaw and 'after a little conversation the PRA [President of the Royal Academy] of the future was telling Norman Shaw RA of his experiments in the type of building suited to agricultural enterprise; just mud-encased on wooden piles, roofed with heather, resistant to wind and weather, warm in winter, cool in summer, conforming with the surroundings...with what he called "my fixed principles" (this made Shaw smile) and those were that anything put up by man should harmonize with what Nature, who had been there first, should dictate. Materials should be drawn from those obtainable in the area and foreign elements strictly eliminated. "Very interesting, my boy, but not always feasible", interrupted the great man. "All right for cowsheds, but human beings demand something a little more in keeping with the age in which we live, and if you had my experience you would find that the newly-rich, who are after all the patrons of today, demand replicas of something they have seen in other countries they have visited"'.[7]

Shaw, the early Shaw of Old English style, was Lutyens's model when he set up on his own at the age of 20 after a couple of years at school and another two in the office of Ernest George & Peto. Lutyens's early houses are rather clumsy, heavy with brick, half-timber and great tile roofs. He found Webb's work in the early '90s and became an immediate disciple. He recalled, of his first sight of Webb's Joldwynds: '"That's good...I wonder who the young man is". The freshness and originality which Webb maintained in all his work, I, in my ignorance, attributed to youth'.[8]

Another strong influence on the young Lutyens was Gertrude Jekyll. Munstead Wood, which Lutyens built for Jekyll in 1896, was made with all the thoroughness and attention to tradition that Webb would have wished. Miss Jekyll commented that 'the architect has a thorough knowledge of the local ways of using the sandstone that grows in our hills, and that for many centuries has been the building material of the district, and of all the lesser incidental methods of adapting means to ends that mark the well-defined way of building of the country, so that what he builds seems to grow naturally out of the ground...I hold as a convincing canon in architecture that every building should look like what it is'.[9] The tiled roof comes right down to the top of the doors and is relieved by large gables containing the first floor rooms; windows are strips of oak-framed casements with leaded lights – a Voyseyish composition, but Munstead Wood is Voysey

Lutyens. Munstead Wood (1896), for Gertrude Jekyll

Lutyens. Homewood, (1899). The influence of Webb's Joldwynds

made particular: virtually every detail is derived from precedents to be found in Surrey vernacular.

It was the first of a succession of lovely Surrey houses in which, while being faithful to vernacular motifs, Lutyens began to show his powers of invention. Deanery Garden, Sonning, built in 1899 for Edward Hudson, managing editor of *Country Life* (to which Miss Jekyll contributed gardening articles) is a fine example. Lutyens took the room-and-a-corridor plan and cranked it round three sides of a courtyard (he was one of the first Arts and Crafts architects to bend the plan in this way and often used three- and four-sided courtyards later). But, even more inventive, he carried the south-eastern corridor straight through from back to front of the house, making a partly open, partly covered route for the family from entrance to garden with stairs, sitting room and hall (a big drawing room in country house tradition) opening straight off it. This convenient, economical, yet grand plan was given walls of small local bricks, roofs of sandy tiles (to attract lichen) and a great double-height square bay in the hall made of oak with pegged joints and leaded lights. The main (south-west) front would have been virtually symmetrical about the hall bay if it had not been breached by the arched opening of the corridor which was balanced by a large Webbian chimney (much bigger than it need have been to serve three small fireplaces).

Such changefulness soon began to fade. In that year Lutyens completed Homewood. The house owes much to Webb's middle period, with boarded gables similar to those at Joldwynds, and symmetrical elevations. And for the first time, Lutyens introduced overtly Classical detailing on the outside: the timber gables are, curiously, supported on walls enriched with rusticated Classical pilasters. As Roderick Gradidge has pointed out in his perceptive analysis,[10] it is significant that this first emergence of the orders* was in an Arts and Crafts house executed for a Vicereine of India – Lutyens's mother-in-law, the wife of Lord Lytton, one of the odder Viceroys.

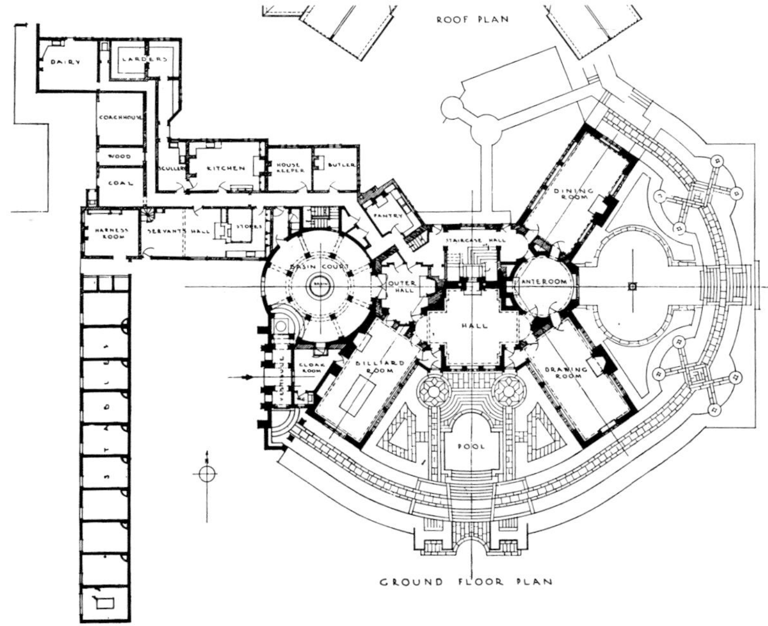

Top: Lutyens. Papillon Court, nr Market Harborough, Leicestershire (1903, now destroyed)
Above: Ground floor plan

Symmetry became increasingly important to Lutyens. His finest work of the early 1900s is in vernacular style, set to symmetrical plans: for instance Marsh Court near Stockbridge in Hampshire (1901), and his variant on Prior's butterfly plan, Papillon Hall near Market Harborough (1903 – now demolished).

The introduction of symmetry was not without problems. As A. S. G. Butler explained in the Lutyens Memorial,** 'the deliberate disorder cultivated by romantic-minded architects of his youth did not appeal to him...He preferred increasingly to avoid a rambling plan, to constrain the wings of a house into a balanced form and even to fold them back neatly within a rectangle, roofing the house as he could. For it is difficult to accomplish exact symmetry in a domestic building and, at the same time, house the inmates quite as they should be...It postulates nearly always some sacrifice of convenience by the owner'.[11] How Pugin would have agreed.

But, Butler emphasized, symmetry 'does provide the only channel

*Classical detailing was to be seen in Lutyens's *interiors* at least as early as Fulbrook (1897).
**A large three-volume work full of detailed drawings and photographs. No other British architect has ever been so quickly and magnificently memorialized.

Below: Lutyens. Heathcote, Ilkley, Yorkshire (1906). His first full-blown Classical design
Right: Ground floor plan

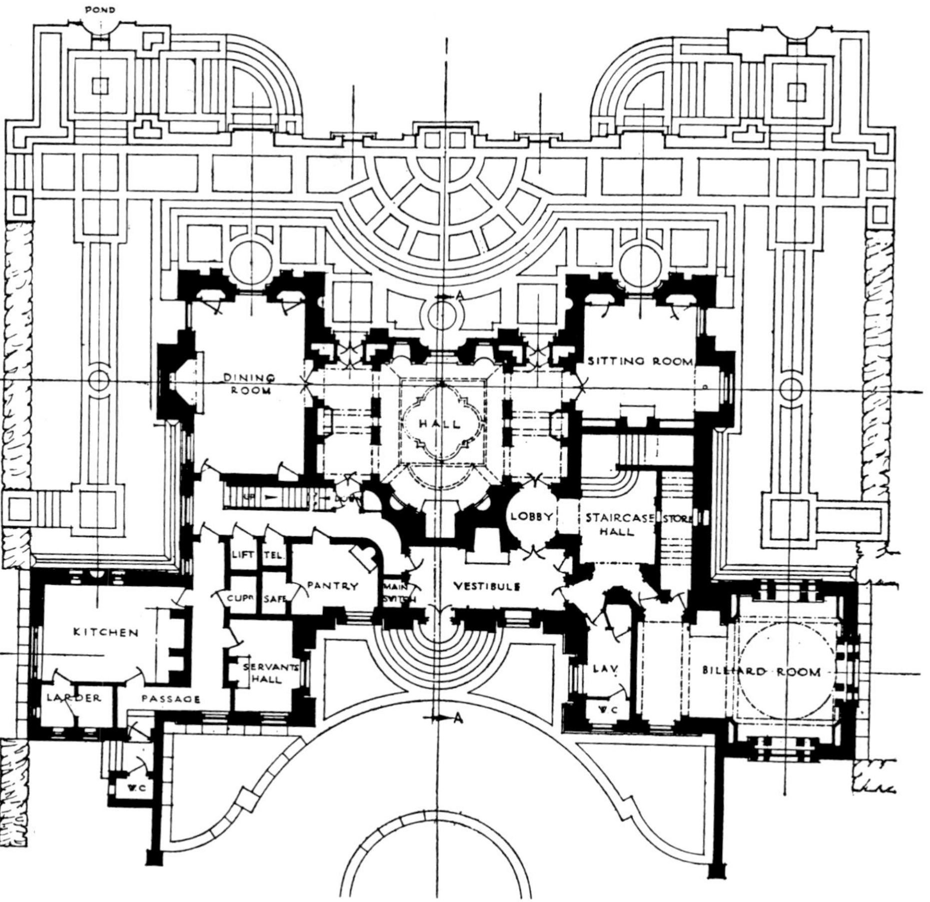

through which an architect may touch the highest performance. For if, through all the intricacies of modern requirements and the technicalities of up-to-date building, he can produce a work which can be enjoyed in detail when explored both inside and out, and, at the same time, can be appreciated in one delightful glance from any direction or distance, he is supreme'.

Inside Papillon was a round basin court, hugged between two of the diagonal wings, in which the roof of the cloister was supported by impeccable Tuscan columns and pilasters. Next year, Lutyens came out with the full blown Neo-Classical elevation of the *Country Life* building in Covent Garden, totally symmetrical and formal with a high tiled roof, rusticated ground floor and stone dressings to the brick upper floors, all in a lively Wrenian fashion.

Lutyens was becoming a convinced Classicist. In 1903, he wrote excitedly to Herbert Baker, 'in architecture Palladio is the game. It is so big. Few appreciate it now and it requires considerable training to value and realize it. The way Wren handled it was marvellous...It means hard thought all through. If it is laboured it fails...it is a big game, a high game'.[12]

In 1906, Lutyens completed Heathcote, a villa in the suburbs of Ilkley in which for the first time he embraced the full panoply of Roman Doric, not just a few columns or pilasters but metopes, guttae, triglyphs – the lot. The plan is fiercely symmetrical with the sitting room balancing the dining room across a country house hall on the main front. Lutyens knew he had been daring. A few years later, he wrote to Baker, 'I have been scolded for not being Yorkshire in Yorkshire. The other view – have a window for this, a door for that etc – a pot-pourri of ornithological details. The result is futile, absolutely unconvincing. My house stands there plumb. I don't think it could have been built anywhere else! Would Wren (had he gone to Australia) have burnt his knowledge and experience to produce a lame marsupial style, though it reflect the character of her aborigines? He would surely have done his best...In modern work – unlike the old – the thinking machine is separated from the labour machine so that the modern architect cannot have the same absolution as we give the old men when the thought and labour was the same individual...The thought and design should, in that they are specialized, become super-thought – and, in that we specialize – must be in advance and distinctly beyond the conceptions of the architect's fellow men'.[13] It was the architecture of authority, of an Empire which stretched from Ilkley to India.

As a Viceregal son-in-law and author of some of the most distinguished Classical buildings in England, Lutyens was an obvious choice for his greatest work – the Viceroy's House in Delhi; a commission he gained in 1912, though the vast building was not completed until 1930. In its overpowering symmetry and blend of Classical and Indian detailing, its endless corridors and jokey incidents, the palace summarizes the worst – and the best – of the last decades of Empire.

The job ensured Lutyens's continuing popularity among the upper and upper middle classes. In the '20s and '30s Lutyens rarely returned

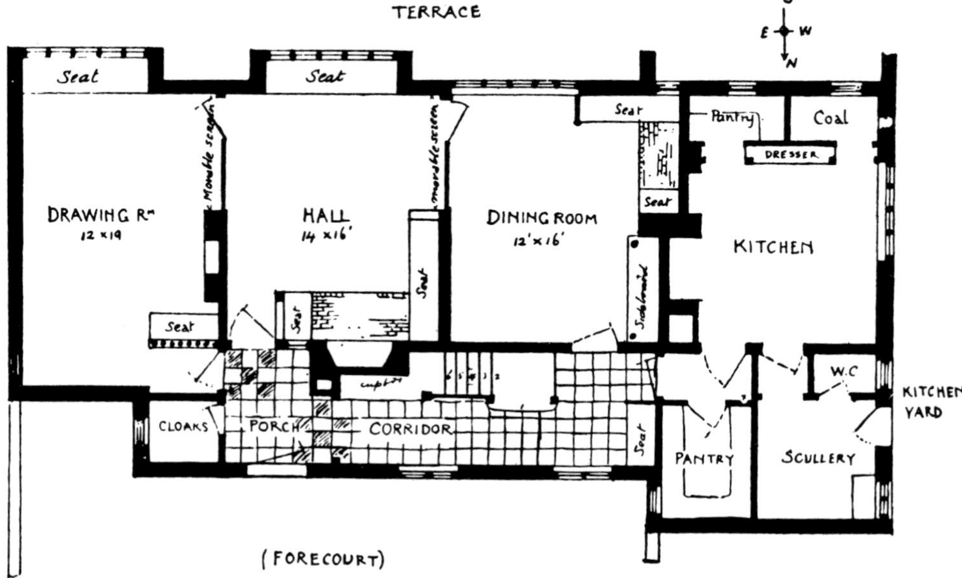

**Above and right:
M.H. Baillie Scott.
An ideal house,
published in *The Studio*
1894. Folding screens
separate principal rooms**

to the full blown Classicism of Heathcote but preferred a more gentle Neo-Georgian, used inventively in many country houses and spread lamentably thinly over Park Lane and the City. But he never wholly forgot his Arts and Crafts origins: many of the later country houses, though almost always symmetrical, are informed by local vernacular.

And, in India, he was brought back to a closer relationship with craftsmen. He advocated making the Delhi works 'a training centre of craftsmanship, a kind of technical university, not only for carvers and painters but engineers and plumbers; and not merely for the immediate needs but as the missing counterpoint to the immense material and intellectual benefits brought to India by the English. For he felt strongly that whilst the raj had suppressed abominable practices, given India the finest engineering in the world, medicine and sanitation and virtually abolished famine, it had destroyed the Indian arts though not more than we have done in England'.[14] The British, said Lutyens, had taught the Indians 'all our evil bureaucratic tricks and little else'. His proposals had no more success than Ashbee's a decade before. They were turned down out of hand by bureaucracy.

Mackay Hugh Baillie Scott (1865-1945) would have applauded Lutyens's idea for a school of craftsmanship for, throughout his long life as a practising architect, he never abandoned the pursuit of craftsmanly architecture or the teachings of Ruskin and Morris.

Baillie Scott was born near Ramsgate, the son of a minor but wealthy Scottish aristocrat. He was originally trained at Cirencester agricultural college with a view to running the family's sheep stations in Australia. But, though he passed all the examinations in 1885, he decided on no very clear grounds* to become an architect. In 1886 he was articled to Major Charles Davis, the city architect of Bath who was responsible for the ungainly Empire Hotel which, until the desecrations of the last three decades, was one of the few cancers in Bath's Georgian fabric.

After this inauspicious beginning, Baillie Scott left Bath and settled on the Isle of Man in 1889 – again on an apparent whim. John Betjeman, as a young *Architectural Review* editor, was told by Baillie Scott that, 'I went to the Isle of Man for a holiday. I was so seasick I couldn't face the journey back so I set up in practice there'.[16]

His first buildings were mostly heavily half-timbered variants of the Old English style, owing little to their surroundings and much more to the early Shaw and to Ernest George. Inside, they were not so conventional. In his own house, the Red House in Douglas (1892-93), Baillie Scott invented a new way of planning in which the living room/hall was separated from the drawing and dining rooms by folding screens allowing all three to be thrown together into one large irregular space or separated into individual rooms. Living halls modelled in miniature on those of country houses, and folding screens allowing interconnected spaces, were to be Baillie Scott's passions, despite their multitudinous disadvantages for families with children.

*For lack of personal papers, Baillie Scott's personality and private history remain shadowy, despite the attentions of James D. Kornwolf who has written down everything there is to know about Scott and a great deal more.[15]

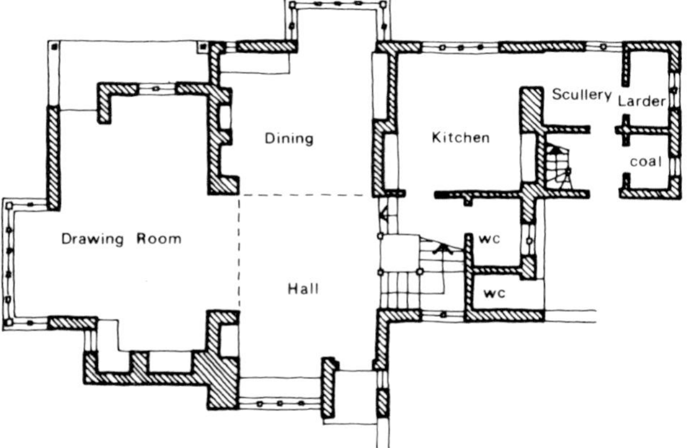

Far left: Baillie Scott. Oakleigh, Douglas, Isle of Man (1892-93). Old English transported. Left: Baillie Scott. Plan, Red House, Douglas, Isle of Man (1892-93). In his own house Baillie Scott attempted a daring fusion of space. (Dotted lines indicate folding screens)

Baillie Scott. Dining room for Grand Duke of Hesse, Darmstadt (1897). Perspective from *Building News*

In 1894, Baillie Scott wrote an article in *The Studio* in which he described the virtues of a hypothetical house* in which a high hall flanked by drawing and dining rooms, all separated by folding screens, were stretched in Arts and Crafts fashion along a corridor where 'to get some idea of its general effect I must transport you to some old Cheshire farm house, somewhere in the country where people have not yet grown to be ashamed of plain bricks and whitewash'.[17] The hall itself had an inglenook over which Baillie Scott placed a small gallery in much the way that Shaw slung his study over the dining room inglenook in his own house – but with much less practical purpose; the gallery was intended to house musicians who would entertain the family taking its ease round the fire, or strike up for a dance when the three main rooms would be thrown into one by folding back the screens. The idea of a late nineteenth-century mini-Medici living in suburban splendour complete with a court band now seems preposterous, but it was sufficiently attractive and credible at the time to earn Baillie Scott many commissions.

The finest manifestation of Baillie Scott's characteristic inglenook and gallery is at Blackwell, a large country house near Bowness in Cumbria (1898-99) where he adopted a northern style: white harling punctuated by strips of stone-mullioned windows under a slate roof with high almost Scottish gables. The half-timbering was brought inside, where it ran rather Teutonic riot round the hall which contained a giant inglenook supporting a half-timbered gallery. The drawing room – a space which Baillie Scott thought ought to be 'dainty' – was all white and delicate. Slender columns were topped by hemispherical foliated basket capitals supporting a thin shelf which ran round the whole room under a plaster-work frieze in which Baillie Scott swirled mountain ash motifs with Art Nouveau-like energy and grace.[18]

The drawing room in particular had some of the fine-drawn Mackmurdoish elegance of Mackintosh at Hill House three years later. As Muthesius remarked, 'In Baillie Scott's work each room is an individual creation, the elements of which do not just happen to be available but spring from the overall idea. Baillie Scott is the first to have realized the interior as an autonomous work of art'.[19]

In the same years, Baillie Scott was building the White Lodge at Wantage in Oxfordshire for the chaplain of St Mary's Convent. Externally the house could easily be mistaken for the work of Voysey until you notice the absence of strong horizontal string courses and the slightly elongated proportions of the mullioned windows – it is a Voysey house yawning. Inside there was yet another decorative approach in the first floor drawing room, which had a white semi-circular vault beneath which were elaborate and unclerical paintings of colourful peacocks and flowers.

This richness is an echo of Baillie Scott's work for the Grand Duke of Hesse at Darmstadt. In 1897, Scott and Ashbee were separately commissioned by Grand Duke Ernst Ludwig to design interiors for the

*Just as Voysey got his first commission after publishing hypothetical work in *The British Architect*, Scott's earliest commissions from England and the Continent followed his articles on ideal houses in *The Studio*.

Baillie Scott. Blackwell, nr Bowness, Cumbria (1898-99).
Above: Garden front – the iron stair was added when the house was converted to a school
Right: Drawing room with foliated basket capitals and bay windows

palace. Baillie Scott designed the white-panelled dining and drawing rooms which were made rich with embossed leather friezes of Voysey-like birds and flowers executed by Ashbee's Guild of Handicraft. In the perspectives published in *Building News* the furniture looks over-carved and lumpen. Yet, in fact, most of the forms were simple. Perfectly flat surfaces bore painted or inlaid floral ornament which like other Arts and Crafts work, however luxuriant, had a certain heraldic stiffness.

Darmstadt was the foundation of a flourishing Continental practice for Baillie Scott which, though commissions never again reached the magnificence of the Grand Ducal palace, included the interiors of a tree house for the Crown Princess of Romania (a Hesse offspring) and several large aristocratic mansions in and around Germany.

At home, life was more humdrum. To be near J. P. White's Pyghtle works for which he designed furniture, Baillie Scott moved in 1901 from the Isle of Man to Bedford, one of England's least romantic country towns, where he adapted a large cottage and worked in rural ease. His Voyseyish style continued well into the decade, and Baillie Scott was not afraid to confess his admiration for the older architect. 'If one were asked to sum up in a few words the scope and purposes of Mr Voysey's work', he wrote in 1908, 'one might say that it consists mainly in the application of severely sane, practical and rational ideas to home making.'[20]

One of Baillie Scott's largest white buildings was Waterlow Court, an Associated Home for Ladies, in Hampstead Garden Suburb. It is a courtyard surrounded by flats. Here, as *The British Architect* enthused, 'Mr Baillie Scott has shown that our old type of almshouse design, built in quadrangular form, may be dealt with in a sensible modern spirit so as to make economical and artistic housing a possibility. A lady may live here with a companion in charming rooms at a cost as low as four and threepence per week'.[21] The quadrangle is all white-washed brick (one of his favourite aphorisms was 'when in doubt whitewash').[22] Big round arches form the cloister above which strips of Voyseyish windows nestle under the eaves of the steep, red-tiled roof. Outside, the block is less severe with a half-timbered first floor on top of dusky reddish-purple brick.

By the time Waterlow Court was built in 1909, Baillie Scott had started to move away from Voyseyish austerity. At Bill House, Selsey on Sea (1906-07), he relieved the white roughcast with jolly chequered patterns of local brick and stone. The Cloisters, Regents Park (1912-13, now demolished) was one of his largest houses, all diapered brickwork enclosing a great half-timbered hall and sumptuously panelled living rooms. It was built for Sir Boverton Redwood, a petrol magnate, and it was so consciously anachronistic that even Lawrence Weaver, one of the most faithful protagonists of Arts and Crafts architecture, had a few qualms: 'Redwood', he wrote, 'can shut his door, entrenched in the Middle Ages tempered by bath taps (h and c) and electric light...As to whether the Cloisters represents him and his contribution to civilization as well as it represents Mr Baillie Scott's devotion to the spirit of

Baillie Scott. Blackwell, inglenook and gallery in hall

Baillie Scott. White Lodge, Wantage, Oxfordshire (1898-99). A Voysey house yawning?

Baillie Scott. The Cloisters, Regents Park, London (1912-13, now destroyed). Sumptuous mansion for petrol magnate

Baillie Scott. Waterlow Court, Hampstead Garden Suburb (1909). Cloistered housing for indigent ladies

medieval craftsmanship is one of those difficult questions which it would be impertinent to explore'.[23]

Only a year after the Cloisters was finished, Baillie Scott designed his first Neo-Georgian house: he had stood out against the new fashion as long as he could. The house was an ordinary little red brick box with a plan contorted to allow the windows to be arranged in regular rows. It was the antithesis of everything Baillie Scott had stood for up to that time. He had increasingly adopted symmetry throughout the previous decade, but the planning had been linear and free and all his forms had been derived from local models.

Neo-Georgian was to be one of the several styles between which Baillie Scott alternated in the '20s and '30s. He continued to preach against machine production and regularity, developing his theme that 'instead of the callous, brutal methods of the modern factory, art makes the workshop into a school, where materials may be "educated" in the literal sense. And the chief aim of this education is not to force the material into the strait waistcoat of preconceived forms, but so to deal with it that, having first sympathetically discovered its character, that character may be expressed properly subordinated to the fulfilment of practical functions'.[24]

But Baillie Scott, though he seems to have had no financial compulsion to go on working (he owned, among other property, the Kensington Palace Hotel), continued to attract clients, and he had to fall in with their taste, which in many cases was for Neo-Georgian discipline. Occasionally, as in his house at Mudeford Green, Hampshire (1924), he achieved a clumsy originality by changefully disposing Georgian elements in a style similar to Queen Anne. But usually, his houses were small, well-mannered brick boxes. The Tudor derived style continued and there were other idioms too: a flat-topped, white-walled bungalow in Hong Kong and flat-roofed, castle-like houses in Cornwall.

Whatever the style, contemporaries still respected his craftsmanship. In 1925 John Clarke wrote, 'His plain brick wall is a joy. There is the same difference between it and the average brick wall that there is between a Persian rug and an Axminster carpet. It brings us back again to the old question that has been discussed and debated so often. Can we with our modern machine-made materials and machine-like labour hope to produce as satisfying work as was produced before machinery came to curse or bless us? Mr Baillie Scott says "No". His answer is: "A study of old building one finds in...villages, suggests that it is not only better than any modern building, but has some essential difference...This difference largely consists in the character of the workmanship which, like handwriting, conveys personality instead of being a lifeless mechanical formula"'.[25]

So Baillie Scott retained his beliefs, however much his clients demanded Neo-Georgian and the bye-laws required him to use fire-resistant fake half-timbering rather than the real thing. Yet his talent had been eaten away. Even his best architecture rarely achieved the originality of Voysey, Prior, Lethaby or Lutyens; after the War, he became a pasticheur of whose work the chief characteristic was, according to Clarke, '...charm. There is no other word that describes it so well. It is all charming, whether it be Tudor or Georgian. It is pookish, unexpected. It has the same quality that appears in Barrie's plays; a quality that is at the moment held lightly'.[26]

It still is. Baillie Scott's later houses were a part of Barrie's Never-Never Land, owned by middle-aged Wendies – a sugary upper middle class realization of Morris's Nowhere.

Arts and Crafts architecture had descended to scene painting. Yet Baillie Scott should not be judged too harshly. He did his best but the times were against him. As A. L. N. Russel wrote towards the end of Scott's long career, surely few architects 'have built so much all over England and done so little violence to its amenities'[27] – not a bad epitaph for a man who loved the countryside and lived in it all his life.

1 *Blomfield, R.* A Short History of Renaissance Architecture in England, *George Bell, London, 1900, p296.*
2 *Blomfield, R.* Memoirs of an Architect, *MacMillan, London, 1932, p113.*
3 *Blomfield, R.* The Mistress Art, *Edward Arnold, London, 1908, p10.*
4 Ibid, *p85.*
5 *Lethaby, W. R.* Philip Webb and his Work, *Oxford, 1935, p76.*
6 *Macleod, Robert* Style and Society, *RIBA Publications, London, 1971, p101.*
7 *Stuart-Wortley, Violet* Grow Old Along With Me *(1952), quoted in Saint, Andrew,* Richard Norman Shaw, op cit, *p311.*
8 *Hussey, Christopher* The Life of Sir Edwin Lutyens, *Country Life, London, 1950, p26.*
9 *Jekyll, Gertrude* Home and Garden, *Longmans, London, 1900.*
10 *Gradidge, Roderick 'Edwin Lutyens' in* Seven Victorian Architects, *Thames & Hudson, London, 1976, p127.*
11 *Butler, A. S. G.* The Architecture of Sir Edwin Lutyens, *Vol I, Country Life, London, 1950, p30.*
12 Ibid, *p34.*
13 Ibid, *p33.*
14 *Hussey, Christopher*The Life of Sir Edwin Lutyens, op cit, *p347.*
15 *Kornwolf, James D.* M. H. Baillie Scott and the Arts and Crafts Movement, *Johns Hopkins Press, Baltimore and London, 1972.*
16 *Betjeman, John* Journal of the Manx Museum, *Vol VII, 1968, p78.*
17 *Baillie Scott, M. H. 'An Ideal Suburban House',* The Studio, *Vol IV, 1894, p127.*
18 *The best modern account of the house is in Hitchmough, Wendy 'Lake Poetry',* The Architectural Review, *Vol CXCIII, 1993, pp72-78.*
19 *Muthesius, H.* The English House, op cit, *p51.*
20 *Baillie Scott, M. H. 'On the Characteristics of Mr C. F. A. Voysey's Architecture',* The Studio, *Vol XLII, 1908, p19.*
21 The British Architect, *Vol LXXII, 1909, p19.*
22 *Kornwolf* op cit, passim.
23 *Weaver, Lawrence* Small Country Houses of Today, *Second Series,* op cit, *p94.*
24 *Baillie Scott, M. H. 'Ideals in Building, False and True' from* The Arts Connected with Building, *Batsford, London, 1909, p142.*
25 *Clarke, John D. 'The Work of Baillie Scott and Beresford',* The Architects' Journal, *Vol LXI, 1925, p60.*
26 Ibid.
27 *Russel, A. L. N.* The RIBA Journal, *Vol XL, 1933, p636.*

Quietly home

14

'There is a boom coming for Garden Cities', Lutyens wrote to Herbert Baker in 1909. 'I am in the train for Tavistock to lay out a building estate for the Duke of Bedford. I have an estate to lay out at Romford*...and then there is the Central Square at Hampstead.'[1] Most Arts and Crafts architects were trying to catch similar trains.

The Garden City movement had begun to take shape six years earlier at Letchworth under the guidance of Barry Parker (1867-1947) and Raymond Unwin (1863-1940). Parker and Unwin were half cousins, both born near Sheffield, though Unwin was brought up in Oxford. Their relationship was made closer when Unwin married Parker's sister Ethel in 1893 and, three years later, the two teetotal socialists went into partnership as architects and planners.

Late in life Mrs Parker remembered, 'As I see the partnership, Unwin had all the zeal of a social reformer with a gift for speaking and writing and was inspired by Morris, Carpenter and the early days of the Labour Movement. Parker was primarily an artist. Texture, light, shade, vistas, form and beauty were his chief concern. He wanted the home to be a setting for a life of aesthetic worth.

'I always felt the Parker, Unwin partnership was an ideal one; each had a deep affection for the other and admiration for each other's gifts – so profoundly different and yet complementary.'[2]

Unwin had attended Ruskin's lectures in Oxford and he was a friend of Edward Carpenter,** probably through whom he met William Morris. Unwin became a socialist and an enthusiastic contributor to Morris's *Commonweal*. His first job was as apprentice engineer for the Stavely Coal and Iron Company, for which he worked on miners' housing.

Parker was articled in 1889 to G. Faulkner Armitage, who, besides having a drawing office, owned a workshop and smithy – an excellent training ground for a young Arts and Crafts architect. When Parker first set up on his own at Buxton in 1895, he, like Voysey 14 years before, earned most of his living from designs for textiles, wallpaper and furniture rather than architecture.

The first big commission gained by the Parker and Unwin partnership was at New Earswick near York, where in 1901 the chocolate magnate Joseph Rowntree bought an estate on which to house his workers. It was to be a philanthropic model village, in the tradition of Port Sunlight and Bournville, created by Rowntree's fellow Quaker cocoa kings, the Cadburys.† The roots of the tradition ran deep – one strand went at least as far back as Saltaire, Bradford, the model village built for his workers by Titus Salt in the mid-nineteenth century; another tributary touched the bosky tastefulness of Bedford Park.

Geoffry Lucas. Detail, 9 Willifield Way, Hampstead Garden Suburb (1909)

*In the event neither of these jobs came to much.

**Edward Carpenter (1844-1929) was ordained but broke from the church to spend his life working with the poor. He set up as a market gardener at Millthorpe in Derbyshire near Sheffield and became an influential figure in the socialist circles of the '80s and '90s. He also made sandals on the Indian pattern: they were so popular that they became the hallmark of a whole class of English intellectuals. He shared with his friend Ashbee an enthusiasm for homogenic love (idealized homosexuality).

†The master plan for Port Sunlight, Lord Leverhulme's model village for soapworkers, was implemented by Thomas Mawson, the Arts and Crafts landscape architect, on the formal lines of an Arts and Crafts garden. Its cottagey rows of houses were to be built in a blend of Old English and Voysey.

Parker & Unwin. New Earswick, nr York (from 1901): model houses for model workers

At New Earswick, Parker and Unwin started a series of experiments in layout which were to continue throughout their association (which formally ended in 1914). The aim was to reduce the amount of expensive road needed to give access to all houses on a site while giving every house a pleasant garden and view. They were particularly vehement about the horror of the back yards created by the parallel rows of bye-law housing, the standard for working people. In a 1902 Fabian tract Unwin wrote, 'It does not seem to be realized hundreds of thousands of working women spend the bulk of their lives with nothing better to look on than the ghastly prospect offered by these back yards, the squalid ugliness of which is unrelieved by a scrap of fresh green to speak of spring, or a fading leaf to tell of autumn'.[3] Sunlight was vital too. 'It must be looked upon as an absolute *essential*, second only to air-space.'[4]

Parker and Unwin solved the problem of view and sunlight by abolishing the old cottage parlour and making a living room which ran from front to back of the house. This allowed the cottages to be made in terraces and yet attract sunlight, no matter how they were turned. The planners were convinced that, when building cheap houses for the working classes, 'however desirable a parlour may be, it cannot be said to be necessary to health or family life'.[5]

The through living room was developed in 'Cottages Near a Town'[6] shown by the partners at the 1903 Northern Art Workers' Guild exhibition in Manchester.* They illustrated plans for semi-detached cottages, with long living rooms, enhanced by a bay at one end and incorporating a snug inglenook round the range. They were to be laid out in a chequered pattern so that street fronts alternated between pairs of cottages and pairs of gardens; the streets were parallel but the effect – houses set among greenery – was intended to be the antithesis of the corridor-like bye-law layout.

In October of the same year, Parker and Unwin were asked to compete with a combination of Lethaby and Ricardo, and with two local architects for the post of planners for the first Garden City at Letchworth. The Northerners won and so became the chief interpreters of the new movement.

The idea of Garden Cities had originated in *Tomorrow: A Peaceful Path to Real Reform*, published in 1898 by Ebenezer Howard, in which the solution to late Victorian urban problems was suggested to be a series of new towns. They would counteract the pull of the cities by offering all the amenities of urban life as well as the pleasures of living in a balanced, semi-rural community. Each Garden City was to be defined in size and surrounded by a belt of agricultural land sufficient to feed the predetermined maximum population.

Howard's vision of houses set in gardens in the countryside was very similar to that of *News from Nowhere*, but it was firmly tied to the practicalities of the late nineteenth century. For instance, in *Garden Cities of Tomorrow* (1902), the successor to *Tomorrow: A Peaceful Path to Real Reform*, a ring of Garden Cities was to surround each great

*The scheme was originally designed for a real site at Starbeck near Harrogate in 1902. A prototype pair was built.

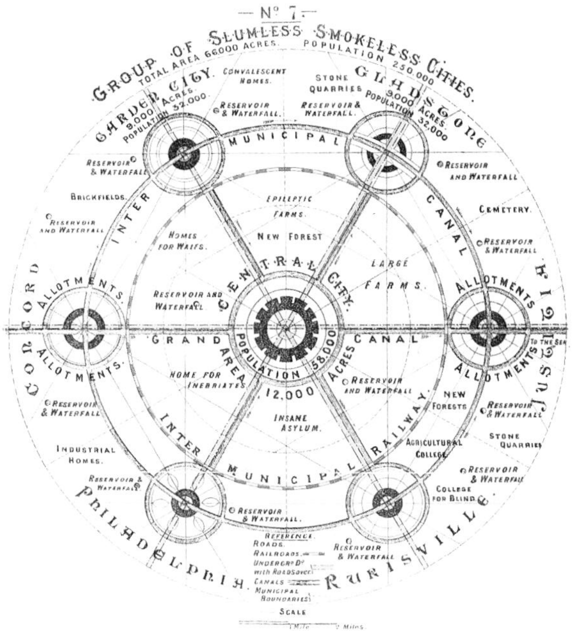

Ebenezer Howard's ideal diagram for Garden Cities round a central city (1898)

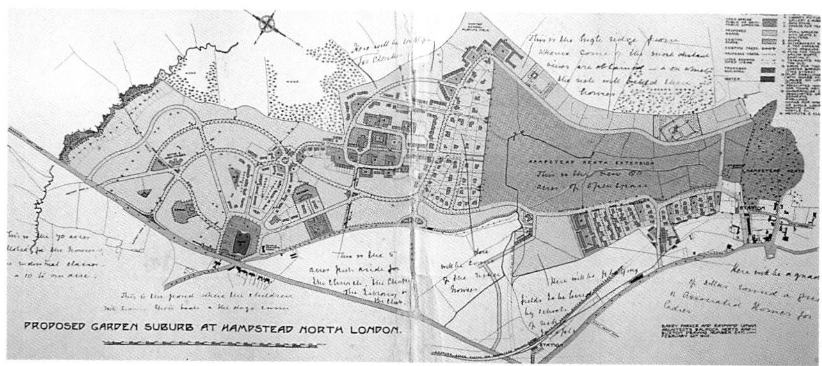

Raymond Unwin. Hampstead Garden Suburb masterplan (1905)

metropolis, connected to it radially and to each other in a circle by fast railways. In *News from Nowhere*, the railway, like all other machines Morris hated, had become obsolete.

At Letchworth 3826 acres were purchased by a joint stock company set up by Howard's disciples and, in January 1904, Parker and Unwin started work. They took 1300 acres for the town,[7] leaving the rest as the agricultural belt. Their design bore more than passing resemblance to Howard's diagrams of the ideal Garden City, in which central public buildings were surrounded by a park, and then rings of houses and gardens, all girdled by a railway and factories on the edge of the agricultural belt. But, as Mervyn Macartney recorded in *The Architectural Review*, when Letchworth began to take shape, 'The present plan...is much more rational. The centre of the town will be taken up by the municipal buildings upon which a number of straight roads converge like the spokes of a cycle upon the hub, and round the centre will be conveniently grouped such buildings as the public hall, institute, museum, school, post office, and so forth. This part of the town all lies south of the G.N.R. [Great Northern Railway] which runs right through the middle of the estate, and half a mile or so eastwards come the factories. By this arrangement the factories not only gain direct access to the main line through their goods station and sidings, but also are so placed that their smoke, smell and noise will be carried away from the town by the prevailing wind'.[8]

Typical of the south of the town are streets edged with broad belts of grass planted with flowering trees; then there are footpaths, the hedges of the front gardens and the houses well set back, usually in semi-detached blocks or short terraces, behind which are ample back gardens. The avenue was common in the affluent suburbs of large manufacturing towns like Leeds and Birmingham in the '90s but through Parker and Unwin's planning, its amenities became accessible to relatively poor people.

To the north of the railway, the layout is more economical, lacking so many tree-lined roads but still with sizeable front and back gardens. This was the area in which a cheap cottage competition was held in 1905; several Arts and Crafts architects entered, including Smith and Brewer, Troup, Baillie Scott and Randall Wells.

The layout of the more formal part, south of the railway, is remarkably like an Arts and Crafts garden. While virtually all the houses (by Parker and Unwin and other architects) are based on irregular vernacular models, the streets show the love of vista, axes and order that Prior had so strenuously advocated in garden making. It is a gentle irony that the layout now focuses on a grand symmetrical design of tall poplars which outline the plan of formal municipal buildings many of which were never constructed due to lack of funds.

Unwin shared Prior's horror of landscape gardening, believing that 'any attempt to copy nature must be futile, for the conditions of natural growth are so complex as to be quite beyond the power of the gardener to understand or reproduce'. Yet formalism could go too far, for 'the formalist needs to remember that his design is subordinate to the site, that the undulation of the ground and the presence of

Parker & Unwin. Letchworth (design 1903) from the west. Formal avenues focus on town centre (top right)

natural features of beauty worth preserving will frequently require some departure from the regularity of his treatment'.[9]

Planning, like gardening, should take a middle way between formal and naturalistic. Unwin was sceptical of attempts to recapture the picturesque interest of old irregular village streets which had grown up over a long period of time. In any case, he believed that 'the relationships of feudalism have gone, and democracy has yet to evolve some definite relationships of its own, which when they come will doubtless be as picturesque as the old forms'.[10]

A degree of order in the main features of a town plan would make it easier to understand but excessive symmetry, for instance, could result in inconvenience, and over-rigid imposition of formal rules could lead to the destruction of natural features such as trees and hedgerows which would help to relate buildings to the site.

Raymond Unwin got another chance to test his planning theories when, in 1905, he was made planner of the Hampstead Garden Suburb. The idea of the suburb originated with Mrs Barnett, a lifelong worker in the East End slums who was instrumental in setting up the Whitechapel Art Gallery, later given its permanent home by Townsend. An extension of the underground railway made development possible on the northern approaches to Hampstead Heath, which until then had been countryside. Mrs Barnett was determined to preserve at least part of the country as open land and, beyond that, to create an area where working men, at the expense of a twopenny tube fare, could enjoy a life of semi-rural freedom among gardens and tree-lined streets.

Centre of Hampstead Garden Suburb from the west (final plan 1912), with Lutyens's church as focus

Mrs Barnett secured her piece of countryside, a long thin strip running north from the Heath, and Parker and Unwin were required to work out development in the long thin tongues of land surrounding it and on the hill which terminated the extension to the north. The first plan was full of informal curved roads snaking round the top of the hill on which Mrs Barnett was determined to build an Anglican church as the community's focus. In the long western tongue of the development land next to the Heath extension, the planners proposed a small area of the chequered housing they had exhibited at the 1903 Northern Art Workers' Guild exhibition.

The final plan (1912) was more formal, with a fan of avenues stretching east from Lutyens's central square and its two churches, Anglican and Free. On the westward slope, development was more irregular along gently curving streets. To the north, across Lyttleton Road, was an area of semi-detached houses for workers' families on long cul-de-sacs (for which a special Act of Parliament had to be passed to overcome the bye-law insistence on through streets). In the troublesome western strip against the Heath, the planners elaborated cul-de-sac plans by placing courtyards at the end of each. (Baillie Scott's Waterlow Court was the most complete of these.) The aims, as usual, were to allow maximum use of the site for minimum road length and to provide all dwellings with sunlight and garden views, both front and back.

Other than in this strip, the Suburb (carefully so-called because it did not have the urban amenities of a Garden City) was laid out to

Hampstead Garden Suburb, view from the Heath today dominated by Lutyens's St Jude's Church

Parker & Unwin. The Homestead, Chesterfield, Derbyshire (1903-05): based on Voysey's Broadleys

Unwin's rule that there should be no more than 12 houses to the acre. The rule was based on sound economic principle, elaborated in Unwin's pamphlet *Nothing Gained by Overcrowding*, in which he showed to his own satisfaction* that, except where land was unusually expensive, such developments 'cause the cost of roads to outweigh the saving in cost of land which results from there being more than 12 houses to the acre'.[11]

This low density was later to produce some of Britain's dullest housing estates from the drawing boards of local authorities and speculative builders in the inter-war years. But the Garden Suburb as seen from the long north slope of Hampstead Heath is a complete Arts and Crafts village, rising sharp out of the green, though not quite as crisply as Unwin (who advocated a great town wall which was only partly built) would have liked. It is tight-knit, yet leafy, with tile pitch piled upon brick gable until the whole composition is crowned by the leaded spire of Lutyens's superb Gothic-cum-Georgian church – wonderfully picturesque, but scarcely the image of a new democracy for which Unwin was searching.

The style of the church is symptomatic of the suburb in which the alteration in Arts and Crafts inspiration from vernacular to Georgian is frozen at the point of transition. Parker and Unwin had learned from the experience of Letchworth that some kind of visual control was necessary over development. At Letchworth, in theory, the company was to build virtually everything, but actually lack of capital necessitated involving many other developers and their architects, resulting in a great variety of architectural expression. For all the strong planning, Letchworth is architecturally chaotic, often no better than a low-key, low-density suburb. At Hampstead, care was taken over eaves lines, roof pitches and textures, unifying the composition. Yet below the eaves, architects were more or less free to do what they liked, vernacular or Georgian, within a restricted palette of materials. As well as Parker and Unwin, many distinguished Arts and Crafts architects contributed housing.

Parker and Unwin themselves usually stuck to vernacular models. From the first, they were committed Ruskinian Goths, working from the inside out. Parker, in an 1895 lecture, urged the virtues of large living rooms in small houses, then usually stuffed with small rooms modelled in miniature on houses of the rich. The number of rooms should, he urged, be reduced, 'keeping such rooms as we do retain, large enough to be healthy, comfortable and habitable...But if your big room is to be comfortable it *must* have recesses. There is great charm in a room broken up in plan, where that slight feeling of mystery is given to it which arises when you cannot see the whole room from any one point in which you are likely to sit; when there is always something *round the corner*'.[13] This is as clear a description of changefulness applied to domestic planning as the Arts and Crafts movement ever produced, and it has echoes in buildings as far back as the drawing room of the Red House.

*Mervyn Miller has demonstrated that Unwin was wrong: either he muddled his sums or he purposely confused calculations to project a model that was more humanly rewarding than the bye-law one. [12]

**Parker & Unwin.
A living room
(from *The Art of Building a Home*, 1901)**

Equally clear is the echo of Morris's teaching. 'The true method of making a room beautiful is to make all the necessary and useful things in it beautiful; so much is this true that it becomes almost impossible to design a really beautiful room that is to have no useful work done in it or natural life lived in it.'[14]

The combination of these two principles created living rooms of subtlety and simplicity of construction – white walls, exposed beams with rugs on simple timber or tiled floors: the 'decorative properties inherent in the construction and in the details necessary to the building',[15] which Parker, following Morris, dearly loved.

It was the vernacular cottage idiom but adopted, so Parker and Unwin claimed, not for sentimental but for practical and artistic reasons. Even the beauty of the leaded light windows they favoured 'has nothing to do with [an] old fashioned look, with romantic associations or quaintness of effect; it is simply an inherent property of all leaded glazing; due to the wonderful and never ending charm of the play of light and shade on different panes, each one catching the light slightly differently from any other, some glistening brightly, others dead and sombre, and the rest occupying every tone between the two'.[16]

Furniture should, as far as possible, be built-in to avoid the clutter of miscellaneous ornament and achieve the sensation of 'reposefulness' which was the architects' main goal. The largest pieces of built-in furniture were the settles round the inglenooks, a device favoured by very many Arts and Crafts architects, which Parker and Unwin incorporated in virtually every house, no matter how small. These inglenooks were one variety of recess used to elaborate and add variety to the basic rectangle of their living rooms. Elsewhere, the architects rarely lost an opportunity to make a bay window or a niche for a piano. No effort was spared to catch a view or a ray of sunlight by opening small lights wherever needed. The living rooms and living halls are the high point of Parker and Unwin houses. They are as spare as Voysey's spaces, yet more snug; they are as spatially inventive as Baillie Scott's without (except when compelled by economy in houses for the poor) adopting the impracticalities of his open planning.

Yet for all their spatial and constructional ingenuity, the outsides of Parker and Unwin houses are often disappointing. Part of the disappointment is caused by lack of originality, part by the ham-fistedness that bedevils most young architects' work, but which the cousins never entirely outgrew. Originality was consciously eschewed by Parker and Unwin. Parker was insistent that contemporary architects should 'do nothing different from what we have done before, until we feel it to be better than what we have done before'.[17] By the time that Parker and Unwin started to practise, a good deal *had* been done before by the Arts and Crafts architects born in the '50s. To architects of Parker and Unwin's generation, they were models of inspiration.

Voysey was the main early influence,* yet externally Parker and Unwin's houses rarely achieved his serenity. For instance, their

*Other influences ranged from Old English and Baillie Scott in his heavier moods to, curiously, Hoffmann. There is a design for a girls' club in Manchester (c1909) which is plainly derived from Hoffmann's Palais Stoclet.

Parker & Unwin. The Den, Croft Lane, Letchworth (1905)

Parker & Unwin. Laneside/Crabby Corner, Letchworth Lane, Letchworth (1904). Unwin lived on the left, Parker on the right

Homestead at Ashgate Road near Chesterfield (1903-05) is plainly derived from Voysey's Broadleys (1898-99) – it has the same double-height curved bays, the steeply pitched hipped roof and the buttresses. But the Parker and Unwin version suggests a couple of bays of Broadleys with the rest lopped off. The roof comes down only just beyond the top of the bays, instead of engulfing them in Voysey's generous hug, so the eaves are high, making the house stilted and vertical. The awkwardness is enhanced by the material: rough ashlar instead of Voysey's smooth harling.

A similar gawkiness is seen in the semi-detached houses the partners built for themselves in Letchworth Lane, Letchworth (1904). Here they had the courage to carry the tiled roof all the way down to the top of the ground floor bay which projects uneasily in brick from the harling of the rest of the mass. The roof is sprigged with spiky gables, and the building terminates unhappily to the south in a tower with vestigial half-timbering on the upper floor.* More coherence was achieved in the Den, Croft Lane, Letchworth (1905) where a complicated series of white wall planes is tied together by a cosy of thatch which swoops down to near head height over the veranda – a kind of outdoor inglenook. One of the best houses of this period was 102 Wilbury Road, Letchworth (1908), designed for Stanley Parker, Barry's artist craftsman brother. The white walled, stone trimmed influence of Voysey is very clear, yet the manner is used with much more confidence than Parker and Unwin had achieved before. And the result, roofs sweeping down to ground floor round a high gable with staggered fenestration, is something that Voysey would never have attempted but which achieves much of his clarity and calm.

In the Hampstead Garden Suburb, Parker and Unwin amalgamated vernacular and Georgian in red brick houses which, under their steep, hipped roofs, combined strips of mullioned leaded lights from the seventeenth century with brick string courses and quoins from the eighteenth. Despite their disparate origins, these semi-detached houses achieve a quiet four-square elegance which, though never reaching the heights of Arts and Crafts work, shows what an excellent second eleven the movement could field, given the opportunity.

Of the little non-domestic work produced by the partnership, the shops at the entrance to Hampstead Garden Suburb are the most dramatic example. High and Hanseatic, the buildings were intended to be a formal gate to the suburb, but, instead of choosing Classical forms to make a monumental statement, Parker and Unwin stuck to their ideals and produced a group in brick, topped with hipped gables and a little tower. It was a monument in the Gothic spirit though the architects turned to Germany for inspiration.

Parker was one of the very few Arts and Crafts architects able to pursue the movement's ideals relatively free of commercial and stylistic pressures long after the War.

*The tower was added by Parker in 1914 to provide a sleeping balcony, a very popular feature in Letchworth. The timbering framed glazing which could be thrown open on three sides to let in the health-giving night air.

Parker & Unwin. 102 Wilbury Road, Letchworth (1908), for Stanley Parker

Parker & Unwin. Shops at entrance to Hampstead Garden Suburb. Formal gate to interior from Finchley Road (1909-11). Now destroyed

In 1901 Parker had dictated that 'the influence of machinery on art is one of the most degrading we have to contend with, for every advance made by machinery must mean a corresponding retreat on the part of art'.[18] But by 1925, he accepted that 'the introduction of machines into art and craft has changed everything. The machine has come to stay and we must accept it. It is useless to hark back and demand only things made by hand. As a work of art, a thing which can be made as well by a machine as it can be made by hand is equally good made either way'.[19] If the machine was accepted, the quietness of Parker's designs was unaffected. His clumsy gentleness continued in buildings like the Royston Cottage Hospital (1924-28) and the library and dining hall of King Alfred's School, Hampstead (1927-29).

By the time he was working on King Alfred's, Parker was a man out of his time. Most architects had accepted the rule of the Orders. A few were struggling to establish the fledgling Modern Movement, which was to subject architecture unequivocally to the ethos of the Machine.

H. S. Goodhart-Rendel summed up the inter-war mood of many: 'In the present market...Victorian liberty is depreciated, and the few traditions the Victorians did not sever are at a premium. We cannot understand why when Adam had perfected orderly planning the Puginists must innovate disorderly planning: why when Cockerell had brought to England the independent doctrine of the French rationalists, Ruskin must force architecture to become the unquestioning handmaid of Protestant morals: why when at last secular Gothic was systemized by Waterhouse and Street, it was necessary to turn from it and woo Queen Anne with bric-a-brac. We cannot understand these reactions because the memory of the actions that produced them has faded away. We have been born to freedom and find it cheap and unsatisfying; we see it against no background of broken tyranny; we see it rather as a heritage of outlawry, as the curse of the wandering Jew. We feel that we need not a Rousseau but a Mussolini'.[20]

The great Arts and Crafts architects lingered on, disdainful alike of Neo-Georgian and the Modern Movement. Lethaby jeered at 'ye olde modernist style' then appearing on the Continent. Voysey, who was hailed as a father of the Modern Movement, railed against the Movement's 'vulgarly aggressive' proportions, its 'mountebank eccentricity in detail and windows lying down on their sides'. Baillie Scott spent much of his later years attacking the Modern Movement's pretensions in yards of waffly invective. Ashbee retired to keep a cynical eye on curious new developments from deepest Kent. When he met Voysey in the street in the late '30s, he 'asked him how, as he looked so down and out, he was getting on. He, who had built more houses than any of us, shook his head ruefully and said "Any house is good enough to start a car from"'.[21] (Voysey had been reduced to literal begging from Alexander Morton in the late '20s, claiming that without £200, he would 'have to leave my flat, sell all my furniture and bury myself in a slum'.)[22]

Yet it was precisely in the houses from which the cheap cars were started that the Arts and Crafts tradition lingered longest. Abandoned by architects, the forms were adopted by speculative builders and

**Parker & Unwin.
Rushby Mead, Letchworth
(1907-11)**

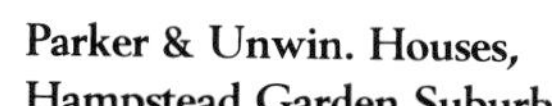

**Parker & Unwin. Houses,
Hampstead Garden Suburb**

local authorities. Round every sizable town in England there is a ring of Arts and Crafts suburbs where, following planning rules drawn up by Unwin, behind laburnums and flowering cherry trees, the architecture of Voysey, Baillie Scott, Parker and early Lutyens lives on in endless copies of hips and gables, half-timbering and harling, mullions and leaded bay windows, with here and there an inglenook. The builders did what the architects, for all their high ideals, failed to accomplish. They brought Arts and Crafts to the people. The image is not so very different from that seen by the man who brought *News from Nowhere*. Cheap transport and the builders' crude copies of Arts and Crafts architecture offered a new life of individuality and freedom to multitudes who escaped from deprivation in the hearts of cities. For a movement which had started with the ideals of Ruskin and Morris, the inter-war suburb was not an ignoble ending.

1 *Hussey, Christopher* The Life of Sir Edwin Lutyens, *Country Life, London, 1950, p187.*
2 *Mrs Parker, letter to Walter Creese, 25 March 1960, Parker papers.*
3 *Unwin, Raymond* Cottage Plans and Common Sense, *Fabian Tract 109, London, 1902, p4.*
4 Ibid, *p3.*
5 Ibid, *p13.*
6 *Parker, Barry and Raymond Unwin* Cottages Near a Town, *pamphlet in the RIBA.*
7 *Creese, Walter L* The Search for Environment, *Yale University Press, New Haven and London, 1966, p205.*
8 *Macartney, Mervyn 'The First Garden City',* The Architectural Review, *Vol XVIII, 1905, p15.*
9 *Unwin, Raymond* Town Planning in Practice, *T. Fisher Unwin, London, 1909, p119.*
10 *Unwin, Raymond 'Co-operation in Building', in Parker and Unwin* The Art of Building a Home, *Longmans Green, London, 1901, p95.*
11 *Unwin, Raymond* Nothing Gained by Overcrowding! or How the Garden City Type of Development may Benefit both Owner and Occupier, *Garden Cities and Town Planning Association, London, 1912.*
12 *Miller, Mervyn* Raymond Unwin: Garden Cities and Town Planning, *Leicester University Press, Leicester, London and New York, 1992.*
13 *Parker, Barry 'The Smaller Middle Class House', lecture 'delivered before an audience of architects in 1895', printed in Parker and Unwin* The Art of Building a Home, op cit, *p3.*
14 Ibid, *pp17-18.*
15 *Parker and Unwin* The Art of Building a Home, op cit, *Introduction, p11.*
16 *Parker, Barry 'The Dignity of All True Art' in* The Art of Building a Home, op cit, *p32.*
17 *Parker, Barry 'The Smaller Middle Class House',* op cit, *p9.*
18 *Parker, Barry 'The Dignity of All True Art',* op cit, *p30.*
19 *Parker, Barry 'Art in Industry', lecture delivered at Balliol College, Oxford, 3 October 1925, p7, Parker papers.*
20 *Goodhart-Rendel, H. S.* The RIBA Journal, *Vol XXXIII, 1926, p468.*
21 *Ashbee, C. R.* Memoirs, op cit, *Vol VII, p333.*
22 *Durant, Stuart* C. F. A. Voysey, *Architectural Monograph 19, Academy Editions, London, 1992, p20.*

Californian idyll

15

The suburbs, not of England but in the United States of America, were the setting of one of the most ingenious and integrated Arts and Crafts building experiments. Gustav Stickley (1857-1942) was a Wisconsin man who moved east to train as a furniture maker and stonemason. After a visit to Europe in 1898, during which he met Voysey and Ashbee, he changed the name of his firm to Craftsman Workshops and tried to reorganize it much on the lines of Ashbee's Guild of Handicraft.

In 1901, he founded a magazine, *The Craftsman*, the first two issues of which were taken up with panegyrics on Morris and Ruskin. *The Craftsman* was partly a means of publicizing Stickley's products but it quickly expanded to cover all aspects of crafts, decorative arts, architecture and Morrisian socialism. In May 1903 the magazine published the first 'Craftsman Home' design, a two-storey rubble house, illustrated with plans and a brief description of its construction. Stickley urged subscribers to apply for information on 'processes or details incident to the building, furnishing, or decoration of the "Craftsman House"'.[1] From January 1904, until the magazine's demise in December 1916, Stickley published monthly details of detached residences 'of which the cost should range between two and fifteen thousand dollars'.

The houses were usually four-square in plan, compressed in the American tradition to avoid corridors. Living rooms often had inglenooks, and the stairs frequently ascended directly from them. It was the kind of economical planning that Parker and Unwin thought suitable for working class families, but was often on a rather more opulent scale.

Bernard Maybeck. Roos House, San Francisco (1909). Detail of gable window

Externally, the houses were undistinguished and derivative of a mass of origins ranging from Californian Mission, New England farmhouse and log cabin to Old English, Voysey and even, here and there, the Tyrol. Stickley and his architects (a group working under Harvey Ellis) were consciously pursuing a native American architecture which necessitated variety appropriate both to a democracy in which 'every man should have the right to think out the plan for his house to suit himself' and to a vast and varied countryside: 'A house that is built of stone where stones are in the fields, of concrete where the soil is sandy, of brick where brick can be had reasonably, or of wood if the house is in a mountainous, wooded region, will from the beginning belong to the landscape'.[2] The Puginian doctrine of fidelity to place had reached a new frontier.

For a decade, Stickley's enterprises were remarkably successful. There can have been few who built a Craftsman Home who did not wish to furnish it with the simple products of the Craftsman studios. If they could not afford the objects themselves, members of Stickley's Home Builders' Club were provided with free designs for wood, metal and leatherwork. In 1910 he founded the Craftsman Home Building Company which built houses in the New York area. An estate agents' wing was founded; advice was offered on landscaping and education. A large building was acquired near Fifth Avenue, New York to house the whole range of Arts and Crafts enterprises.

Right and below: Craftsman Home designs as illustrated in Stickley's magazine, *The Craftsman*: appropriate residences for every type of climate and landscape

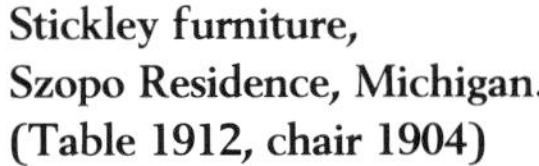

Stickley furniture, Szopo Residence, Michigan. (Table 1912, chair 1904)

By 1915, Stickley claimed that, in that year alone, 20 million dollars-worth of homes were built on Craftsman principles from Alaska to the Fiji Islands.[3] But in 1916, Stickley was bankrupt; he had tried to do too much at a time when big firms were producing cheaper imitations of the products of the Craftsman Workshops, which were the economic mainspring of the whole operation. Stickley had met the same fate as Ashbee: he was unable to cope with competition from big capital. Yet his curious marriage of commercial Arts and Crafts with individualistic socialism for the suburbs was the most successful of all twentieth-century attempts to popularize true Arts and Crafts principles, and, if it never produced great architecture, the Craftsman movement left its stamp all over the American continent and gave many thousands of families a glimpse of Morrisian idealism.

The Craftsman was never simply a vehicle for promoting Stickley's housebuilding enterprises. The work of architects considered sympathetic to the Craftsman ideal was frequently featured – there was a series of articles by Parker on Parker and Unwin, for instance. In a more than usually adulatory article, the magazine reported the work of Greene and Greene of Pasadena as exemplifying 'the type of home that abounds today in California – a type in which practical comfort and art are skilfully wedded...It is a vital product of the time, place and people, with roots deep in geographical and human needs. It has a definite relation to the kind of climate and soil, the habits of the people and their ways of looking at civilization and nature. It is equally rich in historic traditions and in provision for present needs. Based on the Old Mission forms...modern Californian architecture has nevertheless made those traditions servants, not masters'.[4]

When the brothers Charles Sumner Greene (1868-1957) and Henry Mather Greene (1870-1954) set up their Pasadena architectural practice in 1893, their first work was a medley of Old English, Spanish Mission, Queen Anne and Colonial themes. By the early years of this century, their architecture began to acquire a characteristic stamp. It was a style in which complexity was built up from elements of great simplicity; an architecture of timber in which beam was piled on beam, rafter on rafter to form ordered nests of smooth sticks with great overhanging eaves and projecting balconies to provide shade from the sun. Every member and every joint is made explicit. The sources are as diverse as the Anglo-Indian bungalow and the simple peg and tenon joints of Stickley's furniture. (The brothers furnished the James A. Cuthbertson house, Pasadena, with Stickley furniture within months of the first appearance of *The Craftsman*, to which they were subscribers.)[5]

On his visit to California, Ashbee thought 'C. Sumner Greene's work beautiful; among the best there is in this country. Like Lloyd Wright, the spell of Japan is upon him, he feels the beauty and makes magic out of the horizontal line, but there is in his work more tenderness, more subtlety, more self effacement than in Wright's work. It is more refined and has more repose. Perhaps it loses in strength, perhaps it is California that speaks rather [than] Illinois'.[6]

Ralph Adams Cram enthused in *American Country Houses of Today*

Charles S. Greene's own house, Oakholm, Pasadena (begun 1901). As Ashbee remarked, 'the spell of Japan is upon him'

Greene & Greene–designed furniture, Irwin House

Greene & Greene. Dining Room, Irwin House

(the transatlantic equivalent of Lawrence Weaver's books) that 'there are things [in Greene and Greene's architecture] Japanese; things that are Scandinavian; things that hint at Sikkim, Bhutan and the frontiers of Tibet, and yet it all hangs together, it is beautiful, it is contemporary, and for some reason or other it seems to fit California. Structurally it is a blessing; only too often the exigencies of our assured precedents lead us into the wide and easy road of structural duplicity, but in this sort of thing there is an honesty that is sometimes almost brazen. It is a wooden style built woodenly'.[7]

Cram was not entirely correct. As Edward Ford has shown, though the Greenes often expressed the structure of their houses direct (particularly in work for less affluent clients), in the grander ones they would conceal the Oregon pine frame members behind ceilings of plaster on wood laths and then recall them with slips of beautifully finished finer wood, teak for instance, that reflected the lines of the hidden rough-sawn structure. Sometimes slips were imposed at right angles to those showing the real structure to make a decorative grid which concealed rather than emphasized the construction of the house. In some of their later work, they used concealed steel beams clad in plaster and timber.[8]

Greene and Greene often experimented with the thin one-room-and-a-corridor plan, sometimes wrapping it round a planted courtyard in the manner of a Californian Mission. But the Gamble House (perhaps their best-known building) at Westmorland Place, Pasadena, has a much more compact lay-out. A hall penetrates a basically rectangular form with, on one side, the living room and den and, on the other, the kitchen and dining-room. The rectangle is eroded and added to so that each room is articulated and the fundamental simplicity of the plan is enriched with much changeful incident.

Greene & Greene. Irwin House, Pasadena. Enlarged 1906 by the Greenes. North-west front with covered terrace and sleeping balcony

The internal woodwork and the furniture are typical of mature Greene and Greene houses: each visible piece of timber is smoothed and slightly rounded with sandpaper so that the teak's ruddy resonance is beautifully expressed. Smaller items like the living-room inglenook seats are pegged together with square dowels (sometimes the square pegs hide screws), and in the larger structures, like the staircase, the tongued ends of the treads and risers are clearly exposed in the thick horizontal planks which provide support. Throughout, the rectilinear geometry of simple timber construction is softened by the gentle curves of Japanese architecture – for instance at the ends of corbels and in the decorative structure that encloses the drawing-room inglenook. Oriental too are the metal straps which hold the timber elements together; these are apparently tightened by a pair of counterposed wedges which, when driven together seem to lock the structure rigid, though its members are probably really held together by concealed screws.

Outside, the structural emphasis is continued. Some of the beams, rafters and purlins smoothed with almost the meticulous care of the timbers of the interior are exposed. Elsewhere, the Greenes used what

Greene & Greene. Gamble House, Pasadena, California (1908): stair detail Below: Ground and first floor plans

Ford calls an 'analogous system that parallels the real structure that it conceals',[9] which is similar to the decorative teak truss which defines the inglenook. There is a real bearing member in there above the opening, but its presence and importance are heightened by applied poetic gesture – not a move of which the purest Arts and Crafts theorists could have approved. But Webb, that paragon of purity, had used concealed steel at Standen, and the Greenes' strange use of apparent structure is a development of practice that had many, if less elaborate, precedents. It was certainly accepted by perceptive critics like Cram and Ashbee (or perhaps it simply took them in).

The Gamble House largely takes its character from the horizontal striations of the sleeping balconies of the three main bedrooms, each under a generous overhanging roof. Walls are clad in wooden shingles which harmonize with the structural timber yet, by their plain shagginess, emphasize the frenetic elaboration of the apparent structure.

There is a wilder kind of shagginess about the retaining wall for the terrace on the west side of the house. Its battered, curving lines grow out of the ground from boulders found on the site. These gradually give way to brickwork in which the dark, irregular heavily-fired bricks at first respond to the boulder base, then gradually enclose individual stones, then become the material of the parapet, forming a ragged but plainly man-made division between the tamed world and that of the seemingly natural lawn.

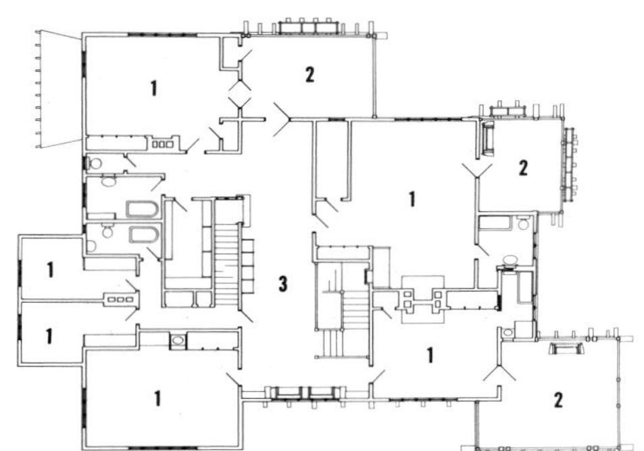

FIRST FLOOR
1: Bedroom
2: Sleeping porch
3: Hall

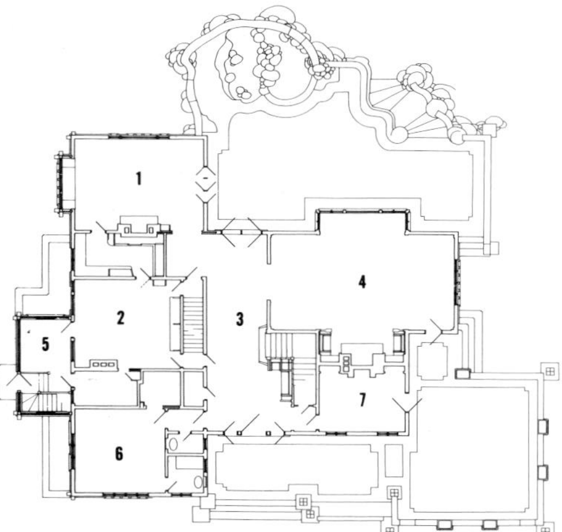

GROUND FLOOR
1: Dining room
2: Kitchen
3: Hall
4: Living room
5: Screened porch
6: Guest bedroom
7: Mr Gamble's den

The Greenes used such picturesque plinths, with overtones of Devey and Prior (though the work of these English architects was probably little known to the brothers) on many of their houses. Other Californian architects of the period were as interested in savage masonry. George Harris (born in 1867) was one of the most extreme. He was interested in buildings made to look as if they had been 'fashioned by nature...an intuitive, spontaneous impression suggested to our minds by the natural environment, heredity and the long, loving association with nature in its many phases'.[10] His masterpiece, Bolton Hall, Tujunga, was built in 1913 as the centrepiece of a utopian community. In it, he said that 'the stones were gathered from the hillside and selected and placed in natural positions such as they might assume when falling down from a cliff and settling in their own natural position...Bolton Hall was built almost entirely without plans, it being a growth, an evolution directed by the materials and the surroundings and made to harmonise with them'.[11] The resulting texture had a curiously organic nature, like the skin of a huge ossified alligator. Inside, the creature's bones were exposed in the roof structure, where the trusses were made entirely of unsawn tree trunks, round and barely de-barked, which were woven together to turn their natural shapes into support for a surprisingly conventional clay tile covering.

Up in the San Francisco Bay Area, Ernest Coxhead (1863-1933) had made much more organic roofs, the shingle skins of which swooped and rolled over his buildings. Coxhead, an English immigrant, was capable of producing churches, like St John's at Del Monte (1891), that almost rival Lethaby's at Brockhampton in intensity and delicacy of detail. It is almost as if Coxhead had brought the Cotswolds to

Gamble House from garden

George Harris. Bolton Hall, Tujunga (1913). Built, almost without drawings, from materials found on site

northern California, picking up a little H. H. Richardson on the way, before reinterpreting his lessons in local materials through Craftsman spectacles and craftsmanship.

In the '90s and early years of this century, Bernard Maybeck (1862-1957) explored a Craftsman-like approach in a series of houses, mainly at Berkeley, where fine craftsmanship is brought into conjunction with an exciting spatial sense that transposed volumes with great dexterity unusual in the Californian Arts and Crafts (interestingly, Maybeck had studied at the Beaux Arts in Paris and later in his career went on to produce the Neo-Classical Palace of Fine Arts for the 1915 San Francisco Exposition).[12]

Maybeck's masterpiece was the First Church of Christ, Scientist in Berkeley. He was commissioned in 1910 by ladies of the local congregation who had seen his houses and decided that his blend of domestic decency and honesty to materials was what they needed for their newly evolved faith. He responded by offering them a building 'the same on the inside as the outside without sham or hypocrisy'.[13]

The church was not small, but the budget was not great, and Maybeck used the products of American industry with the verve and ingenuity that Frank Lloyd Wright had suggested in his essays but had not yet achieved in practice. The main cladding is asbestos cement sheeting, screwed to timber supports through red squares of the same material set at 45 degrees to the horizontal, making a pattern of structural decoration of which Pugin would surely have approved.

Gamble House. Inglenook with decorative teak truss

Ernest Coxhead. St John's Episcopal Church, Del Monte (1891). The Cotswolds in northern California

Bernard Maybeck, First Church of Christ Scientist, Berkeley (started 1910)
Below: Roof detail
Right: Ground and first floor plans

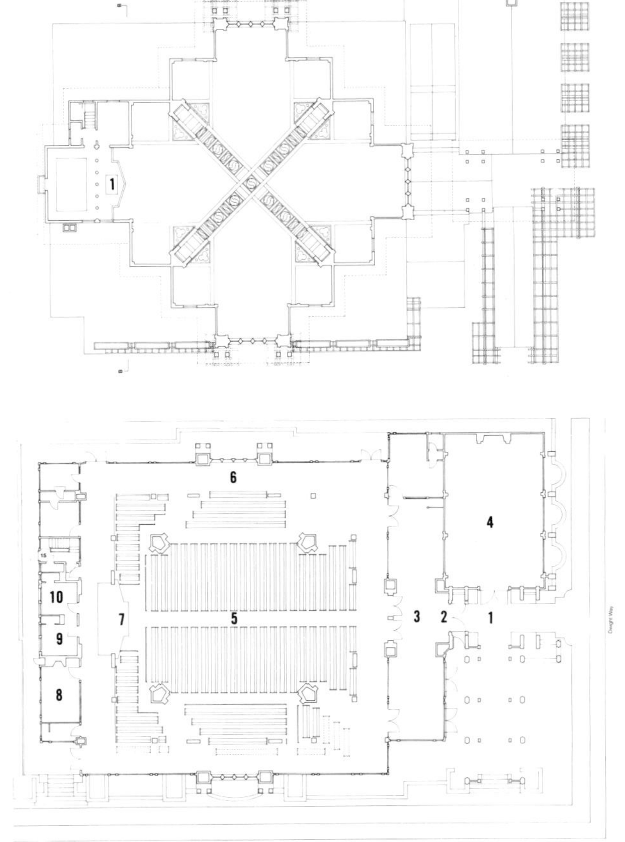

FIRST FLOOR
1: Organ gallery

GROUND FLOOR
1: Portico
2: Entrance
3: Narthex (lobby)
4: Sunday School (now called Fireplace room)
5: Main auditorium
6: Aisle
7: Reader's desk
8: Board of directors' room
9: First Reader's room
10: Second Reader's room

Asbestos cladding then had none of the health threatening implications that it carries for us; it was a simple industrial material, considered even by its makers as too ignoble a product for incorporation into a church. The makers of the stock steel factory sash windows (glazed with hammered glass) had similar objections to the use of their materials in a religious building.[14]

Maybeck used these commonplace things to make a space of great dignity and presence. The church stands four-square on a corner of suburban Berkeley, just south of the university campus. You enter through a dramatic portico. Then there is a low, top-lit narthex, almost Japanese with its rigorous gridded walls of translucent glass and exposed timber roof structure. The church itself explodes beyond the double doors at the end of the narthex. It is based on a square, around which clerestories pour light into the middle of the space. A lower perimeter square eases the transition from narthex to the sacred place and emphasizes its majesty. The construction is all clearly expressed and heightened by touches of clear colour at crucial points. Four massive concrete columns define the central space; they are hollow and act as the main hot air ducts and as the exhausts for used air (which is taken in at their bases and ejected through the roof). This degree of integration of structure and services had precedents in a number of buildings in Victorian England, but was rarely explored in Arts and Crafts work (partly because so much of it was on a small scale – Voysey's chimneys are a curious exception).

The Berkeley church is a great building, innovative, noble in its dimensions and its volumes. But Maybeck never had quite the confidence of his English contemporaries to renounce applied decoration as a means of generating a sense of the holy. Prior at Roker and Lethaby in the Orkneys and at Brockhampton had showed how Gothic could be abstracted to essential principles. Maybeck used Decorated Gothic tracery inside his steel windows, and he was rather less than direct when he claimed that 'summing it up, to build a church edifice can be done by being strictly honest, *ie* make no forms other than those needed for the construction and furnishings, make no ornaments and no color, except those needed and of the form suggested by the need. Avoid all hiding of unpleasant forms. Do not borrow from history, but use form and color as you do words and music'. [15]

A Californian contemporary who must have been disturbed by Maybeck's references to medieval Northern European precedents was Irving Gill (1870-1936). Like most of the other architects, he was an immigrant from the east, and he finally settled at San Diego in the far south of California in 1902. There, he was much influenced by the clear white architecture of the Spanish Missions. 'The Missions', he wrote in *The Craftsman*, 'are a part of [California's] history that should be preserved and in their long, low lines, graceful arcades, tile roofs, bell towers, arched doorways and walled gardens we find a most expressive medium of retaining tradition, history and romance.'[16] Virtually the only idiom the Greenes and Gill held in common was the pergola derived from Mission architecture.

Maybeck. First Church. The great space

that they might
have life, and
that they might
have it more
abundantly
Christ Jesus
85
255
206
85
255
206

Maybeck. Guy Hyde Chick House, Oakland, California (1914). One of his best Bay Area houses

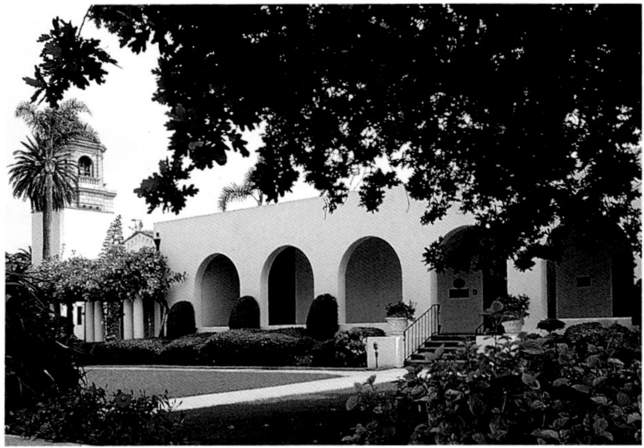

Irving Gill. La Jolla Women's Club, La Jolla, California (1913). Advanced concrete construction evoking Spanish Southern California

Gill's architecture was as simple and solid as the Greenes' was complicated and carpenterish. In his houses, Gill said in *The Craftsman*, 'walls are finished flush with the casings and the line where the wall joins the floor is slightly rounded, so that it forms one continuous piece with no place for dust to enter or lodge, or crack for vermin of any kind to exist. There is no moulding for pictures, plates or chairs, no baseboards, panelling or wainscoting to catch and hold the dust'.[17] The remark recalls *The Studio*'s comments on Voysey's Chiswick house 25 years earlier.

In this simplicity and in his affection for the locus of his architecture, Gill was an Arts and Crafts architect. But in his methods, he was more a forerunner of the Modern Movement. He bought from the US Army machinery for producing prefabricated barracks, and with his tilt slab system of concrete construction he built such elegant minor masterpieces as the Women's Club La Jolla (1913), a white, flat-roofed, arcaded building, surrounded by pergolas covered in lush plants.

The tilt-slab system was developed during the Spanish-American war. It consisted of a gigantic table which could be tilted at 15 degrees to the horizontal. Onto it were laid metal strips to act as reinforcement and barrow-runs for the concrete pourers. Thickness was made up with hollow pots laid on the table. When the concrete was cured and finished, the whole wall could be pulled vertical with a small engine. Crude as it was, the system was much more sophisticated than almost everything tried by the European architects of the machine worshipping Modern Movement in the '20s and '30s. Gill had understood the nature of the local adobe architecture, and translated it into a modern mud construction in one of the last of the many Arts and Crafts experiments with concrete.

1 *Stickley, Gustav* The Craftsman, *Vol IV, 1903, p92.*
2 *Stickley, Gustav Introduction to* More Craftsman Homes, *1911, in Sanders, Barry (ed)* The Best of Craftsman Homes, *Peregrine Smith, Santa Barbara and Salt Lake City, 1978, p7.*
3 *'California's Contribution to a National Architecture: its Significance and Beauty as Shown in the Work of Greene and Greene Architects',* The Craftsman, *in Sanders, Barry (ed)* The Craftsman: an Anthology, *Peregrine Smith, Santa Barbara and Salt Lake City, 1978.*
4 Ibid, *pvii.*
5 *This and much other information about the sources of Greene and Greene architecture is given in Makinson, Randall, L* Greene and Greene: Architecture as a Fine Art *and* Greene and Greene: Furniture and Related Designs, *Peregrine Smith, Santa Barbara and Salt Lake City, 1977 and 1979. Current, Karen* Greene and Greene: Architects in the Residential Style, *Amon Carter Museum of Western Art, Fort Worth, 1974, adds further detail.*
6 *Ashbee,* Memoirs, *typescript in the Victoria and Albert Museum,* op cit, *Vol III, p106.*
7 *Cram, Ralph Adams* American Country Houses of Today, *1913, quoted by Makinson, Randall L 'Greene and Greene', in McCoy, Esther (ed)* Five Californian Architects, *Reinhold, New York, 1960, p146.*
8 *Ford, Edward R.* The Details of Modern Architecture, *MIT Press, Cambridge, Mass. and London, 1990, pp135-159.*
9 Ibid, *p147.*
10 *Quoted by McCoy, Esther in* California Design *1910 eds Timothy J Andersen, Eudorah M. Moore and Robert Winter, Peregrine Smith, Santa Barbara and Salt Lake City, 1980, p110.*
11 Ibid, *p111.*
12 *See Anderson, Tim in* California Design, op cit, *p132.*
13 *Maybeck, Bernard Ralph, correspondence quoted in Cardwell, Kenneth H.* Bernard Maybeck Artisan, Architect, Artist, *Peregrine Smith, Santa Barbara and Salt Lake City, 1977 p122.*
14 Ibid, *p126.*
15 Ibid, *p129.*
16 *Gill, Irving J. 'The Home of the Future: the New Architecture of the West',* The Craftsman, *May 1916, in Sanders, Barry* The Craftsman, op cit, *p314.*
17 *Quoted in McCoy, Esther* Five Californian Architects, op cit, *p69.*

FOR
AND

Ruskin in the Mid-West

16

Gill's technical innovations and the simplicity of his style were unrecognized in Europe, where the Modern Movement emerged. On the international scene, much the most influential American Arts and Crafts architect was Frank Lloyd Wright (1867-1959). Gill had worked with Wright in the Chicago office of Adler and Sullivan, where Wright served his time as apprentice from 1887 to 1893, when he set up on his own. Wright's first office was in the loft of Steinway Hall, an 11-storey office block in central Chicago, where he shared a draughting room and secretary with a group of young architects, Harold Perkins, Robert Clossen Spencer, and Myron Hunt. Other architects gradually joined the group, either actually on the premises or in spirit, to form what became known as the Prairie School – the Arts and Crafts movement's manifestation in the Mid-West.[1]

That Chicago should have preceded New York and California as the birthplace of US Arts and Crafts architecture seems odd at first. But, by the '90s, the city was more generally wealthy than the west coast, while avoiding the stylistic predilections of the established east. Critic Arthur C. David noted in 1903 that the clients of the Prairie School 'the well-to-do western gentlemen for whom the houses are built, do not seem to demand the use of European styles and remnants to the same extent as do the eastern owners of expensive buildings'.[2]

Walter Crane, the socialist, illustrator and friend of William Morris, lectured and exhibited at the Chicago Art Institute at the turn of 1891/2. Ashbee's Guild first exhibited at the Chicago Architectural Club in 1898, and Ashbee himself gave 10 lectures in the city in the winter of 1900. It was then that he formed a lifelong (though sometimes acrimonious) friendship with Wright who agreed to be the local secretary of the National Trust (the body which had sent Ashbee to America to drum up transatlantic support and funds).

Other English influences were through *The Studio*, which was published in America as *The International Studio*, and *The House Beautiful*, which, published in Chicago, illustrated the work of Voysey, Baillie Scott, Townsend (and Wright) before the turn of the century. But Wright was very much a man on his own and direct references to the work of others in his architecture are rare. He once designed a neo-colonial house, once a neo-Cotswold terrace, the Roloson Houses and once a full blown but very individualistic essay in half timbered Old English – the Nathan G. Moore residence at Oak Park (1895). After such fumblings in the '90s, Wright began to evolve a style of his own. The Moore house's open planning recalls Baillie Scott's experiments* and its horizontality is occasionally reminiscent of Voysey. Here and there is a dash of Japanese. But the Prairie houses that Wright evolved in the first decade of the century were as original, consistent

Frank Lloyd Wright. Unity Temple, Oak Park, Illinois (1906): poured and hard-finished concrete made into a noble material

*There was a tradition of open planning in America that dated back at least to the early '80s. Vincent Scully in *The Shingle Style* has shown how the nineteenth-century English tradition of the great central living hall was developed into a continuous space embracing the functions of reception, drawing and dining rooms. The American middle classes seem to have cherished privacy less than their British contemporaries, and in general their houses were rather smaller, so that a living hall would have been too poky for sensible use.

and influential in America as were (in a completely different way) Voysey's houses in England.

Wright's typical grand Prairie houses, built in the new Chicago suburbs for a banker or businessman, are two, sometimes three, storeys high but the chief impression is of horizontality and lowness. (Wright, like Voysey, liked to restrict the height of his rooms, and Voysey-like, he believed 'the horizontal line is the line of domesticity'.)[3] In the Ward Willits residence at Highland Park, Illinois (1902), the plan is cruciform with access to the heart of the house from the entrance off the porte-cochère. In the middle of the plan is a massive set of interlocking fireplaces and inglenooks from which the wings containing the dining and living rooms, and the service wing, shoot out into the garden under their long low roofs. Construction is of stucco on metal lath over a timber frame that is helped to achieve wide spans by steel insertions. Internally, the presence of the steel members within the first floor is signalled by applied timber beams, similar to those in the Gamble House.[4] These members, though, are clean planed by machine and not hand rubbed like those of the Greenes.

Wright's Old English essay, the Nathan G. Moore house, Oak Park, Illinois (1895, rebuilt 1923)

The Robie House in Chicago (designed in 1906 and completed in 1909) sums up the Prairie style at its finest and calmest. The ground floor is a long, low podium of Roman brick capped with simple concrete copings; it contains the entrance hall, and billiard and play rooms. The main spaces are on the first floor: living room and dining room are one great volume separated by a mighty brick fireplace that is more than halfway to becoming an inglenook. The street front is a continuous band of large casement windows opening onto a balcony. The brick piers between the windows prop up the edge of the hipped roof that surrounds the house with wide eaves, and sails out at each end in fantastic (for the time) cantilevers to form generous open porches. The daring spans of these beams are made possible by the inclusion of steel channels concealed in the roof of the first floor rooms which bear on the central brick mass and on brick piers.[5] The second floor, containing the family bedrooms, has an equally sweeping hipped roof, carried on mullions, which sails at right angles across the thrust of the two big spaces below. The whole composition is tied together by the rectilinear vertical bulk of the chimney which serves the fireplaces – symbolically and formally the pivot of the plan.

Wright. Edward R. Hills Residence, Oak Park, Illinois (1900-06)

Those wide eaves were characteristic of Wright's work, even in the early '90s, when he was using much steeper pitched roofs. They caused some disquiet to contemporaries. Wright's fellow Chicagoan, Robert Spencer, asked in the Boston *Architectural Review* what the justification was for 'these almost unvarying broad eaves...It will not do to say that their use in the north gives a quaint and pleasing southern air to a building. That would be frank condemnation, surely. There are at least two points in their favour. Practically they exclude the sun from the upper rooms only during the hotter hours of summer days...[And] the soffits are treated in light reflecting tones, giving the second storey rooms a glow as agreeable as it is surprising to those who expect to find the rooms darkened by the eaves'.[6]

Spencer's 1899 review of Wright's architecture was an extraordinary accolade for 'a young man's work, a boy's work, perhaps, as he is

Wright. Ward Willits House, Highland Park, Illinois (1902): the Prairie School repertoire emerges
Right: Ground floor plan, flowing spaces round a massive fireplace cluster

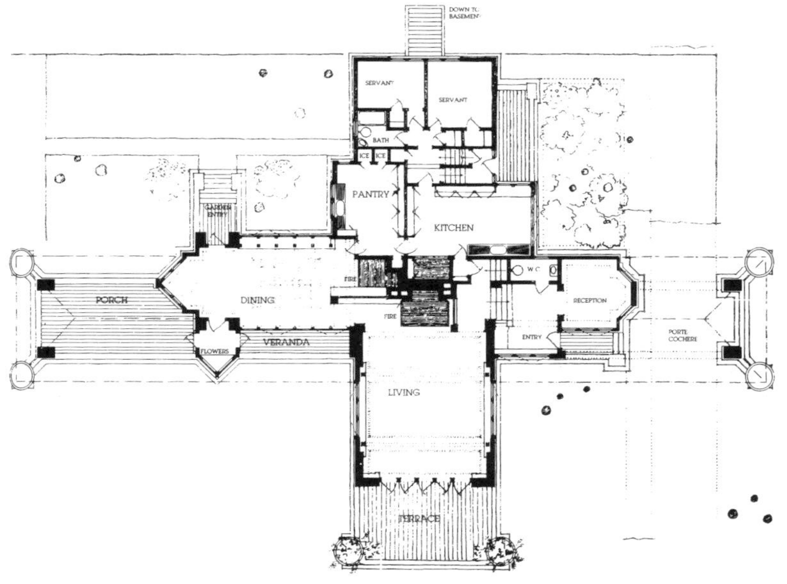

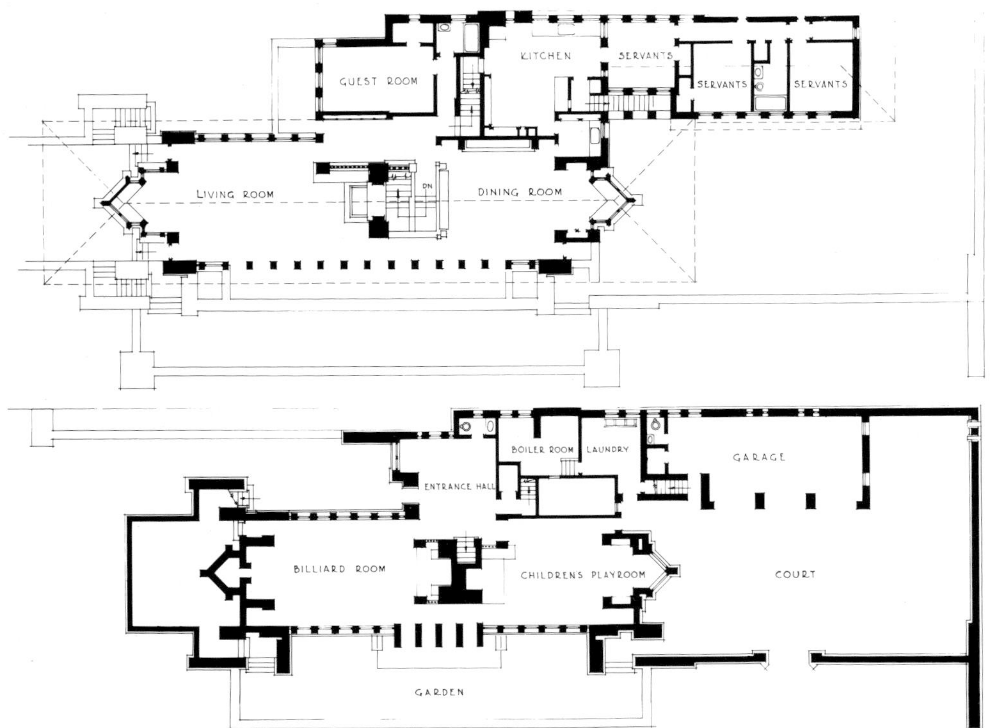

Wright. Robie House, Chicago (1906)
Above: Ground and first floor plans
Right: Living room with its continuous openings onto the balcony. The furniture is new

but 32',[7] which acclaimed that 'it is a pleasure to see how style may be given to the cheapest structure...when dull or useless precedent is abandoned and materials are handled not merely with a sound knowledge of the basic laws of planning and structure, but with a keen poetic insight into the subtle sources of beauty...Our beautiful buildings must not be the forced fruits of an artificial civilization, but must be the natural bloom of a hardy native growth with its roots deep in the soil'.[8] Pugin's philosophy had found yet another new frontier.

Wright was steeped in the theories that produced the English Arts and Crafts movement. Ruskin's *Seven Lamps* was one of the first books he owned on architecture and Morris was one of his early heroes. When working for Sullivan, he would stay in the office into the night arguing for revival of 'the Gothic spirit in the Middle West'.[9]

But in one key aspect he departed from his English masters. He attacked Ashbee in 1900 saying: 'My God...is Machinery, and the art of the future will be the expression of the individual artist through the thousand powers of the machine – the machine doing all those things that the individual workman cannot do. The creative artist is the man who controls all this and understands it'.[10]

Wright's resolution of the Puginian paradox was brutal, and Ashbee, the (theoretical) protagonist of freedom for craftsmen, made what seems to have been the feeble riposte that the 'individuality of the average had to be considered in addition to that of the "artistic creator" himself'.[11]

Wright was plainly not impressed, for a few months later he gave a speech at Hull House* on 'The Art and Craft of the Machine' in which he sang the praises of the machine that 'by its wonderful cutting, shaping, smoothing and reinterpretive capacity has made it possible so [to produce] without waste that the poor as well as the rich may enjoy today beautiful surface treatments of clear strong forms that...Sheraton and Chippendale only hinted at, with dire extravagance, and which the Middle Ages utterly ignored'.[12]. Wright had a good deal of sense on his side, for by the beginning of this century, power tools had made life a good deal more tolerable in the carpenter's workshop than the scene of often backbreaking toil described by George Eliot in *Adam Bede*. While Wright was preaching the virtues of the machine, friends of Ashbee like Ernest Barnsley were getting men to cut planks in a sawpit, dreadful labour to achieve a picturesque finish to appeal to the rich.

Yet Wright's buildings of the early years of the century are not notably more products of machines than those of many English contemporaries, for instance Voysey with his characteristic smooth, square-sectioned stair balusters. Even in Wright's big buildings of the period (he was one of the few Arts and Crafts architects to obtain large commissions in the first decade of the century), there was little sign of machine manufacture. True, his headquarters building for the

Wright. Robie House, Chicago: huge cantilevers made with concealed steel

*Hull House, founded by Jane Addams, was based on the example of Toynbee Hall in Whitechapel, the University settlement where Ashbee had lodged and taught as a young man, and which had itself been founded by Canon and Mrs Barnett, patrons of Townsend and of Parker and Unwin.

Wright. Interior of Unity Temple, Oak Park, Chicago: the bath of light made possible by concrete construction

Entrance to Unity Temple. Wright achieved a nobility and grandeur, for which lesser Arts and Crafts architects turned to Classicism

Larkin household goods mail order company in Buffalo (1903, demolished 1950) had sealed, double-glazed, plate glass windows and a sophisticated (for its time) form of air conditioning. But in both the use of large areas of glass and in mechanical ventilation, he had been anticipated by Mackintosh in the northern block of the Glasgow School of Art.[13] Neither the Buffalo nor the Glasgow building was dominated by the machine aesthetic of smoothness and repetition. The Larkin building was clad in brick and the Glasgow one in stone – the most ancient and labour intensive building materials.*

The Larkin building was Wright's first important commission outside the Mid-West. One of the co-founders of the company was Elbert Hubbard (1850-1945) who had met Morris on a trip to England and who, in the '90s, set up the Roycroft community at East Aurora, New York State. Ashbee, who visited the Roycrofters in 1900, thought their work – furniture and printing – promising but untutored and ugly.

But Hubbard was far from being an innocent idealist. He was a self-publicist on a monumental scale. Through his magazines, *The Fra* and *The Philistine*, he promoted himself, the Roycroft ideals, and the magnificence of turn-of-the-century American capitalist culture in sickeningly adulatory articles on magnates like John D. Rockefeller and Henry Ford. His own capitalist activities were rather less well publicised. By the time of Wright's commission, Hubbard was retired from active interest in the firm and the connection came through Darwin D. Martin, an executive of the company who was the brother of one of Wright's Chicago clients, for whom Wright was building one of his most successful and elaborate Prairie houses in Buffalo at the same time as the Larkin.

The Larkin headquarters was a large abstracted Classical rectangular building, built of dark red brick and cinnamon coloured stone which carried reinforced concrete floors. Large plain slabs of brickwork enclosed the vertical ventilation shafts, from which air was distributed internally under the floors between supporting paired beams. Wright called it 'a simple, dignified utterance of a plain, utilitarian type, with sheer brick walls and simple stone copings'.[14]

Internally, there was a big volume with balconies on which the packers worked surrounding the lower floor where administrators used Wright's specially designed standardized steel furniture. The whole great volume was bathed in light from the roof, under which the workers were organized in serried ranks. It was a temple to scientific management, and it is hard to think of Morris being happy with it. Certainly Janet Ashbee (C. R.'s wife) had strong reservations about the work of this period, 'Lloyd Wright is a strange delightful soul', she wrote, 'a radical original thinker working out his ideas consistently, as an artist, in his architecture not bothering about the "sociology" of it ("it destroys the art") putting up building after building in queer square blocks with squares and long straight lines for decoration'.[15]

Wright's other temple of this period was at Oak Park, Illinois. Unity Temple (1906) had a more spiritual purpose. It is constructed of

*But the building's furniture which Wright specially designed was innovatory. It was made of standardized steel components.

Wright. Larkin Building, Buffalo (1903, demolished 1950). Temple to mail order capitalism

poured concrete, the pebbles of which give the outside the texture of a great block of striated stone. Its eaves project like those of Prairie houses and are propped in the same way by piers between clerestory windows. The square internal space derives much of its character from these windows with their rectilinear pattern of coloured glass, but its effect of being in a cubical bath of light could not have been achieved without the glass laylights between the beams of the concrete roof.

Concrete was chosen as the material for Unity Temple because of its cheapness ($35 000 was the price limit). Structurally the concept was not innovative, and concrete was used in the cheapest possible way – then, as now, a sort of mud was poured by unskilled labour into wooden boxes, themselves prepared with the simplest carpentry and later thrown away. So the contribution to design of the individual labourer was reduced to the absolute minimum – in complete contrast to the way of handling concrete envisaged by Lethaby and his team in their virtually contemporary Liverpool Cathedral competition design. If that had been built, elaborate craftsmanship would have been needed to construct its complicated curves and tapers. The Liverpool design was turned down on the grounds not of the expense of its handwork, but of style. At Oak Park the building process could not at the time be carried out by machine, but Wright was determined to make it as machine-like as possible.* Perhaps it was the vague Neo-Classicism of the result that made it acceptable to a proper middle class congregation.

Wright's productive career spanned a prodigious period – from the 1890s to the late 1950s. He left Oak Park in October 1909, abandoning his family and office in what at the time was a scandalous elopement to Europe with Mamah Cheney, the wife of one of his clients. He received few commissions for some 25 years, but in the late '30s his practice picked up again and, after the Second World War, he was venerated as the greatest living American architect and enjoyed a correspondingly large practice and large ideas – one of his last projects was for a mile high skyscraper. But he never quite forgot his Arts and Crafts origins and preached truth-to-materials and relevance to place to the last. In the lean years of the early '30s, Wright set up the Taliesin Fellowship, a community based on craft teaching and agriculture that rather resembled Ashbee's Chipping Campden Guild (except that most members had to pay Wright for the privilege of belonging to the Fellowship). And, at the same time, he began to evolve proposals for Broadacre City, a low density interweaving of town and country with '*little* farms, *little* homes for industry, *little* factories, *little* schools, a *little* university going to people most by way of their interest in the ground'.[16] It was a (never realized) translation of *News from Nowhere* into the language of middle America: a city in which 'quality is in all, for all, alike'.

Walter Burghley Griffin. Ralph D. Griffin house, Edwardsville, Illinois (c1910)

*It is only fair to point out that this was exactly Voysey's approach. He achieved similarly simple effects by coating crude brick walls with render – a type of construction that requires no initiative on the part of workmen.

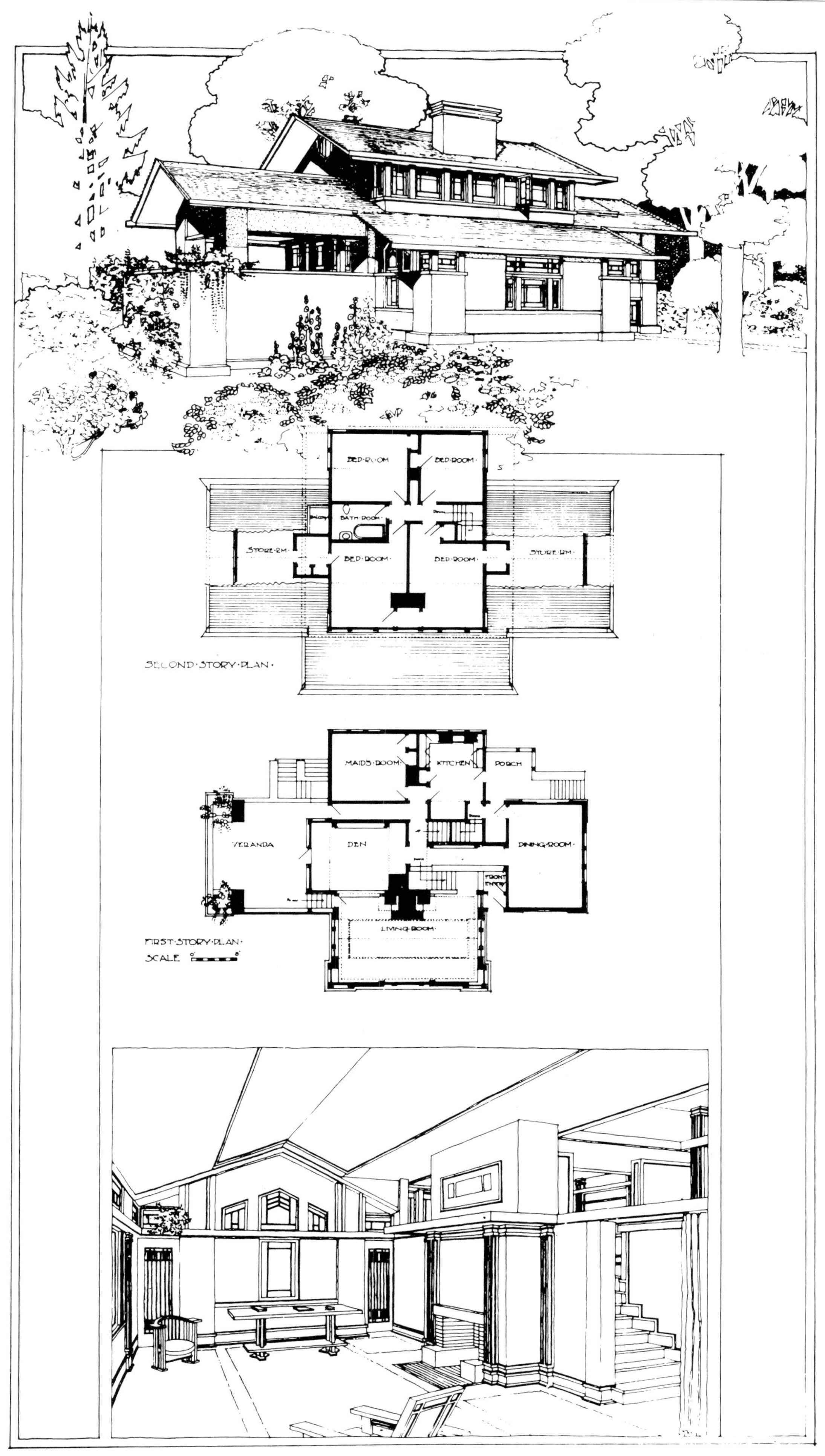
BED·ROOM
BED·ROOM
BATH·ROOM
STORE·RM·
BED·ROOM·
BED·ROOM·
STORE·RM·
SECOND·STORY·PLAN·
MAIDS·ROOM
KITCHEN
PORCH
VERANDA
DEN
DINING·ROOM
FRONT ENTRY
LIVING·ROOM·
FIRST·STORY·PLAN·
SCALE

Walter Burley Griffin and
Marion Mahoney Griffin.
J.G. Melson house,
Mason City, Iowa (1912)

Walter Burley Griffin.
Own house, Winnetka,
Illinois (1912)

Marion Mahoney Griffin.
Perspective of Rock Crest/
Rock Glen, Mason City,
Iowa (c1912)

However wayward he may have been in his later years, in the first decade of the century Wright's influence on architects of the Mid-West was clear. His open plans and sweeping roofs with great eaves supported by the mullions of a band of windows became trademarks of the Prairie School. Even Wright's old master Sullivan adopted the idioms in his later domestic work when his practice was declining.

The people most directly influenced by Wright were the assistants at his Oak Park Studio. His office was almost as fertile a breeding ground of talent as Shaw's had been 20 years before. Of all Wright's assistants of those years, Walter Burley Griffin (1876-1937) developed the most individual approach. He was Wright's chief draughtsman until they parted after a quarrel in 1905, when Griffin set up on his own to produce a series of houses often distinguished by wide overhanging gables and strong vertical elements, more overtly Japanese than Wright's work. In 1911 Griffin married Marion Mahoney (1871-1962), one of the first women architects in the USA, an assistant who executed many of Wright's renderings and some of his furnishings: she also had a small practice of her own, which sometimes overlapped with her work for Wright.

In 1912, Griffin won the competition for planning Australia's federal capital, Canberra, with a design that had all the formal qualities of an Arts and Crafts garden. Griffin left America before the Prairie School's decline had become serious, but over the next 10 years it quietly faded just as the movement in Britain had a few years earlier. The reasons were much the same: an increasing affection for Classical and other historical styles in a client class ever more concerned with order, economy and obvious respectability.

By 1910, Wright had optimistically argued that 'A revival of the Gothic spirit is needed in the art and architecture of modern life; an interpretation of the best traditions we have in the world made with our own methods, not a stupid attempt to fasten their forms on a life that has outgrown them. Reviving the Gothic spirit does not mean using the forms of Gothic architecture handed down from the Middle Ages. It necessarily means something quite different.'

But by 1914, his world had changed and he was bitter. 'I...am heartily sick of being commercialized and traded in and upon; but most of all I dread to see the types I have worked with so long and patiently drifting towards speculative builders, cheapened or befouled by senseless changes, robbed of quality and distinction, dead forms, or grinning originalities for the sake of originality, an endless stream of hacked carcasses, to encumber democratic front yards for five decades or more.'[18]

1 Much information on the foundation and work of the Prairie School is given by the school's historian Brooks, H. Allen in The Prairie School, *University of Toronto Press, Toronto and Buffalo, 1972.*

2 Ibid, *p16. The quotation is from* Architectural Record, *Vol XV, 1904, pp362-363.*

3 Wright, F. L. Introduction to Ausgeführte Bauten Und Entwürfe, *Wasmuth, Berlin, 1910, reprinted as* Studies and Executed Buildings by Frank Lloyd Wright, *Architectural Press, London, 1986, p15.*

4 Ford, Edward R. The Details of Modern Architecture, *MIT Press, Cambridge, Mass. and London, 1990, p179.*

5 Ibid, *pp194-197.*

6 Spencer, Robert C. Jr 'The Work of Frank Lloyd Wright', The Architectural Review, *Boston, Vol I (new series), 1899, p68.*

7 Ibid, *p72.*

8 Ibid, *p62.*

9 Farr, Finis Frank Lloyd Wright, a Biography, *Cape, London, 1962, p46.*

10 Ashbee, C. R. Memoirs, *typescript in the Victoria and Albert Museum,* op cit, *Vol I, p242.*

11 Ibid.

12 Wright, F. L. 'The Art and Craft of the Machine', lecture delivered 6 March 1901 at Hull House, printed in Wright, F. L. Writings and Buildings, *ed Kaufmann, E. and B. Raeburn, Horizon, New York, 1960, pp65-66.*

13 Banham, Reyner The Architecture of the Well-Tempered Environment, *Architectural Press, London, 1969, describes both systems pp84-91.*

14 Wright, F. L. 'In the Cause of Architecture', Architectural Record, *March 1908, reprinted in* Frank Lloyd Wright Collected Writings 1894-1930, *ed Bruce Brooks Pfeiffer, Rizzoli, New York, 1992, p93.*

15 Ashbee, Janet in Ashbee Journals, *King's College Library, Cambridge, cat 325/1908. Quoted in Ford,* op cit, *p163.*

16 Wright, F. L. 'Broadacre City: a New Community Plan', Architectural Record, *Vol LXXVII, 1935, p247.*

17 Wright, F.L. Studies and Executed Buildings, op cit, *p11.*

18 Wright, F. L. 'In the Cause of Architecture: Second Paper', Architectural Record, *May 1914, reprinted in Pfeiffer,* op cit, *p130.*

Northern roots

17

Wright lived at Fiesole for a couple of years and his work was published in 1910 and 1911 by Wasmuth of Berlin who had issued Muthesius's *Das englische Haus*. Wright asked Ashbee, his closest European friend, to provide an introduction, and in it the English architect wrote 'in a comparison of the work of Frank Lloyd Wright with modern work in England and Germany...a certain kinship is significant...In Germany the names of Olbrich, Hoffmann, Moser, Bruno Paul, Möhring suggest themselves. In England those of us who are sometimes called the Arts and Crafts men, Lethaby, Voysey, Lutyens, Ricardo, Wilson, Holden, Blow, Townsend, Baillie Scott. We feel that between us and him there is a kinship. We may differ vitally in manner of expression, in our planning, in our touch, in the way we clothe our work, in our feeling for proportion, but although our problems differ essentially, we are altogether at one in our principles. We guard in common the lamp of truth'.[1]

Between 1890 and 1910 artistic links between Britain and the German speaking countries were particularly close, and, to some extent, architecture followed parallel courses in the offshore island and in northern and central Europe. These developments were part of a rejection of the various forms of Classicism that swept Europe in the second half of the nineteenth century.* The reaction undoubtedly owed something to Ruskinian theory and to the example of Morris, Mackmurdo and their followers. Architects as different as the Dutch romantic H. P. Berlage[2] and the French leader of Art Nouveau, Hector Guimard,[3] paid tribute to Ruskin, and Morris's designs were well known on the Continent by the '90s. Another source of anti-Classicism was the writings of the great French Goth, Eugène-Emmanuel Viollet-le-Duc (1814-79).

H. P. Berlage. Amsterdam Stock Exchange (1898-1908)

Viollet-le-Duc's analysis made Gothic out to be a much more scientific and rational system of construction than Ruskin had suggested, and he proposed various ways of using iron structures according to Gothic principles. His polemics had great influence throughout the Continent and in America where the young Frank Lloyd Wright was one of his many disciples. In England, there was a vogue for Viollet-le-Duc's theories in the '70s and '80s.

By 1900, the European anti-Classicists could be divided broadly, and with many exceptions on each side, into two camps by a line running roughly along the Dutch/Belgian border and down through Munich to Vienna. To the south was the territory of Art Nouveau with its sinuous intertwined curves; its profusion of elaborate ornament; its structures curved and twisted to take the shapes of bones and plants. To the north, a much more protestant spirit prevailed. Structures were simple, straightforward and clearly expressed; ornament was restricted and, where it was used, it tended to follow the

*In America, there was a similar reaction in the Shingle Style and the work of Henry Hobson Richardson (1838-1886). Richardson's last work was extremely changeful and bore a powerful personal stamp – great simple planes of rough ashlar penetrated by giant semi-circular arches round the major openings. His buildings were published spasmodically in Europe and were said to have influenced architects as different as Townsend and Sonck – though sometimes the evidence seems a little stretched, as there are few if any references to his work in the writings of the architects who were supposed to have been under his influence.[4]

Martin Nyrop. Copenhagen Town Hall (1892-1905). One of the first National Romantic monuments

Arnstein Arneberg. Restoration of Akershus Castle, Oslo. Such restorations were very important to the National Romantics

stiff, heraldic forms of the English Arts and Crafts movement. In England, Art Nouveau was regarded with some horror. The *Magazine of Art* held a colloquium on the subject in 1904 to which architects as diverse as Jackson, Voysey and Blomfield were united in decrying the southern movement. Voysey, the most eloquent, welcomed 'the condition that has made *"Art Nouveau"* possible', but he savaged the manifestation as 'distinctly unhealthy and revolting'. 'Is it not', he thundered, 'merely the work of a lot of imitators with nothing but mad eccentricity as a guide; good men, no doubt, misled into thinking that art is a debauch of sensuous feeling, instead of the expression of human *thought* and feeling combined.'[5]

Jackson described the characteristic feature of Art Nouveau as 'the Squirm'. It is easy to see how the proper, rather priggish Englishmen were revolted by Art Nouveau's total wilfulness, profusion of decoration and overt sexuality (naked women figured large in Art Nouveau design, sometimes even forming the structure of chairs): all so alien to ascetic Arts and Crafts folk.

Art Nouveau architects were consciously trying to achieve a new style, derived from nature, in which particularly metal and glass achieved a writhing plasticity never seen before. The northern architects were much more conscious of their past. Like many Englishmen they turned to late medieval domestic architecture as the chief source of inspiration.

In Scandinavia, echoes of the past were pursued in an attempt to achieve nationally identifiable architectures. All four Scandinavian countries were seeking identity, and all four evolved varieties of what came to be known as National Romanticism.

Denmark had a national cultural revival after the loss of Slesvig-Holstein in 1864 and was the first in the field. Martin Nyrop (1849-1923) designed country houses in local styles throughout Denmark but he also received public commissions,* the largest of which was Copenhagen town hall (built 1892-1905). Based on Siena's Palazzo Pubblico, it was a celebration of brick – the material in which seventeenth-century Copenhagen was constructed – in dramatic contrast to the stuccoed Classical public buildings of the previous 80 years. Basically a giant courtyard divided in two by the council chamber, the building's mass was saved from symmetry by the great tower with its copper covered spire. The lessons of Pugin and Morris had arrived in the north. Copenhagen town hall heralded a generation of urban brick buildings, irregular and changeful, by architects such as Ulrick Plesner and Aage Largeland-Mathiesen. The influence was felt in the suburbs and country too in houses like Povl Baumann's 11 Marienlyst Allé, Helsingør; built in 1907, its irregular brick outline would have been perfectly at home in Hampstead, with Danish touches becoming apparent only on close inspection.

Norway, which gained independence from Sweden only in 1906, was as usual quieter than the other Scandinavian countries. Arnstein

*Unlike the English Arts and Crafts people, who rarely received public work, the architects of the National Romantic movements did get large public commissions precisely because their work was identified with national aspirations. Their success is an indication that, had the British architects been given a chance, a great civic architecture could have been evolved out of Arts and Crafts principles.

Arneberg (1882-1961) was one of the first to bring the techniques of traditional timber farm building to the suburbs. He spent many years restoring the mighty Akershus castle, hard by Oslo harbour, on principles that would have delighted the British Society for the Protection of Ancient Buildings. On the west coast, Frederik Konow Lund (1889-1970) had a rural practice round Bergen, where he continued to build Arts and Crafts influenced country houses that reinterpreted local timber and granite construction according to Morrisian principles well into the '20s.[6]

Finland was trying to establish separation from Russia at the turn of the century, and one of the major forces in the struggle was Finnish culture. There was a spectacular revival in all the arts with Jean Sibelius leading the way in music and Akseli Gallen-Kallela in painting. Three young architects, Herman Gesellius (1874-1916), Armas Lindgren (1874-1929) and Eliel Saarinen (1873-1950), who had started in practice in 1896, won the competition for the Finnish Pavilion at the Paris Exhibition of 1900. This was a rather wild cocktail of traditional Finnish elements, with a strong infusion of Dragon Style, the mixture of Swiss cottage and Viking memory which had become popular in Norway and Sweden in the '70s.

Fortified with the fees for the Pavilion, and from the commissions that followed it, the three started to build a group of houses for themselves in the virgin forest at Hvitträsk near Helsinki in 1901. Lindgren built his house to the north of the site, on the edge of the steep bank that falls sharply down towards the lake shore. It was dominated by a central square tower made of logs which carried a viewing platform and a spire. This rather Wild West element was surrounded by two-storey wings with hipped roofs over log walls. The pantiles on the hips were continued over the single-storey common studio which separated Lindgren's house from Saarinen's at the other end, where they rose and swooped in a complicated series of roof forms over the balconies, terraces and bays that changefully express the magnificent interlocking family spaces inside.

From the bank side, the whole range seems to grow out of the Finnish soil. There is a base course of irregular lumps of granite from the site that meets the smoothly rendered masonry of the entrance level in an irregular line that is strongly suggestive of Devey in its intimation that the complex has been built over the ruins of a far more ancient structure. Quite early on, the log upper floors of both houses were covered in shingles reminiscent of those used on sixteenth-century Finnish churches; perhaps the aim was to increase insulation.[7] Lindgren's house burned down in 1922, and was replaced in rather less dramatic style by Saarinen, who had come into ownership of the whole site. But even today, the group hovers over the lake, a magical place linked to the past by its roots in the land and myth, and to the future by its optimism.

The complex was intended to be a focus for all the arts and crafts, and the debt to English thinking of the previous generation was overt. For instance, when Lindgren became artistic director of the Helsinki School of Applied Arts in 1902, he commented that 'there gathered around Ruskin a group of artists, the Pre-Raphaelites, and soon the

Gesellius, Lindgren and Saarinen. Finnish Pavilion at the Paris Exhibition 1900, one of the first fruits of the partnership. A Finnish National Romantic manifesto

Below: Hvitträsk, dining room with ryijys, traditional Finnish rugs, used as sofa and floor coverings
Bottom: traditional materials in new configuration

movement spread to even wider circles, largely because it was not restricted to the three main fields of art, architecture, painting and sculpture, but embraced with burning passion and enthusiasm the "applied arts", crafts, home arts. The most commonplace of things, the simplest of household articles, were through their form and decoration to express the search for truth, simplicity and stability, the watchwords of the new movement'.[9]*

When they built in town, the three partners were equally changeful and concerned with truth. Before the practice broke up in 1905, they completed a number of blocks of flats in central Helsinki, remarkable alike for the variety of their elevations and their plans which offered many different dwellings in each block. In more monumental buildings, for instance in the National Museum, Helsinki (competition won in 1902, and finished by Lindgren in 1910), the partners adopted a tougher style. The museum has a massive base course of squared granite rubble and the two courts are pinned down at their conjunction by a tower capped with brick and copper which is not unlike that of Copenhagen town hall (perhaps not coincidentally – Martin Nyrop was on the competition jury).[10]

The impression the museum now gives was foreshadowed in a pamphlet *Vårt Museum* written by some of the liveliest younger architects of the time, including Gesellius, Lindgren and Sonck, which was presented to the Finnish Senate in 1900 as part of the successful campaign to set up a competition. An imaginary visitor is writing about a visit to the museum in 1910: 'In the great building complex, peaceful yet picturesque in silhouette against the sky, rose a Gothic grey stone church in the style of a massive crown and an antiquated tower like that of a medieval castle. And immediately as one came closer, one could admire the unique and intimate simple detail of this highly novel building which appeared to consist of styles borrowed from a number of ages and yet produced a remarkable unity and clarity in proportion and line. I could feel my heart bursting with pride as I realised that it was my country, slender in resources, that had fabricated this work of art, that it was the history of my fellow countrymen that had inspired the architects' work and the people's great sacrifices'.[11] This is one of the few examples of an accurate description being written of a building before it was designed, and has a strange echo of Morris's description of the Hammersmith Guest House.

Lars Sonck (1870-1956) was even more austere in his urban work than the three partners. He started his practice with wooden houses in the countryside, initially in the Dragon Style, but later, for instance at Ainola built for Sibelius in 1903, in a more rational way. His St John's, Tampere (1902-07), is externally in a form of rationalized Gothic with austere planes of squared granite rubble** topped by needle-like

*J. M. Richards has pointed out that links with England were quite strong during the '90s, principally through Alfred William Finch Finch, the Anglo Belgian who taught at the Helsinki School of Applied Arts and commented regularly on the English scene in the *Ateneum*, the Finnish cultural magazine founded in 1898.[8]

**In looking for a material for their new architecture, the Finns found native granite to be more appropriate and cheaper than the brickwork common to the rest of Scandinavia. In seeking to find the best ways of using the stone, Hugo Lindberg (a member of the Tampere church competition jury) visited Aberdeen and produced a pamphlet on its uses in that city. Sonck's use of the material was based on Lindberg's findings.[12]

Gesellius, Lindgren and Saarinen. Hvitträsk, nr Helsinki, Finland (1901-03), growing out of the body of Finland. Saarinen's house in foreground

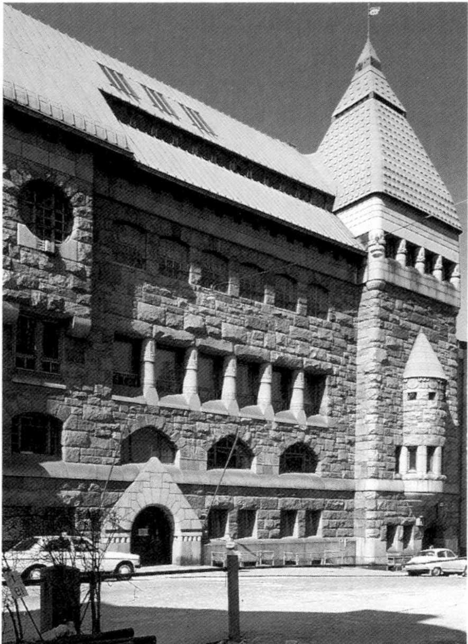

Lars Sonck. Telephone Company offices, Helsinki (1905). Granite was seen to be the national material

Gesellius, Lindgren and Saarinen. Finnish National Museum, Helsinki (1905-12). A built manifesto for a nation struggling for independence

towers. Internally, the whole space is one, dominated by a shallow and daring brick vault. The interior is richly decorated with powerful symbolic frescos by Hugo Simberg and Magnus Enckell, and all the fittings were designed by the architect, the artists or artist-craftsmen, in a similar creative relationship to the one set up by Prior at Roker.

Sonck's rough squared granite was used in his Helsinki telephone exchange (1903-05) where it seems quite brutal in the politely stuccoed street. The asymmetrical elevation with a copper roofed tower at one end is banded horizontally by rows of windows. They were either arched or, on the main floor, capped with rectangular lintels propped by circular columns, the abstracted capitals of which bear almost the whole of the building's simple deeply incised geometric ornament. There is irony in the Romanesque overtones of this building and of the National Museum, for Finland had no Romanesque tradition. National Romantic architects were not only fired by Puginian fidelity to place, they were quite happy to take and reinterpret themes from the architecture of other nations: even Nyrop's Copenhagen town hall was consciously modelled on Siena's Palazzo Pubblico.

In Sweden, the new architecture was powerfully expressed in the Engelbrektskyrkan, Stockholm (1912) by Lars Israel Wahlman (1870-1952). It stands awe-inspiringly high on a bluff, a group of tall brick volumes topped by tiled roofs and dominated by a high brick tower with an elaborate gilded copper crown. The brick was founded on a roughly tooled granite base and is relieved by panels in sandstone by Arthur Gerle and Tone Strindberg. Inside, there is a feeling of medieval precedent, but the timber roof of the nave is carried on parabolic arches, and the whole, although outwardly seeming Gothic, is a single great columnless space like Sonck's Tampere. Some of the stone reliefs are gilded in contrast to the lightly plastered walls, through which the brick is allowed to give its texture. There is a great fresco in the choir by Olle Hjortzberg. The whole place was intended to be a simultaneous celebration of the generosity of Lutheranism and an evocation of the nature of Swedishness. Wahlman believed that 'The church asks only to be honest to itself...Not a single unnecessary mass is there, every stress, be it of wall or framework, is conveyed by a well calculated route down to the firm rock. Each material displays its nature. Practically nothing is dressed and nothing seeks to appear finer than it is. That is the Nordic, the basic Gothic principle in the art of building (though the style is not Gothic)'.[13] Pugin's teachings had been reinterpreted for the northern cultures in a more scientific age.

There are several other virtually contemporaneous churches of almost equal majesty in Sweden, notably the Masthuggskyrkan in Gothenberg by Sigfrid Ericson and the Höglandskyrkan in Stockholm by Ivar Tengbom. The new free-style was vigorously applied to secular buildings as well, for instance the Gothenberg telephone exchange (an important new building type in the early twentieth century) by Hans and Björner Hedlund in which a very changeful brick superstructure was made over a tough, solid granite base, just like the churches.

But the most splendid of all the northern secular works was the

Lars Sonck. St John's, Tampere, Finland (1902-07). Now the Cathedral

Tampereen
Johanneksen Kirkon
Piirustus

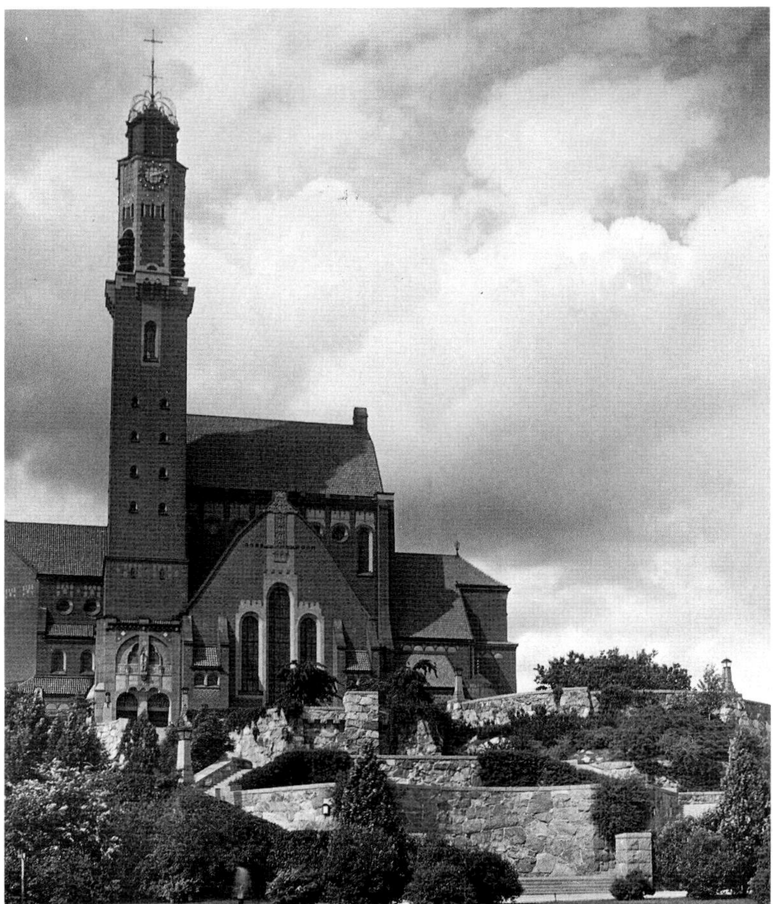

Lars Israel Wahlman. Engelbrektskyrkan, Stockholm (1912). A celebration of the generosity of Lutheranism and the nature of Swedishness

Stockholm town hall, built between 1909 and 1923 by Ragnar Östberg (1866-1945). Like Arneberg, Östberg was a devoted restorer of old buildings (for instance the hall of state in Uppsala castle). In the Stockholm building he mixed much traditional Swedish detail with themes from Gothic and Byzantine architecture.

The ceremonial centre of civic life stands reflected in the waters of lake Mälar, a four-square block of plum coloured brick on rows of Byzantine arches that open the court to views of the lake. Capped with a curving green copper roof, it is pinned down by a huge tapering tower in one corner. (Nyrop was on the jury again, but the shape of the tower is supposed to have been influenced by Sonck, who was a friend of Östberg).[14] Inside, the glory of many splendid spaces is the Golden Hall, a secular cathedral lined with glowing gold mosaic which focuses on a great hieratic mosaic figure of the Queen of the Mälar (Stockholm) by Einar Forseth, stiff and powerful in both Byzantine and Arts and Crafts traditions.

The process of building this magnificent monument would have delighted Morris. Östberg recalled that 'studios and workshops for sculpture, painting, iron and copper-work, wood-carving, the designing of textiles, furniture patterns, decorative work and models of the building, all these were fitted up in the interior of the building. As all these various workers, architects, sculptors, painters, art workers in copper and iron, designers of textiles, carpenters and stone masons were working in close contact with the building under erection and its various premises, their co-operation yielded the most happy results. The lighting, the proportions, the relative positions of the rooms could be considered in conjunction, and could receive their due in the general designs. The close proximity of the model studios and the art workshops to the architect's office and the building site facilitated continuous unity of operations. Work of wrought iron and hammered copper as well as stone sculpture was tested in model form on the very spot before final execution in the workshop. Moreover, the iron and copper workshops were often supplied merely with designs giving the measurements and the general lines of composition, it being left to them to determine the execution in detail'.[15]

Östberg had made possibly the finest public building that Arts and Crafts thinking ever produced: a fusion of all the visual arts in which individual craftsmen had their freedom; a reinterpretation for the twentieth century of Swedish myth and tradition enriched by a deep understanding of materials and their proper expression. It is ironic that many of the glories of the Stockholm town hall were made possible by donations from Swedish businessmen who had been enriched by the First World War, which finally killed the Arts and Crafts movement in Britain.

In the three decades from 1880, links between Dutch and Scandinavian architecture were quite strong. For example, the pivotal architect of the Dutch anti-Classical movement, Hendrik Petrus Berlage (1856-1934) worked initially for the engineer Theodore Sanders who had built in Copenhagen in 1881.[16] Though he practised for a time as a Renaissance architect, then as a formalist Goth, Berlage

Ragnar Östberg. Stockholm town hall (1909-23), the Golden Hall with mosaic of the Queen of the Malär by Einar Forseth

evolved a much more abstract, changeful and savage style in the '90s.

In the Amsterdam stock exchange (built 1898-1908), Berlage married the brick techniques of traditional Dutch architecture with thin metal trusses which carried the glazed roofs on the three main halls. Externally, the building is a large rectangle, anchored, like the Stockholm and Copenhagen town halls, by a big tower in one corner. But the fenestration of Berlage's building is much freer, with the shape and size of windows (generally) dictated by what was going on inside. The south and west elevations were decorous and appropriate for the texture of the old Amsterdam in which he was building. But Berlage let himself go on the east (service) side where a very changeful range is dominated by the chimney and ventilation tower. Internally, the masonry is modulated by strips of blue and yellow glazed brick, and by stone accents that highlight moments of drama in the structure. The recipe is very similar to that of Nyrop's town hall, but without the richness of detailed paintings and sculptures which told tales of the history and myths of the Danish people.

Berlage's use of brick in the '90s was a conscious return to roots and rejection of the architecture of stucco or stone. It was an inspiration to National Romantics of the next generation like Michel de Klerk (1884-1923), Piet Kramer (1881-1961) and Johan van der Mey (1878-1949). These architects came out of the office of Eduard Cuypers (1859-1927), Berlage's rival, an architect much influenced by the British movement, who had modelled his studio on the ideals of Morris and the Arts and Crafts workshops and who was building (pre-Classical) Norman Shaw influenced villas and country houses in the late 1890s.[17]

The young men, who with their friends were later to be collectively termed the Amsterdam School, were well aware of developments in England and Scandinavia. Michel de Klerk visited England in 1906 and tried unsuccessfully to get a job. In the same year, van der Mey went to Copenhagen, where he must have visited Nyrop's town hall, the most prestigious building of the time. On his own visit to the Danish capital in 1910, de Klerk sketched the stone story-telling sculpture and reliefs on the town hall.[18]

In 1912, van der Mey won the commission for the Scheepvaarthuis, the Amsterdam shipping office (completed 1916). He called on help from de Klerk and Kramer, and together they created a building that has some of the feeling of its counterpart in Copenhagen. It is encrusted with stone reliefs and sculpture which evoke myths of the sea all growing of and out of an austere brick backdrop. A great grey knobbly metal dragon-back caps the composition. The interiors and furniture, mainly by de Klerk and Kramer, blended English sensibilities with more curvaceous lines reminiscent of those used by the Belgian Art Nouveau architect Henry van de Velde.

The Scheepvaarthuis was van der Mey's masterpiece, and his later work was never as impressive. But his contemporaries flourished. Like the Scandinavian countries (except Finland, still a Grand Duchy of the Czar), the Netherlands were neutral in the First World War, and though resources were limited, building continued. Social housing in particular was developed with great originality. In a series of large

Östberg. The picturesque towers of Stockholm town hall

Johan van der Mey. Scheepvaarthuis, Amsterdam (1912-16). Encrusted with myths of the sea

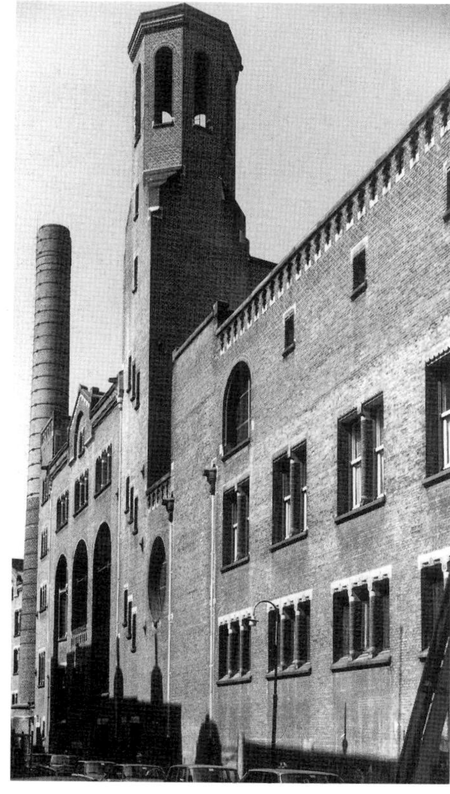

Berlage. Amsterdam stock exchange (1898-1908). Service side

Michel de Klerk. Housing Spaarndammerplantsoen (third block), Amsterdam (1917-21). Giving mass housing a sense of place

blocks on the Spaarndammerplantsoen, de Klerk evolved a new way of building for the working classes. The third block (1917-21) gave a great deal of individual variety (there were 15 different kinds of dwellings) which at the same time provided a strong sense of place for the whole community. In the court, the scale sometimes becomes almost cottage-like, but on the street sides, there is a more formal presence which, while giving due emphasis to individual dwellings, expresses the communal nature of the block and, with its strong horizontal lines, emphasizes the fact that it consists of flats. Accents and flourishes in, for instance, the post office at the apex of the plan and the thin brick tower at the other end, help to give the block memorable presence in the townscape. All is made in excellently crafted brickwork in the Dutch tradition. In its humanity, its changeful understanding of how to make social housing with a sense of place for both the individual and community, and its respect for building tradition the block is one of the last and most impressive examples of Arts and Crafts influenced social idealism in architecture.

At the same time, Amsterdam School architects were beginning to experiment with a wider palette of materials and range of building types. There was an estate of villas at Bergen started in 1917 where architects like C. J. Blaaw and F. J. Staal showed wonderful understanding of the sculptural properties of thatch.[19] After the War, large-scale housing developments were built in south Amsterdam which was being developed to municipally commissioned plans by Berlage,[20] with contributions by de Klerk, Kramer, Staal and other members of the school. In 1922, experiments started in Betondorp, a large housing scheme which suggested that concrete construction could be given a sense of individuality and the particular.[21]

F. J. Staal. Country house, De Bauk, Park Meerwijk, Bergen (1917-18). The sculptural properties of thatch

Work at Betondorp continued until 1926, but Michel de Klerk had died on his 39th birthday in 1923. The spark that had lit the Amsterdam School's fire was extinguished and the spectacular blaze died down quite quickly. The School's magazine, *Wendingen*, staggered on until 1931, but by then, Dutch architecture was dominated by the *sachlich* rigours of the De Stijl movement.

1 *Ashbee, C. R. 'Frank Lloyd Wright: a Study and an Appreciation' reprinted in Kaufmann, Edgar* Frank Lloyd Wright, the Early Work, *Horizon, New York, 1968, p7.*

2 *Singelenberg, Pieter* H. P. Berlage, Idea and Style, *Utrecht, 1972, p149.*

3 *Guimard, Hector* Architectural Record, *Vol XII, 1902, p127. Guimard was identifying the sources of Art Nouveau for an American audience.*

4 *For the argument on Richardson's influence on European architecture see Eaton, Leonard K.* American Architecture Comes of Age. European Reaction to H. H. Richardson and Louis Sullivan, *MIT Press, Cambridge Mass and London, 1972.*

5 *Voysey, C. F. A. in 'L'Art Nouveau: a Symposium',* The Magazine of Art, *Vol II, 2nd series, 1904, p212.*

6 *Grønvold, Ulf (ed)* Frederik Konow Lund, arkitekten som moret seg, *Norsk arkitekturforlag, Oslo, 1989.*

7 *Pallasmaa, Juhani (ed)* Hvitträsk, the Home as a Work of Art, *Museum of Finnish Architecture, Helsinki, 1987, gives a detailed history of the genesis and subsequent life of the house on pp115-120.*

8 *Richards, J. M,* 800 years of Finnish Architecture, *David and Charles, Newton Abbot, 1978, pp116-117.*

9 *Lindgren, Armas in* Teknikern, *Vol CCLXXXVII, 1902, p229. Quoted in Nikula, Riitta,* Armas Lindgren 1874-1929, *Museum of Finnish Architecture, Helsinki, 1988, p148.*

10 *Nikula,* ibid, *p154.*

11 *Vårt Land, 1900 quoted in Nikula,* ibid, *p153.*

12 *Pallasmaa, Juhani (ed),* Lars Sonck 1870-1956, *Museum of Finnish Architecture, Helsinki, 1981, p49.*

13 *Lind, Sven Ivar and others (eds)* Verk av L. I. Wahlman, *AB Tidskriften Byggmästaren, Stockholm, 1950, p194.*

14 *Pallasmaa,* Lars Sonck, op cit, *p121.*

15 *Östberg, Ragnar* The Stockholm Town Hall, *P. A. Norstedt & Söner, Stockholm, 1929, pp28-30.*

16 *Polano, Sergio (ed)* Hendrik Petrus Berlage, Complete Works, *Butterworth, Guildford, 1988, p103.*

17 *For English (and other) influences on Cuypers, and for his on his pupils, see Searing, Helen 'Berlage or Cuypers? The Father of Them All', in* In Search of Modern Architecture: A Tribute to Henry-Russell Hitchcock, *ed Helen Searing, MIT Press, Cambridge, Mass. and London, 1982, pp226-244.*

18 *For connections between Scandinavia and the Amsterdam School see de Wit, Wim (ed)* The Amsterdam School, Dutch Expressionist Architecture 1915-1930, *Cooper-Hewitt Museum, New York and MIT Press, Cambridge, Mass. and London, 1983, pp126-128.*

19 Ibid, *pp59-63.*

20 *Polano,* op cit, *pp165-168.*

21 *The housing work of the school is summarized in Gaillard, Karin* The Amsterdam School and Public Housing, *in de Wit,* op cit, *pp145-158.*

6 7 8 9 10 11 12 1 2 3
6 5 4 3
DER TAG GEHT
ÜBER MEIN GESICHT
DIE NACHT SIE
TASTET LEIS VORBEI
UND TAG UND NACHT
EIN GLEICHGEWICHT
UND NACHT UND TAG
EIN EINERLEI
UND EWIG KREIST
DIE SCHATTENSCHRIFT
LEBLANG STEHST DU
IM DUNKLEN SPIEL
BIS DICH DES SPIELES
DEUTUNG TRIFFT
DIE ZEIT IST UM
DU BIST AM ZIEL

The central problem

18

In the middle of all these nationalistic architectural movements was Germany, and by the early 1900s, there too, many were calling for an architecture which could clearly be identified as German. Hermann Muthesius, for example, ended his introduction to *Das englische Haus* by urging his countrymen to 'face our own conditions squarely and as honestly as the English face theirs today, to adhere to our own artistic tradition as faithfully, to embody our customs and habits in the German house as lovingly'.[1]

Muthesius's own architecture in the years following his return to Germany was a blend of English and German. He rapidly built up a flourishing country house practice in which he incorporated abstractions of local traditional idioms.[2] His plans were based to some extent on English models, often with double-height halls, but he never used the long thin layout beloved of the Arts and Crafts people, and the hall tended to become a focus for circulation rather than a living room in itself. For instance, his mansion built for Hermann Freudenberg at Nikolassee, Berlin (1907-08) appears at first sight to be a Prior butterfly house covered with north German timbering and high tiled roofs. But inside, the layout is quite different from the English type; much more compacted, and given to German grandiose gestures. Before the War, Muthesius had extended his practice to factories and workers' housing; terraces of the latter in Hellerau Garden City bear more than a passing resemblance to Voysey's cottages at Whitwood, but are modified with local German details.

Joseph Maria Olbrich. Mosaic sundial, Hochzeitsturm, Matildenhöhe (1906)

Even while Muthesius was writing his great book, architects like Paul Schultze-Naumburg (1869-1949) and his pupil Heinrich Tessenow (1876-1950) were designing simple villas and cottages in the north German tradition with white walls, pierced where necessary by shuttered windows, sometimes tied together by simple rectilinear half-timbering. These deliberately humble and atavistic buildings were expressions of the northern European romantic search for roots that had started with Old English 40 years before. In 1904, Schultze-Naumburg was one of the founders of the Bund für Heimatschutz, an association devoted to preserving and fostering traditional ways of life and building throughout the newly formed empire. It was opposed to the culture of large cities, which it castigated as non-German, and was keen to ensure that buildings were made with local materials and methods to preserve local economies and ways of life.

It had remarkable successes in promoting conservation legislation, particularly in Prussia, and in craft education. Results in architecture were naturally very varied, ranging from the chaste north German work of Tessenow to, for instance, the Town Hall at Löwenberg in Silesia by Hans Poelzig (1869-1936). This fitted admirably into the medieval higgledy-piggledy pattern of the sleepy little Silesian country town with its great sweeping tiled roofs over a low arcade of round arches. Everything was derived from local precedent, yet abstracted and combined with a flair for plastic handling of form that presages Poelzig's flowering in the '20s as an Expressionist architect. Similarly in Hamburg (though a great city), Fritz Höger (1877-1949) was experi-

Hermann Muthesius. House for Hermann Freudenberg at Nikolassee, Berlin (1907-08)
Right: Floor plans. Butterfly planning with a Prussian accent

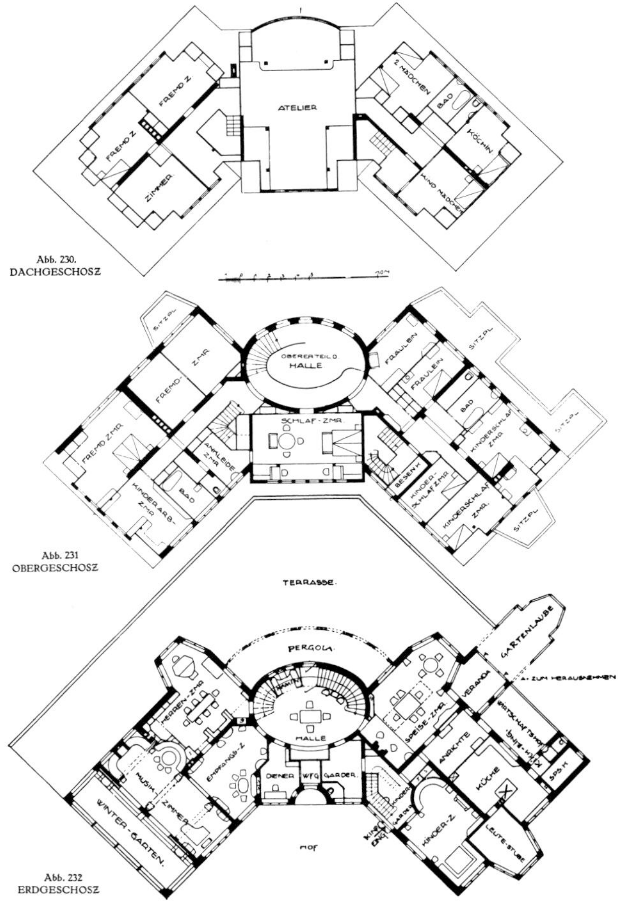

menting with ways of making commercial and residential buildings based on traditional Hanseatic models which were to lead to his amazingly rich post-war brick office blocks.

Heimatschutz thinking plainly had many parallels with the teachings of Pugin and Morris, though these were largely ignored or suppressed in a movement which eschewed foreign influences. There were much more direct links between Britain and the German-speaking countries at the turn of the century. Baillie Scott and Ashbee were working on the Grand Duke of Hesse's palace in Darmstadt in 1897-98. Their designs and those of Voysey and Mackintosh were illustrated in German and Austrian magazines. In 1899, Mackintosh exhibited in Munich, and in November 1900, he and Ashbee showed work (Mackintosh and the Scottish group had a whole room) at the Vienna Secession exhibition.*

In December the same year, the Darmstadt magazine *Zeitschrift für Innerndekoration* launched a competition for a house for an art lover *'ein herrschaftliches Wohnhaus eines Kunstfreundes'*.[3] No first prize was awarded but Baillie Scott got the largest premium, even though his elevations, which incorporated Scottish baronial drum towers, half-timbering and curious, elegant parabolic gables were judged to be lacking in the modern spirit. They made a butterfly plan of no great size look like a castle. Mackintosh was awarded a special prize, though he did not submit enough drawings to qualify (or even with enough consistency to make a coherent building). His elevations were a development of Windyhill: austere planes of white harling punctuated irregularly by windows all of which had small square panes. The plan was basically rectangular: a compressed and elegant version of the long, thin Arts and Crafts layout extending sideways from a double-height gallery hall.

The interiors of the two schemes were radically different. Scott used dark internal half-timbering (as he had done in the Blackwell hall) enlivened by a simple, diagonal, coloured pattern on the edges of the beams, and flowers and painted figures on the walls – very much in the Morris tradition. Mackintosh's music room was white and fine-drawn with tapering pilasters and an elaborate thin, Celticly curving, yet symmetrical screen over the piano, the focus of the space.

There was a clear affinity between the work of the British and Secession designers. Josef Hoffmann (1870-1956) was at this time in his career closest to the British. His first house, the Villa Henneberg near Vienna (1900), echoed the plane walls and irregularly placed small paned windows of the English school. It even had a (partly) double-height hall, though the plan was compressed into a square round it rather than being strung out in the British fashion. In 1901, Fernand Khnopff remarked in *The Studio* (which was very much aware of events abroad as well as at home) that Hoffmann 'is essentially rational and reasonable in all he does. His compositions are never extravagant, never intentionally loud, as are those of his more Western

*The Secession was an association founded in 1897 by artists like Klimt, Olbrich, Moser and Hoffmann in rebellion against the academic management of the Kunstlerhaus. It included virtually all the Austrian artists of the Jugendstil (the Germanic contemporary of Art Nouveau), and its exhibitions were similar in content to those of the Arts and Crafts Exhibition Society.

confrères. He confines himself to...proportion and decoration, and thus is enabled to add to the beauty of the original lines of construction without addition and without alteration'.[4] One of Hoffmann's clearest debts to Britain is shown in his Haus Moll II (1904), built in Hohe Warte, a northern suburb of Vienna. There, a pyramidally-topped two-storey block, clad in hung slates, is in the process of engulfing an early version of Voysey's Bedford Park tower house, shaved of its bay but complete with smoothly rendered white walls, shallow curved metal roof and small paned windows pressing up against the eaves.*

Hoffmann's closest personal links were with Mackintosh. Hoffmann and Mackintosh designed rooms for Fritz Wärndorfer's house in 1902. The two architects corresponded, and Hoffmann visited Mackintosh in Glasgow. On the trip, he went to see Ashbee's Guild of Handicraft at Essex House and, full of the experience, he set up the Wiener Werkstätte in 1903. His partners were Koloman Moser (1868-1918), who taught with him at the Kunstgewerbeschule, C. O. Czeschka and D. Peche. Their sponsor was Wärndorfer. Mackintosh wrote to Hoffmann on 17 March 1903, a couple of months before the organisation was launched, saying that 'If one wants to achieve an artistic success with your programme...every object which you pass from your hand must carry an outspoken mark of individuality, beauty and most exact execution. From the outset your aim must be that every object which you produce is made for a certain purpose and place. Later...you can emerge boldly into the full light of the world, attack the factory-trade, and the greatest work that can be achieved in this century, you can achieve it: namely the production of objects of use in magnificent form and at such a price that they lie within the buying range of the poorest...

'Yes – the plan which Hoffmann and Moser have designed is great and splendidly thought through...all I can say is: begin today! – If I were in Vienna, I would assist with a great strong shovel!'[5] The nearest Mackintosh got to the shovel was the design of an elegant colophon for the Werkstätte.

Two years later, the *Arbeitsprogramm der Wiener Werkstätte* by Hoffmann and Moser announced that the organization's message was 'a welcoming call for those who invoke the name of Ruskin and Morris...We cannot and we do not wish to compete with cheap production; this above all is made at the worker's expense, whilst we consider that our first duty is to give him happiness in his work, and a life worthy of a man'.[6]

The Werkstätte's most important commission was far from being within the buying range of the poorest. The Palais Stoclet was built in Brussels between 1905 and 1911 for a rich art collector who had lived in Vienna. Externally, the house was changeful, building up to a rectilinear stair tower. It continued Hoffmann and Mackintosh's theme of small paned windows set in plain white walls. But the planes were cre-

*British influence in Austria spread further than the Secessionists. One of the sternest critics of Secessionist wilfulness, Adolf Loos (1870-1933), whose ingenious space planning and hostility to arbitrary ornament earned him the reverence of Modern Movement architects of the next generation, designed cosy interiors complete with inglenooks and (often fake) exposed ceiling beams. Even his Haus am Michaelerplatz (1910), a block of flats on top of a store in the middle of Vienna's old city, has a row of Mackintosh-like small paned recessed bay windows between the giant Tuscan columns of the ground floor and the smoothly stripped upper storeys.

Muthesius. Silk factory for Michelk & Cie, Nowawes, nr Potsdam (1912)

Mackintosh. Entry for *'Ein herrschaftliches Wohnhaus eines Kunstfreundes'* competition (1900)

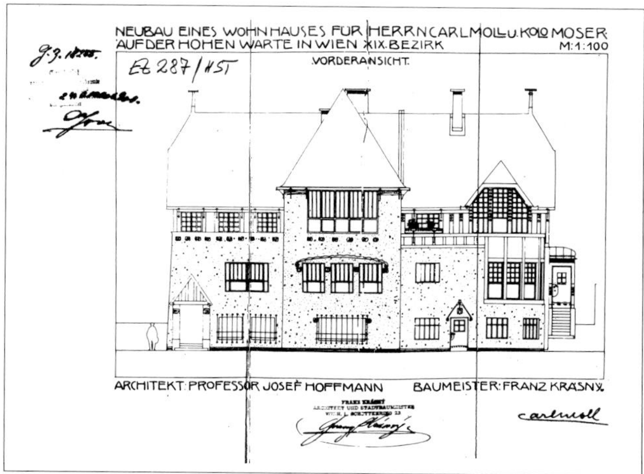

Hoffmann. The Moser and Moll houses, 6-8 Steinfeldgasse, Hohe Warte (1900-01). Street front

Hoffmann/Wiener Werkstätte. Palais Stoclet, Brussels (1905-11)

Palais Stoclet, Brussels. One of the most luxurious houses of its age. Dining room with Klimt mosaics

ated in sheets of sawn pale grey Norwegian granite, not simple Scottish harling, and the whole building was tied together by an ornate bronze band which ran round every corner of the complex silhouette. The regular vertical windows of the main block give the impression that Palais Stoclet is basically a Classical building, carved up and added to rather against its will, instead of one which has grown out of the clash of inner functions which Mackintosh expressed so beautifully in his entry for the Haus Kunstfreundes.

Inside, the plan has some resemblance to Mackintosh's. The Werkstätte skills were used to their full in the most luxurious of materials, marbles and woods from all over Europe. An etiolation and refinement, similar to Mackintosh's but stripped of his sinuous curves, tapers and witty incidents, form the dominating impression. The furniture and wall surfaces have the overriding rectilinearity of Hoffmann's work except in the dining room, which is enlivened by the complex geometry and brilliant colour of two mosaics by Hoffmann's fellow Secessionist, Gustav Klimt. The house was a *Gesamtkunstwerk*, a total work of art. From the garden to the knives and forks, everything was designed by the partners and made by the hundred craftsmen the workshop was employing by this time.

The Wiener Werkstätte was one of many communities in Germany and Austria. Some, like Karl Schmidt's Dresden Werkstätte für Handwerkskunst (founded 1898), were businesses like the Morris Firm – others were much more idealistic like Ashbee's Guild.

In 1899 Ernst Ludwig, the Grand Duke of Hesse, always indefatigable in his pursuit of the Arts and Crafts,* decided to form an artists' colony at Matildenhöhe in Darmstadt to act as an inspiration for German design. He called on an Austrian, Joseph Maria Olbrich (1867-1908) to act as chief architect for the colony and for the exhibition held in 1901 to celebrate its foundation and hopes for the artistic future of Hesse.** Olbrich was a Secessionist and had designed the group's exhibition gallery in Vienna. He was responsible for the Darmstadt colony's houses and the Ernst Ludwig building, a combination of studios and bachelor quarters in the middle of the complex. W. Fred, reviewing the colony's exhibition, *Ein Dokument Deutscher Kunst*, in *The Studio*, enthused that 'For the first time we are able to take a survey of the extent of art-handicraft. For everything, from the architecture of the exterior to the laid out table and the coverlet of the bed in every house, has been entirely designed by the artist and executed under his supervision'.[8]

Besides Olbrich, the colony included Peter Behrens (1868-1940),

J.M. Olbrich. Ernst Ludwig Haus, Darmstadt

*Ernst Ludwig was a grandson of Queen Victoria, who after the early death of her daughter, made herself responsible for his education, so he spent part of nearly every year in England when he was young. Alfred Lichtwark, the director of the Hamburg art gallery described him as having the 'urbanity of a German officer of rank and the artistic culture of an English gentleman'. [7] How the Grand Duke became aware of the English Arts and Crafts movement is unclear, when it was totally ignored by the British Royal Family, and indeed by many English gentlemen. But his decision to involve Ashbee and Baillie Scott in his own palaces doubtless came from his close connections with Britain, and from that choice followed much of his own development as a patron.

**Olbrich was another Anglophile – for instance, he managed to spend half his Rome scholarship travelling in England. He and Hoffmann were close; both studied under Austria's Norman Shaw, Otto Wagner (1841-1918), and when Olbrich moved to Darmstadt, Hoffmann took over his commissions for houses at Hohe Warte.

Olbrich. Ernst Ludwig Haus, Matildenhöhe. The centrepiece of the 1901 Darmstadt exhibition

painter, designer and architect (he was the only other artist who designed his own house), two sculptors, a designer and two painters. Fred emphasized that 'Education by means of art-handicraft, not by dilettantism, but by the daily use of household furniture and utensils, is the special desire of those who in Germany and Austria are fighting for the new art'.[9]

Olbrich. Hochzeitsturm (Wedding Tower), Matildenhöhe (1906). Ernst Ludwig's most striking addition to the Matildenhöhe complex, to celebrate his second marriage

Olbrich's houses varied from free reinterpretations of traditional German styles, with big gabled roofs of blue slates and red tiles on top of white walls relieved by stencilling in chequerboard and stylized tree patterns, through an almost Art Nouveau freedom to a severe rectilinear essay in which small paned windows irregularly pierced smooth walls, themselves capped with pronounced mortar-board roofs. His Ernst Ludwig Haus was a composition in strong horizontals with small paned windows symmetrically set about a great, ornate semi-circular door which was flanked by giant free-standing nude statues of a man and a woman.

The Darmstadt colony was crowned by the Hochzeitsturm (wedding tower) designed in 1906 to celebrate Ernst Ludwig's second marriage. It is topped with the abstracted shape of the upraised palm of a hand, with curved copper cascading round the fingers at the top. The square brick shaft is strapped in a most changeful manner with horizontal bands of windows partially wrapping round the structure and stands above a delightful formal grove of plane trees on a terrace enriched with reliefs and statues by Bernhard Hoetger. It was Olbrich's most original work and one of his last.

Grand Duke Ernst Ludwig's aim in setting up the Darmstadt colony was to improve the quality of art and design in Hesse – and thence in all Germany. Another German ruler, the Grand Duke of Saxony, made a bid for design leadership when he appointed the Belgian Art Nouveau architect and designer Henry van de Velde (1863-1957) as head of the school of Arts and Crafts at Weimar in 1902. This grand-ducal competition was not just a matter of late feudal one-upmanship.* Germans regarded good design as vital for the future of the fatherland. Like Britain, Germany was facing tariff walls, but Germany lacked the enormous resources of the British colonies to feed on and sell to. So German products had to sell on quality – but their reputation was not high.

Muthesius commented in 1907 that 'in architecture we rank as the most backward country in Europe, because German taste in general is regarded as being at the very bottom of the ladder. In fact our artistic reputation has sunk so low that "German" and "bad taste" have become practically synonymous'.[11]

In the same Berlin speech, Muthesius pointed out that 'helping the modern movement is by no means a commercially unsound proposition. The large number of industrialists who followed the new path as a logical decision have obtained significant financial success. It is enough to mention the Dresdener Werkstätten für Handwerkskunst, which in the space of eight years developed from very humble begin-

*Nor was it limited to these two grand dukes; as Wolfgang Pehnt has pointed out, Karlsruhe, Düsseldorf and Berlin merged their academies of art and their schools of craft at about the same time as Weimar.[10]

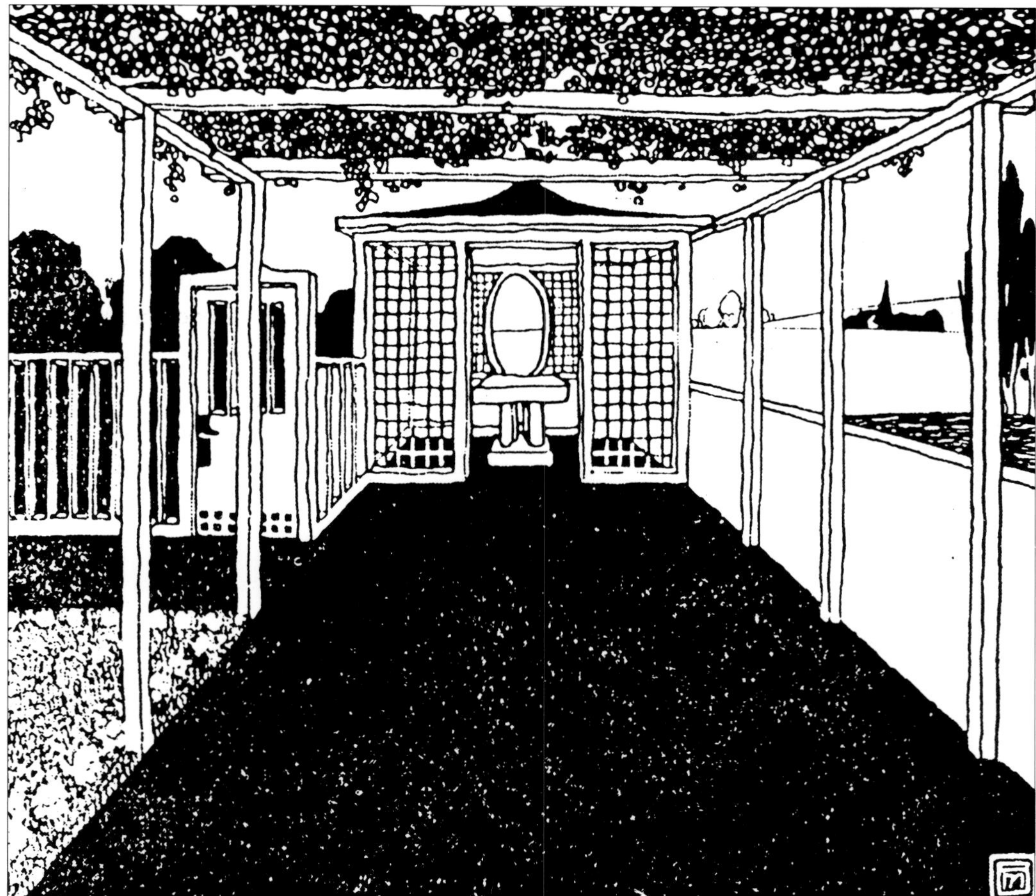

Max Benirschke. Sketch of a garden (c1905). Austrian adaptation of English theme by a member of the Hoffmann school

nings into a concern with a colossal turnover, capable of employing hundreds of carpenters'.[12]

Later in 1907, Muthesius, Olbrich and others were instrumental in founding the Deutscher Werkbund, an organization which brought together architects, artists, designers, industrialists and men from the Werkstätten with the expressed aim of improving German products. In the same year, Peter Behrens of the Darmstadt community was appointed as design consultant to one of the Werkbund's strongest industrial supporters, the great Allgemeine Elektrizitäts Gesellschaft of Berlin. Besides design of the buildings and the products, he was made responsible for all visual aspects of the company's efforts, down to even the writing paper.

There was little question that machinery should not be used to the full. Morris's teaching that working with machines made men into slaves was rejected in the pursuit of economic success for the German nation. Indeed, most members of the Werkbund held that the workers' lot would be greatly improved by an efficient and profitable industrial base. But the arts and crafts were held for a while in high regard as test-bed for product design and as a sort of conscience. In 1907, Muthesius believed that 'the arts and crafts are called on to restore an awareness of honesty, integrity and simplicity in contemporary society'.[13]* But by 1914, there was a huge row within the Werkbund between a party led by van de Velde which believed that the focus should be on the individual artist and craftsman, and an opposing group under Muthesius, which argued for the primacy of industry and the machine. The organization nearly broke up, but the imminence of war helped Muthesius's side to gain the upper hand.

In the 1913 edition of the Werkbund's yearbook, a young architect member, Walter Gropius (1883-1969) urged that 'The artist has the power to give the lifeless machine-made product a soul; it is his creative force that will live on, actively embodied in its outward form. His collaboration is not just a luxury, generously thrown in as an extra, it is an indispensable part of the industrial process and must be regarded as such'.[15]

Gropius was deeply interested in factory design, believing that 'a worker will find that a room well thought out by an artist, which responds to the innate sense of beauty we all possess, relieves the monotony of the daily task and he will be more willing to join in collective undertakings. If the worker is happy, he will take more pleasure in his duties and the productivity of the firm will increase'.[16] If workers were not to be freed of the tyranny of machine processes, they could at least be kept in order with the new architecture. A new factory building could be good for business too. Gropius was sharply critical of 'distorting the true character of the building by allowing it to masquerade in borrowed garments from an earlier period which have absolutely nothing in common with the sterner purposes of a factory. The good name of the firm can only suffer from a building got up in

*The attitude was common in the years just after the turn of the century. Even a machine worshipper like Wright believed that the Arts and Crafts shop should be the 'experimental station that would represent in miniature the elements of the great pulsating web of the machine'.[14]

Peter Behrens. Own house, Matildenhöhe, Darmstadt (1901). Behrens's first essay as an architect

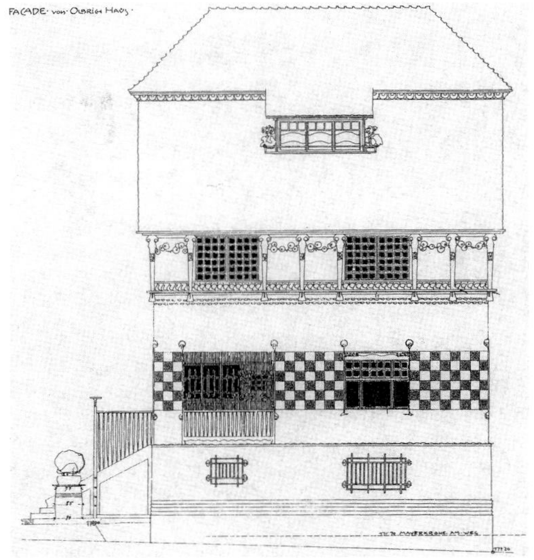

Olbrich. West elevation of own house in the Matildenhöhe colony (1901)

fancy dress'.[17] Gropius built several industrial buildings before the war, including a model factory at the Werkbund's big exhibition at Cologne in 1914. That was mostly of steel and glass – machine-made elements with craftsmanship reduced to an absolute minimum.*

But when Gropius was made successor to van de Velde at the Weimar School of Arts and Crafts in 1919** and turned it into the Bauhaus, the most renowned art school in the twentieth century, he put great stress on teaching the crafts. The first rule of the school was that the 'thorough training of all students in the crafts provides the unifying foundation'.[18] It was one of the last manifestations of the notion, shared by Ashbee, Wright and Muthesius, that the crafts should be the conscience of industry: the early Bauhaus was in many ways a direct descendant of Lethaby's Central School. Nevertheless, Gropius was wedded to machines, so much so that in 1922 he wrote to his fellow Bauhaus masters praising the work of 'young artists...beginning to face up to the phenomena of industry and the machine. They try to design what I would call the "useless" machine'.[19]

*Apart from contributions by Gropius with his partner Meyer and one or two other architects who built with new materials and an understanding of their potential, most of the other Werkbund pavilions at Cologne were vaguely Classical. Hoffmann, Behrens and even Muthesius, who had so sorrowfully chronicled Norman Shaw's conversion to Classicism, all produced buildings with overtly Classical elevations. Hoffmann's conversion to Classicism had begun some years earlier. For instance his Haus Ast (1910), next door to Haus Moll II, is fluted like a flattened out Doric column pierced by regular rows of windows and topped with a Classical cornice covered with curving Celtic ornament.

**Eckhart Muthesius, Hermann's son, told me that Gropius owed his position to Muthesius's recommendation. Eckhart, incidentally, was godson of Mackintosh and Frank Newbery (head of the Glasgow School of Art in the first decade of the century).

So the wheel had turned, and William Morris was stood on his head. Instead of the machine being the hated brutalizer of humanity, it was held to be the prime focus of artistic inspiration. The Modern Movement in architecture was being born, and, over the next 50 years, standardization, machine worship and distrust of the craftsman gradually became some of the dominating themes of architecture, particularly in the *sachlich* wing of the Movement, dominated by rationalist architects from the Netherlands and Germany. By 1927, Ludwig Hilberseimer (who was about to become a senior master at the Bauhaus) could say that 'the necessity of moulding a heterogeneous and often gigantic mass of material according to a formal law equally valid for each element involves a reduction of architectonic form to its most modest, necessary, and general requirement: a reduction, that is, to cubic geometric forms'.[20] All sense of place, history and individuality was to be denied in the struggle to make a world suitable for the smooth running of industrialized culture.

Though gentler principles like fidelity to place were eschewed, a few Arts and Crafts ideals were taken on board by even the tough side of the Modern Movement. Changefulness, for instance, was embraced by some Modern Movement architects, and when the Bauhaus moved to Dessau in 1925, the new building was carefully designed by Gropius to show the difference between living quarters, studios, offices and workshops in a Manx wheel plan with three thin limbs spreading from an ill-defined centre.

The Modern Movement took over the Arts and Crafts dislike of

Olbrich. Dreihäusergruppe. The only permanent building from the 1904 Matildenhöhe exhibition. The group actually consisted of four houses

Aldolf Loos. Living room design (1899). Loos, though he attacked the British-influenced Secessionists, was himself devoted to Arts and Crafts motifs

Heinrich Tessenow. House for an artisan (1906). Simple rural Heimatschutz

period styles (though not its reverence for tradition). Modern Movement architects became fanatical in their hatred of overt expressions of the past. But in their dominant idea that form should follow function, which had been so clearly spelled out by Pugin in his doctrine of propriety, they continued the Arts and Crafts horror of shams – at least theoretically (though many early Modern Movement buildings were built of brick made to look like concrete, just as many Arts and Crafts buildings were given fake half-timbering). And the Movement inherited a kind of social idealism; but, while the socialism of Morris had been concerned to liberate everyone, that of the Modern Movement was concerned with standardization and minimal norms, with only the architect free to decide how people should live. The Puginian paradox was finally and brutally resolved, with the designer in complete control and the craftsman reduced to the status of fitter and machine minder.

In the '30s, the Modern Movement was largely banished from Germany* by the Nazi government which, in reaction, reintroduced some of the ideas shared by the Arts and Crafts movement and the National Romantics of the turn of the century.

Art and architecture were, of course, subject to close supervision by the Nazis, perhaps closer than other branches of intellectual endeavour, because of Hitler's own artistic pretensions. He took the arts very seriously: 'I am convinced that art, since it forms the most uncorrupt-

*Leading lights of the Modern Movement fled to England, then to America, where they found their machine worship remarkably acceptable in the land of Henry Ford.

ed, the most immediate reflection of the people's soul, exercises unconsciously by far the greatest influence on the masses of the people'.[21] Translated into Nazi jargon, echoes of Morris are clear.

The notion of the people – the *Volk* – was of great importance to the National Socialists who favoured two styles of architecture which were supposed to be easily understood by everyman. There was a stripped Classical style used for great public buildings by architects like Speer – a kind of architecture in which Hitler took particular interest. And, of less interest to party leaders was *völkisch* architecture, intended for the houses of the masses and based on the vernacular building of rural Germany.

The housing programme was almost identical to that of the Bund für Heimatschutz, which from its earliest years had been chauvinist and slightly racist. Schultze-Naumburg became an enthusiastic Nazi supporter, glorying in the peasant house as 'a reservoir of all genuine *völkisch* qualities', whose form was 'bound to the blood'.[22] Winfred Wedland, a professor at the Berlin Academy, celebrated the small house as 'the seed core of the *Volk*', in which 'everyone who builds...must feel the duty to do a small service for art, something to give a house a more beautiful character. This does not always have to be figures for the garden or a painting. A pair of carved beams or a carved door will do'.[23] It was a version of Lethaby's brown bread and dewy morning vision of architecture translated to Hansel and Gretel nightmare.

Many small *völkisch* houses were built all over Germany, often in small new settlements laid out on Garden City principles, but the most celebrated *völkisch* building was much grander. At Hermann Goering's Karinhall shooting lodge north of Berlin, a courtyard was enclosed by a thatched roof over white walls liberally besprinkled with antlers. The main reception room was a great German hall, focusing on a mighty fireplace complete with inglenook quite in the Arts and Crafts fashion.

Modern Movement critics of the Arts and Crafts have sometimes made play with similarities between the work of Arts and Craftsmen and Nazi architects, implying some sort of guilt by association. Yet evil men may sometimes embrace noble ideals – that does not besmirch the ideals, it improves the men. *Völkisch* architecture can scarcely be added to the catalogue of crimes perpetrated by the Nazi state. Providing good, simple housing for the people was one of the few decent things that the Nazis did.

The same critics imply that, because the *sachlich* side of the Modern Movement was execrated by the Nazis, it is in some way essentially virtuous. But it was that strain of Modernism that housed ordinary working people in factory-like barrack blocks,* which so closely embraced the tyranny of the early twentieth-century machine, and wanted to reforge man in quite a new image, free of all the inherited detritus of the past. The final, paradoxical irony of the Arts and Crafts movement is that, devoted as it was to freedom and individuality, it should have been the reservoir for two such authoritarian streams as *völkisch* architecture and *sachlich* Modernism.

*I do not wish to suggest that the Nazis who tried to house the Volk in decent dwellings, yet slaughtered millions and kept starving slaves in work camps to help achieve that end, were in any way the moral peers of the protagonists of sachlich Modernism.

---

1 *Muthesius, Hermann* The English House, *trans Janet Seligman, Crosby Lockwood Staples, London, 1979, p11.*
2 *See* Landhäuser von Hermann Muthesius, *F. Bruckmann AG, Munich, 1912.*
3 *Kornwolf, James D.* M. H. Baillie Scott and the Arts and Crafts Movement, *Johns Hopkins Press, Baltimore and London, 1972, has a detailed discussion of the competition, pp216-238.*
4 *Khnopff, F.* The Studio, *Vol XXIV, 1901, p264.*
5 *Quoted by Seckler, Edward F. 'Mackintosh and Vienna',* The Architectural Review, *Vol CXLIV, 1968, p456.*
6 *Quoted by Godoli, Ezio in Russell, Frank (ed)* Art Nouveau Architecture, *Academy Editions, London, 1979, p251.*
7 *Quoted in Windsor, Alan* Peter Behrens, Architect and Designer, *Architectural Press, London, 1981, p14.*
8 *Fred, W.* The Studio, *Vol XXIV, 1902, p26.*
9 *Ibid, p95.*
10 *Pehnt, Wolfgang* Expressionist Architecture, *Thames & Hudson, London, 1973, p109.*
11 *Muthesius, Hermann 'The Meaning of the Arts and Crafts', lecture at Handelshochschule, Berlin, 1907. Translated in Benton, T. and C.* Form and Function, *Crosby Lockwood Staples, London, 1975, p40.*
12 Ibid, *p39.*
13 Ibid, *p38.*
14 *Wright, F. L. 'The Art and Craft of the Machine', in Frank Lloyd Wright* Writings and Buildings, *ed Kaufmann, E. and B. Raeburn, Horizon, New York, 1960, p70. This is the first full printing of the speech given at Hull House, Chicago on 20 March 1901.*
15 *Gropius, W. 'The Development of Modern Industrial Architecture'* Jahrbuch des Deutschen Werkbundes, *1913. Translated in Benton* op cit, *p53.*
16 Ibid, *p54.*
17 Ibid, *p53.*
18 *Gropius, W. 'The Statutes of the Staatliche Bauhaus in Weimar', translated in Wingler, H.M.* Bauhaus, *MIT Press, Cambridge, Mass. and London, 1978, p44.*
19 *Gropius, W. 'The Viability of the Bauhaus Idea', 1922, in Wingler* ibid, *p51.*
20 *Hilberseimer, Ludwig* Grossstadtarchitektur, *quoted in Tafuri, Manfredo* Architecture and Utopia, Design and Capitalist Development, *MIT Press, Cambridge, Mass. and London, 1979, p106.*
21 *Taylor, Robert R.* The Word in Stone, *University of California Press, Berkeley and London, 1974, p31. Taylor is quoting a 1933 remark.*
22 Ibid, *p224. The quotation is from a 1934 book by Schultze-Naumburg.*
23 Ibid, *p221. The quotation is from* Kunst und Nation, *1934.*

Postscript: looking back

There was a half century between the dark night of Nazism and the bright dewy English mornings of the 1880s and '90s when Arts and Crafts architecture was born. By the mid 1930s, the whole world had changed. Ideas of freedom had either atrophied or been transmuted into aids to prizing open the doors of Hell. Arts and Crafts architectural achievements had either been forgotten or commercialized and vulgarized in the suburbs.

Was Arts and Crafts architecture any more than a fashion of the rich: rich architects and designers toying with idealism and rich clients in search of a grand, yet undemonstrative, setting for their lives? Even Morris's own idealism verged at times on the absurd. Ford Madox Brown's grandson, Ford Madox Hueffer, recalled a meeting at Kelmscott House 'brought to an end by someone – I presume an Anarchist – putting red pepper in the stove. Poor William Morris, with his enormous mop of white hair, luxuriant white beard and nautical pea-jacket used to preside...He disliked the violence that was creeping into his beloved meetings. He had founded them solely with the idea of promoting human kindness and peopling the earth with large bosomed women dressed in Walter Crane gowns and bearing great sheaves of full-eared corn. On this occasion his air was most extraordinary as he fled uttering passionate sneezes that jerked his white hairs backwards and forwards like the waves of the sea'.[1]

There were no Walter Crane gowns and precious few ears of corn for ordinary building workers. Ruskin and Morris's ideals of free craftsmanship had little direct effect on the lives of most of the poor. Owen, the hero of *The Ragged Trousered Philanthropists*, Robert Tressell's semi-autobiographical novel of life in the building trade, explained the realities of life to his workmate Easton: 'when there's no work, you will either starve or get into debt. When – as at present – there is little work, you will live in a state of semi-starvation. When times are what you call "good", you will work for 12 or 14 hours a day and – if you're very lucky – occasionally all night. The extra money you then earn will go to pay your debts so that you may be able to get credit again when there's no work...

'In consequence of living in this manner, you will die at least 20 years sooner than is natural, or, should you have an unusually strong constitution and live after you cease to be able to work, you will be put in a kind of jail and treated like a criminal for the remainder of your life.'[2]

Owen was working for a jobbing decorator who never got contracts from anyone as grand as an Arts and Crafts architect. But the life of building labourers who did work on Arts and Crafts houses does not seem to have been very different. H. G. Wells was horrified by the work he saw on his Voysey-designed Spade House: 'It is a house built by hands – and some I saw were bleeding hands – just as in the days of the pyramids'.[3]

Of all the Arts and Crafts architects, only Ashbee made serious and consistent attempts to improve the lot of workmen. His effort failed because, to keep the work (so he believed) as interesting and creative as possible, he held machinery to a minimum and put a premium on handwork. So the products and buildings of the Guild of Handicraft were expensive and could only be bought by the rich. And then the rich turned away from modern work to buying antiques or to commercially made imitations. As D. S. MacColl, the editor of *The Architectural Review* wrote in 1903, 'It is not the inventor who usually gets the benefit of his idea. It is the shops, which straightway set their own designers or facile students from South Kensington to parody anything in which there seems to be a chance of money'.[4] Ashbee was in a trap: he could sell less and less to the rich, whose taste was changing, yet he could not fully embrace machine production and compete commercially – that would have been a betrayal of everything he believed in.

The conundrum was just as incapable of solution in architecture as it was in artifact production. Arts and Crafts architects usually charged extra for their special features like individually made ironwork, decorative schemes and furniture.* This meant that clients were paying a double premium – for having items made by hand which could (without sacrificing convenience) have been more cheaply bought from a mass produced range, and for the architect's special designs (usually charged as a percentage of the cost of production). Or the architect could reduce the client's bill by waiving charges for special designs – but if he did so, he could not make ends meet, as Goodhart-Rendel pointed out.

It was the individualness, the specialness, which stemmed from Ruskin's precepts of savageness and changefulness that priced Arts and Crafts architecture out. The wealth of the upper middle class was gradually being eroded and the systematic approach of the Classicists became cheaper (for one thing, its standardized details were capable of being produced by machines). The really International Style of the '20s and '30s was not the Modern Movement, as some historians have made out, but Classicism in different guises, ranging from the people's palaces of Russia and Germany to the quiet Neo-Colonial and Neo-Georgian of Anglo-Saxon suburbs. It was not until after the Second World War that the Modern Movement was victorious, when its apparent economies, achieved by elimination of hand labour whenever possible, were desperately needed in the labour-hungry former combatant nations.

Wells foresaw the change after his experiences at Spade House. In 1903, he called for a revolution in building with prefabrication, synthetic materials, electric central heating and self-making beds.[6] His vision was an early example of the building science fiction that dominated much Modern Movement thinking. Yet as we now see, and as Morris and many of his followers saw perfectly well at the time, substitution of crude machine production for handwork could improve life for workers little, if at all. Certainly it did away with the awfulness of the Rodmarton saw-pit. But, as building was increasingly made to approximate to machine production, workers fared little better than Tressell's contemporaries. Semi-starvation was obviated by increasingly humane legislation, yet workers were still subject to the demands of a notoriously erratic industry. And increasing systemization and mechanization ensured that they lost any opportunity for personal creativity. Even Tressell's Owen was allowed to work up and carry out occasional decorative schemes himself, one of the few things that made his life not absolutely bleak.

The only way in which Owen could have had a fundamentally better life and in which Ashbee could have escaped from his trap, the only hope of long term survival of Arts and Crafts building, was the revolution preached by William Morris. Arts and Crafts architecture flourished, briefly, in a time when labour was cheap. Only if labour could have been made free, as it was in *News from Nowhere*, could it have achieved full bloom. But none of Morris's immediate disciples backed his revolutionary socialism to the hilt. Even Ashbee held back. Morris himself remained a (benevolent) capitalist. Most Arts and Crafts people must, like Voysey, have shared with their clients a horror of radical social change.

If the Arts and Crafts movement had any coherence at all, it was concerned with the quality of life. The movement had no manifesto. It was far too varied in expression and approach to have a coherent style, for it encompassed Lethaby's Brockhampton church, Prior's Home Place, Mackintosh's art school, Voysey's Sanderson factory and Townsend's Horniman Museum. Yet virtually every Arts and Crafts architect would have agreed with Lethaby when he said that 'what I mean by art...is not the affair of a few but of everybody'.[7]

The Arts and Crafts people knew that quality of life depends on all five senses, and that it is to do with the experience of making and using artifacts. To improve quality, work and leisure, instead of being separated into different compartments as they were by the Industrial Revolution, should be more related to each other. Thinking and making should be brought closer together.

Everyone's ideal of the quality of life must be different. From that understanding sprang the great Arts and Crafts emphasis on individualness. The triumph, first of Classical architecture, then of the post-war Modern Movement with its emphasis on standardization and norms, ensured that individualness became less and less important, even ridiculous in an age of mass produced objects. The same emphasis on standardization and universality meant that the Arts and Crafts respect for locality and humility towards old buildings became regarded as sentimental whimsicality.

Now, some of the basic premises of the early Modern Movement are being questioned. The vandalism and decay associated with many post-war housing estates throughout the Western world are one indication of the falseness of that Movement's belief that satisfaction of people's material needs would in some way automatically ennoble humanity. The realization that supplies of materials are not infinite seriously calls into question the Movement's implicit belief that the whole world would be rebuilt in its image. The end of cheap energy must cast doubt on some of the Movement's theories of building production – for instance, centralized manufacture of bulky building components must become increasingly uneconomic as transport costs rise and pollution abatement becomes increasingly important.

* For instance, on the Waldbühl house, Baillie Scott charged no less than £560 worth of expenses and fees for special designs on top of the basic fee for the design of the house.[5]

While resources dwindle, machine production is entering a new phase. At last the subjugation of man to machine, which formed the Arts and Crafts movement's objection to machinery, may be nearly over. There is hope that people need no longer be at all involved in producing chains or planks or refrigerators or television sets. William Morris would surely have welcomed the microchip. In 1883, he wrote: 'I want modern science, which I believe to be capable of overcoming all material difficulties, to turn from such preposterous follies as the invention of anthracene colours and monster cannon to the invention of machines for performing such labour as is revolting and destructive of self-respect to the men who now have to do it by hand'.[8]

But while the new technology offers freedom from drudgery, it threatens to force millions into dole queues. At the moment, Western societies have no answer to the threat of vast unemployment – except that output will increase so greatly that somehow there will be enough machines for everyone to supervise. The prospect seems increasingly unlikely in an age of diminishing resources.

Against such a future, the Arts and Crafts belief in quality and individualness again seems relevant. The Arts and Crafts integration of work and leisure could be a basis for a humane future. In a small way the new life is already growing with the increased middle class interest in craftwork, cooking and gardening. The do-it-yourself explosion (though largely consisting of the assembly of crass commercial decorative products) is another and much more widespread example of a new attitude to work and leisure.

The roles of architect and designer in this kind of future would be much more advisory than directive. The need for very large new buildings will probably be much reduced in an age of advanced telecommunications (which are quite inexpensive in energy terms). So will the need to organize large teams. Sometimes by their own artistic example, more often by smoothing the path, architects and designers would help others to realize their own potential for creativity. To conserve resources, materials would be drawn from more local sources and old buildings be gently adapted, extended and cherished.

But there are many problems, and while we can learn from the ideals and practice of the Arts and Crafts movement, they must be continuously reinterpreted. For instance, the notion of regionalism, the idea that in a sea of homogenised commercialism, vigorous and satisfying cultures can be informed by local tradition, grew out of the Arts and Crafts belief in fidelity to place. It has many creative aspects, but as events in Northern Ireland and Bosnia have shown, there is a terrifying dark side to the ideal.

The proposal that technology will be able to relieve us of disagreeable tasks has in part proved true. But the increased productivity that cybernetics offers has largely been used to reduce the workforce and increase unemployment to levels which even a decade ago were unimaginable. At the same time, a culture of greed and quantity rather than quality (particularly in Britain) makes a decent society seem even further away than it was.

Where anything has been taken from the Arts and Crafts movement, it has usually been pretty forms, commoditized and applied without integrity to conceal the deficiencies of the most absurdly reductive buildings.

Yet we must not despair. It has become clear that certain strains of Modernism, particularly those most influenced by the Arts and Crafts movement, have much to offer in making humane and ecologically sustainable places to live and work in.

Architects cannot do much to influence society as the experience of the Arts and Crafts movement showed. But if we cease tending the flame of hope and drop the lamp of truth, we will betray our calling, which, as Pugin, Ruskin and Morris explained so well, is to improve the lot of humankind with imagination and love.

---

1 *Ford, Ford Madox 'The Spirit of an Age: the Nineties', originally published in* Return to Yesterday, *1932. Republished in the* Bodley Head Ford Madox Ford, *London, 1971, Vol V, p147. Ford Madox Hueffer changed his name to Ford Madox Ford during the First World War.*

2 *Tressell, Robert* The Ragged-Trousered Philanthropists, *Lawrence & Wishart, London, 1955, p139. Tressell died in 1911 of the deprivations he described so graphically.*

3 *Quoted in Mackenzie, Norman and Jean* The Time Traveller, *Weidenfeld & Nicolson, London, 1973, p149.*

4 *MacColl, D. S. 'The Arts and Crafts Exhibition',* The Architectural Review, *Vol XIII, 1903, p189.*

5 *See the back end papers of Medici-Mall, Katherina* Das Landhaus Waldbühl, *Gesellschaft für Schweizerische Kunstgeschichte, Bern, 1979.*

6 *Mackenzie* op cit, *p149.*

7 *Lethaby, W. R. 'Town Tidying', paper delivered to the Arts and Crafts Society, 1916, reprinted in* Form in Civilization, op cit, *p15.*

8 *Morris, William 'Art, Wealth and Riches', lecture 1883 to the Manchester Royal Institution,* Collected Works, op cit, *Vol XXIII, p160.*

Craftsmanship at Lutyens's
Folly Farm

Bibliography

ADAM, Peter. *The Arts of the Third Reich*, Thames and Hudson, London 1992
Architecture seen against the much less discussed painting and sculpture of the Nazis.

Allibone, Jill. *George Devey, Architect 1820-1886*, Lutterworth Press, Cambridge 1991
First biography, with catalogue of work.
– *Anthony Salvin, Pioneer of Gothic Revival Architecture* Lutterworth Press, Cambridge 1988
Catalogue raisonné with introductory chapters.

Andersen, Timothy J., with Eudorah M. Moore and Robert W. Winter (eds). *California Design 1910*, Peregrine Smith, Santa Barbara and Salt Lake City 1980 (reprint of 1974 edition by California Design Publication)
Somewhat chaotic but informative ramble round the first decade of the century Arts and Crafts in California. Catalogue of an exhibition held at California Design 1974.

Anscombe, Isabelle and Charlotte Gere. *Arts and Crafts in Britain and America*, Academy Editions, London 1978
Conventional but very well illustrated survey of the craftwork. Very little on buildings.

Arts and Crafts Exhibition Society. *Arts and Crafts Essays*, Rivington Percival, London and C. Scribner's Sons, New York 1893
Lectures delivered to the Arts and Crafts Exhibition Society by its leading members.

Ashbee, C. R. *A Book of Cottages and Little Houses*, Batsford, London 1906
Elegant exposition of the architect's country work. Presumably published to attract clients.
– *A Few Chapters on Workshop Reconstruction and Citizenship*, Guild and School of Handicraft, Essex House, London 1894
An early polemic on the virtues of handwork.
– *Craftsmanship in Competitive Industry*, Essex House Press, London and Campden, Gloucestershire 1908
A step in Ashbee's theory of the relationship between the crafts and industry.
– *Memoirs*, typescript in the Victoria and Albert Museum, London (6 vols) (nd)
The Memoirs are a version of Ashbee's diaries at King's College, Cambridge, edited by the author in old age. Ashbee is a most informative Virgil to the Inferno of turn-of-the-century architecture from California to Darmstadt.
– *Should we Stop Teaching Art*, Batsford, London 1911
Ashbee's most sophisticated attack on Edwardian capitalism and his clearest development of Morris' theories.
– *The Trivialities of Tom, Being Reflections on a Victorian Boyhood* typescript in the Victoria and Albert Museum 1940-41
A semi-autobiographical novella.
– *Where the Great City Stands: a Study in the New Civics*, Essex House Press, London 1917
Relatively late Arts and Crafts thoughts on town planning.
– (ed). *The Transactions of the Guild and School of Handicraft*, London 1890
Published and printed by the Guild, the Transactions are the first published report on the Guild's activities.

Atterbury, Paul and Clive Wainwright (eds). *Pugin, a Gothic Passion*, Yale University Press with theVictoria and Albert Museum, London 1994
Essays published in conjunction with major exhibition. Throws new light on life and many aspects of work.

BAILLIE SCOTT, M.H. (and others). *Garden Suburbs, Town Planning and Modern Architecture*, Fisher Unwin, London 1910
Essays by Arts and Crafts Garden City enthusiasts (including Unwin) in the first flush of apparent victory.
– *Houses and Gardens*, G. Newnes, London 1906; 2nd edition with A. Edgar, Beresford 1933
Essays, photographs, perspectives and plans which explained and publicized the firm's work. Buildings are not dated.

Baker, Herbert. *Architecture and Personalities*, Country Life, London 1944
Autobiographical sketches.

Beattie, Susan. *A Revolution in London Housing: LCC Housing Architects and their Work, 1893-1914*. GLC and Architectural Press, London 1980
The influence of Arts and Crafts idealism on mass housing.
– *The New Sculpture*, Yale, New Haven and London 1983
Survey of English Arts and Crafts sculpture, an exciting and sensual school, previously neglected. Biographies and bibliographies of sculptors.

Belcher, John. *Essentials in Architecture: an Analysis of the Principles and Qualities to be Looked for in Buildings*, Batsford, London 1907
Principles of architecture and building, taken principally from Classical examples.
– and Mervyn Macartney. *Later Renaissance Architecture in England* (2 vols), Batsford, London 1897-1901
A key to the Wrenaissance.

Belcher, Margaret. *A.W.N. Pugin: an Annotated Critical Bibliography*, Mansell, London and New York 1987
Exhaustive and very well researched.

Benson, E.F. *Queen Lucia*, Heinemann, London 1970 (reprint of first 1920 edition)
Punishingly ironical fictional description of arty-crafty ideas and behaviour.

Benton, Tim and Charlotte with Dennis Sharpe (eds). *Form and Function: A Source Book for the History of Architecture and Design, 1890-1939*, Crosby Lockwood Staples, London 1975
Extensive, though quirky, collection of contemporary essays and manifestos, some translated for the first time.

Blomfield, Reginald. *A History of Architecture in England, 1500-1800*, London 1897
Ammunition for the Classical argument.
– *A Short History of Renaissance Architecture in England 1500-1800*, George Bell, London 1900
An abridgement of the author's *History of Renaissance Architecture in England, 1500-1800*
– *Memoirs of an Architect*, Macmillan, London 1932
Autobiography of a Norman Shaw disciple who started life as an Arts and Craftsman but changed to being one of the chief early twentieth-century proponents of Classicism.
– *The Mistress Art*, Edward Arnold, London 1908
Lectures on Classicism to Royal Academy students.
– *Richard Norman Shaw*, Batsford, London 1940
The first biography by a (Classical) acolyte.
– and F. Inigo Thomas. *The Formal Garden in England*. Waterstone, London 1985 (reprint of original 1892 edition)
The Arts and Crafts love of formal gardening explained by one of its best practitioners.

Brandon-Jones, John (and others).*C.F.A. Voysey: Architect and Designer, 1857-1941*, Lund Humphries, London 1978
Catalogue of a major Voysey exhibition first held in Brighton. Well illustrated, it covers the whole of Voysey's work in essays.

Brooks, H. Allen. *The Prairie School: Frank Lloyd Wright and his Midwest Contemporaries*, University of Toronto Press, Toronto and Buffalo 1972
The fullest description of the School.
– *Prairie School Architecture*, University of Toronto Press, Toronto and Buffalo 1975
Edited studies from the contemporary *Western Architect*.

Brooks, Michael W. *John Ruskin and Victorian Architecture*, Thames and Hudson, London 1989
Excellent analysis of Ruskin's arguments against contemporary thought.

Brown, Jane. *Gardens of a Golden Afternoon, The Story of a Partnership: Edwin Lutyens and Gertrude Jekyll*, Allen Lane, London 1982
Analysis of the partnership, mainly from secondary sources. Has detailed descriptions of genesis of major gardens and complete list.
– *Vita's Other World, a Gardening Biography of V. Sackville-West*, Viking, Harmondsworth 1985
Vita Sackville-West continued the Arts and Crafts gardening approach well into the twentieth century.
– (ed). *Fulbrook* Libanus Press, Marlborough 1989
Sumptuous private press presentation of original documentation of one of Lutyens' great houses. Includes correspondence with client and specification. How an Arts and Crafts house was made.

Buchanan, William (ed). *Mackintosh's Masterwork, the Glasgow School of Art*. Richard Drew, Glasgow 1989
A mosaic of essays, old and new photographs and original drawings bring the masterpiece to life on page (foreword by Eckart Muthesius, son of Hermann and Mackintosh's godson).

Burkhardt, Lucius (ed). *The Werkbund. History and Ideology 1907-1933*, Barron's, New York 1980
Overlapping essays by different scholars form a perceptive collage.

Burne-Jones, Georgiana. *Memorials of Edward Burne-Jones* (2 vols), Macmillan, London 1904
Adoring, detailed, gentle portrait. First volume charmingly describes setting up the Firm and early friendship with Morris.

Butler, A.S.G. *The Architecture of Sir Edwin Lutyens* (3 vols), Country Life, London and C. Scribner's Sons, New York 1950
The Lutyens' memorial volumes, magnificent compilation of Lutyens' main works in drawings, photographs and descriptions.

CALDER, Alan. *James MacLaren 1853-1890: Arts and Crafts Architect*, RIBA Publications, London 1990
Small pamphlet: only publication on this interesting but short-lived architect.

Campbell, Joan. *The German Werkbund. The Politics of Reform in the Applied Arts*, Princeton University Press, Princeton and Guildford 1978
Thorough coverage of the Werkbund from 1907 to 1934.

Cardwell, Kenneth H. *Bernard Maybeck, Artisan Architect, Artist*, Peregrine Smith, Santa Barbara and Salt Lake City 1977
First biography.

Cassell, John (publisher). *The Illustrated Exhibitor*, Cassell, London 1851
Popular guide to the Great Exhibition; originally published in parts, copiously illustrated.

Clark, Kenneth. *The Gothic Revival: an Essay in the History of Taste*,John Murray, London 1928
Written under the spell of Geoffrey Scott's reductivist criticism of Ruskin, but very entertaining. Later editions acknowledge the bias.

Cobden-Sanderson, T.J. *The Arts and Crafts Movement*, Hammersmith Publishing Society, London 1905
Cobden-Sanderson coined the term 'Arts and Crafts'; this long essay is an exposition of the movement's early principles.

Comino, Mary. *Gimson and the Barnsleys: 'Wonderful Furniture of a Commonplace Kind'*, Evans, London 1980
Covers whole lives, not just Sapperton period. Main focus on furniture.

Coleman, Stephen and Paddy O'Sullivan(eds). *William Morris and News from Nowhere, a Vision for our Time*, Green Books, Bideford 1990
Modern reassessment of many aspects of Morris' thought, particularly good on ecological strands.

Cooper, Jeremy. *Victorian and Edwardian Interiors: from the Gothic Revival to Art Nouveau*, Thames & Hudson, London 1987
Scholarly and well illustrated, from Pugin to Heal.

Cram, Ralph Adams. *American Country Houses of Today*, 1913
Cram was Weaver's transatlantic equivalent.

Crane, Walter. *An Artist's Reminiscences*, Methuen, London 1907
Memoirs of snobbish socialist. Describes origins of Art Workers' Guild from painters' side.
– *Ideals in Art*, G. Bell, London 1905
Credo of an Arts and Crafts designer.

Crawford, Alan (ed). *By Hammer and Hand: the Arts and Crafts Movement in Birmingham*, Birmingham Museums and Art Gallery, Birmingham 1984
Covers all aspects of a vigorous local school with separate chapter on each. Architecture section by Remo Granelli.
– *C.R. Ashbee: Architect, Designer and Romantic Socialist*, Yale University Press, New Haven and London 1985
Magisterial description of all aspects of life and work.

Creese, Walter L. *The Search for Environment: the Garden City: Before and After*, Yale University Press, New Haven and London 1966. New edition, Johns Hopkins University Press, Baltimore 1992
Covers the origins and development of the Garden City; focuses on Howard, Parker and Unwin.

Cumming, Elizabeth and Wendy Caplan. *The Arts and Crafts Movement*, Thames and Hudson, London 1991
Brisk survey of all visual arts, covering roughly same period and geographical range as this book.

Current, Karen (with William R. Current, photographer). *Greene and Greene: Architects in the Residential Style*, Amon Carter Museum of Western Art, Fort Worth 1974
Beautiful and revealing photographs of some of the best work, text not as scholarly or comprehensive as Makinson.

Curry, Rosemary J. and Sheila Kirk. *Philip Webb in the North: the Architecture of Philip Webb and Furnishings by William Morris 1836-1990*, Teesside Polytechnic Press and Teesside Branch of the RIBA, Middlesborough 1984
Exhibition catalogue covers, rather sketchily, Arisaig in Scotland and work in north-east England. Original photographs.

DAKERS, Caroline. *Clouds, the Biography of a Country House*, Yale University Press, New Haven and London 1993
Detailed portrait of the inception (Webb and his clients), life and decline of the house.

Davidson, Raffles (ed). *The Arts Connected with Building*, Batsford, London 1909
Essays by leading Arts and Craftsmen including Voysey and Baillie Scott.

de Wit, Wim (ed). *The Amsterdam School, Dutch Expressionist Architecture, 1915-1930*, MIT Press, Cambridge, Mass. 1983
Catalogue of an exhibition at the Cooper-Hewitt Museum, New York. Essays cover aspects of development of work of de Klerk and colleagues.

Dixon, Roger and Stefan Muthesius. *Victorian Architecture*, Thames and Hudson, London 1978
Outline from Pugin to Mackintosh.

EASTLAKE, Charles Locke (ed). *A History of the Gothic Revival* (introduction by J. Mordaunt Crook), Leicester University Press, Leicester and Humanities Press, New York 1970 (second revised edition of original 1872 edition)
Still the most comprehensive history.

Eaton, Leonard K. *American Architecture Comes of Age. European Reaction to H.H. Richardson and Louis Sullivan*, MIT Press, Cambridge, Mass. and London 1972
Makes most of contemporary references and modern inferences.

FARR, Finis. *Frank Lloyd Wright, a Biography*, Cape, London 1962
Wide-eyed.

Fawcett, Jane (ed). *Seven Victorian Architects*, Thames and Hudson, London 1976 and Pennsylvania State University Press, University Park 1977
The essays on Bodley (by David Verey) and on Lutyens (by Roderick Gradidge) are particularly relevant to the Arts and Crafts movement.

Fellows, Richard A. *Sir Reginald Blomfield, an Edwardian Architect*, A. Zwemmer, London 1985
Life and architecture from early idealism through neo-Georgian to heavy classical post-war work.

Ferrey, Benjamin. *Recollections of Pugin*, Scolar Press, London 1978 (reprint of the first 1861 edition)
The first biography by an architect ecclesiologist friend.

Ford, Edward R. *The Details of Modern Architecture*, MIT Press, Cambridge, Mass. and London 1990
Modern analysis of architects' constructional intentions from their drawings. Most revealing chapters on the Arts and Crafts in USA and UK.

Ford, Ford Madox. *The Bodley Head Ford Madox Ford* (5 vols), Bodley Head, London 1971
Not the collected works, but the next best thing. Reminiscences of the Pre-Raphaelite world surrounding Ford Madox Ford in volume five.

Franklin, Jill. *The Gentleman's Country House and its Plan 1835-1914*, Routledge and Kegan Paul, London 1981
Development of English country house planning from Salvin to Maufe. Chapters on social structure and life in houses. Excellent comparative plans (not always scaled).

GEBHARD, David. *Charles F.A. Voysey, Architect*, Henessy and Ingalls, Los Angeles 1975
Selection of Voysey's writing and pictures of his designs.

Geretsegger, Hans and Max Peintner. *Otto Wagner, 1841-1918: the Expanding City, the Beginning of Modern Architecture*, Pall Mall, London 1970 and Academy Editions, London 1979 (translation of original German edition 1964)
Analysis of urban work.

Girouard, Mark. *Sweetness and Light: the 'Queen Anne' Movement 1860-1900*, Clarendon Press, Oxford 1977
Definitive, scholarly and entertaining.
– *The Victorian Country House*, Oxford University Press 1971 (revised and enlarged edition, Yale University Press, New Haven and London 1979)
Covers the 1830s to the 1890s. Particularly useful on Devey, Shaw and Webb.

Goodhart-Rendel, H.S. *English Architecture since the Regency*, Constable, London 1953
Elegant and ironic analysis ranging from 1820 to 1934 (when the lectures on which the book is based were given). Particularly good on the Picturesque origins of Victorian Gothic designs.

Gray, A. Stuart. *Edwardian Architecture: a Biographical Dictionary*, Duckworth, London 1985
Invaluable biographical dictionary of British architects practising in first decade of twentieth century. Focus on Classicism but Arts and Crafts well covered.

Greensted, Mary. *The Arts and Crafts Movement in the Cotswolds*, Alan Sutton, Far Thupp, Stroud 1993
Covers both Ashbee's enterprise and the Gimson Group. Continues story of Arts and Crafts activity in area to present day.

Grønvold, Ulf (ed). *Frederik Konow Lund: arkitekten som moret seg*, Norsk Arkitekturforlag, Oslo 1989
Excellent late Arts and Crafts in west Norway.

HAIKO, Peter (ed). *Sketches, Projects and Executed Buildings by Otto Wagner*, The Architectural Press, London 1987
Reprint of the magisterial record of works by the mentor of Hoffman and Olbrich published in German between 1889 and 1922.
– (ed). *Joseph Maria Olbrich, Architecture*, Butterworth, London 1988
Reprint of original plates selected by Olbrich for publication in three volumes between 1901 and 1914.

Haslam, Malcolm. *Arts and Crafts Carpets*, David Black, London 1991
Patterns and means of production.

Henderson, Philip. *William Morris, his Life, Work and Friends*, Thames and Hudson, London 1967
Particularly good on the life, with many previously unpublished letters.

Hessisches Landesmuseum und Kunsthalle Darmstadt. *Ein Dokument Deutscher Kunst 1901-1976*, exhibition catalogue (5 vols), Darmstadt 1976-7
Description in detail of the Darmstadt school and of Jugendstil in general.

Heuffer, Ford Madox, see Ford, Ford Madox

Hitchcock, Henry Russell. *Architecture: Nineteenth and Twentieth Centuries*, Pelican, London 1958; Penguin Books, Harmondsworth 1968
Still the most comprehensive single volume on the two centuries.

Howard, Ebenezer. *Garden Cities of Tomorrow* (2nd edition), Swan Sonnenschein, London 1902
Theoretical basis of the Garden City movement. The first edition (published 1898) was called *Tomorrow: a Peaceful Path to Reform*.

Howarth, Thomas. *Charles Rennie Mackintosh and the Modern Movement*, Routledge and Kegan Paul, London 1952; 2nd edn. 1977
The best biography. Particularly good on life and contemporaries.

Hoare, Geoffrey and Geoffrey Pyne. *Prior's Barn and Gimson's Coxen*, privately published by the authors, Seaforth, Little Knowle, Budleigh Salterton 1978
The best descriptions of these two Devon buildings.

Hussey, Christopher. *The Life of Sir Edwin Lutyens*, Country Life, London 1950
The only biography by an author who knew Lutyens.

IRVING, Robert Grant. *Indian Summer: Lutyens, Baker and Imperial Delhi*, Yale, New Havenand London 1981
Imperialism and the conquest of Arts and Crafts idealism by Classicism. Includes work by eg W.S. George and A.G. Shooshmith.

JACKSON, Frank. *Sir Raymond Unwin, Architect, Planner and Visionary*,A. Zwemmer, London 1985
Life and work from partnership with Parker to influence of planning theoryin USA.

Jackson, Neil. *F.W. Troup, Architect 1859-1941*, Building Centre Trust, London 1985
Only, and useful, monograph, based on an exhibition.

Jackson, T.G. *Recollections* (ed Basil H. Jackson), Oxford University Press, 1950
Memoirs of a very successful late Victorian architect.
– *The Renaissance of Roman Architecture* (2 vols), Cambridge University Press 1922
The first volume traces the history of Renaissance architecture in Italy, the second does the same for England. Surprisingly, the conclusion is more like Lethaby than Blomfield.

Jekyll, Gertrude. *Home and Garden*, Longmans, London 1900
The Jekyll philosophy of building, living and gardening.
– *Wood and Garden*, Longmans Green, London 1904
Evocative month-by-month description of the new, free garden (Munstead Wood).
– and Lawrence Weaver. *Gardens for Small Country Houses*, Country Life, London 1912
Wide-ranging description of free and formal gardens from the first decade of the century. Includes plans, photographs, details of work by Jekyll, Mawson, Lutyens etc.

Jewson, Norman. *By Chance I Did Rove*, privately published 1973
Account of the heroic days at Sapperton by Barnsley's son-in-law.

KAPLAN, Wendy (ed). *The Art that is Life: the Arts and Crafts Movement in America 1875-1920*, Museum of Fine Arts, Boston 1987
Exhibition catalogue with useful essays on all sides of movement.

Kaufmann, Edgar. *Frank Lloyd Wright, the Early Work*, Horizon, New York 1968
Survey includes most of Ashbee's original introduction to Wright's 1910 Berlin description of his own work.

Keeler, Charles. *The Simple Home*, PeregrineSmith, Santa Barbara and Salt Lake City 1979
Reprint (with modern introduction by Dimitri Shipounoff) of pamphlet by Maybeck's first client and disciple extolling turn-of-the-century Morrisian life in the Bay Region.

Kornwolf, James D. *M.H. Baillie Scott and the Arts and Crafts Movement: Pioneers of Modern Design*, Johns Hopkins Press, Baltimore and London 1972
The only, and exhaustive, biography.

Komonen, Markku (ed). *Saarinen in Finland*, Museum of Finnish Architecture, Helsinki 1984
Essays analyse all aspects of work.

LANE, Barbara Miller. *Architecture and Politics in Germany 1918-1945*, Harvard University Press, Cambridge, Mass. 1968
Very thorough from Jugend to Nazism.

Larner, Gerald and Celia. *The Glasgow Style*, Astragal Books, London 1980
The craftwork of a powerful local school.

Latham, Ian. *Olbrich*, Academy Editions, London 1980
Commentary on plates from collected works (see Haiko) and modern photographs.

Lethaby, W.R. *Architecture*, Williams and Norgate, London 1911
The history of architecture written by an Arts and Craftsman for laymen.
– *Architecture, Mysticism and Myth*, The Architectural Press, London 1974 (new edition of the first 1892 edition) The cosmology of a young, brilliant, self-educated Arts and Crafts architect.
– *Form in Civilization*, Oxford University Press 1957
Collection of some of his most important essays.
– *Philip Webb and his Work*, Oxford University Press 1935
Still the only biography. Lethaby shows himself to be Webb's devoted disciple.
– (ed). *Ernest Gimson, his Life and Work*, Stratford, Oxford and London 1924
An obituary panegyric to Gimson by friends.

Lind, Sven Ivar (ed). *Verk av L.I. Wahlman*, AB Tidskriften Byggmästaren, Stockholm 1950
Memorial volume to a neglected National Romantic architect.

Long, Helen. *The Edwardian House*, Manchester University Press, Manchester and London 1993
How Arts and Crafts architecture was transmuted for ordinary people by developers. Good on building trade.

MACARTNEY, Mervyn (ed). *Recent English Domestic Architecture*, special issues of *The Architectural Review*, bound specially, London 1908-11
Chronicles the growth of neo-Georgian.

Macaulay, James. *The Gothic Revival 1745-1845*, Blackie, Glasgow and London 1975
History of Picturesque Gothic Revival and its relationship to theory and literature.

MacCarthy, Fiona. *The Simple Life: C.R. Ashbee in the Cotswolds*, Lund Humphries, London 1981
Loving, detailed account of Ashbee's heroic attempt to set up his crafts community.

McCoy, Esther. *Five California Architects*, Reinhold, New York 1960
Essays on Maybeck, Gill, Greene and Greene and Schindler.

Mackail, J.W. *The Life of William Morris* (2 vols), Longmans Green, London 1899
The first biography, weak on politics, useful on life and art.

Mackmurdo, A.H. *A History of the Arts and Crafts Movement*, nd, typescript in the William Morris Museum, Walthamstow
A rather chaotic collection of notes made by an old man.

Macleod, Robert. *Charles Rennie Mackintosh*, Hamlyn, Feltham 1968
Well illustrated guide to the work.
– *Style and Society: Architectural Ideology in Britain 1835-1914*, RIBA Publications, London 1971
Lively guide to the theory.

Madsen, Stephan Tschudi. *Sources of Art Nouveau*, H. Aschehoug, Oslo 1956
Useful (particularly for its time) theoretical overview of Europe at the turn of the century, and of differences between English and Continental habits of mind.

Makinson, Randell L. *Greene and Greene: Architecture as a Fine Art*, Peregrine Smith, Santa Barbara and Salt Lake City 1977
The most comprehensive book on the buildings so far.
– *Greene and Greene: Furniture and Related Designs*, Peregrine Smith, Santa Barbara and Salt Lake City 1979
Both Makinson's books are well illustrated and are the best available accounts of the architects' work.

Manson, Grant Carpenter. *Frank Lloyd Wright to 1910*, Van Nostrand, New York 1958
Particularly good on the earliest designs.

Massé, H.J.L.J. (ed). *The Art Workers' Guild 1884-1934*, Shakespeare Head Press, Oxford 1935
Essays by the original members of the Guild and their close followers.

Mawson, Thomas H. *The Art and Craft of Garden Making*, Batsford, London 1907
The most elaborate work by a contemporary on Arts and Crafts garden making.

Medici-Mall, Katharina. *Das Landhaus Waldbühl*, Gesellschaft für Schweizerische Kunstgeschichte, Bern 1979
Painstaking description of Baillie Scott's Swiss house.

Miller, Mervyn. *Letchworth: the First Garden City*, Phillimore, Chichester 1989
Theory, inception, development and story to present day.
– *Raymond Unwin: Garden Cities and Town Planning*, Leicester University Press, Leicester, London and New York 1992
Authoritative analysis of planning theory and practice – shows mathematical fallacies in density calculations.
– and A. Stuart Gray. *Hampstead Garden Suburb*, Phillimore, Chichester 1992
Like the Letchworth book. Contains useful biographies of architects who built there and location of their buildings.

Moon, Karen. *George Walton: Designer and Architect*, White Cockade, Oxford 1993
Only life of a curious designer, neither Arts and Crafts nor Glasgow School but influenced by both.

Moorhouse, Jonathan, Michael Carapetian and Leena Ahtola-Moorhouse. *Helsinki Jugendstil Architecture 1895-1915*, Otava, Helsinki 1987
Comprehensive: theory, plans, modern photographs.

Morris, May. *Works of William Morris*, see Morris, William
– (ed). *William Morris, Artist, Writer, Socialist* (2 vols), Basil Blackwell, Oxford 1935
Much otherwise unpublished work by Morris, and anecdotes about him collected by his daughter. An introductory essay by G.B. Shaw.

Morris, William. *The Collected Works of William Morris* (ed May Morris) (24 vols), Longmans Green, London 1910-15
Comprehensive coverage of the literary works but lacks some essays and lectures (see above).

– *The Unpublished Lectures of William Morris* (ed Eugene D. Lemire), Wayne State University Press, Detroit 1969
Ten further lectures including 'Art and Labour' and two on the Gothic Revival.
– *William Morris* (ed G.D.H. Cole), Nonesuch Press, New York 1974
Useful collection of some of Morris's most revealing writing, not all printed in the *Works*.

Morton, Jocelyn. *Three Generations in a Family Textile Firm*, Routledge and Kegan Paul, London 1971
Details of Voysey's relationship with his manufacturing patron.

Muthesius, Hermann. *Das englische Haus* (3 vols), Wasmuth, Berlin 1904-5. The first English edition (based on the second German edition, 1908-11) is *The English House* (1 vol), Crosby Lockwood Staples, London 1979
A good translation by Janet Seligman but foolishly truncated.
– *Die englische Baukunst der Gegenwart: Beispiele neuer englischer Profanbauten*, Cosmos, Leipzig and Berlin 1900
Large-format illustrated essay. Norman Shaw is already the hero.

Muthesius, Stefan. *The High Victorian Movement in Architecture, 1850-1870*, Routledge and Kegan Paul, London and Boston 1972
Analysis of relationships of the theories of Pugin, Ruskin, Street, Butterfield etc.

NAYLOR, Gillian. *The Arts and Crafts Movement: a Study of its Sources, Ideals and Influences on Design Theory*, Studio Vista, London 1971
A pioneering modern work which covers the crafts well but scarcely mentions architecture.

Newton, W.G. *The Work of Ernest Newton, R.A.*, The Architectural Press, London 1925
Life and work by Newton's son.

Nikula, Riita. *Armas Lindgren 1874-1929*, Museum of Finnish Architecture, Helsinki 1988
The only biography, well illustrated. Parallel texts in Finnish and English.

ÖSTBERG, Ragnar. *The Stockholm Town Hall*, P.A. Norstedt & Söner, Stockholm 1929
Architect's account of creation of a National Romantic masterpiece.

PALLASMAA, Juhani (ed). *Lars Sonck, 1870-1956* Museum of Finnish Architecture, Helsinki 1981
Parallel texts in Finnish and English make this the only detailed non-Finnish source on Sonck.
– (ed). *Hvitträsk, the Home as a Work of Art.* Museum of Finnish Architecture, Helsinki 1987
Essays analyse a masterpiece of National Romanticism from many angles.

Parker, Barry, and Raymond Unwin. *Cottages near a Town*, pamphlet, nd (probably 1903) in RIBA British Architectural Library.
Expounds an early type-plan evolved by the partnership.
– and Raymond Unwin. *The Art of Building a Home*, Longmans Green, London 1901
Essays on architecture, art and planning by the two partners.

Pehnt, Wolfgang. *Expressionist Architecture*, Thames & Hudson, London 1973
The first thorough attempt to recognize expressionist architecture. Focusses on Germany and Holland.

Pevsner, Nikolaus. *Pioneers of Modern Design, from William Morris to Walter Gropius*, Penguin Books, Harmondsworth 1960
A revised and largely rewritten edition of *Pioneers of the Modern Movement* (Faber and Faber, London 1936), originally the first re-evaluation of the turn of the century. Forces Arts and Crafts into being pioneer of the Modern Movement.
– *The Buildings of England series*, Penguin Books, Harmondsworth 1951 onwards (46 vols)
Pevsner, as one of the first explorers of the Arts and Crafts movement, has, in his own volumes in this series, a keen eye for its buildings, particularly in the later guides.

Phillips, R. Randal. *Small Family Houses*, Country Life, London 1924
Post-war Arts and Crafts building. Many examples of neo-Georgian and neo-vernacular.

Polano, Sergio (ed). *Hendrick Petrus Berlage, Complete Works*, Butterworth, Guildford 1988
Drawings, contemporary photographs, includes Berlage's essay, 'Modern Architecture'.

Powell, Alfred. *Country Building and Handicraft in Ancient Cottages and Farmhouses*, Society for Protection of Ancient Buildings, London 1948
The gospel of repair according to Society for Protection of Ancient Buildings.

Prior, E.S. *A History of Gothic Art in England*, George Bell & Sons, London 1900
Gothic as seen by the generation of Shaw's pupils. Illustrated by Horsley.
– *The Cathedral Builders of England*, Seely & Co, London and E.P. Dutton, New York 1905
Introduction explains why literal Neo-Gothic was unsatisfactory to Arts and Crafts people.

Pugin, A.W.N. *An Apology for the Revival of Christian Architecture in England*, London 1843, reprinted in facsimile by St. Barnabas, Oxford 1969
Continues the attack started in *Contrasts*; accepts 'modern inventions'.
– *Contrasts*, London 1836, reprinted in facsimile by Leicester University Press, 1969
Pugin's first and most savage attack on Classicism and Protestantism.
– *The True Principles of Pointed or Christian Architecture*, London 1841. Reprinted in facsimile by St. Barnabas, Oxford 1969 and Academy Editions, London 1973
Detailed prescription of how to design and build in Gothic.

QUENNELL, Marjorie and C.H.B. Quennell. *A History of Everyday Things in England* (3 vols), Batsford, London 1919, 1934
An Arts and Crafts history of design.

REILLY, Charles H. *Representative British Architects of the Present Day*, Batsford, London 1931
Covers Baker, Blomfield, Dawber and others who were still alive when the book was written.

Richards, J.M. and Nikolaus Pevsner (eds). *The Anti Rationalists*, The Architectural Press,London 1973
Essays on individual turn-of-the-century anti-Classicists written in the 1960s and early 1970s.

Richardson, Margaret. *Architects of the Arts and Crafts Movement*, Trefoil Books, London 1983
Very well illustrated with drawings from the collections of the RIBA's British Architectural Library; covers roughly same ground as British chapters of this book with useful analysis of architects by office of apprenticeship (eg Sedding, Arthur Blomfield).

Robertson, Pamela. *Charles Rennie Mackintosh, the Architectural Papers*, White Cockade and Hunterian Art Gallery, Glasgow 1990
The few papers, thoroughly annotated.

Robinson, William. *The English Flower Garden*, John Murray, London 1883
The first advocate of horticultural naturalness (in the Ruskinian sense), Robinson strenuously opposed clipping and pleaching. The book ran into many editions around the turn of the century.

Royal Institute of British Architects. *Directory of British Architects 1834-1900*, Mansell, London 1993
Comprehensive but necessarily uneven biographical (and in some cases bibliographical) guide to almost every British architect recorded in practice during that period.

Rubens, Godfrey. *William Richard Lethaby, his Life and Work 1857-1931*, Architectural Press, London 1986
Covers whole work, architectural and theoretical. Has bibliography of Lethaby's writings.

Ruskin, John. *The Complete Works of John Ruskin* (ed E.T. Cook and A. Wedderburn) (39 vols), London 1903-12
Complete.

Russell, Frank (ed). *Art Nouveau Architecture*, Academy Editions, London 1979
Survey of turn-of-the-century architecture from Austro-Hungary to USA. Excludes Scandinavia. Essays vary in quality; illustrations are excellent.

Russell, Gordon. *Designer's Trade*, Allen and Unwin, London 1968
As a boy, Russell observed the north Cotswold Arts and Crafts school at work and grew up under its influence.

SAINT, Andrew. *Richard Norman Shaw*, Yale University Press, New Haven and London 1976
The definitive, endlessly entertaining and informative biography.

Savage, Peter. *Lorimer and the Edinburgh Craft Designers*, Paul Harris, Edinburgh 1980
Perceptive account of the work; draws extensively on previously unpublished correspondence.

Schorske, Carl E. *Fin-de-Siècle Vienna*, Alfred A. Knopf, New York 1980
Rich ruminations on relationships of different aspects of Viennese cultural life. Surprisingly light on Wagner's pupils.

Scully, Vincent J. Jr. *The Shingle Style and the Stick Style*, Yale, New Haven and London, revised edition 1971
Guide to the American contemporary of the Queen Anne style.

Sedding, John Dando. *Art and Handicraft*, Kegan Paul, Trench, Trübner, London 1893
Essays based on lectures expounding the approach of this early, contradictory Arts and Crafts architect who believed that buildings should be allowed to speak for themselves, unadorned, yet who produced one of the most decorative Arts and Crafts churches.
– *Garden Craft Old and New*, Kegan Paul, Trench, Trübner, London 1891
A posthumous book which crystallizes late 1880s architectural sensibilities on garden design. Was influential in subsequent two decades.

Service, Alastair. *Edwardian Architecture: a Handbook to Building Design in Britain 1890-1914*, Thames and Hudson, London 1977
Handy guide to the period. Useful short biographies with addresses of buildings.
– *Edwardian Interiors*, Barrie & Jenkins, London 1982
Arts and Crafts seen in Edwardian social context.
– *London 1900*, Granada, London 1979
Wide-ranging review of London architecture in the first decade of the twentieth century.
– (ed). *Edwardian Architecture and its Origins*, Architectural Press, London 1975
An extensive quarrying of contemporary *Architectural Review* articles on turn-of-the-century architects, with essays by modern scholars.

Shaw, R.N. and T.G. Jackson (eds). *Architecture: a Profession or an Art*, John Murray, London 1892
The artistic architects' counterblast to increasing professionalism of the RIBA.Essays by leading Arts and Crafts architects.

Simpson, Duncan. *C.F.A. Voysey, an Architect of Individuality*, Lund Humphries, London 1979
Summary of the architectural work.

Singelenberg, *Pieter H.P. Berlage, Idea and Style: the Quest for Modern Architecture*, Haentjens Dekker & Gumbert, Utrecht 1972
The best description of Berlage in English.

Spencer, Brian. *The Prairie School Tradition*, Whitney Library of Design, New York 1979
Record of an exhibition. Has some previously unpublished drawings.

Spencer, Christopher and Geoffrey Wilson. *Elbow Room, the Story of John Sydney Brocklesby, Arts and Crafts Architect*, Ainsworth & Nelson, London 1984
The only work on this late Arts and Crafts architect whose practice continued until the late 1920s.

Stamp, Gavin. *Robert Weir Schultz, Architect, and his Work for the Marquesses of Bute*, Mount Stuart 1981
Schultz's work for the Butes. Explains some of the Arts and Crafts fascination for Byzantine architecture.

Stanton, Phoebe. *Pugin*, Thames and Hudson, London 1971
Particularly useful on relationships with manufacturers. The only modern biography with much previously unpublished material.

Street, Arthur Edmund. *Memoir of George Edmund Street, R.A. 1824-1881*, John Murray, London 1888; reprinted by Art Book Company, London 1976
Biography by Street's son.

TAYLOR, Robert R. *The Word in Stone*, University of California Press, Berkeley and London 1974
Nazi policies on architecture extensively described from original sources.

Thompson, E.P. *William Morris, Romantic to Revolutionary* (2nd edition), Merlin Press, London 1977
Exhaustive on the politics – the second edition is more sympathetic to Morris's liberterianism than the first.

Thompson, Paul. *The Work of William Morris*, Quartet Books, London 1977
Systematically analyses each aspect of Morris's creative work.
– *William Butterfield*, Routledge & Kegan Paul, London 1971
The only biography, curiously organized.

Trapp, Kenneth R. (ed). *The Arts and Crafts Movement in California, Living the Good Life*, Abbeville Press, New York, London, Paris 1993
Essays published in conjunction with major exhibition cover whole phenomenon; rather stronger on crafts than architecture.

Trappes-Lomax, Michael. *Pugin, a Medieval Victorian*, London 1932
Fiercely Catholic biography.

Tressell, Robert. *The Ragged-Trousered Philanthropists*, Lawrence and Wishart, London 1955
Autobiography in fictional form of a building worker who died in 1911.

Triggs, H. Inigo. *Formal Gardens in England and Scotland*, Antique Collectors' Club, Woodbridge, 1988
Reprint of the 1902 Batsford edition in which Triggs illustrated some of the most important old formal gardens in photographs and drawings. Some modern photographs.
– *The Art of Garden Design in Italy*, Longmans Green, London 1906
Lavish presentation of some of the great Italian gardens: an attempt to reinforce the formal movement in England.

UNWIN, Raymond. *Cottage Plans and Commonsense*, Fabian tract 109, London 1902
Plea for hygiene, sunlight, greenery in working-class housing.
– *Nothing Gained by Overcrowding! or How the Garden City Type of Development may Benefit both Owner and Occupier*, Garden Cities and Town Planning Association, London 1912
The economic arguments for low densities.
– *The Legacy of Raymond Unwin* (ed Walter L. Creese), MIT, Cambridge Mass. and London 1967
Collection of essays, lecture notes and some extracts from previously published work.
– *Town Planning in Practice*, T. Fisher Unwin, London 1909
Monumental manual of picturesque and practical precepts for planning practitioners with illustrations of ideal townscapes. There is a new edition from Princeton, with an introduction by Walter Creese, 1994.
– and Barry Parker. *See* Parker, Barry.

VARNEDOE, Kirk. *Vienna 1900, Art Architecture and Design*, Little Brown, Boston 1986
Similar to Vergo.

Vergo, Peter. *Art in Vienna 1898-1918*, Phaidon, London 1975; 3rd edition, 1993
The Secession and its effects on all the arts.
Voysey, Charles F.A. *Individuality*, Chapman and Hall, London 1915
More about Voysey's philosophy than his architecture and design.
– *Tradition and Individuality in Art*, unpublished manuscript 1923, RIBA British Architectural Library
Attack on the regrowth of Classicism by a late Puginian.

WEAVER, Lawrence. *Houses and Gardens by E.L. Lutyens*, Antique Collectors' Club, Woodbridge 1981
Reprint of 1913 Country Life edition which covered many of the great works.
– *Small Country Houses of Today*, Country Life, London, first series nd (1909?), second series 1919
Weaver was a great and well informed protagonist of Arts and Crafts country work.
Windsor, Alan. *Peter Behrens, Architect and Designer 1868-1940*, Architectural Press, London 1981
First account in English of life and work.
Wingler, Hans Maria. *Bauhaus: Weimar, Dessau, Berlin, Chicago*, MIT Press, Cambridge (Mass) and London 1969
Vast collection of Bauhaus materials, including much not otherwise previously published or translated. Originally published in German, 1962.
Woolf, Virginia. *Roger Fry, a Biography*, Hogarth, London 1940
Fry's Omega workshops were a late example of Arts and Crafts Guild Association, though Fry disliked Arts and Crafts styling.
Wright, Frank Lloyd. *Ausgefürte Bauten und Entwürfe*, Wasmuth, Berlin 1910
Extensive compilation by Wright of his early work with a valuable introduction by Ashbee.
– *Collected Writings* Vol 1, *1894-1930* (ed Bruce Brooks Pfeiffer), Rizzoli, New York 1992
First volume of projected six includes all best known published writings, and some from manuscript.
– *Writings and Buildings* (eds Kaufmann, E. and B. Raeburn), Horizon, New York 1960
Compilation of Wright's writings from different periods.

MAGAZINES During the nineteenth and twentieth centuries, Britain has had anunrivalled range of periodicals on architecture, and these are usually the freshest sources of contemporary ideas. *The Builder* (founded 1842) chronicled the Gothic Revival and the battle of the styles. *The British Architect* (founded 1874) was particularly helpful to the young Voysey. The magazines of the 1890s – *The Studio* (founded 1893) and *The Architectural Review* (1896) – were, in their early years, solidly for the Arts and Crafts movement. *Country Life* (1897) is particularly good on early Lutyens. *Academy Architecture* (1889) shows the changing taste of the turn of the century. Other useful British magazines include *The Architect's Journal* (founded as *The Builder's Journal, an Architectural Review* 1895), *The Architect* (1869), *Building News* (1857), and the *Journal of the Royal Institute of British Architects*. Useful American magazines include *The Craftsman, The American Architect*, the *Architectural Review* (Boston) and *Architectural Record*.

Index

Note: Page numbers in italics refer to illustrations
Page numbers followed by n indicate footnotes

Acknowledgements

t = top b = bottom c = centre l = left r = right

AKG Berlin 234; Peter Aprahamian, photographer 147, 202, 203; Arcaid (photo Alex Bartel) 228, (photo Richard Bryant) 170, 198, 208(t), 208(b), 210, 211, 222(tb), 223, (photo David Churchill) 52, (photo Mark Fiennes) 103, 152, 153, (photo Lucinda Lambton) 124, (photo Clay Perry) 23; Architectural Association (photo J Greenwood) 58, (photo Petra Hodgson) 191(l), M. Morrison 108; courtesy Architectural Review 51, 76, 83, 86(b), 92(l,c), 110, 114, 115(b), 117(t), 119, 120(l), 122(b), 142(r), 148(r), 158, 160(c), 162(l), 171, 172, 178(c), 186(l), 213, 224; Art Institute of Chicago 216(b); Ashmolean Museum, Oxford 54; Jan Asplund, photographer 227; Richard Barnes, photographer 192, 204(t); de Beurs van Berlage (photo Morad Bouchakour) 218; Edward Bosley 201tb; Bridgeman Art Library (Cheltenham Art Gallery and Museum) 156tb, (William Morris Gallery, Walthamstow) 56, (courtesy of the Trustees of the Victoria and Albert Museum, London) 2, (Christopher Wood Gallery) 14; British Architectural Library, RIBA, London 15(t), 17(t), 57(b), 62, 80(r), 90(t), 91, 93(t), 96(l), 97(r), 98, 106(t), 109(t), 112(r), 113(t), 120(r), 159, 160(l,r); by permission of the British Library (LR414r15) 57(t); Cambridgeshire Collection, Cambridgeshire Libraries 81; Are Carlsen, photographer 220(r); Martin Charles, photographer 6, 20, 21, 38, 40(t), 41, 45, 46, 69, 70, 71, 72, 73, 74, 75, 78, 84(r), 85, 88, 94, 95, 100, 112(l), 118, 142(l), 143, 145(r), 149(l), 166, 169, 176(l), 176(r), 177, 178(b), 247; Peter Cook 140; Country Life 106(br), 173(l); Peter Davey 17(b), 18, 19, 22, 24, 32, 42, 43(l), 48(l), 50(b), 59, 66, 80(l), 82(bl), 84(l), 86(t), 90(b), 92(c), 93(b), 97(l), 102, 105, 108(r), 113(b), 116, 117(b), 121, 122(t), 141, 145(l), 148(l), 149(r), 150, 153(r), 161(r), 162(c,r), 178(t,b), 182, 186(r), 188, 189, 229; Jan Derwig, photographer 229(t), 231; Edifice (photo Gillian Darley) 92(r), 128, 129; (photo Philippa Lewis) 60(t); Mark Fiennes, photographer 111; Museum of Finnish Architecture 221, 225, (photo Kari Hakli) 224(l); First Garden City Heritage Museum, Letchworth Garden City 183(l); Archive of the Guild of Handicraft Trust, Chipping Campden 157; Hampstead Garden Suburb Archives Trust 183(r); Courtesy Holy Trinity Church PCC (photo Peter Smith) 61; Angelo Hornak, photographer 30(tc) (courtesy Hon. David Erskine), 35(t); Alastair Hunter Archives 138; A F Kersting, photographer 10(t), 34, 35(b), 44, 96(r); Balthazar Korab, photographer 194(r), 204(b), 206; Helga Lade (photo E Bergmann) 220(l), (photo Joke) 237, 238, (photo Krecichwost) 232; Andrew Lawson, photographer 126, 127, 131, 132(b), 164; Frank Lloyd Wright Foundation, Scotsdale, Arizona 214; Mathildenhohe Institute, Darmstadt 240(l), 241; National Museums and Art Galleries on Merseyside (Walker Art Gallery) 55(t); National Trust Photo Library (photo John Blake) 36, (photo Eric Crichton) 133, 136; (photo Andreas von Einseidel) 26, 30(tr), 31, (photo Andrew Lawson) 134, 135(b), (photo Nick Meers) 33; Francesca Odell, photographer 60(b), 180, 191(r); Courtesy Oxford Union Society (photo C W Band) 29; Garrick Palmer, photographer 64, 67, 154, 163; Royal Commission on the Historical Monuments of England, Crown Copyright 82(t), 146; Collection of the Guild of St George, Ruskin Gallery, Sheffield 55(b); Scotland Street School Museum (photo David Morrison) 151; Stichting Beeldrecht, Amsterdam 230; Tim Street-Porter, photographer 195, 196, 197(l), 197(r), 199, 200; Swedish Museum of Architecture 226; Courtesy of the Board of Trustees, Victoria and Albert Museum, London 76; Charlotte Wood, photographer 28, 40(b).